The Last Division

Also by Ann Tusa

THE NUREMBERG TRIAL (with John Tusa)
THE BERLIN BLOCKADE (with John Tusa)

THE LAST DIVISION

Berlin and the Wall

Ann Tusa

Hodder & Stoughton

British Library Cataloguing in Publication Data
Tusa, Ann
    The last division : Berlin and the wall
    1. Berlin Wall, Berlin, Germany, 1961–1989   2. Berlin
    (Germany) – History – 1945–1990   3. Berlin (Germany) -
    Politics and government – 1945–1990
    I. Title
    943.1'55'087
    ISBN 0 340 52972 5

Typeset by Hewer Text Composition Services, Edinburgh
Printed and bound in Great Britain by
Mackays of Chatham PLC, Chatham, Kent

Hodder and Stoughton
A division of Hodder Headline PLC
338 Euston Road
London NW1 3BH

Contents

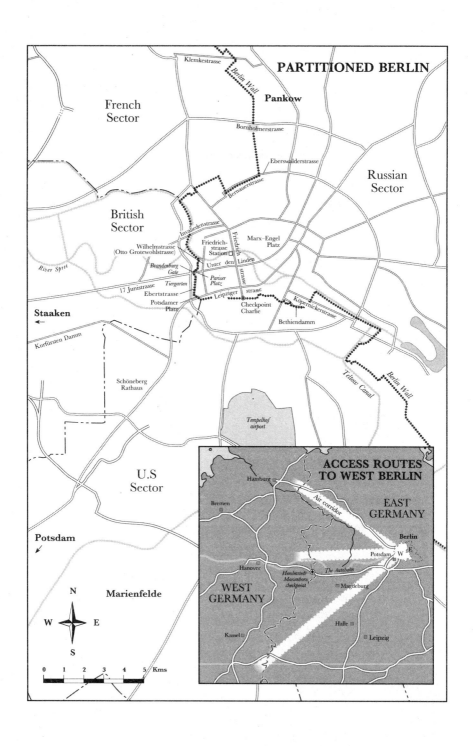

PARTITIONED BERLIN

French
Sector

Klemkestrasse

Pankow

Bornholmerstrasse

Eberswalderstrasse

Russian
Sector

British
Sector

Bernauerstrasse

Invaliedenstrasse

Wilhelmstrasse
(Otto Grotewohlstrasse)

Friedrich-
strasse
Station

Friedrichstrasse

Marx–Engel
Platz

River Spret

Brandenburg
Gate

Unter den Linden

17 Junistrasse

Tiergarten

Pariser
Platz

Leipziger strasse

Köpernickerstrasse

Staaken
←

Ebertstrasse

Potsdamer
Platz

Checkpoint
Charlie

Bethiendamm

Kurfürsten Damm

Schöneberg
Rathaus

Tellow Canal

Berlin Wall

Tempelhof
airport

U.S
Sector

ACCESS ROUTES
TO WEST BERLIN

Hamburg

Air corridor

EAST
GERMANY

Bremen

Berlin

Potsdam
↙

Hanover

Potsdam

The Autobahn

WEST
GERMANY

Helmstedt/
Marienborn,
checkpoint

Magdeburg

N

Marienfelde

Kassel

Halle

Leipzig

W   E

S

0   1   2   3   4   5 Kms

Illustrations

———⇒►◄⇐———

ILLUSTRATIONS

East Berliners try to escape through windows on Bernauer Strasse (*Landesbildstelle Berlin*)

A Vopo tries to stop the escape of a 77-year-old woman (*Hulton Deutsch*)

Twelve-year-old Erwin Schake goes to school with one scoutcar in front and another behind (*Landesbildstelle Berlin*)

Lucius D. Clay, Vice-President Johnson and Willy Brandt (*Landesbildstelle Berlin*)

A balloon laden with adults and children attempts an escape in 1979 (*Hulton Deutsch*)

A tunnel under the Wall in 1962 (*Landesbildstelle Berlin*)

Six refugees crammed into this cable drum in 1965 (*Landesbildstelle Berlin*)

Kennedy visits West Berlin, June 1963 (*Hulton Deutsch*)

East German refugees in Hungary, September 1989 (*Associated Press*)

Crossings through the Wall had opened but the Brandenburg Gate is still blocked, November 1989 (*Landesbildstelle Berlin*)

The Wall open and unmanned, January 1990 (*Landesbildstelle Berlin*)

Honecker on trial, November 1992 (*Associated Press*)

Celebrating the removal of Checkpoint Charlie, June 1990 (*Landesbildstelle Berlin*)

Foreword

W olfgang Grund rang me from Berlin in November 1989 when the Wall began to crumble. "You have to be here," he insisted. "You must see it." He took no excuses. He even managed to find me a plane ticket at a time when it seemed the whole world wanted to be in Berlin to watch and celebrate. Thanks to him, I talked to Berliners as the Wall fell, heard what it had done to their lives, saw the significance of its end through their eyes. This experience galvanised me into writing this long-considered book.

On that occasion, as on others, I relished the warm hospitality and kindness of Michael and Henrietta Burton in Taubertstrasse. A few months before, General Robert Corbett, the British Military Commandant, had sent me in a helicopter to see the Wall in its full, frightening extent. At that time it had seemed impregnable and permanent. I am fortunate to have seen divided Berlin from the air and on the ground, and then to have watched the transformation.

In the lonely, obsessive business of research I have been cheered by all those I interviewed. Their names are listed at the back of this book. Here I would like to express my gratitude for the time they spared me, for the memories they shared which gave life and meaning to the bare facts, and for the sense they communicated of how events looked and felt to those who lived through them. In East Berlin, Hans Jacobus and his friends helped me to view the Wall from the other political side. In West Berlin I was put in touch with many witnesses to the city's partitions by the Senate, that civic model of help and efficiency. One of the contacts it made for me was with Günter Dittmann, who provided me with copies of the police records for the crucial period of the building of the Wall – a treasure trove of information about a great drama, and an accurate framework on which to pin the chaotic events of troubled, complex days.

Research was a particularly time-consuming and frustrating business in the period when the Soviet bloc, like the Wall, was collapsing. Telephone communications with Eastern Europe were tenuous at best and often required the arcane arts of international operators, stringing connections through improbable exchanges and setting up professional conspiracies with counterparts in faraway places; institutions often shared a few phones between several offices, so even if you got through to them it might take half an hour to get the person you wanted; names and numbers were not listed in directories and came from personal contacts or as a result of umpteen calls. Emily Kasriel took over my phone and showed admirable persistence in setting up visits to East Berlin and Moscow. Kostya Sakharov drew up an impeccable programme for me in Moscow then remade arrangements time and again as interviewees changed them. In addition he interpreted with skill and nannied me through the political complications and the Metro. Tanya Krasavchenko took me into her flat, sight unseen, fed me, cosseted me and made me laugh until my sides ached.

Back in London Sue Davison risked her health on my smoke and black coffee, and translated German. The BBC World Service team who made the series *The World that came in from the Cold* was generous with ideas and contacts, and allowed me to read the transcripts of all their interviews with key figures of the post-war period. Deborah Rogers and David Miller gave encouragement when it was needed and must have permanently damaged their lips by biting them rather than nag for a faster rate of work; Roland Philipps too showed remarkable patience and an acute, sensitive editor's eye. Professor Lawrence Freedman told me that King's College, London had acquired the National Security Archive dealing with Berlin (thus saving me goodness knows how many expensive journeys to the United States) and the Basil Liddell Hart Library provided cosy, peaceful conditions for reading the microfiches.

Access to documents is not always so easy and agreeable. When I needed them neither East German nor Soviet papers were available to non-official outsiders. Soviet Foreign Ministry documents might have been read and summarised for me by Russian researchers, but at a stiff price. Gratifying though it would have been to support young Russian historians whose grants were meagre and likely to dry up, I decided that there was no substitute for doing one's own work and from the raw material. Thanks to hard work in united Germany and recent cooperation, funding and equipment from international bodies to help the Russians prepare their archives for the public, the documents I could not see will soon be available to others. They will fill the gaps I left, substantiate or disprove my guesses, provide other perspectives from which to view the story. I envy future researchers.

Readers may appreciate as I do information supplied by the Bank of England on the relative values of currencies in the period covered by this book. Give or take a few decimal points the pound sterling in 1950 was worth $2.8; the Deutschmark was not quoted until 1953 by which time it stood at 11.7 to the pound. Inconceivable as it seems in more troubled financial times, the relative values had not changed by 1960. A sadder story is revealed by the decline in the purchasing power of the pound: £1 in 1950 was worth £12.8 in 1960 and £17.8 in 1995.

No one but myself can understand how much help, support and sympathy I have received from my husband, Johnny; only he knows how intolerable living with me and this book has been over the last few years. I cannot thank him adequately. All I can do is to dedicate the book to him and state that his name ought to be on the cover.

Ann Tusa

INTRODUCTION

Berlin: November 1989

————◆————

F or four days and nights the people of Berlin cheered, sang and danced to the music of popping champagne corks and honking car horns on a ground bass of rumbling bulldozers and tapping hammers. It was, everyone said, the longest, biggest, happiest street party in history.

They were celebrating the breaching of the infamous Wall, which had been an impermeable barrier across their city since it was built by the East German government in August 1961. For twenty-eight years Berliners had lived with its ugliness and endured its brooding threat: twenty-nine miles of concrete slabs, each nine to twelve feet high; on the East Berlin side a Death Strip of raked sand set with mines and electric alarms, patrolled by armed men with dogs, tirelessly scanned by watchtowers and machinegun emplacements, and harshly exposed by the merciless glare of floodlights. The Wall had severed a living city in half: cut communications between East and West and sundered families for a generation. At each end it met the frontier of East Germany with West Germany – itself already the most impenetrable border in Europe. This bisected an entire nation. Furthermore on either side of it Europe was split into two hostile camps which at any time might engage in nuclear war. The first shots in such a cataclysmic conflict would almost undoubtedly be fired at the point where the enemies confronted each other face to face – in Berlin itself. No wonder Berliners came onto the streets as the news spread on the evening of 9 November 1989 that the Wall was opening.

It had been a year of political upheaval and staggering change in

Europe, but no one had dared imagine that the Wall would collapse. A middle-aged man crossed from East to West Berlin, then burst into tears: "To think that it could happen in my lifetime." Another walked over, then turned round to look the way he had come: "I have lived for twenty-eight years with my windows looking on this side of the Wall. I wanted to see what it looked like from the other side." Huge crowds danced all night in the heart of the city where the Wall was thickest and most fortified – at the Brandenburg Gate. With them was a sixteen-year-old lad from West Berlin. He had never before stayed up all night. His parents had never allowed him to go to a disco – they thought he was too young. Tonight they had encouraged him to go to the Gate. There would never be another night like this. More than most people, they understood what it meant. They had known war, invasion, occupation. The boy's father had lived in this city through a year of blockade by the Russians, a year of cold, hunger and fear; he had humped precious sacks of coal brought in by the western airlift to earn one meal a day so that his mother and her other children could share his ration book and eat dehydrated potatoes by the light of a candle. The boy's mother had watched the Wall go up and lost her family behind it. Surely tonight marked the start of something better. Young Alexander must bear witness to new hope.[1]

As Berliners celebrated, the rest of the world shared their joy. For the disintegration of the Wall was of international significance. It was all summed up by a pocket cartoon in *The Times* on the morning of 10 November, showing a man's head popping through a hole, gratified and agog. "Ich bin ein Berliner," he said. He said it all. Those words, "I am a Berliner"*, first used by President Kennedy, were a reminder that everyone outside was involved in Berlin's fate. The city had been the hub of Europe since the end of the Second World War in 1945. It had been the pivot of the Cold War. On it centred the fundamental conundrum of strategists, diplomats and politicians: "Solve the Berlin problem and you solve the European question"; "You can't resolve the Berlin situation until you find a settlement for Europe". No one had managed to answer this puzzle. So all the political difficulties which it summarised had been buried under the Wall. Thereafter, the Wall, like the Bomb, had served as a disgusting deterrent to even more obscene violence.

The story which follows will explain these paradoxes. It will also suggest why the joyous days of November 1989 were followed by less happy months of disillusion and wrangling, and why the first rapture as the Wall fell gave way to sobering realities.

---

* Or to be linguistically accurate, "I am a doughnut."

I

The Division of Berlin, Germany, Europe

The building of the Berlin Wall in 1961 was only the final act in a long series of divisions of the city from 1945 onwards. The first split had been planned by the coalition which was led by the United States, the Soviet Union and Great Britain and was engaged in the Second World War against Nazi Germany. These allies set up the European Advisory Commission (the EAC), which began work in London in January 1944 and had three members: John Winant, the American ambassador in Britain, his Soviet counterpart Fedor Gusev, and the Permanent Under-Secretary at the Foreign Office, Sir William Strang. Its job was to plan the terms of German surrender and the nature of the subsequent occupation regime. Its assumption was that allied military government would be short-lived: once the German armies were disbanded, civil institutions denazified, and industry put on a peacetime basis, a German civilian regime would be created and power would pass rapidly into politically and morally cleansed German hands. The victorious Powers would then impose a peace treaty and evacuate their forces.[1]

The EAC worked according to instructions which had been sketched in only the broadest of brushstrokes. While the battles were fought from 1939 to 1945, the allies were too stretched by the demands of war and too uncertain about its outcome to consider seriously how Germany would be treated if they ever achieved final victory. That was why the British Prime Minister, Winston Churchill, warned a joint session of the US Congress in 1943: "We must beware of every topic, however attractive, and every tendency, however natural, which diverts our minds or energies from the

3

supreme objective of the general victory of the United Nations." What he could not admit publicly was that any discussion of post-war policy exposed fundamental disagreements in the alliance and threatened to wreck it. Furthermore, it seemed sensible to postpone an itemised scheme for the peace until the war was won and actual conditions in Germany could be assessed – as the American President Franklin D. Roosevelt put it: "I dislike making plans for a country we do not yet occupy."

So just a few basic principles were established for the EAC to develop. It had been agreed by the coalition that Germany must surrender unconditionally: there must be no revival of the post-1918 myth that potentially victorious German troops had been "stabbed in the back" by politicians. Once the body politic was purged of Nazism and militarism by occupation forces, the victors would impose a peace settlement to ensure that Germans could never again wreak havoc in Europe. It was also determined that Germany would be kept intact, give or take some frontier adjustments. Throughout the war each ally had toyed with schemes for dismemberment of Germany, for destroying once and for all the country which had caused two world wars of unparalleled ferocity in twenty-five years. The US Secretary of the Treasury, Henry Morgenthau, had gone even further: he wanted to "pastoralise" Germany – to dismantle all industry and create an impotent and impoverished population barely able to subsist, let alone disrupt the peace of Europe. Opponents of dismemberment gradually won ground in the final stages of the war. They argued successfully that enforced partition and consignment to pariah status would ultimately provoke German revanchism and new aggression, that a reasonably prosperous Germany was an essential trading partner for her neighbours and a vital source of coal and steel for rebuilding a shattered continent, and that a thriving but carefully supervised German industry would create goods which could be seized as reparations by those who had suffered such destruction from Nazi invasion and looting.

It was therefore immediately agreed by the EAC that Germany should be run as a single unit. For ease of administration, however, the country would be divided into three military zones of roughly equal size and resources – one each for the Americans, Russians and British. The three Military Governors would meet in an Allied Control Council to devise common policies. Initially, Sir William Strang suggested that the zonal boundaries should be drawn and the ACC set up wherever they converged – Leipzig seemed geographically likely. But Berlin had always been the government centre of a united Germany, and would no doubt be the capital of a reunified Germany. Berlin, logically, must be the seat of the Allied Control Council. And the city, like the country, would be subdivided into three administrative sectors but run according to common policies drawn up by the three Military Commandants in an Allied Kommandatura. Into these tidy, bureaucratic arrangements the EAC had inadvertently built a booby-trap. Common policies required unanimity in the ACC and Kommandatura: a veto had been given to each member. Yet this potentially destructive device aroused no immediate suspicion or comment. It was an item of faith in the period that peace would nurture the cooperative spirit of the wartime alliance and that the institutions for maintaining that peace must be based on consensus (which is why a veto was also plumbed into the Security Council of the United Nations Organisation). Even Churchill – highly sceptical about the ambitions and motives of the USSR and pessimistic about the chances of preserving collaboration once the common Nazi enemy was defeated – shared the prevalent belief that the maintenance of peace and the rebuilding of a shattered Europe could not be achieved without Soviet help. He wrote, "I felt bound to proclaim my confidence in Soviet good faith in the hope of procuring it. Our hopeful assumptions were soon to be falsified. Still, they were the only ones possible at the time."

There was a second danger in the occupation plans. This stemmed from the decision that the lines of the occupation zones would not meet at Berlin: the city lay too far to the east, and was well inside the designated Soviet area. How would the American and British commanders keep contact with their garrisons there; how could the Military Governors in the Control Council maintain communications with their zones? Junior American officials in the EAC were keen to make the Russians specify road and rail links for western use and provide written guarantees of access. Gusev merely waved away the request: there would be "no difficulty" over access, he assured them; "of course" the allied presence in Berlin automatically meant a right of communication. John Winant was unwilling to press the access point. He argued with one of his team, Robert Murphy, that he had "established a personal relationship with Ambassador Gusev after months of patient effort and had gained the Soviet envoy's confidence . . . The Russians", he declared, "were inclined to suspect our motives anyway and if we insisted on this technicality we would intensify their mistrust." He told Murphy he "would not do it." In Winant's opinion, pursuing this matter against Soviet resistance risked wrecking EAC agreements made so far and aborting others. Strang took much the same view and, in addition, reckoned that a written guarantee would be broken by the Russians just as easily as a verbal promise if and when it suited them. He also upheld the legal judgement, frequently quoted in civil and military circles, that specific arrangements on access implied a denial of movement over any and all routes. Only years later did Strang decide that the western representatives on the EAC had made a fatal mistake, that they should have held out for a tightly defined access arrangement: "the possibility of such an agreement", he wrote in his memoirs, "did exist then, and perhaps only then."

Unfortunately, however, those who wanted to secure allied access to Berlin got no backing from higher authority. The US War Department insisted that it was up to the military, on the spot and at the time, to decide what communications would suit their needs; the State Department had no wish to insult their coalition partners, the Russians, by suggesting that a Soviet word was not a bond. Supreme Headquarters, Allied Expeditionary Forces in Europe took no interest in the question at all: there were many more urgent problems to settle in the final months of the war. Indeed, when the EAC's proposals finally arrived at SHAEF about a week before D-Day, the Chief of Staff, General Walter Bedell Smith, confessed that he "gave them only the most casual inspection": he was a busy man, the EAC's terms for the peace looked like "counting chickens" before the war had even reached its crucial stage. Not least, the recommendations came from under the names of three diplomats, not the combined chiefs of allied forces or heads of government, so he assumed they were tentative suggestions, which would be analysed and adjusted for months to come.* The Supreme Commander, General Dwight D. Eisenhower, had many too many immediate problems on his mind and he always made a very proper distinction between military matters, which were his business, and general policy, which he regarded as the responsibility of politicians.[2]

Post-war policy for Germany was a responsibility shirked by the Big Three, the leaders of the United States, Soviet Union and Britain, when they met at Yalta in February 1945. Absorbed as they were in holding together their coalition and winning the war they nodded through the agreements drafted by the European Advisory Commission. They paused only to grant an occupation zone to France – to be carved out of American and British territory. This was at the insistence of Churchill, who wanted a Continental counterweight to the Soviet Union in Europe but who diplomatically put it that the French were needed to share the burden of occupation of Germany. Access to Berlin was not even mentioned at this conference. It should have been thoroughly discussed and settled.

Because the western allies had blithely put themselves behind what

---

* Such was the importance attached by SHAEF to documents coming from the EAC that Headquarters forgot it had ever received the Commission's painstakingly drafted terms of German surrender and its staff spent three days and nights cobbling together its own version when Nazi generals were about to arrive and lay down their arms.

would soon become enemy lines, their Berlin garrisons, as well as the seat of the military government for Germany and the administration of the capital were all 120 miles inside the Soviet Zone with the West's communications totally dependent on Soviet goodwill – and that was already an evaporating asset. Western presence in Berlin was an essential element in the occupation of Germany and the final settlement of Europe. Yet that presence was painfully vulnerable. If the Russians decided to hinder access, it could not be maintained: the western garrisons, the symbol of occupation rights, would be turned into hostages. Berlin's role as a post-war Pandora's box had been created even before the fighting stopped.

When the Big Three met again, at Potsdam from 17 July to 2 August 1945, the pernicious results of neglecting the access question were already manifest. The German armies had capitulated in the first week of May. From that moment, according to the decisions of the EAC approved at Yalta, all four victorious powers should have established quadripartite government in their capital, Berlin. This had not happened. Worse: the western Powers were not even admitted to the city until early July. The Russians kept them out.

Soviet forces alone captured the German capital. General Eisenhower had allowed them to do it, for what seemed good military reasons. The Red Army had broken on to German soil in January 1945 and by March was within thirty-five miles of Berlin; western forces, on the other hand, were still 200 miles away. Eisenhower was influenced by intelligence reports that Hitler would order a last stand in the south and that nuclear weapons were being developed in the same area. His staff assured him that an assault on Berlin might cost 100,000 men. Why, Eisenhower kept asking, "should we endanger the life of a single American or British soldier to capture areas we soon will be handing over to the Russians?" Why encourage his forward units to press on to Berlin when he could not yet give them infantry or air support? So Eisenhower overrode the protests of several of his own generals, ignored the repeated appeals of Churchill to "shake hands with the Russians as far to the east as possible" and did not push on to Berlin. He also swallowed a lie from Stalin: that the city was not the prime strategic target and the Red Army would concentrate on a grand meeting with the western allies at Dresden. Once Ike's attention was distracted, Stalin attacked Berlin and took it on 8 May. The Russians had certainly achieved a military triumph. They had also stolen a political march.

They used their position in the capital to keep western forces out until it was convenient to admit them – and on terms favourable to the Soviet Union. A month after the four-Power Allied Control Council should have

7

begun work, Eisenhower and his British and French colleagues were grudgingly allowed to pay a visit to the Red Army commander, Marshal Georgi Zhukov, in Berlin on 5 June. The Marshal argued, as if a patient and reasonable man, that it was improper to start quadripartite government until American units were withdrawn from Saxony and Thuringia in his Zone, into which the impetus of their advance had propelled them. At this point Eisenhower could, and probably should, have replied that he would not move his forces until the Soviet Union fulfilled its international agreements and allowed the entry of the western allies into the capital and the establishment of the ACC. Instead, he persuaded himself that there would be "grave misunderstandings, if not actual clashes" with the Russians unless he withdrew. His colleagues shared his fears and were equally determined to start four-Power government of Germany on amicable terms with their Soviet ally. As the future Military Governor of the American Zone, General Lucius D. Clay, put it in May 1945: "If the four of us cannot get together now in running Germany, how are we going to get together in an international organisation [the UN] to secure the peace of the world?" Clay was perfectly aware that collaboration was going to be difficult but he explained later, "I thought then *and I still do*, that we had an obligation to try and make it work – and that if it failed, it wasn't going to be our fault." So the western allies meekly accepted Zhukov's arguments and hoped against hope that concession would earn Russian cooperation.[3]

It did not – then or later. Once the United States promised withdrawal of its troops into the American Zone on 21 June, Stalin insisted that allied entry into Berlin would have to be delayed until the city was "cleared of mines"; he ignored requests from the United States and Britain for free access by road, rail and air. Washington decided to leave the matter to be settled by the military authorities in Germany, and when the western commanders again visited Zhukov on 29 June, their requirements were hardly exorbitant: four rail links between Berlin and the western zones, two roads – one for the British, the other for the Americans – and two air lanes. Zhukov reacted as if they were absurd: few means of communication in his zone were in a fit state of repair, he explained, and western control of routes through his territory would "create an extremely difficult administrative problem". Surely, he pleaded, one railway, one road and a single air lane would be more than enough to supply the small garrisons in Berlin. In any case, he added, proper transit arrangements could be drawn up later by the Allied Control Council (not reminding them of his veto).

The western commanders took Zhukov at his word – they always saw him as an admirable officer and charming gentleman, not as the servant of the tyrannical, devious and mendacious Stalin. They settled for the access he offered, however unsatisfactory. Field Marshal Bernard Montgomery explained three years later that they believed they had "a sort of friendly agreement, rather loosely defined. It was accepted that we would all do our stuff and no one would abuse" the arrangement. Clay took the tougher line – "we were sitting over there with the greatest army that had ever been seen, nobody was concerned about anybody blocking us on roads and railroads" – and could not imagine that within six months American troops in Germany would have been cut to a division and a half. In the meanwhile the western military leaders assured themselves that once they were teamed up in Berlin and applying sound military common sense to their problems, all the wrinkles would be ironed out.[4]

Far from it. And even before the western Powers got into the city the Soviet Union had tied them in further knots. On 7 July Zhukov presented the western commanders with another démarche: their sectors of Berlin could not be fed from the surrounding Soviet Zone. His reasons sounded plausible, indeed they engaged sympathy: food supplies in eastern Germany had been destroyed in the recent fighting, the Red Army was sacrificing its own rations to keep Berliners alive, the Russian people were starving and could do nothing to help. Faced with such a heart-rending story how could the West refuse to bring in food, even though they would have to do so from 120 miles away and on one railway line and one road? Yet again the allied commanders assumed this was a temporary arrangement which could be sorted out in due course. But while they were still victims of Soviet pathos and their own optimism, Zhukov added a further onerous stipulation: they must also provide their sectors with coal from the Ruhr since the city's traditional source, Silesia, was now under Polish control. This indeed presented considerable logistical difficulty. Berlin's public utilities alone consumed about 6,000 tons of hard coal a day for gas and electricity. In addition, householders needed coal for their fires and boilers and for some solid fuel ovens. Once the western commanders got their breath back, they appealed for the Russians to provide 1,500 tons a day of brown coal, lignite, for domestic use. This point, at least, the Russians gracefully conceded.

They could easily afford to do so. In the course of just a few weeks the Soviet Union had made sure that the West's presence in Berlin would always be insecure because it depended on tenuous and inadequate access routes which could be cut at will by the Red Army. Furthermore, if the West chose to fight for its right to stay in Berlin it would not only hazard its garrisons but the lives of two and a half million Berliners in the western sectors whose heat, light and food were now their responsibility. The

West's high risk gamble – sacrifices to win Soviet collaboration – did not even gain a quick entry to Berlin. Only in the first week in July did the Russians finally and reluctantly admit western troops. The Allied Kommandatura, in which the four Military Commandants were to run Berlin, was set up on 11 July. The Allied Control Council for Germany did not meet until 20 July. By then, the Soviet Union had the city in a tight grip.

Though the western allies had neglected, indeed deliberately avoided, the details of their own policy for Germany while the war lasted, the Soviet Union had not been so casual. In February 1944 a commission of German exiles in Moscow began to examine the political, economic and ideological framework of occupation. Twelve months later it was ordered to plan the work of "anti-Fascists" in the future Soviet Zone. The talks were under close Soviet supervision, all decisions depended on ultimate Kremlin approval. The key figure in the work, however, was a German – Walter Ulbricht.[5]

He was uniquely well-qualified. He had been a dedicated Communist since joining the youth movement in 1908 when he was fifteen years old, a full-time Party official since 1919. He was trained at the Lenin School in Moscow in the mid-1920s and was a Communist deputy in the Reichstag (the German parliament) from 1928 to 1933. The rise of Fascism broadened his experience and honed his talents. After fleeing from the Nazis in 1933, he worked for the Party in Paris and Prague, then made a name for total ruthlessness in the Spanish Civil War, exterminating anti-Stalinists in the Republican Army. In Moscow from 1938 to 1945 his reputation for implacable orthodoxy was substantiated – he never lifted a finger to help the fourteen top German Communist officials who were executed and was merciless in "purifying" the exiled Party of any who veered from the straightest of ideological lines. Ulbricht was much more than a zealot, however. He was an apparatchik with an insatiable appetite for work and an exceptional capacity for organisation. He had no rhetorical talent; he was renowned for spreading gloom over any event he attended; he won no affection and never showed any. It was easy to mock or mimic his castrato voice and the Saxon accent which Germans find so hilarious. Cartoonists delighted in his goatee beard which was no doubt intended as a loyal tribute to Lenin but which went only too well with his bleating tones. But Walter Ulbricht was no laughing matter. He was a chilling, remorselessly efficient, Party machine.

Given his qualities and experience, Ulbricht was an inevitable choice to head one of the three groups of German exiles which the Kremlin decided would move into Germany with the Red Army in April 1945. These were tiny cadres – ten men in each – but every member had been picked and trained for his work. One group was destined for Saxony, one for Mecklenburg, and the third, under Ulbricht, for Berlin. They were to make the first political assault: build up an anti-Fascist (though not necessarily a Communist) bloc, purge Nazism, and set up information media to preach cooperation between the local population and the Soviet forces. Waiting for them were local Communists with information on activists and particular enthusiasm for their duties. Held in reserve were about 150 more German émigrés in Moscow as well as German troops who had been indoctrinated in the prisoner-of-war camps. The first task of the cadres, after the surrender of the German High Command in May, was to make contact with anti-Nazis of every hue – politicians of all parties as well as public-spirited citizens – to enlist their help in wiping out the Nazi state and restoring public services.[6]

In Berlin, they faced an appalling task. The city was a scene of ghastly destruction. Western bombing, Soviet artillery, and vicious street fighting had pulverised it: 12 per cent of all buildings had been razed to the ground, 76 per cent were in ruins; there were only 8,500 hospital beds remaining from a previous 35,000; 128 of the 150 bridges were smashed. There was no public transport, no gas or electricity, no water supply. The sewage system had been out of action for months and dysentery and typhus had reached epidemic proportions. Air Marshal Arthur Tedder decided in May 1945 that the "city is completely dead. One drives for miles through desolate smoking ruins and finds nothing habitable. It can never be reconstructed." Clay, on his first visit to Berlin in June, found "my exultation in victory was diminished as I witnessed this degradation of man".[7]

Yet within a week of arriving in the capital, Ulbricht's Moscow group and its workers had restored limited services for buses and trams, the district surface railway (the S-bahn) was working and some lines of the flooded underground railway (the U-bahn) had been pumped out and begun operation. For the ideological task of propaganda Radio Berlin had gone on the air again, and two newspapers had begun publication: the *Berliner Zeitung* and a Soviet Army publication, the *Täglische Rundschau*. Small shops had reopened to sell the very limited stores of food and guards had been posted at depots to prevent looting; by 15 May ration cards had been printed. While army engineers struggled to repair electricity and gas supplies, standpipes were set up in the streets to provide buckets of water for the weary, grimy queues of Berliners. On 26 May there was enough order and normality for the Berlin Philharmonic to give its first post-war concert. All in all it was a remarkable achievement.

Most impressive of all was the speed with which a new Berlin administration was created. It was in place by 17 May. The principle on which it was based was brazenly but privately expressed by Ulbricht: "It's got to look democratic, but we must have everything in our control." At the head of the Magistrat, the eighteen-man Berlin executive, a figurehead was appointed as Mayor – Dr Arthur Werner. His anti-Nazi record and innate decency made him publicly acceptable; his lack of any political convictions or personal assertiveness meant he was no threat to the Soviet authorities. His deputy, Karl Maron, on the other hand was a member of the Ulbricht group and had been a Communist émigré in Moscow since the '30s. Several departmental positions were held by non-political experts: for example an eminent surgeon was in charge of public health, an architect was to deal with housing. But seven other departments were given to Communists and of these Education and Personnel were to be run by members of the Moscow group. The same process of camouflaging Party officials with specialists and political neutrals was applied to the local governments of the twenty Berlin Bezirke or boroughs. The structure of Party control was finally capped in June by the appointment as Chief of Police of Colonel Paul Markgraf, fresh from political training in a Soviet POW camp since his capture at Stalingrad. The machinery for running the whole of Berlin – the three western sectors included – had been designed to ensure a prevailing Communist influence and, through it, Soviet control.[8]

With so much accomplished, Marshal Zhukov could now confidently allow the western forces into the capital. He claimed to have "cleared land mines" from the roads through his Zone; in fact he had dug a political pit in Berlin. The western Powers obligingly fell straight into it. On 11 July the four Military Commandants met for the first time in the Allied Kommandatura and without any western discussion, let alone objection, they signed a decree, drafted by the Russians, accepting and legitimising "all existing regulations and ordinances". As a result, they were now harnessed by Soviet ideological decisions which had pre-empted true quadripartite government. The western Powers were blinkered too: they preferred not to notice the almost derisive way in which they had been hoaxed, and to persist in the fallacious belief that they could win Soviet good faith by demonstrating belief in Soviet good intentions. There were practical considerations mixed with their naïveté: given the appalling state in which they had found Germany, they could see no other option but to struggle for four-Power unity at any cost to tackle the enormity of their problems.

For Berliners, on the other hand, the experience of the last two and a half months, during which the Red Army took and held Berlin, had been a trauma which damaged irreparably their relations with the Russians and with the Communist Party. The final assault on their city had been devastating. At least 300,000 Russians and 100,000 Berliners were killed in the last weeks, and no one could count the German military dead. The stench of putrefying corpses lingered for months beneath the twenty-five million cubic metres of rubble. Yet it was not the horror of war which hardened Berliners against their invaders. It was the nightmare of debauchery, looting and havoc which followed once the guns were silent. Little girls, young women, grandmothers were raped. Hundreds died of wounds because there were no hospitals to treat them or of venereal diseases for which there was no penicillin. Watches were snatched from their owners or hacked off with the hand if resistance was offered. Day and night, carpets, china and glass were looted; furniture and paintings were smashed or burned by drunken soldiers.

Stalin was puzzled that anyone should complain "if a soldier who has crossed thousands of kilometres through blood and fire and earth has fun with a woman or takes some trifles". The Red Army authorities made no attempt to discipline their brutal hordes – the bacchanalia was seen as justifiable revenge for German barbarity in the Soviet Union for years on end. Indeed, the Red Army engaged in its own carefully organised and deliberate rapine: stripping Berlin of anything and everything which might be used in the Soviet Union to repair the destruction of Nazi invasion and occupation. Russian troops raided factories and removed their machinery, stocks, raw materials, blueprints; if they found good engineers or research scientists, they took them too. They tore out electrical fittings, telephones, wash basins, filing cabinets and piled them on to trains for despatch to the Soviet Union where the engines and rolling stock would be kept as well as their contents. Having transported their booty home, the Soviet Military Administration sent the lines on which it had travelled – by the end of 1945 over half of all East German railways were single track. No one stopped to consider whether all this rail equipment would fit Soviet gauge; nor was there any mechanism for distributing or making use of the captured goods – for years, overland travellers to Moscow would pass mountains of German industrial equipment, crumpled and rusting by the wayside.

The Soviet Union paid dearly for what it took so freely. When a young member of the Moscow group expressed horror at the scenes of wholesale pillage in Berlin in May and June 1945, a political commissar told him: "This will cost us a million roubles a day. Political roubles." The depredations of the Soviet soldiers did, as he prophesied, ensure that Berliners would forever oppose them and their local sympathisers.[9]

For the moment, however, Berliners were in no state to take sides actively. They were totally absorbed in a desperate struggle for survival. Through the autumn of 1945 and the bitter winter which followed they fought against starvation and cold. The official rations could seldom be met, thanks to the destruction of agriculture and transport, and people were driven to barter for black-market food with their last remaining personal possessions. Foreign visitors were shocked to see Berliners slowly stumbling across streets in front of oncoming traffic – they were, in fact, too hungry and exhausted to move out of the way; their children were riddled with rickets. There was little or no work to be had: the German civil service had been Berlin's major employer but it no longer existed; industry had been wrecked by the Red Army's invasion and looting and now had no coal to start up again. The population was living in rubble: in damp cellars or in roofless rooms tented with a sheet, shivering in the dark, coughing with TB, and sniffing the foul air compounded of mildew, blocked drains and rotting flesh. It was the time they called Stunde Null – Zero Hour – when everything had stopped dead. Whether or not anything would ever start again and, if so, in what direction it would move was out of German hands. It was up to the four Powers to decide.

Berlin's misery reflected the destitution in the whole of Germany. Most cities had been shattered by air attack and artillery bombardment: 53 per cent of all buildings in Hamburg were reduced to rubble, only 44,000 out of 177,000 houses still stood in Frankfurt; Dresden and Stuttgart were in ashes after firestorms. A British official driving across the country in the early weeks after the Nazi surrender decided that "Everything which modern man considers necessary to the maintenance of life in a civilised society had disappeared. There was no governmental authority, no police. No trains, trams or cars; no factories working, no postal service, no telephones, no newspapers, no banks. No shop was open and it would have been impossible to buy a loaf of bread, a glass of beer or an aspirin." The roads were potholed by shells, railways contorted by bombs, river bridges lying in the water and blocking the barge routes. As a consequence, what little food was produced could not be distributed; the few factories still intact could not get raw materials or fuel to start work.[10]

Even without transport, however, Germans were on the move, trudging across the country with suitcases, or a few possessions bundled on handcarts or bicycles. They were city dwellers who had fled to the countryside to escape the bombing and now had no homes to go back to, or people from eastern Germany who had fled before the advancing Red Army and were afraid to return to Soviet occupation. With them traipsed Displaced Persons – mainly those who had been brought by the

Nazis to Germany to work as forced labourers and could not or would not go back to the Russian-held East – there were over two million of them in the American Zone alone. They were joined by millions more refugees from east Europe. Many of these were racial Germans whose families had lived in the Slav lands for hundreds of years. It had been decreed at Potsdam that they could be deported together with the hated new settlers who had arrived in the wake of the German armies. The rest were exiles from former German territory east of the rivers Oder and Neisse. This area had been handed to Poland by Stalin, without any consultation with his western allies, while the Soviet Union absorbed East Prussia. In so doing, the Soviet Union had dared to impose two frontier adjustments in advance of a peace settlement and carried out a unilateral dismemberment of Germany. Still, even faced with such provocation, the western Powers were not prepared to face a war with the Soviet Union having just ended one with Germany. After a weak splutter of protest, they were content with a clause in their Potsdam communiqué which put the Oder-Neisse territory "under Polish administration" until a "final settlement". They might as well have set the date at the Greek Kalends.

It is impossible to estimate with any accuracy how many people this decision added to the drifting, homeless masses in Germany in 1945 and 1946. Given the collapse of administration, no proper figures were compiled. One guess is that by 1950 a total of 7,978,000 refugees had arrived in West Germany. They were a distressing burden on an already shattered land; they would ultimately be an incalculable economic asset as the labour force which rebuilt it. Already they served as political indicators: a high proportion of them preferred to stay in the West. The story of the events that led to the building and the collapse of the Berlin Wall has refugees as its leitmotiv.[11]

For the moment, however, refugees were simply seen as extra mouths to feed – and Germany was frighteningly short of food. Agriculture was neglected during the war when the populace lived off what was looted from occupied Europe; there was now no fertiliser, and no chemicals or coal to start production. The country could not afford to import the 30 per cent of food on which it always relied in peacetime. By United Nations calculation, an adult needed to consume 2,650 calories a day. In the western zones of Germany in late 1945 and early 1946 the best that could be provided was 1,500 calories. Conditions were rather better in the Soviet Zone where officials, intellectuals and manual labourers were guaranteed 2,485 calories a day, but those categorised as "useless" – that is to say the old, the unemployed and the politically incorrect – were lucky to get 1,248. In March 1946 west zonal rations had to be cut even though the British and

Americans were importing food at their own expense – what the British Chancellor of the Exchequer called "paying reparations to the Germans". No wonder that TB was rife, typhus and dysentery endemic, and that miners in the Ruhr who used to produce 1,547 tons of coal per shift in 1938 were now only averaging 711.

Clearly it was not just a humane duty to feed the Germans. It was also in the interests of the occupying Powers to do so. As General Clay put it: "there is no choice between becoming a Communist on 1,500 calories and a believer in democracy on 1,000 calories". German diseases could spread to allied troops, German coal and industry were essential to rebuild devastated Europe, and it was difficult enough to denazify and demilitarise without also having to deal with hunger marches in spring 1946 and a strike of Ruhr miners for food. Yet the Allied Control Council could agree on no quadripartite policies for agriculture or food distribution: the Russians refused to pool resources or accept a joint export–import programme so that food could be bought from abroad. According to the agreement of the four Powers at the Potsdam Conference, Germany was to be run by the Allied Control Council as a single economic unit and to be administered by German departments acting under its close supervision. But from the very first meeting of the four Military Governors in Berlin on 20 July 1945, the ACC was castrated by the veto built in to its constitution.

It was the French not the Russians who first used that veto consistently and destructively. They could not forget that France had been invaded by Germany three times since 1870 nor forgive the recent humiliating and vicious occupation by the Germans. They were now determined to prevent a resurgence of German military power and to secure a strong eastern frontier by detaching from Germany the Saar and the Rhineland. They were ready to hold up all ACC business until they achieved their aims. So in 1945 the French blocked the creation of a central German transport agency or indeed any German administrative department and they prevented the federation of trades unions and the formation of national political parties.

By a terrible irony, almost the only common policies the ACC devised made the situation worse. In March 1946 it accepted the recommendation of an international commission on reparations and fixed the overall level of German industrial output at half that of 1938, with a total ban on the manufacture of armaments and building of aircraft and ships, and a limit on steel production to about a third of pre-war output. For the moment the diktat was pure fantasy – industry was incapable of reaching even the low level set – but it was still a harsh settlement, smacking of vengeance and bordering on Morgenthau's plan for pastoralisation. In the longer term, it was economic nonsense: ignoring Europe's need for German exports and preventing Germany from earning enough to buy food. It certainly was in contradiction to the allied requirement for reparations. At the Potsdam Conference it had been agreed that each occupation power would take reparations from its own zone. At first they came from dismantling armaments factories then, once the Level of Industry Plan was in operation, from any surplus productive capacity. In recognition of the dreadful losses the Soviet Union had suffered in the war, it had also been decided that the USSR would receive a further 15 per cent of all industrial equipment dismantled in the West in exchange for raw materials from the Soviet Zone, and another 10 per cent without counter-deliveries. No final total had been fixed. While politicians argued about it, the Russians simply stripped their zone without rendering any account and took deliveries from the west without payment in raw materials. In the absence of an overall economic policy, the four occupying Powers were plucking a goose which might one day lay golden eggs and letting it die slowly of hunger and cold.

Faced with this dangerous and self-destructive situation, the Military Governor of the American Zone, General Lucius D. Clay, called in May 1946 for Germany to be treated as a single economic unit with shared resources and sufficient exports to buy food. Yet again the Russians refused to cooperate, and Clay's patience snapped. He sent no more reparations from the American Zone and stopped dismantling "until the economic unity on which reparations are based has been achieved". He furthermore warned Washington that currency reform was essential for the revival of German industry and trade: inflation which had been drifting steadily upward since before the war was now galloping, thanks to liberal Soviet use of captured Reichsmark printing plates to pay their occupation costs.

The Soviet authorities in Germany were unmoved by Clay's protests and new tough measures. Rather than work for economic unity they forged ahead in creating a separate system for their Zone. They took control of the banks, and impounded all gold, silver, foreign currency and valuables on deposit. Not content with removing about 45 per cent of all industrial equipment as reparations (the total was around 8 per cent in the western zones) they also took reparations from current production, including the entire output of the East German uranium mines. Having reduced their zone's productivity to 42 per cent of its 1936 level, they then grouped up to a third of the industrial concerns into SAGs – Soviet Limited Companies, two-thirds of whose products were sent to the Soviet Union with transport costs paid by the East Germans. By spring 1948 these SAGs employed about a fifth of the entire labour force. Similar Soviet methods were applied to agriculture. First the Russians took over Nazi and former State property, then the estates of the Prussian landowning aristocracy, and finally any land in excess of a hundred hectare holding. A third of all confiscated land was collectivised. The rest, however, was distributed to small farmers – a popular move, of course, but an agricultural disaster, since there were now too many smallholdings for efficient production. That, indeed, was probably the intention: poor farmers would be driven to join collectives.

The Russians found it more difficult to establish a political grip on their Zone. After a campaign of coaxing and bullying, all the zonal parties were forced to join the Communists in April 1946 in a new Socialist Unity Party of Germany – the SED. It fared badly in the Soviet Zone elections that autumn and failed to get a majority in any of the five eastern Länder (or provinces). After that, authorities would permit only a single list of candidates in any election; opposition was abolished. The big stumbling block to Soviet political ambitions, however, remained Berlin. Here the local branches of the democratic socialist party, the SPD, resisted all pressures to join the SED. On 31 March 1946 they held a referendum in the city on the issue of party merger. This, for the first time, drew the western allies and the Soviet authorities into open political confrontation. The western Commandants were persuaded to provide newsprint for the SPD and guards for West Berlin polling stations; the Russians arrested SPD speakers in their sector, allowed their police to beat up SPD activists and finally closed the Soviet Sector polling booths. Even so, of those able to vote 82 per cent came out against party merger and the Berlin SPD was saved. In the Berlin municipal election in October 1946 the Russians and German Communists used old tactics of intimidation and physical violence and added new inducements such as distribution of free food and cutting the electricity supply to the western sectors. To no avail: the new city Assembly had 63 SPD members, 29 Christian Democrats and 12 Liberals; the SED won only 26 seats.

Berliners in all sectors were proud of the democratic stand they had made. The experience had stirred them out of political apathy and confirmed their loathing for the Soviet authorities and their German Communist henchmen. The lesson they drew from it was to look to the West for support: to national party organisations in the allied zones and to the western occupation forces. In the middle of the Soviet Zone there was now a city divided not just by the occupation authorities but at the political grass roots, and determined to build up an alternative to the Soviet system. Berlin was also on the fault line in the seismic rending of Germany and Europe.

For as the Soviet Zone increasingly diverged from any shared occupation assumptions, so too the western zones branched off into separate development, driven less by ideological imperative than by the urgent need to stop the disastrous drift into starvation and misery and to provide German materials to rebuild Europe.

The impetus to "go it alone" came from the Americans. On 11 July 1946 the US Secretary of State, James Byrnes, told the three other occupying Powers that, pending uniform quadripartite policies for Germany, he was "ready to enter into an agreement with any other zone for the treatment of the two zones as an economic unit". The Soviet Union, of course, made no response. Nor did France, for whom any prospect of German revival still seemed a threat to her security. The British, on the other hand, agreed to economic union with the American Zone. But Bizonal fusion seemed to have come too late. During the frozen winter of 1946–47, over a thousand Berliners died of cold, 40,000 others were treated for hypothermia and more deaths than births were recorded in the city. The meagre ration in the western zones fell to 900 calories a day, in most areas there was electricity for only a few hours a week, and in every city there were hunger marches and deaths from starvation and cold – all in spite of huge food and fuel deliveries from Britain and the United States. Ex-President Herbert Hoover warned Washington that the food deliveries must be increased immediately "if we want peace, if we want to preserve the safety and health of our army of occupation and if we want to save the expense of an ever larger military force to preserve order". Not least, he pointed out, "The productivity of Europe cannot be restored without the restoration of Germany as a contributor."

In spring 1947, the American and British Military Governors agreed that economic fusion did not go far enough to revive the life of their zones. German cooperation and expertise had to be exploited. So in May – with a repeated invitation to the Russians and French to join in zonal integration – they set up a German Economic Council with representatives from all their Länder to take charge of economics, finance, transport, food and agriculture. In July they revised the Level of Industry quotas to nearly 75 per cent of the pre-war level and with emphasis given to exports. From August coal production was entrusted to German management under allied supervision. None of these measures could brake the disastrous economic decline. By autumn 1947 Bizonal industrial production was barely 47 per cent of its 1936 total, only half the pre-war output of coal was being mined, rations were seldom 1,000 calories a day; an anguished occupation official knew that the western zones were "living from ship to ship" of food aid. The Americans and British fired one of the few remaining shots in their depleted locker: they recommended independent German political institutions to complement the new economic structures and foster a German will to fight for reconstruction. The two Military Governors of the Bizone insisted that their policy was merely a remedy for economic malady, and that it permitted Soviet participation whenever wished. The SMA (Soviet Military Administration) recognised the political lurch to a separate west German state and responded in kind. They, too, set up a German Economic Commission for their Zone.

Clearly quadripartite government of Germany had become meaningless and the split between the western and eastern zones was becoming institutionalised. The West was developing on parliamentary and capitalist lines and the East into a single-party state with nationalised means of production. A sudden stream of refugees arriving in western Germany from the Soviet Zone was a vote between the two systems. The prospects were alarming: two rival power blocs confronting each other across the German divide and Berlin a potential battleground.

Perhaps the collapse of wartime aims and the breakdown of the peacetime coalition in Germany could have been averted had the four Powers been able to reach any agreement at the level of heads of government. In fact the Potsdam conference in 1945 was their last meeting for ten years. In between times they handed responsibility for Germany and a post-war settlement to their Foreign Ministers. A series of meetings of the Council of Foreign Ministers (CFM) from 1945 to 1947 merely exacerbated the growing antagonism between governments. There was stalemate on all the basic issues. The Soviet Union adamantly blocked any progress by demanding $20 billion of reparations and a share in four-Power administration of the Ruhr. The French played off both sides in the hope of a favourable settlement of the Saar and Rhineland until the Moscow meeting in 1947 when Russians would give them no more backing. Thereafter France threw in her hand with the West and began negotiations for a Trizone in Germany – to a volley of Soviet accusations that the western Powers were turning their zones into a base "to take over Europe". Each CFM had rapidly descended into acrimony and had closed in sterility. No one expressed disappointment when the final meeting in London from November to December 1947 adjourned without fixing a date for another.

By then this façade of four-Power unity had long been unable to conceal the harsh reality of two hostile blocs in a divided Europe. As the Red Army advanced into Germany in 1945 it positioned troops in all the countries of eastern Europe. In its wake, the Soviet Union built up Communist parties, fostered them in elections, and finally supported their seizure of power. By late 1947 Rumania, Bulgaria and Hungary were one-party states and the democratic leader of Poland had been forced to leave the country, in

February 1948 Czechoslovakia would be taken over by the Communists. In a speech at Fulton, Missouri in March 1946, Winston Churchill had warned that the Russians had set up an Iron Curtain across the Continent. Their ambitions, in his opinion, would not be satisfied with the absorption of eastern Europe; the Russians did not want war but they did want "the fruits of war and the indefinite expansion of their power and doctrines". US President Harry S. Truman had by then lost his early belief that he could "do business" with the Kremlin and abandoned hope of Soviet collaboration: "I'm tired of babying the Soviets," he exploded.

On the most sympathetic of interpretations, the Russians had created a buffer zone along their western frontier to give permanent security against German attack. By a more sceptical or ideological analysis they had carried out their Marxist-Leninist duty to world revolution. The western Powers finally decided that the Russians were more interested in expansion than security when the Soviet Union supported the Communists in the Greek Civil War from September 1946 and began to increase their influence in Turkey. In March 1947 President Truman told the US Congress: "It must be the policy of the United States to support free peoples who are resisting attempted subjugation by armed minorities or outside pressure." His Doctrine was a gauntlet thrown down to the Soviet Union.

The United States had not yet, however, abandoned all hope of Soviet cooperation in Europe: if they could not win it, perhaps they could buy it. General George Marshall, Byrne's successor as US Secretary of State, saw at first hand the helpless misery of Europe and the Soviet Union in the spring of 1947 and was aghast. On 5 June he announced his Plan for American aid to any state "willing to assist in the tasks of recovery". He was at pains to emphasise that this assistance was "directed not against any country or doctrine, but against hunger, poverty, desperation and chaos". His munificent offer was seized on eagerly by the west European states; it was denounced by the Soviet Union as a weapon of imperialist expansion and turned down flat – not just on its own behalf but that of all the Soviet satellites of eastern Europe.

This was one of the major decisions of post-war Europe and the repercussions would be felt for more than two generations. Thanks to Marshall Aid, the west European states now had the hope of prosperity and a chance to preserve free, democratic institutions under the protection of the United States; the eastern states had been denied a sorely needed transfusion of capital, cut off from the liberal, parliamentary West, and even more tightly bound by Moscow's control and the closed market of the Soviet bloc. The political division of Europe was doubly underlined by this economic split. "This really is the birth of the western bloc," whispered the

British Foreign Secretary Ernest Bevin, at a conference to decide how Marshall Aid would be deployed; the Soviet bloc set up Cominform in September 1947 "to take the lead in resisting the plans of imperialist expansion and aggression". And the difference was deeply scored across Germany. The western zones and sectors were included in the European Recovery Programme. They had a chance to revive, thanks to the aid and the developing markets of the West; the Soviet Zone would remain the milch-cow of the Russians.

The demarcation line of divided Europe ran through Berlin. As the western sectors of the city became a showcase for capitalism and democracy, could the Soviet Union tolerate this advertisement for alternatives in the centre of its zone of occupation? From the end of 1947 western observers thought not. Bevin warned that the Russians would soon apply pressure in the city: the western presence was "fatal to any plans which they may have for the political assimilation of the Eastern Zone". He was uncomfortably aware that any attempt to "squeeze us out by direct pressure on our communications or by cutting off our supplies in Berlin would be very risky and might even lead to war". Yet as the American ambassador in Moscow pointed out: to "think in terms of appeasing the Russians in order to maintain our position in Berlin seems to me to ignore what experience in dealing with [the] Soviet government should have taught us".

In spite of the alarming certainty that an attack on Berlin was inevitable the western allies were not deterred from pursuing their contentious policies in their zones of Germany. As Clay was well aware: "Appeasement of [the] USSR will continue the present unsatisfactory administration of Bizonal Germany and make economic reconstruction difficult if not impossible." Reconstruction was vital: a public opinion poll in the British Zone in January 1948 revealed that 46 per cent of the inhabitants believed that "starvation and wrecking the economy" were the deliberate objectives of allied occupation (though in the British Sector of Berlin only 19 per cent of respondents took that view and 44 per cent reckoned the allied aim was "building democracy and fighting communism"). Overhauling the administrations and staffing them with Germans now seemed more urgent if good use were to be made of Marshall Aid.[12]

So in January 1948 the American and British authorities in the Bizone recommended that the German Economic Council be given the right to levy taxes and that an elected Legislative Council and a High Court be established. West German politicians were frightened by the prospect of a nascent government and by the reduced chances of a united nation.

Soviet-controlled newspapers gave ominous warnings that such flagrant violation of the Potsdam agreement on running Germany as a single unit must lead to changes in the running of Berlin. To bring home that message, the Soviet military drew attention to the precarious foothold of the western Powers in the city: they held up western trains bound for Berlin or turned them back at the border of the Soviet Zone.

Still undeterred, the governments of the United States, Britain and France decided to hold a conference in London on the future of Germany. They invited Belgium, Holland and Luxembourg to take part, but emphasised their will to continue with separate west German development by excluding the Soviet Union. On the agenda were all the issues thought most necessary to revive Germany, but also most likely to inflame the Russians: French merger with the Bizone, west European control of the coal and steel of the Ruhr, and the setting up of a German government. The Communist coup in Prague in February edged these same six western states into discussing other matters. In March they signed the Treaty of Brussels, promising mutual assistance against any armed aggression, and they began talks with the Americans and Canadians on extending that union into an Atlantic pact.

The Russians again reminded the western Powers of their vulnerability in Berlin, this time by interfering with German civilian traffic across the Soviet Zone. Freight for the city dropped to a quarter of its usual total, and food was soon in short supply. The moment it became clear that the London talks would reach agreement on a German constituent assembly to draw up a constitution for a West German state, the Soviet Union replaced warnings with a body blow. On 20 March 1948 the Soviet Military Governor announced to his western colleagues in Berlin that the Allied Control Council "no longer exists as an organ of government". He walked out of the ACC and ended quadripartite government of Germany.

In the three months that followed, the Soviet occupation authorities gradually tightened a noose around Berlin. Allied access to the city was interrupted by insistence on examining individual travel documents of every car or train passenger; western supplies were not allowed through unless each item had a separate Russian permit; rail traffic was turned back when western military guards refused to let Soviet soldiers on board to inspect travellers' papers and remove German passengers. A stranglehold was put on German traffic: coal barges with cargoes for Berlin were tied up awaiting "new Soviet transit regulations"; food lorries were held up for days on end while drivers applied for "new special permits" and their meat and vegetables rotted before they were inspected at Soviet checkpoints. In the city's factories goods piled up for lack of transport to the western zones and future production was threatened by shortage of raw materials. All the while, Berlin politicians with known western connections were kidnapped and taken to the Soviet Sector – forty-nine of them from the American Sector alone in March and April; Soviet Zone politicians who tried to keep contact with West German headquarters were threatened with loss of their homes and had their ration cards downgraded.

The crisis culminated in June 1948 when three strands of western policy were woven together. First the London talks agreed that a West German constitution would be drawn up. Then on 11 June the US Senate approved the principle of American association with European defence pacts. The Soviet Commandant walked out of the Berlin Kommandatura and ended four-Power administration of the city. Finally, on 18 June the western Powers announced currency reform in their zones: the inflated Reichsmark was to be replaced immediately with a new West mark, the Deutschmark.

That was the last straw for the Russians. They themselves issued a new East mark and commanded that it should be the sole legal tender for the whole of Berlin. When the City Assembly met on 23 June to back Mayor Ernst Reuter's call for a united city under quadripartite control with both currencies in circulation, a mob of SED (the Socialist Unity Party of Germany) and Communist trade unionists howled down the debate and beat up members as they tried to leave. And in the early minutes of 24 June the SMA stopped all traffic in and out of the western sectors and cut their electricity supply. West Berlin, with an allied garrison of 12,000 men, was under siege by a force of 300,000 Soviet troops. Two and a half million Berliners in the western sectors were hostages; the price of their survival was a western ransom – the abandonment of all the policies for West Germany and western Europe which would mean collapse into political and economic disaster. The only alternative seemed to be a new world war, with Berlin as the flashpoint.

No one at all expected the western sectors to hold out for more than a few weeks under the Berlin Blockade. They depended on 12,000 tons of supplies a day, brought along the one road and one railway from the western zones; even for bare subsistence, they needed 4,500 tons. There were, however, stores of food for thirty-six days and coal for forty-five. That gave the western Powers a month to find a diplomatic settlement with the Russians – yet in four years since the war negotiation with them had achieved nothing.

There was perhaps one way to gain a little more time for talking: an airlift. But that seemed little better than a counsel of despair. In the whole of Germany the British had only six transport aircraft – Dakotas; the

Americans had a hundred of their equivalent – the C-47. Each aircraft could carry merely two and a half tons. They could not fly round the clock, because they would have to be serviced, and they would be grounded by bad weather. Their route to Berlin crossed 120 miles of Soviet-controlled eastern Germany and was confined to the three air corridors which had been allocated to the western Powers by the Soviet Union in 1946. Each corridor was just twenty miles wide; they converged on Berlin where there were only two short runways for landing. The air transport experts of the United States and Britain were unanimous: it was impossible to supply the western sectors by air. The United States Air Force thought the scheme folly: a "diversion from planning for the war which might well develop from the current crisis" and a misuse of aircraft which would then be needed anywhere in the world. President Truman's Chief of Staff warned that an airlift was, in itself, "a dangerous enterprise" and could well "spark military conflict" with the Soviet Union; the British Chiefs of Staff agreed that anything but quiet diplomatic activity "would almost certainly lead to an incident and the opening of World War III".

The air force professionals, however, were overruled by the politicians. First Ernest Bevin, the British Foreign Secretary, then Harry Truman, the President of the United States, decided that an airlift must be set up and they would commit every available aircraft to it. They knew they could not supply the western sectors indefinitely nor provide an acceptable standard of living, but they calculated that every hour would strain Soviet determination to maintain the Blockade, every day give a chance to try negotiation. They knew that they were risking war but backed their hunch that the Soviet Union was no more willing than they were to face renewed fighting and destruction. They were certain that if the western Powers were driven out of Berlin the embryonic recovery of western Germany would be aborted and hopes for European reconstruction would die. They were intent on staying in Berlin: Bevin told the House of Commons that Britain could not "abandon those stout-hearted Berlin democrats who were refusing to bow to Soviet pressure"; Truman decided that the United States was "going to stay – period", and Marshall added "we are not going to be coerced." Britain and America would refuse all concessions over currency, constitutions or the Ruhr, but they were well aware that their right to stay now depended on Berliners' willingness to endure suffering.

The West staked everything on the Airlift and they won – but only just. It took from June to September 1948 before the basic 4,500 tons a day could be delivered to Berlin. During that time there was filthy weather and a desperate shortage of aircraft, let alone the machinery and tools to keep them airworthy; there were no proper procedures to control take-offs and landings or movement along the air corridors; there were too few dispatch airfields, little or no connection between them and the west German roads and railways which delivered the goods, and the runways in Berlin were too short and were cracking up under the heavy traffic; world stocks of dehydrated food (which was lightweight and took up less room in the holds) had been stripped and factories had still not geared up to provide new supplies; there was not enough capacity to carry the minimum amount of coal needed in the western sectors, not even an adequate supply of bags to pack it in (dust corroded aircraft controls and electric connections) or lashings to stop it shifting during a flight (so it upset the trim of an aircraft and could well cause a crash). By September Clay knew "we are not quite holding our own". Even after only a couple of months of siege, the average Berliner was 8.5 pounds underweight and struggling along on 1,600 calories a day; the British Military Commandant warned that it was "highly improbable that the western sectors could hold out through a winter on this basis" and that given yet more hunger, dark and fear the people "would prefer to have the Russians".

At last, in October, big capacious American C-54s began to arrive and brought a brief spurt of hope that they could carry enough to sustain life in the western sectors. (A young pilot asked: "Will the C-54 ever replace sex?") Yet it was January 1949 before there were enough heavy transport aircraft plus the organisation and supplies to lift 5,500 tons a day and guarantee a daily ration of merely 1,500 calories. Berlin only survived that winter thanks to a meteorological freak: there was little frost or snow and clear visibility for three months so that every aircraft that could fly packed supplies into the city round the clock.

And, in the final analysis, the success of the Airlift and victory over the Soviet Blockade was a triumph of Berliners' morale: if the people had not found the endurance to stand up to privation, the western allies would have been obliged to hand over their sectors to the Russians. Berliners' courage never wavered. "Faith", said a taxi driver, "came by our ears": as long as they heard the steady drone of allied aircraft they could fight on. They withstood a year of siege – the Blockade which began in June 1948 was finally lifted in May 1949. They never tasted fresh fruit or vegetables; they clogged their tonsils with dried potatoes (and Berliners love a real potato). They had only four hours of electricity a day, so if power came on in the middle of the night that was when the cooking, washing and ironing had to be done; they shivered in front of twig fires but refused to chop down the city's trees (Berliners love their woods as much as their potatoes). They darned socks by the light of a candle stump; turned the collars and cuffs on shirts for the umpteenth time; cut bands of cloth from old dresses and stitched them on to the bottom of skirts for growing children; made wooden clogs because there were no nails or leather to repair shoes; and they had their teeth filled by dentists who worked by candlelight with foot-pedalled drills. They laughed, mordant Berlin laughter: "Have a cup of Blumen-kaffee" – coffee so thin you could see the flower at the bottom of the cup; "Things could be much worse. Think if the Americans were blockading us and the Russians were running the Airlift".

Through the dark, cold, frightening months, West Berliners resisted any form of pressure to surrender. They refused Soviet offers of rations. They fought off repeated attacks on their democratic institutions. In August the City Assembly, which met in the Soviet Sector, was invaded by Com-munist agitators; in September it was besieged for over twenty-four hours by a mob backed by Soviet Zone police. City officials worked with Soviet officers at their desks; their phones were cut off, their staffs sacked; they were threatened with loss of home and ration card; some were kidnapped, others were interrogated by East Sector police night after night, several were slapped into solitary confinement for weeks at a stretch. Until December they clung on to their posts in the East and to the principle of a single administration for a united city. Then, one by one, departments moved to the western sectors taking their files, desks and typewriters with them. When the city's university – on Unter den Linden in the Soviet Sector – could no longer maintain freedom of thought and scholarship against a relentless Soviet campaign of "purging" liberal teachers and compulsory lectures in Marxist dialectics, the students moved west too. They took their books and laboratory equipment stuffed into their overcoats and trousers, and in two rooms they founded the Free Uni-versity.

In response to every assault, freedom-loving Berliners came out on to the streets in hundreds of thousands to demonstrate that they would stand for their rights and would not waver. Their beloved mayor, Ernst Reuter, spoke for them when he told General Clay in the early days of the Blockade that the western Powers could leave if they wished but Berliners would fight to the end. He put their feelings into words when he told a mass meeting that Berliners would "build a dam against which the red tide would break in vain". He transformed their misery into a battle cry when he said "The struggle for Berlin is a struggle for the freedom of the world." The world heard the cry and took sides.

By April 1949 the Airlift could carry nearly 8,000 tons a day and was obviously expanding. Stalin, ever the realist, faced the facts. The Blockade of Berlin was lifted on 11 May. The city was now sharply divided – not as a symbol of four-Power occupation as intended in 1945, and not for temporary administrative convenience, but as a reflection of two rival power blocs. The mood was noticeably altered too. East Berliners remained apathetic and resentful; West Berliners had been politicised by the siege, had grown in pride and now regarded the western Powers not as invaders but as allies. One thing remained the same: access to Berlin from the West was still vulnerable. The Soviet Union, in the formal agreement to lift the Blockade, which was signed in Paris in June 1949, had guaranteed unimpeded access, but had conceded no extra roads or railways. Few people had confidence in these paper promises and they had just experienced the ease with which the Russians could cut off the city.

Conspicuous changes had taken place in Germany, too, during the Blockade. On 8 May the Parliamentary Council had approved the Basic Law – a constitution for the western Länder which joined them in the Federal German Republic where Germans would run their own affairs and the three Military Governors would hand residual powers to civilian High Commissioners. The Basic Law had been drawn up reluctantly by the West German politicians: it was a painful admission that a united Germany was now postponed. It had been carefully drafted so that the federal structure could include the five eastern Länder some day; it called on the entire German nation "to accomplish by free determination the unity and freedom of Germany". The hope that the division of Germany would only be temporary was emphasised in the choice of a capital for the Federal Republic: Bonn – provincial, geographically peripheral and deficient in facilities – was merely a stop gap for a provisional state. The aim was a united nation with its capital in Berlin.

That, of course, had been the declared intention of all the four Powers in 1945. Yet in the four years that followed they had created a situation in which it was no longer possible, and the projected post-war settlement had collapsed. In its place was a very different makeshift settlement which would, in fact, last for forty years because no one could find an alternative. The coalition against the Nazis, which should have drawn up a treaty with Germany and rearranged Europe to prevent future aggression, had disintegrated. With the split, Germany had been partitioned – in the East, the German Democratic Republic (the GDR) was proclaimed in October 1949 – and Europe divided into two blocs which threatened the peace. The Soviet Blockade of Berlin had acted as a catalyst in bringing the United States and Canada into alliance with the European states who signed the Brussels treaty. On 4 May 1949 they entered into the North Atlantic Pact, promising mutual assistance in case of armed attack on any member – and "on the occupying forces of any party in Europe". This clause made Germany an inevitable battleground in hostilities between NATO and the Soviet Union. It turned Berlin into the front-line city of the Cold War.

2

Abnormal Normality

===▶●◀===

"Berlin", a Foreign Office official once said, "resembles a bridal trousseau, with two of almost everything". From 1949 there were two separate Kommandaturas in the city: one for the Soviet sector, the other for the three western sectors where the only reminder of quadripartite government was a portrait of the last Soviet Military Commandant. There were two currencies and two local governments – East and the West; two police forces, two fire and ambulance services, two gas and electricity suppliers. In 1950 and 1951 the West Berlin mayor, Ernst Reuter, tried to reunite the two sides and called for free all-city elections. The East Berlin Magistrat refused to take part. When a United Nations commission came to investigate the question in 1952 it was refused admission to the Soviet Sector. By then, Berliners had learned to live with two disparate systems.[1]

At first this made little difference to many aspects of their lives. In 1949, despite the divisions, Berlin was still an open city. Trams, buses, the U-bahn (the underground railway) and the S-bahn (surface rail) ran across sector borders without hindrance; tickets could be bought in either West or East marks. The telephone system connected both sides of the city and bills were paid in the currency of the subscriber's sector. There were plenty of official crossing points in and out of East Berlin, with few barriers and little checking of documents. No one was obliged to use an official crossing point anyway: the Soviet Sector border was sometimes marked only by a white line painted across the road and frequently not indicated at all, especially across the tracts of rubble in this war-ravaged city. So Berliners lived, worked, and moved where they chose. West Berliners went east for hair cuts, tailoring, shoe repairs – services were cheap if you paid in West marks, which were worth up to five times the number of East marks on the black-market exchange. East Berliners went west for better quality clothes and shoes, and for more varied food than they found in local shops.* They enjoyed the cinema and theatre in West Berlin: expensive, given the rate of exchange, but free of the political hectoring which spoiled the fun of a night out in the East. West Berliners, on the other hand, appreciated the brilliance of acting and production by Bertolt Brecht's Berliner Ensemble, and ignored the Communist message.

Travel in and out of the city was not difficult, and it came as a relief to West Berliners who sometimes felt claustrophobic on their "island" in the Soviet Zone. Pan Am, British European Airways and Air France ran regular flights along the allied air corridors. West German drivers could use twelve crossing points to the city and were free to travel in any direction, though they were often stopped by the police or military in the Soviet Zone for document checks. West Berliners used many more crossings into the Zone, official and unofficial. Train services were good and people who travelled on a western military train were spared the irksome Soviet headcounts and scrutiny of papers at checkpoints: they sat back while the train commander handed over passenger lists and argued about the details with the Russian soldier on the platform. Thanks to the agreement on lifting the Blockade which the Soviet government had signed in Paris in June 1949, Berlin now received sixteen freight trains a day and an unlimited number of lorries and barges. Transporting freight, however, was a wearisome and exasperating business: drivers and skippers were held up for hours or even days if the Russians decided to question their waybills or cargoes.

Delays and sudden, almost capricious, changes in Soviet procedures at the checkpoints were a constant reminder of West Berlin's isolation and vulnerability. So too were the access arrangements for western troops and occupation officials. They had not changed since 1945: three air corridors, one railway line and one road – the Autobahn from Berlin to the Soviet Zone frontier at Marienborn, 120 miles without a café or a garage. A few lone voices had argued at the Paris Conference that western access must be renegotiated and derestricted while the Soviet Union was in a weak position thanks to the success of the Airlift. They met the same fate as the

---

* There was a doleful joke which could raise a smile in Berlin for forty years and more because it was always true. Q: How do you recognise an East Berliner? A: By his shoes and his sandwich.

original critics of the EAC's access arrangements in 1944. Their masters ignored them, and pursued a general settlement of Berlin's civilian communications at the expense of their own.

In Berlin itself, the western allies had to cope with the oddities of their hasty administrative partition of 1945. The occupation forces had drawn sector boundaries on maps and assumed they would avoid problems by following the lines of the old Bezirke (borough) limits. These, however, meandered and created small western enclaves which jutted into the Soviet Zone – reminders of bygone days when the city authorities owned farms in the countryside. The British Sector, for example, included a tiny settlement at Eiskeller: not much more than a few holiday cottages on the north west tip of the Spandau Forest. The Americans had Steinstücken: homes for about sixty families, a general store, and a sandy access path 1,200 metres long through Soviet Zone woods. Both enclaves could be bitten off and digested by the Soviet Zone if ever the Russians wished – unless the western Powers decided they were a good cause for a just war. The British Army barracks at Kladow was an even more peculiar anomaly. It was legally Soviet property but was let out on permanent lease. It was a source of innocent merriment for years. An official British report in 1954 chirpily described "the annual incident", "a traditional feature of Christmas time in Berlin". On 30 December, the Soviet Army announced that it would send a daily patrol through the barracks. Next morning a small Russian unit broke through the perimeter fence and grabbed three British soldiers. The British colonel immediately protested to Soviet headquarters at Karlshorst, and within hours the soldiers were released and the fence neatly repaired. No more Soviet patrols were seen until the next festive season. Such miniature dramas were a regular occurrence on the borders with the Soviet Sector and Zone; a welcome way to cheer the routine of garrison life and thoroughly enjoyed by both sides. Or that is how they were treated. Deep down, everyone knew they were evidence of a serious problem: the Russians were testing the western allies' determination to hold on to every inch of territory, and reminding them of the weakness of their garrisons should they attempt to fight for their rights.[2]

The Russians were also trying to shake West Berliners' confidence in the ability of the western Powers to protect them. That is one reason why they held tenaciously to two toeholds they had established in the British Sector in 1945 and been allowed to keep when western troops arrived in the city. Rundfunkhaus was a striking pre-war building faced with glazed burgundy bricks which housed the old studios of Berlin Radio. Soviet troops manned it, even during the Blockade, to the fury of West Berliners who wanted them expelled. The British always argued that forced evacuation of heavily armed men was dangerous and might escalate into something much nastier. Berliners thought that the attempt would be well worth a few British lives but doubted the Russians would put up much of a fight. Similarly they resented the presence of Russian troops at the Soviet War Memorial – known locally as "The Tomb of the Unknown Plunderer". This marble structure, made from slabs taken from Hitler's Chancellery and decorated by a real T-34 tank, stood in the Tiergarten just west of the Brandenburg Gate. Every day a Soviet detachment drove through the Gate and changed guard at the memorial with a good deal of high kicking and boot stamping. Every so often West Berliners would be maddened by the ceremonial reminder of Soviet invasion and occupation and then British patrols would be sent to guard the guards. The nonsense went on until 1990 – solemnly justified by the western allies as fulfilment of their four-Power agreements of 1945.

In reality, of course, quadripartite government and agreement were patently dead by 1949, though the four Powers still shared some vestigial duties because it suited them to maintain contact. For instance, they ran Spandau jail where seven Nazi leaders were imprisoned after being found guilty of war crimes by the Nuremberg Tribunal in 1946. Each Power took responsibility on a monthly rota for the cavernous building, and supervised at vast expense the dwindling group of increasingly elderly and infirm prisoners. (Even when only one remained – Rudolf Hess – the Soviet government refused to change the system or move to a cheaper jail.) Once a month the acting governor gave a lavish and liverish lunch to his colleagues, and handed on the command. At times when tensions between East and West ran high these occasions gave a rare chance to meet and pass hints and messages from one side to the other. In the Berlin Air Safety Centre, representatives of the four Powers worked together daily at a practical, less political level, exchanging information on flight plans for the civil and military aircraft in the three allied air corridors and on air movements in the twenty-mile safety zone around the city. Four men, with one office, a kitchen and a darts board continued to carry out their duties until 1990 on the ground floor of what was still called the Allied Control Building but was nothing more than a gloomy echoing edifice with 549 empty rooms, two or three of which were occasionally dusted for a quadripartite party.

Such social and administrative leftovers from four-Power occupation demonstrated that, as yet, neither side was willing to accept openly the permanent division of Germany. Furthermore, four-Power responsibility for Berlin, even when it had become a pallid shadow of cooperation, was piously invoked because it signified ultimate collective responsibility for the final post-war settlement of Europe. For the western allies, their very presence in the city was justified by its quadripartite status.

That is why in 1949 they struck out the sentences in the draft Basic Law which referred to Berlin as a Land, a province, of the Federal Republic: they would not permit the Federal government to claim the eastern sector and they were anxious to avoid a legal split of the city, which would destroy its unique standing and their own rights in it. The western Military Governors insisted that the city "shall possess none of the attributes of the twelfth Land" – a deliberately ambiguous phrase which might or might not mean that Berlin was a Land even though it had none of the characteristics of other Länder in the West German federation. To stress the city's special position they forbade standard representation of the western sectors in the Bonn parliament. Instead West Berlin was allowed to send eight (later twenty-two) delegates to the lower house, the Bundestag, and four to the upper chamber, the Bundesrat. They were entitled to take part in debates and sit on committees, but not to vote on legislation.

Similarly, the western Military Commandants suspended Article 1 of the West Berlin constitution, drafted in 1948, which called the city (the whole city) a Land and stated that all federal legislation applied there. They stipulated that federal laws would only apply in the western sectors if first adopted by a vote in the City Assembly and if not vetoed by their tripartite Kommandatura. In 1951 the Commandants speeded things up by conceding that federal legislation would be automatically valid in West Berlin within a month if passed under a covering law (a Mantelgesetz) and not rejected by the Assembly. They themselves would only use their veto in such matters as security, defence and civil aviation. The whole process was intentionally fuzzy and it grew incomprehensible as the volume of legislation increased over the years and those involved interpreted the details to suit their own needs. It had its comic side too, as when the West Berlin Statute Book adopted completely irrelevant regulations for wine-growing or the activities of North Sea pilots. The procedure was acceptable, however, because it worked. It was quick and avoided friction between the High Commissioners and the Bonn government and between the western Commandants and the Berlin Senate (the new thirteen-man city executive). It avoided naming the city a West German Land while actually giving the western sectors most of the "attributes" they needed; it preserved a role for the Commandants which justified a western presence. The Soviet authorities found it hard to prevent the insidious legislative tying of the western sectors to the Federal Republic, though they protested – sometimes successfully – when laws too blatantly contravened everyone's understanding of Berlin's quadripartite position.[3]

Once West Berlin was slotted into the legislative machinery of the Federal government, it was inevitably incorporated administratively. Federal courts had jurisdiction in the city, and civil and criminal appeals went to the higher court in Karlsruhe. Gradually from 1949 Federal agencies opened branches in the western sectors. By 1959 there were over thirty of them, ranging from offices for taxation, social security and labour matters to the Federal Statistics Office, the Archaeological Institute, the Patents Office and the Biological Institute for Agriculture and Forestry. Each office was like a flag staking Bonn's claim to the city; each was denounced by the Soviet authorities as a step to Federal take-over. The western Commandants publicly argued that every agency operated under their control so did not breach quadripartite agreements, while privately leaving them to get on with their business undisturbed. Occasionally they put their foot down when they feared the Russians would be provoked beyond endurance – for instance they vetoed a Federal instruction to arm all customs officials.

The first Federal agencies to open in West Berlin were all financial and they were essential for the sectors' preservation. The war had left the city in ruins and the Blockade had destroyed it economically. During the siege West Berlin survived on interest-free credits from the western Powers and zones and by overspending its budget. Prospects for financial recovery looked bleak indeed: no revenue would come in from the 400,000 unemployed, little if any from the pensioners who made up over a quarter of the population; industrial production was stuck at 20 per cent of its 1936 level and order books were blank. Yet by the end of 1949 several West German firms had been persuaded to resume production of radios and cars, and Siemens – historically the city's biggest employer after the civil service – had decided to rebuild some of its plants. Most importantly, Marshall Aid was in the pipeline and would be allocated for housebuilding, small as well as heavy industry, and public communications systems – all overdue investment which would also create jobs. The results soon showed promise, though they also indicated the depth of the economic trough: by 1954 West Berlin's output had risen to 70 per cent of its pre-war level and unemployment was down to 158,000. The western sectors' exports rose tenfold over the period and most of them went to West Germany – tying the not-quite Land more closely to the provisional Federal Republic and weaving interdependence. This was a process guaranteed to disturb the Russians. They knew, however, that they could cut West Berlin's road and rail links at will and its prosperity would vanish overnight, damaging that of the Federal Republic into the bargain.

There was a related reason for Soviet unease. Burgeoning western affluence was an all-too-obvious contrast to the economic depression and austerity of the Soviet Zone, the new German Democratic Republic. In 1936 (even if Berlin was excluded from the figures) it had produced half of all the country's machine tools, 33 per cent of vehicles, 82 per cent of office machinery; during the war it experienced a boom as factories moved there to escape western bombing. By 1949, however, plant had been stripped by the Soviet occupation forces, over 60 per cent of production was concentrated in badly managed state enterprises and two-thirds of output had to be exported to the USSR. Human resources were drained too: by 1953 about 10,000 physicists, engineers and technicians had signed "voluntary" contracts and gone with their families to the Soviet Union. All the essentials for recovery were lacking: the East Germans had no surpluses for export to pay for purchases abroad, no Marshall Aid or alternative finance; they had lost access to West German steel and had to pay through the nose for Polish coal and Soviet gas and oil.[4]

Political conditions in the GDR were equally dispiriting for the majority. The trappings of the state were those of national confidence and unity. Its 1949 constitution stated that it was adopted by "the German people", ignored the disagreeable fact of a divided nation and proclaimed "an indivisible democratic Republic". The East German state flew the same flag as the West: the red, gold and black bands of nineteenth-century nationalism (the compasses, hammer and corn wreath were not added until 1959). Nevertheless, patriotic decorations could not conceal the structure. This was a state run in obedience to directives from the Kremlin and it was not recognised outside the Soviet bloc. Nor could incessant propaganda about the "anti-Fascist democratic alliance" hide the reality of a one-party system where all key posts were held by Communists. The blossoming of this state and the withering of democracy were marked by the purge of the SED – the Socialist Unity Party – from 1948. Old SPD comrades were thrown out; "Trotskyists", "Titoists" and all who strayed from the ideological straight and extremely narrow path to Socialism were denounced and expelled. Anyone who had been in western exile or prisoner-of-war camp or who had relatives in the West became "politically suspect" and lost employment in the civil service and nationalised enterprises.

For a few inhabitants of the GDR, a restricted economy and a rigid polity were positively desirable. Old Communists who had been champing at the bit for years – in prison, concentration camp or abroad – raced down the course to true Socialism like steeplechasers: took the hurdles of double-speak, mismanagement and repression in their ideologically trained stride; relished the Party's whip and rein as expert guidance in the Marxist Stakes.

Young Party aspirants threw the energy and altruism of their age group into "building a better world" and, with the confidence of youth, believed they could make a better job of it than their parents. Like the older Party members they viewed the state and the outside world through a Communist prism: drab conditions, confiscations, new economic organisations were "necessary stages" towards a richer and fairer life; criticism of the Party and resistance to directives sprang from the "self-interest" of the few who prevented the well-being of the majority; Soviet occupation and asset stripping were a punishment for Nazi wickedness and compensation for the valiant struggle and suffering of the Soviet people. For Communists the present dismemberment of Germany was a check to chauvinism and an encouragement to international brotherhood; it repressed the German original sin of aggression and guaranteed world peace. Within the narrow confines of the GDR they felt they could work for a way of life in which goods were shared, no one was exploited, the poor and ill were cared for, and the state provided the necessities and decencies of life.

Such aims tapped a rich vein of idealism in non-Communists. Many people were prepared to accept present sacrifices and drawbacks in the hope that some Party promises would be fulfilled. Years of Nazi extremism had made it difficult to conceive of a spectrum of moderation – perhaps, they thought, Communism must be tolerated as the only alternative to Fascism; capitalism, after all, had supported and armed Hitler. There were those, too, for whom a Communist state offered freedom from guilt. In it they could be born again, repress memories of shooting women and children and herding queues into gas chambers, throw away their SS badges and start a new purifying life. Some might even join the Party: membership was certainly the best way to get privilege and promotion, and they did not have to believe all the slogans, just mouth them and do as they were told – quite like the old days, really.

For the vast majority of East Germans, however, all these political arguments had no interest or relevance. For them, the German Democratic Republic was simply the place where they happened to live. The state aroused no loyalty or respect, only fear. It had no legitimacy: the government was not elected on a free vote, it had no independence from the Kremlin, it would not survive for a week without the backing of 300,000 Soviet troops. They just had to put up with it and try to keep out of trouble. They told themselves: "You have to howl with the wolves if you want to stay alive", or "I'll be a little grey mouse in a dark corner where no one will see me". These people clung to their homes, familiar surroundings, family and friends. Sometimes they hoped that this regime, like the last, would be overthrown one day, perhaps with help from the West. For the most part they were glad if the daily struggle for food and warmth left them too tired to think about much else.[5]

Those who could not lump the GDR left. From 1949 to December 1951, 492,681 refugees arrived in the Federal Republic. A sprinkling still came from eastern Europe, but most were East Germans. Of these 150,000 had gone first to West Berlin. It was so easy to cross the sector borders, and anyone who travelled light and alone ran little risk of being questioned. They were a mixed bunch: militant anti-Communists; teachers who resented Party interference in education; businessmen and smallholders whose assets had been seized or who faced nationalisation; young men avoiding service in the People's Police or the uranium mines; Nazis hoping to hide in a new home under a new name; young and old looking for pay and pensions in Deutschmarks and a higher standard of living; parents who wanted their children's minds to grow through discussion not dialectic. Legally, they could stay in the western sectors only if they were officially recognised as in danger from political persecution; then they qualified for citizenship and full social and pension benefits. Over the period, 73,000 fell into this category of whom 18,500 were flown on to West Germany. It was difficult to sift through the mixed motives for seeking asylum and many refugees were not given official status but were allowed to stay all the same – living in camps, given occasional jobs clearing rubble, or finding casual, uninsured, work on building sites. Others were forced, or chose, to return to the GDR, but an uncountable number went to ground in West Berlin, lived off charity or their relatives, and sometimes contributed to the rising crime rate.

Refugees settled fairly easily into West Berlin: no language problems or great cultural shock. Their new neighbours accepted them, on the whole – they were "Germans, not foreigners". Berlin had always been an immigrant city. There is an old saying that true Berliners are not born there, they come from Pomerania or Saxony. But the sheer volume of arrivals was a financial and administrative headache for the West Berlin authorities. Refugees added to the unemployment figures and the housing shortage. Two hundred officials had to be appointed to cope with them. In autumn 1952 the Federal government took a lot of the strain. The Emergency Reception Law was extended to West Berlin and thereafter central government funded a camp to hold applicants and paid the air fares to the West for 80 per cent of those recognised as refugees.[6]

Once there the immigrants were distributed between the Länder of the FRG for resettlement, with much of the expense born by the Federal budget. The Bonn government had learned important lessons from the earliest refugees from eastern Europe. These had tended to congregate in large numbers in small areas, seeking comfort from each other's familiar dialects, cooking and ways of life. This had stirred resentment among the locals (West Germans did not have Berlin's experience of immigrants and often saw Germans from the East as foreigners) and created huge problems and expense for the few local governments responsible for finding houses, jobs, schools and medical care for the new arrivals. There had been a political danger too. These refugee groups expressed militant views about the fate of former German lands from which they had been driven and provoked Soviet accusations of intended aggression and reminders from the western High Commissioners that foreign policy was under allied control and a final settlement of Europe's frontiers would be made by the victorious coalition against Hitler.

Recent East German refugees, well scattered, caused no such difficulties. For a year or two they added to the FRG's housing shortage and pushed up unemployment figures to 10 per cent. From 1949, however, there was more and more money to throw at such social problems. West Germany was beginning its Economic Miracle – the magic result of currency reform, zonal fusion, Marshall Aid, higher ceilings for the Level of Industry Plan, careful fiscal and monetary policies to prevent inflation, to keep down export prices and restrain domestic consumption, and sheer hard work. West Germany's post-war disadvantages were transformed into industrial virtues. Thanks to allied dismantling, factories could re-equip with state of the art machinery; thanks to bombing, obsolete buildings were demolished and could be replaced by purpose-built structures. Refugees provided an endless supply of cheap labour. Since the Federal Republic was forbidden to make armaments or build ships, plant and skills were released for other manufacture. Given a stable currency and growing demand, agriculture revived. Better fed miners could keep up with the demand for coal and iron from domestic and West European consumers and what they earned from sales abroad bought food to top up home production. None of these economic wonders happened overnight, yet each year the increase of prosperity was perceptible. West Germans, unlike their East German cousins, could see that sacrifices paid dividends; they were confident that the recovery would continue and that its benefits would accrue to those who worked for them.

Presiding over the creation of this wealth and assurance was the hawk-like figure of the Federal Chancellor, Konrad Adenauer: still, alert and focused, with sharp eyes darting at the slightest political movement and constantly scanning the international horizon. He had been elected by the Bundestag in September 1949 by the narrowest of margins: one vote, his own. He revelled in that questionable, precarious start. It could in no way shake his total conviction that he had unique qualities and authority for his position.[7]

The man chosen to run the new-born state was already seventy-three years old when he took office; he had been formed by the nineteenth century. He was born in Cologne in 1876 and was brought up as a devout Catholic in a hard-working, disciplined home where there was little money and also, one suspects, little display of affection. His family could not afford to send him to university, so he worked for two years in a bank before winning a scholarship to study law. He then followed in his father's footsteps and became a middle-ranking public servant, as counsellor in the city government, before becoming mayor in 1917 – a post he held until removed from power by the Nazis in 1933. This long term of office undoubtedly strengthened his belief that he served the public weal rather than narrow party interests, and developed his taste for stability and authoritarianism. Years of life and work in the city of his birth also confirmed Adenauer as a Rhinelander: Catholic, west European, and resentful of Prussian centralism imposed by unification in 1871 on the historic freedoms of an ancient German confederation. As Mayor of Cologne, he was an ex officio member of the Prussian First Chamber, but he hated attending meetings in Berlin. "Europe", he once said, "stops at the Elbe", and he claimed that if obliged to travel to the capital he pulled down the blinds of his railway compartment at Magdeburg, "so that I did not have to see the steppes of Asia".

This was hyperbole, of course, but Adenauer's jibes expressed strong and enduring attitudes. For him, Berlin and the east of his country were indeed alien: Protestant, Prussian, and the heartland of Socialism; a pole drawing Germany towards the Slav lands from which Christian Europe had once been threatened by paganism and barbarism and where now lay the menace of atheism and Communism. When Bonn became the Federal capital in 1949, people said the choice was Adenauer's: he wanted to stay in his beloved house at Rhöndorf and look down on the Rhine. The decision, however, had not been his alone, and it pleased him for more than domestic reasons. He had insisted in an interview in *Die Welt* soon after the end of the war that the German capital should be sited "where Germany's windows are wide open to the West"; "whoever makes Berlin the new capital will be creating a new spiritual Prussia" and damning Germany forever in the eyes of the world.

It was an opinion with great appeal in the Federal Republic. People wanted to sweep their experience of Nazism under the carpet and make a fresh start. Bonn distanced them symbolically from their past and geo-graphically from Soviet expansionism. Many shared Adenauer's view that ties with the Atlantic alliance offered security and that membership of West European supra-national institutions would restrain their own worst instincts of rabid nationalism and aggression. The Social Democrats, on the other hand, bitterly complained that the Chancellor's policy of refusing any negotiation with the Soviet Union condemned East Germans to Soviet rule. Willy Brandt, a later Chancellor, put it that "opting for the West meant abandoning reunification until further notice". For Berliners Adenauer was Chancellor of a mere "Rheinbund", a narrowly defined, backward-looking Confederation on the Rhine. Nonetheless, enough West Germans were satisfied with mere lip service to the cause of national unity. Like Adenauer himself they could not forget the seventeen million East Germans living in the Soviet-dominated GDR, but they preferred not to incur the wrath of the Soviet Union or the suspicions of the West by striving on their behalf; they did not wish to hazard new-found prosperity and alliance or to restrict the pluralism of their state by compromise with Communism. The Chancellor told them to be satisfied for the time being with half a nation – half a loaf to be cast on western waters. This was certainly better than no bread, which was literally what they had had in 1945.

Adenauer could call for such sacrifices because he embodied Germans' recent experience: the destruction of two wars, the humiliation of defeat and international loathing, economic collapse and the failure of democracy, the temptations and disasters of Nazi dictatorship. West Germans trusted him to avoid such catastrophes and to build a framework in which they became decent citizens with some justifiable pride and acceptance by their European neighbours. Their Chancellor was a father figure, perhaps, but not an all-loving, all-forgiving Papa. He was stern, demanding and frequently contemptuous. He despised West Germans' sacrifice of ideals to materialism, but understood their fear of idealism which had been so easily perverted by Nazism and knew that material satisfaction would provide political stability. He mistrusted people's sudden conversion to democracy and spoke scathingly of the German love of a great leader, right or wrong. He told the story of being in a concentration camp (he had, in fact, never been in one, though he was interned twice) and asking his guard why he was working for the Nazis. "Because I am a German", was the reply. "There," said Adenauer, "you can't trust the Germans." Yet West Germans did not resent such criticism: they mistrusted themselves and felt more confident under the disciplines and chastisement which Adenauer imposed – an authoritarian certainly, but not a tyrant.

The Chancellor had a gift for communicating with his people simply and directly. He came from a humble background and never lost the common touch. His speeches were delivered in a high voice, with a Rhineland accent, and in a monotone which came as a relief to listeners sickened by high-flown Nazi rhetoric. He conveyed a few basic ideas in homely, rather inelegant language. His arch-rival, the Social Democratic leader Kurt Schumacher, once sneered that Goethe had a vocabulary of 29,000 words but Adenauer had only 500. A woman colleague immediately retorted "if he had 200 more, he wouldn't use them. That is his strength." He also knew how to make an audience laugh – not with wit but by sarcasm and sharp thrusts below an opponent's belt. His jokes were earthy, often coarse, and they were relished. Though his manner and opinions smacked of a previous age, Adenauer was adept at using the political tools of the twentieth century. He cultivated the media with skill: press affairs were kept under his personal supervision in the Chancellor's own office, his frequent tea parties for foreign journalists were an essential element in his foreign policy. He was a conservative in his political views, yet his party, the Christian Democratic Union (CDU), was committed to social welfare and spreading some of the profits of capitalism to help the needy. Domestic policy was designed to weld all classes in the new state and, as Bismarck would have put it, to "taking the wind out of the sails" of the Social Democrats, the SPD.

Adenauer was wily and, as Willy Brandt well knew, he "thought more subtly than he spoke". Foreign politicians and diplomats were impressed by the speed with which he got to the nub of any problem, by the stamina with which he wore down opponents in negotiation. His face was striking: waxen skin stretched tightly across high cheekbones, a small raptor's beak between wide-set eyes. Everyone saw it as "Mongolian" or "Asiatic" – unfortunate adjectives for a man who, in his cups, once referred dismissively to the East Germans as "the Chinese". His features were the product of nature emphasised by accident: a car crash in 1917 when his driver had fallen asleep at the wheel had pushed up the cheeks and flattened the bridge of the nose. They perfectly suited his cunning and inscrutability. His bearing was dignified and assured, his back and shoulders were always parade-ground straight. Dean Acheson, President Truman's Secretary of State, who met Adenauer many times over the years, noted: "The control is absolute . . . He moves slowly, gestures sparingly, speaks quietly, smiles briefly, and chuckles rather than laughs when amused." The brief smile was usually ironical or malicious; the most contented chuckles were at the expense of others. Though Adenauer could show great kindness to his tiny inner circle, he had few intimates. He had been twice widowed. His affection was reserved for his grandchildren, the Rhine, wine and his roses.[8]

In 1949 the Chancellor had personal authority and political mastery in the Federal Republic but he did not have charge of many of the activities which characterise a sovereign state. The three Western Powers – the United States, Britain and France – still controlled foreign affairs, trade and exchange through the reserved powers of their High Commissioners who had taken over from the Military Governors in Germany and had the right to resume total authority if security or democracy were threatened. The Federal Republic had no army or nationally organised police force and was forbidden to manufacture goods classified as potential war matériel; its frontiers were ill-defined and awaited determination by others in a general peace settlement. West Germany had no Ministry of Foreign Affairs or even consulates abroad but, even so, Adenauer had a foreign policy. His aim was to gain a national voice, acceptance in the society of free nations, and integration in western institutions and alliances – all leading to full sovereignty.

He built on the solid foundations of a trusted currency and expanding trade in western Europe first by seizing an invitation in April 1950 to become an associate member of the Council of Europe, then by welcoming enthusiastically the idea of a European Coal and Steel Community put forward by the French Foreign Minister, Robert Schuman, in May. Meanwhile, he cultivated relations with the Western Powers – not in a subservient manner, for all Schumacher called him the "Chancellor of the Allies", but speaking on equal terms so as to win eventual equality. His message to them was that the FRG was a reliable ally, with a political and economic contribution to make. He played on western fears by emphasising the FRG's need for defence against the Soviet Union yet also suggested that West Germans could assist in the defence of Western Europe – at the political price of more freedom to manoeuvre abroad and run their own affairs at home. His big opportunity to establish a new role came with the outbreak of the Korean War.

When North Korea invaded South Korea on 24 June 1950, the attack projected a horrifying Asian image of troubling European problems. Korea, after all, had been divided like Germany since 1945 and had two opposed governments and systems (Communist in the North and capitalist in the South) each of which could call on a European bloc for aid. The invasion seemed to justify long-felt western fears of expansionist Communism and growing anxiety about the flimsiness of the defence of Western Europe. This had relied since the defeat of Hitler on the Atom Bomb – virtually an American monopoly. All the western allies had demobilised and disarmed since 1945 and had substituted a cheaper nuclear strategy for expensive conventional forces. In July 1949, however, the Soviet Union exploded its own Bomb and the West knew that, before long, first use of nuclear weapons would provoke instant, destructive Soviet retaliation. Even so, the western alliance was locked into its nuclear strategy: by 1951 NATO had barely eight divisions, and estimated (probably over-estimated) that they faced 175 Soviet divisions in Europe. Only the temporary nuclear superiority could redress that conventional imbalance. For the long term the United States was developing a Hydrogen Bomb and acquiring bases from which the US Strategic Air Force could launch nuclear strikes at the military and industrial centres of the USSR. For the immediate future, however, urgent action must be taken to build up conventional strength – not least because West Europe could not be left so feebly defended whilst American and allied efforts were concentrated in Korea.

An obvious way to stiffen western defence was with units from the FRG – the state in the front line of any European war, on whose protection other NATO countries were spending vast sums while it waxed fat with new-found prosperity. In September 1950 at the NATO Council meeting in New York, the United States recommended West German rearmament. Adenauer named his price: he would not accept "Foreign Legion" status in NATO; West Germans would be equal partners or remain non-combatants. He got it. On 19 September, the three western Powers agreed to end the state of war with Germany, recognised the FRG as the only legitimate German government with a right to speak for the German people in international affairs, and authorised Adenauer to establish a Ministry of Foreign Affairs and enter into diplomatic relations. There was a swift response from the Soviet bloc. On 20 October its Foreign Ministers, meeting in Prague, demanded a four-Power ban on the remilitarisation of Germany, an immediate peace treaty followed by the withdrawal of all occupation forces within a year of signing it, and the setting up of an all-German Constituent Assembly to draft a constitution for a united state.

This was a clear Soviet alarm bell. But was it intended to frighten the West or to indicate a Soviet wish to compromise? As so often with Soviet diplomacy, the strident tone suggested that reasonable negotiation was impossible. And one stipulation stuck in western gullets: Soviet insistence on equal representation for East and West Germans in the Constituent Assembly – an equal number of delegates for the GDR which had a third of the population of the FRG. The West drew the conclusion that the Soviet Union was only interested in retarding West European defence and West German independence. On that same assumption, the three Powers also rejected proposals in two Soviet Notes, on 3 November and 15 December, that a four-Power conference should discuss Germany and demilitarisation. They insisted that such matters could only be dealt with in the wider context of East–West relations and a European settlement. Perhaps they had missed an opportunity to open talks and to push their aims while the Soviet Union felt vulnerable.

The proposal to rearm the Federal Republic had come as a shock to many members of NATO, who had so recently been at war with Nazi Germany, but by October 1950 the French had found a way to calm their fears and save their money. The Pleven Plan (named after the French Prime Minister) proposed a European Defence Community, to which the West Germans would contribute units, and in which the forces of all members would have common uniforms, pay and training and serve under an integrated command. In 1951 negotiation on the EDC began in earnest, particular attention being paid to the nature and size of the West German contribution. Chancellor Adenauer made sure that the FRG gained from every stage in the discussions. In September 1951 the three western Powers agreed they would replace the Occupation Statute and discuss a new relationship. In the following February they were reminded that West German military support might save defence expenditure but would not come cheap: the Bonn parliament approved the principle of taking part in the EDC, but only as a sovereign and equal partner.

It is conceivable that events in Berlin in 1950 had no connection with these rapid political and military changes in the West, that they were just "the usual incidents" in the Soviet campaign of probing and seeing what they could get away with. Certainly that is how they were interpreted by the West. The British High Commissioner dismissed Soviet interference with military traffic on the Autobahn at the end of 1950 (checkpoint hold-ups and attempts to turn back allied cars with German drivers or passengers) as "minor vexations". No one saw special political significance in August 1951 when the East Germans closed all their city crossing points and put up road barriers in the Zone to stop their citizens visiting a World Youth Festival in West Berlin: this was standard practice whenever there was a major event in the western sectors. Never mind that 10,000 members of the East German youth movement (the FDJ) were allowed through the barricades to march on West Berlin and throw stones at the police in their own version of a youth festivity: they were soon dispersed with water cannon and the West Berlin government was much more worried by the sharp increase in the number of young East Germans who dodged the roadblocks and applied for asylum. The occupation of the American Sector settlement at Steinstücken by East German police on 18 October could be seen as just another instalment of the endless enclave saga. The inhabitants did not enjoy being told they must not use Deutschmarks, and they were put out when their postman was forbidden to collect and deliver letters, but after a week and an American protest the People's Police withdrew, the postman came back, and the West Berlin police moved in for a few days until everyone felt better.[9]

All these happenings, unimaginable in any other large modern city, were everyday occurrences in Berlin – people called the constant crises "Berliner Wetter", Berlin Weather. It is very likely, however, that Soviet obstruction of civilian traffic to and from Berlin in 1951 was something more: a deliberate attempt to influence developments in the western alliance and Bonn along the lines of the early stages of the Blockade of 1948. The hold-ups began in May when Soviet guards at the East Zone checkpoints demanded certificates of the origin of all materials in goods exported from West Berlin – allegedly to prevent illegal use of East German resources. Lorry drivers, backed by the western authorities, refused to comply. As a result, they could not get Soviet stamps on their waybills so could not drive to the FRG, and by July goods worth DM70 million were piled up in West Berlin. First the commercial airlines then the western Powers mounted airlifts to clear the backlog. The sense of impending siege of the western sectors intensified in September. The parcel post was blocked so packages had to be flown out by the allies. Several rail wagons a day were turned back by the Russians on the grounds that they were badly loaded. On 6 September the GDR announced heavy tolls for all West German registered vehicles crossing the Soviet Zone. West Berliners were incensed and called on the allies (in vain) for retaliatory measures such as tolls on the waterways through the western sectors.[10]

Meanwhile, the annual negotiations between the East and West Germans on the Interzonal Trade Agreement ground to a halt while both sides wrangled about the traffic interference, and the Russians refused to issue transit permits for barges – which left the western sectors short of coal. In response to western complaints about the delays, a Soviet spokesman put forward an argument little discussed at the time: that the regulation of traffic and all other Berlin problems should be handed to German authorities. This was undoubtedly an attempt to get recognition for the government of the GDR – a policy of growing importance in the crises of the coming years. For the moment it was not pursued, and suddenly Soviet pressure relaxed. By the end of the year, the trade and barge agreements had been signed, traffic seemed to be running fairly normally, the East Germans reduced their road tolls, and the western allies began to wind down their airlift having cleared most of the blocked goods and post.

Significantly, the West had not insisted on its demand that a clause guaranteeing freedom of all traffic should be written into the next Interzonal Trade Agreement. They had merely sent a letter to the Soviet authorities stressing that the allies must have free access. This was a weak stance at a time when Soviet interference could have been countered by an expanded airlift. It put the short-term aim of getting traffic moving above the longer-term vital principle of general access to maintain western presence and the survival of West Berlin through ties with the FRG. Ominously, at the end of 1951, thirteen of the fifty-five barriers erected by the East German police at city crossing points during the Youth Festival were still in place; sixty-three of the Soviet Zone roads which connected Berlin with the outside world were also closed. No one – ally or West Berliner – made much protest about this; they resigned themselves to using other routes. They took it for granted that normal life in this abnormal city involved adjusting to major inconvenience and occasionally turning a blind eye to flagrant Soviet breaches of agreement. It could well be argued that by so doing they handed the Soviet Union a knife for salami slicing. How many more closures could the Soviet authorities get away with? Would the Western Powers ever take a stand or a risk to defend the basic principles of occupation of the city – principles on which their own presence and the survival of the western sectors depended?[11]

In 1952 the complex components involved in the construction of western defence began to click into place. At a NATO conference in Lisbon in February, new force targets were set at fifty divisions and 4,000 aircraft – unrealistically high, as it turned out, but a strong and public commitment to rapid build-up. On 26 May, in the Bonn Convention, the Western Powers revoked the Occupation Statute and agreed to replace their High Commissioners in the Federal Republic with ambassadors. The next day the EDC treaty was signed in Paris and Britain, who had decided not to join, promised to keep four divisions and an air force on the Continent. Only formal ratification by member parliaments was now required before the Community could be established – and no one realised what a farce that process would be. On 25 July the European Coal and Steel Community was set up, weaving West Germany into the West European economy and sowing the seed of a Common Market. In November the United States exploded its first Hydrogen Bomb. There was every reason for the West to feel more confident and, indeed, more assertive. Viewed from Moscow, on the other hand, these developments were dismaying. They opened the prospect of Germany permanently divided with the FRG under arms and safe from Soviet intrusion within the western alliance; of secure democracies defended by growing armed forces and the American nuclear umbrella; of rapid West European economic growth with which the Soviet Union could not compete and which would be on daily show to East Germans in the shop windows of West Berlin.

On 10 March 1952 Stalin launched a major political offensive. He sent a Note to the United States, Britain and France proposing four-Power discussions on a peace treaty to be negotiated with the government of a united and sovereign Germany – a state with the right to defence forces, which guaranteed the freedom of speech, the press and religious worship and which permitted free activity by political parties. These were tempting concessions indeed. It did not take long to spot the hooks in the bait, however. Stalin stated that Germany's eastern frontier would be the Oder-Neisse Line, claiming deceitfully that this had been "agreed" at Potsdam; he wanted all occupation troops withdrawn within a year of a treaty and Germany to be neutral and forbidden to enter any military alliance, which would create a vacuum waiting to be filled by East or West and would knock EDC plans on the head; and he called for a ban on all organisations "hostile to democracy and to the cause of peace" – a woolly phrase read in the West as a clause to justify Soviet meddling in German affairs on the slightest pretext. The Western Powers were leery about even discussing Stalin's proposals. They preferred to get on with their West European arrangements. An exchange of exploratory Notes with Moscow finally brought the West to a sticking point: the Soviet Union would not concede secret free elections under UN supervision for an all-German government – under four-Power supervision maybe, but everyone had seen Soviet "supervision" of elections in Berlin in 1948. Stalin's agenda was turned down flat; no talks took place.

Did the West miss a historic opportunity in 1952? Could the Cold War have been ended and the costly, frightening arms race averted? Many Soviet officials interviewed in the early 1990s thought so. Stalin's Note, they said, expressed a genuine wish for a German and European settlement; it was an indication of his fears which could have been exploited to extract further concessions; it put the most generous terms the West would ever be offered. But even if their interpretation is correct, it is not enough to blame the Western Powers alone for missing a chance. It also has to be said that the March Note was an example of poor Soviet diplomacy: timed to look nothing more than an attempt to wreck the Bonn and Paris agreements, and framed in a manner which increased western anxieties about a weak Germany vulnerable to Soviet pressure. As far as the western allies were concerned Stalin himself had missed more than one historic opportunity – by turning down the American offer of a mutual security pact in 1946, stymieing every Council of Foreign Ministers meeting from 1945 to 1948, and refusing Marshall Aid. They themselves now had an opportunity to build up their own prosperity and defence, and they had no intention of being diverted from it.[12]

In any case, the West was in no mood to trust in the honesty of Stalin's intentions. The Soviet authorities and the East Germans were conducting a bullying campaign in Berlin throughout 1952 that caused considerable alarm. Unlike the events of 1950 and 1951, this fresh assault on the western sectors could not be dismissed as "the usual incidents"; it was all too reminiscent of the attempt in 1948 and 1949 to prevent West German economic and political development, and for many months there were fears it might develop into a full-scale blockade. It is perhaps a pity that on this occasion the West did not display the robust reaction that had preserved their sectors during the previous siege.

By January 1952, traffic to and from West Berlin was flowing so smoothly that British and Americans assumed they could soon stop their airlift from the western sectors, which was now down to two aircraft a day. Then suddenly there were troubling signs that all was not well. At the end of January the Russians held up barges for cargo inspection; six of them were stuck for two weeks or more. Next, in the first week of February only half the lorries from West Berlin to the Federal Republic had their waybills stamped. The Bonn government wanted to take a stand: trade with the GDR must go on to a barter basis until traffic restrictions were lifted. The Western Powers argued that if the West Germans took such a provocative line, they must also take on the costs of an inevitable expansion of the airlift. While the debate went on, another blow to West Berlin was struck, this time in the city itself. On the night of 4–5 March the electricity supplied from the eastern to the western sectors was cut – a nasty reminder of June 1948 when West Berlin was plunged into darkness and the Blockade began.[13]

In itself this loss of current was not a major problem. It amounted to only an eighth of West Berlin consumption and this could easily be provided in the western sectors by the new generating station built during the Blockade with components delivered by the Airlift. Indeed, many West Berliners thought the break in supply offered a delightful chance to irritate the Russians. They wanted to disconnect their own supply to Rundfunkhaus and to the Soviet War Memorial (for which the Russians had not paid the bills for years), but the western Commandants could not bring themselves to touch these sacred quadripartite cows. Possibly there was no immediate link between the electricity cuts and outside developments. Many West Berliners and allies thought that the cuts were, as a British official put it, "part of a long-term plan to sever all connection between the western sectors and the surrounding territory" – to increase West Berlin's sense of isolation and to reduce the allies' repertoire of retaliation should the western sectors come under pressure or attack. Back in July 1951 the East Germans had opened an Outer Railway Ring, south of Berlin, to bring trains from Saxony and Thuringia straight into East Berlin without touching the western sectors; since then they had spent enormous sums on a northern rail bypass, an Autobahn Ring, a north-western canal, and a new water supply from Potsdam.[14]

Seen in the context of interference with traffic earlier in the year, however, the electricity cuts had to be taken seriously. And lest anyone doubt that the western sectors were under pressure, further blows were struck in May 1952. Six of the road connections between the western zones and the East (one half of all major roads) were closed by the Soviet authorities. The Russians then announced that a five-kilometre prohibited area would be established along the whole border between the GDR and the Federal Republic; troops began to seal 1,381 kilometres of the frontier with wire and mines – a "Wall" between the two halves of Germany. On 26 May, the telephone service connecting West Berlin with East Berlin and East Germany went dead, and several of the circuits with the FRG were cut. Three days later one hundred streets leading from East to West Berlin were barricaded.[15]

It was perfectly clear that these frightening moves against the western sectors' links with the outside world were part of a co-ordinated plan and were staged to coincide with the final signing of the Bonn and Paris agreements. Disturbing though they were, the Western Powers feared there was worse to come while the two agreements were ratified. When the US Secretary of State, Dean Acheson, met the British Foreign Secretary Anthony Eden and the French Foreign Minister Robert Schuman in Paris on 28 May, he pleaded for allied agreement to respond to each and every Soviet move with prompt and appropriate counter measures. He called for an immediate protest about communications to be made directly by the three High Commissioners to the Soviet authorities without wasting time on consultations with the capitals; should that fail to get the recent restrictions lifted, then he recommended that the whole matter should be taken up by the western governments with the Kremlin. Acheson more than most knew the effectiveness of resolute action faced with siege measures in Berlin: during the Blockade he had worked closely with the British Foreign Secretary, Ernest Bevin, and seen the success of a combination of airlift, diplomatic pressure, and readiness to take risks to uphold western rights and Berliners' freedoms. That past experience and victory, however, did not impress his colleagues now. Eden, in particular, took the view that the "virtual independence" of the Soviet Sector made retaliation "difficult", that protest to Moscow would allow the Russians in Germany "to wash their hands" of the whole business – in other words he did not want to do anything at all.[16]

The one thing agreed on in Paris was that a full-scale airlift could be reconstituted if need be. On 29 May the Federal government promised to give the West Berlin Senate DM500,000 to cover its share of the cost. Assessments in June suggested that the western sectors had a six-month supply of necessities already stockpiled and that this could be topped up with a daily 8,600 tons brought in by air. The British were short of aircraft in Germany but could lift 300 tons a day with their present capacity and, given adequate warning, would charter civilian transporters. They checked ground facilities (most of the dispatch airfields from the 1948 Airlift were in their Zone) to see what updating was required for a major operation and decided that the Germans would have to help to run them. Then they sat back with the agreeable thought that the US Air Force in Germany "could carry enough to keep Berlin going indefinitely at an austere standard without any assistance from us at all". In the first two weeks in June it looked as if the Americans would have to do just that. Soviet interference with the Autobahn traffic increased noticeably and on 12, 13 and 14 June not a single waybill was endorsed.[17]

No Berlin crisis, of course, could be worthy of the name without an enclave incident. This time it was the turn of Eiskeller in the British Sector. On 1 June Soviet troops blocked the track which led to the tip of the peninsula where twenty-nine West Berliners lived and others came to holiday cabins. They dug a ditch across the path, then six men and a corporal manned it and told residents they must have a Soviet pass to come and go. The British military hesitated to take direct action for a few days (no one was sure how many more Soviet soldiers lurked beyond the ditch) but they gave pleasure to West Berliners by blocking Soviet access to Rundfunkhaus. Finally on 9 June a British detachment advanced up the path and staged not so much an assault as a comedy. The officer in charge drove off the track and bogged down in a drainage channel. Forgetting that his job was to drive the Russians out, he allowed them to pull him out. For a moment the Eiskeller inhabitants thought he was being arrested. It might have been more glorious if he had been. In the event, the Russians rendered a double service: righted the car and left the enclave. In return, the siege of Rundfunkhaus was lifted. (In 1956 the West Berlin authorities negotiated a full Soviet withdrawal.)[18]

Amusing though this Eiskeller drama had been, it cannot detract from the true seriousness of the mini-blockade of 1952. The Soviet Union had demonstrated yet again the vulnerability of the western sectors and the ease with which they could be made pawns in a wider international game. Furthermore, most of the measures taken over the months remained permanently in force: the closed roads were never opened, the cut telephones were never connected, and the fortification of the East German frontier became even more intense. In July the East Germans made further spiteful moves to increase the discomforts and constraints of the western sectors. They announced that from now on all trams must stop at the Soviet Sector boundary; tickets for a cross-sector journey were still valid, but passengers must disembark and change vehicle. West Berliners were also forbidden to visit the small properties they owned on the perimeter of the city, just inside the Soviet Zone. There were 40,000 of these: small allotments where flowers and vegetables were grown and where families stayed for a night or two to escape from hot, cramped flats and enjoy the fresh air and countryside. Worse, and pitiably, West Berliners were told they must apply for a special permit to visit eleven cemeteries just outside the city boundary – that meant a trip to an East Berlin police station, waiting in queues and filling in forms, for those who wanted to tend one of the 10,000 family graves.[19]

Throughout these sorry months the Western Powers had taken no effective counter measures. No airlift was mounted to demonstrate western determination and superior resources, and remind the Soviet Union of the failure of the 1948–9 Blockade. Instead innumerable protest letters were sent by the Commandants and High Commissioners to their Soviet counterparts. Many of them went unanswered; none produced a result. Protest was a bankrupted activity. The Americans had suggested a "barge war": interfering with the GDR's canal traffic as a reprisal for the blocking of West Berlin's communications. Neither the French nor the British supported the idea. Firm united action seemed beyond the wit or will of the West. To be fair, the allies were very aware that assertiveness could lead to conflict and danger to Berlin and the rest of Europe. It would be no easy matter for three democracies to convince their citizens that the closure of a few Berlin streets justified the risk of nuclear war. The Western Powers also had a tendency to think they must reserve strong measures for graver situations. It could be argued, to the contrary, that firm action would pre-empt major crises. It might further be claimed that the West's resigned acceptance of recent Soviet moves in Berlin gave the Kremlin confidence to make more: the salami knife had been sharpened for them.[20]

The mini-blockade of 1952 gave the Soviet Union a loss on the international roundabout: it did not break the West European pro-cesses. On the other hand it produced definite Soviet gains on the Berlin swings: huge increases in the constraints for Berliners, East and West, and proofs that the ratchet of restriction could be applied at will. These gains, however, had been achieved at a price – in people. In May 5,000 East Germans crossed into West Berlin; in June 7,000; in July over 10,000. The sharp increase in refugee numbers was clearly a response to the crossing closures: people were getting out while they could and Berlin offered the easiest escape route as the state border was increasingly wired. The influx was a terrible burden for the West Berlin city government. There was already a huge backlog of refugees to be flown to West Germany. By August at least 40,000 East Germans were waiting for registration and nearly all of them were dependent on financial and material assistance from the city: 22,000 had found private accommodation, but 17,000 were in camps and living in squalor; existing buildings had run out of space and many families were sleeping in the open. The Red Cross and Senate issued appeals for blankets, crockery, cutlery and medical supplies. The Allied Kommandatura immediately responded with money to buy basic necessities, and the Americans and French released bedding and cooking equipment from their military stores. British officials in Berlin were anxious to follow suit: "the need is very serious", they cabled to London. For Whitehall, however, the prime need was always to hand the bill to someone else: Rhine Army asked the War Office for permission to open stores; the War Office would only give it if the Foreign Office bore the costs of depreciation (£2,700, they gasped); the Foreign Office threw the problem to the Treasury, who failed to find anyone else to pass it on to. It was late October before British help was available. By then many refugee families were housed in bombed out ruins, living in filth and with no heat or protection from the elements as winter drew in.[21]

Stories of dirt and cold could not deter East Germans determined to leave for the West. Far more potent for them was the daily news of the sealing of the GDR frontier. The original wire was being strengthened with high fences; homes and businesses inside the five-kilometre prohibited zone were being demolished and mines laid in the wasteland. By February 1953 only two crossing points for pedestrians were open along the entire outer border between the Soviet Zone and West Berlin; the rest had been blocked by trenches or mounds of earth. Would-be refugees rushed to squeeze through the remaining gaps in central Berlin. In January 1953 25,340 crossed; in February 39,962; in March 48,724. Among them were East Berliners who worked in the western sectors and whose ration books had been confiscated by their city government. Fewer people crossed in April – only 33,647, but the figure soared again in May to 41,938.

For once the refugee barometer was not responding to an abrupt change in the political climate. On 3 March 1953 Stalin had died. It was said in Imperial Russia that the people wept at the death of a Tsar: they feared his heir would be worse. Few shed a tear for Stalin: surely anyone else would be better. East Germans, indeed, felt a tingle of hope. Reading between the lines of newspaper editorials and noting the minute variations in the vocabulary of political speeches, they sensed that Stalin's successor, Malenkov, was not in full command and that the Kremlin's reins would slacken as rivals jockeyed for position. Party member and officials began to hear rumours that Ulbricht and his comrades were under threat from their only supporters – the Soviet government. In later years, evidence surfaced to substantiate these stories. It seems that the death of Stalin uncorked debate on Europe and Germany. There were those in the Kremlin who argued for buying détente by selling the GDR government down the river: agreeing to unification on something close to western terms and letting the East German Party go into opposition. One of the most vociferous, it is said, was the dreaded secret police chief, Lavrenti Beria. According to the memoirs of Andrei Gromyko, there was a Politburo meeting in Moscow at which Malenkov talked of the importance of the GDR in Soviet policy and Beria snarled "The GDR? What does it amount to, the GDR? It's not even a real state. It's only kept in being by Soviet troops, even if we do call it the German Democratic Republic." If correctly reported, this was a crude expression of the disagreeable reality which few others dared to put into words. Beria's attitude to the "first workers' and farmers' state" was certainly used to warrant his arrest and execution later in the year.[22]

Such debates took place in the utmost secrecy. A wider public became aware of a shift in Soviet policy and the danger for Ulbricht's government in August 1953 when, in reply to western soundings, the Russians agreed to a four-Power Foreign Ministers' meeting to discuss a German treaty, a provisional government for a united state and even free elections. The East German youth leader, Erich Honecker, was aghast at the very mention of elections. "We shall fight and if the worst comes to the worst we shall go under fighting like heroes," he nobly cried. The story went round that whenever he came into his office in a bad temper, he had dreamt the night before that Adenauer had accepted the Soviet proposals. East German politicians well knew that if there was reunification on democratic terms, they would not have an office to go to; they would be lucky to get a job stoking a prison boiler.[23]

Their regime was secured, however, and, paradoxically, as a result of one of its greatest crises: the East Berlin Rising. This began when, under pressure from the Kremlin, the Ulbricht government made painful concessions, intended to defuse opposition at home and build up respectability abroad.

The New Course, announced in July 1953, promised to lessen discrimination against independent farmers and craftsmen, withdraw recent price rises, increase the food ration, reduce ideological pressures on teachers and intellectuals, release 4,000 political prisoners and pardon émigrés if they returned to the GDR. One vital inducement was left out of the bribe: there was to be no slackening in the latest work norms on which wages were assessed and which amounted to 30 per cent more work for no more money. The patience of the overworked and underpaid snapped. On 15 July labourers on East Berlin building sites downed tools. Next day they were joined by thousands of other workers in a protest march. On 17 July there were strikes all over the country and calls for free elections by secret ballot. It was an alarming moment for the state: insurrection at the very time when the Soviet Union seemed ready to abandon them. In the event, the rising saved them: Moscow could hardly permit the example of successful political agitation in their bloc; Soviet tanks suppressed the revolt.

The protesters had won a reduction of their work norms and a tribute from the people of West Berlin – the main road through the Tiergarten was renamed 17 July Street. More significantly they had learned a bitter lesson: they could not look to the West for liberation from the Soviet Union. The Western Powers had sent no help, had made no attempt to remove barricades which blocked every crossing from the Soviet Sector, and had turned down Mayor Reuter's plea for a show of armed strength and talks with the Soviet Commandant. Their passivity implied that East Berlin was solely a Russian charge, that for all the talk of "quadripartitism" the West felt no responsibility there. It was a stance which the Kremlin could interpret as encouragement to take further unilateral action in the Soviet sphere. The crisis had tightened the grip of the Ulbricht regime: shattered the spirits of the opposition, given an excuse for a stringent purge of critics and non-enthusiasts in the Party, and convinced Moscow that the GDR must be bound even more tightly into its political, economic and military strategy. At the 1955 Party Plenum Ulbricht had the confidence to reject the New Course.

Nineteen fifty-three was the year of high refugee tide. Over the twelve months, 331,390 East Germans crossed to the West; the GDR had lost the equivalent of the population of a major city. The new fortified frontier would restrict the flood for years to come. Yet Berlin was still a relatively open city. There were fewer sector crossings and more East German guards, but the brave or desperate could slip through. There are stories that at about this time Erich Honecker complained to his deputy that the Berlin gap should be sealed; that an official from the East German State Planning Commission smuggled to the West government papers including studies for erecting barriers and watchtowers along the Soviet sector border but that Bonn did not take them seriously. In fact it was obvious to any observer that the East German government must be weighing the political risk of closing its Berlin border against the economic problem of loss of manpower, and wondering if the Soviet Union would give permission. Closure was a great temptation, but as a British official put it, "This, it appears, is a step which, much though they might like to do so, they are still not prepared to take." Not yet.[24]

It was assumed that 1954 would be the year when the last pieces of a western settlement would slot into position. Everyone was waiting for French ratification of the Paris Agreement on the EDC. Paris society was riven by the issue of German rearmament; passions raged, a French diplomat noted, on a Dreyfus scale and opponents and proponents of a German army could not be invited to the same dinner party. West Berlin braced itself for a violent Soviet reaction. East Germans poured out to the West in the expectation that a new Berlin crisis would close all the sector crossings again. Moscow and the western capitals made final diplomatic attempts to find some agreement on the problems of Germany and security.[25]

On 25 January the Foreign Ministers of the four Powers met in Berlin to see if they could reconcile their views on these two fundamental matters. It was clear from the start that there was no wish to meet half way: the two sides could not even agree on where to hold their meetings, so they took place in the old Allied Control Council building in the American Sector and at the Soviet Embassy in East Berlin on alternate days. The East Germans assisted the talks by reconnecting two telephone cables across the city – but only for as long as the conference lasted. They made every effort to impress their western visitors: there was plenty of shiny paint on buildings along the route to the Soviet embassy, almost desirable goods appeared in shop windows, the great new Stalinallee with its two miles of shops, restaurants and workers' flats trumpeted Socialist achievement and concern for welfare, and no one yet knew how soon its plastic facings would turn yellow and drop off. Yet westerners were most struck by the drabness and oppressive atmosphere of East Berlin, by the silence and poor clothing of its people – a startling contrast with the lights and relative comfort of West Berlin. A few steps either way across the Soviet Sector border and one entered a different world.

The proposals of East and West at the conference were worlds apart too. Anthony Eden, the British Foreign Secretary, put forward a plan for reunification by stages: starting with free and externally supervised elections throughout the country, followed by the drafting of a constitution by an all-German government which would negotiate a peace treaty and be free to join or reject alliances with other powers. On the other hand, his Soviet counterpart, Vyacheslav Molotov, refused to consider elections until there was a German government made up of representatives of both states. True to his revolutionary alias ("Molotov" means "hammer") he banged out the same insistent phrase which a French visitor to the last three days of the talks reckoned he heard twenty-five times: "We are opposed to the EDC which is provoking a rebirth of German militarism."[26]

When the Berlin conference broke up on 18 February having found no common ground, the Western Powers were more determined than ever to persist with the Bonn and Paris agreements. They were not deflected by a startling suggestion from Moscow on 31 March that the Soviet Union should join NATO: it seemed nothing more than a diversionary tactic. They were, however, shattered on 30 August when the French National Assembly voted against ratification of the plan for the EDC. After five years of negotiations, amendments, and rebuffs to Soviet approaches, the West was now faced with the wreck of all its plans. Diplomatic sophistry by Eden salvaged them. At his suggestion the Federal Republic was made a full member of the West European Union and could then be invited to join NATO, though forbidden to manufacture atomic, biological or chemical weapons, or to use force in the pursuit of reunification and the modification of its borders. The arrangement fell far short of a truly European army: there would be no integration of national forces and the United States would continue to provide the nuclear shield. It was far better than nothing. European aspirations and energies were now to be channelled into a Common Market instead. Adenauer was well satisfied with a role and voice in West Europe.

Moscow kept up the struggle to prevent the new agreements coming into force. In October 1954 the Soviet Union offered to reconsider the question of free elections in Germany; in January 1955 it said that the only block to free elections and reunification was West German entry into NATO; next month it suggested that all the western plans could be put into effect if a four-Power conference were held and West German rearmament cancelled. All to no avail. So the Soviet Union made the best of its bad job and set up the Warsaw Pact in May (though as yet no other bloc power was willing to give the East Germans full membership), then gave "sovereignty" to the GDR in September (a fine word which did not disguise the fact that the Kremlin's grip was as tight as ever). To give an impression of East German independence the Soviet deputy Foreign Minister Valerian Zorin and the GDR Foreign Minister Lothar Bolz agreed in an exchange of letters that East Germany would be responsible for West Berlin's lines of communication through the GDR but added that control of the traffic of the western garrisons "will temporarily be exercised by the command of Soviet troops in Germany, pending the conclusion of an appropriate agreement". This was an attempt to make Bonn deal with East German authorities on matters of civilian traffic. It was a decisive step in the Soviet policy of securing recognition of the GDR regime, which was to be a fundamental cause of the crisis which led to the building of the Berlin Wall.

For Berliners, the new settlements of East and West rubbed salt in the city's wounds: reunification and a united capital now seemed the remotest of possibilities; Soviet attempts to abort western agreements had considerably reduced communication within the city and with the outside world. Yet Berliners reacted as they so often did to their "Berlin Weather" and its storm damage: "Na und," they said, "So what?" They had learned to live with the difficulties of their peculiar city; they were untroubled by the anomaly that it was the last remaining area of allied occupation in Germany. The abnormal was, after all, normal life in Berlin, and people prided themselves on the cheerful way they coped with each extra burden and the stubbornness with which they resisted pressure. West Berliners even felt some relief that the situation was not worse: they had expected a physical assault on their sectors when the Bonn and Paris agreements were finally implemented in May 1955, but the East German press and politicians had contented themselves with hurling abuse against the agreements and no bones were broken. Furthermore there were indications that the future could be bright. Industrial production and exports were booming (and the West German government agreed to take on the costs of a huge increase in freight charges imposed by the East Germans in May 1955); fat subsidies from Bonn fed the well-being of the western sectors. West Berlin had institutional ties to the democracy and freedoms of the Federal Republic. The Paris Agreement had promised that western troops would stay in the city and that the three Powers would "treat any attack against Berlin from any quarter as an attack on themselves", a declaration with which NATO had associated itself. Perhaps West Berliners had reason to feel confidence in their survival.

Was confidence misplaced? The survival of the western sectors still depended on the vulnerable road, rail and canal links with the Federal Republic and the exiguous western garrisons of 12,000 men. It hung by the wispiest of threads. The NATO guarantee meant that the West would retaliate if its sectors were subject to outright military attack: in practice, that the western garrisons would meet a quick death and the western sectors be reduced to rubble again while NATO decided whether to fight for the city on another battleground and with nuclear weapons. Like western strategy in general the policy for the defence of Berlin was dismally lacking in intermediate, measured and conventional means to deter and respond, or to contain a crisis. And surely Moscow had proved by its actions in the city in 1951 and 1952 that there were plenty of ways to kill the Berlin cat besides sending tanks across the sector border: small, gradual measures to stifle the western sectors which would meet no resistance from the Western Powers. In those two years, indeed, the West had allowed the Russians to make all the running in the city and to retain nearly all the gains they had made. Fear of a worse crisis, dread of precipitating war are understandable, yet failure to come up with pre-emptive measures or any response stronger than formal written protests must be deplored. After all, those with responsibility for Berlin at this time had already experienced the deadly consequences of a policy of appeasement when it was applied to Hitler. When Berliners learned to "put up with", "live with", "make the best of" the changes forced on their city, they were showing courage; when the West accepted the increasing abnormality of normal life there, it was surely a dangerous political error. It is not unreasonable to suggest that by 1955 the ineffectual and timorous behaviour of the Western Powers had fed Soviet ambition and confidence, sapped the West's position in Berlin, and left the western sectors exposed to the far worse crises that were to come.

3

Stagnation and Shock

———————

For the next three years, however, Berlin did not face any major crisis. Once the West European settlements of 1955 were in place there was quiet in the city, though it was not true peace but the torpidity of stagnation. The four Powers were diverting their antagonism and ambition to other channels and the brackish waters of Berlin were unstirred for a time. East and West had recognised that the twin problems of Berlin and Germany were insoluble except by compromises that neither side was willing to make. They had reached an impasse, and their position was confirmed by the Summit Conference at Geneva from 15 to 21 July 1955.

This was the first time the heads of government of the four Powers had met since Potsdam in July and August 1945. The term "summit" was new – probably coined by Churchill in one of his last speeches in the House of Commons when he called for a "parley at the summit" to find ways of relaxing the tensions with the Soviet Union. Perhaps he envisaged the kind of meeting which the leaders of the allied coalition had held during the war: private and intimate, with deals struck behind closed doors and the fate of nations decided by pencil strokes on sketchmaps. Peacetime requirements were very different. There was widespread distaste, especially in the United States, for secret diplomacy and ruthless bargains of the wartime kind. World leaders now travelled with plane loads of advisers and assistants. Those from the West thought as much about the electorate at home as they did about proposals on a conference table. The media expected, and often got, thorough briefing on the details of discussions and plenty of leaks for interpretation and titillation.

The novelty of Summits seized the public imagination. There was an expectation that, after years of post-war diplomatic futility and rancour, the men who held ultimate power and responsibility could establish goodwill by personal contact, ignore the hair-splitting of their bureaucrats, and solve international problems by a few days of plain speaking and mutual understanding. This was a simplistic belief. It ignored the real gravity and complexity of problems, overlooked the value of careful preparation and skilled negotiation, and was blind to the disagreeable probability that tangled disputes can only be unknotted with time and patience and that lasting solutions are more likely to be achieved by gradual adjustments. The rarefied air at Summits went to the heads of politicians. They, too, tended to believe they could score instant successes where experts had failed for years. The darting microphones, blazing arc lights and clicking cameras encouraged them to reduce intricate issues to simple formulae suitable for a fireside chat on radio, a strong headline for the newspapers, or a stabbing gesture at a globe in a television studio. It is questionable whether elderly men, with many other foreign and domestic affairs on their minds, performed effectively at conference tables after long, slow journeys in bumpy, noisy aircraft and between strenuous wining and dining sessions.

Be that as it may, the Geneva Summit of 1955 was the first of its kind and opened to great optimism and excitement. The western delegations had been impressed by recent statements from the Kremlin that all problems were susceptible to negotiation, and by Soviet alacrity in accepting the invitation to these talks. That sense of opening possibilities was reinforced by the relative ease and speed of four-Power agreement on 15 May 1955 to the Austrian State Treaty, which restored Austrian sovereignty, ended allied occupation, and guaranteed that the country would remain neutral. Never mind that the Soviet Union could well afford a gesture in Austria where no real sacrifice of interest or strategic position was involved, or that neutrality for Germany was unacceptable to the West because it would create a dangerous vacuum in the heart of Europe and deprive NATO of the Federal Republic's troops. At least one post-war worry had been allayed, and to the satisfaction of all concerned. Perhaps this presaged progress on more troublesome matters.[1]

As an additional benefit, Geneva offered the western delegates the intriguing chance to meet and assess the new Soviet leaders. Malenkov had been replaced in February by a diarchy: Nikolai Bulganin as Chairman of the Council of Ministers and Nikita Khrushchev as First Secretary of the Communist Party. First impressions were good. Seasoned negotiators, used to stony-faced, hard-eyed and relentless Russians, were relieved to encounter smiles and occasional willingness to listen. The general public warmed to the press stereotype of the two as cuddly teddy bears, "Krush and Bulge", just as it had been deceived by the cosy wartime image of the cruel despot Stalin as "Uncle Joe". People enjoyed the spectacle of these portly, waddling, jovial men, in silly hats with upturned brims, brightly coloured suits with voluminous jackets billowing over the paunch, and eighteen-inch trouser bottoms flapping round the ankles. (Vladimir Nabokov once pointed out that Soviet suits were not intended to be sartorial achievements but advertisements for the productivity of the State worsted industry.) It was not clear which of the two was in charge. Bulganin was the titular head of delegation and did most of the talking in formal sessions; Khrushchev, on the other hand, took over at dinners and receptions. It was realised later that Khrushchev was on his best behaviour at this meeting, and was curbing his usual ebullience and flares of bad-tempered polemic. He was, perhaps, overawed: the peasant and mining mechanic at table with world leaders; the Russian, born and bred in a closed society, out in the great world. He certainly recorded in his memoirs that the Soviet delegation "found itself at a disadvantage from the very moment we landed at Geneva airport. The leaders of the other three delegations arrived in four-engined planes and we arrived in a modest two-engined Ilyushin."

At the conference many observers of Khrushchev noted only the outward appearance and were not impressed. The French Prime Minister, Antoine Pinay, commented with disdain on the "coarseness" of "this little man with his fat paws". The British Foreign Secretary, Harold Macmillan, who was accompanying the Prime Minister, Anthony Eden, asked snobbishly "how can this fat, vulgar man with his pig eyes and ceaseless flow of talk really be the head – the aspirant Tsar – of all those millions of people?" He was confusing the qualities needed in a Soviet leader with those for membership of White's or Boodle's. Eisenhower's judgement of Khrushchev was more perceptive: "rotund and amiable but with a will of iron only slightly concealed".

General Eisenhower had been President of the United States since 1953. The problems he used to leave to the politicians were now his. Dominant among them was the obesity of the national budget – US government spending stood at $80 billion in his first year of office, was slimmed back to $57.1 billion by 1955, but swelled thereafter – which meant he had to levy high taxes. Defence expenditure devoured well over a third of all revenue. The situation was repugnant to a Republican president and irrational to the mind of a soldier. "Excessive spending", Eisenhower wrote, "helps cause deficits, which cause inflation, which in turn cuts the amount of equipment and manpower the defence dollar can buy. The process is circular and self-defeating." A second vicious circle interlocked with it. This was strategic. The Bomb, atom or hydrogen, was excessive for many military needs, and its use was virtually suicidal as the Soviet Union became capable of replying in kind. The US armed services, therefore, wanted flexibility for response at various levels. But more specialised troops, a variety of weapons, sophisticated missile delivery systems, increased transport capacity all meant even higher military expenditure. For Eisenhower the defence budget was money badly spent: "Every gun that is made, every warship launched, every rocket fired, signifies, in the final sense, a theft from those who hunger and are not fed, those who are cold and are not clothed." Like all good soldiers he hated war. His experience had shown that it caused pain and havoc beyond bearing or reason, wasted lives and resources, and was the penalty paid for political failure. Nuclear war, he well knew, would be exponentially worse. The United States had the power to win a nuclear war against the Soviet bloc but, the President asked his Joint Chiefs of Staff in 1954, "Gain such a victory, and what do you do with it? Here would be a great area from the Elbe to Vladivostock . . . torn up and destroyed, without government, without its communications, just an area of starvation and disaster." There had to be a better way to resolve disputes.[2]

In the hope of reducing international tension and allaying the suspicions and fear which could lead to war, Eisenhower proposed at the Summit an "Atoms for Peace" programme and called on the Soviet Union to exchange with the United States "a complete blueprint of our military establishments from beginning to end, from one end of our countries to the other". He recommended an "Open Skies" policy: the provision by each state of "facilities for aerial photography" to double-check the blueprints and to give assurance that no surprise attacks were being prepared. As the President finished his speech there was a sudden clap of thunder and all the lights went out. "Well," he said, "I expected to make a hit, but not that much of one." For the rest of the session he believed he had made a big hit with the Soviet Union: Bulganin commented that his proposals had "real merit" and would be given sympathetic study. But as they left the conference room, Khrushchev murmured "I don't agree with the Chairman", implying that his would be a policy of skies closed to all but bombers, missiles and spy planes. In so doing, he had also given Eisenhower the strong impression that the First Secretary, not the Chairman, would make the fundamental decisions.

Khrushchev was rather disappointed by this first meeting with Eisenhower. He wrote later that Stalin had always spoken warmly of the

General, of his "decency, generosity and chivalry in his dealings with his allies". (He also noted, seemingly without irony, that Stalin believed "if it hadn't been for Eisenhower, we wouldn't have succeeded in capturing Berlin.") At Geneva Khrushchev decided that the President lacked toughness and was too dependent on his Secretary of State: John Foster Dulles was constantly passing notes and it looked as if Eisenhower "was letting Dulles do his thinking for him". Khrushchev had misjudged – as so many did. It was easy to underestimate Eisenhower, with his goofy grin and self-deprecating remarks: "I'm just a simple soldier", or "just a farm boy from Kansas". Journalists, wishing to sound sophisticated, scoffed at a man whose literary interests extended only as far as westerns and whose replies at press conferences were stumbling or incoherent (few of them could have matched the lucidity and punch of his written style). The young told each other he was senile: "The President has stopped work for the day," they giggled. "His lips were tired from reading official papers." Radicals prophesied that he would be golfing while the world burned in a nuclear holocaust. By contrast, those who worked with Eisenhower knew he was canny and efficient. General Clay, for example, had learned he was a hard task master and ruthlessly disposed of anyone who did not live up to the job. Clay would have known why Dulles was so busy at Geneva: the President, he was well aware, "had a philosophy of administration in the White House. He believed that his Secretaries were responsible for their departments and they had to make the decisions"; "he kept his mind and his desk free from clutter". It was a technique which had served Eisenhower well in the war. His staff officers beavered at the routine problems and were expected to take the initiative in their allotted tasks; the Supreme Commander listened, assessed the information he was given, then gave rapid and confident orders.

During the 1952 presidential election campaign President Truman had jeered "The General doesn't know any more about politics than a pig knows about Sunday." It was an electioneering jibe rather than a discerning estimate of the man Truman had admired as Chairman of the Joint Chiefs of Staff and recommended as Democratic presidential candidate in 1948. Eisenhower was not a votary of one party or another and was certainly not a machine politician. As President he was anxious to keep above the mêlée and to preserve the dignity and prestige of his office from the taints of partisanship. Yet he was capable of astute political judgement and had long experience of political process, domestic and international. He had lobbied for the armed services in Washington before the war, appeared before Congressional committees and served the White House with the JCS. He had held together the wartime coalition and earned the respect of Churchill, de Gaulle and Stalin for the way he did it. His role at NATO had required diplomatic skill and sagacious handling of politicians as well as officers.

For much of his career he had dealt with Europeans and European problems – few of his compatriots had such deep knowledge of them. His attitude to the Soviet Union had always been unnuanced and it swung with the weathercock of contemporary opinion. During the war he, like everyone else, marvelled at the courage of the Russian people, admired the vital contribution of the Red Army and ignored the hostility of the Soviet political creed. (He retained his respect and affection for Marshal Zhukov and was delighted to meet him again at Geneva, in his new role as Minister of Defence. They enjoyed a private lunch, mulling over old victories, but the President was disappointed to find that his old ally had lost his cheerful confidence and had no political influence.) Eisenhower, like most Americans, had assumed at the end of the war that Soviet cooperation was vital to the peace and could be won by conciliation. In keeping with the general mood, his views had soon hardened. By September 1947, when he was a keen supporter of the Marshall Plan, he wrote in his diary of the Soviet Union's "damnable philosophy" and ambition "to communise the world" by promoting "starvation, unrest, anarchy". As the Cold War chilled, he decided that the conflict with Communism was a "war of light against darkness, freedom against slavery, Godliness against atheism".

These were Manichean words which might equally well have been spoken by his Secretary of State. John Foster Dulles had come to his office as a crown prince comes to the throne: the post had previously been held by his grandfather and uncle. Much of his life had been training for it: he attended his first international conference at the Hague in 1907 when he was nineteen years old, was a legal counsel for the American delegation to the Reparations Commission at Versailles after the First World War, and a political adviser at the Council of Foreign Ministers meetings in London in 1945 and Moscow in 1947. He had known over a dozen Secretaries of State personally and worked for eight of them; his career as a corporation lawyer had been largely concerned with international cases, he had travelled widely and met many major European figures. Yet what distinguished Dulles at the State Department was not so much his diplomatic expertise as his moralising analysis of foreign affairs. To his worldly, political inheritance there was added a Calvinistic patrimony and he himself was a church elder. His creed had taught him to fight depravity with the perseverance of the saints, with the confidence of the divinely elect, and in the knowledge of inevitable grace – or, to put it in secular terms, he thought he was right and

66

would prevail. In Dulles's political cosmology, Evil's gospel was Communism and its devilish avatar was the Soviet Union. He armed himself to combat it by zealous study of Stalin's *Problems of Leninism* – there were copies, together with the Bible, at the bedside of each of his homes and in all his offices, dog-eared from use and well-annotated in pencil. The West personified Good and must struggle to defeat Evil by moral vigilance, intellectual commitment, economic superiority and "a deterrent of massive retaliatory power".[3]

His doctrines of "rollback" of Communist power and "massive retaliation" against any Soviet threat made the Secretary of State the bugaboo of the Left, the Liberal, the cautious, and the subtle the world over. What they found most hair-raising was his tactic christened "brinkmanship": going to the very edge of war to show the enemy the seething chasm of destruction awaiting anyone who did not step back. Dulles explained the technique in 1956 in words he used with lawyers' precision: "The ability to get to the verge without getting into war is the necessary art . . . if you are scared to go to the brink, you are lost." "Without getting into war" was the key phrase and his critics never believed he would be able to pull back in time. Significantly his enemy, Khrushchev, shared Dulles's belief that he knew when to stop: "he had the common sense never to overstep that 'brink' he was always talking about."

Khrushchev also praised Dulles as "a worthy and interesting adversary . . . It kept us on our toes to match wits with him" even though (or perhaps because) he was a "chained cur of imperialism" and a "faithful dog of capitalism". Ideologues feel comfortable with ideologues; they are ill-at-ease with compromise and shading. That is why Dulles thought Molotov, whom most people regarded as intolerably hide-bound and pig-headed, one of the world's greatest negotiators. At the other end of the political spectrum, Adenauer delighted in Dulles's views. Both men ruminated ponderously on the great abstractions and the broadest historical sweeps; both saw themselves as warriors against a heathen abomination; neither believed in compromise. They could only hold a conversation with the help of an interpreter, but they spoke the same political and ethical, black and white language.

Their mutual respect and understanding was reinforced by Dulles's sympathy for Germany: he condemned the Versailles Treaty in 1919 for its harsh allegations of German war guilt and its reparations policy, he became a staunch champion of Bizonal fusion then Marshall Aid for Germany after witnessing the misery of Berlin in 1945, and had called for the defence of the city and the tying of the Federal Republic to the West ever since flying the Airlift in 1948. Those convictions had been strengthened in 1949 during his attendance at the Paris Conference to negotiate the raising of the Blockade, and at the Berlin Conference in 1954. No wonder so many Germans trusted and admired him. Many non-Germans did not share that view. Harold Macmillan judged him to be a man "whose vanity more than equalled his talents". When Eisenhower persuaded them to get better acquainted he conceded that "with all his faults – his agonisingly slow speech, his unwillingness to look you straight in the face, his deviousness of manner – there was something engaging about him . . . His rare smile had great charm." Smiles and charm were equally rare. His usual demeanour was sombre, his thin lips drooped down. He could be tetchy: he had frequent back pain and attacks of gout, and he suffered other agonies from those he thought fools or critical. He loomed: standing with his arms thrust deep into his pockets, sitting back from a table with thumbs tucked into his waistcoat or crouching forward to doodle hard-edged triangles and squares on a yellow legal pad. (Molotov was driven to distraction whenever he paused to sharpen his pencil with a pen knife.) He seemed joyless, judgmental, pompous and a prig; "dull, duller, Dulles", they said in Washington. He talked of righteousness, but Selwyn Lloyd noticed that he "would not begin a negotiation about the line to be pursued without an escape clause. He would say one thing and do another." Yet Dulles had the esteem of the one man who really mattered to him: the President. Eisenhower knew his Secretary of State was totally loyal and shared his own reverence for the Presidency. He could rely on Dulles's selfless devotion to duty, his assiduous dispatch of business, his mastery of detail, his willingness to bear responsibility. "There's only one man I know," said the President happily, "who has seen more of the world, talked with more people and knows more than he does – and that's *me*."

Khrushchev was wrong to think Eisenhower was dominated by his Secretary of State, but it would be true to say that sometimes he was influenced by him. Before the Geneva Summit, Dulles persuaded the President to abandon a tentative idea for calming Soviet fears of a reunified Germany by creating a belt of neutral but armed states in central Europe (though Eden developed the idea during the talks). Dulles could never see virtue in neutrality towards Marxism and in this case saw a threat to the defence of Western Europe; Adenauer agreed and added the argument that he would not accept reunification if it meant leaving NATO. At the Summit, Eisenhower denounced the existing disunity of Germany as "a grievous wrong" to the German people and "a basic source of instability in Europe". He proposed reunification with a government based on free elections and given the right to bear arms and enter alliances; once that was accomplished, matters of European security could be discussed. The Soviet delegation put the argument the other way round: first there must be a halt to German rearmament, withdrawal of all foreign troops, a security agreement to replace NATO and the Warsaw Pact; then perhaps arms limitation, though without the sanction of inspection; finally the German problem, already partly solved by this process, could be tidied up through negotiation. The two sides were miles apart and each was unwilling to take a step towards meeting half way.

The final communiqué from Geneva reaffirmed the "common responsibility" of the four Powers for the settlement of the German question "by means of free elections". This was relatively easy to write. It was most unlikely that it would ever come into effect. The Soviet Union would never countenance a democratic poll: as Khrushchev put it to Eisenhower: "The German people have not yet had time to be educated in the great advantage of Communism." The communiqué also referred to the "close links between the reunification of Germany and the problem of European security". Security was defined by the West either as NATO (unacceptable to the Soviet Union, especially when it included the Federal Republic) or as the Bomb (where the Soviet Union was still at a disadvantage but catching up fast) or as an area of demilitarisation and disengagement (as suggested by Britain but opposed by the United States and the Federal Republic) or as an arms limitation pact supervised by inspection (and Khrushchev told Eisenhower that his "Open Skies" proposal was "a very transparent espionage device", though he did not admit that the Soviet Union lacked the necessary technology). If reunification and security were indeed closely linked, then neither issue could be resolved.

It was deadlock. Deadlock it would remain. The public in the West still had high hopes of summitry; was delighted to hear that the Foreign Ministers of the four Powers would hold subsequent talks in Geneva on European questions and disarmament; enjoyed Macmillan's typical resort to old songs in his triumphant announcement to the press on return to London: "there ain't going to be no war." Headlines and speeches extolled "The Spirit of Geneva" and a new atmosphere of cordial, rational pursuit of answers, forgetting that spirits befuddle judgement and soon evaporate. It took only a few days for cold sobriety to set in. Khrushchev stopped in East Berlin on his way home from Geneva and warned that "mechanical reunification" was "unreal" and that the "working people of the GDR" could not agree to unity at the expense of abolishing their "political and social achievements" and "democratic transformation". Two weeks later the Soviet Union began a series of H-Bomb tests. In November Molotov told East Berliners that reunification was "primarily a matter for the

69

Germans themselves" not the four Powers. So much for Summits, their spirit and communiqués. In reality there could be no solution to the German problem without a significant slackening of East–West tension. For the moment both sides preferred that tension to any concession.[4]

A two-minute silence had been observed in West Berlin to mark the opening of the Geneva Summit. Perhaps it would have been more appropriate as mourning for its end. Berliners, East and West, well knew that the final communiqué offered no hope of a speedy reunification of Germany which would heal the wounds in their city. "Na und": they soon got used to the idea that the road to unity would be slow and hard. They learned to live with the new adjustments to their daily routines.[5]

In accordance with the Bolz–Zorin letters of September 1955, the East Germans took over control of civilian traffic in and out of the western sectors at the end of the year. This made little practical difference. There were still many Soviet personnel at the crossing points for the Eastern Sector and the GDR; the rules and regulations for transit did not change. Interference with traffic was not much worse than it had ever been – indeed, for three years West Berlin's trade suffered rather less than usual. There were, however, variants on the "usual incidents". In late 1955 and early 1956 the East Germans confiscated 278 tons of scrap metal being exported from West Berlin by road and fined lorry drivers for "false declarations" about its origins. In October 1957 there was a flurry of nervousness when the East German police held up mail trains and searched for "anti-Communist propaganda", but by the following month mail was moving normally. Barge traffic experienced periodic crises. In 1955 there was a long delay in renewing the annual transit permits before the GDR assumed responsibility for them. In May 1958 the East Germans imposed a toll of DM3 per ton for all West German barge freight, alleging that a new Federal dam on the Elbe was damaging East German farms. The skippers refused to pay and water traffic came to a standstill until June when the Bonn government finally promised to reimburse them. Lorries and trains had coped efficiently with the water freight in the meanwhile (it was about 30 per cent of the sectors' usual imports), and barges never recovered all their old customers.[6]

West Berliners were not impressed by allied handling of any of these problems. In late 1955 the Mayor, Otto Suhr, told the Military Commandants that the only way to deal with the Russians and East Germans was to get tough; in May 1956 he criticised the Western Powers for their limp response to Communist moves and made unfavourable comparisons with allied resolution in 1948 and 1949. In April 1956 he showed them how things should be done. There was another Steinstücken drama. For several weeks the fridge in the enclave shop was broken and the East German police refused to let West Berlin repair men in to mend it. Suhr decided to assert the rights that the Western Powers would not defend. He gave twenty-four hours' notice then drove to the barrier across the access path and demanded passage. The East German police told him to apply for a DM3 pass for "transit across the GDR". He reminded them that Steinstücken was in the American sector, that all access in Berlin was technically free, and that even to cross to the Federal Republic West Berliners needed only an identity card. The policemen would not budge. Still, the Mayor thought he had made his point so retreated, promising the enclave a new fridge at the Senate's expense. The van which delivered it was allowed through without any delay or argument.[7]

There were few interruptions to free passage in Berlin itself through the stringently reduced number of crossing points, though in 1957 there were sporadic customs and currency checks by the East Berlin police at the inter-sector border. More noticeable and sustained was the tightening of security on the GDR frontier, but this was recognised as a campaign to pen in East German refugees rather than as an attempt to strangle West Berlin communications. Rumour had it that Ulbricht wanted to be stricter about movement in the city itself, but was being restrained by the Russians who did not want a confrontation with the western allies.[8]

In actual fact the Soviet authorities were perfectly ready to provoke the Western Powers elsewhere – by interfering with their military traffic to and from the Federal Republic. Trouble started on 17 November 1956 when the Soviet officer commanding the railway checkpoint at Marienborn on the GDR frontier accused the allies of carrying unauthorised German passengers on their trains. He insisted that in future individual travel orders and identity cards must be produced and that his men would board the trains to check the papers against the occupants. Five days later, one French and three American west-bound trains were delayed until their commanders did indeed provide all the papers called for, but a British train from Hanover refused to comply or let a Soviet officer on board and even so was finally let through. The allies protested to the Soviet military authorities, more trains were held up and some were boarded and some were not, but eventually all three Powers agreed to present the required documentation, though not to allow Soviet checks of the passengers. That did not help them for long. By January 1957 all military trains were stopped automatically at Marienborn for thirty minutes. The excuse was that a pause was needed for cleaning them (and the brown coal they burned did indeed make them filthy). In practice the time was being used by the Soviet soldiers for peering into the compartments, trying to get inside, and arguing about whether or not there was a right to stamp civilian passports. Meanwhile, several military convoys on the Autobahn had been stopped and searched, or sent back if permission was refused. The Americans wanted to stage a demonstration of the right to free passage: send a convoy from Berlin, refuse identification, push through if possible, or return day after day to wear the Russians down. There was no support for the idea from the British or the French. By the end of the year the West had negotiated a new movement order with the Soviet authorities, conceding rights over papers but not inspections, and transit was speeded up.[9]

The allies had let the Russians get away with breaking their previous agreements on movement procedures and made little protest about accepting alternatives: offered a few slices of salami for the sake of a quiet life. Just as destructively, the basic principle of free access had been significantly eroded. Western willingness to negotiate it away had surely convinced the Russians that it was always worth putting on pressure: the West would yield to it sooner or later.

There were other ways in which the Russians might threaten western military traffic – ways that could advance a major Soviet aim in Germany. The Soviet Union had long wanted full diplomatic recognition for the GDR from the international community: the Kremlin – let alone Pankow (the Berlin borough where the government had its offices) – was tired of the accusation that the East German government was nothing but a puppet, accepted as a legal and independent regime only by other Soviet bloc countries. The western allies were anxious to avoid full, de jure recognition which would contradict their oft-repeated demands for German self-determination and free elections and knew only too well that a second German state would further impede national reunification along the lines they had insisted on. Much of the pressure to ostracise East Germany, however, had come from Adenauer.

Back in September 1955 he had accepted an invitation to visit Moscow and, in a very bad bargain which was the only agreement he could salvage from a hostile Khrushchev, had agreed to establish diplomatic relations with the Soviet Union in return for a mere 10,000 German prisoners-of-war still in Russian camps. (The Red Cross estimated that there were more than 130,000 of them; the Soviet authorities would only admit to between nine and ten thousand, all of whom they classified as "war criminals".) Recognition of the USSR was as far as the Chancellor was prepared to go – and some people thought he had gone too far. Under no circumstances would Adenauer countenance official dealings with the East Germans, let alone recognise the regime. If business had to be done, it must be through subordinate agencies. In practice there were plenty of contacts. Various court and administrative bodies wrote to each other; the East and West German police were in constant touch by letter or telephone; there was daily cooperation between telephone operators and maintenance teams on either side of the frontier and a shared office in Berlin for international post and telecommunications; the East German Reichsbahn ran the railway stations in West Berlin, collected the money for tickets and controlled the trains which transited the city. There were also occasional, discreet dealings at a higher level: in 1958 officials from East and West met in Thuringia to discuss Bavarian frontier control and hydro-electric schemes on rivers which crossed their borders; the annual Inter-zonal Trade agreement could hardly be categorised as "low-level administration". Even so, the myth of non-contact was resolutely upheld in Bonn to avoid any taint of recognition of the GDR.

Furthermore, Adenauer was adamant that his allies must abide by it. He enforced what came to be known as the Hallstein Doctrine (though his Foreign Minister, Dr Walter Hallstein, complained that his name was attached to it by his enemies): the FRG would break relations with any state which entered into them with the GDR. This terrorised the Western Powers. Their officials in Germany were forbidden the sort of contacts the West Germans themselves had with East Germans. They even contorted their vocabulary to fit Bonn's straitjacket. They tried not to refer to the "GDR" (or even to the "DDR" as it was translated into German by westerners to stress that it was a foreign fiction and not a state); they spoke instead of "East Germany" or even "east Germany" to give the impression of a geographical area rather than a political entity (and then got tied in knots when they felt the phrase included land beyond the Oder-Neisse). The old-fashioned or those who wanted to stress East German subservience stuck to "Soviet Zone". The East German government had to be called "the Ulbricht regime", or "Pankow" or the "so-called East German government". It was all ludicrously convoluted in theory and irritatingly inconvenient for daily business. As they well knew. On one occasion the French ambassador in Bonn arrived late in Berlin for a meeting and apologised, explaining that as he drove across the "so-called GDR" his car had been hit by a "so-called tree".

On 9 January 1958 David Bruce, the US ambassador in Bonn, wrote to the State Department warning that, as a first step to full recognition, the Soviet Union would gradually give the East Germans authority over allied traffic, to force the Western Powers into direct dealings with Pankow (breaking every existing agreement including the Bolz–Zorin letters of 1955). The handover, Bruce suggested, might take the form of requests for

German translations of documents, insistence on GDR visas for transit, or East German inspection of allied papers and vehicles. At what point would the allies have to make a stand? And how would they do it? How could the general public in the West be persuaded that a stand must be made when the measures seemed so slight? Furthermore, he alerted his government to the strong possibility that the Russians would try to gain the same degree of control over the air corridors that they had achieved on the ground, and be able to hamper an airlift in the event of any blockade. Berliners, he pointed out, were worried that the Western Powers were uncertain of their air rights and might not be willing to defend them. It was a prescient message, and the western capitals should have started planning for just such a situation. It was also a reminder that even when life in Berlin seemed quiet and traffic was flowing freely, fears of blockade nagged just below the surface of normality.[10]

And one aspect of "normal" life in Berlin never varied: the refugees always flowed through from East to West. After the high tide of 1953 when there were 331,390 arrivals in the Federal Republic, the current had slackened noticeably. In 1954 only 184,191 had crossed, thanks largely to the new fortification of the frontier; in 1955 the total rose to 252,870; it went up again in 1956 to 279,189; then it dropped in 1957 to 261,622. During these four years just over a half of all emigrants left via Berlin. The GDR government had tried different ways to deter them. For several months at the end of 1955 young people were taken off long distance trains bound for East Berlin and escorted to a police station for questioning; ticket offices in East German stations were told to report twice a day the number of tickets they had sold to young people. In 1956 the regime held the first public trials of those who encouraged or aided the "crime of fleeing the Republic"; in 1957 Ulbricht denounced those who left as "traitors to the working class" and a new passport law imposed a three-year jail sentence on anyone making an unauthorised trip to the West. Any such government move of course resulted in political hostility and roused fears of even tighter restrictions – so more people wanted to get out.[11]

The East German government would have been better advised to concentrate on improving material conditions: a major proportion of emigration was inspired by economic rather than political motives, by the attractions of the Golden West's high wages and well-stocked shops. Yet Ulbricht had failed to take advantage of real opportunities to raise the standard of living. In 1954 the USSR had decided to take no more reparations and to hand back the SAGs (the Soviet-owned companies); East German goods, coming from the most technologically advanced country and the most skilled labour force in Eastern Europe, were prized in the Soviet bloc; industry was experiencing a relative boom, with steel and brown coal production doubling in five years. Even so, wages were low and the prices of many desirables were high. It took an East German worker 195 hours to earn enough to buy a bicycle whereas a West German only had to work for 88; the East German put in 65 hours of labour before he could afford a pair of shoes, the West German laboured for 18. There was an acute housing shortage in the GDR (though if a family could find a home, rents were low). Rationing of meats, fats and sugar continued until 1958, but a ration was no guarantee of a supply – there were chronic food shortages, especially just before a harvest. An experienced observer of refugees, who was a constant visitor to the Marienfelde reception camp in West Berlin, noted in 1956 how poorly clothed and fed East German agricultural workers were: they looked as shoddy and drawn as Germans had been in 1945 and many of them told him they had been forced to leave because wages of 120–140 East marks simply could not support them. They were in constant fear of collectivisation and under the pressure of unrealistic delivery quotas. No wonder there was a shortage of food.[12]

The same observer noticed that many refugees came from the lowest income groups who thought they could hardly be worse off in the West. There were fewer highly trained or professional workers arriving for the moment: the regime wanted to keep these valuable citizens so was less insistent on Party activity or attendance at indoctrination lectures, and more reluctant to punish negligence in factories or failure to reach production targets as "acts of sabotage caused at the instance of a class enemy". A lot of the young men leaving the GDR claimed they were escaping conscription into the new People's Army, though the press-ganging of "volunteers" had actually ended in the autumn of 1955 and conscription in the FRG would soon start. There was also a continued flow of church members. From summer 1954 pastors had been harassed, religious literature and meetings banned, and the state was insisting that all adolescents should go through a secular confirmation service (the Jugendweihe) with a course of preparation classes to wean them from the spiritual influence of their families and priests.[13]

Overall, however, by 1956 it seemed that East German illusions about the delights of the West were fading. Some refugees went back (the GDR claimed 100,000 in 1954). They were not just homesick but disheartened by difficulty in finding homes and jobs, especially if they were unskilled. Some of those considering emigration changed their minds at the time of the Geneva Summit: they had taken western promises of "rollback" and imminent reunification seriously and were disappointed when there was no real commitment to them. It was also clear from interrogation reports at Marienfelde that many East Germans were coming to terms with the regime, and were prepared to make allowances for its less agreeable features. They were in favour of sensible nationalisation and land reform, they approved of their social security system. "The East Zone inhabitants are gradually developing into a different German nation," thought the observer, "not only as regards their political and social structure but more importantly as regards their outlook on the outer world." They had a "highly developed sense of social responsibility" and saw western materialism and individualism as greed and selfishness. What they disliked at home they softened with jokes: "An old lady in Leipzig wrote to Ulbricht on his birthday saying 'I wish you everything that the German people have been wishing you for years'. Next day she was arrested for incitement to murder." "A beggar cursed the regime and was arrested. 'Can't you see he's mad,' bystanders shouted. 'No, he isn't,' said a policeman, 'he's talking sense.'"[14]

In 1956 and 1957 Berliners, so often the focus of world attention as victims of East–West rivalry, were spectators of crises elsewhere which preoccupied the Powers and left the city a backwater for a while. Yet, however remote these crises seemed at the time, each and every one would eventually have an impact on Berlin itself.

The Soviet Union was engaged in struggles in the Party and against separatism in Eastern Europe. In February 1956, at the Twentieth Party Congress, Khrushchev delivered a searing attack on Stalin, hitherto the unchallengeable embodiment of every human and revolutionary virtue, and denounced him as the founder and chief priest of the cult of his own personality. Just as startling, Khrushchev implied that there might be "different roads to Socialism" from the Stalinist route: condemned the theory of the inevitability of war with capitalism, and suggested that it was possible to achieve "peaceful coexistence" with ideological enemies without compromising the ultimate victory of Marxism-Leninism in the class struggle. Khrushchev's words, leaked to the world by the CIA, were then put into bold measures: de-Stalinisation to purge the Party and rehabilitate those formerly condemned as heretics; decentralisation to encourage local initiative. In July 1957 Khrushchev fought off the challenge of the so-called "Anti-Party" (in fact anti-Khrushchev) group, which included the former Foreign Minister, Molotov. He then rewarded Marshal Zhukov for providing military transport to bring his supporter to Moscow, with dismissal and disgrace – the charge was "Bonapartism". Khrushchev now had control of both the Party and the armed forces.

By criticising Stalinism, he had, however, inadvertently called into question the very foundation of Communist authority and Soviet domination in Eastern Europe. After riots in Poznan in 1956 the Polish government demanded, and achieved, greater control over its internal affairs, and the Soviet Union was forced to recall the Red Army marshal it had imposed on Warsaw as Defence Minister, though Soviet troops remained in the country as "Warsaw Pact allies". In Hungary, nationalist and anti-Communist riots swelled into full revolt by October 1956. The Party lost its supremacy in government and a new Prime Minister tried to negotiate the evacuation of Soviet troops and renounce the Warsaw Pact in favour of neutrality. Such defiance could not be borne by the Kremlin. On 4 November Red Army tanks rolled into Budapest. In West Berlin angry crowds draped the Soviet War Memorial with a black flag for the death of Hungarian liberty, and smashed the windows of a bus carrying Russian guards to Spandau prison. They were briefly diverted to a silent protest outside the Rathaus but their anger and frustration soon erupted again. They called for a march on the Brandenburg Gate. Only quick thinking and a stirring speech from the local SPD leader, Willy Brandt, prevented a confrontation with the East Berlin police and inevitable bloodshed. He persuaded enough of the crowd to follow him to the memorial for the 1953 East Berlin uprising, well away from the Soviet Sector border. The rest were held back from the Gate by West Berlin police and their ardour doused with water cannon.[5]

In Berlin the Hungarian uprising had created contempt for the western allies and profound scepticism about the guarantees they had given for the defence of the western sectors. The Western Powers had stood by as the last anguished appeals for help were broadcast from Budapest and merely watched as 200,000 Hungarians fled the country and over three thousand died in street fighting against the tanks. Where was the military might of NATO when it was needed? Did all the fine words about "liberation" and "rollback" mean nothing? In fact, as President Eisenhower knew to his chagrin Hungary "was as inaccessible to us as Tibet". He faced the mortifying dilemma that western slogans could only be given reality by nuclear means, and "to annihilate Hungary . . . is in no way to help her". How, then, would he help Berlin? Were all the western promises and guarantees of defence for the city just so much hot air too?

By an appalling mischance, the crisis in Hungary coincided with another which involved two NATO members militarily and threatened to shake the alliance politically for a long time to come. The British and French colluded with an Israeli attack on Egypt at the end of October 1956 as an excuse for invading to regain control of the recently nationalised Suez

Canal. The British had not only reverted to gunboats in an ill-organised revival of nineteenth-century imperialist power politics but had foolishly misjudged American reaction. Harold Macmillan, the Foreign Secretary, had deliberately not informed Washington of the plot with the French or of the intention to land at Suez; had taken for granted Britain's "special relationship" with the United States; and had, furthermore, assumed that his "old friend" Eisenhower would give support once action was taken. Eisenhower did not see friendship as a one-sided asset to be exploited nor was he a sucker. When there was a run on sterling in November, he instructed the IMF to deny funds to Britain. Once the financial plug was pulled, Britain deserted the French and gave up the Suez operation. Any British reputation for moral authority, or diplomatic and military competence, had been lost; claims to be a superpower were exposed as pretension; the alliance with the United States was painfully ruptured. For the French, the Suez débâcle had acidulated resentment of American strength and influence in Europe, and peppered traditional antipathy for perfidious Albion with new misgivings about British dependability in any joint venture. Significantly, Adenauer was in Paris at the moment of ceasefire in Suez. He conjured visions for the French Prime Minister of a strong new European community. Neither man would be too unhappy if Britain were excluded from that picture; the French would be delighted if European partnership toned down American primacy.

NATO was in disarray. In March 1957, however, Eisenhower and Macmillan (now Prime Minister) met in Bermuda, re-established their personal relationship and patched up something of their political amity, with the United States promising delivery to Britain of sixty Thor missiles to be controlled by a "two-key" system. But at exactly the same time, six West European states signed the Treaty of Rome under which the European Economic Community would be established – and Britain, with 43 per cent of her trade based on the Commonwealth and a refreshed "special" status vis-à-vis the Americans, stayed on the sidelines.

There were not only political rifts to trouble NATO; military problems remained intractable. The alliance was still tightly bound by its nuclear strategy, in spite of theoretical argument and the recent Hungarian experience which suggested that "massive retaliation" was inappropriate for most of the crises it was likely to confront. Conventional defence was simply not feasible. French troops were increasingly committed to a colonial war in Algeria. The West Germans, who had euphorically promised 500,000 men, had only provided 120,000 by 1957; they wanted to reduce conscription, so unpopular with the electorate, and to have nuclear weapons instead. A British Defence White Paper in April 1957 recommended the complete abolition of National Service (which would cut the armed services by virtually a half) and reductions in the troops and tactical air force stationed in Germany; since Britain could no longer afford a grandiose military posture, she must crouch under the American nuclear umbrella. The United States was by now spending nearly 60 per cent of its budget on defence so there were attractions for Eisenhower in a proposal by the chairman of the Joint Chiefs of Staff to slash conventional forces and rely on cheaper nuclear weapons.

There was a widespread public belief that the way to cut the nuclear knot and reduce taxes was an international agreement on general disarmament. In addition, as nuclear arsenals grew so did public fear of accidental explosions and minor incidents escalating into mass destruction, or of maniac Dr Strangeloves unleashing a holocaust with one touch of a crazed finger on the nuclear trigger. There was panic from 1957 about "fall-out" from nuclear explosions plunging the world into eternal darkness, poisoning the atmosphere, spreading cancer and putting bone-rotting Strontium 90 into children's milk. Americans clamoured for a national fall-out shelter programme; the British middle classes thought they would be just as safe, and infinitely more cosy, in a cottage in Wales. Campaigns for Nuclear Disarmament were organised in every NATO country. Unfortunately disarmament talks between the Western Powers and the Soviet Union from 1956 to 1958 came to nothing. The Russians would never agree to inspection in the Soviet Union which would have reassured the West that there were no covert tests or preparations for surprise attack; the West would not countenance American withdrawal from bases on the Continent which would leave Soviet tanks with a clear ride across it. The West wanted to reduce ground forces, in which the Soviet Union had superiority, whereas the Kremlin was interested in cutting down on nuclear weapons with which the West had a head start. When attempts were made to prevent further research into nuclear weapons, each side tended to propose a ban only when it had just completed a successful test series; when there was a brief moratorium, it was broken by whichever side felt it was lagging behind.

Given this impasse over disarmament, interest grew in schemes for "disengagement", "demilitarisation" and "neutralisation". In March 1956 the Soviet Union first suggested a nuclear-free zone in central Europe and in October they backed a proposal from the Polish Foreign Minister, Adam Rapacki, for a non-aggression agreement between the Warsaw Pact and NATO and a nuclear-free band across Poland, Czechoslovakia and both Germanies – which, in effect, would have meant neutralising the whole area. Western governments were unwilling to discuss such measures, on the grounds that Germany would remain divided and the Federal Republic would be insecure, NATO would lose its forward position in Europe and still be vulnerable to Soviet long-range missiles.

Yet there was growing support for such ideas from government opponents. The West German SPD had always argued that arming the Federal Republic meant freezing the division of Germany, making Germans the Poor Bloody Infantry of NATO, and turning the country into an atomic battlefield. Now they called for an atom-free area, disengagement, and replacement of existing alliances by a collective security system. The leader of the British Labour Party, Hugh Gaitskell, in speeches at Harvard and the Free University in West Berlin, called for the military evacuation of central Europe and the gradual creation of a disengaged zone which might extend to Bulgaria and Rumania. George Kennan, an esteemed American diplomat and expert in Soviet Affairs who had previously argued strongly for containment of Communism, put forward similar ideas in his BBC Reith Lectures in 1957. (Interestingly, though less sensationally at the time, Kennan drew attention in his lectures to the dangers of the "extremely precarious and unsound arrangements which now govern the status of Berlin".)

The nature of this debate, the unsteady balance of power in Europe and even the basic assumptions of international relations were all abruptly shifted on 4 October 1957. A "bleep . . . bleep . . . bleep" on radio told the world that the Soviet Union had launched the world's first satellite into space: Sputnik I, the "travelling companion". This remarkable technological achievement came as a total surprise to the United States and a dreadful blow to American self-confidence. It was, said Dr Teller, father of the H-bomb, a greater defeat than Pearl Harbour. Suddenly, the nation which had believed itself the richest, most powerful, most advanced in the world felt inadequate and vulnerable. No one was cheered when the satirist Mort Sahl said: "Don't worry; all Sputnik proves is that the Russians captured better German scientists than we did"; there were few American laughs when Sputnik II was launched with Laika the dog on board and Downing Street was snowed under with letters from the British public incensed by cruelty to animals. To add to humiliation and fear, the Gaither report, from a committee of businessmen and academics, estimated that the Soviet Union would have strategic superiority by 1960 and that a massive civil defence programme would only cut likely American casualties in nuclear war from 120 million to 55 million.[16]

Eisenhower could have dismissed such dramatic warnings. Since the failure of his "Open Skies" proposal, U-2 spy planes had been flying over the USSR and their intelligence made it clear that there was no "Missile

Gap" nor was there likely to be. But the President chose to keep this information to himself: the U-2 missions were secret and he was alternately too embarrassed by them and too afraid of Soviet reaction even to hint at what they revealed. He could at least soothe something of the public alarm (and keep defence costs down) by deploying Inter-Continental and tactical Intermediate-Range Ballistic missiles in Western Europe, where the warheads would be stockpiled under the supervision of the Supreme Commander of NATO and the allies would make joint decisions on their use. Militarily, fiscally, politically and diplomatically the move to nuclear rather than conventional forces seemed irresistible. And the problems of Germany and Berlin were tightly bound in to it.

The deployment of nuclear missiles in Western Europe inevitably provoked the Soviet Union. In mid December 1957 Bulganin sent letters to all the Western Powers repeating the call for a non-aggression pact between the West and East, and recommending the denuclearisation of both Germanies, together with a ban on atomic tests for two or three years and renunciation by all of the use of atomic weapons. He followed this with another letter on 8 January 1958 suggesting that his proposals should be discussed at a Summit together with such topics as troop reduction so as to "help create conditions favouring a rapprochement of both German states". In an exchange of Notes the Western Powers stuck to their long-agreed policy: negotiations on arms and demilitarisation must be held in conjunction with discussions on German reunification – and reunification not by rapprochement but by free elections for an all-German government.

The Soviet Union had been thwarted. Worse: synchronised with the decisions to provide ICBMs and IRBMs for NATO had come the news that the alliance would consider equipping the armed forces of the Federal Republic with nuclear missile carriers. It was a prospect which quickened every Soviet fear and trauma: atomic weapons at the heart of Europe and in the hands of Germans. No matter whether the warheads would be under American control. Possession of the artillery itself gave Adenauer what he had worked for and what the Kremlin had dreaded: a strong political and military German voice in the western alliance.

The Russians struggled to abort the delivery of the carriers. On 12 December 1957 Bulganin wrote to Adenauer warning that "the equipment of Western Germany with atomic weapons, by harnessing it still more closely to the North Atlantic bloc, would bar the only way to the re-establishment of Germany's unity", which was agreement between the two German states. In March 1958, while the Bundestag debated whether to accept tactical nuclear weapons, Otto Grotewohl, the East German Prime

Minister, gave notice that such a step "makes peaceful unification completely impossible" and that "counter-measures by the States threatened will follow with no long delay". At the end of April Anastas Mikoyan paid a visit to Bonn, ostensibly to sign a trade agreement with the Federal Republic. This wily Armenian was a member of the Party Presidium, survivor of every Soviet war, coup, purge and ideological tussle and, incidentally, the former minister responsible for dismantling in the Soviet Zone. Foreigners usually found him the most pleasant and flexible of his comrades, a cliché disarming carpet salesman in economic negotiations and an amusing social companion. On this occasion he was brutal and splenetic in high Kremlin style. For four days he berated the Chancellor, ministers and civil servants for their nuclear policy, starting at the opening dinner where he left his formal speech to be read by an interpreter while he used his own energy in tirades at all present until, as the British ambassador reported, the "whole party broke up in a thoroughly unfriendly atmosphere, the Germans giving as good as they got".[7]

It was inconceivable that the USSR would have suffered in silence West Germany's further, and nuclear, armament – the Soviet reaction to the events of 1948 and the strengthening of the western alliance in the early 1950s proved that. Given the rebuff to all Moscow's recent proposals for disarmament and reunification, it was entirely predictable that the response would be fierce and dangerous. And, in any case, by 1958 the Kremlin was spoiling for a major confrontation with the Western Powers. The launching of Sputnik I had put the finishing touch to new Soviet confidence. The Russians, long inferior to the West in military science and technology, now had the Atom Bomb, the Hydrogen Bomb, Intercontinental Ballistic Missiles and a lead in satellite development. Surely, they argued, the balance of power had tilted in their favour? Surely this should be acknowledged by a shift in western attitudes? Nikita Khrushchev typified the mood of assertion. He was, indeed, positively bumptious. The man who had been born in poverty, wiped his nose on his sleeve and never worn shoes from spring to autumn, now sat in Stalin's office in the citadel of the Tsars, ruled an empire and controlled the biggest army in Europe. Not that his position was unassailable. He had domestic enemies who feared that his de-Stalinisation would cause instability in the one-party state and the Soviet bloc and that his readiness to negotiate with the West would endanger security. Khrushchev had to prove that true Soviet principles underlay his unorthodox polices; he had to deliver triumphs to underpin his standing.[18]

And it was not in Khrushchev's nature to accept meekly the stalemate which Soviet foreign and military policy faced by 1958. He was energetic, enthusiastic, bull-headed. He had ridden roughshod through the technical difficulties of building the Moscow Metro in the 1930s (when he had never even heard the word "escalator") and brought Donbass miners to hack the tunnels by brute force; faced more recently with the rigidity of the Stalinist system he had smashed the bureaucratic machine; impatient with the chronic sterility of Soviet agriculture, he called for the ploughing of the virgin lands. Dynamism plus quick, slick answers to complex problems – that was Khrushchev's style. On occasion he would act on a whim. Painstakingly drafted speeches might be flung aside once he found an audience to play to; he would extemporise, brighten prosaic official pronouncements with "old Russian proverbs" (many of which he minted himself), and construct in public policies he had scarcely sketched in private. Yet his was a calculating mind (even his "impulsiveness" was sometimes carefully planned). Khrushchev was a cunning political infighter and an unscrupulous wielder of power. He could watch his own back and find the weakest spot between an opponent's shoulder blades. He acted the cheery little fat man, and a State Department assessment pointed out how successfully he posed as a "handshaking, back-slapping, grassroots politician who could draw a good vote in any democracy". But the bonhomie was often cracked by explosions of rage and brow-beating, and whatever the novelty of his slogans he was, as Foy Kohler of the US State Department warned Dulles, "a true believer" whereas Stalin had been a "cynical and cautious realist". This made him more dangerous. His readiness to put faith before reason in policy, his impetuosity and his reckless gambling constantly wrong-footed pragmatic, circumspect opponents.

He was proud and prickly: the uneducated peasant with cocksure opinions on anything from cotton planting to nuclear physics; the self-made man determined to be honoured as leader of a world power and ready to throw his weight about if he was not; a Russian who demanded respect for his country's achievements but who feared contempt and suspected the motives of others; a Communist who was convinced that one day soon the world would experience the victory of his creed but would meanwhile do anything to prevent it. In a brash mood Khrushchev would crow that the Soviet Union had the whiphand in military technology and that American nuclear weapons and bombers belonged "in a museum". He knew this was untrue, and was ashamed of the many other areas in which his country lagged behind. Just after Sputnik II went into orbit, the British ambassador in Moscow was driving about thirty miles outside the capital. He watched two women, shouldering ox yokes with dangling buckets, trudge 500 yards through the snow to a river where they broke the ice to draw their household water. Khrushchev would try to conceal such backwardness by swagger and boasts of "firsts" and "records", but he yearned for western technology and know-how to expunge national inferiority and to confirm Marxist pre-eminence.

In his *Last Testament*, Khrushchev described United States policy since 1945 as "calculated to provoke and bully us from a position of strength". By 1958 the Soviet Union would not, could not, be bullied and Khrushchev wanted to provoke the Americans to talk. And to him, personally. He had no patience with professional preparation and preliminary agreements by Foreign Ministers. As he told the West German ambassador: "These gentlemen want to chatter for weeks. They can't make decisions all the same, because that is the business of heads of government"; given a Foreign Ministers' conference, "I will keep my minister on a chain". He was anxious to discuss the full range of European problems, especially nuclear and troop reductions. By his reckoning a Soviet division abroad cost twice as much as one at home. Nuclear research and manufacture absorbed millions of roubles and gave "our adversary an opportunity to exhaust us economically, without war, by forcing us to compete with them in a never-ending arms race" – words which could just as well have been written by Eisenhower. Money spent on soldiers and weapons could be diverted to industry and raising the standard of living; it could be invested in agriculture and, as Khrushchev was fond of saying, "Love of Communism passes through the stomach." Peaceful co-existence would encourage trade and develop the economy, give a chance to acquire western technology. There was no contradiction in Khrushchev's mind between peaceful co-existence and his threat to the West "we will bury you": this was war conducted by other means.

The Yugoslav ambassador in Moscow, Veljko Mićunović, decided in January 1958 that the Soviet Union was "becoming convinced that there can be no victors in the cold war"; but there was a chance of winning a few battles before a truce was called. He recorded in his diary on 26 January Khrushchev's wish for recognition of the European status quo: specifically the political split and Soviet territorial gains at the end of the war (but probably also the division of Germany – though the Soviet Union spoke publicly of reunification and proposed a loose confederation between the GDR and the FRG, Khrushchev may have already decided what he later said in private: that he preferred to have seventeen million East Germans under Communist rule than seventy million neutrals on the loose). On 29 January Mićunović commented that the Russians were "betting heavily" on the damaging effects of the present disagreements between Britain and the Continental powers, France and Germany, and between Western Europe and the United States. Khrushchev could also play on continuing American shock at Sputnik and fear of nuclear fall-out. All in all, this was a good moment to exploit Soviet strength. Furthermore, Khrushchev seems to have genuinely believed that the West owed him concessions. Since 1955 Soviet armed forces had been cut from five and three-quarter million men to four million; the USSR had collaborated over the Austrian State Treaty, closed its naval base at Porkkala in Finland, withdrawn troops from Rumania in May 1958. (Better forget Hungary, or claim freedom of action in a Soviet sphere of influence.) He expected his de-Stalinisation policies to earn western approval and trust and his disarmament and test ban proposals to be treated as sincere. By his calculation, what he had done required matching adjustments by the West. He was asking not for a favour but for his due.[19]

The fulcrum against which Khrushchev could apply his strength to obtain maximum leverage in the present situation was, of course, Berlin. Here the Western Powers were at their most vulnerable, with tenuous communications and poor defence for a client of NATO whose loss could shake the alliance. Here, too, was what he called "a bone in the throat" for the Soviet Union: a model of western democracy and capitalism in the centre of the Soviet Zone, a destabilising force for the GDR. Soviet residents and visitors hated West Berlin's bright lights and consumer goods; they saw them as propaganda designed to shame and annoy them. They loathed the RIAS radio station which all East Germans listened to and which the regime could not jam. They bitterly resented the fact that, with West marks exchanged at one to five with East marks, the few attractive goods in East Berlin shops were snapped up by western buyers. It rankled with Soviet diplomats that just behind their embassy in East Berlin was a hairdresser whose establishment grew more and more resplendent every year with marble pillars and cut glass chandeliers: all his customers were West Berliners; they were the only people who could afford his prices. They were riled too by the extent of allied and Federal spying and subversive activities directed from the western sectors. It was no solace that they themselves were quite as busy with espionage and infiltration in the West, or that their agent George Blake, who was also employed by the British SIS, had kept them informed about the 1,000-yard Anglo-American tunnel from which Soviet military and intelligence telephones at Karlshorst were tapped so that the KGB could stage a propaganda coup in April 1956 by "discovering" it. The Soviet Union was exasperated that penetration of East German government departments by western agents not only revealed GDR secrets but gave clues about what was going on in Moscow as well. That, for the secretive and paranoid Kremlin mind, was defilement.[20]

There was, too, some growing Soviet awareness of the political and economic embarrassment for the Ulbricht government of the West Berlin escape hatch for refugees. Overall, the refugee figures for 1958 showed a significant drop: 204,092 East Germans left for the West by comparison with 261,622 in the previous year. Even so, by August 1958 the Communist authorities still had cause for concern. Up to two-thirds of all refugees were crossing via Berlin and a significant proportion of them came from the professional classes. From January to August they included 250 university professors and 619 school teachers; the First Rector of Jena left just as his university was about to celebrate its 400th anniversary. There was a "doctors' revolt", sparked by recent political pressure but kindled by long-standing resentment of bans on access to western conferences and professional literature and by discrimination against their children when applying for university places. Industry, too, was losing trained specialists. In late September, the owner and sixteen directors of a hydraulics firm went to the West taking all their blueprints with them, when the East German government was ready to nationalise their factory. The Ulbricht regime tried to back-pedal. On 18 September the Politburo declared that non-Marxist doctors must not be subjected to political harassment and promised to investigate their grievances. On 26 September Ulbricht confessed in a speech that the GDR was experiencing real difficulties as a result of the flight of professionals, scientists and skilled production workers. He criticised Party workers for the insensitive methods they used to "persuade" others of the "advantages of Socialist thinking" and, mindful of 1953, insisted that industrial norms could be raised only after consultation with workers.[21]

A regime which was losing its population could hardly be said to be in charge of the country. Its image and effectiveness were further damaged by the fact that it was only officially recognised by the states of the Soviet bloc: at the very least, acceptance by outsiders might bring a degree of acquiescence by insiders. And the simmering question of recognition came to the boil when, on 2 July 1958, the Bundestag in Bonn challenged the very survival of the GDR by calling on all four Powers to set up a committee to prepare proposals for "a solution of the German problem" – in other words, for national unity, which would wipe out East Germany as a separate state and swamp its system in the larger, capitalist and democratic, federation. The Western Powers immediately realised that the governments in Pankow and Moscow would interpret the proposal as provocative. They persuaded the West German government to delay any action, but it was clear that Adenauer would soon have to succumb to the Bundestag's strong feelings and that there would be pressure on the West to fulfil its responsibility for reunification.

To increase western unease, the Bundestag resolution had, in itself, given a handle to the Communist allies. On 5 September the Czech Foreign Ministry insisted on delivering an East German Note to the three western ambassadors in Prague. This caused a flurry in diplomatic dovecotes. Could a GDR communication be officially accepted? Was it sanitised by passing through the hands of a third party? Would they be criticised by the Federal Republic for studying it and reprimanded by their own governments if they did not? (Ambassadors faced with this dilemma on other occasions sometimes ostentatiously dropped the East German communication into the wastepaper basket while the messenger was present, then fished it out again once he left.) The three decided to open the Note. It repeated the usual things about the need for a confederation, a nuclear-free and alliance-free zone, troop withdrawal from Germany and closure of foreign military bases in Europe. Its main point, however, was that a peace treaty must precede reunification, and that German representatives must share responsibility for it with the four Powers and have their own commissions to deal with their economic relations, matters of currency and trade, transport and the easing of inter-zonal travel. The fact that the initiative had come from the GDR, not the Kremlin, and included a demand for a part in the negotiating process gave a clear indication that, if nothing else, the East Germans were making a play for recognition. How could the western allies even reply to the Note without conceding them some? As a Foreign Office official minuted with exasperation: "It becomes increasingly inconvenient to abstain from dealings with the GDR Government which does, after all, exist."[22]

Diplomatic discomfiture was avoided, however, thanks to the Soviet Union weighing in behind the GDR with a Note on 18 September turning down the Bundestag call for reunification and purely four-Power responsibility for a treaty. The West could now bypass Pankow and reply directly to Moscow, insisting on free elections for an all-German government before any treaty negotiations. The Bundestag was delighted by this evidence of allied support. In October it met in Berlin for a four-day session – a yearly event to remind itself and everyone else that Berlin would one day be the capital of Germany, which the *Times* correspondent compared to "a band of nature-lovers annually walking a footpath to keep open the right of way". At this meeting the members again called for their 2 July proposals to be put into effect. The German problem, tucked out of sight or at the end of an agenda for three years or so, had now come back to the forefront.[23]

And it was a further piece in the international kaleidoscope which Khrushchev was ready to shake. Ulbricht gave the first slight touch. On 27 October in a speech in East Berlin he claimed that in 1945 Berlin had not been made a fifth occupation zone: it was always a whole city which was first a part of the Soviet Zone and now was "situated in the territory of the GDR" and belonged to its "sphere of authority", though he recognised that by the agreement of 1955 Soviet forces still controlled the movement of allied garrisons to and from the western sectors. There was nothing new in any of this: East German politicians had often referred to the whole of Berlin as their capital. But Ulbricht went a stage further. The western allies, he alleged, had lost their right to be in the city by failing to honour the Potsdam agreement to liquidate Nazism and militarism; indeed, by forming the West German state and including it in the western alliance they had "undermined the legal basis for their presence in Berlin and forfeited all legal claim and every moral and political justification for continuing the occupation of Western Berlin".[24]

The immediate allied reaction to Ulbricht's speech was unruffled. British officials in Berlin merely thought it "quite interesting" that GDR claims were being extended and that "Ulbricht himself has given public expression to them for the first time". When Dulles was asked at a news conference on 7 November whether the speech was a threat to the security of Berlin, he answered that it was not, because the West was committed to hold the western sectors by military force if need be – and that, it was to be assumed, would deter any Communist move from words to deeds. It took a sharp Berlin eye to spot the new menace in Ulbricht's words. A German press analyst, who had worked for the US Mission in Berlin for twelve years, read the full text with care, then underlined in red a phrase which referred to the need to "neutralise" the western sectors. It was the first time she had seen that concept of western withdrawal, and she did not like it. She asked her boss "Will the Americans take my husband and me out of Berlin by airline if things go bad here?"[25]

Things were certainly about to get worse. On 10 November Khrushchev addressed a Soviet–Polish Friendship Rally in Moscow. "The reunification of Germany can only be decided by the German people themselves," he told his audience (in contradiction to what had been agreed in the Geneva Summit communiqué), though the peace treaty was still a matter for the four Powers. The Western Powers, he asserted, had broken the Potsdam agreement by allowing West Germany to become a major military power, to receive nuclear weapons from the United States and to become a major steel producer. (Not surprisingly he did not mention any of the numerous Soviet infractions, not least over freedom of movement between the occupation zones of Germany.) All that remained of the Potsdam Agreement, he declared, was "the so-called four-Power status of Berlin" and, in his view, the "time has clearly come for the Powers which signed the Potsdam Agreement to renounce the remnants of the regime of occupation in Berlin and thus make it possible to create a normal situation in the capital of the GDR". The Soviet Union was ready to hand over all its functions in the city to the "sovereign GDR" (and that presumably meant the control of allied traffic). If the three Western Powers had any questions about the city they should address them to the East German government (which, of course, would involve recognition). Then he issued a warning against extreme attempts to resist the new arrangements: "If any forces attack the GDR . . . we shall regard this as an attack against the Soviet Union and against all countries belonging to the Warsaw Pact." Finally a new threat: the Western Powers, he alleged, have used their sectors for subversive activities against the GDR, the Soviet Union and the Warsaw Pact. To do so they "still use the right of uninterrupted communication between West Berlin and western Germany by the air corridor(s), by rail and road, and by the waterways of the GDR which they still do not wish to recognise".[26]

In speaking as he did, Khrushchev challenged just about every western historical assumption about Berlin. He launched a crisis which would culminate in the building of the Berlin Wall. It was a crisis which the Western Powers had known would happen sooner or later, which they had tried to stave off with concessions to the Soviet authorities in the early 1950s, but which they had made no preparations to counter. Khrushchev had not so much stirred up the stagnation of Berlin as thrown in a bombshell.

4

Ultimatum

———————————

Convulsive though Khrushchev's bombshell was, West Berliners reacted with the calm closing of ranks which they had perfected over the years of threat. Basically Berliners love crises. They know they are good at them and they enjoy being the focus of attention. Some of them now dismissed Khrushchev's speech as "the usual stuff"; most argued that the Soviet Union did not want war so his threats were bluff – all the Western Powers had to do was to stand firm and call it. But few people underestimated the gravity of the situation: this was not routine Soviet probing and harassment; by the standards of "Berlin Weather", it was undoubtedly a storm. After a week or so, morale in West Berlin wavered: the stock market dropped about 10 per cent, bank withdrawals exceeded deposits for a few days and some accounts were transferred to West Germany, but there was no panic selling, no mass exodus from the western sectors, no hoarding of food. There was a scare on 14 November 1958 when an American convoy refused to be searched at the Berlin end of the Autobahn and was then surrounded by a ring of heavily armed Soviet troops for over eight hours before turning back. For a moment it had looked as if a new blockade might begin, or shooting would break out. (There would have been an even bigger scare had the public known that a US battle group was put on alert.) But traffic, military and civilian, soon flowed normally again and everyone relaxed. People were greatly reassured by newspaper stories (planted by the Pentagon) that the Americans had 600 aircraft standing by to fly in supplies. Poor Berliners: the story was totally untrue. But false hope is better than none. Schadenfreude is a great help too, and by the third week in November many West Berliners had persuaded themselves that the allies and not the western sectors were Khrushchev's target; the allies, they thought, could perfectly well look after themselves.[1]

Such consolation was all very well for the man in the street. West Berlin officials and businessmen, on the other hand, were not quite so sanguine. On 13 November Willy Brandt, the SPD Mayor who had been elected in 1956, told the US Deputy Commandant (the Military Commandant's political adviser) that Khrushchev's attack on the Berlin status quo enabled the East Germans to reduce the refugee flow by hinting that West Berlin would no longer be a safe escape route and, most dangerously, to shake the economic stability of the western sectors by scaring off investors and customers. He assumed that the East Germans would not be satisfied by control of traffic, nor even by eventual recognition of their regime; they would use their new powers to throttle West Berlin's communications with the Federal Republic. Indeed, since the destruction of West Berlin was their main aim, Brandt expected them to turn the sector boundary in Berlin into an international frontier so as to get a complete stranglehold on the western sectors. He told Sir Christopher Steel, the British ambassador, that when that happened the allies would no doubt protest, but "he knew that this would not be effective and that the de facto situation this created would have to be accepted." Brandt had not used the word "wall", but he had prophesied with horrible accuracy the forcible division of his city in 1961 and the impotent western response.[2]

The business community was more preoccupied by the immediate possibility of disruption of its traffic with the FRG: there were rumours from 15 November that the next Soviet move would be against commercial carriers. This was an alarming prospect. The western sectors received about 700,000 tons of supplies and raw materials a month and exported 100,000 tons of finished goods. Few businessmen believed that trade on that scale could be kept going for long by an airlift. For the moment, though, business confidence was not badly shaken. Private orders declined a little by the end of November, but the Bonn government then steadied morale by placing a few contracts with West Berlin firms and prolonging some tax concessions which were due to lapse. Such was the buoyancy of the economy and the overall optimism of Berliners that by the end of the year unemployment in the western sectors was down to 91,503 – a drop of over 16,000 from the previous December.

One vital ingredient for maintaining West Berlin's morale was, however, hard to come by: evidence that the Western Powers would stand up to the Kremlin and assert their rights in the city. Brandt's deputy, Franz Amrehn of the Christian Democratic Union, called for a prompt allied response to Khrushchev's speech, to be delivered to the Soviet embassy in East Berlin and to the Soviet government in Moscow. He wanted it to emphasise that East German control of allied communications with Berlin was unacceptable. Brandt agreed with the need for a speedy approach to the Kremlin and also suggested that spirits would be raised if the United States sent a few prominent visitors to the city as tokens of support. Neither suggestion was taken up. In fact an allied diplomatic move in Moscow was delayed until December and even West Berlin leaders themselves had to wait until 15 November, five days after the Khrushchev speech, before General Barksdale Hamlett, the American chairman for the month of the western Kommandatura, came to give them official reassurance that the Western Powers would stick to their guarantees to the western sectors – a dilatory formal response, one might think, however many informal contacts there had been before.[3]

And the effect of that reassurance soon rubbed off. Brandt and Amrehn were appalled to learn from the three Deputy Commandants on 20 November the details of allied standing orders on checkpoint procedures should East Germans ever replace Russians in the control of military traffic. These had originally been drafted as a more or less theoretical exercise in 1954 and updated in 1957; they were merely intended to postpone a "self-imposed" blockade. They stated that, if East Germans took over rail and road checkpoints, allied documents would be shown to them and a stamp accepted, though with a protest on the spot and another to the Soviet authorities later. Only if new documentation was introduced or the East Germans tried to impose customs duties and tolls on military traffic would vehicles and trains turn back. This policy, exclaimed Amrehn, meant "the occupiers are submitting to control by the occupied", and Brandt called in the Deputy Commandants to argue forcibly that any submission to East German controls would "destroy the Western allied position in Berlin". It might look like a minor technical adjustment, he explained, but in the context of the threat to the allied status in Berlin and the economic survival of the western sectors it would be a dangerous and possibly fatal step. Indeed, he added, if the Russians did hand their responsibilities to the GDR, he personally would rather see the Western Powers asserting their rights in the west of the city and the "sector boundary converted into a Chinese Wall". Cassandra words again – and this time "wall" was among them.[4]

His worries about accepting East Germans as Soviet "agents" for the control of allied military traffic fed nascent American doubts about the policy. On 20 November, the US Commandant in Berlin cabled the

Department of the Army in Washington and warned that submission to GDR traffic control would be "the first step in the wrong direction". The alternative was, of course, to stop allied traffic by road and rail which, as General Hamlett was well aware, would mean losing garrison supplies and communications with the allied authorities in the Federal Republic. Even so, he argued that if "we are not ready for the eventual showdown, at least a self-imposed blockade will be a far stronger action than de facto recognition of the GDR through the 'agent' fallacy". His views were taken seriously in Washington. The Joint Chiefs of Staff and representatives of the Departments of State and Defence, began to reconsider the contingency plans for access.[5]

Western officials in Berlin were also worried about the third means of allied communication: the air. What if East Germans turned up at the Berlin Air Safety Centre to replace the Soviet air controllers? Standing orders forbade East German substitutes – interestingly a more rigid policy for air traffic than for land communications. But the Deputy Commandants spent a lot of time on 17 November mulling over what to do if the Russians kept control over military flights (so stuck to the letter of their agreements on western air access) but insisted on the GDR dealing with civilian traffic. The East Germans and Russians had claimed for years that the air corridors had been provided for garrison needs only, and the Western Powers had often felt the argument was valid, even though they did not admit it. It was obvious now that the GDR would welcome the chance to block civilian flights to West Germany as a way of stemming the refugee flow. The British inclined to the view that sooner or later East Germans would have to be allowed into the BASC under the "agency" theory. The US Mission in Berlin, to the contrary, was determined to avoid any degree of recognition, and it was backed by General Lauris Norstad who commanded US troops in Germany. He told the JCS on 23 November that if East Germans tried to replace Soviet air controllers they should "be asked to leave and, if need be, escorted out". The JCS agreed with him. So, after a bit of persuasion, did the British and French. It was finally decided that any East German who turned up at the BASC would be shown the door; the Russians would be told that they were still responsible for all air traffic control, flight plans would be put on their (empty) desk, and flights would continue with or without their say so. Should there be any threat to civilian flights over the GDR, the airlines would be given extra insurance or military pilots and, if dangerous interference occurred, military aircraft would be substituted.[6]

Meanwhile in Washington, Paris and London there had been a great deal of diplomatic speculation about Khrushchev's speech of 10 November, but little or no progress towards a detailed policy for preventing or countering Soviet moves in Berlin. In spite of the fact that the allies had long known that this was a crisis waiting to happen, they had prepared nothing but contingency plans for preserving their own access, and these were in need of review in the light of existing circumstances. In the absence of strong, immediate measures, the Western Powers fell back on defensive, reactive responses to any Soviet initiative. Even these proved slow to come.

This sluggishness was dignified by worldly-wise injunctions to "sit tight", "wait and see" and "do nothing rash". After all, Khrushchev had not set a timetable or specified what he would do. And the signals from the Communist side were confusing. For example, on 12 November the East German Prime Minister, Otto Grotewohl, told a press conference that "Berlin is not the main question"; if it became necessary to change the agreements on allied access, the adjustments would be made in the context of a general settlement. On the same day the official Party newspaper, *Neues Deutschland*, stated that Khrushchev's remarks had been "hypothetical". All this could be interpreted as watering down the threatening tone of the speech and suggesting that the Communists too wanted to "wait and see" – to test western reactions before deciding what to do next. By contrast, Khrushchev himself rattled the occasional nuclear sabre. When the Swedish and Austrian ambassadors asked him on 10 November what would happen if the Western Powers refused to deal with the East Germans he replied confidently "They won't; our rockets are pointing the right way." He told the graduates of Soviet Military Academies on 14 November that Dulles's threats to use force to hold West Berlin "bounce off us"; the USSR, he boasted, "commands remedies that can bring any aggressor to his senses". In that same speech, he announced that his government was "preparing an appropriate document on the question of Berlin". That was a good enough excuse for the western capitals to wait a little longer.[7]

And there were even some indications that Khrushchev might eventually climb down. On 11 November the West German ambassador in Moscow, Hans Kroll, asked the Soviet Foreign Minister when Khrushchev would carry out his new policy. Gromyko was evasive and said he was not in a position to answer. A "Soviet source" (and Kroll had an ever-open door for Kremlin gossips) then hinted to the ambassador that Khrushchev's speech had sparked off a lively debate in the Presidium and that several senior members opposed too aggressive a stance. (Over thirty years later Sergo Mikoyan, son of the former deputy Foreign Minister, named his father as one of them and thought he might even have resigned over the issue but decided to stay on as a rare bird who actually dared to argue with the

Soviet leader.) The British ambassador, Sir Patrick Reilly, noted on 24 November how quiet everything had been for the past two weeks – nothing more from Khrushchev, no Soviet press comment: "It is all pretty odd and not at all in Khrushchev's normal style." Perhaps the initiative "had not been worked out in detail", perhaps the Kremlin was finding it complicated to hand over not just duties to the East Germans but the whole job of putting pressure on the Western Powers. Was the Soviet leader having second thoughts?[8]

Many people wondered if Khrushchev had been pushed by Ulbricht further and faster than he wanted to go. Brandt said on 13 November that the East Germans reckoned they were the driving force behind the new initiative and the Soviet ambassador had assured them of support. There was tittle-tattle on the diplomatic cocktail circuit too. By December American officials in Geneva and Prague had picked up stories from Soviet and GDR diplomats that Khrushchev had staged the crisis at the insistence of the East Germans who felt their regime could not cope any longer with the drain of refugees and wanted a major change in the status of Berlin. Would he finally decide that the East German game was not worth the Soviet candle?[9]

There was, indeed, a hint that not even the Soviet authorities in Berlin knew what would happen next. In the second week of November the three Western Powers realised they had not received the usual invitations to the annual Russian celebration of the October Revolution – all the more surprising since for weeks past Soviet officials had been promising them a particularly good party. Was it that the Russians were reluctant to entertain those they had just described as "illegal occupiers of Berlin"? Or did they think that the crisis would have escalated by then and everyone would be more in the mood for shooting than champagne? Or did the Soviet authorities imagine that their buildings as well as duties would be handed over so quickly to the East Germans that there would be nowhere to hold the yearly beanfeast?* The social storm soon blew itself out. By the end of the year Russians and East Germans were avidly seizing invitations to western parties and, after a few drinks, hinting heavily that Khrushchev had taken considerable risks to oblige Pankow – which supported the argument that Khrushchev might well drop the initiative.[10]

All these reports and rumours provided nothing more than a chance to read Soviet policy from blurred runes and predict Kremlin moves by

---

* The party did take place – and the Norwegian Military Mission were the only westerners to be asked to it. Willy Brandt had returned to Berlin after the war as a member of that mission. Did Soviet social secretaries have extremely out of date guest lists?

examining the entrails of a small mouse. Those were the only mechanisms the Western Powers ever had to work with, since contacts with Soviet officials, let alone leaders, were few and far between and the heavily censored Soviet press shed only the light which had been narrowly beamed by those in charge. (Until Soviet and East German archives have been fully opened and deeply ploughed, the historian is not much better equipped.) The very vagueness of the situation of course encouraged the allies to stay vague too. It was also an excuse to avoid the hard graft and potential divisiveness of agreeing on strategy and tactics. This was dangerous: would the Kremlin interpret the western stance as "dignified silence" or as proof that the West had been winded by a well-aimed blow?

When Eisenhower heard the news of Khrushchev's speech on 10 November, his son and aide, John, observed that: "The Boss, seeing nothing to react to immediately, held his tongue." As the President himself explained later: "Too much eagerness to counter Khrushchev's statement would give the impression that our government was edgy." In Eisenhower's view, western rights in Berlin were firmly based, the allied sectors were secure given the West's frequent and public promises to defend them, and the Soviet Union had no more wish for war than he did. The only decisive action needed was to restrain his own military. When the American convoy was held up on 14 November General Norstad, with the full approval of the JCS, announced his intention of sending a battle group down the Autobahn to force the lorries through; if the battle group in turn were detained he would get it out by the "minimum force necessary". However "minimum" that force would be, it was too much for Eisenhower. He refused to give the go-ahead, and insisted that no move be made without prior approval from his allies. He was not going to start a war on his own; he preferred not to start a war at all.[11]

His whole approach was approved by the Acting Secretary of State, Christian Herter, who was minding the shop while Dulles was out of Washington. He recommended the President on 13 November to avoid "actions which might over-dramatise the present situation". His calm was in line with a report from his Department's Bureau of Intelligence and Research which suggested it was "unlikely that the USSR plans at the present time to use force against the western position or to blockade the city", let alone "undertake a substantial risk of war over Berlin", though "the West must expect a serious increase of tension". The State Department briefed its embassies to avoid conveying "the impression of excitement or undue anxiety" and to regard the recent Soviet move as "a probing attempt in the war of nerves". When Herter telephoned Dulles on

13 November he admitted that he himself found it difficult to tell if "this is just probing or business". The Secretary of State had no doubts: "It is probing," he declared confidently. Nor was Dulles ruffled by the question troubling others: whether East Germans could be accepted as Soviet agents at checkpoints. He told the West German ambassador, Wilhelm Grewe, on 17 November that he did not feel strongly one way or the other about dealing with GDR officials – after all, his government dealt with the Communist Chinese over practical matters, even though the United States did not formally recognise the Republic of China.[12]

Eisenhower's immediate foreign policy advisers might be imperturbable, but the US ambassador in Moscow, Llewellyn Thompson, called Khrushchev's speech "a most dangerous move": an expression of frustration at not getting talks with the Western Powers and an attempt to exploit tension to force recognition of the GDR. Thompson's view had to be taken seriously. He had studied the Kremlin since he first went to Moscow as Second Secretary in the American embassy in 1940 and stayed at his post, observing the Soviet scene, when most of the staff left following the German invasion of the USSR. Since then he had broadened his experience in Washington and in the negotiations for the Austrian State Treaty before returning to Moscow as ambassador in 1957. By comparison with most diplomats he had a close relationship with Khrushchev – he was one of the few westerners to be asked to stay at a Khrushchev dacha. This was a tribute to his discretion, to the combination of guts and good manners with which he stood up to the First Secretary's hectorings, and the sincerity with which he worked for mutually acceptable solutions to Russo-American problems. It was also a help that Thompson came from a poor Colorado ranching family and he and Khrushchev could swop jokes about herding sheep in their younger days. His wife, Jane, made a big contribution too. Khrushchev enjoyed her charm, candour and spontaneity; he treasured a glass she once gave him which looked large but was so solid that even a drop of alcohol made it seem full – she suggested he would find it useful for the endless toasts at receptions.[13]

On 14 November Thompson urged the President to make a speech confirming western rights in Berlin and stressing the importance of allied communications. In the following week, he warned that, although the Soviet Union would like to avoid armed conflict, once it had handed its functions in Berlin to the East Germans it "would take great risks rather than back down in the face of our counter action." So the best policy would be to act before the Kremlin did; the worst "would be one in which there is any uncertainty as to what to do". That meant getting agreement from Britain and France on the use of force to maintain the Berlin position and allied access, then telling Moscow what had been decided "promptly but confidentially". Clearly for Thompson there had to be a clear distinction between "over-dramatising" and muffing a cue.[14]

Allen Dulles, John Foster's brother and Director of the CIA, was also arguing that the Russians would carry out their threat to hand over responsibility in Berlin to the East Germans, that this would "create the most complicated situation in Berlin since the end of the Blockade" and that preparations must be made to face it. The US Embassy in Bonn was equally certain that the GDR would soon take on Soviet functions and challenge western rights in the city. Not least, Eisenhower was aware of the Federal Republic's need for reassurance. On 20 November Adenauer wrote to Dulles (as well as to Paris and London) expressing concern at the gravity of the situation and warning against the slightest allied concession. The West German press was calling for a firm stand, so were Bonn officials.[15]

By 21 November Eisenhower had decided "the time had come to make some sort of low-key announcement that the United States would stand on its commitments" – but so low-key that it was made by his Press Secretary, Jim Hagerty, at a routine press conference, and in the most general terms ("our firm intentions in West Berlin remain unchanged"), refusing to spell out what they meant. At the same time the President gave way to Dulles's calls for scotching press rumours of a split in the allied camp and soothing Bonn's worries: he accepted a State Department draft for a Note to be delivered in Moscow by the three allies. He confided to Herter on the phone that "his instinct was to make a very simple statement to the effect that if the Russians want war over the Berlin issue they can have it", but he then laughed the matter off and said he would not actually say that, but wait for further developments.[16]

In the event, he would have to wait until 31 December before his allies agreed on the text of the Note to Moscow. Other joint decisions would take even longer – and many of them were never reached. The Western Powers were divided, not just on details but on their whole approach to the crisis.

The most predictable western reaction to the Soviet initiative of November 1958 – and, indeed, the most consistent policy for the next three years – came from the Federal Republic of Germany. The West Germans were convinced that, given a resolute and united stand by the West, the Kremlin would back down. When he first heard of Khrushchev's 10 November speech, Chancellor Adenauer wondered if it had been off-the-cuff, in which case it might be nothing more than a whim or an audience grabber and have no consequences. Once he learned that Khrushchev had spoken from a prepared text, Adenauer had no doubts at all: this was a dangerous situation, dangerous not just for the FRG but for the world. On 12 November his Press Office issued a warning that any unilateral renunciation by the USSR of international agreements on the four-Power occupation of Berlin would sharpen international tensions. It added that the Federal government and people of Berlin had every confidence in western assurances on the defence of the city. This was a case of "wishing will make it so": Bonn was, and would remain, deeply dubious about the reliability of its allies and their readiness to keep their promises. Adenauer and his government had the reputation within the alliance of an irritating, insatiable, craving for reassurance. On this occasion, as is so often true with whining and demanding children, they had every reason to feel insecure.[17]

At least the Federal Republic knew where it stood with the Soviet Union. The Soviet ambassador, Andrei Smirnov, spent an hour on 20 November telling Adenauer frankly, and even rudely, that the Soviet Union would not be deterred from handing over its responsibilities in Berlin. The message, like the manner of its delivery, was brutal but the Chancellor had long expected it and had a policy for dealing with the inevitable crisis. On the assumption that his allies were not as well prepared, a long memorandum was sent to them from Bonn two days later stressing that no one should enter negotiations "with the Soviet Zone regime" because all experience proved that these would only produce "a temporary and artificial solution" followed by further demands, a process which would weaken world confidence in the alliance and in NATO. Privately Heinrich von Brentano, the Federal Foreign Minister, expressed concern to the US ambassador and others that any concession – and he specifically mentioned the showing of allied military travel documents to East Germans at checkpoints – would start an avalanche of capitulation. Unless the Western Powers reacted to the earliest Soviet move with total firmness, they would "have lost the first bloodless blow of the Third World War".[18]

That was very much the approach that the French wanted. Paris, like Bonn, believed that the Soviet handover of control of access to the East Germans would be done in slow stages, making it difficult to know where to make a stand. Better, France believed, to stick to the principle that the Soviet Union remained responsible for allied traffic and to refuse any dealings at all with East Germans at checkpoints. This may not have been the line which the French Foreign Minister, Maurice Couve de Murville, would have chosen. He commented to the British ambassador on 17 November that the West faced the dilemma of risking war rather than implying recognition of the GDR – and, as far as he was concerned, it was a great mistake not to have recognised the GDR long before. Whatever his personal misgivings, however, Couve was corseted by the inflexible strategy of the man who had led the French government since May 1958 and who would become the President of the Fifth Republic in December – Charles de Gaulle.[19]

Germany was a central issue in de Gaulle's foreign policy and the Berlin crisis offered an opportunity to achieve several of his aims. Germany, indeed, had been central to his life. He was well read in German literature, philosophy and history; he spoke German better than English (well enough to talk to Willy Brandt in German with only occasional explanation of nuance by an interpreter). De Gaulle's father had been wounded in 1871 during the Prussian siege of Paris, at the climax of the unification of Germany. He himself had fought the Germans in the First World War, been wounded twice, and spent thirty-two months as a prisoner-of-war in their hands. He fought them again in the Second World War – as commander of a tank division, as Under-Secretary for National Defence for twelve brief days before France was overrun, then as leader of the Free French in London. When he returned to liberated Paris in August 1944, the city was still within German artillery range. He set up a national government before the German army was driven from French soil.[20]

A lifetime of enmity towards Germany had not, however, left de Gaulle enamoured by those who had fought at his side. For his allies he reserved a separate category of hostility. Where, he asked, were the Americans in 1914 or 1939? Who had cried "Halt" in 1918 and ended the war "at the very moment when we were about to pluck the fruits of victory"? The Anglo-Saxons. Who had dominated the Versailles conference and denied France the reparations she deserved? The United States. Who had backed the Vichy regime throughout the next war, withheld recognition of his own government until three months after the liberation of Paris, had the insolence to plan an occupation administration for France and the stupidity to imagine that training the staff for it would only take two months? Again: the United States. Who had dared to contemplate the surrender of Alsace to the Germans during the Ardennes offensive and had told de Gaulle he would be denied petrol and ammunition if he tried to defend Strasbourg? The American general, Eisenhower. Who attacked the French fleet at Mers el-Kebir and landed in Corsica without so much as a warning to him? The British. Who had told him in 1944: "Any time we have to choose between Europe and the open seas we shall always be for the open seas . . . Every time I have to choose between you and Roosevelt, I shall chose Roosevelt"? The British Prime Minister, Winston Churchill.

Wartime exile in London had rubbed the salt of humiliation in de Gaulle's wounds of defeat. Harold Macmillan was probably right to suggest years later that "Things would have been easier if southern

England had been occupied by the Nazis – if we'd had Lloyd George for Pétain; then we would have been equal." As it was, de Gaulle felt himself and his nation patronised. Dependence on American military might to free his own country kept his wounds painfully open; exclusion from most of the allied councils of war made them fester. Already by 1943 he had announced "I have no more confidence in the Anglo-Saxons. From now on my policy will be based on the Russians, and perhaps on the Germans." But even when peace came, he was stuck in the western alliance; all he could do was to make his position more palatable with the formula he had used throughout the war: "The weaker I am, the more intransigent I shall be." And obduracy was constantly called for as he faced the ignominy of his country's post-war status. France was excluded from the Yalta and Potsdam conferences, condescendingly tossed an occupation zone in Germany and a sector of Berlin, given only temporary support by the Soviet Union in her claims for the Saar and the Rhineland and none at all by the Western Powers. She was deserted by the British and checked by the Americans in Suez; never even informed of the Anglo-American invasion of the Lebanon in July 1958. The country was drained by colonial wars in South-East Asia and North Africa. The General himself, who had been branded a deserter by a French court in 1940, was rejected by his people in elections in 1952. Once more he went into exile, this time to his home, La Boisserie, in the tiny village of Colombey-les-Deux-Églises. Here he walked three times a day, brooded, lived on a colonel's pension, played simple games with his severely handicapped and beloved daughter, and crafted his eloquent and magisterial memoirs. Six years, seventeen Prime Ministers and twenty-four wobbly ministries later he was recalled to power.

He took power as his right. The cartoons which showed the General as Saint Joan of Arc or Louis XIV encapsulated his almost mystic assimilation with France and the noble role he believed that he and his country must play. De Gaulle was "convinced that France is true to herself only when she stands in the front rank; that only great enterprises can neutralise the poisons of disunity which her people carry in their veins; that our country, such as it is, in the world as it is, must hold itself erect and look to the heights if it is not to fall into mortal peril. To sum it up, France cannot be France for me without grandeur, and not France unless she is great."

The world as he analysed it in 1958 was haunted by fear of conflict between the United States and the Soviet Union – a conflict which would be fought on the European battlefield. The Atlantic alliance "amounted to the military and political subordination of western Europe to the United States of America" which prevented détente with the USSR. Germany was the pawn of the two opposed sides. There could be no true European union without Germany, no lasting peace until there was a settlement acceptable to its "great people"; yet Germany's "evil genius" had to be restrained. France must take the lead in establishing a new order: encourage the interdependence of the continental states through the EEC, create a "European" ("American-free") Europe, develop détente and then entente with the East, and maintain the Atlantic alliance "as an ultimate precaution" while detaching from "the integration under American command" which NATO had brought about. To do all this France must be independent – and her independence could only be assured if she had her own nuclear weapons, the means of defence against mightier aggressors and the ticket for a place at the conference tables of the great Powers. Not for de Gaulle the ignoble nuclear posture of Britain: the English, he told one of his diplomats in 1960, had become satellites of the United States and were "truffés d'armes" (as perhaps a capon might be studded with truffles), American arms over which they had no control. He himself proudly rejected Dulles's offer in July 1958 of American weapons under the double-key arrangement which had so gratified Macmillan; later he would refuse to allow the Americans to base nuclear weapons on French soil. These were grand gestures indeed from the head of a state which did not test its own first nuclear device until January 1960. They were demonstrations of the intransigence which turned France's weakness into strength.

And it was with the confidence of the strong, and not in the spirit of the weak groping for support, that President de Gaulle agreed to meet Chancellor Adenauer on 14 September 1958. With matching self-assurance, he invited the Chancellor to stay not in a great palace but in his own home in Colombey-les-Deux-Églises. It was a simple, family house, inelegantly furnished and always cold, for all that rudimentary central heating had been installed in 1948 and the General himself constantly stoked open fires. Madame de Gaulle, quite as proud and stubborn as her husband when she chose, refused to titivate her home to impress their great visitor; he must take them as he found them. They had both reached an intuitive understanding of how best to please him. Adenauer was moved by the very personal consideration shown him, impressed by the simplicity and naturalness he found in de Gaulle, and honoured by his exquisite courtesy. This was a historic meeting: a coming together of enemies, the start of a revolution in European politics. It was possible because both participants had pride in themselves and their countries, had known personal and national degradation but triumphed over it, would not stoop in their private relations or their public policies, and could disagree with each other's views without feeling threatened by them.

They did indeed disagree on many fundamental questions. They had a different vision of Europe. Adenauer was in favour of close integration, of encouraging political bonds to develop from the economic partnership of the EEC; de Gaulle did not believe that Europe could or should be a political entity. Neither wanted to include Britain in their Community while she still maintained strong ties with the Commonwealth and United States and insisted on broadening the concept of Europe by adding seven peripheral states to create a free trade area rather than a common market. De Gaulle made clear his distrust of American influence in Europe and his intention to leave NATO eventually; Adenauer stressed the Federal Republic's need for American protection and won the President's sympathy plus the promise of French defence. For the Chancellor, of course, NATO gave not just security but partnership. The President, on the other hand, was not satisfied with equality for all. Two days after this meeting, he wrote to Eisenhower and Macmillan and recommended that the three of them should control the alliance's policy. France's future membership, he warned, would depend on this change being implemented. Ironically, de Gaulle was calling for tripartite authority just when a major crisis was about to break in Berlin – the one place where tripartitism was embodied and where it would be tested and often found wanting.

On the problem of Germany de Gaulle did not spare his guest's feelings: the country's division, he said, was artificial, but reunification could only be accepted if Germany renounced nuclear weapons and resigned herself to the present frontiers; national unity would only be possible in the remote future and the Germans must wait for it "with unremitting patience". The Chancellor accepted this bleak prospect with surprising calm. De Gaulle wrote later that he sensed that this Catholic, Conservative Rhinelander represented the Federal Republic's misgivings about incorporating the Prussian, Protestant, Socialist East. He himself did not admit to embarrassment in dashing German nationalist hopes. In 1962 he haughtily told the then Austrian Foreign Minister, Bruno Kreisky: "We have brought Germany the friendship of France, and that must be worth at least as much as reunification."

At the end of the meeting at Colombey-les-Deux-Églises, the two men had established a rapport which would be strengthened by talking again on 26 November at Bad Kreuznach, a small spa town on the Nahe. Their relationship was maintained thereafter by over a hundred hours of conversation during fifteen other encounters and a correspondence of forty letters – letters which de Gaulle always wrote by hand, a courtesy deeply appreciated by Adenauer. The rapprochement of the two states was accelerated by their shared views of the Berlin crisis. There would be no formal treaty between France and West Germany until 1963, but the growing national and personal accord was dramatically and emotionally demonstrated in 1962 when the two leaders prayed together in the cathedral at Strasbourg, a city which their countries had so often fought over.

The development of Europe in the second half of the twentieth century, let alone the handling of the Berlin crisis from 1958, would have been so very different had the British been capable of the vision and magnanimity of de Gaulle and Adenauer. But Britain, who had not suffered, as France had, two defeats and three invasions by the Germans in the course of seventy-four years nor a recent degrading and savage occupation, was incapable of burying the hatchet. Hostility to Germany, developed in two world wars, was nurtured thereafter by virulently anti-German British media, especially the Beaverbrook press, the public's appetite for war memoirs and prisoner-of-war escape stories, and a cinema seemingly devoted to a monoculture of films about a brave British hero single-handedly seeing off Nazi hordes, thanks to his own stiff upper lip and Jerry's lack of a sense of humour. Tales of past glories distracted the British people from their new poverty, loss of Empire, and need to replace obsolete industry and outdated trading patterns. The attempts of successive post-war governments to straddle the United States and the Commonwealth, while keeping one toe on the very edge of Europe, were precarious to the point of political hernia or diplomatic multiple fracture. For several years after 1945 the British Foreign Office allocated up to one half of its entire staff to the occupation of Germany but for nearly a decade had no European department. No wonder that perceptions of the Germans, even at this supposedly sophisticated level, were warped and those of the future of Europe and Britain's place in it remained so unrealistic.

If anything, Britain's relations with Germany deteriorated when Harold Macmillan became Prime Minister in 1956. As his biographer, Alistair Horne, put it: "Like so many of his generation, he could never quite overcome his distrust and dislike of Germans or of anyone who supported them." He bore the wounds of fighting them in the First World War: a damaged right hand which crabbed his writing and gave him a flabby handshake; bullet fragments in his pelvis and lower leg which caused pain all his life and a shuffling walk which many dismissed as a lasting Balliol affectation. Those who lost nearly all of their contemporaries in the terrible battles of 1914–18 carried bitter feelings and loneliness to their graves. Macmillan's conventional upbringing had done nothing to encourage understanding of Europeans in general. He was born at a time when the British looked beyond the Continent to the Empire; he was educated in the classics, not modern languages; he preferred a holiday on a moor to a trip abroad; he came from a nation which historically only involved itself in European affairs to restore the balance of power then willingly withdrew to its island. His major concerns as Foreign Secretary then as Prime Minister were with Britain's remaining worldwide commitments and colonial responsibility, which had to be carried out with diminishing resources and a chronically weak currency.[21]

Macmillan disliked Adenauer and feared a German domination of Europe which Britain had fought two major wars to prevent. The Chancellor, in turn, had deep-rooted prejudices – few men had more or deeper.* He never forgot or forgave the fact that a British brigadier sacked him as Mayor of Cologne at the end of the war on the grounds that he had not shown "proper supervision and energy". (It was the Americans who reinstated him.) Since then he had been pained to see Britain standing aloof from Europe after Churchill's initial enthusiasm and had somehow managed to persuade himself that Britain was behind France's refusal to ratify the agreement to form a European Defence Community. He believed that the 1957 Defence White Paper presaged withdrawal of British troops from Germany, feared that fashionable British talk about disengagement in Europe would lead to enforced German neutralisation, suspected that London would happily settle with the Soviet Union at the price of a permanent division of Germany, and saw Macmillan's zeal for adding seven peripheral nations to the European Six as a malign attempt to sabotage the Common Market and convert it into a free trade area for the sole benefit of Britain and its Commonwealth and at the expense of European unity.[22]

As if all that were not bad enough, Adenauer was maddened by the reporting of the Federal Republic in the British press; according to the British ambassador he found it "hostile, unfair, vindictive and outdated". He was even angrier that his constant complaints about it produced no improvement and assumed that the biased coverage must be inspired by the British government. Yet rancorous though Adenauer could be, he was easily won over by even the slightest personal approach, and a full-scale meeting would give him a rosy view of its participants for months on end. Alas, the British government could seldom bring itself to make such gestures. The Foreign Office official responsible for relations with the

---

* The French ambassador in Bonn described him as "tenant toujours ouvert le cahier de ses doléances" – keeping ever-open a list of grievances of the kind pre-Revolutionary French deputies would present to the King to inform him of the complaints of his subjects.

Federal Republic played to Macmillan's aversions by calling any response to Adenauer's need for reassurance "running after the Germans". All in all, the recent Anglo-German relationship and the personal bias of the two heads of state did not bode well for cooperation in facing the Berlin crisis.[23]

Much the same could be said for the interaction between London and Paris. Macmillan had a slightly better rapport with de Gaulle than with Adenauer, but that was not saying a lot. The Prime Minister gleefully recalled that the General's wartime code-name had been "Ramrod" – a reminder of "a man who was alleged to have all the rigidity of a poker without its occasional warmth". And that rigidity, which others found a unique strength, Macmillan could only see as exasperating. Macmillan was occasionally prepared to acknowledge some of the President's personal virtues: "He has extraordinary dignity and charm," he wrote in November 1961, " 'unbends' delightfully, is nice to servants and children and so forth." Yet "he does not apparently listen to argument . . . He merely repeats over and over again what he has said before." And: "He talks of Europe and means France." Conversely, of course, de Gaulle did actually listen to what Macmillan said and did not like what he heard about Britain's colonial duties, American ties and special trading needs – it all added up to anti-Europeanism as far as he was concerned. The Suez adventure and Britain's subsequent concentration on repairing the ties with the United States had inevitably opened a rift between France and Britain. By September 1958, with the startling French rapprochement with the Federal Republic and de Gaulle's threat to leave NATO unless a triumvirate were set up, that rift had widened to a chasm.

The contrast between the frosty relations with the continental Powers and the warmth of Macmillan's feelings for the United States owed much to the political advantages which Britain had gained from the partnership for several generations and a little extra from the Prime Minister's own background and character. His mother had been born in Indiana. He himself, as he confessed to his biographer, was "a strange, very buttoned up person" yet he could relax in response to Americans' open friendliness and unpretentiousness. He was never as comfortable in British company, let alone European. His Edwardian country house manners, the actor-manager's expertise in hogging centre stage and timing effects for maximum theatrical impact, the skilfully painted image of effortless superiority and majestic calm, all concealed boiling emotions and the constant fear of attacks of Black Dog – paralysing fits of despondency which he airily pooh-poohed as easily remedied by strong doses of Jane Austen. The man the public loved or loathed as a toff also suffered profound social ill-ease. He took pride in his marriage to the daughter of a duke (though was anguished by her love for another man); when it suited him, he claimed to be the grandson of a Scottish crofter (though his grandfather left the croft at eleven years old and established an extremely successful publishing house, which gave Harold a comfortable income and a "gentleman's profession"). He did not quite fit anywhere. This, together with his emotional repression, left him with few friends or intimates, though his dry wit, flashes of charm, stocks of beautifully told and maliciously detailed stories made him clubbable.

If he lacked the social half of Aristotle's definition of a man, he was certainly very much a political animal. David Bruce, who became US ambassador in London when he left Bonn, judged him to be "shrewd, subtle in manoeuvre" and, in spite of his occasional "air of Victorian languor", he could "featly spring onto his toes like a ballet dancer" and perform the most intricate political choreography. He was a connoisseur of the House of Commons, a specialist in its moods and likely shifts of opinion. He was an expert performer there, too, though his polished speeches took days of preparation and he was acutely nervous before making them. Unflappability (a French interpreter once translated the word as "macmillanisme") was not a natural characteristic but a political weapon. He hid his strong political ambition in the cloak of a Whig grandee.

His Foreign Secretary, Selwyn Lloyd, was the ideal man for the job as defined by Macmillan: loyal, hard-working, honest, with few original ideas and little confidence or persistence in pushing those he had. He could be given high office without becoming a political rival – his standing in the Party and the House was too low for that. Macmillan delegated to him the technical aspects of foreign policy, in which he himself took no interest, and the slog of mastering details of briefs from the Foreign Office, which he tended to wave aside as "a lot of fuss by officials". Lloyd was a ready butt for the snobbery in which Macmillan hid his own social ambivalence: "a middle class lawyer from Liverpool", he called him, suggesting the kind of provincial attorney in the nineteenth-century novels Macmillan loved, who was only asked to dinner if there were thirteen at table. The Prime Minister was amused by his Foreign Secretary's humble gratitude for a permanent suite at Chequers, the official country residence which Macmillan tended to shun on the grounds that he did not "like weeding other people's gardens" and to which he could find much smarter, even ducal, alternatives for the weekend. The *Observer* once unkindly suggested that Lloyd's "great asset to the Prime Minister is that when he is dropped no one will notice his departure"; when he was finally dismissed from the Foreign Office he was in tears at the sight of the staff lined up to bid him farewell, so fortunately was too moved to notice that when the Permanent Under-Secretary called for three cheers they could only raise enough enthusiasm for two. This subservient, diligent, safe pair of hands offered no challenge to Macmillan's intention to be his own Foreign Secretary; he got on with the drudgery while his master dealt directly with the "top people" at the "top table". Unfortunately Lloyd could not fill any of the gaps in Macmillan's sympathies or understanding. Just as bad, he backed away from argument even when his instincts were perfectly sound.[24]

There was a disastrous example of this weakness and of the blind spots in British foreign policy right at the beginning of the Berlin crisis. Sir Anthony Rumbold Bt, the Foreign Office official in charge of German affairs, penned a six-page memorandum which was sent as telegram 8113 on 15 November to Paris and Washington for discussion with the other two Western Powers in Berlin, and passed for information to British posts in Moscow, Bonn, Warsaw, Prague, Geneva and at NATO and the United Nations. This telegram could be easily mistaken for a statement of British government policy and had a wide circulation long before American or French reaction to it could be tested. It opened with an analysis of Khrushchev's possible motives for the 10 November initiative: an attempt, in Sir Anthony's view, to stop West Germany getting American nuclear weapons, an inducement to the Western Powers to negotiate on Germany and disengage in Central Europe; hoping to build up the GDR and oblige the West to recognise its regime, and to consolidate the Soviet satellite empire. Nothing remarkable so far: most people concerned had the same ideas and stressed one or the other according to taste. Rumbold, however, leapt from that ruminative position to arguing that it would "be foolish not to proceed on the assumption that Khrushchev is going to do more or less what he says he is going to do": hand over Soviet functions in Berlin to the East Germans. From there he jumped to an even more pessimistic opinion: "We cannot stop him from doing this. The main question for us to decide is therefore how to react when he does it." Sir Anthony had not paused to consider whether Khrushchev might be "trying it on", whether a firm and united stand in public, or in private as Thompson had suggested, might pre-empt further moves. He was prepared to remain passive and let the Kremlin make the running.[25]

By the middle of his second page Sir Anthony rallied a little from his mood of gloom and doom and managed a rather more spirited paragraph: "We must naturally proceed from the basis that we will under no circumstances withdraw our forces from Berlin or abandon the West Berliners whom we are pledged to support." Rather than let Berliners starve under blockade "we would resort to force" because the alternative "would be as fatal to NATO as it would be dishonourable". Stirring stuff.

But what he said thereafter made it clear he would avoid using force at all costs. And the price he was willing to pay for continued allied presence in Berlin and avoidance of a blockade of the western sectors was recognition of the GDR. After all, he argued, the Federal Republic and West Berlin authorities dealt with East Germans, and the GDR already controlled the city's civilian traffic. If the western military refused to submit to East German personnel at checkpoints, the GDR would put the screws on civilian access, leaving the West to maintain their sectors by air – and "our preliminary examination of the technical problems involved suggests that we would not repeat *not* be able to supply Berlin by airlift for more than a year." QED: an airlift was not an option, the only choice was between force or dealing with the GDR. He took head-on the current metaphor that dealing even on minor matters "would bring us rapidly on to a slippery slope at the end of which would lie full and formal recognition of the DDR". Not for Sir Anthony a slow traverse; he closed his skis and schussed straight down. It might be possible, he admitted, to draw up rules for behaviour at checkpoints, "maintaining the theory" that the Russians were still responsible for allied access, but in his despondent opinion "we ought not to be under any illusion that such a modus vivendi would be allowed to operate for very long, if at all"; the Western Powers would soon be faced with an icy, precipitous downhill run and be obliged to choose between recognition or a blockade which could only be broken by force.

Selwyn Lloyd was given the Rumbold memo on 14 November, on the evening before it was sent off as a telegram. He minuted his agreement that Berlin could not be abandoned and added that "Dealing on a de facto basis with the East Germans is a reasonable course and I would not much mind if it ended up with the recognition of the DDR Government." Thus far, capitulationist. But he was much readier than Sir Anthony to take the slippery slope in slow stages, on the off-chance that a plunge into the chasm at the bottom could be avoided. He spotted the point that if the experts thought the western sectors could be supplied by air for twelve months, then "in practice, that means indefinitely", because "I refuse to believe that human ingenuity would not be able to protract it." In that case, of course, the whole Rumbold argument collapsed: there was at least one middle way which avoided the stark alternatives of recognition or war, or which at least could stave them off for a considerable length of time.

It was for these very reasons of widening options and buying time that the former Foreign Secretary, Ernest Bevin, had argued so passionately for an airlift during the blockade of Berlin in 1948–9. He had always believed in the need to boost Berliners' morale and show defiance of the Soviet Union. More than that: even if "the Russians held the cards . . . we could bluff them out of their hands by convincing them that we meant business" and the longer the Soviet Union tried to starve to death two and a half million people, the more criminal it would look in the eyes of the world and the greater the political pressure to raise the siege. (The only time limit for Bevin was how long Berliners themselves thought they could hold out.) He was also ready to gamble that the Russians would not use force against an airlift because they would not risk war; to remind them how high the stakes were, he encouraged quiet but observable military preparations for a conflict he had every intention of avoiding. And Bevin had forced his policy through when his allies were very dubious that it would work, when all the experts assured him that it was absolutely impossible to maintain a large civilian population by air, when Berlin's stockpiles were low and the Western Powers were painfully short of transport aircraft. Now, in 1958, the air forces could promise twelve (or even fifteen) months' supply, were ready to start a mini-lift straightaway to top up comfortably full warehouses in the western sectors, and had experience in running the successful previous operation with the added benefit that, this time round, the West Germans could contribute to the financial costs.

What Bevin had always appreciated was that there is never one single, instant solution to a political dilemma. An airlift offered what the JCS had termed "a cushion of time": to forge a stronger alliance, test Soviet will, try any number of non-military manoeuvres, reject unsatisfactory compromises and wait for the best settlement. How odd that Sir Anthony Rumbold, a professional diplomat, demonstrated no belief that diplomatic process might help to avert this particular crisis or contribute to its solution. Selwyn Lloyd in turn had noticed that an airlift made time available, but had not suggested political action to fill it. Had either of them remembered what had happened a mere ten years ago (or had the intellectual curiosity to find out) they might have been a little more confident in their own crafts. Indeed, they might have decided that the Soviet Union had learned the lesson in 1949 that blockades did not work and would try something else this time. In that case what was needed now was new analysis and fresh policies, not pat, worst case answers to outdated scenarios.

As it was, telegram 8113 was despatched to Washington, Paris and elsewhere, minus the Foreign Secretary's rider about the possible effectiveness of an airlift (though a cover letter did contain a phrase about what "ingenuity and effort" could do to extend the period of supply). It was received as a stink bomb. At a discussion in the State Department on 21 November Foy Kohler, Deputy Assistant Secretary for European Affairs, analysed some of its more noisome elements. Dealing with the GDR to buy a temporary period of peace and quiet, he argued, would not avoid the slippery slope but actually push the Western Powers on to it, leading to full recognition, and damaging the relationship with the Federal Republic and allied prestige in Europe; the bottom of that slope was not, in any case, recognition but the West Germans having to leave NATO. Far better, in his view, to stabilise the present situation (which Khrushchev was trying to break up) by a display of strength followed by negotiations. American officials, near and far, were equally horrified by the telegram. The ambassador in London was quick to point out to Selwyn Lloyd that recognition would end the quadripartite status of Berlin, stripping the legal basis for the western presence in the city. The US embassy in Bonn condemned Rumbold's thesis as "defeatist" and complained of the "simplistic" argument of British diplomats in the city that the public would never agree to die for the principle of non-recognition of the DDR – after all, said the embassy, the public in 1939 had been willing to die for Danzig, once the issues had been properly explained to them.[26]

The British Deputy Commandant in Berlin, Edward Peck, suggested to the British embassy in Bonn that the trouble with the telegram was its implication that recognition of the GDR would have to come almost immediately: "I doubt if this is really meant by the author." ("Yes, it was so meant," Sir Anthony proudly scribbled in pencil on the copy of the cable which arrived on his desk.) Instant recognition, thought Peck, was "abandoning the battle before it has begun". He did, however, think that his American counterpart Findley Burns was "unrealistic" in believing that not even half an inch should be given to the Russians; his own long experience in Berlin suggested that one had to find "a good foothold a little lower down" the slippery slope, having made "every conceivable protest and noise before loosing our upper handholds". (What he described was very much what had happened in the city throughout the 1950s. Some might argue that the slow slide, whatever noises had been made on the way, had weakened western ability to find a good grip now.) But Peck certainly believed that "an inflexible front will make the Russians think twice" and agreed with Burns's tactics: a garrison airlift and resistance to East German attempts to stamp documents. When he later expanded on the need for "a robust reaction" Rumbold pencilled on his cable "extremely interesting and intelligently written" and thought he would like to talk the ideas over.

It was much too late in the day to hold a seminar on The Berlin Problem, Its Cause and Cure. The damage of Sir Anthony's telegram had been done. When it was given, together with an explanatory memo, to the Federal Republic's Foreign Minister on 20 November the American embassy in Bonn said that Brentano "visibly found them most distasteful" – non-recognition of the GDR was a cornerstone of Federal foreign policy and the yardstick of allied support. He was "horrified" by the telegram and called those who had drafted it "grossly ignorant" of the implications and consequences – and of course he assumed the drafters were the British government. There was not quite such a horrified reaction in Paris: Couve de Murville, after all, had no objections to recognising the East German regime. But Quai d'Orsay officials thought the memo weak and certainly going too far too fast.[27]

The British government tried frantically to carry out some patchy repairs to its damaged relations with the allies. Diplomats scurried round various capitals stressing that the telegram had only been intended as a discussion document. When Jock Hay Whitney, the US ambassador, communicated American anxiety about its defeatist tone to Selwyn Lloyd on 18 November, the Foreign Secretary not only denied that it was policy, but – breathtakingly – said that he had not read the whole document before it was sent to Washington. Was this a downright lie? An embarrassing confession that he did not supervise the work of his department? Or an admission of idleness? (It is worth noticing that, even if he had found reading six pages rather a strain, he had had the energy to get as far as page three where Rumbold had dismissed the idea of an airlift, and by that stage the basic argument was clear.) Whatever the answer, Whitney was not impressed by Lloyd's excuse; he believed that the infamous telegram "had a lot of his thinking in it".[28]

It was on 18 November, three days after telegram 8113 was sent out and assumed to be an official statement, that the Cabinet met to decide what its policy really was. Selwyn Lloyd at last spoke out: he was still in favour of some kind of arrangement with the East Germans over access but felt that the best way to get a satisfactory one would be to make it clear that western rights would be maintained by airlift if need be. His colleagues agreed with him. There was a general feeling that interference with an airlift was an act of war and the Soviet Union would avoid it. Everyone was reluctant to give way to Soviet pressure by recognising the GDR. Faced with the Cabinet decision and the international brouhaha, Macmillan was moved to action. Ever since Khrushchev's speech on 10 November he had wondered whether to send a personal message to Adenauer (but had obviously decided not to "run after the Germans"). The Chancellor himself had written on 20 November asking for British representations to be made in Moscow and all the cables from Bonn showed how alarmed the West Germans were by telegram 8113. The Prime Minister now came up with a way to avoid seeming too fussed by Federal agitation, to demonstrate

British firmness to all and sundry, and to go right to the top where he felt happiest: on 22 November he wrote to Khrushchev (copies to all allies) warning that his speech was "difficult to reconcile with your many previous expressions of the desire to reduce tensions in the world" and affirming that the Western Powers would uphold their rights in Berlin.[29]

Whatever impression his letter made on the Kremlin it did something to help Macmillan's standing in the western alliance. Only a little, however. Telegram 8113 poisoned Britain's relationship with her allies permanently. Whatever Macmillan said or did in future would be judged from the standpoint of Rumbold's memo – and much of what he said and did would confirm the suspicion that the memo "had a lot of" the Prime Minister's thinking in it.

Seemingly the last of Macmillan's allies to hear about British appeasement, as recommended by Sir Anthony Rumbold, was Eisenhower. He read of the telegram on 27 November in a bundle of government situation reports which his son brought from Washington to the golf course in Augusta, Georgia where the President was on holiday and handling the duties of state from a little office above the pro's shop. In no time at all he was on the telephone to Dulles: "Until this morning I didn't know of the existence of this British paper and I'm astounded by its arguments." (John Eisenhower wrote later that his father had said "What the hell are the British up to?" which certainly conveys the tone.) The President went on to tell Dulles that it looked as if the British government was ready to say to the Kremlin "we will do what you want"; to make matters worse, Couve de Murville whom "I had always considered a stout-hearted individual" was ready to do the same. The Secretary of State calmed him down by confirming that telegram 8113 was a working paper from "the lower echelons of the Foreign Office" and pointing out that Macmillan had disavowed the document and shown a very different attitude in his letter to Khrushchev.[30]

But, by an extraordinary and most unfortunate coincidence, Eisenhower was now in something of the same mess that Macmillan had just begun to dust off – and not a mess created by "low echelons" of his administration. John Foster Dulles himself had made it. At a press conference in Washington on 26 November he had given a series of resolute replies to journalists' questions about the Berlin crisis: it was the Soviet Union's obligation to ensure access to the city, he told them; the West would use "any and all means" to maintain that access; "we do not accept any substitute responsibility in that situation." But under close questioning about whether the Western Powers would accept East Germans as Soviet agents at checkpoints he replied "We might, yes", pointing out how often there were dealings in practical matters with "people that we do not recognise diplomatically" and that the Federal Republic itself dealt with East Germans on routine business. Would all three Powers accept East Germans, he was asked. "I think it is agreed between us that we might", but it depended on circumstances. Note how carefully Dulles had avoided implying recognition, even de facto; remember, too, that he used the term "agent" with a lawyer's precision and had insisted that if dealing with agents involved "acceptance of the substitution of the GDR for the present obligation and responsibility of the Soviet Union, then that, I take it, we would not do". It was no use him being so correct and circumspect. The journalists leapt at "the agent theory", and made that their story, ignoring all the qualifications.[31]

West Germans read only the newspaper version and not the full transcript which would have shown Dulles's caution. In Berlin the reaction was reported as ranging "from disbelief to dismay and downright anger". The presumed Dulles policy "had caused consternation in Bonn", the British embassy reported (no doubt chuffed that for once they were not themselves getting the Federal flak). This Bonn reaction was surely more than a little disingenuous: the West Germans had been told the details of allied contingency plans for dealing with East Germans at checkpoints; these had been confirmed by Dulles in his conversation with the Federal Ambassador on 17 November and in a letter to Adenauer on 24 November. Even so, it was perhaps one thing for the allies to consider such a policy in private and quite another to announce it to the world's press and the Kremlin. The Federal government did not know that Eisenhower had refused to accept the contingency plans and insisted on rigid avoidance of any trace of recognition; that the State Department was redrafting the instructions on procedure. Confidence as shallow-rooted as the West Germans' was easily disturbed and, after this incident, it would never quite bed down again. Bonn's faith in the strength of its vital alliance with the United States had been jolted just at the very time when it was most needed – the moment when a new stage of the Berlin crisis was upon them.[32]

For, by yet another dreadful coincidence, on 27 November 1958, the very day Eisenhower was talking to Dulles from Augusta, the day when he had to assess the damage his Secretary of State had done to US–West German relations and was shaken by Britain's rickety stance, Khrushchev at last delivered the written statement on Berlin he had promised during his speech to the Soviet Military Academies on 14 November. It was Thanksgiving Day and there was not a lot to be thankful for.

A twenty-four-page Note was handed to the American and British ambassadors in Moscow by Gromyko. Khrushchev claimed he had drafted it personally (he certainly was able to recite long passages from it by heart weeks later). Its tone was more moderate than the speech of 10 November; the British ambassador thought the style was "by Soviet standards one of seriousness and respectability". The substance, however, was challenging and alarming. Quadripartite agreements on the occupation and administration of Berlin, announced Khrushchev, had "lost force" and the Soviet government would discuss the transfer of its functions to the GDR at an "appropriate moment". The most "correct and natural solution" of the Berlin question, he suggested, would be to join both halves of the city and make them "part of the State on whose land it is situated" – East Germany. But, given what he termed "the present unrealistic policy" of the Western Powers to the GDR, he was willing to discuss turning the western sectors into a "free city", under the United Nations' protection, which would be permitted to trade with East and West (the Soviet Union was ready to deliver raw materials and to place orders) and be demilitarised and neutral like Austria. The GDR, he promised, would guarantee free access – in return for a West Berlin undertaking to stop "hostile and subversive activity" against the East German state. If his proposal were rejected by the West, then Khrushchev warned that "no subject remains for negotiations between the former occupying Powers on the Berlin question" – which was tantamount to saying "take the package whole or leave it". However, to give the West time to examine this settlement, the Soviet Union would not "introduce any changes in the existing manner of military transport" to and from the city for six months. If no agreement was reached in that period, complete sovereignty would be handed to the GDR, including full control of land, water and air communications, and all contacts would end with western representatives in Berlin. And that was as good as saying "take it or leave the city".[33]

Khrushchev had offered the Western Powers only Hobson's Choice, since neither a "free city" nor willing abandonment of the western sectors was acceptable to them. And he had given six months for that choice to be made – or else face total East German control of access and the likelihood of being forced out. At a press conference that evening he denied he had issued an ultimatum; the deadline, he claimed, merely defined a period for discussion of his proposal. At a reception in the Albanian embassy two days later he tossed off the remark that the Soviet Union would take no unilateral action as long as the West began, rather than completed, negotiations within six months. But there was no denying the menace in the Note. It warned against "reckless threats of force" by the West: "Only madmen can go to the length of unleashing another World War over the preservation of privileges of occupiers in West Berlin." Lest

Potsdam 1945. The Big Three smile to conceal discord and shake hands on agreements all the Powers will invoke but break. *From the left:* Winston Churchill (soon replaced as Prime Minister by Attlee), Harry Truman and Joseph Stalin.

In Berlin, meanwhile, the rubble is cleared from the shattered city and thousands live in the skeletal buildings which still stand.

The first coal is delivered by the Airlift to blockaded Berlin on 7 July 1948, packed in kitbags because there are no sacks available. The German workers get pay and, what is better, a hot meal every day.

The Foreign Secretary, Ernest Bevin, and US Secretary of State, Dean Acheson, who amicably co-ordinated allied policy during the year-long Blockade.

Selwyn Lloyd and Foster Dulles in London, February 1959.

Harold Macmillan, in the hat which caused such hilarity or offence, is greeted on arrival in Moscow by Khrushchev, February 1959.

De Gaulle and Adenauer,
who remained allied and
stubborn in the face of
Khrushchev's ultimatum.

Eisenhower and Macmillan,
August 1959, at a time when
gentlemen still dressed for
television as well as dinner.

The Foreign
Ministers at the
Geneva
Conference.
From the left:
Brentano (in
profile), Lloyd,
Couve de Murville,
Herter, their Swiss
counterpart, and
Gromyko, almost
smiling.

Khrushchev, with
Mrs Khrushchev
and Frank Sinatra
on the set of *Can
Can* – temporarily
admiring Shirley
MacLaine's legs,
but soon to make a
scene of his own.

Macmillan, at the end of
the Paris Summit, failing to
persuade Eisenhower and
de Gaulle that the
conference should struggle
on.

Khrushchev arrives in
Berlin from Paris to tell
Ulbricht (*right*) that the
Soviet Union will not sign
a separate treaty with the
GDR.

Khrushchev greets Kennedy at the Soviet embassy in Vienna on 4 June 1961. (Gromyko between them).

The western Foreign Ministers in Paris, 5 August 1961, preparing for a Berlin crisis which does not happen while the Soviet Union and the GDR get ready to build the Wall. *From the left:* Brentano, Home, Rusk and Couve de Murville.

Willy Brandt (with a Senate official) sees the barricades at the Brandenburg Gate on the morning of 13 August 1961.

Facing him, East German police and troops. The sign marks the precise boundary of the western sectors.

ACHTUNG
Sie verlassen jet
WEST-BERLI

anyone imagine that the GDR could be bullied, notice was given that aggression against any Warsaw Pact country "will be the cause of appropriate retaliation by all". To rub that message home, Ulbricht told an American interviewer that an allied airlift, mounted to defy the transfer of traffic control to the GDR, would in itself constitute a military threat. The version of the Note sent separately to the Federal Republic stressed the danger of "incidents" in Berlin and pointed out that the whole of West Germany could be destroyed by one H-bomb if the area became a theatre of war.[34]

The perils of the six-month deadline and the choices available frightened Macmillan. "We shall not be able to avoid negotiation," he wrote to Selwyn Lloyd on 28 November. And not just on the Berlin issue, either. He saw this new crisis in the context of all the other problems bedevilling East–West relations and dividing the western alliance: disengagement, nuclear test negotiations, European Free Trade. "We must think of all these problems together," he decided, then quailed at the difficulty of doing so when "the groups of powers in this strange quadrille keep changing." Still, he extracted one nugget which gave some personal pleasure: "It may be that Khrushchev is really working for a Summit conference . . . In that case, it would certainly not be bad politics for me to take the lead in suggesting it." Not bad domestic politics, perhaps. But would his offer of a Summit to Khrushchev please his allies? Surely they would say: if he is prepared to concede such a major Soviet aim, what else will he surrender?[35]

French diplomats saw hardly any possibilities for negotiation. As one of them put it to Foy Kohler, in Khrushchev's Note "brutality is masked behind an apparent suppleness" which suggested there would be no Soviet bending at a conference and the "free city" idea was nothing but a verbal disguise for eventual annexation of West Berlin. De Gaulle himself took the most uncompromising line: there was no point in negotiating since there was no offer the West could make which Khrushchev would accept. The President admitted that it was anyone's guess what the Soviet Union would do once the six-month time limit had expired, but it was his personal belief that there would not be war. That being the case, de Gaulle advised that a form of immobilism was the only suitable reaction to the Soviet Note: "stay in our trenches" – a redolent metaphor from the General who had written long ago on the virtues of the tank as opposed to the static strategy of the dug out. From that point on, as long as the crisis lasted, de Gaulle would take the lordly view that since the Russians had caused all the trouble and danger, it was up to the Russians to find a way out, and no one should stoop to help them. The French President and the British Prime Minister were clearly not going to see eye to eye on Berlin policy – or anything else for that matter.[36]

On the other hand, de Gaulle would prove to be Adenauer's staunchest supporter. The Chancellor had no objection in principle to negotiations with the Soviet Union but he would not agree to talks under the pressure of a six-month deadline nor on any agenda involving disengagement, neutralisation, recognition of the DDR, or reunification without a prior free election. That meant no negotiations in practice. His government was quick to reject the proposals in the Soviet Note: a "free city" would mean the division of Germany into three; it would have no real guarantees of access or security (and who knew better than Germans how ineffectual international agreement can be if a power decides to annex territory). For those same reasons, the Soviet proposals were equally abhorrent to Willy Brandt: a "Danzig-on-Spree" he called the "free city", demilitarised but surrounded by Soviet divisions, cut off from the Federal Republic and sucked into economic dependence on the Soviet bloc even before being gobbled up by the GDR. For once he and Adenauer were in the improbable and embarrassing position of agreeing with each other. Brandt was marginally more in favour of talking to the Soviet Union than was the Chancellor: on 29 November he told Ambassador Bruce that the Russians had presented a maximum not a minimum programme, which suggested he thought they could be beaten down. He was, however, convinced that the Berlin problem could not be tackled in isolation: as he was to put it in speeches in 1959 this crisis was "the effect and not the cause of hostility in international politics"; "Berlin", he said years later, "could not be seen as a down payment on détente but as a touchstone of it."[37]

So by the end of November 1958 two German political enemies were united, two Continental Powers (France and Germany) were in agreement, one ally (Britain) was at loggerheads with them, and the West Germans were suddenly uncertain about American intentions over the GDR. The President of the United States sat by the Augusta National Golf Course, contemplated this muddle, and listened to the summary of the Soviet Note which his Secretary of State was relaying to him on the telephone. He told Dulles that back in the days when Berlin had first been divided and he was not a politician, he had pointed out what a trouble it was going to be but Roosevelt and Churchill had said "Oh, we can get along with Uncle Joe"; now he "had been worrying late at night as to what the eventual fate of Berlin would be". He felt no enthusiasm for the concept of a "free city": it was only feasible if both parts, east and west, were included, if access were guaranteed by the United Nations, and if the Federal Republic agreed to it – and that last condition, he knew, was more than a little unlikely. He took

Dulles's point that Khrushchev's deadline could be seen as a postponement of any Soviet moves in Berlin for six months, but he commented afterwards to his son, John, that if no agreement had been reached by May 1959, the West "presumably would be faced with a far more serious crisis". Meanwhile it was clear to him, as he put it later, that the very length of the ultimatum held its own dangers: "we could be sure that the Russians would use every weapon in their arsenal to divide the West and to play on the already taut nerves of some of its leaders. There seemed to be no avoiding a showdown because Khrushchev had apparently laid his prestige on the line." He chewed the ear pieces of his reading glasses, looked at the first tee, and mused that it was now up to the United States to make sure that this crisis did not split the West.[38]

That was no easy matter. He was to find it just as difficult as confronting the Soviet Union.

5

Divided They Stand

————————

I n some ways Khrushchev's ultimatum came as a relief to West
Berliners. They had been waiting since his speech on 10 November
to see what specific form the Soviet threat would take. Now they knew
where they stood. They were like actors with a favourite and familiar part –
the heroic role they had played during the Blockade. Observers saw them
ready to perform it again to an international audience. They knew their
lines. "If we can survive the Blockade, we can survive this ultimatum,"
everyone was saying. Or, at least, that was what they were saying in public.
Privately, some individuals had doubts. Would morale hold for six months?
Would it be snapped by tension? If there were negotiations before the
deadline was reached, would the Western Powers make concessions to the
Soviet Union at Berlin's expense? Above all, would the allies stick it out in
the western sectors, come what may? Back in the epic days of the Blockade
Berliners had said "Cheer up, allies, we're in front of you." It was a typical
sardonic Berlin joke. In all seriousness, people knew then that the allies
supported them, would supply them and would stay with them. Today
there was not that certainty. The western stance looked very much more
rickety. Without a firm western stand Berlin could not hold out for long,
however courageous Berliners might be.[1]

So there were more withdrawals of savings from banks than after
Khrushchev's 10 November speech; the price of shares on the stock
exchange dipped; several firms planned to transfer their operations to
West Germany and some of them actually packed up and left. Parents were
particularly worried: should they send their children to the West to stay

with relatives? If they did, would they ever see them again? Ought they to go too and give them a secure life away from these endless Berlin tensions? Furniture vans and plane tickets were booked for the spring, for the days before the deadline ran out – "just in case". But politicians and the general public damned or rallied the faint-hearted. Rumours soon spread that all the advance bookings had been made by Communists to spread panic, and that puffed out Berliners' chests again. Business confidence was propped up by a Bundestag vote to increase financial aid to West Berlin, by West German orders, by firms in the FRG expanding their local branches, and by an announcement from Siemens, that DM36 million would be invested in their Berlin production. The unemployment figures told the story of sustained hope of survival: by March 1959 they were 20,000 down on those of the previous year.

Clearly if Khrushchev hoped to bring West Berlin to its knees economically, he was going to have a hard time of it, short of blockading the city all over again. And blockade was something most Berliners did not expect: they doubted the Russians would play the same game twice, not after losing the first one. Nor was Khrushchev going to score an easy political victory. Most West Berliners rejected the "free city" proposal out of hand: there was nothing "free", they thought, about the western half of the city being cut off from the Federal Republic and deprived of the allied garrisons who defended its rights and freedoms. When a reporter from the East Berlin radio station, Radio Berlin, did a vox pop in the western sectors he could find no one in favour of the scheme; even the "friends" he interviewed in the expectation of a good Socialist soundbite expressed no enthusiasm for Moscow's "solution". Yet Willy Brandt seems to have been virtually alone in his instinct that if Moscow rejected a blockade and the West turned down a "free city", there might be Soviet action to seal off West Berlin at the zonal and sector borders, leaving only tenuous connections with the Federal Republic. He told a CBS journalist in an off-the-record interview in January 1959 that he was mulling over counter measures, such as calling on the East Germans to aid the western sectors by strikes or go-slows. Some people, though, thought there might be an open military assault to take West Berlin. But most Berliners, in East and West, reckoned that Khrushchev would not dare to act violently; that he was bluffing, trying threats to see what would happen, hoping to break the will of Berliners and the nerves of the Western Powers before the six-month ultimatum was up. He would never risk war. They themselves were willing to take that gamble. Were the Western Powers?

West Berliners gave their allies a lesson in resolution on 7 December. They went to the polls in their local election and treated the occasion as a referendum on the "free city" proposal. Only 1.9 per cent voted for the SED and the Moscow line; 52.1 per cent voted for the SPD and its slogan "security for Berlin". The CDU got only 37.3 per cent of the poll – thanks, in no small part, to the intervention in the campaign of the Chancellor himself. Adenauer, who avoided Berlin like a plague spot under normal circumstances, had turned up on 4 and 5 December. No one believed he had come to give them ready help in times of trouble: it was too obviously an electioneering move and even regular CDU voters found it distasteful. The CDU mayoral candidate's election slogan – "A vote for me is a vote for Adenauer" – backfired painfully.[2]

The election result was an act of defiance against the Soviet Union. It was, in addition, a strong endorsement for the personality and policies of the sitting Mayor, Willy Brandt. In later years Brandt fell from grace in the eyes of many Berliners: he left the city to become Federal Foreign Minister, then Chancellor (and Berliners think there is something seriously wrong with the judgement of a man who thinks those are better jobs than being their Mayor); he divorced his wife (she was popular, and divorce was not with stern, unbending Prussian Protestants); he negotiated with the Soviet Union, winning concrete advantages for both sides of the city and the Nobel Peace prize (but some Berliners sucked their teeth at "supping with the Devil"). In 1958, however, he was at the height of his political stature in the city. Since 10 November he had spoken out bravely against Soviet threats and said what Berliners wanted saying: the future of the city must depend on the freely expressed views of its people, East and West, the position of the Western Powers must not be weakened, the ties with the FRG must remain and be strengthened, any negotiations with the Soviet Union must deal with the city as a whole and in the context of Germany as a future nation state. Brandt never spoke with the eloquence of his predecessor as Mayor, the late and loved Ernst Reuter; he seldom touched the heart. He lacked Reuter's warmth and common touch. He suffered too from being thought "young" – forty-five years old in 1958, not the father figure Reuter had been – and many people thought wisdom came with years. Yet Brandt had earned respect since taking office. People knew he was trusted and admired by the western authorities in the city, and allied good opinions were vitally needed in this crisis. They saw how well he put Berlin's case to the international press: as an ex-journalist and a relaxed, unpompous man with intelligent views, clearly and openly expressed, he was ideally suited for spreading their story to the world.

Most western officials and politicians agreed with Berliners that a second full-scale blockade of Berlin was unlikely. Khrushchev, they calculated, would remember the failure of the first siege and would try something new to force the Western Powers to accept his terms. Slow, gradual interference with West Berlin's land communications with the Federal Republic seemed most probable: each step so slight that a strong western response would seem unwarranted, yet every measure designed to sap morale and slowly stifle the western sectors. Even on that calculation, however, it was prudent to brush up plans for a major airlift. It might just be needed. A mini-lift certainly had to be ready, to supply the garrisons in Berlin if the Western Powers decided to make a major stand against accepting East Germans at checkpoints; it could be expanded to top up civilian stores if interference with land traffic became severe. An airlift of any size would make a political statement, act as a show of strength, postpone the evil day when concessions might have to be made or outright force used. In any case, the Western Powers had not decided on any diplomatic or political strategy and they had no counter measures prepared for putting retaliatory screws on the Soviet economy or communications. At least there were airlift plans of a sort already available.[3]

Ever since 1949 the western sectors had kept large stores of necessities and the western allies had regularly reviewed ways to supplement them by air and to maintain their own garrisons. It had long since been decided that British Zone airfields would be used for any major operation to reduce flying time. Up to the summer of 1952 storage targets for West Berlin were based on a six-month "balanced stockpile" (something of everything in the warehouses); thereafter on a "staggered stockpile" (plenty of coal and other bulky items in store, so that the initial lift could concentrate on more easily transportable goods). In autumn 1953 it was assumed that 1,248 tons a day could be carried at short notice, mainly by US C-124s already available in Germany; that the British would bring twenty-five Hastings aircraft into operation within six weeks, to deliver an extra 8,400 tons a month, and would then charter civilian aircraft to fly in difficult and dangerous loads such as liquid fuel. Once additional aircraft were brought from the United States, the operation would peak within 180 days and supply a regular daily 6,500 tons. All this looked good on paper. Unfortunately, however, the three Powers had not actually made a firm political commitment to running a joint airlift (and the French had a chronic shortage of transport aircraft, so it would have to be a two-Power show); the Federal Republic was more than a little reluctant to make any financial contribution to the stockpile or the transport costs; and there were considerable doubts about whether 6,500 tons a day would be adequate to fuel Berlin's recent economic recovery or maintain the standard of living so dramatically improved since the Blockade.

Other problems became apparent from 1956. Several airfields in the British Zone were being handed over to the new NATO ally, the Federal Republic, and the RAF was reluctant to let the Americans use those it had left. More worryingly, the Soviet Union had acquired technology it had crucially lacked in 1948 and 1949: it could now jam navigational and air traffic control radar aids. At an allied meeting in Washington in February 1958 Admiral Radford of the JCS dismissed all airlift planning as impractical: the needs of West Berlin, in his view, could never be met with available resources. The impracticality was greater than he thought: planning was still based on 1954 figures for population, production and living standards; only after Khrushchev's 10 November speech was it realised that the stockpile intended for twelve months would only last for 120 days.

Nevertheless, by the end of November, the allied air forces had licked the plans into shape and reached much more cheerful conclusions. A mini-lift could be launched within twenty-four hours to supply the garrisons and fly out refugees. Aircraft were now so much bigger than during the Blockade that even if they flew only in good weather and daylight, to dodge Soviet radar jamming, they could still deliver the tonnage achieved by the round the clock operation of 1948–9. If the Americans provided thirty extra C-124s, they could carry 45,600 tons a month with these resources alone. Thereafter, they could use their fifteen C-130s, already in Germany (which could lift 15 tons or take 65 passengers) and five C-119s (18 tons or 85 seats) and bring over more aircraft to reach or surpass the target of 6,500 tons a day. All in all, there would be the capacity to keep West Berlin's warehouses topped up with food and the refugee camps regularly cleared, though there were worries about whether enough coal could be delivered to maintain industry for long. There were other, faster and bigger US transport aircraft, but for the moment runways in Berlin were too short for them. The FRG had still not agreed to make any financial contribution, but the air forces were told in December to keep accounts in case Bonn eventually decided to be generous. The fact was, as Ernie Bevin used to say, the costs of a whole year of airlift were infinitesimal compared with the cost of one day of war.[4]

Unfortunately there were no such ready-reckoner answers to other fundamental questions raised by airlift planning in 1958. How long could West Berliners hold out under siege conditions? Their food would be rationed; there would be little fresh fruit or vegetables and much less than the 115,000 tons of meat they consumed every year, because of the difficulty of flying bulky and perishable items. The western sectors would be cold and dark: electric light and all forms of heating would have to be cut because of the huge airlift capacity needed for coal. Private cars would be taken off the roads; fuel carriers would concentrate on diesel for public transport, but buses already used about 16,000 tons of it a year and once they had to carry more passengers the airlift might not be able to keep up with demand. In 1948 Berliners were well used to hunger, cold and deprivation. What were their limits of endurance now? Industry would be badly hit by a new blockade, however gradual. Once output was hit by shortage of raw materials, fuel and spare parts, and finished goods could not get to market in the West, businesses would fail and workers would be on the dole. Was feeding and defending the western sectors nothing more than dragging out their misery and staving off the inevitable moment when they collapsed economically? Did it not make more sense, as the three western ambassadors in Moscow or Sir Anthony Rumbold in London recommended, to recognise the East German regime and avoid subjecting the western sectors to a lingering death? And, as if the Berlin dilemma were not worrying enough in itself, the military raised the same frightening question they had put in 1948: what if this crisis led to general war? Was it not folly to put all the air transport eggs into the tiny Berlin basket when they might be needed anywhere in the world?

Given all the logistical, political, and military problems, opinion was hardening in some quarters against any airlift at all. In Washington, there was increasing enthusiasm for showing the Soviet Union at the earliest opportunity the Western Powers' determination to defend their rights in Berlin whatever the price; once that demonstration was made, the argument went, there would be no more interference with traffic, so no need for air supply of the western sectors. What was being urged was the despatch of an armed convoy up the Autobahn the moment access was blocked. This was a strategy much bruited in 1948 and 1949 but always rejected. It had been the pet scheme of General Lucius D. Clay, the then US Military Governor. Clay, to this very day, appears in bas relief profile on a bronze plaque at Tempelhof airport over the words "Father of the Airlift". "Would-be Abortionist" is perhaps a more accurate title. He never believed an airlift could break the Blockade but as a good soldier he obeyed orders to mount one. Given the choice, Clay would have sent a convoy with about 6,000 men – a regimental combat team with armour and artillery plus an engineer battalion with bridging equipment – to the west end of the Autobahn, prepared to force their way through the Soviet checkpoint at Marienborn if need be, and to shoot their way to West Berlin if they met resistance en route. If large forces were encountered, Clay's Air Force colleague, General Curtis Le May, was ready and willing to launch a strike on Soviet airfields. It had been Clay's firm belief (and he never changed his mind) that this show of force was all that was needed to dissuade the Soviet Union from blockading Berlin; that a symbol of military strength and resolution was enough to make the Kremlin back down.[5]

He was never given the chance to prove it. The Joint Chiefs and the US government unanimously agreed in 1948 that the experiment did not justify its considerable risk of war. The British thought the scheme little short of barmy: a force that small could never push up the 120 miles of road, they argued; the convoy would grind to a halt at every dynamited viaduct or bridge and it could be pinned down by minimal Soviet forces unless huge tracts either side of the road were secured by infantry and air cover. If it was forced to retreat, it would do so in ignominy and the prestige of all western forces would be damaged, shaking the confidence of Europe. Even if the convoy got through, what then? Was the next consignment of a dozen tons of supplies to be accompanied by several thousand tons of artillery and pontoons? And the next, and the next? How many divisions would it need to keep the Autobahn permanently open?

Even Clay himself finally admitted to his biographer that he was never sure that he could force a convoy to Berlin without massive air cover and control of the surrounding terrain. "I wanted to do so for pride," he confessed. And he was a very proud man with a lot to be proud of, not least his country's strength and virtue which he felt were being mocked by the Russian siege of Berlin. He had a long career behind him as a first-class administrative soldier and an outstanding political Military Governor. But he had never seen action. He was a military engineer in peacetime, building dams and airfields; after Pearl Harbour, he went first to work on procurement for the War Department then became Director of Matériel. Throughout the war he constantly requested active duty; in 1943 he tried to resign (for the umpteenth time) and was willing to drop rank from major-general to colonel if he could go to the front. He came very near to it in 1944 when he was sent to unblock the flow of supplies from the port of Cherbourg to the invading allied armies; but he was then sent back to Washington, protesting loudly, to do the even bigger plumbing job of moving artillery ammunition to Europe. Late in life, Clay still resented his career which others thought so distinguished: "I'd been through the First World War without seeing combat and to go through the Second as a professional soldier without seeing combat was about as humiliating as anything I could think of. And I'm still ashamed of it." Given all due caution against the perils and folly of amateur psychologising, it is tempting to speculate that Clay, the desk general, saw the armed convoy as a balm for hurt pride and a last chance to do some real fighting.

Yet whatever Clay's personal motives in 1948 and whatever the objections raised then to his scheme, there were people in 1958 still in favour of sending an armed convoy up the Autobahn, though to make a show of force and probe Soviet willingness to resist it rather than shoot through to Berlin. Many of them were in high military places – and they enlisted the press to their aid by leaking to journalists. There was a string of stories in the American newspapers from mid-November 1958 that armed convoys would take on any East German attempt to block western access to Berlin. By December, Joseph Alsop, the most influential and best connected of columnists, was telling the British ambassador in Paris, Gladwyn Jebb, that the US government was "sold on the idea" and the Russians would give up at the first shot. He wrote a fully fledged piece for the *Washington Post* claiming that the three Powers had rejected "the easy way out that was taken last time, the resort to an airlift" because that implied "acceptance of a Soviet right to impose a land blockade at will", because the Soviets could jam radar, and Berlin could not be supplied by daytime and fair weather flights only. None of this was true. There was no belief in any Russian "right" to blockade the western sectors; just a fear they would try to. Britain and France were still keen on an airlift, and air transport planners thought it perfectly feasible.[6]

Alsop also asserted that the US government was planning an armed probe as well. What was nearer the truth was that some elements in government were, but they were faced with stiff internal opposition, never mind resistance from the allies. By 11 December the State and Defence Departments had agreed that the use of "limited military force to show our determination to maintain surface access" was just one of several options, including a diplomatic démarche in Moscow and various gradations of airlift, which they should discuss with Britain and France. On 12 January the JCS approved a policy paper which included a recommendation to test East German resolve by an armed convoy with combat escort which would "push through any opposition encountered using force until stopped by force". David Bruce in Bonn and General Hamlett, the US Military Commandant in Berlin, on the other hand, feared that limited force would be made to look ridiculous by the first blown bridge or small detachment of East German troops it encountered. They preferred sending what Bruce called "a souped-up division to Helmstedt to show we really mean business". Significantly however, General Norstad, who as Commander-in-Chief in Europe would be ultimately responsible for such an operation, wrote to the JCS on 23 November that he favoured a sharp but private nudge to the Kremlin: "In my view, it is essential to inform the Soviet government immediately and preferably without public announcement that we do not intend to recognise a deal with the GDR, that we will not allow the GDR to impede the exercise of any right we presently hold, that we will not accept any control by the GDR over our movements to and from Berlin, and that we will use force if necessary to enforce our rights."[7]

What was correct in Alsop's story – and what suggests one of his sources for it – was that Robert Murphy, Assistant Secretary in the State Department, had recently been given the job of examining the feasibility of the armed convoy scheme. Murphy had been Clay's Political Adviser in the US Zone at the time of the Blockade and had passionately argued the case for a convoy. He had never ceased to believe that it would have called the Soviet bluff and prevented twelve months of siege. He went further in his memoirs in 1964 and said that Washington's refusal to employ the convoy had "caused Soviet leaders to downgrade American determination and led, I believe, to the subsequent Communist provocation in Korea". Macmillan, who had worked closely with Murphy as Eisenhower's political adviser in North Africa, scribbled in angry red on a minute about Alsop's article: "I have no doubt that Murphy and Co. have inspired this line in the Press. This is Algiers form. They are angry with Dulles and the President" – who, whatever their own views on the scheme, could not launch a convoy unless they had total backing from their allies. And Britain and France had not given approval to the idea by mid-December, indeed they were appalled by it. It very much looked as if Murphy, probably with the help of the Pentagon and the JCS, was trying to squeeze Eisenhower and Dulles into support.[8]

The British and French were alarmed by the idea of using an armed convoy for the very reasons they had opposed it in 1948: it would either provoke the Soviet Union into war because that was what the Russians actually wanted, or it would spark off the kind of small incident where a young, nervous soldier or would-be hero opens fire and everything gets out of hand. As Sir Patrick Reilly pointed out from Moscow, if the convoy were stopped, the onus was then on the Western Powers to use force and this involved "the risk of war, which given Khrushchev's temperament we must, I think, take seriously". This fear of full-scale conflict was fuelled by a strident declaration by Tass, the Soviet news agency, on 12 December that any attempt to break through to Berlin by force would be regarded as an attack on the GDR and its Warsaw Pact allies; in the fighting which followed, both sides would go "right up to nuclear and rocket weapons". Dulles, on the other hand, saw the use of a convoy as a classic brinkmanship tactic: if the Western Powers demonstrated determination to uphold their rights, the Soviet Union would understand the dangers of opposing them and back down to avoid war. General Twining of the JCS declared almost nonchalantly: war "is coming anyway", so "force the issue on a point which we think is right and stand on it". What he chose to ignore in his seventh heaven of fatalism was that Berlin was certainly not the best place to start a war: stuck inside enemy territory in the GDR, defended by 12,000 allied fighting men and a few armed police who faced four Soviet divisions round the city itself and a total of thirty in East Germany (315,000 men in all, it was usually estimated), who could be further strengthened by troops from other Warsaw Pact bases.[9]

There was no hope of a limited war, either. In 1957 General Norstad had proposed thirty NATO divisions on the Central European front to contain Soviet forces and avoid immediate recourse to nuclear weapons. He had not got them: no one in NATO was willing to pay the increased tariff for conventional forces. As a result, it was reckoned that the Commander-in-Chief's forces could just about cope with the East Germans alone – seven divisions, about 145,000 troops. If the Russians intervened, as they undoubtedly would, then the West could only rely on massive retaliation. That meant nuclear war, and general nuclear war over a wide front. At that point, so soon reached, no one wanted to have forces pinned down to maintain Berlin's access. In fact, by then, Berlin would probably have been smashed to smithereens and its defenders massacred. Those in the general public in the 1950s who were scared that John Foster Dulles would unleash mayhem and slaughter would have been utterly petrified if they had known how General Twining's mind worked. Those privy to military secrets certainly got a whiff of his thinking. No wonder the British and French were so chary about using an armed probe.

Not the least of the allies' handicaps when they came to assess the merits of armed convoys, airlifts, or any alternative tactics was that they had no central organisation to focus their thoughts and co-ordinate decisions and action.

When the Blockade was imposed in 1948 there was already machinery to deal with it. The three western Military Governors had been working together closely for three years and their basic views were meshed. Their powers in Germany were proconsular: they commanded men and resources, had full authority over the local populations and institutions, and little need to gain political consensus or carry public opinion. They had wide latitude from their governments, and could move incisively and fast; they were left to run day to day affairs in Germany, supervise the Airlift and watch over the creation of a West German state. Meanwhile the broader political and diplomatic co-ordination of the allied response to the emergency was directed from London. Within two days of the start of the Blockade, Ernest Bevin had set up a committee to handle the details: Sir William Strang of the Foreign Office, and the French and American ambassadors René Massigli and Lewis Douglas. Strang and Massigli had, of course, known the Berlin problem ever since being members of the European Advisory Commission in 1944 (it would be unkind and untrue to say they had caused it). Douglas contributed experience of working with Clay for several months in the US Zone and attending the London Conference on Germany in 1948. The personalities of the three men gelled in a small, professional unit through which all aspects of the crisis were channelled. They swopped cables from each other's governments, and jointly drafted the necessary diplomatic notes and agendas. London had reasonably convenient communications with Germany and Paris, though poor Lewis Douglas spent many a restless night on a sofa in his office waiting for telephone conferences with Washington, five hours behind European time. Hovering over the committee and sniffing the political wind from every capital was Bevin himself.

By 1958 nothing was as simple or clear. The Military Governors in Germany had been replaced by ambassadors who visited Berlin not as their seat of government but as a peculiar military island where the civilian writ did not run and standard diplomatic formulae did not apply. These ambassadors were accredited to a sovereign power; they could only listen and suggest, they could not command. Yet they and their governments did not always treat the Federal Republic as an equal or as an ally whose support must be won and whose views must be taken seriously. The old "occupation" mentality still flickered. For example, the three Powers kept Bonn in the dark about contingency planning for Berlin and military strategy for Germany. It was 18 November before German representatives were first shown plans for an airlift (no wonder the Federal government was reluctant to pay for a pig in such a thick poke) and all three allies preferred to consult each other about Berlin policy, then merely inform Bonn of their decisions. When Selwyn Lloyd read the draft of a cable to Washington on 14 November about some such tripartite talks, he asked: "Won't that all cause the Germans mortal offence?" Typically he showed a sound instinct but weakened his point by framing it as a question. The Germans were indeed offended, frequently and increasingly, at being barred from the debate about their future capital and the prospects of a war to be fought over their territory. Adenauer was always accused of being paranoid, but he was right to suspect that there was a lot going on behind his back: conspiracy without him rather than against him.[10]

Partly to ease relations with the Germans, partly to use local expertise, and mainly to concentrate allied thoughts and effort, the British pressed throughout November and December 1958 for a co-ordinating committee of ambassadors to be established in Bonn. Not the least of Bonn's attractions was that, as a Foreign Office official pointed out: "The Americans have got a first-rate Ambassador there in the person of Mr Bruce." Sir Christopher Steel, his British counterpart, wanted the committee to have a German representative to avoid the embarrassment of making decisions which the Germans then rejected. Not so Sir Anthony Rumbold: "it is the three Powers who have responsibility in Berlin" and this was a "golden opportunity" for tripartite consultations "by way of giving a sop to General de Gaulle" who wanted them in NATO. Nor Couve de Murville, who warned against giving the impression of "being led by the nose by the Germans". Crucially, the Americans rejected Bonn. They wanted to co-ordinate policy in Washington. This was hardly surprising: the United States, after all, made the major contribution of men and money to the alliance and would be called on for an even bigger one if the crisis led to war. So a committee of representatives from the State and Defence Departments plus the British and French ambassadors, first set up in Washington in November, finally became a formal Working Group in February 1959, and occasionally graciously admitted the Federal German ambassador to its meetings. Yet Washington was remote in geography and time zone from Berlin. In consequence other liaison groups proliferated, ad hoc and propter hoc, in various capitals and at different times. Allied control of the crisis remained diffuse, and jumbled by Chinese whispers.[11]

It was symptomatic of the organisational muddle and political cross purposes that the allies could not even agree on a tripartite Note to the Soviet Union to counter Khrushchev's allegations and proposals of 10 and 27 November. Eisenhower had a State Department draft in his hands by 21 November. By 24 November all three western ambassadors in the Soviet Union agreed that a triple démarche should be made in Moscow – and the sooner the better. The French government refused to join in. Couve criticised the Note as a "sign of nerves", "so undesirable", and his President agreed with him. Llewellyn Thompson said that the British and Americans should publish their own drafts regardless: they would boost morale. By the end of the month the Foreign Office was arguing that since the Note was so important it must not be rushed; the French had suddenly decided that it was so vital it must be drafted by the three Foreign Ministers themselves; Washington seems to have given up the drafting struggle and suggested sending the whole business to Bonn. There, David Bruce was so fed up with trying to revise contingency plans when his British colleague wanted no change and his French counterpart had to await

Paris's approval to change each comma, that he saw no point in trying to draft a joint Note with them. He too recommended that it be left to the higher political level.[12]

It was just as well that the Foreign Ministers were due to meet anyway in December, at a NATO ministers conference in Paris: someone had to get the allied ball rolling and it clearly needed a hefty push from the top. Here were the Western Powers facing a six-month ultimatum and after nearly a month of it they had not decided whether to accept East Germans at checkpoints, whether to press on with airlift planning, whether to try an armed probe, whether to negotiate with the Soviet Union and if so on what agenda and with what fall-back positions and sticking points, let alone on whether or not to send a Note to Moscow. They had strained their relations with the Federal Republic and to make matters worse, they had so far failed to inform their other NATO partners about what was going on. And NATO was more than a little miffed about its support being taken for granted – the Secretary General, Henri Spaak, in particular. He was, furthermore, extremely alarmed about the whole Berlin crisis by early December, and deeply suspicious that the Western Powers might abandon Berlin in which case, as the British representative at NATO reported, "He did not dare to think where the retreat would end, probably in catastrophe."[13]

The meeting in Paris from 14 to 16 December 1958 did little to calm him down and not much more to advance western policy on Berlin. Dulles, Selwyn Lloyd and Couve de Murville met privately on the first day. "Foster", Lloyd remarked, "looked only fairly well." In fact he had come to Paris against doctors' orders, having walked out of hospital after five days of treatment for a severe inflammation of his intestine. The three men quickly agreed on a joint declaration affirming "the determination of their Governments to maintain their positions and their rights with respect to Berlin, including the right of free access". That bit was easy. The difficulties started when they discussed how to do it all. They finally decided to send similar but separate replies to the Soviet Note, though they reached no decision on a delivery date. They were all willing to discuss Berlin with the Soviet government as long as talks did not take place under duress and covered the whole German problem, but just how the Kremlin could be persuaded to accept those two stipulations was not examined. The recently up-dated airlift plans were nodded through, but without any analysis of when and why they would be implemented. There was a debate on what to do about East Germans at checkpoints which ended with a decision to accept them as "agents" but not as "substitutes" for the Soviet authorities. This no doubt made good legal sense to Dulles, but Selwyn Lloyd thought it was a ruse to permit full dealing with East Germans and ignored Dulles's explanation that it was intended to avoid it; Couve seemed to understand that "agents" were not "substitutes" but was not really willing to do business with either. The three allied delegations were impressed when Willy Brandt addressed them at their afternoon session, stressing that the recent city elections proved West Berlin's confidence in itself and its allies and promising that the people would endure any hardship as long as they were sure of allied backing. Brandt too was impressed when Dulles then walked round the table and said "we won't let you down". Quite what they were going to do to help was far from clear.[14]

Lots of items could be ticked on the agenda; issues had been raised and decisions taken. But no awkward question had been tackled, for the simple reason that, as with the wartime coalition, any fundamental argument would have widened the divisions between the allies. Selwyn Lloyd sounded relieved when he cabled back to London that there had been no discussion of "hypothetical situations" and "a curious reluctance on everybody's part to get involved in the really controversial issues". Perhaps he should have been worried: dodging problems did not get rid of them. The most controversial issue – that of using an armed convoy as a demonstration and probe – had been touched on lightly, dropped the moment the British and French had shown themselves opposed to it, and was then reserved for "further consideration". In the event it was taken up by the Working Group in Washington, at a sufficiently low level not to disturb the Foreign Ministers for the moment. This typified the limited aim of all three Powers: merely to paper over the cracks between them.

At least the NATO ministers had been sufficiently mollified by this meeting to issue their own supportive declaration on 16 December, asserting that "the renunciation by the Soviet Union of its inter-allied agreement on Berlin can in no way deprive the other parties of their rights or relieve the Soviet Union of its obligations"; western presence and free communications for the western sectors must be maintained; and the Berlin problem must be settled within the context of Germany as a whole. Finally there was a reminder that NATO had responsibilities "in regard to the security and welfare of Berlin and the maintenance of the position of the three Powers in that city". This statement clearly irritated the Soviet Union. A *Pravda* article made the "Miss Manners" point that the Soviet Note had been addressed to the three Powers so ought not to have been discussed by the NATO Council, then added the accusation that this very discussion proved that the West saw Berlin as a military confrontation not a political problem. Bonn, on the other hand, was said to feel "slight relief" after reading the two declarations. For this "slight relief not much thanks", perhaps. Certainly not in West Berlin where people soon spotted that the three Foreign Ministers and the NATO Council had found no solutions to the Berlin crisis. Some West Berliners were probably glad they had booked their plane tickets and furniture vans for the spring.[15]

The Foreign Ministers in Paris had at least given the diplomats the go-ahead to complete one outstanding formality: to prepare replies to the Soviet Note of 27 November. Gone were the happy days of 1948 and 1949 when such matters were sorted out by three men sitting round a table in London. Now whole teams laboured in Paris, making separate drafts, amending their own and each other's, struggling to harmonise all the versions while leaving some individual national chords, submitting intermediate suggestions to their capitals and incorporating the changes and insertions sent back after yet more discussions with the other groups. They were soon bogged down in an interminable, near terminal, morass of terminology. "DDR", someone wrote, and immediately the German observer stated a case for "so-called DDR", "the Pankow regime", "the SED regime", "the regime in force on German territory behind the iron curtain" – anything but "DDR". The Americans invented "the regime which the Soviet Government refers to as the GDR", which might have sounded better as a German compound noun. The French liked "Pankow regime"; the British did not and suggested "East" or "Eastern Germany" at which the Germans pointed out that these days it was more correct to say "Central Germany" because true "East" Germany was the area beyond the Oder-Neisse line in Poland. Once the vocabulary was established, final versions had to be submitted for NATO approval – another hazard everyone was spared during the Blockade. It is quite amazing that under those circumstances, drafts were eventually polished and three western notes were delivered in Moscow on 31 December.[16]

A Note is governed by Newtonian law: it has an equal and opposite reaction in the form of a Note in reply. The Soviet response on this occasion was sent on 10 January (Moscow clearly spent less time on semantics). It said all the expected things about handing over Soviet functions to the East Germans, added what Eisenhower found "a long tedious argument" for a German peace treaty (with draft enclosed), suggested a peace conference in Prague or Warsaw, and pressed for reunification through negotiations by the two Germanies rather than free elections. There were also a few proposals for troop withdrawals, but even Macmillan, usually an enthusiast for such schemes, thought these had only "a certain specious attraction". Back went the western replies on 16 February. The French and American versions responded a little to Soviet arguments; the British did not deign to discuss them. The contents of all these missives, and most of those which followed for the next two years, hardly matter. They were steps in a diplomatic minuet, making the same moves over the same narrow area. They did not address, let alone answer, the basic question: what is everyone going to do to find a mutually acceptable settlement?[17]

There was an omission in the 10 January Soviet Note. It was remarked on in the West and thought potentially more interesting than anything actually said. There was no reference to the six-month deadline for negotiations. When Mikoyan arrived in the United States in the first week in January for what he described as "a holiday", everyone waited to see if this hint became a louder word to the wise. It did. Mikoyan told Dulles that the 27 November Note had not been an ultimatum; the six-month period was suggested as a reasonable time for the West to accept the handover of Soviet duties in Berlin to the GDR, for the two parts of Germany to make approaches to each other about gradual reunification and for negotiations on a treaty. He did not shift ground on any of the Soviet proposals but, without actually mentioning a Foreign Ministers' meeting or a Summit, he gave Dulles the strong impression that the Soviet Union wanted talks with the West. This point was made publicly and more clearly when Mikoyan held a press conference on his return to Moscow (unusual behaviour for a holiday-maker): "We have not issued any ultimatums to anyone and have not threatened anyone . . . The main thing in our proposal is not the date for ending the talks but the talks themselves, the necessity of their being held."[18]

Was there anything worth talking about? Certainly no one in the West was prepared to accept the Soviet agenda as laid down by Khrushchev on 10 and 27 November and repeated recently by Mikoyan. East German control of western access to Berlin was a point still being debated by the allies themselves; recognition of the GDR, the "free city" and the present reunification and troop withdrawal proposals were all objectionable. So could the West make any concessions or counter-proposals which would tempt the Soviet Union away from its major demands without compromising western rights?

At the beginning of January the British military chiefs and the Foreign Office embarked on a major review of existing plans for German reunification and European security. They found little room for manoeuvre over the basic principles which had governed western policy so far. Reunification and security, for instance, had to be linked: to guard against too strong a Germany or permanent division as the major cause of instability in Europe, to keep a German contribution to NATO and to prevent a neutral Germany being tugged by West and East. Nevertheless, it seemed possible to ease the present tightness of that link. Complete reunification and security agreements did not have to be reached at one and the same moment; each could be achieved by gradual and concurrent stages, each synchronised and strengthening confidence to continue.[19]

A variety of possible ingredients for this phased plan was put forward. For example, a narrow strip on the FRG-GDR border could be partly demilitarised by the withdrawal of non-German forces. If that proved satisfactory, there might be thinning out of NATO and Warsaw Pact forces over a wider area and an agreement on inspection to prevent surprise attack. The West might ban the production and possession of nuclear weapons in the Federal Republic if Poland and Czechoslovakia were to renounce them too; there could be a prohibition on the basing of IRBMs (Intermediate Range Ballistic Missiles) in Germany. The Soviet Union was more likely to accept such proposals if the West promised to recognise the Oder-Neisse Line. (The Foreign Office had the impression that Adenauer would agree to this proposal, even though he would not say so publicly.) All these ideas, however, would have to be introduced into negotiations to coincide with stages in the reunification process. Here again, the British were unwilling to concede the fundamental tenet of policy: free elections in both parts of Germany as the essential element for the establishment of a united state. But, they asked, did elections have to be the first stage? Why not start by building up German contacts over matters of mutual interest, or set up a three-Power body to discuss unification and security and invite German representatives to take part in the discussions? If such dealings proved fruitful, then they could be followed by the establishment of an all-German body, with one representative from each of the Länder, which could discuss a constituent assembly and decide when to hold elections.

None of these proposals, of course, would automatically solve the Berlin problem. The hope was that it would lose its urgency given a general slackening of tension. If nothing else, detailed negotiations on reunification and security would distract attention from the narrow and dangerous area of Berlin and postpone Soviet action against the western sectors. The Foreign Office did not necessarily want to negotiate about the city at all. In spite of all the known drawbacks to the Berlin arrangements, the status quo still seemed better than any of the alternatives until the city became the capital of a free and united Germany. All that was needed in the interim was a Soviet guarantee that the GDR, acting as Soviet agents, would provide exactly the same access as before. If that were refused, perhaps the United Nations could be asked to take over traffic control, or move some of its agencies, even its headquarters, to the western sectors and become involved in preserving their liberties; if western presence became untenable, the UN could take over all three-Power responsibilities. If all else failed there might be some leeway in offering to limit allied propaganda and espionage activities from the western sectors in return for a Soviet and East German guarantee of free movement for refugees.

The British review had reconciled the need to find new approaches, a genuine agenda for negotiation, and relatively safe concessions with the preservation of basic freedoms and allied rights in Berlin. Perhaps its recommendations were too vague: it did not specify the exact correlation between the security proposals and the reunification stages or the order in which they should be carried out. But perhaps this was a virtue: a mix and match policy could be constantly adjusted to suit circumstances. Certainly the British suggestions fell far short of the Kremlin's demands: the full Rapacki neutralisation, an immediate peace treaty, reunification by a German assembly with equal representation of East and West and recognition of the "political and social achievements" of the GDR, and a "free city" of West Berlin. And would the other western allies accept them? For the moment the British were far from certain that they would. And for that reason the review was kept under wraps. Macmillan himself recognised that the proposals might well be seen as "evidence of weak-kneed British unreliability" and decided to hold them in reserve, at least until any negotiations on Berlin were breaking down and the six-month ultimatum had virtually run out.

Meanwhile, in Washington in January, State Department officials had also been reconsidering policy on Berlin. They dusted off some old ideas and kicked around a few new ones, but without much confidence in any of them. How about an appeal to the Security Council, they asked, to put the western case to the world and explore all peaceful possibilities before resorting to force? They knew the answer: it would be a long procedure, much longer than the six-month deadline (if that still applied) and the Soviet Union had friends and a veto on the Council. Take the case to the International Court of Justice? Possibly even more long-winded, and the Soviet Union had never accepted its jurisdiction. Unify Berlin under a city government of its own choice? That would still leave the city isolated in the Soviet Zone and no one could believe the East Germans would allow free elections. Make West Berlin a Land of the FRG and a NATO responsibility if western troops had to withdraw? That would break quadripartite agreement on Berlin and, anyway, Bonn opposed the idea. Put West Berlin under UN trusteeship? What if the United Nations recognised the GDR? Reduce some of the western intelligence and propaganda activity in Berlin? Well, that would please the Russians and East Germans, but would they make any reciprocal gesture? All these ideas raised difficulties rather than hopes. And they were only tinkering at the edges of the problem. No one, either side of the Atlantic, had come up with anything as fresh and radical as the suggestion of a Frankfurt banker: buy the East Zone from the Russians. (He thought that a milliard Deutschmarks paid over ten years was a fair price and perhaps in his line of business he knew how to raise it.)[20]

It was John Foster Dulles himself who was ready to go to the core of the problem. Shockingly in the eyes of many, he was willing to make major concessions and, furthermore, to make them publicly and in advance of any negotiations with the Soviet Union. At a press conference on 13 January 1959 he was asked: "Mr Secretary, is it our position that free elections are the only method of reuniting Germany. In other words do we say 'No free elections, no reunification'?" This had indeed always been the western position, but Dulles replied: "Well, we never have said that. The formula of free elections was the agreed formula" (note the past tense) and it "seems to us to be a natural method. But I wouldn't say that it is the only method by which reunification could be accomplished." Without consulting his allies, Dulles had loosened a previously rigid western principle: made free elections only one, though perhaps the preferred one, of a whole range of possibilities rather than the sacrosanct method. Bonn was appalled, and no wonder. When Bruce saw Adenauer and Brentano the next day he described their "expressions as little short of violent" and reported that he had been quite unable to calm them down.[21]

Dulles had another nasty surprise in store for them. On the day of his press conference he saw the British ambassador. Sir Harold Caccia (who stressed he was speaking "without instructions", but who was undoubtedly conveying the views of his government very accurately) explained that in this British election year no party could possibly stand on the slogan "Vote for us and a war for Berlin": the voters, he explained, would want to see a real effort at negotiations with the Soviet Union before force was used to uphold western rights. Dulles chuckled then admitted confidentially that he had an idea which he had not yet thought through: could Germany be reunified in a confederation, a loose union of East and West which would preserve much of the systems in both parts? This method, he suggested, would appeal to that vast majority of East Germans who did not support the present regime and it would give the West Germans a chance to dominate and perhaps ultimately to absorb the East. He did, however, acknowledge that the "trouble in all this was Adenauer", who stuck to existing principles. That was putting it mildly.[22]

Confederation was in the air. Ulbricht had talked about it at the SED Central Committee's Plenum on 15–17 January and recommended a Council of a hundred members drawn from the national assemblies of East and West on a basis of equal representation for each side and with the addition of members of "mass organisations", which in GDR vocabulary meant Communist. This Council would advise the two existing governments until there was a peace treaty, followed by reunification, then by elections for one national government. The sudden American interest in the confederation device soon leaked to the press. There was an article in *Newsweek* claiming a "Murphy plan" for it; the West German newspapers were full of rumours and speculation but total disapproval. A gleeful Foreign Office minute noted that Dulles's recent comments on free elections and confederation showed he was softening up and "This is probably no bad thing." But the British kept their heads down, and their recent policy revisions secret. It must have been rather nice to sit back and watch the Americans take the lead in the appeasement stakes for a change.

And Dulles stuck his neck right out at his next press conference on 27 January. He dismissed Ulbricht's specific confederation proposal as "obviously designed . . . to perpetuate the partition and division of Germany". Yet he went on to say: "You can have a confederation which is, in fact, of very considerable progress to reunification." And although he admitted that the word "confederation" was one "around which emotions revolve" and one which he himself preferred not to use, he went on to recommend that all ways to promote reunification "can and should be studied as resourcefully as possible".

That really put the cat among the Bonn pigeons. By the end of January Adenauer was reported to be utterly opposed to any Summit meeting with the Russians. Not surprisingly: the ideas Dulles had been sounding out recently were ideas Adenauer did not even wish to have thought, let alone negotiated on. Even so, the Chancellor was realistic enough to face the unpleasant fact that there might be negotiations whether he liked them or not – and if the Russians really had abandoned their six-month deadline he no longer had an excuse for refusing to take part. His Foreign Ministry secretly began to reappraise Federal policy, though the Chancellor himself believed there was little room for amendment.

While others came to terms with the inevitability of talks with the Soviet Union and struggled to find a negotiating position, the alternative approach to the Berlin crisis – the use of force – had been kept simmering. From 5 to 11 January, the British and French ambassadors in Washington, Caccia and Alphand, wrangled with Robert Murphy over the plan to send an armed convoy up the Autobahn to assert the allied right to ground access and show readiness to fight for it. The British and French were unwilling to make any advance commitment to the plan; they preferred to wait until exact circumstances were clear. The British stuck to their belief that an airlift was the best response to any blocking of ground access; Murphy was adamant that the 1948 lift had been a mistake, that a challenge to ground access must be met on the ground. The Continental allies would not yield an inch.[23]

That did not deter the Joint Chiefs. Indeed their plans for an armed convoy had expanded considerably from their early intention to use "limited force". On 15 January Dulles was sent their recommendation: "we will not evade the issue" of blocked ground access by setting up an airlift and must "accept the risk of general war" by using military force to restore it. They suggested that once the GDR took control of the Autobahn checkpoints there should be an immediate probe of Soviet and East German intentions by a small convoy accompanied by an armed escort of platoon size. If that were barred, a division would force it through. Since deployment on that scale could well lead to what they euphemistically called "further military operations", they proposed the evacuation of non-combatants from Berlin as well as partial mobilisation in the United States, and that NATO should be made ready for war.

The JCS had overstepped the mark. At a meeting in the White House on 29 January General Twining came under fire from the President and the Secretary of State. Eisenhower did not even accept the military aspects of the plan. A division, he insisted, was too small to reopen communications; if the convoy were stopped it must turn back and there must be no further attempt to get to Berlin until world opinion had been mobilised and diplomatic pressure brought to bear on the Kremlin. He drew Twining's attention to the political dimension of his plan. The American people, he pointed out, had to be convinced that the issue justified the action taken: it was far from certain that they would want to fight over the recognition of East Germany let alone the "shape of the helmet" of the man who held the checkpoint; they must first understand and sympathise with the need to protect the rights of the allies and the two million Berliners they were responsible for. Not that he was averse to a display of military strength. He approved "quiet preparation and precautionary military measures", such as increasing patrols on the Autobahn and guards on allied trains or bringing forces in Europe up to full peacetime strength and changing the deployment of units in Germany – measures which would not alarm the public but would show Soviet Military Intelligence that force was available and could be used if pushed to it.[24]

Nor was Eisenhower opposed to the use of an airlift – certainly to top up garrison supplies. He did, however, defer to Dulles's opinion that air supply would not maintain West Berlin's economy for long. Never mind: it gave time for diplomatic and political action. The President also gave enthusiastic approval to Dulles's recommendation that there should be talks on Germany with the Soviet Union by about April and that these talks should give the Russians a chance to withdraw their ultimatum and modify their proposals without loss of face. Only if all these measures failed to produce any result would the President reconsider the use of force.

The developing American ideas on talks, negotiating positions, and contingency planning were tested in the three allied capitals when Dulles flew to Europe at the beginning of February. In London he found Selwyn Lloyd and Macmillan keen on an early Foreign Ministers' meeting with the Russians and relieved by the scaling down of the armed convoy plan. He listened politely to the Prime Minister's views on thinning out forces in Central Europe, though did not agree with them and later called the explanation "rather rambling". He was, however, far from pleased to find the British still keen on a major airlift and shocked by their readiness to accept East Germans as Soviet substitutes at checkpoints – a point he imagined had been cleared up in Paris in December. De Gaulle, on the other hand, told him firmly that the French had no intention of dealing with East Germans. The President, indeed, regretted the softening of the convoy plans: he was all in favour of instant use of force to maintain access, a zeal which Dulles attributed to "the fact that it is we who would have to make most of the military effort" since the French had so few troops in Germany. In Bonn, Dulles finally persuaded himself that Adenauer accepted a Foreign Ministers' meeting on Germany, but only on the "theory that 'silence gives consent'". He did his best to reassure the Chancellor that any negotiations would meet Bonn's recently coined formula "no concessions without counter-concessions", but could do little to calm his fears that the British were ready to recognise the GDR. And he had not fully restored Adenauer's trust in the United States after his recent alarming press conference: a week later, the American embassy in Bonn reported that the Chancellor's confidence was still badly shaken.[25]

On the whole, Dulles had reason to be pleased with his European tour. Personal contact had eased relations with his allies and although minds did not meet on every subject at least everyone had a clearer view of what was in them. Thanks to the consensus he had found on the need for talks with the Soviet Union, a joint three-Power Note was sent to Moscow on 16 February proposing a conference at which East and West Germans could take part as advisers. These gains, however, must have been made at terrible personal cost in terms of pain and exhaustion. Macmillan had recorded in his diary on 4 February when Dulles arrived in London: "I was shocked at his appearance . . . it was clear to me that he was a very sick man." And on 10 February Dulles went into hospital for what was said to be a hernia operation. Cancer was discovered. He was a dying man.

Though Dulles had filled many of the cracks in the alliance which had merely been papered over at the Paris meeting in December, one fissure had actually widened during his tour: that between Britain and the other Western Powers. Harold Macmillan had ignored the need for tripartite policy and joint action and had announced that he would go to Moscow for personal talks with Khrushchev in late February.[26]

It was a decision he had been talking himself into for a year at least. The idea first came to him during a Commonwealth tour in January 1958. At that time, he thought in terms of discussions about holding a Summit. The Cabinet disapproved of the scheme, and it was dropped. But once the Berlin crisis began in November, Macmillan revived it. He became preoccupied with thoughts of 1914 and memories of the Great Powers drifting into war without trying to prevent it by negotiation. Not for him the analogy both Spaak and de Gaulle were drawing at this time: that a seizure of Berlin by Khrushchev would resemble Hitler's occupation of the Rhineland and must be forcefully resisted to pre-empt further aggression. Nor did he wonder whether a visit to the Kremlin would turn out to be as pointless and shameful as Chamberlain's trip to Munich. Instead, he asked himself in his diary on 5 January 1959 "Are we really prepared to face war over Berlin?" He certainly was not. He did not see the issue as one of rights, or threat to the freedoms of West Berliners, of resistance to bullying in international relations, let alone as a crucial battle in the Cold War. He understood it only in the narrowest of terms – access, and only military access at that, since civilian traffic was already controlled by the East Germans. Given his analysis, he doubted "whether we can make the question of whether the Russians or the East Germans approve the bills of lading or punch the railways tickets into a casus belli". If the cost of a military journey up the Autobahn was recognition of the state which appointed the checkpoint official, Macmillan was happy to pay.

He could find plenty of justification for a visit to Moscow which avoided thinking of it as a mission of appeasement. From his first Commons debate in 1946 he had preached that the Soviet quest for security could only be met by "direct and personal negotiation". The British press was bewitched by summitry, the public believed the Berlin question should be settled by sensible talking and not by fisticuffs. He loved to be loved by both, and there was no better time to woo affection than an election year. There must have been the thought at the back of his mind, too, that Britain, no longer a Great Power, might still play the honest broker between the two Super-Powers. He knew perfectly well that the Federal Republic would oppose a personal initiative in Moscow. But Macmillan had regarded Adenauer's rejection of his EFTA proposals for adding another Six to the Seven states of the EEC as a personal betrayal, and he resented the way the allies were tied by Bonn to support for reunification and avoidance of dealings with the GDR. He found the Chancellor's belief in total disarmament in Europe as the prerequisite for settling all other problems quite as unreasonable as the rest of his policy. In his own view, gradual thinning out leading to disengagement would relax tensions and create the atmosphere in which all issues could be rationally discussed; it was a pity that his allies tended to see such ideas as an unacceptable Rapacki Mark II.

By the second week in January 1959 Macmillan had persuaded himself that it was his duty to see Khrushchev and avert a dangerous confrontation over Berlin. He told his diary that discussion of the crisis was permissible because the Soviet ultimatum had been dropped and that there had been "a sort of outstanding invitation" from the Russians ever since Khrushchev and Bulganin had been to Britain in 1956. A diary is such a comfort: like Selwyn Lloyd as Foreign Secretary, it does not answer back. Selwyn was, in fact, not in favour of a Moscow visit – he once said that "summitting is an occupational weakness of any incumbent of Number 10" – but he did not argue. The Foreign Office was sceptical. Sir Patrick Reilly, the ambassador in the Soviet Union, was downright critical of the idea. In private he thought the plan was a cheap electioneering gambit; officially he explained that the Russians would use Macmillan's presence to drive a wedge into the western alliance and to isolate Adenauer as chief obstacle to a German settlement. Macmillan took no notice. On 23 January Sir Patrick was instructed to suggest to the Kremlin a visit of a week or ten days, starting on 20 February. Gromyko "listened intently but made no comment", Sir Patrick reported. There was then a long wait for a Soviet response.

Meanwhile, the Prime Minister had to square himself with the Americans. Sir Harold Caccia put the case for a visit to Moscow as convincingly as he could and on 22 January the US government accepted the scheme, though warned of the risks of talking to the Russians before there was an agreed allied policy. That warning had no effect. Macmillan sent an effusive message of thanks, saying he was "touched by the confidence which the President and Mr Dulles have shown in him and his judgement". In fact, they had little in either. The log of the phone call between the President and Secretary of State on 21 January shows that they disapproved of Macmillan's proposed visit but did not think they could tell him not to make it; the nicest thing Eisenhower could say about Macmillan was that he "was the best friend in the PM spot that we had" – which may suggest that he, too, thought the chief aim of the Prime Minister's Moscow venture was to win the forthcoming election.

On 31 January Macmillan described himself as "rather depressed and frustrated" as he waited for a Soviet invitation. He was finally put out of his misery on 2 February when the Kremlin accepted the date and length of visit he had suggested. Suddenly, and rather late in the day one might think, he began to "have some qualms", to think that the trip was "a perilous undertaking" and to realise he must "avoid negotiation" over Berlin because he had no authority from his allies and there was no agreed policy anyway. At long last he told France and the Federal Republic of his intentions. The French were polite though not very impressed. Adenauer was hopping mad. Was this, he asked Sir Christopher Steel, "an election manoeuvre"? He then held forth at angry length on the importance of western unity in the face of the Berlin crisis, the suspicions Macmillan was creating among his allies, "the hopelessness of dealing with Khrushchev", and the undesirability of running to the Russians to negotiate about a problem they themselves had caused by renouncing their agreements. He at last simmered down enough to remark that if the visit "meant that the Conservative Party would win the election there was some point in it". Clearly Macmillan's arguments about duty convinced only himself.

Taxpayers and students of international relations might suppose that before a major meeting between statesmen, all efforts are directed to preparing agendas, briefings and negotiating positions. Not so. Throughout the ages, the best minds, the greatest diplomatic expertise and inordinate sums of public money have been devoted to one vexing question: what presents shall we take? Before Macmillan's trip to Moscow, long lists were compiled of Russians who must be given something. Soviet ministers and departmental heads? Yes. Their wives? Some of them. Children and grandchildren? A few. Secretaries and interpreters? Certainly. But don't forget embassy staff, drivers and guards. Sir Patrick Reilly, an enthusiast for the latest design, cabled to say this was an area where the Soviet Union lagged behind and suggested asking the Council for Industrial Design for ideas. A modern British painting (but not "too modern", he cautioned) would flatter Khrushchev by implying that he could understand it. Shivers of horror from the more conservative sections of the Cabinet and Foreign Office: modern rubbish? Minutes and memos poured out urging nice antique furniture and silver. Beware, said someone who had "once lived in Moscow": the Russians do not appreciate simple elegance; make sure everything is very elaborately decorated, the more florid the better. How about a Rolls-Royce for Khrushchev? – after all, Lenin had one. And a sports car for Master Khrushchev, Macmillan added generously, but Selwyn Lloyd drew the line at expensive gifts for private individuals. Embassies were asked to find out what other states took to the Soviet Union and to enquire discreetly what the presents had cost. The Queen was asked for her opinion. She thought Mr Khrushchev would like a lion (he and Bulganin had given her two horses and the Prince of Wales a "small" bear in 1956). The President of the Board of Trade, who was said to be "very interested in the subject", gave a lot of thought to the problem then recommended taking gifts from all parts of the United Kingdom: whisky in porcelain bottles from Scotland, sporting guns from England, linen from Ulster, and . . . and . . . and . . . But, try as he would, he could not think of anything from Wales.[27]

Finally, two silver candlesticks and an antique bureau-bookcase were chosen for Khrushchev. (Since, according to their son, Mrs Khrushchev never allowed him to keep expensive presents, it is probably lying mildewed and warped in some Kremlin cellar.) Mrs Khrushchev was given a silver tea service, tray, china and table linen – suitably over-decorated, one hopes. Quantities of leather luggage, more china and silver were bought for top brass; the lower orders were provided with silk scarves, pens, lighters and shavers. Watches were taken for children – no point in taking toys, someone pointed out, the Russians make such good ones. Buy fifty dictionaries, was a last minute suggestion: people are always grateful for them. Whisky? Macmillan intended to take plenty, but was worried to hear that Khrushchev kept making speeches about excessive drinking. Several dozen cashmere sweaters were bought for ministry secretaries – seemingly by a tidy-minded bureaucrat (they were all the same size) and obviously by a man who had never seen a fine specimen of well-fed Soviet womanhood (they were all size 36 and presumably the poor, disappointed girls had to give them away to children). One might have thought that, after three weeks of frenzied list-making, argument and shopping, every person and every eventuality had been thought of. But no sooner had the British party arrived in Moscow than an urgent cable was sent to London: please send by Comet half a Stilton for Mikoyan; he is a cheese fancier.

Macmillan and his entourage stepped out of their own, cheese-less, Comet at Moscow on 21 February, wrapped and furred for the Russian winter, and were met by a guard of honour and most of the Soviet leadership similarly swaddled – "*Boris Godunov*, Act II", a diplomat muttered. The Prime Minister was not a sartorial success. With the parsimony of his class he had borrowed his father-in-law's old fur coat and dug out a fur hat he had bought in Finland in 1940. This once white object was now yellow with age and perched a foot high on the top of his head as if just landed from the air. It produced hoots of laughter in Britain when the newspaper photographs were seen, and caused immediate offence in the Soviet Union: it was a Finnish hat, so national pride was hurt; it had been bought during the Soviet war against Finland so must be intended as an insult. (A proper Russian black hat replaced it for the rest of the trip.) He was far from well – he had a chest infection, and his doctor doubted that he was fit to travel – but was excited, and enjoyed greeting everyone, having decided that the Russian word for "good day", "dobrodjen", could be pronounced "double gin".[28]

Before leaving the airport, he tried to repair some of the damage the announcement of his trip had caused. In a short speech he made it clear that he had not come to negotiate (that was a sop to his suspicious allies) but hoped to improve East–West understanding and "alleviate some of the cares that at the present time bring anxiety to the world" (reassurance to the Russians who had been affronted when he told the House of Commons he was going to Moscow for a "reconnaissance", a word which in Russian means an "espionage mission"). That afternoon he and Selwyn Lloyd paid a courtesy call on Khrushchev; there was an early and unusually quick dinner in the Kremlin, then the British party drove to a Soviet government dacha in Semenovskoye to spend the night.

Here and in the British Embassy, work suffered from the usual drawback in the Soviet Union – the knowledge that the KGB would be listening. The ambassador's office was thought to be relatively secure: it was draped with a tent inside which tapes of running water and cocktail party noise were played to distract the bugs. Safe it might be, but inhibiting and irritating all the same. In the rest of the house and in the cars which ferried the party there could be no free chat, and Macmillan decided it was safer not to keep his diary up to date. At Semenovskoye, all serious conversations had to take place in the freezing open air, and that meant pulling on layers of thick clothing first, then avoiding trees because security experts reckoned they were festooned with microphones. The dacha offered some relaxation, though. Between the formal talks with Khrushchev, Gromyko, Mikoyan and Malik on the first day, there were troika rides in the snow, clay pigeon shooting, and lots of boisterous fun sliding down a huge ice mountain. Macmillan and Khrushchev squashed together in a round wicker basket which spun as it slithered to the bottom – not the "slippery slope" of current metaphor.

In that first day of discussion the British came in for a lot of Soviet hard pounding. Khrushchev accused the West of trying to impose "rollback" and "liberation" by force; of creating an atmosphere of war in the hope of getting Soviet concessions. He was adamant that the problems of security, disarmament, a peace treaty and a "free city" must all be treated separately; other disputes must wait until these matters had been settled. When Macmillan tried to suggest that "unless we could work to a solution of the whole problem we should find great difficulty in dealing with particular aspects of it", Khrushchev complained that the Western Powers were trying to "bring together questions which were ripe for settlement with others which were not" and their agenda "looked like an attempt to draw the Soviet Union into a labyrinth of negotiations which might last for five or ten years". Germany, he insisted, was a matter for the Germans, not the four Powers; the two German states had "completely different systems"; Dulles's recent comments about elections and confederations, he said approvingly, "gave some hope of a settlement". He seemed, for a moment, to offer a small concession on Berlin: "free" West Berlin could retain western troops as a "police force". Then it was snatched away: Soviet troops would be based in the western sectors too, though a quadripartite force in East Berlin, the "capital of the GDR", was not permissible. He dismissed the question of western access as though it were trivial (guarantees could be registered at the United Nations, he said airily) but warned that any attempt to maintain access by force would lead to the "loss" of the western garrisons (and that undoubtedly meant their deaths).[29]

For most of the meeting Macmillan listened rather than spoke – he was given little option. But at one point he commented worriedly that "the situation was very serious and if the Soviet position was indeed as Mr Khrushchev had described it, it was very dangerous." He was undoubtedly expressing his own fear. This was not how his Soviet listeners understood him. On this occasion, and on others when members of the British delegation tried to point out the "danger" of a clash over Berlin, the word was taken to mean "a danger to the Soviet Union", in other words, a threat. Macmillan's anxious remark, instead of coaxing Khrushchev into a more reasonable frame of mind, toughened an already hard Soviet line.

The meeting in the Kremlin next morning did nothing to soften it. A formal dinner at the British Embassy gave no opportunity for private approaches or fishing for openings – and the Russian interpreters' habit of loudly translating every comment by the leaders for the benefit of the whole room made it as drear socially as it was fruitless diplomatically. The following day, however, there was a visit to the Nuclear Research Institute at Dubna. (Macmillan wore a Brigade of Guards tie for the occasion. He did not bump into Bruno Pontecorvo, the British nuclear traitor who was thought to work there.) The two-hour drive gave Selwyn Lloyd the chance for a quiet talk with Gromyko, so he popped into his mind the possibility of limiting armaments in a restricted area and warned that the Americans would use force if their access to Berlin were blocked.[30]

But while the cats were away, Khrushchev played an alarming political game. He went to an election meeting in Moscow that afternoon and delivered a barnstorming speech, attacking the western position on Berlin, opposing a Foreign Ministers' meeting on the subject, threatening that any violation of the GDR's frontiers would be "the outbreak of war", lambasting Eisenhower and Dulles, and excoriating the Federal Republic as "a capitalist state where militarism is being revived and plans for revenge are being nurtured" by Nazi generals. He warned Adenauer, "this so-called Christian": "you will have to face the judgement of the Lord one day" and "your policy contradicts the teaching of Christ". It was quite a performance. Thinking about it later, Reilly decided that it was a normal speech by Khrushchev's standards and had probably been drafted before the British arrived in Moscow. The fact that he delivered it while they were there may have been "a typical example of Mr Khrushchev's blindness to the effect of what he says and does on other people"; on the other hand it could be seen as "standard Soviet tactics of turning nasty and increasing pressure in the middle of a discussion or negotiation".[31]

Whatever the explanation, such an intemperate and abusive outburst could not be ignored by the British. Llewellyn Thompson cabled to the State Department that "the greatest contribution Macmillan could make to peace would be to pack up and go home immediately", but he speculated that Khrushchev was testing the Prime Minister to see how much he could get away with, reckoning that Macmillan was so anxious to make this visit a vote catcher in Britain that he would not dare to break off the talks. And when Khrushchev arrived at a large reception in the British embassy that evening, looking very pleased with himself, no comment was made about the speech. There was much forced jollity and heavy badinage, but at one point Macmillan felt faint and had to go out and rest for twenty minutes. He blamed the heat in the rooms, but may well have been feeling the strain of keeping his temper and worrying about how to handle the situation: he was never as unflappable as his image. After the party, the British left for their dacha. Next morning, 25 February, they held a council of war and planned the details and tone of the reproach they felt must be made to Khrushchev about his behaviour.

When he arrived for lunch he looked grumpy. Reilly suspected he felt guilty about his speech. Macmillan delivered a carefully phrased statement, solemn rather than angry and very firm. He emphasised that the British could not be separated from their allies by attacks on their leaders; he appealed for serious discussion of the whole range of pressing problems faced by East and West so as to "take the poison out of the international situation"; he stressed the danger of the Berlin situation which had resulted from the Soviet initiative in November, a danger which he warned could "develop into something tragic for us all". Khrushchev began his reply as if bewildered: what did the Western Powers want from the Soviet Union? Why were they trying to maintain a state of war with Germany? What would they lose by a "free city"? Why did they not take Soviet proposals seriously? Then he began to boil as Selwyn Lloyd talked of a Soviet "ultimatum" over Berlin and "threats of war" if the sovereignty of the GDR was infringed. He turned on Macmillan when the Prime Minister condemned the Soviet unilateral renunciation of its obligations in Berlin. "If the West wish to maintain a state of war, the responsibility lies on them," he shouted. "History will condemn them." On and on went the argument, round and round the same stubborn points. Tempers frayed. But by the time the meeting broke up for tea and vodka, the British party believed they had shocked Khrushchev out of his belief that they were an easy target. They were relieved to find him particularly friendly and hospitable at the ballet that evening. Perhaps he had come to terms with the new balance of the talks and would begin to discuss rather than bullyrag.[32]

No such luck. Next morning in the Kremlin Khrushchev delivered a statement which Reilly, like everyone else, found "offensive both in tone and substance". He made derogatory remarks about the British role in Suez, complained that the British had been threatening him, and warned that if NATO tried "to impose their will on the Soviet Government, the latter would reply with all the means in their possession". (Seemingly the references from Macmillan and Lloyd the previous day to "danger" and "threats" had again been interpreted as aggressive and Khrushchev was giving as good as he thought he had got.) As if this was not damaging enough to the prospects for fruitful talks, Khrushchev added a final, near fatal blow to the whole Macmillan visit. As the British delegation rose to leave, he announced that he would not accompany the party to Kiev next day – he was going to the dentist to have a tooth filled. It was a very nasty moment. Breaking the Kiev arrangement, and on such an excuse, was clearly a deliberate insult. And Mikoyan rubbed the insult in: he would not join the party in Leningrad thereafter – he had to go to "an election meeting" in Rostov. To cover the shocked British retreat to the door, there was some ponderous joking about whether Prime Ministers were any use without teeth, and unpleasant metaphors from Khrushchev about keeping his teeth strong and sharp and using "science and technology in this".[33]

When Eisenhower read the account of this meeting he commented that he personally would have "gotten in the plane and headed home". That was the immediate instinct of the British, too. On second thoughts they decided to carry on regardless: the main party would go to Kiev and Leningrad but Reilly and two Foreign Office officials would stay in Moscow to see if Khrushchev developed his attack in public and to decide what to do if he did. The hope was that Khrushchev's behaviour that morning was a cover for his guilt at his election speech or a spontaneous emotional reaction to the firm line the British had taken over it. Conceivably the crisis might blow over if both sides kept apart for a few days.

The tactic worked. After an afternoon in Kiev trudging round an exhibition of "socialist achievement", the British found that Khrushchev's daughter had turned up for dinner – obviously as a gesture of reconciliation. When they moved on to Leningrad, Gromyko and a suddenly election-free Mikoyan were there to greet them. This was more than a gesture. The two men had come to do business. For during the Kiev stay, Selwyn Lloyd had buttonholed Kuznetsov, the First Deputy Foreign Minister, and made clear how worried the British were about the recent atmosphere in their meetings with Mr Khrushchev and how important it was to start talking seriously: a "collision was impending with disastrous consequences". He gave a candid British view of what had gone wrong: they had come not to negotiate but to explore the Soviet viewpoint and to put their own; Khrushchev had merely hammered at the old points, and not responded in any way to British suggestions about a Summit or arms limitation. Macmillan, he explained, had been obliged to protest at the "election" speech and had done so courteously, but Khrushchev had been so "rough and belligerent" next day that the Prime Minister and Foreign Secretary "had with difficulty kept our tempers"; the business about the tooth was "childishness". Kuznetsov admitted that he had heard this meeting had gone badly. (Accustomed though they were to Khrushchev's outbursts, Soviet officials were frequently embarrassed by his fits of temper in front of foreigners.) He asked questions about British views on various Berlin problems, then disappeared to make a telephone call. When he came back he said that Khrushchev was willing to meet the Prime Minister on Monday 2 March and particularly wanted him to know that his tooth was now better – his dentist had used a special English drill.[34]

So by the time Selwyn Lloyd settled to talk privately to Gromyko in Leningrad on the morning of 1 March, the air was already clearer. The two held a post mortem on what had gone wrong so far, the Foreign Secretary repeating everything he had said to Kuznetsov. Gromyko explained that from a Soviet point of view Macmillan had seemed to be issuing threats at the dacha lunch on 25 February; the British constantly used words like "disaster" and "calamity" and that, he complained, was threatening language. Selwyn Lloyd suggested that a "kind of pathological difficulty underlay the question of who was threatening whom"; the Foreign Minister did not demur. Having cleared more air, they got down to a sensible discussion on nuclear testing. That evening at dinner Gromyko said that he had spoken on the phone to Khrushchev who wanted to explain that the delivery of his "election" speech during the British visit had been "pure coincidence", but was perhaps "unfortunately timed". The improved atmosphere was demonstrated when Gromyko then gave the Foreign Secretary an advance copy of a Soviet Note, to be delivered to the Western Powers next day, agreeing to talks. This readiness to meet was a major step forward – the British reckoned that they could claim credit for it with their allies and that it justified their visit. They took the overnight train to Moscow in very much better heart.[35]

The three days away had shown Selwyn Lloyd at his best. He was not a great political figure or foreign policy visionary, but he had undoubted talent for smoothing ruffled feathers, patiently unknotting tangled emotions, conveying trustworthiness, and coaxing the recalcitrant into reason. Reilly had been impressed and decided he was underrated. He wrote later that the Foreign Secretary was "the ideal second" for Macmillan, was "always sensible, calm and a steadying influence during the bad times of the visit" and had played a great part in its success, not least by his handling of Gromyko and Kuznetsov. Perhaps he had also given evidence to critics of summitry that a lot more business can be done by private chats between Foreign Ministers than by highly publicised heavyweight contests between heads of government whose prestige and vanity are on the line.[36]

Thanks to the spadework in Kiev and Leningrad, the talks in the Kremlin on 2 March went smoothly and cordially. Khrushchev kept plugging his "free city" and peace treaty proposals but indicated that the 27 May deadline for a settlement was not significant (the West could "name a date", he said). He also suggested that formal recognition of the GDR was less important than de jure acceptance of its frontiers. He hardly nibbled at Macmillan's fly of force limitation, but made a little speech about his tooth and the English drill which Reilly thought "came as near to an apology as perhaps a Communist leader can". That evening Macmillan made a speech on Moscow television which any Minister of Propaganda would have been proud of: claiming that the British invented just about everything but the wheel, had the most mechanised agriculture in the world, phenomenal export success, with all the delights of free speech and a free judiciary into the bargain. The hit of the evening, however, was Macmillan's interpreter, Mr Morgan, with whom countless young ladies in the audience fell in love at sight. (They rang up after the programme to ask all about him.)[37]

A joint communiqué was signed next morning. The Russians had cut from the British draft a phrase about "a dangerous situation arising" if present disagreements were not settled, on the grounds that it would frighten the Soviet people. What remained still had a very British tone, with phrases to reassure the allies about no negotiations having taken place. Significantly, the communiqué also suggested that "further study could usefully be made of the possibilities of increasing security by some method of limitation of forces and weapons" in a small and inspected area. That was not going to please Britain's allies one little bit. The Foreign Office quickly put the message about that "limitation" did not mean "neutrality" or "disengagement", that it might result in NATO forces staying at the same level while Warsaw Pact forces were reduced, and that, of course, this was just "one of many" avenues to explore.[38]

Macmillan returned to London bringing not so much peace with honour as some assurance for the public that the Soviet Union might talk rather than fight. Privately he felt that the people would be readier to support tough action over Berlin because he had made the effort to avoid it, and he told the Cabinet that, though he would prefer to get a negotiated settlement, "I will be no Mr Chamberlain" and there must be no humiliating climb-down. He would find it difficult to convince his allies that this was his stance: for all that he had written several times to Eisenhower, de Gaulle and Adenauer from Moscow, swearing that he had made no deals with the Soviet Union, they were suspicious and thought he was capable of negotiating away his own grandmother. So after a gruelling trip, he now had to plan three more to the allied capitals. The alliance must be restored. And given the forthcoming talks with the Soviet Union, there were agendas, negotiating positions and tactics to plan. If, by any chance, the Soviet six-month ultimatum was still in force, the West had already lost three months of it. The drifting had to stop.

6

Geneva and Camp David

———————

Macmillan's trip to Moscow had not only confirmed his belief that there must be negotiations with the Soviet Union to prevent a disastrous conflict over Berlin. He had also seized on a remark Khrushchev made at the first formal meeting in the Kremlin on 23 February: that disputes should be settled by heads of government, working out principles between themselves then directing their Foreign Ministers to sort out the details. "Lock them up with a limited supply of bread and water," he had said, "and tell them to reach agreement." The Prime Minister's experience of the Soviet leader had transformed his initial snooty impression at Geneva in 1955 of a man unfit to be Tsar. "Mr Khrushchev is absolute ruler of Russia," he wrote in his diary for 4 March 1959, "and completely controls the situation." Having decided that he was "the boss", it followed that "no meeting will ever do business except a Summit meeting".[1]

The other western leaders were far from convinced. They believed that one of Khrushchev's aims in precipitating the Berlin crisis had been to force a Summit. Ergo: he did not deserve one, especially while there was still the whiff of a threat to the city. All of them thought there was no point in talks between heads of government unless substantial progress to an agreement was reached first by the Foreign Ministers. They were willing to meet to sign a settlement, not to waste their time haggling item by item. They would certainly not risk failure at such a high level. Unlike Macmillan, his allies did not believe that Khrushchev would go over the brink and into war. Faced with a firm response, they calculated, he would back down. By their logic, rushing into talks was merely a sign of fear – and fear would be exploited by the Kremlin.

Furthermore, their doubts that the Soviet Union would make any of the concessions needed to justify negotiations were confirmed by Khrushchev's speeches during a visit to the GDR in mid-March: these all repeated his standard demands for a peace treaty, a free city of Berlin, and the end of the western "occupation regime". The only sign of flexibility came in his comment that the period for reaching a settlement might be extended for a month or two: if the Western Powers "talked reasonably", he suggested, "we are not in a hurry". But most people, other than Macmillan, saw this as just a tactical shift: creating more time for fears to prey on western minds and splits to develop in the alliance.[2]

Only West Berliners took much comfort from the extension of the ultimatum period – and it was a poor sort of comfort at that. A British official reported in April that they felt "they can look forward about as far ahead today as they have ever been able to do since their island existence began". They were far from optimistic about the outcome of any negotiations with the Soviet Union: they saw the British as capitulation-ist, the French as too militarily weak to convert tough words into deeds, and the Americans as likely to waver now that Dulles was ill. If there had to be negotiation then West Berliners thought it was dirty work, best left to the Western Powers, however unreliable they might be. There was great relief in the western sectors when Willy Brandt (mainly as a result of American pressure) turned down an invitation to see Khrushchev while he was in East Berlin in March. There was derision for Erich Ollenhauer of the Federal SPD who did go to see the Soviet leader and was then inveigled into signing a joint communiqué full of Communist slogans but no western rhetoric about free elections or reunification. And there was more contempt for the SPD when two of its luminaries, Carlo Schmid and Fritz Erler, went to Moscow to visit Khrushchev on 16 March. They found him completely uninterested in their party's offer of security agreements and a slowing down of rearmament in return for Soviet concessions on Berlin and reunification; they returned to Bonn depressed by his stubborn determina-tion to carry out his existing policies. "Serves them right", was the general reaction. West Berliners thought it wrong to make offers to the Kremlin; they wanted a resolute stand, whatever dangers and hardships it brought them. Secretly, and rather shame-facedly, their leaders sometimes wished people were a bit more frightened: some food hoarding would relieve pressure on crammed city warehouses but, as a member of the US Mission noted, the city fathers "don't quite know how to suggest such private stockpiling without causing panic".[3]

So all in all, Macmillan faced stiff political opposition and more than a little opprobrium as he set off on a tour of the allied capitals to repair some of the damage caused by the Moscow trip and to argue his case for an early Summit. His first call was on de Gaulle on 9 and 10 March. The French ambassador in London had already told Selwyn Lloyd that any meeting with the Russians was distasteful: likely to confirm the existence of the GDR regime and bound to get bogged down in discussion of the totally unacceptable Soviet draft treaty. The French, he explained, wanted to see some Soviet cards on the Foreign Ministers' table and a whole range of agreements reached before heads of government got involved. In Paris, Macmillan got the impression that de Gaulle was rather more pliable than his officials and noted with pleasure how embarrassed they were when the President said there could not be nuclear war over the question of whether a Russian or an East German sergeant "signed the pass to go along the Autobahn". But Macmillan was surely the victim of his own lordly metaphor and shallow understanding of the Berlin problem. He did not give sufficient weight to the comment de Gaulle added: that the justification for such a war would be blockade of the western sectors – implying (for those who wished to hear) that force should be used to uphold the important principles at stake in Berlin. It was no good Macmillan writing that the French were "trying to pretend that we are weak and defeatist and that they are for 'being tough'." There was no pretence about it, though there was self-delusion on the Prime Minister's part. And although his visit did something to allay the French suspicion that he had secretly negotiated in Moscow and did a little to clarify the British distinction between "thinning out" and "disengagement", it gave the French government new anxieties: about British recklessness in rushing to a Summit and a sudden willingness to abandon the present legal basis for western presence in Berlin (based on conquest) for a new contractual agreement with the Soviet Union (which Couve de Murville and the Prime Minister, Debré, castigated as a climb-down).[4]

The British visit to Bonn on 12 and 13 March fared little better. To prepare for it, Adenauer had burnished his grievances. There were plenty of them: British readiness to deal with, and even recognise, East Germany at the expense of reunification, the fact that he had not been consulted about the Moscow trip, the reference in its communiqué to what sounded very like "disengagement". Steel described the Chancellor as "so suspicious that I can hardly have any conversation with him without his twisting it to fit his phobia of the moment". To make his mood worse, Adenauer had recently been to Paris where de Gaulle had stoked his worries about Macmillan's willingness to make concessions over Berlin. The Prime

Minister and Foreign Secretary spent the first meeting trying to explain that they had offered no deals to Khrushchev, had not let the Kremlin drive a wedge into the western alliance, had never mentioned "disengagement" and did not believe in it anyway. After a three-hour stormy session Brentano muttered to Lloyd in the hall that he himself understood and was satisfied by the account of the Moscow talks and communiqué. Not so the Chancellor, who regarded any limitation of arms, even if it was called "thinning out", as dangerous avoidance of the only true solution to Europe's problems which was controlled disarmament, and who considered Macmillan's call for "flexibility in tactics" during negotiation as a euphemism for surrender of principles. When his officials talked to Selwyn Lloyd next day they were not impressed when he dismissed tough talk and military preparations as dangerous bluff (they were all in favour of using an armed convoy to restore communications with Berlin) and they were appalled when he referred to right of conquest to justify allied presence in West Berlin as "flyblown" (maintaining the present Berlin situation, they insisted, was very much safer than risking something worse by negotiating changes). They themselves would be satisfied with a temporary truce on existing terms.[5]

The best the British could get from their talks in Bonn was Adenauer's acceptance that if, or probably when, a Foreign Ministers' conference failed, there should be a Summit – though Khrushchev, he insisted, should pay for it by agreeing to a five-year preservation of the status quo in Berlin. Macmillan saw this concession as "a great thing" and imagined the West Germans would now persuade the Americans to attend a meeting of the four heads of government. In fact it should have been clear to him that the West Germans would do no such thing. The Chancellor (aged eighty-three) had told him that Eisenhower (aged sixty-nine) was not quite up to a Summit and had been "absolutely unwilling to discuss any political questions at all" when they last met.* Could Mr Nixon, he mused, represent the President? Might Mr Macmillan raise the whole delicate matter when he went to Washington? Clearly the Chancellor had added the American President to his ever-growing list of unreliables.

---

* Western statesmen increasingly behaved like elderly gentlemen at memorial services: making rude comments on each other's decrepitude and preening themselves on their own virility. After Adenauer and de Gaulle (sixty-nine) met at Colombey-les-Deux-Églises each commented that the other was managing remarkably well "for his age". Macmillan wrote in his diary in April 1959 that the Chancellor was senile and had gone "a bit potty" which was enough explanation for his political animus to Britain. David Bruce was interested that Eisenhower pointedly asked on one occasion if Adenauer showed signs of senility; Bruce had not noticed any, which was probably disappointing.

And the British visit to Bonn had given him a few new suspicions of Macmillan.

When Macmillan reached Washington he did not find Eisenhower in the best of moods either. From the start of March, the President had been under fire from Congress and the press: Khrushchev's 27 May deadline was fast approaching and there could well be war over Berlin, yet the US government had ordered no military preparations and was still cutting the armed forces. Herter, as acting Secretary of State during Dulles's illness, was called to defend the policy before the Senate Foreign Relations Committee. When Eisenhower was asked at a press conference on 4 March why he had not put the armed services on a war footing he asked in turn "did you ever stop to think what a general mobilisation would mean in a time of tension?" and warned of the dangers of creating a garrison state. The following week he told the White House press corps that there was no point in calling for more troops ("we are certainly not going to fight a ground war in Europe") but did not rule out nuclear war ("we will do what is necessary to protect ourselves but we are never going to back up on our rights and our responsibilities" in Berlin). That was a message not just to the press but to the Soviet Union as well, and it came with the reminder to all that war could not "free anything. Destruction is not a good police force." Meanwhile, the President was still being badgered, by General Twining and others, to approve the armed convoy plan whatever the risks. When the proposal was brought up yet again at a White House meeting on 5 March Eisenhower's devoted assistant, Ann Whitman, noted his reply: "You might as well go out and shoot everyone you see and then shoot yourself." That, she reckoned, "indicated a remarkably depressed view for him to take".[6]

Given his worry over growing hostility to what he had intended to be a calm but firm stand and his sense of widespread ignorance of the issues and risks of the crisis, Eisenhower took up a suggestion from Vice-President Richard Nixon and called in Congressional leaders, senior members of both parties, and representatives from the Armed Services, Senate Foreign Relations and House Foreign Affairs Committees for a briefing on 6 March. Again, he was criticised for "failure" to mobilise or cut military expenditure, and had to bat down calls for immediate military action with or without allied support. But at the same time he also had to quench the hopes of those optimists who thought it would be easy to negotiate a way out of the crisis or to win a conventional ground battle for Berlin. Some of the questions put to him were frightening proof of the ignorance he had suspected – and they came from supposed military or foreign affairs "experts": Is Berlin part of NATO? You have to go through East

Germany to get to Berlin? Surely we can "clobber" the East Germans? (And a horrified response when it was pointed out that the problem was not a few East Germans but 300,000 Soviet troops.) But the politicians were careful to avoid party point scoring and anxious to help the President. Indeed Eisenhower had to beg them not to pass Senate resolutions or whip up press and public support for him – he did not want any alarm or rocking of the alliance boat; just quiet backing.[7]

Useful though this meeting had been in easing some of the President's domestic political problems, it did not answer any of the grating questions about the Berlin crisis to which he, as leader of the western alliance, had the ultimate responsibility for finding answers. As he went to see Dulles in hospital that day he told Ann Whitman that he had "never been as tired". Dulles's absence, while undergoing X-ray treatment, was undoubtedly an extra burden for Eisenhower, let alone the probability that his Secretary of State would never recover and resume his post. Furthermore, a strong presidential address on radio and television on 16 March did not have the effect he had planned. He denounced the Soviet "free city" proposal ("It is by no means clear what West Berlin would be free from, except perhaps from freedom itself"), refused to "purchase peace by forsaking two million free people of Berlin", to accept a permanent division of Germany or to "negotiate under a dictated time limit or agenda". But next day, to his fury, he discovered that the press interpreted his remark that a Summit would be justified by agreements at a Foreign Ministers' conference as meaning that he would go to a Summit as long as a preliminary (and presumably pro forma) Foreign Ministers' meeting was held first. That was a very Macmillan view, and one with which he had no sympathy.[8]

The President was, indeed, increasingly irritated by the British and their Summit obsession. It seemed obvious to him that Macmillan's up-beat reports of his visits to Paris and Bonn had been misleading (or misled). Those from de Gaulle and Adenauer showed that they were far from happy with the British analysis of the crisis and the strategy to tackle it. He reckoned that Macmillan was making a serious mistake, even from the narrow domestic viewpoint, in rushing into talks with Khrushchev without demanding a quid pro quo first. How long, Eisenhower asked testily, would the British public "stand for continued insults at the hands of the Soviets?" He was riled to hear that Caccia had commented at a dinner that the British would not be "atomised over the stamping of papers" – a remark which he said in his memoirs showed "a lack of appreciation of the implications of seeming trivialities". Just as the Prime Minister and his party were about to arrive in Washington Eisenhower grumbled to a small group that too much time was wasted in vague procedures such as "informing each other of our thinking". Not the best frame of mind in which to receive Macmillan.[9]

But it was John Foster Dulles who opened the attack against the visitors. Macmillan and Lloyd went to see him in Walter Reed Army Hospital on their first full day in Washington, 20 March. He was in bed and in pain; Selwyn Lloyd was shocked by how "thin and frail" he looked. There was nothing feeble about the views he expressed. Time and again he insisted "there's going to be no war"; if the western allies were firm, the Soviet Union would give in. The western position in Berlin, he affirmed characteristically, was "legally and morally impeccable" and to assume that merely because it was challenged by the Kremlin "we have to seek a compromise, is all wrong". He made it absolutely clear that he was not persuaded by the arguments for an early Summit: Khrushchev seemed unwilling to pay a proper price for one or to hold out prospects of an agreement; everything Macmillan told him about the Moscow talks made him doubt the usefulness of negotiation. What was wrong, he asked, with the present situation in Berlin? Why change it just because the Soviet Union wanted to? Why spend $40 billion dollars a year on a deterrent power if people tried to buy peace with compromises every time the Soviets threatened? "If that is going to be our attitude, we had better save our money." Lloyd's record of the meeting suggested that Macmillan eventually got a word in edgeways but that Dulles was "not well enough for a sustained argument"; Macmillan himself later regretted having argued at all with a dying man. The fact was that, dying or not, Dulles had been in good fighting trim for fifty minutes non-stop. The only sign of his condition is that the initials he put to the memo on the meeting, which he dictated immediately afterwards, are poignantly faint and unsteady.[10]

Undismayed by Dulles's barrage, Macmillan and Lloyd went off to see Eisenhower at Camp David still determined to hold their positions. The President showed he could match Dulles's firepower when he chose. The discussions about a Summit were heated: Eisenhower refused to meet Khrushchev unless and until he was satisfied by preparatory agreements at Foreign Minister level, the British party argued that the Foreign Ministers would only make progress if there was a prior arrangement for a meeting of heads of state. Macmillan raised the emotional temperature by plaintive references to the First World War, which he argued could have been avoided if the British Foreign Secretary of the time had talked instead of going fishing; Eisenhower retorted tartly that Chamberlain had gone to talk in Munich and had not prevented the Second World War – and that, said the President, was not "the kind of meeting with which he intends to be associated". Macmillan then tried to argue that he had a duty to go to a Summit because eight Soviet nuclear bombs could kill twenty million British people; Eisenhower snapped back that his own people would want a Summit to be justified, and that seventy million US lives were at risk. There were further spats about contingency planning for Berlin. Macmillan was clearly irked when Murphy insisted that stamping of documents by East Germans was unacceptable (he decided in his diary that Murphy had just been on the telephone to Dulles). Watching a film, *The Great Country*, that evening did nothing to jolly the Prime Minister along. He described it as "inconceivably banal". (A three-hour western sounds much more Churchill's cup of tea.) Relations between both sides were strained throughout and Ann Whitman noticed that the British party, who had given an account of being bugged in Moscow, now seemed "a little suspicious of us". "They huddle in groups outside." Eisenhower might be said to have won the battle honours: it was agreed that a Note to the Kremlin, proposing a Foreign Ministers' meeting in May, should make it clear that a Summit depended on developments at this level. With that gained, the President could be generous: he promised to be elastic in his definition of progress.[11]

Macmillan seemed unperturbed by the opposition to his policies from every capital on his grand tour – and he could certainly feel gratified by the approval of his domestic press and electorate, who felt his time had been well spent. But the fact was that the main result of all his air miles and arguments had been to unite the other Western Powers against him. When reports of what he had said to Eisenhower about force limitations got back to Bonn, Adenauer – rightly – spotted that his proposals would involve denial of IRBMs to the Federal Republic. The Chancellor worked up an alarming head of steam. Macmillan quickly sent a reassuring message. It did no good. Steel reported on 31 March that the "Chancellor's suspicions of us are not only alive but more rampant than they have ever been"; the atmosphere in Bonn was "potentially explosive". And it did not improve. In late April Adenauer was still seething when David Bruce went to see him during his holidays on Lake Como: certain that Macmillan had done a secret deal with Khrushchev in Moscow and dreading British behaviour at any conference. The French were in less of a flap but no more convinced by any of Macmillan's reasoning. De Gaulle haughtily scorned the Prime Minister as "marqué" by his Moscow trip. Couve de Murville had no patience with the British demand for "flexibility" in negotiations; expected a Foreign Ministers' conference, let alone a Summit, to fail so saw no reason for talking to the Russians at all; agreed with Herter that Macmillan's defence proposals for Central Europe "seemed vague and unsatisfactory" and thought a new contractual agreement for western presence in Berlin would be an inadequate substitute for the present "clear rights". Dulles lay in hospital lamenting that the old Anglo-Saxon collaboration "seems to be over". One of Macmillan's few sympathisers was the American ambassador in London, Jock Hay Whitney. He assured the State Department that Britain was not really in "Munich mood" and that the Prime Minister would, in the end, stick to western rights in Berlin and the alliance. They could only hope he was right.[12]

Britain's relations with her allies were strained yet further when on 14 April Khrushchev sent a nine-page letter to Macmillan which even the Prime Minister could see was "a somewhat crude attempt" to split him off from the western alliance. It praised British efforts for "peace" and vilified various American and West German "warmongers" and "adventurist circles". Macmillan was quick to keep his nose clean. He passed on edited, less personally abusive, versions of the letter to all three leaders. De Gaulle sent a formal acknowledgement but did not stoop to comment. Eisenhower warned that the tone of the letter suggested that Khrushchev would use a Summit for propaganda purposes. Adenauer tartly advised that "an exchange of letters with Khrushchev at this moment seems to me a bad idea". This was advice that Macmillan did not take: he wrote back to Khrushchev on 29 April and thus began a lengthy correspondence.[13]

On 30 March the Soviet Union agreed to the western proposal to hold a Foreign Ministers' meeting in Geneva, starting on 11 May. The Kremlin expressed some disappointment that the Western Powers would not accept Czech or Polish representatives at the conference – something they had been urging for many months in an attempt to broaden the four-Power responsibility for a post-war settlement and to get East–West equality of delegations. The British and Americans had always opposed the idea. If Czechs and Poles were let in, the Yugoslavs would claim a right to take part as victors against Nazi Germany. Let the Yugoslavs in and how could anyone exclude all the other former enemies of Hitler, from Brazil to India with most of Europe and the whole British Commonwealth in between? There would be too many snouts at the trough, too many conflicting interests. It was quite enough to have agreed that East and West Germans could attend as advisers. The Western Powers, in any case, wanted to focus on Berlin and Germany before the proceedings were expanded to a general peace settlement.[14]

Even before the invitation to a conference had been sent or a date fixed, the western negotiating positions were under discussion. A four-Power Working Group in Washington in early February agreed that the aim of the talks must be an interim agreement on Berlin – to last until reunification – which would preserve the freedoms of the western sectors and allied presence and access. It had also been decided that the issues of reunification and free all-German elections must slip down the timetable of a settlement: the Soviet Union was clearly going to oppose both and unless the West slackened its position, there was a strong possibility that the Russians would hand over their responsibilities in Berlin to the GDR and sign a separate treaty, making an interim Berlin agreement impossible. Since it was also felt that any security arrangement in Central Europe must be tied to reunification, that too slid down the list of priorities. Even so, some relaxation of tension in the area seemed feasible: the West Germans had confirmed that they were willing to recognise the Oder-Neisse Line, have diplomatic relations with Poland, and to consider non-aggression pacts with other Eastern Bloc states (though these were cards they preferred to keep up their sleeves until it was seen if the Soviet Union was ready to offer compromises in return). Once this general outline had been sketched in Washington – showing significant loosening of the western principles held since Geneva in 1955 – another Working Group was set up in Paris, on 9 March, to fill in some details.[15]

Here, the British lost their argument for a new quadripartite agreement to replace occupation as the basis for the right of presence in Berlin. The others insisted that the old arrangement was legal and still binding and that any new contract would be more easily bent or broken by the Russians. There was a lot of discussion about ways of persuading the Kremlin to preserve the present status of Berlin: a four-Power agreement by which the GDR was accepted not as a government but as a Soviet-designated authority; United Nations' supervision of access, refugees or propaganda activities; an all-Berlin government. Enormous efforts were made to draw up a phased plan for reunification, security and a peace settlement, but even the British, on whose old Foreign Office paper it was based, had to admit that the result was "hideously complicated" and "would not be accepted by the Russians". Bonn was driven to distraction by the elements of the plan which dealt with German reunification: an all-German committee with two representatives from each Land to draft an electoral law and take on quasi-governmental duties, followed by elections for a constituent assembly, then by the formation of a national government. One senior Federal official was said to be in "a state of nervous exhaustion". Brentano protested that the proposals were no better than those put forward by Khrushchev and Ulbricht, that no West German would work with East Germans who were nothing more than Soviet stooges and the only proper way to unity was through free elections. In fact, however, it was obvious that he was personally uncomfortable with the rigid 1955 posture that the Chancellor was forcing him to adopt.[16]*

The next Working Group, in London from 13 to 23 April, toned down the reunification proposals: limited the all-German committee to drafting an electoral law and co-ordinating contacts between East and West; built in a plebiscite on the electoral law; suggested a poll under international supervision for a national assembly to draft a constitution. These discussions were tightly controlled by all four capitals. Everyone had strict instructions on each point in the agenda and Pentagon representatives breathed down the necks of the State Department officials throughout. A simpler, but still ill-fitting, phased plan was drawn up. No one was satisfied with it; no one could decide whether the package could or should be split into smaller packets or would have to be taken or rejected whole by the Soviet Union.

Fortunately the Foreign Ministers of the three Powers met in Paris on 29 April and managed to break through most of the tangles. They picked out of the Group's report some basic principles which could be used as opening proposals at Geneva, and put all the detail to one side to be used if appropriate once the Soviet line was known. There was little dispute at this meeting. The Foreign Ministers were acutely aware that allied unity was the paramount need. After all, the Geneva Conference was due to begin in less than a fortnight's time.[17]

For twenty-four hours, from 10 to 11 May, it looked as if the conference would never open. With all the problems outstanding since the Second World War to be settled and a potential nuclear conflict to be averted, there was a major East–West confrontation – over placement. On the evening of 10 May Gromyko stamped his foot and declared that the two German delegations (invited as advisers and observers) must sit at the table with the four Powers and speak whenever they wished. He turned down the suggestion that this

---

* Brentano was no more likely to argue, however, than Selwyn Lloyd. David Bruce once described him as "not master in his own house" and "moving unsteadily in the shadow of the Chancellor". Everyone respected him as a good negotiator, but reckoned that he was tied to Adenauer's brief. According to an old Bonn story, the Foreign Minister had once got into a lift with the Chancellor, pressed the button to go up a few floors, and was then ignominiously taken down to the basement. That, it was said, was the last time he was allowed to take an initiative.

could be discussed at the first session and insisted that the Germans must take part from the very beginning. The Western Powers realised that the East German delegation would be encouraged by the Russians to make all the running on German topics, at one and the same time getting de facto recognition and advancing the argument that reunification was a matter solely for the two Germanies. An informal meeting of the four Foreign Ministers was held to decide how everyone would be seated and under what rules the Germans would speak, the western speakers doing their best to make sure that the Germans would be kept at a distance and as quiet as possible. There was no agreement that evening. Next morning the ministers met again. This time they set to work with paper and pencil and drew diagrams of seating plans with all the passion of interior designers. Selwyn Lloyd was in favour of a half-moon table for the four Powers and a separate table at each horn for the Germans. Others played with permutations of round tables, oblong tables, small squares alongside, small circles above or below. Finally: a breakthrough. It was agreed that the four Powers would sit at a round table with the two German delegations at small oblongs a little apart. So far, so good. But how far apart? More argument, more diagrams. Mr Gromyko's sketch was the winner. It was fastidiously detailed. He drew the exact measurement of the gap between the main table and the two satellites: the width of six pencils precisely.*

Progress indeed. Now all that had to be settled was the question of who would speak when. It was finally agreed that the Germans were only advisers but could participate in discussions if they applied for permission from the chairman and there were no objections from other delegations. At last the first formal session of the Geneva talks could be held – at 6 p.m. rather than 3.30 as originally scheduled. This session revealed a new complication: the tables had been placed to everyone's satisfaction but not the chairs. There were ten at the main table for the four Powers and only six for all the Germans. Gromyko demanded equality. And more: he called for chairs for Polish and Czech advisers too. As Herter cabled to Eisenhower: "If today's haggling [is] any indication of days to come, patience and then some will be a very necessary requisite." The wretched conference secretary, who was af-flicted with responsibility for furniture, very sensibly removed all the extra

* The six sketches which got into the final round are preserved at the Public Record Office at Kew (FO371 145884). Each is illegibly marked to show whose idea it was and at what time it was suggested. They are in a blue folder – of very much better quality than the standard instantly dog-eared issue – with a cover note: "This should provide good material for some Harold Nicholson [sic] of the year 2000." Thank you.

seats until the Foreign Ministers thrashed the matter out. That took three whole days. Finally Gromyko grudgingly accepted that there would be only six chairs for the Germans and no representation for the eastern bloc. The conference was at last out of the procedural wood and into the substantive forest.[18]

For the next two weeks the proceedings were taken up with the formal reading of prepared texts laying out the eastern and western positions: speeches rather than negotiation, with just an occasional comment or grouse to relieve the tedious predictability. For a lot of the time the two sides might just as well have been sitting in separate rooms – their proposals were so at odds it was as if they were working on different agendas. The Soviet and East German delegations presented the same demands they had made since the beginning of the crisis: a peace treaty (as in the draft attached to the 10 January Soviet Note) to be signed by the four Powers and both parts of Germany, a loose German confederation with parity of representation to establish contacts and deal with practical matters, and the replacement of the "occupation regime" in West Berlin by a demilitarised "free city".[19]

The western phased Peace Plan tabled by Herter on 14 May was totally incompatible with this Soviet programme. As simplified by the Foreign Ministers in Paris, it envisaged two parallel sets of measures. One group would lead to German reunification in four stages: starting with the integration of Berlin, followed by the establishment of a mixed German committee to draft an electoral law, then elections for an all-German government, and finally the signing of a peace treaty between the new state and the four Powers. The other group consisted of a graded series of security measures (including the renunciation by both Germanies of biological, chemical and nuclear weapons), culminating at the time when an all-German government was formed in the creation of a zone of equal size and depth within which eastern and western forces would be reduced to an agreed size. Once a peace treaty was signed, all foreign troops would withdraw from the zone if asked to do so by the governments in the area. The new German state would have the right to join NATO or the Warsaw Pact and, if it took either option, forces along the new frontier between the alliances would be adjusted to prevent a clash.

Neither side showed any inclination to deviate from its pre-determined route to a settlement. The Western Powers argued that their Plan already conceded enough: offering an instant all-German body, postponing elections for at least two and a half years, and promising guarantees of security to the Soviet bloc. The Soviet and East German delegations denounced western refusal to recognise the GDR as an equal partner in a purely German settlement of national unity, and accused the West of trying to "liquidate socialism" and perpetuate a state of war by delaying the treaty. "Adenauer was the real author of the Plan", claimed Gromyko; it permitted the remilitarisation of the Federal Republic. The Soviet plan, replied the western Foreign Ministers, was for an imposed treaty, which would be unjust, would not last, and would prevent full reunification. Each side vilified the other for stubbornness in refusing to split its package and deal with individual items; each alleged that the other was trying to create deadlock. After two weeks the talks were getting nowhere.[20]

They had certainly not been helped by the conditions in which they were held. The sessions were attended by anything from 120 to 150 people; in the early days there were 1,800 journalists milling about outside and even when many of them got bored and went home the rest needed 800 copies of every statement and were nourished by gossip and leaks from the huge delegations which could not be fitted into the conference room. The Americans and French were acutely suspicious of British readiness to capitulate or unwrap the western package. ("One can sense this", Sir Anthony Rumbold wrote to the Foreign Office edgily, "almost in the way they look at us and from the way one can see them talking to each other in corners.") Both German teams were sulking because they resented sitting at a lower table ("Cat's table" in German). Lothar Bolz, the GDR's Foreign Minister, piped up constantly on German matters to stake his claim to represent a true state, but seethed at perpetual western references to the "so-called GDR". In all the time he was at the talks he was said to have received not one single directive from his own Ministry so made do with those from Moscow. To reassert themselves, the East Germans tried to hold press conferences. Never having had a proper press conference (or press, for that matter) they handled them extremely badly, and shouted down any journalist who had the impudence to ask a pointed question. The Federal Foreign Minister, Brentano, refused to sit in the same room as his East German would-be counterpart, so lurked outside, frustrated, while Bonn's point of view was put by Wilhelm Grewe, of the Foreign Ministry, a man with an admirable grasp of detail and devotion to accuracy but no political acumen, eloquence or social grace.[21]

Since formal talks were obviously bogged down, the western Foreign Ministers decided that the only chance of progress lay in private meetings with Gromyko: informal discussions in their villas, well away from the hordes of officials and journalists, and concentrating on matters where some agreement might be found. Their wish to salvage something from the talks, and possibly to build on accord, was understandable. It was a dangerous move, however. Once the western package was loosened, was it possible to stop the Russians grabbing the bits they fancied and wrecking the whole? Would the quest for some positive result lead to excessive concessions?[22]

By regrettable coincidence there was a sudden opportunity to explore prospects for these private talks. On 24 May John Foster Dulles died. Though his allies and enemies had so often disagreed with him in life, in death they must honour his indisputable stature. A recess was called at Geneva and all the Foreign Ministers flew to Washington for Dulles's funeral on 27 May. That was, of course, a momentous date: the day when Khrushchev's ultimatum for a Berlin settlement ran out. What with the hurried journey and the preoccupations of the Geneva talks, the significance was hardly noticed.

President Eisenhower paid his last respects to his trusty Secretary of State and conducted personal diplomacy. He got up to date with Herter and insisted that the Berlin problem must not be settled outside the whole German question, that any interim agreement was too low a price for a Summit, and there must be no wavering over western rights in the city. He braced Adenauer, who was going through an acute phase of phobia about the British, with assurances that Macmillan would be firm once the showdown came. He stiffened Selwyn Lloyd by promising to go anywhere, any time, for a Summit once there was real progress at Geneva. The next day at lunch he told the four Foreign Ministers to start talking turkey. In fact he threatened to order the pilot who flew them back to Geneva to stay in the air until they found a basis for agreement; "I will provide the services of an American tanker airplane to extend your flight indefinitely." They took the hint and on the return journey talked seriously and at length about Berlin. There was little new in what they said. Gromyko could not resist trying to tug Britain and her allies apart by suggesting that existing western rights should be replaced by a new contract for presence in Berlin, but the western ministers closed ranks and insisted that their rights were inalienable.[23]

That aircraft discussion set the style and topic for most of the activity in Geneva for the coming two weeks or more. There were still some formal sessions with full delegations present and a lot of gnawing at old bones. But the four Foreign Ministers met regularly and privately at each of their villas in turn. Much of their talking was done during or after dinner. Nearly all of it was devoted to Berlin. The conversation shifted round four central issues: rights, troops, access, and subversive and propaganda activities, with the topics overlapping but being separately emphasised from time to time as one side probed the position of the other.

The matter of four-Power rights in Berlin, with the corollary of their responsibilities, boiled down to all the old arguments. Gromyko declared the right of occupation obsolete, ideally wanted western withdrawal and a "free city" but would settle for a new contract on presence; the West countered that the four-Power status of the city must remain until it was the capital of Germany and that no party could unilaterally renounce its duties, though the allies were ready to "supplement" existing rights by new arrangements "without prejudice" to the old ones. From the western assertion of rights in Berlin flowed their argument for continued presence and access. Gromyko kept calling the allied garrison a "threat" to the GDR and a "danger to peace"; the three other Foreign Ministers replied that their troops in the city were "symbolic", wanted by the West Berliners, and could not be joined by Soviet units. But after days of this argy-bargy, the West went into a perilous retreat by allowing discussion on cutting the size of their forces and fixing a ceiling of 7,500. That risked making the garrisons "symbolic" indeed – limiting their police work on public order and against East German incursion as well as their patrols to protect communications by road and rail. Any cut would give the Russians a political victory and damage West Berlin morale. As far as access was concerned Gromyko continued to argue that the Soviet Union must soon hand over control of all routes to East Germany – and as a sovereign power, not as a Soviet agent. The western ministers insisted on agency and refused to accept the Soviet offer of a guarantee for access since Gromyko intended to associate the GDR with it, which would clearly involve some degree of recognition for the Pankow government. They were not tempted by his suggestion that a four-Power commission could settle access disputes with the East Germans – though that did imply that the Russians would retain some of the responsibility which they claimed they were handing over.

Weaving in and out of all these other Berlin topics was the question of subversion and propaganda activities in the city. It was a problem sometimes dismissed by Gromyko as "a minor matter" (but he kept coming back to it) and on occasion treated by the other Foreign Ministers as if it were a thread to guide them out of the maze of complications into which the other aspects of their talks had trapped them. Subversion and propaganda had the advantage of being matters of complaint by each side rather than issues of principle. Perhaps that might make them easier to deal with.

On 1 June Herter read a paper detailing alleged anti-western activities conducted from East Berlin. He claimed that at least 20,000 people were engaged in civil and military subversion in the western sectors; he listed pages and pages of front organisations which were believed to be bases for Communist agents and their covert work (anything from the local SED offices or trade union cadres through to youth groups, commissions for women's affairs or cultural societies). He described at least sixty-three kidnappings from West Berlin since 1945 as well as hundreds of attempts; false rumours and slanders spread against western leaders (himself included); a whole range of treasonable and infiltration activities which were planned and directed from the East. Everything he said was undoubtedly true. If anything he underestimated the scale of the problem: every West Berliner had dozens of stories of Communists planted in their offices or factories to stir up trouble, of blackmail attempts, of approaches from friends or relatives working for the East German State Security with threats to family members living in the GDR unless help or information were given. The trouble with the Herter paper, however, was that it was written on the assumption that the West's cause was "good and true" so did not need much evidence to support the charges – and inevitably it avoided any reference to the considerable amount of espionage and propaganda carried out by western agents in the East, so looked like humbug. As a result it was all too easy for Gromyko to comment that the Secretary of State obviously thought that attack was the best defence and to call piously for the Foreign Ministers to "try to rise above this kind of thing". But as the topic kept being revived during the talks, the Western Powers showed increasing willingness to limit their own activities in return for a Soviet quid pro quo.[24]

The propaganda aspect worried Willy Brandt. From an early stage in the Geneva Conference he had warned that what the Soviet Union called "propaganda" could well be described as "free speech" in West Berlin. He did not want the West to negotiate away the western sectors' newspapers and RIAS radio. Nor was he in favour of any reduction in the allied garrisons: they were essential for morale, for support of the police force, and monitoring civilian communications with the Federal Republic. He had always pointed out the danger in detaching Berlin from the wider German question. Now that it was indeed being discussed separately, the western Foreign Ministers seemed ready to make concessions on western sector freedoms in the attempt to get a mere temporary settlement and they were concentrating on their own access rather than that of West Germans and Berliners. To make matters worse, Berlin itself was not represented at the talks, and Brandt was not getting regular reports or many briefing documents from the Federal delegation in Geneva. Not only was the Berlin question detached from the German issue, the western sectors felt cut off, impotent, and vulnerable to their friends as well as their enemies.[25]

In fact the western allies were equally depressed. The private discussions had turned out to be as unproductive as formal sessions, in spite of all the crumbs and occasional thick slices of concession the West had thrown on the waters. In tone, the villa conversations had been perfectly pleasant. Gromyko, who seemed cold, humourless and tight-lipped in Khrushchev's company or impatient, sarcastic and harshly obdurate in a large conference chamber, was more relaxed and forthcoming in these small groups. He showed his mastery of his briefs (western diplomats thought of him as His Master's Voice; Soviet diplomats judged him to be a remarkable professional and an expert on German affairs). He revealed a quick, dry wit; was affable and polite, though as impersonal and reserved as ever. He sometimes gave a flash of ideological hectoring or made a sudden brutal stab at an opponent's argument, but the western Foreign Ministers forgave him; they knew he was on a tight rein from the Kremlin. Whenever he soured, Selwyn Lloyd played his customary role of pacifier, once telling him to "cheer up, go away and have a good lunch, and come back in a more flexible mood". Relations between the western Foreign Ministers had certainly improved in the villas. Herter told Eisenhower that Couve de Murville was "an excellent partner, articulate and forceful", that Lloyd "played the Allied game faithfully" though was "too ready to inject a moderating remark and to profess to see points of agreement with the Soviets when in fact none exists". Herter himself was appreciated by his colleagues for skilled chairmanship and polite doggedness in debate, though Selwyn Lloyd once cabled wistfully to Macmillan: "I do miss Foster."[26]

But a pleasant working atmosphere was not enough. There had been no real progress over the Berlin problem, let alone on the questions of reunification and security which were still being debated in the main conference. Hopes for some agreement were finally snuffed on 9 June. That morning Gromyko denounced a paper summarising western proposals and added that he had "come to the conclusion that the West did not want serious negotiation about Berlin". He then laid out harsh Soviet conditions for a settlement: the western "occupation" could continue for one year, as long as forces and arms in the western sectors were reduced and all propaganda and espionage in East Germany ceased; in that year an all-German committee must be formed, with parity for the FRG and GDR, to work out the terms of reunification and a peace treaty; if all this were agreed, the Soviet Union would guarantee the Western Powers' existing communications and join a four-Power body to deal with access problems; if the proposals were rejected, the Soviet Union would not permit continued "occupation" and would sign a treaty with the GDR.

The western Foreign Ministers were stunned. These were the terms of 10 and 27 November 1958, with a new ultimatum of twelve months. Not only had they failed to shift the Soviet position after weeks of talks, they were now being told to negotiate under a new threat. As they withdrew from the meeting a despondent Herter said he could not stay in Geneva for more than a few days; they discussed an adjournment though no one was willing to bear the responsibility for breaking up the conference. They tried further argument with Gromyko, who denied he had issued an ultimatum but would not budge from the line of his statement.[27]

Though Gromyko was impervious to pressure, Eisenhower was showing signs of succumbing to it. On 3 June he wrote to Macmillan along his usual lines: "A Summit meeting based on nothing more than wishful thinking would be a disaster. The world would interpret such a move as being a virtual surrender, while Soviet prestige would be enhanced." Yet he admitted that when he met the Prime Minister at Camp David he had offered a "rather liberal definition of progress", and he now defined "progress" as at least an agreement by the Foreign Ministers to confirm the "continuing status of Berlin pending the unification of Germany". That in itself was something of a climb-down from what he had said to Herter at the time of Dulles's funeral. And the President's resolution was being buffeted from all sides. Reports from Geneva suggested that the Russians would hold out to force a Summit; news from London showed that Macmillan was likely to invite the American, French and Soviet leaders for "talks" (and whatever these were called, they would be seen as a Summit); there were strong arguments from the State Department that unless Khrushchev was given a token success to counter Party critics of his policies, the Kremlin would drift into an even tougher policy. On 9 June Herter cabled an account of Gromyko's new, frightening démarche and pointed out "we are at the cross-roads, which requires a new initiative on our part." So on 15 June Eisenhower wrote a personal letter to Khrushchev saying there could be no Summit without progress at the Foreign Ministers' level or freedom from threat. But – and it was a major weakening of his position – he only called for enough preparation at Geneva "to suggest the possibility of agreement on significant matters". He was unhappy with this offer but others had driven him to make it. Caccia reported that at a meeting on 16 June the President groaned "what a hell of a world we were getting to if there was no means of carrying on diplomacy except by the President of the United States having to meet one dictator after another."[28]

A last ditch effort was made to save the Geneva conference and stave off a Summit or a worsening of the Berlin crisis. On 16 June the western

Foreign Ministers presented Gromyko with proposals for an interim settlement pending reunification. They offered to stick to a limit of 11,000 men and to conventional weapons for their garrisons in Berlin and to "consider the possibility of reducing such forces if developments in the situation permit". They agreed to accept German personnel at checkpoints "without prejudice to existing responsibilities", and suggested that both sides should avoid activities "which might either disturb public order or seriously affect the rights and interests" of others. They called for freedom of movement from East to West Berlin and accepted the idea of a four-Power commission to settle access disputes.

These were the proposals of desperate men. They came very near to a sell-out. Having already abandoned the attempt to get a wide agreement for Germany and European security, the Western Powers were now recklessly throwing cards on the table to get a temporary Berlin settlement. The offers of troop limitations and future reductions were an open invitation to the Russians to start salami slicing on the allied garrisons, as well as blows to West Berlin morale and the effectiveness of their forces. The access arrangements they accepted were those of April 1959 – way short of the number of crossing points and slacker checkpoint procedures of the early '50s. East Germans would control traffic (and take a step to recognition) without any formal acknowledgement of Soviet responsibility. The clauses on espionage and propaganda had no safeguards for a free press or broadcasting and no mechanisms for monitoring the activities of both sides. It was all very well to insist on free movement in Berlin (and keeping the door open for refugees) but there was signal failure to mention movement between the Federal Republic and the GDR. By omitting any reference to the Western Powers' right of occupation in Berlin, the way had been left open to the Soviet Union to chisel away at presence and access and weaken the basis of the allies' right to frame a final settlement. It was just as well that by accident rather than design these proposals were never negotiated on.

They had been offered contrary to the long-held views and frequent recommendations of the allied authorities in Berlin and were seen by Brandt and his city government as a dangerous threat to the freedom of the western sectors and the allied position. In public Brandt spoke of the new western offers as going to the limits of the tolerable; in private he made it clear they had gone way beyond. He was furious not to have been consulted; the Senate was alarmed that no concessions had been demanded in return. Morale in Berlin degenerated until by mid-July it was described as at "the gloomiest level" since the start of the crisis.[29]

Gromyko professed himself unimpressed by the western paper: the new proposals, he maintained, were little different from the old and prolonged the occupation regime; 11,000 troops, he argued, were not "symbolic" though 3,000 or 4,000 might be (the salami knife was out already). There was then a pause in the talks during which it was assumed he was waiting for instructions from Moscow (where conceivably, as often happened when Soviet politicians were faced with compromise, everyone assumed the concessions were a trap). And in the interval the pressure on Eisenhower built up. On 16 June Macmillan had written to the President suggesting that since the Geneva talks were breaking down he would hold an "informal meeting" of the heads of government. As soon as he read the letter Eisenhower complained that "the more he thinks about the matter, the more impatient he becomes with the stand Mr Macmillan has been taking" and the more determined not to be "bludgeoned" into a Summit; he would not say "please" to Khrushchev to get one. He then worked himself into a fine old paddy saying that, whatever the British public thought, he personally would rather be "atomised than communised", the maintenance of freedom and rights for Berliners was a justifiable cause for war and if the Russians challenged "we must then talk about hitting them". General Twining would have been proud of him. The President did, however, let slip that he had been thinking, just thinking, that he might talk personally and privately to Khrushchev. It looked as if he might have to. On 17 June he got a letter from the Soviet leader: nothing but repetition of the hard line, which made it obvious that there would be no yielding at Geneva. Next day Herter cabled that the western Foreign Ministers agreed that unless there was a fresh and substantial Soviet proposal, the conference must go into recess for a month or so. When on 19 June Gromyko finally offered nothing more than an extension of the deadline for a settlement from a year to eighteen months, the Geneva talks broke up until 13 July.[30]

Macmillan used the interval to press his case for a Summit. Fortified by reading about the start of the First World War, he ignored the opposition of his allies: "None of them", he thought, "seemed to appreciate the dangers of drifting on" to what he believed would be "serious catastrophe, perhaps leading through some folly to war". He wrote to Eisenhower on 23 June: "It would not be easy to persuade the British people that it was their duty to go to war in defence of West Berlin", and for people "who have tried to destroy us twice in this century". The President, conversely, felt duty bound to save West Berlin and the allied position in the city, and to lessen the tension which could so easily result in a dangerous confrontation. On 11 July, therefore, just before the Geneva talks resumed, the President sent a message to Khrushchev, via Frol Kozlov who was returning to Moscow from the UN, suggesting in the most general terms that they should have a quiet meeting and an informal discussion. He hoped that this invitation would produce "some sort of change of attitude" in the Soviet delegation at Geneva.

That was a vain hope – and naïve, perhaps. The Kremlin could interpret his offer as an indication that if they pushed harder at the conference, they could topple Eisenhower into a Summit. Gromyko returned to Geneva with all his fighting irons on. He wrecked the first two or three days by refusing to attend private meetings unless he could bring East Germans with him, then prevented discussions on Berlin by harping on all-German problems. By 17 July Herter had decided that the Soviet Foreign Minister was "not only obstructive but objectionable". Couve de Murville was quite ready to break up the conference – after all, he had never expected anything from it. Selwyn Lloyd was depressed because, whatever his Prime Minister believed, he was now so thoroughly infected by his colleagues that he could not contemplate a Summit without some degree of agreement at this meeting. Everyone struggled on however. Prolonged and intensive negotiations tend to take on their own momentum and to lose sight of the real prospects for success; there is a temptation to lose a grip on basic principles in the quest for anything to put on paper to show that talks have not been a waste of time.[31]

Gromyko seemed to sense western anxiety to avoid total failure and he exploited it. He picked the proposal for all-German negotiations for reunification and a treaty – long since rejected by the West – and made it the condition for an interim Berlin settlement. It was a skilful move. His opponents, who had spent weeks unpicking their own package, were now faced with assembling a new, unattractive one if they wanted to gain anything from Geneva. The West Germans were enraged by the possibility they might have to talk on equal terms with the untouchables from the East. The western Foreign Ministers realised they could not force them to do so, desirable though it was to encourage contacts between both parts of Germany, because the logic of the Soviet plan led from a committee to a loose confederation – and that meant permanent virtual partition. So on 20 July Herter announced that if the committee was the sine qua non for agreement everyone might as well go home. Gromyko butted in: he "was not saying that . . ." and hours and hours of bad-tempered wrangling over all the same old points followed. By 24 July Couve de Murville had a headache. No wonder.[32]

Relief, of a sort, was at hand. On 22 July Khrushchev replied to Eisenhower's letter that he would be delighted to come to the United

States and stay for ten or fifteen days, though he still believed that a meeting "at the highest level" was essential. The President was furious: there was no reference in the reply to his wish for the visit to be linked to progress at Geneva. Why not? The answer was that Robert Murphy, to whom his letter had been entrusted, had failed to deliver to Kozlov the President's verbal rider stressing this link. Murphy claimed he had not understood his instruction. "To say that this view disturbed me", Eisenhower wrote later, "is an understatement." He scourged all around, telling them how Dulles used to send him a memo on every meeting then go over the points by phone to be sure that all instructions were correctly noted. But then, true to form, he took the blame on himself. He decided he had not made his wishes clear so must pay for it by meeting Khrushchev against his better judgement. The formal invitation was sent for private talks at Camp David – with a warning that Khrushchev's reception in the United States would depend on the outcome at Geneva. A second message went to Herter that he must try to keep the talks going.[33]

Macmillan responded to the news with a letter to the President warning that it would be difficult to avoid discussing matters of substance with Khrushchev (quite a nerve after his repeated denials that there had been any such risk during his own Moscow trip) and that French and Federal German suspicions would be aroused (something on which he was an expert). He therefore advised (getting down to the real point of his letter) that a Summit should be announced at the time of Khrushchev's visit. Eisenhower, not surprisingly, slapped the idea down. It was, after all, quite bad enough that he had to put up with Khrushchev's company. A Summit, he told Macmillan firmly, would "run the risk of spectacular failure or unthinkable capitulation".[34]

Meanwhile, at Geneva, the western Foreign Ministers made one last throw for an agreement. Emotion and professional pride demanded it, though clearly matters were already slipping away from them. On 28 July they submitted a paper to Gromyko which was very much a restatement of their 16 June proposals, but with the addition of some clauses to involve the United Nations in supervising an agreement and to allow for a review by the ministers after five years. All they got in response was a repeat of recent Soviet demands. It was deadlock all over again. Several days of dispiriting villa sessions, frustrating one-to-one conversations, and anxious murmuring in corridors did nothing to break it. As Macmillan (no doubt happily) wrote to Selwyn Lloyd on 4 August: "The President has, of course, inadvertently sabotaged the Conference."[35]

Perhaps it did not need wrecking. Perhaps it had always been a defective undertaking and was doomed from the start. Neither side had ever wanted an agreement on the terms of the other or shown the slightest desire to move on to middle ground. The Soviet Union was not even tempted by the compromises, some of them considerable, which the West put forward. Each side was, indeed, happier with the situation as it existed than with any alternatives on offer. The President's new initiative was a perfect excuse to end the whole barren, wearisome manoeuvre. The final communiqué from Geneva was a doleful thesaurus of diplomatic euphemisms for failure: "positions of the participants in the conference were set out", some of them "became closer", there was a "useful exchange of views", and a "frank and comprehensive discussion" on Berlin. If there were any positive results from nearly three months of talking, they were peripheral or virtually exiguous. Khrushchev had squeezed a trip to the United States and might convert that into a Summit. The East Germans had appreciated a few weeks of official involvement, though they had not enjoyed their lowly status and had not advanced their claims to recognition. The Western Powers had at least shown rather more cooperation and harmony than they had previously achieved. The West Germans were relieved that the 16 June western proposals had not been pursued, but dreaded that they still might be. West Berliners welcomed a new breathing space: further Soviet moves against the western sectors were unlikely while Eisenhower and Khrushchev were talking.

Indeed, according to information passed to the Americans in Bonn by a "usually reliable and well-informed source", East German documents on the handover of checkpoints by the Soviet authorities, which had been ready and waiting for early take-over of access control, had now been sent back to Pankow's Department for Legal Affairs. It was reassuring to think they were in a filing cabinet because they were not needed. It would have been very much better to know they had been consigned to the waste bin.[36]

Since, like it or not, President Eisenhower was now faced with a visit from Khrushchev, he wisely decided to pre-empt allied suspicions and went to see each of the western leaders in advance of the Soviet leader's arrival. It was a sensible move, probably benefiting from Macmillan's mishandling of the Moscow trip. By talking calmly and rationally to his allies he got calm and rational support for what he had to do. He also gave them a chance to get a lot of their current worries, unrelated to Berlin, off their chests. The success of the tour was a tribute to the President's persuasiveness and a reminder of what had made him such an effective wartime leader: he was very good at holding a coalition together.

Eisenhower left Washington for Bonn on 26 August. It was his first flight in a jet aircraft and he found it "exhilarating". It was also his first visit to

Germany for seven years and he was impressed by the new prosperity which contrasted so strongly with the misery he remembered. The two days of talks with Adenauer ranged over the problems of NATO, West German fears of American withdrawal from Europe and the Chancellor's latest obsession – the need to help de Gaulle in Algeria. The President was irritated by Adenauer's inflexibility over the German and Berlin problems and called in vain for some fresh initiatives and the development of contacts with the East Germans. That apart, business in Bonn was pleasant and it served the purpose of reassuring Adenauer that there would be no American deals with Khrushchev. The visit to London, Eisenhower's first since Suez and the disastrous rupture of the Anglo-American alliance, was again uncontentious and helped to re-establish an easier relationship with Macmillan. In Paris, Eisenhower found de Gaulle much more agreeable and serene than the prickly wartime leader he remembered, and they managed to discuss equably such thorny issues as France's wish for a tripartite directorate in NATO or refusal to take nuclear missiles without a veto on their use. Then, after a few days of well-earned bridge and golf in Scotland, the President returned to Washington on 7 September to gear up for the Soviet visit.[37]

Khrushchev landed in the United States on 15 September in the highest of spirits. As he said in his memoirs, he regarded the invitation as "a colossal moral victory" and the Federal German ambassador in Moscow noticed that from the moment it arrived he was "radiant". There had been one or two minor anxieties as he planned the trip. Should he take his wife? His instinct was not to (it was, he thought, "unbusinesslike" and "a petit bourgeois luxury") but Mikoyan was strongly in favour. So, never a man to do things by halves, he brought Mrs Khrushchev, his son, two daughters and a son-in-law. What was this "Camp David" where he was asked to stay? No one in the Soviet Foreign Ministry knew; nor did anyone in the embassy in Washington. Khrushchev had a nasty memory of a Soviet delegation, soon after the 1917 Revolution, being received at a place called Prince's Island where, he gathered, "stray dogs were sent to die". He feared Camp David might be on the same lines – but cheered up when he discovered that it was the Presidential dacha.* Thereafter his mood was gleeful. The trip was politically important: it set the seal on his role as a world leader and acknowledged the power of the USSR. For all that he had been in full control of the Soviet Union since 1957, outward and visible signs of his authority were still welcome to combat domestic and

---

* De Gaulle did not think of Camp David as a dacha. He once described it as "un groupe de hutments".

Chinese critics with evidence that "peaceful coexistence" mixed with Berlin threats paid off. He was undoubtedly excited too. The shepherd boy and Donbass mining engineer was going to be the first Soviet leader ever received by an American President; the life-long Communist and isolated inhabitant of the Kremlin with an insatiable curiosity would be in the big, bad capitalist world, seeing for himself things he had only read about.[38]

To put the icing on the cake, his visit coincided with a new Soviet space triumph, one to surpass even the achievement of Sputnik: Lunik II was about to land on the moon. To add a cherry on top, he was flying in a brand-new Soviet aircraft, the Tu-114, a huge, state-of-the-art plane to wipe out once and for all the shame of his arrival at Geneva in 1955 with nothing but two engines. In fact only a truly devoted propagandist for Soviet technology would have been as thrilled as Khrushchev was by this journey. The Tu-114 was so new that this was its test flight. Lying around it were engineers, listening to the engines through headphones. Some of them were asleep. Not to worry, said its designer, if the engines start to fail they will wake up. At that, most airline passengers would demand a parachute and the nearest emergency exit. Not so Khrushchev. He had every confidence in Soviet engineering and complete trust in Tupolev – one of the very few people he ever addressed in the familiar second person singular. (He never got round to calling his son-in-law, Alexei Adzhubei, by his first name; they stayed on "Comrade" terms.) It was a consummate joy that when they landed at Andrews Air Base in Maryland there was no set of steps tall enough to reach the high door of this aeronautical miracle: the Soviet party stepped on to American soil by means of a superior, long Soviet ladder.

Preliminary talks between Khrushchev and Eisenhower took place that afternoon in the Oval Office of the White House. Both men stuck to generalities about the need for peace and the desirability of a Berlin settlement. Presents were exchanged. Khrushchev had brought a model of Lunik II and replicas of the pennants it would leave on the moon as well as a shot gun, a malachite box, gramophone records, vodka and wine. (Several weeks later the secret service was said to be "currently check-ing" the twelve boxes of caviar and the elk head he also presented.*) Then

---

* Later in the trip Khrushchev promised to send Eisenhower some films. By January the following year they had still not arrived but had been named as *The Fate of a Man*, *Penguins* and *The Adventures of Two Bear Cubs*. The Soviet ambassador, Menshikov, had strongly recommended Eisenstein's *Ivan the Terrible* as well. One can only assume he did so out of spite: it is hard to imagine a movie less likely to appeal to Eisenhower, even though Part II does finish with song and dance in colour.

off they all went for a helicopter ride round Washington. This was a dismal failure. The President drew attention to the rush-hour traffic below, no doubt hoping to impress his visitors with the triumphs of the national car industry and the wealth of the American consumer. Khrushchev's hackles rose. He told a reporter when they landed "We are never going to have automobiles like you have in this country, jamming up the highways. Absolutely uneconomic." He probably meant it: Soviet visitors to the West were frequently horrified rather than awed by luxury, and even if they were not, they would bite their tongues rather than admit to being impressed. This little incident was a warning of the unforeseen and adverse reactions Khrushchev would have more than once during his stay. Next day, he spoke at the National Press Club and had tea with the Senate Foreign Relations Committee – an occasion marked by the late arrival of a young senator who made a delightful and breezy apology. It was John F. Kennedy. Khrushchev did not forget him.[39]

With the formalities of a state visit completed, Khrushchev set off on a tourist's dream trip combined with an electioneering politician's whistle-stop tour. For the most part, he had a whale of a good time, asking endless inquisitive questions, winning over crowds with grins and jokes. But Henry Cabot Lodge, who had been made guide and companion, had his considerable stamina, patience and good manners tested to the limit. After New York (with visits to the Empire State Building, the United Nations and the worst Harlem slum the Soviet embassy could find), the party travelled to the West Coast. A Hollywood lunch with the stars (which Ronald Reagan boycotted) gave Khrushchev the chance to grip Marilyn Monroe's hand long and hard. (She decided later: "I guess it was better than having to kiss him.") But the next intended honour backfired. He was taken to the lot where *Can Can* was being filmed and a row of gorgeous girls danced for him. Others would have been enchanted. But not Khrushchev, the product of a puritanical culture. "This is what you call freedom," he shouted in disgust, "freedom for the girls to show their backsides. To us it's pornography."[40]

And then everything went further down hill. Local police, disturbed by a minor incident of tomato throwing at the Soviet party, decided that they could not guarantee security at Disneyland. Khrushchev had set his heart on Disneyland and was deeply upset to be robbed of his treat; he brooded on suspicions of a plot to ruin his visit. The Mayor of Los Angeles made a tactless speech at a civic dinner, attacking Khrushchev's famous phrase "we will bury you" in combative, capitalist terms and he got as good as he gave with the Soviet leader shouting back that this was no way to treat the guest of the President and "Do you want war?" According to a later Soviet

version of this disastrous dinner he had also been angered by the presence
of the deputy mayor, a Jew brought up in Rostov – which suggested that his
family were tsarist toadies since Jews were not usually permitted to live in
the city – and who was proud to have fought with the White Russians
against the Communist Red Army. Whether or not Khrushchev had found
two reasons to take umbrage, he certainly took it. That night he had his
revenge.

Gromyko was ordered to call on Cabot Lodge and announce that the
Soviet leader would cancel the rest of the trip and leave the United States.
"Tomorrow?" asked Gromyko – it was 2 a.m. "Now," said Khrushchev. It
was all a ploy; he had long since calmed down after his therapeutic
shouting match at the dinner and according to his son-in-law played out
the whole scene for the presumed CIA microphones in the hotel room.
Poor Cabot Lodge was got out of bed. He used every ounce of diplomatic
skill to soothe and sympathise, admitted that mistakes had been made,
offered innumerable blandishments and promises to persuade Khrushchev
to stay. Of course, it worked. The party set off the following morning on the
next stage of its itinerary, and Khrushchev savoured the success of getting
his own way when, thanks to firm instructions from Cabot Lodge, the
police and security escort in Santa Barbara allowed him to rush into
crowds to slap backs and act the cuddly Russian bear. The remainder of
the tour was pure pleasure and geniality.

On 25 September the party returned to business: talks with the
President at Camp David. These followed the classic pattern of Soviet
diplomacy: a friendly opening, a long stormy middle section and a last
minute, cliff-hanging reconciliation. The first conversations were amicable
enough, but they added up to nothing more than a review of the opposed
arguments of each side over Berlin. At lunch on the second day the
tempest blew. Khrushchev deliberately revived a row he had had with
Vice-President Nixon in Moscow in July. The two men had visited an
American exhibition where the Soviet leader was shown a model kitchen
with all mod. cons. It touched him on the raw: the machines and labour-
saving gadgets were beyond the wildest dreams of any Soviet householder
(beyond those of a British housewife, come to that). Whether or not he
knew deep down that this was a genuine display of successful capitalism,
he behaved as if the whole thing was a fake designed to disparage Soviet
achievements. As ever when Khrushchev felt a sense of inferiority he
became belligerent. He staged an angry debate with Nixon, starting with
boasts that Russian kitchens would soon have all this equipment, sneering
at a lemon squeezer ("you can squeeze a lemon faster by hand. This kind
of nonsense is an insult to our intelligence"), then goading Nixon into

GENEVA AND CAMP DAVID

admitting that some of the machines were not yet on the market ("You didn't think we'd figure that out") and finally engaging in a vicious exchange about comparative strengths in nuclear missiles ("We are strong. We can beat you"). The incident had continued to rankle with him. He referred to it several times during his American tour – no doubt because much of what he saw reminded him of Soviet backwardness. Now, at Camp David, he picked the scabs of his wounded pride. The Soviet people, he shouted, had not been fooled by the "Miracle Kitchen"; they had a high standard of living of their own; any attempt to lure them to capitalism would fail. Eisenhower tried to distract him with some social chit chat: the phone was always ringing, the President complained. The Soviet Union, Khrushchev retorted, "will soon have *better* phones".[41]

It was beginning to look as if the Camp David talks were actually making relations worse rather than solving any problems. But a trip after lunch to the Presidential farm at Gettysburg cleared the air. Khrushchev enjoyed inspecting the cattle and romping with the Eisenhower grandchildren. The talks resumed in a much more relaxed manner. That is not to say, however, that work the following day was easy or particularly fruitful. At a private meeting in the morning, with only two interpreters present, Khrushchev insisted that a communiqué must be issued. Eisenhower could hardly see the point, since nothing had been decided, and once the two men got down to the details of what would go into a joint announcement, all the arguments so far suppressed came to the surface. Khrushchev called for acknowledgement that the "occupation of Berlin" must end and that the Soviet Union must take unilateral action if no treaty were signed; Eisenhower refused to negotiate any settlement under duress or to go to a Summit without previous progress. Gradually the President nudged Khrushchev into saying that he had never intended to issue an ultimatum in November 1958 and was willing to resume negotiations as long as the West did not try to fix the present Berlin arrangements in perpetuity. In return for those concessions, Eisenhower promised to visit the Soviet Union and agreed to a Summit. That was just enough for Herter, Gromyko and their officials to start drafting a communiqué.[42]

As they struggled over the wording, the rest of the party had lunch. It ended with a reminder that the troubles of dealing with Soviet visitors were never over and that the most important diplomatic attribute is a cast iron digestion. Khrushchev produced a box of chocolates. He explained that they had been given to him by the American pianist, Van Cliburn, who had hoped he would eat them with the President. They were passed round. Khrushchev commented on their good quality. Instant rumble from the Soviet ambassador, Mikhail Menshikov, down the table: Russian chocolates are better. "Don't translate that remark," Khrushchev snapped at his interpreter. But it was too late: Llewellyn Thompson had, of course, understood it. The Soviet leader accused Menshikov of being tactless. The ambassador struggled to reconcile the need for apology with loathing for making one. He rephrased his comment: "personally" he "preferred" Soviet chocolates.[43]

When the draft communiqué was finally produced, Khrushchev was dissatisfied with it. He wanted to cross out a phrase about negotiations on Berlin having "no fixed time limit". This phrase, he said, would be claimed as "a great victory for Adenauer"; it might mean, added Gromyko, that talks could drag on for fifty years. Eisenhower was indignant: Khrushchev was going back on the agreement he had made that morning and reintroducing an element of ultimatum. Without that key passage, the President would not go to the Soviet Union or the Summit. The argument went round and round in circles. At long last an awkward compromise was reached. The phrase was dropped from the communiqué but Eisenhower would use it at a press conference and Khrushchev would confirm publicly that he had agreed to lift his ultimatum.[44]

Each man kept to his side of the bargain. It was more than a little unfortunate, however, that when the President gave an account of the talks to the press on 28 September and announced that the ultimatum had gone, he referred to the Berlin situation as "abnormal". That one word was enough to ruin the effect of the small gain he had made at Camp David. It was Khrushchev's standard description of the status quo which the West had sworn to uphold. The State Department, of course, rushed to explain that it had been a slip of the tongue. But the damage had been done. West Berliners were convinced that the Western Powers must be contemplating a deal at their expense; Adenauer, just back in Bonn after his holidays, was said to be "aggressive, ill-tempered, and lashing out left, right and centre". With a single word, Eisenhower had lost credit for the only concrete result of difficult and disappointing talks which he had never wanted to get involved in and, at the same time, sent a tremor through the alliance which he had painstakingly cemented only a month before.

It was a miserable end to what had been a long, if Napoleonic, retreat by the President. He had only invited Khrushchev to the United States in the hope of saving the Geneva Conference but those talks had broken down; he had met the Soviet leader in the hope of wringing substantial concessions to justify a Summit but had merely been given a face-saver; the Camp David talks had proved that there was little chance of bridging the gap between the Soviet and western positions on Berlin and Germany, yet the President had been driven to commit the West to a Summit. Few believed that such a meeting would produce a satisfactory settlement; many now dreaded that it would result in a diplomatic defeat for the West and the sacrifice of all principles.[45]

7

The Paris Summit

————►●◄————

Like a man who has reluctantly decided he must go to the dentist, President Eisenhower now seemed to want to go to the Summit as soon as possible and get it over and done with. On 9 October 1959 he wrote to de Gaulle and Macmillan suggesting that the meeting should be in December, after a preliminary policy discussion by the western heads of government, and that it should be held in Paris since de Gaulle was due to pay prior state visits to the United States and Britain. In private, he doubted that the Summit would achieve much in the way of major settlements or even an interim agreement on Berlin – neither the Soviet position at the Geneva Conference nor Khrushchev's views at Camp David had indicated areas of possible compromise. What mattered, in the President's opinion, was to capitalise quickly on Khrushchev's willingness to talk and on the slight Kremlin softening shown by the lifting of the Berlin deadline.[1]

Macmillan was rather amused that the President "was now in something of a hurry" to get to the Summit, though he agreed with him that unless talks began soon Khrushchev might "well turn nasty and start sending ultimatums again about Berlin". He was less pleased that the President would be satisfied with minimal results: he himself wanted a Berlin settlement at the very least, and feared that without it there would be a Soviet treaty with the GDR by the end of 1960 with consequent trouble over western access. The Prime Minister's ideal would be a wide-ranging agenda, then an endless series of top-level meetings to improve on any and every decision. He had persuaded himself that the western Powers had done well at Geneva and that it only needed one last heave to get Khrushchev's agreement to their proposals at the Summit.[2]

But the big stumbling block to planning the Summit was not Macmillan but de Gaulle. The French President had always argued that no one should talk to Khrushchev while he was behaving so badly, and now told Eisenhower, "I do not think that it is in our interest to hasten the opening of this meeting with Mr Khrushchev which will lead to the confrontation of irreconcilable policies, but at the same time be decisive." "As for Berlin," he wrote calmly, "there is no hurry." He had never believed that the Soviet Union would risk war over the city, and the conclusion the French drew from Camp David was that the Russians were, in fact, trying to avoid a crisis. Present arrangements in the city suited the West: why change them? Any negotiations about the status quo would lead to western concessions and enhance the status of the GDR: so why bother? There were hard-nosed political calculations underlying the haughty logic. France would test her first atom bomb in February 1960 and did not want any disarmament agreement before then; her President would prefer to sit at the Summit table as the representative of a nuclear power. Furthermore, in 1960 the United States would be entering its Presidential election campaign; with Eisenhower a lame duck and US foreign policy in flux, France could make waves. Even if de Gaulle could not prevent a Summit, he could gain a lot by delaying it. He slipped the proposed schedule by agreeing to host a December meeting of the four western heads of government, but having proposed May or early June 1960 for the Summit he then made sure it could not happen sooner by inviting Khrushchev to visit Paris in March.

Adenauer, no keener than de Gaulle on the Summit and for the same reasons, could not sabotage it but acted as a wet blanket on all the preliminaries. He had not been invited to take part (the four victorious Powers of 1945 guarded their right to make the major settlements). In his isolation he felt resentful and more than usually suspicious of his allies. Even France, the Federal Republic's most trusty supporter, was in the Bonn doghouse: the Chancellor was alarmed by de Gaulle's stand-offish attitude to NATO and refusal to provide bases for its nuclear weapons or join an integrated air defence system; insulted by the French navy's arrest of a German merchant ship, the *Bilbao*, on the (correct) assumption that it was carrying arms to the Algerians; needled by public statements from de Gaulle and Prime Minister Debré that the Oder-Neisse Line should be the eastern frontier of a united Germany (for all he, himself, was privately reconciled to accepting it). His relations with the United States were no better. Adenauer was just as aggrieved by the Camp David talks as he had been by Macmillan's trip to Moscow and a recent spate of complaints from Eisenhower about Bonn's refusal to discuss any new ideas about Berlin and all-German contacts had persuaded him that the Americans were likely to make damaging concessions at the Summit over his head. Britain, of course, and Macmillan in particular, were always deemed untrustworthy. A visit to London from 17 to 19 November did nothing to chip that hardened belief. He did not sense that Macmillan or Selwyn Lloyd had really rejected "disengagement" in Central Europe even though the term they now used was "controlled zones" and the areas they specified were the Arctic and Antarctic. Nor did he take seriously any of their reassurances about avoiding a sell-out in Berlin: Adenauer feared that the western sectors would be treated in isolation so as to dodge the German problem and that their status and security would be compromised. By the time the Chancellor got to Paris his view of Britain was said to be "bitter". And since no grievances were settled during these talks with de Gaulle, his view of France was not much sweeter.[3]

This Paris meeting of the western heads of government in December failed to build up the slightest trust or agreement within the disputatious alliance. De Gaulle kept saying that the West must not admit to any abnormality in the Berlin situation and that it was up to Khrushchev to make proposals for changes since only he wanted any; privately he thought Britain and America were "inclined to do anything to avoid the worst". Eisenhower and Macmillan were perfectly happy to start the Summit with the western package first put forward at Geneva on 28 July 1959; Adenauer thought it the "absolute limit of what was tolerable and left no margin for bargaining". There were rows over what measures should be taken to prevent Berlin being cut off from the West by Soviet or East German interference with communications: de Gaulle and Adenauer preferred to wait and see what happened before making decisions; Eisenhower wanted to settle details here and now. The President was irritated by de Gaulle's attitude to NATO and refusal to talk about test bans or disarmament at the Summit. Eisenhower's patience was finally snapped by the Chancellor's rigidity on all points and at one moment Macmillan thought he was "very firm and almost rude" to Adenauer, who lapsed into silence but not acquiescence.* To add to the general grumpiness, Adenauer was offended by being excluded from many of the meetings – tripartitism may have been

---

* Unfortunately, Adenauer broke his silence after lunch next day with a long monologue about Communism, the World and History. Macmillan admitted that he went to sleep. It is to be hoped that everyone else did too: to judge from the transcript only John Foster Dulles could have endured the sermon.

rejected in the North Atlantic alliance but it operated here in a failed attempt to mollify de Gaulle.[4]

Something was saved from the sorry mess: a time and place were fixed for the Summit. Not that it was easy. Busy men had full diaries. By the time they had added up de Gaulle's state visits, Khrushchev's trip to Paris, an African tour for Macmillan, and the need for Eisenhower to be polite to the King of Nepal in Washington, May 1960 was the first available date. Macmillan quite fancied meeting in Geneva – to "break the curse" on that place "where nothing ever seemed to go right". But de Gaulle demurred: Geneva, he thought, was not "très gai", there was all that "histoire de Monsieur Calvin"; and as for "le lac . . .". So, as he had no doubt hoped all along, Paris was finally chosen. And later in the month Khrushchev agreed to attend.

On 11 January 1960 Adenauer went to West Berlin – a rare excursion to "Asia" during which he addressed the House of Representatives for the first time since becoming Chancellor in 1948. Again and again in his three-day visit he stressed that the Soviet Union had already rejected the 28 July western package and that the status quo was the best the West could expect until reunification. West Berliners were delighted, but allied diplomats writhed at the public challenge to their shaky tactical position. In a most unusual show of solidarity with the city – which was probably as much a demonstration of ill-ease with his allies – the Chancellor endorsed Brandt's stipulations for any new Berlin agreement: upholding the legality of the allied presence, keeping the western sectors in the Federal legal, financial and economic systems, ensuring free and preferably improved access from outside and unrestricted movement across the city, and taking account of the will of the entire population. Not that Adenauer was all sweetness and light during his stay: malice and sarcasm were his more natural modes. The kindest thing he could find to say to Willy Brandt was that he thought of Franz Neumann as his worst SPD enemy; the highest praise for the western sectors was that they made "sound use" of the "very large Federal subsidy".[5]*

Predictably, the presence of the Federal Chancellor in Berlin infuriated the East German regime: Grotewohl insisted that Adenauer had no right to

---

* One evening at dinner the Federal Plenipotentiary in West Berlin boasted that he had some superb Mosel in his cellar – a grave error in the presence of the Chancellor who would brook no rivals in connoisseurship of wine. At the end of the meal the man was encouraged to go off and play cards with his friends. While he was away Adenauer sent a car to his house to fetch a few bottles. When the wine proved as good as its owner claimed, he was summoned back to help drink it. Did he choke?

be in the GDR's "capital". The arrival soon afterwards of the Federal President Lübke for a ten-day official visit kept the anger on the boil. Then, to the rage of the eastern authorities, on 27 January the Bundestag in Bonn gave the first reading to a bill to establish a federal radio authority with headquarters in the western sectors: threatening yet another institutional stake to affirm claims in the city. The Western Powers were not pleased either: the bill had been introduced without consulting them and risked confrontations in the city during the build-up to the Summit (the French and British were even ready to use their reserve powers of veto should it go through). It was just as well that the bill eventually foundered (not because the Bundestag was willing to kowtow to East or West but because they wanted to block Federal control of broadcasting). During the radio row, however, the German Synod of the Evangelical Church was held in East Berlin and Willy Brandt and Ernst Lemmer, the Federal Minister for all-German Affairs, drove to the opening service on 21 February through the Brandenburg Gate with Federal and West Berlin Senate flags on their cars. This was an unprecedented assertion of rights and it was galling to the East Germans. They soothed their feelings a little by accompanying the Synod with preliminary legal proceedings against Otto Dibelius, the Bishop of Berlin-Brandenburg, a hated figure whose diocese straddled West and East and whose message to his flock was encapsulated in his pamphlet *Obrigkeit*: "render unto Caesar . . .". Even so, on 6 March Dibelius preached his regular monthly sermon in the Marienkirche in East Berlin, this time on the theme that Christians must not compromise with active atheism. For the moment, Pankow did not dare to touch him.[6]

Given all these vexations it is perhaps surprising that the East German and Soviet authorities behaved with comparative restraint in Berlin in the early months of 1960. On the other hand, their patience may have sprung from a wish to keep measures in reserve to influence the outcome of the Summit. This was a period of unremarkable "Berlin Weather". In early January a Soviet officer and soldier boarded a US train bound for Berlin (which they had no right to do) claiming they were looking for deserters, but they did as they were told when ordered off. Later in the month a Russian at Marienborn detached a refrigeration car on a French train on the grounds that it had "swastikas" drawn on its side. That having proved successful, another train was stopped in March, this time an American, with the claim that there was an "anti-Semitic drawing" in the dirt on the side of a carriage. When the officer in charge coolly told the Russians they were at liberty to rub it out, they rapidly found a "swastika" as well and sent the whole train back to Helmstedt for thorough cleaning. A French army bus was held up in April when the Soviet officer at the Marienborn checkpoint tried to clamber in to count the occupants. When he was shoved off, he ordered everyone out; when they refused to dismount, he in turn refused to get a chair to do his check through the window and the bus was backed to the West. To be scrupulously fair to this zealous officer and to make it clear that he was in no way vertically challenged, it must be explained that French military buses were very high and that American and British troops travelled in trucks low enough for all the passengers to be checked by peering over the tailboard. Future Franco-Soviet strife was avoided by stopping French buses at the Soviet guard hut so that the officer could stand at the top of the steps and see inside.[7]

Marginally more serious than these trivial "usual incidents" was a campaign in April and May by the East German Transport Police (the Trapos) to inspect documents and question passengers on the S-bahn in the western sectors. When West Berlin police tried to move the Trapos back to the East where they belonged, they got a very stroppy response. At the end of April the East German police tried to dispute the right of western police to patrol S-bahn stations in their own sectors and after incidents of pushing and shoving several of them were arrested. The three Powers stuck to the principle that the East German Transport Police were Soviet agents whose only job was to protect S-bahn rolling stock and rails; they had no authority inside trains or stations in the western sectors. When the East Germans sent a protest note in May about "interference" with their police and claimed full responsibility for all aspects of the S-bahn, the western Kommandatura took no notice since it had been delivered through their embassies in Warsaw. For whatever reason, there was no more trouble with the Trapos.

At the time, the explanation for the raids on the S-bahn was that the East Germans were looking for evidence to present at the Summit that Berlin was a source of dispute and unrest; if they could not find any, they would create some. With hindsight, however, it seems just as likely that they were hoping to intimidate refugees. For the most startling feature of Berlin life in the first half of 1960, and the development of greatest significance for its future, was the marked increase of people leaving the GDR – and doing it via the western sectors. In 1958 a total of 204,061 East Germans had moved to the West. That was a decline from the previous year's figure: 261,622. In 1959 the number dropped again – to 143,917, the lowest since 1949 when proper records were first kept. Seventy-six per cent had crossed first to West Berlin. It was noticeable that the "quality" of refugees had declined too. It was reckoned that during 1958, 4,394 of all emigrants from East Germany came from the most highly educated and expensively trained sectors of the population: management, the professions, the bureaucracy and education. In 1959, this group had contracted to 3,418. It was still a disturbing loss for the GDR, given state investment in training these people and their value to the community and economy. And it came in addition to the fact that the East German population was declining anyway – more as a result of the drop in the birth-rate during the war and soon after than because of emigration. (In 1948 the GDR had 18,388,172 citizens; ten years later it had only 17,311,707.) There was an increasing shortage of workers which was bound to check the ambitious targets of the 1959 Seven-Year Plan for economic growth which envisaged an 88 per cent increase in industrial production. And politically, the flight of refugees was a disaster: a proclamation to the outside world of the regime's failure to earn loyalty, and a potential brake on the speed with which radical measures could be introduced to "socialise" the system more fully.[8]

From the western viewpoint, on the other hand, what had been most noticeable in the refugee figures up to the end of 1959 was the consistent decline. From this, the conclusion was drawn that the GDR regime was improving its grip: its frontiers were now tightly secured with only the single gap in Berlin; the countervailing influence of the churches had been reduced by persecution and prohibitions on religious education; and its most vociferous opponents been driven out or into prison, leaving a docile if sullen populace. Analysts in the West had been surprised and impressed that there had been no unrest during the year in spite of a poor harvest and a prolonged drought in the autumn which had cut back dairy production and led to a shortage of milk and butter in the shops and only erratic supplies of meat. There seemed every chance that the East Germans would continue to stay quiet and stay put. Life in the GDR was drab but there had been a recent perceptible increase in available consumer goods and the Seven-Year Plan promised a rise in real wages of between 60 and 65 per cent – even if that were not achieved, a definite improvement was on the cards. A Soviet–GDR trade agreement signed in November 1959 would mean that for the first time East German imports from the Soviet Union would exceed exports at least up to 1962, and that would boost the standard of living still further.

As it turned out, the western observers had leaped to these conclusions too soon. Already in 1959 there was a rumbling of discontent in the GDR which had not yet registered on the seismograph of emigration, merely bleeped in sporadic rumour and minor news stories. In May there was a report of several hundred farmers rioting for two days in a village twenty-five miles south-west of Berlin: smashing the town hall windows and demolishing the statues of Engels and Thälmann. The violence seemed to be a reaction to a sudden and unreasonable official demand for increased fruit and vegetable deliveries. Then there were accounts of arson on collective farms: when two men in Karl-Marxstadt were given prison sentences in December for setting fire to barns out of "hatred of Communism", it emerged that there had been about 900 such incidents in the third quarter of the year. By March 1960 even the East German press was admitting to 1,273 fires in the Erfurt area alone over the previous twelve months. This was an uncoordinated peasants' revolt against agricultural collectivisation.[9]

By June 1959 something like 40 per cent of all farm land in the GDR had already been collectivised – partly as a result of confiscations of estates at the end of the war, partly by brute force in 1953. At the beginning of 1960 the regime began a campaign to complete the process and by March about 80 per cent of all arable land was under state control. It had been no easy matter. The government had tried to avoid outright violence, but it was dealing with a particularly stubborn and independent group of people. Bands of agitators had been sent to bellow at the recalcitrant by day and night through loudspeakers; some farmers were dragged to as many as sixty "discussion groups" in the space of three weeks or to the local police station where they were told they would be charged with black-marketeering unless they cooperated; wives and children were coaxed or frightened into putting pressure on farm owners; one man was offered a television set and a holiday on the Black Sea if he joined a cooperative, another was promised instant payment for his standing crop. In the early months of the campaign the West was surprised that farmers were not leaving the GDR. Only later did it emerge that many of them had followed their most basic instincts and got on with spring sowing regardless of who would reap; many more were planning to leave but wanted to sell their stock and belongings first or draw out savings from the bank in small sums so as to avoid detection. The full extent of farmers' discontent finally came to light when in March 1960 they began to vote with their feet against the government's agricultural policies. That month 13,442 refugees crossed to the West, and 12.8 per cent of them were workers in farming or forestry plus their families. (In 1959 they had been about 5 per cent of the total.) In April there were 17,183 emigrants and agricultural and forestry workers now made up 14.5 per cent. There was a positive flood of people at Easter, and in West Berlin twice as many registered as over Easter the previous year. Trains from East Berlin were said to have been so crowded that the GDR police could not squeeze inside to check travel documents and a new camp had to be opened in West Germany to cope with the overflow from the two existing reception centres. And in May, the figures went up yet again: to 20,285, with an even higher proportion of farmers. It was assumed that this group would grow still further once the harvest was in.[10]

Collectivisation alone could not account for the abrupt increase in the number of refugees, even though it was a major factor. Small business owners, retailers and independent craftsmen were pouring out too – four times as many of the self-employed crossed in May 1960 as in the same month the previous year. By mid-1959 private enterprise in the GDR produced only about 5 per cent of the gross product, but it was a political thorn in the flesh. To drive private firms out of business or into co-operatives, the state kept them short of raw materials, denied them markets, offered loans in return for a controlling interest in a business then sacked the owner-manager, or sent round tax inspectors to discover "irregularities" then demand back payment to ruin the finances. By the end of 1960, 144,000 artisans had been herded into cooperatives (only 8,000 belonged in 1957) and industrial output from the private sector had dropped to 3.8 per cent. But the regime was already paying a high price for nationalisation. The exodus of the self-employed was disrupting repairs, transport, and the skilled manufacture of specialised items, and would further threaten the targets of the Seven-Year Plan.[11]

The Ulbricht government might feel the worst was over and nationalisation was virtually complete. It could congratulate itself on having checked the outflow of professionals and academics over the past three years or so. Had it, however, learned from this that better salaries and less political pressure were the ways to keep all its citizens passive? Would it use the opportunities of the new trade agreements and Soviet support for the GDR economy to spread benefits to its workers? What conclusions would it draw from the knowledge that by May 1960 it was the young rather than the old who were again emigrating and that over three-quarters of all refugees were now leaving via West Berlin? Could it afford to leave that escape hatch open?

In the two months before the Paris Summit the four western leaders flew hither and yon. They had individual conferences with each other, but little meeting of minds. Macmillan visited de Gaulle on 12 and 13 March and found him still obdurately backing Adenauer's hardest uncompromising line. The French President conceded that some modus vivendi for Berlin might emerge during talks with the Russians but seemed untroubled by the probability that it would not. By then, Adenauer was on his way to Washington to present his own adamantine case. Eisenhower was alternately bewildered and irritated by the Chancellor's calm acceptance that the consequence of refusing to make concessions would be war over Berlin or the slow stifling of the western sectors' economy. He thoroughly resented Adenauer's tendency to dictate what should be on the agenda at the

Summit and was reported to have "stated strongly" to his advisers that *he* would decide what the United States would or would not discuss at these meetings. When Macmillan then arrived at Camp David at the end of the month Eisenhower had to cope with the reverse of Adenauer's intransigence and counter British appeals for compromise with arguments that if the Federal Germans felt let down by the Summit they might turn neutral and that weakness over Germany could shake the western position throughout Europe.[12]

Meanwhile Khrushchev had spent three days being feted in Paris and had toured the provinces to press flesh, beam smiles, crack jokes, and generally create the impression that the Soviet Union was a friendly bear. He was not very successful. No one warmed to his family either: unlike the Americans, the French found Mrs Khrushchev forbidding rather than a huggable granny from central casting. And the head of the East European section of the Quai d'Orsay said that he had seen nothing to compare with the Soviet entourage's rabid nationalism and blatant concern for power since the arrival of the Nazis in 1940. Khrushchev's talks with the President were examples of an irresistible force meeting an immovable object. He himself painted a frightening picture of a new outbreak of German violence unless the FRG was disarmed and the nation kept divided, and vehemently insisted that unless the German question was settled soon he would sign a separate treaty with the GDR and hand over all powers to Ulbricht; de Gaulle frigidly pointed out that such a course of action would not solve the German problem or take the sting out of it by creating détente. When the news of the successful French nuclear test was announced, the Soviet leader made no attempt to congratulate his host: he merely commented "it's very expensive". He returned to Moscow in a noticeably less triumphant mood than from his trip to the United States, grumbling that de Gaulle was cold, reserved and formal. But their differences went much deeper than temperament.

Much more fun was had from de Gaulle's stay in Britain in April – except by the unfortunate people who had to make the arrangements. The complexity and grandeur of state visits make choosing diplomatic presents look like child's play: more government departments insist on being involved, there are even more arguments, misunderstandings and muddles, and the costs are tossed from budget to budget like a frenzied game of pass the parcel. Where were all the French visitors going to stay? Breathtakingly it was claimed that Buckingham Palace only had room for seven members of the party in addition to the President and Mme de Gaulle, and that left everyone dodging the bill for hotel accommodation for the overspill. Should stands be erected at Whitehall for de Gaulle's review of the Household Troops? Most certainly, said the Foreign Office (they could be left there for Trooping of the Colour and charged to the War Office). Where should the grand state lunch be held? The Painted Hall at the Royal Naval College, Greenwich? Well, the journey there was "uninspiring" (undoubtedly the miles of rotting warehouses and decaying docks were not a good advertisement for the British economy). So what about Chelsea Hospital? Big snag: the Great Hall was festooned with the captured French standards of centuries, all labelled in very large gold letters. Back to Greenwich then? No: the ceiling was adorned with scenes of the destruction of the French fleet at Trafalgar. Never mind: there were plenty of monuments in Paris to Bonaparte's victories and Napoleon III had not objected to a dinner in the Waterloo Chamber at Windsor. Perhaps Chelsea would be better though? Yes, but remember that the poor old Pensioners would be deprived of their dining-room, and last time it was used for a state bunfight they had been kept out for four whole days.

Now: music. Well, said the armed services, it would be "difficult" to bring bands to Chelsea (though no one explained why). Pah, said the Brigadier who ran Government Hospitality: "We have got to have a band – there is no argument about it" (no one could mount a guard of honour for the President without national anthems) and "furthermore, we must have an orchestra to play during lunch . . . Can you imagine anything more damned dull without one?" At least the War Office took responsibility for feeding the President's escort (one officer and six other ranks): lunch at three shillings a man was authorised though eyebrows were raised at French insistence on a standard issue of half a litre of wine per meal ("Hic" someone scribbled on a memo and he had not lapsed into Latin). Next: will the President freeze to death in Westminster Hall while making an address? How about sending a diplomatic mission, someone suggested, to warn him to bring woolly underwear? Can the place and the audience be heated up with braziers? Maybe, but can the Ministry of Works be persuaded to pay for them? Yes; but the fools have just printed the programmes for Chelsea with the wrong rank for the bandmaster. De Gaulle is adding to the complications. He does not want to go to Chequers (that would reduce him to a head of government rather than a Head of State) and he refuses to accept an honorary degree from Oxford (because that would set a precedent for all the universities on his forthcoming American tour). He insists on coming by air at whatever the risks to the timing of his reception. Clearly, wrote a weary official, "among the special powers he has now assumed, he includes control of the weather".[13]

All the weeks of work, and even the expense, had probably been worth it. The President seemed to relish every detail of his visit. His memoirs glow with descriptions of the "great splendour" of his reception, which he attributed to British respect for the Free French. He was charmed by the Queen's banquet at Buckingham Palace and the firework display afterwards (the killjoy official estimates had warned that one half hour would cost £5,000). He was delighted by the garlands of carnations which Her Majesty had ordered to decorate the Royal Opera House and as chuffed as only a very grand soldier can be by the honour of reviewing her Household Troops. With scrupulous tact, he avoided any reference to the EEC in his speech at Westminster Hall, which warmed government hearts as effectively as the braziers had warmed the building. With matching consideration, no one drew his attention to the bill for £80 for ambulances and blood kept on standby throughout his visit, though no doubt a few civil service teeth were gnashed. Only after his departure did a row erupt over the trampling of grass and daffodils in Carlton Gardens where he had paid tribute to the statue of Marshal Foch (the Foreign Office successfully argued that most of the damage had been done by journalists during a rehearsal so it was not their fault or charge). Well satisfied, the President returned to Paris for a few days before setting off for Canada and the United States. There he poured cold water on Eisenhower's hopes for some minor agreements at the Summit, argued that since the German problem was not ripe for solution it was better left undiscussed and warned that the United States must not try to act as universal judge and policeman. He was tiresome, maybe, but enviably tireless.

While the western statesmen criss-crossed the world but got nowhere politically, their ministers and officials laboured to construct a negotiating position for the Paris Summit. It was like trying to get up a hill while tied in a small sack. A State Department official bemoaned the fact that there were no new ideas to be found because the Berlin problem had been so thoroughly examined already; given those old ideas, as the Foreign Office soon found, the range of possibilities acceptable to the West was "a relatively narrow one". There was some willingness to jiggle elements in the set pattern. For example, everyone in the alliance, the Federal Republic included, now openly admitted that there was no possibility of reunification in the foreseeable future so solutions to other problems would have to be sought separately. Adenauer would sooner or later accept the Oder-Neisse Line as Germany's future eastern frontier and Eisenhower was ready to push him to other concessions such as establishing contacts with the East Germans.[14]

A four-Power Working Group in Washington from January 1960 to April scrutinised all the stale options. Their discussions only revealed that the British and Americans wanted to get something out of the Summit but did not know quite what or how; the French and West Germans thought the talks a waste of time at best and probably a temptation to capitulation. At one point the Americans tried to frighten the Federal German team into a more flexible stance by showing them some old contingency plans for maintaining access to the western sectors which proved how easily war could break out. Bonn, of course, had always been in favour of going to the brink to give the Soviet Union a fright, so the ploy failed. The Group's final report came to the stark conclusion that since German reunification was out of the question and a Berlin solution was only feasible within the context of a general settlement, the West must either put up with the existing situation in spite of all its dangers or push for the 28 July Geneva proposals. With great reluctance and no belief that any good would come of it, the governments opted for that package as a negotiating tactic. But, and it was a big but, no one thought that any interim agreement would be satisfactory unless western rights were retained at the end of it; few imagined that the Soviet Union would give such a guarantee and stick to it. And would a temporary modus vivendi for the western allies in the city do anything to secure West Berlin freedoms, communications and trade?[15]

With little hope for a breakthrough over Berlin at the Summit, Eisenhower still thought there might be a modicum of progress over disarmament. Adenauer clung to his belief that "little" was as good as "none" and that only a general and comprehensive agreement would create the climate of détente within which other settlements could be reached. Couve de Murville was coming round to the opinion that an interim Berlin arrangement might be desirable ("When we said the same thing months ago", exclaimed Selwyn Lloyd, "we were accused of basic unreliability and of selling the pass"). But Couve was merely Foreign Minister; his President had made French policy and would stick to it: no changes, no concessions. A reunion of the western Foreign Ministers in Washington from 12 to 14 April, and further get-togethers at the Central Treaty Organisation assembly in Teheran and the North Atlantic Council in Istanbul in May threw up no fresh ideas. Only Macmillan, with his manic-depressive view of the Berlin crisis and his obsession with summitry, looked forward to Paris in the belief that "future generations could look back on the meeting as the start of a new era". Everyone else leaped at Eisenhower's suggestion that the talks should be kept as short as possible, and mainly restricted to the heads of government on the off-chance that if Khrushchev were separated from his advisers he might make a few tacit agreements. This put the Foreign Ministers' noses slightly out of joint (they tried to argue that it would save time if they attended sessions so did not have to be briefed on them) but they probably saw advantages in not having to attend public slanging matches.[16]

That was the style which could be predicted from recent statements by the eastern camp. An open letter in the GDR press on 17 April, signed by Ulbricht and addressed to "the West German working class", offered to accept an interim Berlin agreement while "the necessary degree of confidence was being created" in a "free city", on condition that during this period no atomic weapons were stationed in West Berlin, the allied garrisons were reduced, and the western sectors were no longer "misused as a base for sabotage and subversive activities of all kinds". Grotewohl expanded on these themes in the Volkskammer on 11 May and then Ulbricht threw in the demand that, as an element in a temporary agreement, British and American radio stations should be removed from the city. None of this could be dismissed as sabre rattling by Pankow to compensate for not being invited to Paris. On 25 April Khrushchev too made a noticeably tough speech in Baku restating all the hardest aspects of the Soviet line at Geneva and renewing his threat that if the Western Powers refused to sign a treaty with the GDR "they will then naturally lose the right of access to West Berlin on land, water and by air". No one read that as bombast. Sir Patrick Reilly pointed out that such a speech would make it difficult for Khrushchev to accept a negative result from the Summit; Charles Bohlen, a former US ambassador in Moscow who was visiting the city at the time, decided that Khrushchev was not bluffing: "He would suffer an unacceptable loss of prestige as a leader unless he eventually acted." Everyone was sure that the Soviet leader was under heavy criticism from the Presidium for his German policy, that his theory of peaceful co-existence had failed to convince many and that the Soviet Union was engaged in an intense ideological struggle with the Chinese over it which Khrushchev and the Kremlin could not afford to lose.[17]

To avoid swelling the animosity the Russians were patently going to bring to the Summit, and to check a minor source of squabbles with his allies, President Eisenhower decided in March to order a halt to high altitude flights by the US Air Force in the Berlin air corridors. These flights had a long, fretful history – and make a neat little case study in political in-fighting. The Soviet authorities had fixed no ceilings for aircraft when they signed the air agreement in November 1945 to establish the three corridors or when the four Power rules for air safety were codified in October 1946. There was no need: the technical limitations of aircraft at that time kept them low. During the Airlift, when every inch of air space had to be crammed, 10,000 feet was the operational ceiling. But from 1953, the

Russians began to claim that this was the legal rather than technical limit. In 1958 they put that claim in writing and said they would not "guarantee the safety" of flights above it. They were obviously seeing if they could assert as much control in the air as they already had over ground communications. In addition it was suspected that they wanted to keep western aircraft low so as to monitor them easily and to keep the space above 10,000 feet for their own fighters to dart across the corridors unobserved. The Western Powers continued to claim a right to fly at any altitude, but for the time being they did not need to exercise it.[18]

All that changed in 1959: new civil and military aircraft were introduced, and allied planners considered which to employ for an airlift and how best to use airspace. The USAF would have the C-130 turbo prop as its transport workhorse by 1961; service chiefs argued that it could only fly with maximum efficiency at over 10,000 feet. The JCS wanted to test Soviet reactions to high altitude flights – an air version of the contentious ground probe on the Autobahn. For a time, Dulles stopped them: the British and French were averse to the idea and he preferred to get their agreement to other disputed aspects of contingency planning first. The Pentagon kept up the pressure, however, and on 26 March 1959 the JCS ordered immediate flights above 10,000 feet, several times a week; if serious Soviet opposition was encountered these would be discontinued. A C-130 made the first flight next day, in spite of objections by the Soviet representative at the Berlin Air Safety Centre. It went to Tempelhof at 25,000 feet, harassed all the way from the GDR frontier by a single MIG fighter; it returned at 20,000 feet with a bigger but less belligerent escort. The Russians sent a protest note about the flight; the Americans replied with a protest about the inter-ference with it; the British, Herter and David Bruce at the US embassy in Bonn all expressed doubts about the wisdom of the exercise. On 1 April the JCS ordered such flights to cease until further notice, but General Twining recorded his personal objection to "allowing certain allies to pressure us with this defeatist attitude" and Eisenhower hoped that the principle of flying high would be tested from time to time. When it was, on 15 April, an almighty row erupted, and not just from the Russians. The Foreign Office gave an off-the-record press briefing (instantly published in American newspapers) with plenty of colour about Selwyn Lloyd's disapproval and a long smear about the Pentagon triumphing over the State Department. Thereafter, the State Department insisted on blocking high-altitude flights until the Geneva conference was over.[19]

The Pentagon and JCS still argued for the expansion of air space in case of an airlift; they continued to assert that the C-130 must operate at above 10,000 feet; they now wanted to put their fighters at just below 30,000 feet;

they yearned to confront the Soviet Union and prove they would not be kicked about. By early 1960 they were finding allies. Air France introduced Caravelle jets on to the Berlin run in February, but decorously stuck below the 10,000-foot ceiling; the British decided to employ their Comets on the same route. Both aircraft could only operate economically at higher altitudes.* Herter seized the opportunity and opened tripartite talks on a joint policy to push up the ceiling in the corridors. He was on the very verge of an agreement with his allies when Joe Alsop leaked the story in the *Washington Post*. The Russians went wild. And at that moment of all moments, the US Joint Chiefs suddenly decided that the C-130 did not actually have to fly above 10,000 feet at all. Not that they wanted anyone else to know, let alone to abandon high-altitude flights. They now justified them as a good "cold war tactic". They could not have found a worse argument to present to Eisenhower. Such considerations, he snarled, were for the State Department, not the military. But, Herter intervened, there would be trouble with the allies if the United States said it had changed its mind about the policy. No trouble for the President: tell them "we made a mistake", he answered, "and do not wish to compound it"; if necessary he himself would take the rap for cancellation of the flights. And with that, there were no more.

How much difference would it have made if Eisenhower had been as firm with the CIA? By a weird coincidence, just at the time he banned high-altitude flying to Berlin in the run up to the Summit he was being pestered by the Agency to send a U-2 spy plane over the Soviet Union. He had always been cautious about the repercussions of military incidents on political processes: when a US Navy patrol plane was shot down in June 1955 just before the Geneva Summit, he had ordered all aircraft and vessels to steer well clear of Soviet territory until the meeting was over. He was also ambivalent about the U-2. It was an aircraft specially designed for espionage, which photographed Soviet installations from twelve miles above the earth and reassured the Administration that there was no "Missile Gap". All the same, as a straightforward, above-board man Eisenhower would have preferred his Open Skies programme; as a realist he knew that the Russians would react violently to intrusion on their airspace and secrecy. The Soviet Union had spotted U-2s as early as 1956 when no one believed their radar was up to it, but kept their protests to

---

* Someone in the British embassy in Bonn had the spiffing wheeze of sending Lord Mountbatten to Berlin in a high altitude Comet to see what the Russians would do about it. It was rather reminiscent of the old *Beyond the Fringe* sketch in which a hapless young man is told by his commanding officer "The time has come for a useless sacrifice. We have chosen you" – and not at all the conventional treatment for the Chief of Imperial General Staff.

Washington private, presumably to avoid admitting that their artillery could not hit them. The American press learned about U-2 missions in 1958 but kept quiet about them; the official story was that U-2s flew for NASA and gathered meteorological information. Eisenhower, wanting to avoid further risks and future embarrassment and knowing that the United States would soon have spy satellites to do the job, forbade the CIA to send U-2s to look for Soviet ICBM bases in October 1959 and February 1960. But they finally persuaded him to sanction a mission for 9 April. This U-2 was fired at by Soviet ground to air missiles. They missed, but came near enough to convince Eisenhower that there must be no more flights. Yet again the CIA ground him down. They begged for one, just one more mission, probably the last ever. And the President agreed. It nearly never took place: bad weather prevented take-off and Eisenhower had forbidden any attempt in the weeks before the Paris Summit. But on 1 May, his final deadline, Francis Gary Powers piloted a U-2 from Peshawar in Pakistan. This time Soviet missiles hit their target.[20]

Khrushchev was on the reviewing stand for the May Day parade in Moscow when he got the news. And it was even better than expected: the authorities had the wreckage of the U-2 and had captured the pilot alive. Powers had disobeyed orders to eject if he ran into trouble and to press the button which would blow up his aircraft seventy seconds later; he had not taken the poison with which he had been issued, and had failed to empty his pockets of his social security card, driver's licence and pass for facilities on USAF bases. He had been caught red- but not clean-handed. But these were not tidings of unadulterated joy which Khrushchev wanted to spread immediately. Would his opponents, including the Chinese, claim that the flight proved the folly of peaceful co-existence with the United States? Would his critics insist that the Summit could not take place? Should he ignore their arguments in the hope of victories in Paris which would justify his policies and strengthen his grip on power? Should he cover up the U-2 story to maintain secrecy about previous flights and the failures of Soviet defence systems? Was it better to claim a victory over capitalist aggression or to give Eisenhower time to apologise for an "accident" and let the whole business be brushed under the carpet (which is what the Kremlin had done over the 1955 US Navy patrol)? Did Eisenhower, a man he trusted, a man Stalin himself had praised, know about this intolerable violation of Soviet sovereignty just when the Summit was about to begin? If he did, what was his deep motive? Khrushchev wrestled with all these questions. Not a word about the U-2 got out until 4 May when he discussed it privately with the Central Committee.

Then, at a meeting of the Supreme Soviet on 5 May, he announced that the U-2 had been shot down. That was all. There was no mention of Powers or the wreckage, no criticism of Eisenhower. Doors had been left open for the United States. But on that same day, NASA stated that one of its "research" planes on "a meteorological mission" had "crashed in Turkey". Khrushchev had trapped the Americans in blatant lies, but he did not yet slam all the doors on them. On 6 May photographs of wreckage were published – but they were not of the U-2: Washington could still wriggle out. The chance was not taken. Another was offered. On 7 May Khrushchev told the Supreme Soviet that the U-2 pilot was alive – but he went out of his way to say: "I am quite willing to grant that the President knew nothing" about the flight. Was he trying to restore his faith in the man he so respected, or hoping against hope that everyone could get out of their embarrassment? Either way, Washington ditched him, and dug a deep pit for itself. First the Americans denied spying, then that this U-2 flight had been authorised, then that the President knew anything about it. They did not even admit to their allies what had been going on. Eisenhower squirmed under the lies, wanted to tell the truth before it came out willy-nilly, was temperamentally prone to accepting responsibility and resented the implication that he had not been in charge on this occasion. Disastrously he did not follow his instincts; others were allowed to make the running. On 11 May Khrushchev put the U-2 wreckage on display in Moscow and announced that Powers would be put on trial. The United States could cover up no longer. The whole story came out and the President belatedly declared that all U-2 flights had been made with his knowledge and approval.

Did this mean that the Summit would be called off? That was the general expectation. Yet on 9 May Khrushchev had sent letters to Macmillan and de Gaulle complaining about "cold war statements" by the United States, adapted to the "policies and likings of Chancellor Adenauer" and only mentioning the U-2 on page three where its flight was condemned for being "provocative and aggressive", timed to coincide with the "festive celebrations" of May Day, and to "poison the atmosphere" for the Paris meeting. This read more like an attempt to split the western alliance than a cancellation of the Summit. Everyone made their final preparations for Paris uncertain about what would happen. Did even Khrushchev himself know? When he went to the airport, he hesitated for a long time under the wing of his plane, deep in thought. Suddenly: "We're flying."[21]

As soon as he arrived, on Sunday 15 May, he handed de Gaulle a six-page statement which boiled down to saying that he would take no part in the

Summit unless President Eisenhower made a public apology for the U-2 flight, announced punishment for those responsible for it, and promised to dispatch no more. De Gaulle saw this as an attempt to force the Americans into humiliation and into taking the blame for wrecking the conference; he tartly told Khrushchev that there was no better illustration than the U-2 incident of the need to discuss détente. Such superior calm worked Khrushchev into a lather: the USSR's honour was at stake, he cried, but it had the means to crush its enemies. De Gaulle was far from impressed: twice in his lifetime, he replied, he had seen the defeat of a country which had gone to war certain of winning. That afternoon he warned the other western leaders that a Summit was unlikely, and that if one began with bickering over the U-2 it should be adjourned sine die. Eisenhower was still hopeful that the talks would take place, though not about their outcome, and he promised to open them with a conciliatory statement, though not "to grovel". Macmillan's zeal for top-level talking was unquenched when Khrushchev came to see him that afternoon and read the statement previously given to de Gaulle, with an added diatribe on the "bandit philosophy of espionage", his betrayal by Eisenhower who had called him "friend" at Camp David, and the formidable number, power, range of Soviet rockets, ending with an invitation to a demonstration of how they could bring down an aircraft flying at 20,000 metres.[22]

Meanwhile, Eisenhower was chewing over the situation with his advisers, and not enjoying the tastes. He could not understand why Khrushchev had waited so long before blowing his top; he was puzzled that the CIA had never predicted the "emotional, even pathological" attitude of the Russians to their frontiers; he was offended that the Soviet leader had seen de Gaulle and Macmillan but not himself; he was ready to issue a joint East–West statement deploring espionage; he thought the Soviet Union had a perfect right to protect itself against spying and he would cheerfully renounce the use of the U-2, especially as it had reached the end of its working days. But he was damned if he would go as far as Khrushchev wanted and make cringing public apologies and promises. Would it not be better, he asked, to call the conference off here and now? Bohlen reckoned that the Soviet Union would abort the conference anyway (the fact that Khrushchev had read his statement suggested that it had been written in Moscow and that the strategy of breakdown was already planned); others advised leaving it to the Russians to call off the talks. When the three western heads of government and their Foreign Ministers met again at the Elysée in the evening they went round the same houses again, but with Eisenhower adding retrospective to current depression and wondering why the Western Powers ever moved into

Berlin in 1945. Macmillan recommended struggling on for any settlement at all that would last for two years and suggested that a "free city" with a UN guarantee "might not be such a terrible thing". The Prime Minister "went to bed with rather a heavy heart". Unique among his colleagues, however, he was "not without hope".[23]

Just how false that hope was became clear the following day. Over breakfast Macmillan and Eisenhower drafted a statement for the President to make at the opening session which promised that U-2 flights would be stopped immediately and permanently. Much good it did them. When the first formal meeting of the Summit began in the Elysée at 11 a.m., Khrushchev insisted on speaking first, in spite of protests from de Gaulle and Eisenhower. He gave a blistering version of his demands for apology and punishment for espionage, denounced the "war profiteers" and the "small frantic group in the Pentagon" who wanted to wreck the peace, withdrew his invitation for Eisenhower to visit the Soviet Union, and called for the Summit to be postponed since the United States did not "want a settlement". He stormed on for forty-five minutes and at one point, when his thunder was particularly resonant, de Gaulle intervened to say "The acoustics in this room are excellent. We can all hear." Bohlen noticed that Eisenhower's "bald head turned various shades of pink, a sure sign that he was using every bit of will to hold his temper". Eisenhower himself pushed a note to Herter: "I'm going to take up smoking again." (He had stopped in 1948). At long last the President got his chance to speak. With calm and dignity he delivered the statement prepared at breakfast: regretted the "distasteful necessity of espionage activities", announced that U-2 flights had ended and would not resume, and called for an "Open Skies" programme to detect preparations for war. Macmillan, who in de Gaulle's view "exuded anxiety and distress", made flabby appeals for quiet reflection and readiness to let bygones be bygones. De Gaulle was more dispassionate: the U-2 business should have been sorted out before now, he chided. And he was pointed: a Soviet satellite, he reminded the Soviet leader, flew over France eighteen times a day. Khrushchev was soon back on his feet: there must be a public declaration that U-2 flights had ended; Eisenhower had not apologised for them; the President's term of office was nearly over and what was said now did not bind his successor; the Soviet Union would take no part in a Summit until the United States had removed the threat and insult to the USSR. The meeting broke up at 2 p.m. It was not clear whether Khrushchev had accepted de Gaulle's suggestion that it should be reconvened next day.[24]

The Foreign Ministers, with various advisers, went into a huddle at the Quai d'Orsay that afternoon. Herter made it clear that Eisenhower would never accept Khrushchev's terms for a Summit; he personally was sure the Russians meant to wreck it anyway. That was a prospect viewed placidly by Couve de Murville: without a Summit, the perfectly satisfactory status quo in Berlin would continue. He was much more interested in professional details: since the Soviet interpreter had not had a prepared version of Khrushchev's later remarks, did this mean they had been drafted just before the meeting? Had a late message from Moscow put the extra vitriol into the ending? Selwyn Lloyd typically tried to find a bright side to look on: perhaps Khrushchev would come back to the meeting now he had got things off his chest? Would it help if Macmillan and de Gaulle went to see him? Llewellyn Thompson warned that he had never seen Khrushchev in a worse mood and that it would be better not to go near him this evening.[25]

But Macmillan embarked on a personal crusade to save the Summit. Having forewarned de Gaulle (whom he found in "one of his rather cynical moods") and Eisenhower (who seemed "much shaken" but had expressed "in quite idiomatic language what he had thought of Mr Khrushchev and the Russians in general"), the Prime Minister called on Khrushchev at 9.30 p.m. De Gaulle and Eisenhower had not given him much encouragement to do so and his Foreign Secretary had advised against it: Selwyn thought it was better to play for time and that Macmillan was too tired to do a proper job (in any case he was peeved at not being taken along). The meeting at the Soviet embassy lasted an hour and three-quarters. Macmillan pleaded for at least another day of Summit before a "dignified transition" to a new gathering in eight months' time. He made no impact. Khrushchev now sounded perplexed and upset rather than furious. Why did the United States send those planes? he asked. Why would Eisenhower not apologise? Had he signed the orders for the U-2 flight without reading them? Had everything been done by Allen Dulles, because the President reigned rather than governed? Patrick Reilly, who was present, was convinced that Khrushchev spoke more in sorrow than anger or cunning. He thought it just possible that Khrushchev would stay at the Summit, given a sufficiently grovelling gesture from Eisenhower, though he knew that Communist journalists had been briefed by embassy officials that the Soviet party would leave Paris on the 18th.[26]

Any remote possibility that the President would eat humble pie disappeared next morning, 17 May. Khrushchev brought the whole dispute into the open by holding an impromptu press conference at 9.10 a.m. on the pavement outside the Soviet embassy. The Reuter correspondent noted that he was in jovial spirits – but there was nothing genial in what he had to say. The Soviet delegation, he announced, would stay at the Summit only if the Americans admitted that U-2 flights had been deliberate aggression, apologised for the "banditry" and punished those responsible; otherwise "we will leave for home", probably next day. Eisenhower had always sworn to leave Paris if Soviet demands were published and everyone found this public airing of their disagreements singularly bad mannered. At a meeting at 10 a.m. de Gaulle, at the request of Macmillan and Eisenhower, agreed to invite Khrushchev to a Summit session at 3 o'clock that afternoon: to end the conference in proper form if nothing better was likely. Then, since there was no business to be done and no point in sitting around moping, Eisenhower drove Macmillan to Marnes-la-Coquette, where he had lived as Supreme Allied Commander Europe, and they had a chat with his old friend the Mayor.[27]

But where was Khrushchev? Nothing had been heard from him since his press conference, not even an acknowledgement of de Gaulle's invitation. In fact the Soviet leader too had gone to revive old memories. Marshal Rodion Malinovsky, the Soviet Defence Minister, had taken him to the village where the old soldier had been billeted as a machinegunner in the First World War. They thoroughly enjoyed themselves. On the way, Khrushchev hacked at a fallen tree which was blocking the road – no harm, he decided, in showing people that a head of government, whatever his age, could still do strenuous work. In the village they found the house where Malinovsky had lived and the owner was still in residence – once a beautiful woman, Khrushchev recorded with fine Russian melancholy, but now "wrinkled and pinched" as if she "had suffered". They went to an inn and had cheese and wine for lunch, while Malinovsky reminisced about the pretty waitress who used to work there and locals came in to swop stories of his unit and the bear it had kept.[28]

When the western leaders arrived at the Elysée for their 3 o'clock meeting, they found no Russians. Khrushchev claimed in his memoirs that when he got back to Paris from his partie de campagne, Gromyko told him the Summit had been cancelled; an official Soviet statement issued that evening said that Khrushchev had been informed of the invitation to a meeting while in the country, had read it on return, had telephoned de Gaulle to clarify whether he was asked to attend a preliminary discussion or a "unilaterally" convened Summit, but "got no answer". As the heads of government sat, wondering and waiting, Couve came in with a telephone message from the Soviet embassy: Khrushchev would not come to the meeting if it were devoted to general matters; if the U-2 was the topic, he would come at 5 o'clock because he was tired and had "missed lunch". Up with that Eisenhower would not put. He wanted to publish a three-Power statement on what had occurred. Macmillan could not face irreparable breakdown. He called for patience and asked de Gaulle to appeal to

Khrushchev's "sense of duty to the world". That was not at all the French President's style. He replied tartly that the Western Powers had been patient throughout and there was now "no point in beginning an exercise of seduction". Another Soviet telephone message: Khrushchev asked if this meeting was to settle conditions required for a Summit. Eisenhower declared himself "fed up"; he would not discuss terms with Khrushchev.[29]

De Gaulle thought it was time to draft a communiqué announcing the collapse of the talks; Macmillan tried to postpone the inevitable by asking Khrushchev to put his latest request in writing for the record. A third Soviet phone message: Khrushchev would not write, and he wanted a reply to his earlier enquiries. De Gaulle was unwilling to give him one: the Soviet leader had not yet replied to his first letter and merely left it to subordinates to pass on his views by telephone. Eisenhower was "getting sick of the whole thing". Yet another message: Khrushchev had told the press he would go to the Summit as soon as the American President met his demands. In what de Gaulle later described as a "solemn dirge", Macmillan plaintively begged for one more chance for the Summit and bemoaned "the collapse of two years of peacemaking"; by the Prime Minister's own account, he added a plangent reference to "churches and chapels praying for success". His colleagues were not moved. But he wore them down and they agreed to postpone a final communiqué until they met again the following day. That evening Eisenhower did what his wife said he always did when things looked bad: headed for the kitchen. When he heard the news of Pearl Harbour he had made vegetable soup; this time he cooked steaks for an embassy barbecue.

At 10.30 next morning, 18 May, Khrushchev appeared at the British embassy with his full retinue. Obviously aware of the gossip that Malinovsky had been sent to Paris as his minder, he made a heavy joke about the Marshal being present to make sure that Macmillan's diplomatic skill did not sap the Soviet position. There was a stiff, brief conversation. Khrushchev now felt certain that Eisenhower had been responsible for the U-2 flights; the Prime Minister assured him that the President had gone as far as any head of state could in taking responsibility but not apologising, and hoped for a Summit under better conditions in a few months' time. The Foreign Ministers and their advisers held a disconsolate meeting mid-morning, seemingly too drained and depressed to do more than fear the worst (an immediate Soviet treaty with the GDR and a gradual squeeze on Berlin) without knowing what to do about it. At an afternoon chat Eisenhower and Macmillan talked about NATO, the EEC and EFTA – anything except their immediate problems. They went off together to meet de Gaulle at 5 o'clock. While they discussed what was likely to happen in Berlin and how few ways they had to counter Soviet action, news came of a two-and-a-half-hour press conference given by Khrushchev that afternoon. It was a vintage performance: lashing out at Eisenhower and his Open Skies proposal, threatening to shoot down any future U-2s and "strike devastating blows at the places from which they take off". He called hecklers in the hall "riffraff" sent by Adenauer, people who had "escaped the beating at Stalingrad". "I like coming to grips with the enemies of the working class," he shouted; "it is gratifying to me to hear the frenzy of these lackeys of imperialism." Even when he quietened down enough to take questions, he did not tone down his views: western proposals for arms control amounted to the "collection of espionage information"; he would turn West Berlin into a "free city" and sign a treaty with the East Germans to deprive the Western Powers of their occupation rights and garrisons. "When? That is our business, when we consider the time to be right."[30]

It was just as well that everyone was about to go home – though they hung on for a day or so as if not sure what to do with the unexpectedly spare time. (Eisenhower went to see Notre Dame and Sainte Chapelle before his prearranged visit to Lisbon.) Most participants and observers at the Summit had never expected much from it, and once Khrushchev arrived in Paris few had believed it would ever start. Even so they were dismayed by its utter failure. Macmillan, by contrast, had worked for it, argued for it, invested policy and emotions in it, pleaded and crawled for it to continue against all odds. Now, as his private secretary Philip de Zulueta was to remember, he had never been "so depressed . . . this was the moment he suddenly realised that Britain counted for nothing; he couldn't move Ike to make a gesture towards Khrushchev, and de Gaulle was simply not interested." At the final dinner at the British embassy (for which the ambassador Gladwyn Jebb had promised an exceptional claret but for which he produced appropriately less glorious bottles) Macmillan jollied himself along by saying "Well, I suppose to cover up the disaster, we'll have to sack you, Selwyn." (Poor, sad Foreign Secretary whose role at the conference, according to a British official, had been to follow his Prime Minister "making the occasional bleating noise".) But Selwyn Lloyd was spared and his master dosed depression with *Pride and Prejudice*, whose title was perhaps suitable for the Summit just as the contents were an antidote to it. There was no way to fend off outside judgements, however. The headline of the *New York Times* on 22 May read "Summit Casualty – Macmillan"; the article suggested that he had "pursued the role of middleman past the point of diplomatic usefulness", his argument that Khrushchev would be reasonable in private talks had been "blasted and discredited", and "Britain was now even more isolated from Europe than ever".[31]

No one was so harsh about Eisenhower. Macmillan wrote to the Commonwealth Prime Ministers: "I do not believe that a lesser man or the Head of a smaller state could have gone as far as the President did" to meet Soviet demands in Paris. The American public was, on the whole, pleased with his firm and dignified stance, though John F. Kennedy was to argue in the Presidential election campaign that more concessions should have been made to Khrushchev and sections of the press were critical of the whole handling of the U-2 affair. Characteristically, Eisenhower took the blame on the chin and regretted in his memoirs that he had sanctioned the attempted cover-up once the spy plane was shot down. De Gaulle murmured privately to the French ambassador in Washington that the whole situation had required quicker reflexes and less submission to events than the President had shown. But he reserved his more astringent comments for Khrushchev ("so vulgar", giving press conferences "on the pavement", talking like "a cabdriver") and especially for Macmillan ("lamentable"; "il a fait du munichisme larmoyant").[32]*

De Gaulle was, of course, delighted that the collapse of the Summit had prevented changes to the Berlin status quo. So was Adenauer. The East German regime, however, was in for a nasty shock. Khrushchev flew straight to East Berlin from Paris. He arrived looking tired and grim, and was given a "beaming" reception by Ulbricht and Grotewohl who no doubt expected that he would now sign the longed-for treaty. No one had expected this visit, or at least, not so soon: preparations had not been made and most of the street decorations were for the Summit or an international cycle race. At first it was suggested that the Soviet leader would address an immediate mass meeting in the wide open spaces of the Marx-Engels-Platz. Suddenly the arrangements were changed: the meeting was postponed for twenty-four hours, would be held in a hall and before an invited audience. Something was up. But when the *Times* correspondent arrived at the rally he found a crush of happy, confident people outside and 8,000 people in the hall, laughing, cheering and clearly looking forward to good news. Only later did anyone realise the significance of Ulbricht's tight face as he came on to the platform. The first obvious clue that something unpleasant was about to happen came when Khrushchev sat down after delivering the opening paragraphs of his speech and left the rest to be read by his interpreter. This was common practice on routine occasions, but surely not

* On another occasion de Gaulle referred to Macmillan as "ce vieillard lachrymose". The Prime Minister squeezed a tear and impressed the young and naïve like Kennedy or the sentimental and class-ridden British television viewer, but it was not an effect which worked on everyone.

right this evening. Then it gradually dawned on the audience why he had not chosen to speak himself. No treaty was announced. After the ceremonial clichés condemning American aggression and the forces of reaction at the Summit came the declaration that the Soviet Union would do nothing to worsen the international climate: the Berlin situation must remain as it was at least until there was another Summit in six to eight months' time. Khrushchev stood again to promise "We shall not forget the matter" and to warn that Soviet patience was not "inexhaustible" and could not be "abused", but he added "Let us wait", the matter "will ripen". There was little applause from the shattered audience. Their disappointment was reinforced when Khrushchev announced soon after his return to Moscow that there would be no Summit (so no move in Berlin) until the American Presidential election had taken place and a new Administration had settled in. Again he called for patience.[33]

How long could the Ulbricht regime keep it? How long could the GDR survive its present situation?

While the western heads of government had been closeted with each other and with Khrushchev in Paris, their Foreign Ministers had time to look at the state of contingency planning for Berlin. Once the Summit collapsed, the review became a matter of urgency. Postponement of the treaty had spared the West an immediate confrontation in Berlin, but only briefly, and it had not ruled out the possibility of subtler, gradual moves against the western sectors. Contingency plans, it was soon realised, were not adequate to meet either short- or long-term threats.

The first concentrated effort to prepare practical measures for the defence of the western sectors had been made by General Lauris Norstad, Supreme Allied Commander at NATO, when in February 1959 he set up what he called "a small concealed US-only group" to plan military restoration of access to West Berlin should it be cut by the East Germans or Russians. In March, first the British then the French were invited to join; by 14 April there was a tripartite staff at St-Germain-en-Laye for an operation codenamed "Live Oak". From the start its work was bedevilled by the contradictory authorities and competing agencies which confused the rest of allied policy for Berlin. Norstad himself now had to juggle three roles: responsibility for contingency planning, his command of US forces in Europe and his post at NATO. The "Live Oak" group was not technically part of NATO but three of its members were, they answered to its head, and their plans might ultimately need the alliance's forces. Their activities were secret but suspected by their NATO allies who resented the lack of consultation and formation of a de Gaulle-style tripartite nexus within the Organisation but independent of it. Their planning was resented by the West Germans who were not privy to it. Norstad had wanted the group to report directly to the three western ambassadors in Washington, but the British Chiefs of Staff would not accept loss of control over military planning which might lead to European war, so each government was dealt with individually and retained national right of approval. To add to the muddle, there was a further triple blurring of communications. A committee of three ambassadors in Washington (with the Federal German occasionally in attendance) took charge of political planning and overall co-ordination. Their colleagues in Bonn had responsibility for devising checkpoint procedures and then took over the problem of air access – which was more obviously a military matter but had been sidelined by those in Washington who did not want Airlift planning to take precedence over aggressive defence of ground access rights. The allied authorities in Berlin were left to deal with the military defence of their sectors and supplies for the civilian population; they were kept out of the wider issues, for all that they knew more about the city's needs and often had a better understanding of the repercussions of decisions than did Bonn, Washington or "Live Oak".[34]

Within this triangular confusion, each component was riven by sharp disagreement over every aspect of policy. Should Soviet and East German intentions be tested on the Autobahn by an armed probe? With how large a force? At what point should it be launched and under what circumstances should it withdraw? Should access be restored by force? If so, how much? Would East Germans be accepted at checkpoints? Would they be allowed to check documents, stamp them, change their format, search vehicles? Could the western garrisons be supported by air? Could civilians be fed? Could military pilots take over if civil airlines were attacked in the air? Could they fire on Soviet aircraft? Could the western sectors' economy survive blockade? When would each stage of each plan be put into operation? When could the military respond automatically and when must they have political sanction? Given the difficulty in finding answers or tripartite agreement to any of these questions, and given a slackening of effort around the time of the Geneva talks and the lifting of the May deadline for Khrushchev's ultimatum, contingency planning had not got far. The résumé of plans which the Foreign Ministers and then the heads of government examined at the Paris Summit was not a pretty sight.

A few decisions had been made. There were new instructions for checkpoint procedures in the event of blocked western access (East Germans acting as Soviet agents could check allied movement orders and identity papers but not vehicles or trains; they would not be allowed to impose customs duties or tolls). Preparatory military measures "which would not cause public alarm but would be detectable by Soviet intelligence" (such as unit deployments or dispersal, preparations for evacuation of non-combatants) had either already been put into effect or could be implemented the moment Soviet authorities handed over control of access. Drafts had been prepared for protest Notes to Moscow and for public statements on western rights in Berlin. But referral of a Berlin crisis to the UN had been left for last-minute decision. The whole complex range of airlifts for military and civilian supply or evacuation still required political approval (and the question of what part would be played and what proportion of the expense would be taken by the FRG had not been answered).

After all this time, the arguments over a probe on the Autobahn had not been settled even at the military let alone political level. There was a plan sketched for "Operation Free Style" – a tripartite convoy, perhaps with armoured personnel carriers or armoured cars, which would withdraw if obstructed. As yet it had not been agreed at what precise stage it would be dispatched; Norstad reckoned that it would take seven days to prepare, but others thought it would serve no purpose if not sent the moment access was blocked. "Operation Trade Wind", to make the Russians face the imminence of war, envisaged a three-Power force of battalion strength ready to fight its way up the Autobahn. The British Chiefs of Staff judged it would result in "a military débâcle": the Russians could destroy the great bridge over the Elbe or any of the other forty-seven bridges along the route, and once the force was blocked "fore and aft" it would be in an "ignominious position from which it would be difficult to extricate it". Norstad had accepted their point that the force could not be confined to the Autobahn if it was fired on, but no decision had been made on when it should take to the country either side or if reinforcement would be sent; the British gave only formal consent to the scheme as a paper exercise not a course of action and refused to train for it until there was a cover plan. A third level of probe had been considered – a division-sized force – but this had foundered on British objections that if the Soviet military did not take the hint from "Trade Wind" that nuclear war was in the offing then they never would, and that preparing "unsound" plans had an adverse effect on morale and was a waste of staff resources.[35]

And, as if all that were not bad enough, there were numerous likely crises which were simply not covered at all by the contingency plans. Virtually all attention had been devoted to probable western predicaments and military action. That left untouched a multiplicity of problems which West Berliners might face and which, given the failure of the Paris Summit, they could well confront in the very near future. The omissions had frequently been pointed out. In March 1959 the US Mission in Berlin was aware of growing local fear that the western sectors would be cut off from East Berlin and the Soviet Zone so as to stem the flow of refugees. Herter, after talking to his Department's Legal Adviser during the Geneva conference, asked Washington what action would be taken if a separate treaty was signed and the GDR converted the sector boundary into a state border. He was told there were no existing plans to meet this threat and it was "merely a facet" of the general dilemma of what to do if the status quo was unilaterally changed; indeed some people in the State Department took the view that a frontier across Berlin would involve nothing more than tighter controls at crossing points, seemingly something not to make a fuss about, however many international agreements it might break. But the really yawning gap in planning was the absence of measures to counter harassment as opposed to full-scale siege of the western sectors. This omission was not caused by old generals fighting the last war (or in this case the old Blockade) or pointing their guns in the wrong direction (only considering a total cut of communications and not slow suffocation). The likelihood of harassment had been acknowledged. The sad fact was that no one could come up with any satisfactory responses to small but sustained pricks at West Berlin's lifeblood.[36]

Everyone had tried. The Americans had devised tit for tat measures: if an allied plane was buzzed in the corridors, buzz a Soviet aircraft somewhere else; if unacceptable document procedures were introduced at East German checkpoints, insist on similarly disagreeable conditions before Soviet ships could leave allied ports. Trade boycotts and full embargoes were often discussed, though in a desultory way: they seemed more likely to damage one or all of the allies rather than the Soviet Union and its satellites. The British Chiefs of Staff had considered blockades of eastern Bloc ports and even closing the exits from the Black and Baltic seas but it was soon clear that such measures could "only be enforced if the West were prepared to shoot first". It was not. And when it came down to it, all proposed counter measures ultimately relied on the Soviet Union giving way to them or facing war – which was a prospect just as terrifying to the Western Powers. There was an added political problem: how could the public be persuaded to go to war over what would be seen as a trivial matter of vexation or interference? It was precisely this point which made the western Foreign Ministers and heads of government in Paris dread harassment – and assume it was inevitable. When they gloomily reviewed the contingency plans on 18 May all they could do was call for brushing some of them up and for more intensive study of non-military options.

That was very little and it was rather too late. The predictable and oft predicted squeeze on Berlin communications was about to begin.[37]

The East German regime was always glad of excuses to assert itself and to get a firmer grip on travel in and out of the western sectors. It found plenty in June and July 1960. Advertisements appeared in West Berlin for volunteers for an auxiliary police force, matching the Workers' Militia which had existed in the GDR for many years, to guard public buildings, factories, radio stations and telephone exchanges during emergencies. The idea had been bandied about for over a year: it was an obvious way to compensate for any reduction in the allied garrisons (as well as to make up for inadequate recruitment to the regular police force which did not pay well in a city of high employment). The plan leaked to the East Germans in April when Brandt discussed it with newspaper editors. The GDR press then denounced this "terror organisation" and "armed civil war force", and claimed it was being trained with infantry weapons and in street fighting, though it had not as yet been formed, the men were going to be given pistols, and their most dangerous activity was likely to be a promised monthly Beer Evening. Once recruitment began, the East German attack shifted to stories of the units being transferred to the FRG Army and of the US Air Force flying in heavy weapons for them; there was a Soviet protest Note about it all on 30 June, which added complaints about the "misuse" of the Autobahn as well as the air corridors. Then, tension built up over the issue of whether the Federal Bundestag would hold its annual formal session in the western sectors in the autumn. The West Berlin authorities were keen to maintain the tradition: with it went their claim that the city was the future capital of a united Germany and their links with the FRG. The Bonn government and the Christian Democratic Party – no lovers of Berlin or its SPD Mayor – were ready to abandon the meeting for a year at least, arguing that this was a bad moment to stir up the East. The Western Powers tried not to get involved but were dragged in when Khrushchev told a press conference on 8 July that if there was a Bundestag session in West Berlin the eastern Bloc would sign a separate treaty with the GDR at which the Bundestag members would "be forced to ask Comrade Ulbricht for a visa in order to get out of Berlin". Allied embassies in Moscow took that threat seriously and advised against the meeting; western officials in Berlin and the allied capitals took offence and urged that it should take place to make a stand against Soviet bullying.* It may have been pure

---

* The row simmered on, mainly between Berlin and Bonn. On 20 October the FRG affirmed the right to hold a Bundestag meeting in Berlin but postponed fixing a date. In the event, the next session in the western sectors was to be in 1965.

coincidence that on 21 and 28 July West Berlin lorries bound for the Federal Republic were stopped at the Babelsberg checkpoint at the Berlin end of the Autobahn and their cargoes seized – green concrete slabs of a colour sometimes used for camouflage which were said to be war matériel.[38]

But there could be no doubt whatsoever about the deliberation with which Pankow tackled the next "provocation" in West Berlin. In the first week of September the western sectors were the site for a congress of former German prisoners-of-war and relatives of those listed as "missing" which coincided with the annual Homeland Day for German refugees and expellees from beyond the Oder-Neisse Line and the Sudetenland of Czechoslovakia. In the night of 29–30 August the East German Ministry of the Interior issued a decree: "As a defence against the threat to the order and security of the peaceful life" of its citizens arising from these "revanchist" meetings, from the next day until 4 September Federal Germans would only be admitted to the "capital of the GDR" if they had a visitor's permit. West Berlin, the decree continued, did not belong to the FRG whose organisations had no right to operate there; the western Powers were responsible for any "revanchist agitation and all consequences"; the air corridors were provided only for the western garrisons and must not be used by "militarists" from West Germany.[39]

Next morning there were tight controls at all checkpoints in the city, and some West Berliners and nearly all West Germans were refused entry to the eastern sector. (Refugees moved the other way without much trouble for a couple of days until they decided not to risk it.) Almost as soon as the order came into force, a bus with twenty-four delegates to the Homeland Day was turned back at the East German frontier; over the coming days 1,200 West Germans were refused permission to cross. The Senate announced it would pay the air fares for anyone wishing to attend a meeting in West Berlin and some 700 travellers took up the offer; there was no interference with their flights in the corridor. About 15,000 people took part in the Homeland Day (up to 25,000 had been expected) and they engaged in their usual "revanchist, militarist" business of dressing up in their local costumes and singing old songs in dialect. West Berliners were not unduly alarmed by the travel restrictions: there was a feeling that the controls were a practice run for the coming Bundestag meeting. And all the restrictions were lifted, as promised, on the night of 4 September. Sighs of relief: this had just been a brief spell of "Berlin Weather".

Not so. On 8 September the East Germans reintroduced the same conditions for access to East Berlin: those wishing to make a short visit must apply for a permit at one of five crossing points; those wanting to stay several days must get a permit from an East German police station. Pankow then made matters infinitely worse: refused to allow West Berliners to travel through the GDR on a West German passport. At one stroke, residents of West Berlin had been turned into a separate category of citizen (even before the creation of a "free city") and refugees, who had always been issued with FRG papers, had been denied the chance to move to the West by road. No time limit was set to these regulations. They were immediately recognised by the West as the first move from words to deeds since the crisis had begun in November 1958. In an uncommonly quick and tough reaction, the Western Powers suspended issue of Temporary Travel Documents, used every year by about a thousand East German and by other travellers to West Berlin and the Federal Republic whose states and passports were not recognised. Protest Notes were delivered in Moscow on 12 September. The Federal government recommended West German businessmen not to travel to East Germany as long as the new regulations were in force and refused export licences to firms suspected of Communist sympathies. The East Germans were undeterred. All traffic for Berlin was subject to long delays at the checkpoints (lorries from Hamburg accustomed to hold-ups for three hours were now delayed anything from five to eight hours). On 17 September the Papal Nuncio was refused permission to enter East Berlin since the Vatican did not recognise the GDR. On 22 September the US ambassador in Germany was blocked at an eastern sector crossing point site until he showed his identity card – thereby conceding the right of a guard to ask for it and surrendering his own right to unimpeded access.[40]

Was there any other counter-pressure the Western Powers could bring to bear? Bonn was ready to stop all trade with the GDR – if the western allies and preferably all NATO countries did the same – but feared this might bring even tighter measures against West Berlin. The Americans were enthusiastic about an embargo: when a Federal diplomat in Washington warned Foy Kohler of the State Department that the likely result would be full blockade of the western sectors, the reply was "maybe we would have to face that". The French called the approach "exaggerated and over-excited"; the British thought major economic sanctions must be kept in reserve for worse situations because the West had so few cards up its sleeve. The American answer to this was that strong measures now would nip tougher eastern policies in the bud. NATO members were most reluctant to take part in an embargo: they not only stood to lose trade but were probably getting their own back for never being consulted or even briefed about Germany. There was no way at all that western countries outside the alliance could be persuaded to join in and some, like Sweden, would be an excellent source for many of the supplies which the GDR usually got from West Germany.[41]

But while the western allies dithered, Bonn acted without warning. On 30 September the Federal government announced that it would not renew the annual Interzonal Trade Agreement, due to lapse in December, unless "necessary preconditions" were met by the GDR. West Berlin businessmen were upset at this unexpected blow to their trade with the East and there was soon criticism in the western sectors that giving a three-month warning to the East Germans had also given them time to make alternative arrangements for supplies and markets. Ulbricht lashed back: this was an "aggressive act"; it was up to Bonn to open negotiations. He then dripped poison on relations between Bonn and Berlin by offering to discuss a separate trade agreement with the Senate, linked to guarantees of access. The American government refused to issue export licences in October for two large East German orders for steel and magnesium. ("This is *very* silly," noted Macmillan; the whole trade boycott is "quite absurd", his private secretary added.) The screws on West Berlin tightened. In October the GDR refused transit permits for goods (usually building materials) from Poland to the western sectors; in early November two lorries were seized by East German customs officers because allegedly they were carrying radios "for the West German army"; several other carriers were detained for twenty-four hours or more on the grounds that their waybills were inaccurate.[42]

The pinpricks stopped abruptly in mid-November. Secretly, a high ranking official in the Federal Ministry of Economics had had a long talk to his counterpart in the GDR Ministry of Foreign and Inter-German Trade. This was an amazing meeting. West Germans, after all, claimed that they had no contacts and would never establish any with East Germans, and they petrified their allies into doing the same. Everyone knew, of course, that there was plenty of joint activity over practical matters – but this was an intensely political affair. And the conversation took place not in a wild forest on a dark night but in a Berlin restaurant. That opening round was followed by a series of negotiations in the Berlin Treuhandstelle, the Trustee Office for Interzonal Trade, between the West German representative, Professor Leopold, and his East German opposite number, Dr Behrendt. Since they worked in the same building no one could spot what they were up to and although the western authorities got hints from the discussions, everything was played so discreetly that details were only pieced together, by the British at least, the following year. Leopold and Behrendt got nowhere at all at first; then on 13 December the East German offered to lift restrictions on movement to, from and within Berlin in return for the restoration of the International Trade Agreement for a year. It was guessed later that the GDR was already feeling the pinch from loss of special steels and machinery from the FRG which could not be supplied by the Soviet bloc because German tooling and standards were different; it was also suspected that when Ulbricht was in Moscow in late November he was told to avoid major trouble in Berlin until the Kremlin had assessed the new American Administration. Be that as it may, after the initial softening Behrendt froze the negotiations again. It came as something of a shock, therefore, when both sides announced the renewal of the Trade Agreement on 29 December, two days before it was due to lapse. Mystery was added by Bonn's insistence on total secrecy about the conditions of the settlement; the Western Powers were, however, asked to resume issue of TTDs. Tantalised allied observers soon decided that there must be a secret protocol; rumour had it that there were only two copies in the West, one with the Chancellor and the other with Leopold. Much later it was discovered that the East Germans had not only promised to lift their restrictions on West German travellers, but had agreed to inspect goods in transit only once after which lorries and rail wagons would be sealed. The phrasing of the protocol was said to be vague. But Bonn could make the commitment stick: it would not issue waybills for selected (and very desirable) items if the GDR did not keep to its side of the bargain; any more trouble and the following year's Trade Agreement would not be signed.[43]

It took time for all aspects of the settlement to come into force. The Western Powers issued TTDs for trade in early January but kept up the ban on travel documents for people until 15 February because the GDR maintained tight inter-sector controls in Berlin. The sealing of lorries was delayed for some time, which aroused nasty thoughts of GDR reneging until the East Germans finally asked Leopold if he could give them some lead and sealing equipment. From then on, all ground traffic ran more smoothly and quickly than it had done for years. The Western Powers preened themselves a little on the success of their quick protests and counter-measures. But the real lessons of what had been the gravest threat to Berlin since the Blockade were that it was the West Germans who had hit the GDR where it hurt most, that the habit of the West dealing with matters of allied access and neglecting that of Germans must stop, and that threats to the western sectors needed a full range of options and co-ordinated action preferably with full NATO support. Would any of these lessons be learned – and put into practice?

From an East German perspective, of course, there were different conclusions to be drawn from the recent grave crisis. Yes: trade and travel had suffered for a while. Yes: the Ulbricht regime had been obliged to lift its restrictions on Berlin's communications. But hadn't they really scared West Berlin, Bonn and the Western Powers? Hadn't they shown how effectively the GDR could act on its own? Hadn't they been an impressive rehearsal which proved how devastating a full performance could be? Would Pankow have needed to climb down if it had had full backing and economic help from the Soviet Union and Bloc? What had the Kremlin done to give meaning to its standard rhetoric about Berlin being part of the GDR and the East German state having rights over access? Hadn't this crisis lengthened the charge sheet against the Soviet Union: shown yet again that Berlin was an issue the Kremlin exploited when it suited its own purposes but dropped if it did not fit a specifically Soviet aim? Look at the way Khrushchev had handled Berlin at the Paris Summit: he had given Pankow no advance information on his intentions and tactics. Look how he had slapped the GDR in the face by postponing a separate treaty. He called for patience. East German patience was sorely tried.

And it was under severe strain over a problem where the Kremlin seemed to show no understanding or willingness to act. Refugees. The numbers rose steadily in the second half of 1960: 16,343 East Germans left for the West in July (48 per cent more than in July 1959); 21,465 in August (36 per cent up on the same month the previous year); 20,698 in September (again 36 per cent up and this was the period of tight checkpoint controls); 21,150 in October (66 per cent higher than in October '59); 16,427 (a drop, maybe, but there always was when the weather got worse, and the figure was still 68 per cent up on the previous year). These statistics represented a dangerous loss of labour, especially of professional and skilled workers: they would inflict considerable damage on the Seven-Year Plan and the chances of catching up with the living standards of the FRG by the end of 1961. Furthermore, this total did not reflect another, growing, drain on the workforce: Grenzgänger, those who crossed into West Berlin to work. For years past there had been about 40,000 of them, as well as an uncountable number of cleaners and home helps plus "black" workers who did not register for insurance or pay taxes. Between March and September 1960 that number rose to nearly 50,000 (and at the same time West Berliners who crossed to work in the other direction dropped from a steady 16,000 or so to 12,766). Most of the women Grenzgänger worked in textile factories; the men went into metal production, the building trade and transport – all areas where the GDR was short of labour. Their wages came in 40 per cent West marks and 60 per cent East marks; they paid at home for food, rent, and heating with East marks, so could use West marks for high quality goods or conversion to eastern currency at a rate of one for five. Many left consumer durables with friends in West Berlin – ready for the day they decided to cross permanently to the West, where their jobs were ready for them.[44]

Ulbricht was struggling to stem the labour tide. The requirement for teachers to take part in outside political activities was dropped; in December doctors and dentists were told they could hand on their practices to their children and local officials were instructed to curb "bureaucratic arrogance" towards them. Given anxiety about low agricultural production, Ulbricht had back-pedalled at the end of May and criticised "advanced collectivisation" rather than the "elementary" form in which livestock and implements stayed in private hands. He put the brakes on "socialisation" of craftsmen and tradesmen. To lessen the attractions of the Golden West there was a campaign to supply the "thousand and one small things that are missing": nail scissors, drawing pins, fresh vegetables among them. But whatever the regime did it still came in for criticism from its own supporters: at a biennial conference of SED organisations speakers objected to the "breathless rate" of economic change (comments the authorities called "social democratic deviation and capitulation to imperialism"). Yet loyal Party workers were also upset by sudden ideological and policy U-turns. Ulbricht rejigged his government and was said to have replaced some 50,000 junior officials in local organisations to strengthen Party discipline and work on raising morale. He gave his own spirits and position a boost by becoming Chairman of a new Council of State (which made him Head of State as well as First Secretary of the SED), taking powers previously held by the Council of Ministers, and changing his scruffy old clothes for a dark suit, white shirt, silver tie and a couple of decorations in his lapel. His public manner became regal with a dash of paternal benevolence; he entered meetings through a guard of honour and double doors flung wide while those present stood in respectful silence.[45]

No amount of policy shift or personality cult could conceal or cure the political unease and economic strains. And the refugee problem lay at the core of both. In August 1960 the President of the GDR Volkskammer, the People's Chamber, spoke to a journalist, with what was undoubtedly genuine pride, about what had happened in his country since the war: "We had to rebuild our life from its very foundations and under the gravest difficulties. We suffered much more heavily than Western Germany under the burden of reparations. We had fewer resources. We received not one cent of Western financial aid. We have rebuilt by our own strength and by that alone." He believed, and many more who were not even Party members shared his belief, that the GDR was creating a new, better human being, who would live comfortably and humanely by service to the state and fellow citizens, not by western selfish individualism. Given those achievements and hopes, it was intolerable to see the lifeblood of the state draining away.[46]

It would be easy to stop it. Every western official, every Berliner, knew that all Ulbricht had to do was seal the sector border. There was no need to make it airtight – and it would be wise to avoid driving those either side to a violent protest. It could be done simply by tightening controls. Anything more drastic seemed inconceivable to most people. A group of West Berlin students visited Jerusalem in 1960. They saw a wall across the city. Could such a thing ever happen in Berlin? they asked themselves. No, they decided: you could wall off Arabs from Jews but not Germans from Germans. Yet later that year a reader in chemical pathology at St Bartholomew's Hospital in London attended a symposium in East Berlin. From what he heard from GDR colleagues "preparations seem to have been made for the administrative and technical organisation required to seal the East–West German border".[47]

The letter he sent to the Foreign Office was popped into a file without comment. Perhaps what he had heard was just tittle-tattle from the Berlin rumour machine. But if there was any truth in it, new, nasty possibilities had been raised. Did "technical" mean "construction"? Did "seal" imply a complete blocking of all crossing points in the city? If so, the situation was going to be even more alarming than the expected tightening of crossing procedures. And no one had stopped to think, no one had dared to contemplate, what the West would do under those circumstances. Yet allied analysts and Berliners alike felt something would happen soon. Surely as far as Pankow was concerned it had to: the East German state could not tolerate this leeching away of its population; the regime had to control its borders, to save its economy and its political authority. Was there anything the West could and should do to keep Berlin open? Given the complexity of the city's problems and their repercussions on all allied policy, was it easier to ignore the question of Berliners' freedom of movement?

8

Ducks in a Row?

———⇒>●<⇐———

W hen the Paris Summit collapsed in May 1960, so did hopes for a Berlin solution. Everyone had long since run out of ideas; most people were now tired and depressed. Not so Adenauer, who was delighted that the U-2 row had prevented any discussion of Germany and Berlin, and was for once reported to be "in a mellow mood" before leaving Bonn for one of his lengthy holidays on Lake Como. On return he made an early start to the campaign for the election of the Federal Chancellor in September 1961, in which his challenger was Willy Brandt. Herter had decided to "let the dust settle" before taking any further initiative. Eisenhower was ready to leave the next move to the Soviet Union (and since there was unlikely to be one before his Presidency ran out at the end of the year, he could sit back). Macmillan made the best of his particular bad job and told Selwyn Lloyd on 24 May that "if Mr Khrushchev does nothing about Berlin for a year or so, then we shall not have done too badly". A "year or so" was probably wildly optimistic. On 3 June Khrushchev gave a belligerent press conference threatening action in the city if the West did not come to a Summit "to solve ripe problems" in six to eight months' time – in other words soon after the new US Administration took over. Such a time limit was something of a relief to West Berliners. They had been anxious during the Paris meeting and taut after Khrushchev's speech in Berlin. A life expectancy of six or eight months was as good as they were ever promised.[1]

Gradually the western leaders' attention was diverted from Berlin to major problems elsewhere. In April 1961 Macmillan decided to come out of isolation and apply for membership of the EEC; and he was faced by incessant trouble with South Africa and Rhodesia. There was rebellion in the Congo against the Belgians and a civil war with appeals for help to the United Nations, the United States and the USSR. (Macmillan's nightmares of a new First World War switched from Berlin as its cause to the Congo in "the role of Serbia".) There was civil war too in Laos, with the Soviet Union and the United States backing opposing sides and growing American fears of a toppling row of South-East Asian dominoes. De Gaulle held a referendum in January 1961 on Algerian self-determination and thereafter faced terrorism and French resistance to independence.

Khrushchev, it was hoped, also had plenty to distract him. His policy of ploughing the virgin lands to create agricultural wealth was clearly failing; Soviet industrial production was dropping. His quarrel with the Chinese was out in the open and Soviet technicians were withdrawn from China in August 1960. Yet at the same time, he was caught in crossfire from his domestic critics: the U-2 incident had swelled opposition to détente with the West; there were rumours of conflict with Mikoyan and the Party ideologue Mikhail Suslov. And by June 1960 the State Department had reports, "of varying reliability and plausibility", that Ulbricht was "exerting pressure on Khrushchev to initiate unilateral action" over Berlin. Whether or not they were true, whether or not Ulbricht was a tail which could wag the Soviet dog, Khrushchev could not neglect Berlin, even if he preferred to postpone a crisis. On 29 June he warned the Federal German ambassador, Hans Kroll, whom he had taken aside at a Kremlin reception, that the Berlin matter could not stay in suspense for long; a treaty must be signed soon. Kroll drew the conclusion that there would be no move until after the American election but, given the presence of Gromyko at this quiet chat, he felt the message was as much for the Presidium as for the West and that Khrushchev intended to stick to his new six to eight month deadline.[2]

A fresh, vital spirit was injected into the uneasy yet lethargic European truce. John Fitzgerald Kennedy was elected President of the United States in November 1960 and took office in January 1961. He was young: born in 1917 and the only leader of the four Powers to belong fully to the twentieth century. He was free from the ingrained prejudices and weariness of the other elderly, long-serving heads of state. He was wealthy, good-looking, and blessed with an enchanting, elegant wife. He had intelligence, charm and energy in abundance. He brought a refreshing informality to the conduct of affairs: his small children, with or without dogs, trotted in and out of the Oval Office; if he wanted information he was just as likely to telephone the man who had it at his fingertips as send a memo through official channels. He stirred hearts and minds with his eloquence. The words were often written by others, but he chose them with taste, delivered them with conviction and with a simplicity of manner and voice, which was particularly effective on television and gave the sumptuous phrases meaning. He won loyalty and love. The world at large felt, as Charles Bohlen did, "infinite hope that somehow or other he was going to change the course of history".[3]

One quality in Jack Kennedy struck everyone immediately. He had "a voracious appetite for information", said Llewellyn Thompson. He knew how to get it: he was "an excellent questioner and an excellent listener", remembered Livingston Merchant of the State Department; indeed, in George Kennan's view, he was the "best listener I've ever seen in a high position", and resisted "the temptation to which so many other great men have yielded, to sound off himself and be admired". By corollary, Foy Kohler noted the "rapidity and brilliance of his mind in grasping the essential facts". There was, inevitably, an obverse side to Kennedy's éclat and talents. He was a quick reader – but he liked something quick to read: long briefing papers bored him, he had no interest in the geology of a problem, no concern with the history of its development and treatment. Untrammelled by conventional ways of seeing things and intolerant of stale assessments, he was ready for vigorous assaults on seemingly intractable dilemmas. But in the judgement of George Ball, Under-Secretary at the State Department, he was not "profound either in his analyses or his judgements"; he was a pragmatist whose "main concern was action and day to day results"; he tended to postpone decisions in areas where there would not be instant success. His youthful confidence that energy and originality would untie every knot galvanised others, but with it went a hazardous disregard for acquired experience. His policy meetings had the intellectual excitement of a good seminar, but sometimes shared the academic weakness for concepts rather than common sense and decision. Irritated by executive straitjackets and slow procedures, he streamlined the bureaucratic machine; the Departments were often circumvented by Special Assistants; the collective wisdom of full cabinets or broad-based councils was replaced by small collections of the "Brightest and the Best" – men of undoubted brainpower but not always of matching experience or political sagacity.

A central and winning element in Kennedy's election campaign had been defence policy: he had attacked Eisenhower's cuts in the military budget and whipped up a fury at the supposed "Missile Gap" with the Soviet Union. Even when the new President discovered that no such gap existed, he stuck to his belief that defence spending must be increased: both to maintain nuclear strength and also build up conventional forces. The massive nuclear response might ultimately have to be employed, but the President was repelled by its undiscriminating destructiveness – after a briefing on nuclear potential in summer 1961 he commented: "and we call ourselves the human race". A purely nuclear strategy he defined as "bankrupt"; neither side wanted to use its bombs, and nuclear missiles were inappropriate for local wars and salami tactics. What was needed was the capacity for flexible, graded responses to fit the stages and intensity of a wide spectrum of political and military situations. "The greater our variety of weapons," he argued, "the more political choices we can make in any given situation."[4]

Kennedy had provided a manifesto for his foreign policy in a collection of his speeches, *The Strategy of Peace*, published for the election campaign. Here he castigated existing practice as being restricted to "the arms race and the Cold War" and consisting largely in "eleventh-hour responses to Soviet-created crises". As his adviser and Boswell, Arthur Schlesinger, put it, Kennedy wanted to "get the hysteria out of the conflict": drop the Cold War rhetoric, look for points of agreement with the Soviet Union, find a genuine "peaceful coexistence". The President had written that it was "far better that we meet at the Summit than at the Brink", but he wanted to speak from strength. "As long as Mr Khrushchev is convinced that the balance of world power is shifting his way, no amount of either smiles or toughness, neither Camp David talks nor Kitchen Debates can compel him to enter fruitful negotiations." Kennedy was restless in a world ossified by old dissension, obsolete responses and hoary slogans and, as one critic put it, his Administration "much preferred solving problems to living with situations not of their own making or choosing". That raised the question of whether the given situation was sometimes better than any alternative.[5]

For all his impatience with inherited circumstances and methods, Jack Kennedy did not have a slapdash view of international relations. "Domestic policy can only defeat us; foreign policy can kill us." So it was a charge he believed he must take on himself. He felt well qualified to do so. He had travelled and read; his father had been ambassador in London before the war, he himself had been a member of the Senate Foreign Relations Committee since 1957 (though some observers carped that he had spent most of his time there fostering his political career). What he lacked was deep understanding, patience with the details, or practice in international negotiation. He needed a skilled, seasoned Secretary of State. But when Robert Lovett, a wise old man of the Democratic Party, asked whether he really wanted a Secretary or an Under-Secretary, the President replied, "Well, I guess I want an Under-Secretary." Not for him a John

Foster Dulles, to whom Eisenhower had delegated, a Marshall or Acheson whom Truman had trusted to get on with the job. Kennedy picked his own version of Gromyko, Brentano, Lloyd or Couve – a safe pair of hands, Dean Rusk.[6]

He was not the President's first choice, nor an obvious one. All the more heralded candidates for the State Department had been ruled out either because Kennedy did not like them or because their track records made them politically vulnerable. It was greatly to Rusk's advantage that the President had never met him and he was little known on Capitol Hill; the clincher was an article he had written for *Foreign Affairs* arguing that a President must make his own foreign policy. He was reluctant to take the job: it was short term and entailed a drop in salary from his present steady, well padded position as President of the Rockefeller Foundation. These were troubling prospects for a man who struggled out of real poverty as the son of a Georgia dirt farmer. Thanks to intelligence and hard work he had gone to college, won a Rhodes scholarship, been an academic and then a staff officer in the Far East during the war, before spending several years at the State Department. Kennedy was well served by Rusk's loyalty and lucidity, and his grip on the minutiae of international problems. Happily for the President, less fortunately for American foreign policy, Rusk stuck to his views about the nature of his office: the Secretary of State, he believed, "is the creature of the President". He would not argue. He listened patiently to the views of others, though as J.K. Galbraith noticed "with no thought of changing his mind", and was silent at the seminars in the Oval Office. "My own feeling", Rusk recalled, was that "the Secretary of State should not take much part in those discussions"; his opinions "ought to be known to the President in private". There is no evidence that he did make them known (perhaps simply because the informal conduct of business in the White House did not spawn records or minutes).[7]

Convenient though this passivity was to a President who wanted to be his own Secretary of State, it was an irritant to an intellectually curious and combative man. Rusk "never gives me anything to chew on", Kennedy complained. "He always gives me twenty options and argues convincingly for *and* against each of them." So the President surrounded himself with advisers of more congenial mind to brainstorm issues, or called in experts to deal with specific problems. That left Rusk exiled from the Oval Office. He was never on Christian-name terms with Kennedy – he said he preferred it that way – nor one of the charmed circle invited to extended family weekends at Hyannis Port or Palm Beach. (Similarly Gromyko was not asked to Khrushchev's dachas; Selwyn Lloyd spent weekends at Chequers only because Macmillan chose to be elsewhere.) He probably felt at ease in his Department, but Arthur Schlesinger lamented "He seemed actually to prefer State (Department) to fresh ways of saying things" and crossed out striking phrases from a Presidential speech in favour of "weary State formulas". The Department gave him no authority or voice: the President began by mistrusting it as hidebound and prejudiced and was soon maddened by its slow formalities and caution. He complained that the place was "a bowl of jelly", and that giving an instruction was like "dropping it in a dead letter box". Schlesinger blamed much of the weakness of the Department on Rusk's lack of leadership and habitual inscrutability: "since his subordinates did not know what he thought, they could not do what he wanted". Yet it was the President who sapped the State Department by seeking original approaches from a Babel of advisers rather than relying on the measured, tested and professional.[8]

Both the exhilaration and the shortcomings of rejecting past experience were vividly illustrated by Kennedy's handling of the Berlin problem. Everything he had said about it before taking office hinted at readiness to conduct a thoroughgoing re-examination of American policy, but showed lack of knowledge of the complexities involved. In his second TV debate with Nixon during the election campaign he had proclaimed the western right of presence in the city – but called it a "contractual right", no doubt unaware that this was a step on to a British slippery slope of concession. He often stressed the need to uphold "freedom and independence" – but only referred to "West Berlin". (Willy Brandt in a press conference at the end of 1960 reminded the allies that "all Berlin, not just West Berlin, is a four-Power responsibility".) Kennedy told the Senate in June 1960 that a solution to the Berlin problem was "only possible in the context of a solution of the problems of Germany and, indeed, the problems of all Europe", but this was a truism, describing the predicament not the way out, and he offered no real answers to the German or European questions. He suggested that the UN might guarantee western access; in return allied garrisons could be thinned out and so-called "propaganda activities" cut (seemingly oblivious to the reasons why others had rejected such ideas long since). He stepped on the thinnest of ice by referring in an interview to the necessity for the East German government to have "increased status", though admittedly he said on other occasions this would not mean giving it recognition. He spoke of the broad compass of the Berlin crisis: the city was central to the policies of East and West, the Russians were "fighting for New York and Paris when they struggle over Berlin", and argued they must be resisted by force if need be. But the concessions he suggested sounded like retreats and they would have widespread repercussions which he did not recognise.[9]

Before taking office, Kennedy had suggested that: "the Berlin problem and the problems suggested by Berlin are going to be with us for many years"; thereafter he refused to acknowledge its urgency or be deflected from lengthy and painstaking examination of it by the restlessness of others. Khrushchev had made it clear soon after the Paris Summit that he would stay his hand just until the new Administration was settled in. In December 1960, the Soviet ambassador suggested to the President's brother, Robert, that there were no real barriers to resolving disagreements. Kroll was taken aside at a Kremlin banquet the next month to be told by the Soviet leader that he could not hold out for long against pressure "in certain quarters" for a settlement. Even so, Kennedy made no reference to Berlin in his State of the Union message on 30 January. The West Germans were distressed: their Washington ambassador, Wilhelm Grewe, complained to the State Department; the President himself had to assure both Brentano and Brandt that silence did not imply lack of interest but a wish to avoid provoking the Soviet Union into an offensive – a view formalised in State Department instructions to Moscow on 28 February. Llewellyn Thompson recommended dropping a quiet word to Khrushchev that the problem could be tackled after the Federal German elections in September; if no such approach was made he feared Khrushchev would "almost certainly proceed with his separate peace treaty" and begin "the slow strangulation of Berlin". His advice was not taken. Khrushchev's patience began to fray. On 17 February a Soviet aide-mémoire was delivered to Adenauer – politely worded but stressing that "all the time limits have expired for understanding the need to sign a peace treaty". (Adenauer, who had come to terms with the status quo and endured more than one Khrushchev ultimatum, did not bother to reply until July.) No public statement or private approach to the Kremlin was made by the new President.[10]

Kennedy thought Berlin would wait. He had 1,200 executive offices to fill and domestic policy to devise; according to briefings from Eisenhower and his own Departments, Laos was the looming crisis. Attempts to jolt his attention back to Berlin, such as a belligerent speech by Khrushchev on 6 January, merely made him stubborn. He would deal with it in his own time, and in his own way: from scratch, with the broadest possible range of opinion from all the best minds. On 11 February he gathered Rusk, Bundy, and Vice-President Johnson to listen for two and a half hours to a review of Soviet policy in general by Thompson and three former ambassadors in Moscow, Averell Harriman, George Kennan and Charles Bohlen. On 22 February he sent a letter to Khrushchev hoping that "before too long" they might meet personally for an informal exchange of views. Only then did he launch an exhaustive examination of the Berlin problem. The State and

Defence Departments were asked for assessments. As if these might be inadequate, on 15 February Dean Acheson was put in charge of a separate review group. At first glance this was an odd appointment. In many ways Acheson personified the Old Guard Jack Kennedy normally shunned: Truman's Secretary of State and a reject for the post in this Presidency, a soul mate for Bevin in countering the Berlin Blockade, a founding father of NATO, a Cold Warrior, whose spiteful comments on the President and his entourage too often got back to them. On the other hand, Acheson had often spoken in favour of flexible political and military strategies and his hard line views would be balanced by other people. The President was making a thorough approach and showing admirable open-mindedness. But he had begun what was bound to be a lengthy process and ignored Khrushchev's heavy hints about a speedy settlement. Conceivably Kennedy was also not giving enough attention to the distress signals coming from Berlin itself. Problems were coming to a head in the city which would not permit leisurely reflection.[11]

In February 1961 a total of 13,576 East Germans left for the West (38 per cent more than in February 1960); 16,094 followed them in March. The flight of refugees was high on the agenda at the Plenum of the SED Central Committee. Ulbricht told it on 16 March that the drain of people was having a deplorable effect on the GDR's economy. Three days later he produced a tough version of standard demands: immediate negotiations for a treaty, East German control of West Berlin's traffic, liquidation of "espionage" and "sabotage" organisations and a ban on "revanchist and militarist" meetings in the western sectors. These were not just desirable ends in themselves, but means to halt the refugee flood. According to one American newspaper, Ulbricht also got endorsement from a secret session of the Plenum to request Khrushchev's support for sealing the sector boundary between East and West Berlin. (From Willy Brandt's memoirs it appears that he, too, heard that Ulbricht was going to make a direct appeal to the Kremlin.) It is likely that the East German leader did indeed raise the refugee problem in Moscow at the end of the month, at a meeting of the Consultative Committee of Warsaw Pact ministers. The evidence for this is sketchy. Most of it can be traced back to Jan Sejna, the Czech Defence Minister who later defected to the United States and might be suspected of feeding titbits to his interrogators and puffing his autobiography with "vital secrets". He has, however, convinced many that at this meeting Ulbricht poured out his woes and proposed tighter frontier controls including the erection of barbed wire along the entire intersector boundary, but was opposed by the Hungarians and Rumanians who argued that wire was a poor advertisement for Socialism, would be criticised by the international community, and might incite the population either side to riot. Khrushchev is said to have called boundary closure "premature" but to have agreed to preparations being made pending final approval. He may have been sceptical about the whole policy; he may have wanted to avoid any hostile move until he had met the new American President; thirty years on, many well-informed analysts in Moscow wondered whether Ulbricht had merely asked for permission or had wanted twenty Soviet divisions to do the job for him, which would have sparked off a much bigger confrontation with the four Powers.[12]

Nothing of this debate on border closure (assuming it took place) became public knowledge for years. What was soon apparent, however, was that the Kremlin and Soviet bloc were pressing hard for talks about Berlin. The communiqué from the Warsaw Pact meeting was particularly strongly worded in its demands for a treaty and the establishment of a "free city". On 21 April Ulbricht took the same line in a speech for the fifteenth anniversary of the SED and added condemnation of "subversive activities" by the West Germans, among which he included the "trade in human beings" – in other words, helping refugees. (Clearly no one would leave the First Workers' and Farmers' State unless bribed or shanghaied.) Three days later Khrushchev warned Hans Kroll that he had given the new US Administration time enough to settle in and could wait no longer: he wanted a final Berlin settlement within months; unless he got four-Power agreement he would sign a treaty with the GDR and was confident that the Western Powers would not risk war over it. The Poles pitched in: Gomulka gave speeches on 24 April and May Day also stressing that a treaty and a Berlin settlement were now urgent. The rhetoric from all quarters was as intimidating as ever; there was no hint at a slackening of the Communist position. But, given the sustained campaign from the Kremlin and its allies ever since the start of the new US Administration, it might have been worthwhile for the West to take soundings to see if any real negotiation was likely.[13]

President Kennedy, however, was not to be hurried. The State Department's Berlin report was ready on 13 March – or rather, was finished to the Department's satisfaction but far too long to be given to the President. It had to be cut from twenty-seven pages to eleven. That took ten days. The report might have been better received if it had been reworded as well as shortened. Its very opening was bound to infuriate the President: "However impelling the urge to find some new approach to the Berlin problem, the ineluctable facts of the situation strictly limit the practical courses of action open to the West." Thereafter, all the conclusions were negative: the positions of East and West were irreconcilable; nothing could be added to the western Peace Plan which would make it a negotiable basis for a settlement; an interim agreement was unlikely; a "free city" was unacceptable to the allies and would be seen as American weakness; the status quo was the best solution available but would not necessarily be tolerated by the Soviet Union. The State Department was pessimistic about military measures too: contingency plans for reopening access were unsatisfactory and likely to be rejected by the other Western Powers; the Russians "have the capacity, if they wish to use it, to prevent our reopening access" by conventional forces; nuclear deterrence was increasingly incredible and opposed by the allies and NATO; "it is particularly difficult to beat back each minor encroachment on western rights"; there were huge dangers in each side miscalculating the other's readiness for war. Nor did the Department show any confidence in alternatives: none of the economic counter measures so far considered would be "sufficient to deter the Soviets once they have taken the basic political decision" to precipitate a crisis; if the UN were brought in, it might well impose a settlement "whatever the political cost to the West". And with a final despondent whimper: "There is no reason to believe that the Soviets are not in deadly earnest about Berlin" and would not sign a separate treaty.[14]

The President was temperamentally inclined to "get up and go"; the State Department had told him there was nowhere to go to, not even elbow room where he was. He was intellectually committed to flexible, multi-faceted strategies; he now got the exact opposite from Dean Acheson's interim proposals, handed over on 4 April. These dismissed as ineffective all diplomatic and economic pressures on the Soviet Union, warned that readiness to negotiate would be seen as weakness and that the Kremlin saw the Berlin issue as a test of wills. Acheson therefore urged the strongest possible military measures to demonstrate American power and determination. McGeorge Bundy, Special Assistant to the President for National Security Affairs, thought the memo was "first-rate" and, as he forwarded it to the President, added his own beliefs that attempts "to negotiate this problem out of existence have failed in the past" and that "Berlin is no place to compromise".[15]

When Macmillan and his new Foreign Secretary, Lord Home (Alec Douglas Home), were told of the proposals by Acheson himself on 5 April, they were aghast. The Soviet Union, he maintained, would press the Berlin issue this year, and there was no solution to the city's predicament which would not sap the entire western position in Europe. The British tried to argue that Khrushchev might be on a hook and need help to get off. No,

Acheson insisted, the Soviet leader was bent on dividing the West and Berlin was his chosen pressure point. Perhaps, Home tentatively suggested, right of conquest as the justification for western rights was "growing thin". Again, no: in Acheson's opinion it was western power which was "growing thin". Political and economic moves would not adequately demonstrate allied strength, nuclear threats would not be believed, air probes or airlifts would be met by Soviet rockets. So there must be military action on the ground, involving no less than a division with a second in support, to "raise some ugly questions for the Russians".[16]

What Acheson proposed raised very ugly questions indeed for the British, though before leaving Washington they agreed to review contingency planning and authorise training for it. The President too was clearly alarmed by Acheson's entirely military approach and by the possibility that it would run out of control. He called for prompt reports from the Department of Defence and the Joint Chiefs on current Berlin policy and the full range of contingency plans. The first results made bleak reading. The military believed that it would require substantial rather than limited action to reopen blocked access. The Secretary of Defence, Robert McNamara, warned: "Of all the problems the administration faces, Berlin seems to be the most pregnant with disaster" and the most likely cause of war. That meant nuclear war: American strategy was still stuck in a rigid nuclear framework. The President had been told he had no political options; now he had been offered little flexibility in military response. He was peering over the Brink. What he could not see was the political reasoning behind Acheson's seemingly militaristic proposals: that the view might be just as bloodcurdling for the Soviet Union.[17]

And by the time he had reflected on all the most doomladen consequences of a Berlin crisis, President Kennedy had been involved in a quite different disaster. He had approved a CIA and Pentagon plan to support an émigré invasion of Cuba to overthrow the Communist-backed Castro regime. He had been warned against it: Senator Fulbright of the Senate Foreign Relations Committee had prophesied a débâcle, Schlesinger feared a lengthy civil war which would suck the United States into direct intervention; Acheson argued that it did not take Price Waterhouse to work out that 1,500 Cuban exiles would not be as good as 25,000 local Cuban troops; Rusk said nothing, Soviet experts were not consulted. The President himself decided to keep the invasion force small and to deny it air cover. (He told Eisenhower later that if American aid was obvious "the Soviets would be very apt to cause trouble in Berlin".) When the force landed at the Bay of Pigs on 17 April it was wiped out and the popular uprising promised by the CIA did not take place.[18]

The President was devastated. The early confidence and exuberance was knocked out of the Administration. Acheson told colleagues that Europeans had been watching a "gifted young amateur practise with a boomerang when they saw, to their horror, that he had knocked himself out" – an unendearing remark which got back to the President. Kennedy took the blame for the Bay of Pigs on himself, but wanted to understand what had gone wrong and learn from the mistakes. General Maxwell Taylor, a former Chief of Staff of the Army and critic of massive retaliation, was called in to review the whole operation. What struck him was the "lack of team play" in the Administration which seemed to consist "largely of strangers": the President did not know the Secretary of State, the military and civilians did not know each other. Kennedy came to the conclusion that the CIA could not be trusted (its Director, Allen Dulles, was eventually persuaded to resign); that the military must be viewed with suspicion (Taylor was kept on as special adviser on military and intelligence matters and asked to review Berlin planning); and that his own White House staff must exercise much tighter control over all government business (which increased the bias away from the professionals). He undoubtedly learned from the Cuban fiasco – his next Cuban crisis proved that. But it was a slow process. For the moment he had wounds to lick, self-confidence to restore, and a stern test to face – a meeting with Khrushchev himself. It was unfortunately timed. Eisenhower warned the President on 22 April: "The failure of the Bay of Pigs will embolden the Soviets to do something that they would not do otherwise."[19]

Kennedy had written to Khrushchev on 22 February suggesting that they might meet in due course. Thompson then had a Mrs Beaton problem delivering the message: first catch the Soviet leader. He finally tracked him down in Novosibirsk on 9 March. Khrushchev waited until 12 May to reply and agree to talks. (An interesting delay given his other signs of impatience to tackle the Berlin problem.) The President proposed that they meet in Vienna – neutral ground – and a date was fixed to follow his planned visit to Paris starting on 31 May. That did not leave long to prepare.[20]

Both men were undoubtedly agog. Each was intensely curious by nature, and confident in his own powers and cause; each represented a superpower whose policies would be conditioned by the other. Khrushchev was known for prodding for weakness in an opponent; Kennedy had been saying "I have to show him that we can be just as tough as he is. I can't do that sending messages to him through other people." Thompson had always been keen on the meeting: "I found it impossible to convey either in writing or orally what Mr Khrushchev was like, and I felt that the President should find out for himself by a direct encounter." Bohlen and others in the State Department agreed: the President had to "get a feel of the type of man he was dealing with and the type of situation he was confronting". Not so Rusk, who felt "nervous" and "sceptical"; he doubted the value of such personal contacts and was worried that Summits involved "the court of last resort too soon" in a negotiating process.[21]

The President was bombarded, perhaps over-loaded, with advice on how to handle the meeting: letters, memos, briefing papers, psychological and political assessments, and seemingly every transcript of every conversation Khrushchev had ever had with an American. He was told how to create a "Cordial Atmosphere": talk about grandchildren, agriculture and fishing, Sokolovsky's novel *Quietly Flows the Don*; avoid "getting him too tired" (signalled by him speaking more slowly or lapsing into Ukrainian); "Do not challenge him in public" (this causes aggressiveness, forecast by a vein swelling in the left temple). "For a Productive Discussion": avoid the bland or non-committal, be prepared for switches from hearty friendliness to denunciation; do not start a sentence with a hostile phrase (he will not listen to the rest of it); check the translation (his own interpreter "often softens Khrushchev's rude words"). The columnist Walter Lippmann opposed negotiation on Berlin until after the Federal German elections; Thompson was in favour of exploring areas of accommodation; Bundy was not averse to broaching the possibility of a free city of all-Berlin. In the view of Allan Lightner of the US Mission in West Berlin the fact that there had not been a showdown for two and a half years suggested the Kremlin would not stage one if the Western Powers showed readiness to fight: Khrushchev's toughness hid "a large element of bluff", and he must be convinced that his threats were too risky. The Soviet Union could "live with the Berlin status quo for some time" and American willingness to "discuss interim solutions, compromises or modus vivendi . . . would reduce [the] impact of warning Khrushchev of the dire consequences of his miscalculating our resolve". The CIA warned that Khrushchev doubted western willingness to fight and that "a growing number of western leaders consider a nuclear response to Soviet encroachments out of the question".[22]

So there was advice aplenty for Vienna. But there was no agenda. Khrushchev tried to set one. On 23 May he told Llewellyn Thompson that he would attend a visiting American ice revue that evening and hoped the ambassador would be present. During supper in the interval the Soviet leader said "frankly he had seen enough ice shows" and wanted to discuss the forthcoming talks. He then stated bluntly that if there was no general agreement on Berlin soon he would sign a treaty with the GDR, possibly following the German election in September or the Soviet Party Congress in October, after which all western rights would end and the East Germans would control access. When Thompson replied firmly that if force were used to interfere with western communications, it would be met with force, Khrushchev did not flinch: "If we wanted war," Thompson reported, "we would get it." To make doubly sure that the Kremlin message was received, Khrushchev repeated it to the Indian ambassador, paying a farewell call: for ninety minutes he repeated that there would be a treaty and "free city" and that he was confident the Western Powers would not go to war on the issue.[23]

These were disturbing words and many observers believed they were spoken in earnest. They did not, however, impress de Gaulle. When he met Kennedy in Paris on 31 May, he calmly pointed out that Khrushchev had been making threats and issuing ultimatums for two and a half years – and done nothing more. The West, thought the French President, should make no concessions over their rights or the Berlin status quo. If Khrushchev wanted a war, he could have it; an allied airlift should be prepared and if the Russians shot down a plane there would be no ambiguity about their intentions and should be none about the western response. Privately, de Gaulle had expressed fears to his ambassador in Washington, Hervé Alphand, that Kennedy might be tempted in Vienna by a reasonable sounding offer, then Khrushchev would dictate terms to the western world – especially to Macmillan, who "will look for every compromise" – and Berlin would be lost and western prestige damaged. In the event, the three-day Kennedy visit greatly reassured him about the new President and American policy. He found Kennedy firm and clear on all issues from NATO to Laos and was undoubtedly flattered by the close attention with which the young man listened. De Gaulle decided that he had at last found a true "interlocuteur", the first US President with whom he could hold a dialogue (unlike the loathed Roosevelt, mistrusted Truman or "superficial and prevaricating" Eisenhower). The American visitors, for their part, were delighted by the dazzling hospitality they received and the warmth of the public reception. Mrs Kennedy, above all, was a succès fou – thanks to her charm, style (Givenchy as a compliment to her hosts), good French and knowledge of French history.* Jack Kennedy introduced himself to the press as "the man who accompanies Jacqueline Kennedy to Paris, and I have enjoyed it".[24]

---

* Khrushchev was not so bowled over by Mrs Kennedy when they met in Vienna. He thought she did not have "that special, brilliant beauty which can haunt men". (Did Mrs Khrushchev?) But she was "youthful, energetic, and pleasant, and I liked her".

After basking in splendour and popularity, Kennedy now had to brace himself to face Khrushchev – physically, too, since he was suffering acute back pain. He was, thought Schlesinger, hoping to get "a standstill in the Cold War" and persuade Khrushchev that the United States must "not be crowded" over Berlin. Last-minute advice came to him in Paris, recommending less lofty ambitions. Averell Harriman told him not to try to settle anything: talk gently about each other's view of the world, he suggested, be relaxed and make jokes. As the American party set off to fly to Vienna, Thompson added a final warning: "Avoid ideology, because Khrushchev will talk circles round you." The inexperienced President would have done well to pay heed.[25]

For at the very first meeting with Khrushchev, in the American embassy on 3 June, he positively leapt into ideological debate. The talk began pleasantly enough: the two men remembered meeting in 1959 at the Foreign Relations Committee; they exchanged formal phrases about the desirability of peace. Then Khrushchev expressed the opinion that the United States should recognise that Communism existed and had a right to develop. This was clearly not intended as a challenge – he immediately added that he would not try to convert the President and the President should not waste time trying to convert him. But Kennedy tried to do just that. The Soviet Union, he argued, was attempting to eliminate free systems in areas associated with the United States; people should have free choice and the struggle for the victory of ideas must not affect vital security interests. Khrushchev constantly interrupted: the Soviet Union was not trying to enforce its policies, Communism would triumph anyway, the struggle against ideas provoked conflict and history would judge Communism and capitalism by their results. He gave Kennedy a chance to drop the futile dispute: each side believed in its own system, he suggested, and that was not a matter for argument, much less for war. The President did not take the chance. He ploughed on with his thesis. He was patently nettling the Soviet leader; then suddenly, if unintentionally, he provoked him: he warned against "miscalculation" when both sides had weapons of mass destruction. The very word was a red rag to Khrushchev who had been keeping his temper with unusual restraint so far. To Soviet ears it was imbued with threat and suggestions of ineptitude. That was "a vague, misleading term", he snapped, and should not be used; the Soviet Union would defend its interests but did not want war.[26]

Lunch was an awkward affair. The President asked Khrushchev about the medals he was wearing. They were Lenin Peace medals. "I hope you keep them," he commented – not a remark calculated to reduce tension. Khrushchev paid polite tribute to American technology and the youth of the President, but added that at sixty-seven years of age he was not retiring from competition. Before resuming formal talks, Kennedy suggested a quiet walk in the garden, remembering how the Soviet leader had relaxed outdoors at Camp David. Fresh air did not cool the atmosphere. Khrushchev complained about American support for German reunification and explained that his son had been killed by the Germans; so had his own brother, the President flashed back. But when Kennedy tried to lighten the conversation with a little chatter about overworked leaders (forgetting advice about avoiding banalities) and asked how Khrushchev found so much time for American visitors, all he got was a smug rejoinder that the Soviet system was blessedly "decentralised" and that the United States should adopt it. The afternoon talk – private with just the two interpreters present – was as antagonistic as the morning session. The two men argued about Laos and Cuba; Khrushchev accused Kennedy of support for "reactionaries", Kennedy asked what the Soviet reaction would be to a free regime in Poland. And he again referred to "miscalculation" which again provoked a fiery response. When Khrushchev left the US embassy at 6.45 the President asked Thompson "Is it always like this?" "Par for the course," the ambassador assured him. Kennedy should have known. He had talked to the experts, been given so many transcripts. If anything, Khrushchev had given him an easy ride. It might have been even easier if he had accepted advice, not least from Thompson.[27]

He followed a little of it next morning, at talks in the Soviet embassy with full teams present. He asked Khrushchev where he came from, which allowed a long happy boast about the Ukraine and its wondrous resources of iron ore. There was then a useful exchange of views about Laos and Khrushchev agreed that there should be moves to a cease-fire. But stormy winds began to blow when they got down to discussing test bans (the Soviet leader described more than three inspections a year as "espionage") and the UN (which he said had failed to be neutral in the Congo and must now be run by a troika of East, West and non-aligned members). Khrushchev's tempest really raged once the conversation turned to Berlin. Sixteen years had passed since the end of the war in which twenty million Russians had died, he exclaimed; it was time to sign a peace treaty; only German militarists gained from the delay, their generals held office in NATO and threatened a third world war. He insisted that a treaty must recognise the "reality", the existence of two German states; he wanted to sign it with Kennedy, but otherwise would reach a separate agreement with the GDR, and then all existing rights would be invalidated, West Berlin would be a "free city" and allied troops would remain only if Soviet forces joined them. Kennedy tried to explain calmly that the United States had rights in Berlin ("contractual rights" he called them) and had made commitments; that Berlin involved American security; that leaving the city would be regarded as deserting Europe. Khrushchev retorted with the obvious jibe: if American security was involved in Berlin, the Americans might just as well claim Moscow – that would certainly improve their situation.[28]

The President made a firm statement of determination to stay in Berlin – then wrecked it by adding that the situation there was not "satisfactory" and that Eisenhower had called it "abnormal". Khrushchev seized the openings: in that case the United States must show itself willing to "normalise the most dangerous spot in the world"; the Soviet Union wanted to eliminate "this thorn, this ulcer" and impede "those who want war". No force in the world, he declared, could stop him signing a treaty; no delay was necessary or tolerable. Why did the United States want to prolong the state of war? Why did the Americans want Berlin? To unleash war from the city? If a war started over Berlin, the USSR would fight for peace. If the United States wanted war, so be it. The President kept trying to intervene, to argue that the Russians could transfer their own rights to the GDR but not those of others, that the United States did not want to precipitate a crisis. But Khrushchev thundered on.

Kennedy had totally mishandled the exchange. He had admitted that the Berlin status quo was not normal, stated commitment to the western sectors but not to the city as a whole, and he had not taken up several hints from Khrushchev that an interim agreement might be found. By warning the Soviet leader that there must be no attempt to disturb the balance of power in Europe, he had challenged the "inevitable victory" of socialism on the Continent, the military and technological strength of the Soviet Union and Khrushchev's own prickly pride. Yet the argument over this issue was very revealing: Khrushchev was drawn to say that he wanted no change in Europe, just "formalisation of the situation resulting from the war": recognition of the Polish and Czech borders, acceptance of East German sovereignty and frontiers. He had expressed openly what many had long guessed underlay his entire European, and specifically Berlin, policy.

As they adjourned for lunch after nearly four hours of grim set-to, Kennedy told his aides that he wanted a short private conversation with Khrushchev that afternoon to check the Soviet position and make sure his own was fully understood. Lunch itself was disagreeable, with barbed comments from each of the leaders about disarmament, defence cuts and Laos. There was the ritual exchange of presents – a Czech porcelain coffee service for a model of the USS *Constitution*, but perhaps a swop of poisoned chalices would have been more appropriate. The afternoon session was merely a résumé of the morning's conversation but, if anything, couched in stronger, clearer terms. Kennedy expressed the hope that the two countries could avoid confrontation and that the Soviet Union would not present a situation which involved American interests. Khrushchev warned that if the United States insisted on its occupation rights after a treaty and violated the land, water or air borders of the GDR, the USSR would defend its own interests and force would be met with force – it was up to the United States to choose peace or war. The President at last explored a few details of a possible interim agreement. They were far from attractive: it would last only six months, Khrushchev declared, and thereafter all occupation troops must be withdrawn from Berlin and the East Germans would control access. Unless these proposals were accepted, he added, he would sign a separate treaty with the GDR in December. In that case, replied the President, "It will be a cold winter."

Kennedy was shattered by his encounter with Khrushchev and horrified by the prospect of crisis which it had opened up. He drove back to the American embassy that evening patently upset. This personal Summit seemed to have brought both sides to the Brink, and the President, it appeared, had no confidence that his opponent would step back first, no feeling that Khrushchev's bullying and threats were just "par for the course". When he arrived in London next day, Macmillan found him "rather stunned – baffled would perhaps be fairer, and obviously impressed and shocked by Khrushchev's views". Macmillan was the perfect paramedic for such a wounded President: he knew all too well what it was like to be mauled by Khrushchev. They settled down to sandwiches and whisky and a post mortem on Vienna, a cosy chat which set the seal on their personal relationship. Kennedy once told a journalist that he felt at home with Macmillan: "I can share my loneliness with him. The others are all foreigners to me." He appreciated his combination of informality and high aristocratic style. Macmillan admired Kennedy's courage, confidence and courtesy and, as on this occasion, readiness to take blame and responsibility. He relished his own position as the older man holding forth to the attentive, powerful young leader and enjoyed his "quick, well-informed, subtle mind", though sometimes worried that he "proceeds more by asking questions than by answering them".[29]

President Kennedy told James Reston of the *New York Times* that the last session with Khrushchev had been the "toughest thing in my life"; the Soviet leader had decided he was young, inexperienced and easy meat, "so he just beat the hell out of me". (Macmillan wondered if it was the first time the President had ever met anyone on whom his charm failed to work.) For weeks after returning to Washington he read the transcripts of the talks and quoted them at length to visitors. He was still shocked by Khrushchev's brutality, though if he had compared his own experience with those of other victims, he might have drawn the conclusion that Khrushchev had been almost temperate by Kremlin standards. The Vienna experience had been a bitter blow to his self-confidence (so soon after the Cuban débâcle) and to his optimism that he could establish a working relationship with Khrushchev and "take the hysteria" out of the Cold War, indeed it gave the impression that the opposite had occurred. Vice-President Lyndon B. Johnson commented that Khrushchev had "scared the poor little fellow dead". The British ambassador, Sir Harold Caccia, worried about what would happen next: Kennedy had so far used all the right phrases about Berlin but had not created any "co-ordinated central direction and decision" for handling the problem and had failed to prepare the American people for the fact that "they might have to look forward to a national emergency rather than a summer holiday". The President had spoken in Vienna of a "cold winter"; many now expected a painfully hot summer.[30]

By contrast – and contrary to the assumption of the American team who had been in Vienna – Khrushchev seems to have formed a warm opinion of Kennedy. He said in his memoirs he had found him "a better statesman than Eisenhower" (the U-2 was never forgotten or forgiven), but gave as evidence that Rusk had never been consulted throughout the talks as Dulles had been. He paid tribute to Kennedy's "precisely formulated opinion on every subject" and his son remembered that Khrushchev felt he had met "a worthy partner and strong statesman, as well as a simple, charming man to whom he took a real liking", someone "with whom we could do business". (It has to be remembered that the Soviet aim in doing business was always to get the best of the bargain.) On reflection, Khrushchev can hardly have been entirely pleased with the results of their meeting, however enjoyable it might have been to score off the President for a couple of days. His adversary had shown no signs of sympathy for his own version of peaceful coexistence and no desire to turn Cold War swords into ploughshares to aid Soviet technology and trade. He had failed to lure Kennedy into negotiations over Berlin, by which he could have caused ructions in the western alliance and weakened the allied position in the city. He had issued a new ultimatum and, since his threats were beginning to sound unconvincing to many friends and foes alike, he might have to act on it and take major political and military risks. And it is probably true to say that Khrushchev had made a serious miscalculation at Vienna. He had made Kennedy's blood run cold, but after the initial shock the President rallied and resolved to confront Khrushchev in Berlin. He returned to Washington with a clear message: the Administration must "get all its ducks in a row".[31]

The Washington ducks, however, were not components in a simple machine. They were free-range and capricious and needed careful handling to get them lined up and facing in the same direction. It was to take several weeks for policies to emerge, nearly two months before they were co-ordinated. The President himself insisted on supervising every detail: strategic and diplomatic policy, military and economic plans, negotiating proposals and financial estimates. The often floated idea of a Berlin Task Force, to co-ordinate the work of numerous agencies and sift all their material, was resisted by several Departments and not insisted on by the White House. (It was not sanctioned until 17 July.) Instead, according to one old Berlin hand in the State Department: "Kennedy was the Berlin Desk officer. The difficulty was that he couldn't devote full time to it." He was impatient too: officials grumbled that they found it difficult to provide quick but sound answers to half-formulated questions. They also complained about his failure to understand that Khrushchev's Vienna threats were just the latest in a long process of crisis – an official like Foy Kohler at the German desk in the State Department struggled to act as "the continuity factor" and "to explain and indeed defend, the plans which had been developed over the past years". That did not make him popular in the White House.[32]

The immediate task – the one the President expected to be simple – was to reply to a Soviet aide-mémoire, presented at Vienna, which summarised Khrushchev's stark demands. On 15 June Rusk and Home agreed there must be a tripartite response. As joint discussion and drafting went on, Home's advice was taken: "keep Khrushchev in play", leave a door open for further talks with the Soviet leader. It was also realised that, since military action or widespread economic measures might have to be taken, the final reply must be submitted to NATO. Kennedy seemed totally unaware of the complexity and international ramifications involved. He was vexed by the delay. And when he finally read a draft reply on 4 July he was exasperated by what appeared to be "a compilation of stale, tedious and negative phrases", a "turgid rehash" – and infinitely too long for his taste. He asked Theodore Sorensen to rewrite it, clearly and simply. Sorensen knew his President's mind and wrote many of his most eloquent speeches, but was hardly qualified for such a technical job. Once his version was finished, the White House at last grasped that it could not be given draft approval by the allies without repeating the whole consultation process. The final rendering – unliterary, long, circumspect but acceptable to the professionals – was not ready until 18 July. Jack Kennedy, usually so ready to take blame, never forgave the State Department for this pickle, some of which was of his own boiling.[33]

Meanwhile Dean Acheson had been commissioned to write another report, this time on ways to counter Soviet action in Berlin. He took barely two weeks: it was complete by 29 June. Again his premise was that Berlin was a test of resolution. Negotiations should only take place after convincing Khrushchev that the balance of power was not in his favour and they must ensure a permanent, not an interim, settlement. He recommended low-key but open measures to stress the seriousness of American intent: bringing military reserves up to battle readiness and US forces in Europe to full strength with all necessary air support and combat supplies; the navy should be ready to force Soviet ships back into port. SACEUR (Supreme Allied Commander Europe), General Norstad, must have tight control over nuclear warheads to prevent premature escalation; civil defence must be stepped up to cope with possible nuclear hostilities. There must be plans for a NATO trade embargo on the entire Soviet bloc. Acheson wanted his proposals to be implemented in stages to influence Soviet moves up to the Federal German election in September, then to the separate treaty threatened for the end of the year. Full action, in his opinion, should not be launched at the moment the East Germans took control of access – the stamping of documents was not an adequate justification. But if military access was blocked on land, then troops should be moved by air, trading shot for shot if there was interference in the corridors. If civilian access was prevented, an airlift and the full range of economic measures should be introduced. Unless an initial probe by an armed battalion on the Autobahn was quickly effective it must be followed by a substantial force to demonstrate determination – the JCS now reckoned this would involve seven divisions with air support. All this would be expensive. The President must put the case to Congress and obtain the funding. The public must be informed of the full importance and urgency of the Berlin issue.[34]

When Acheson presented these views in person to the National Security Council on 29 June the President, who had spoken of a confrontation over Berlin, was clearly shaken by what it might entail. He addressed few of the points in Acheson's report and instead asked anxious questions about matters which had not been covered: was insistence on German reunification viable? should there be an all-German plebiscite? what would be the effect of military build-ups by both sides? What, he suddenly thought, if Khrushchev proposed a Summit this summer? Acheson had no difficulty with that one: suggest lower level talks first – there were plenty of "elderly, unemployed people like himself who could be sent to interminable meetings", and personally he could talk without negotiating "for three months on end". Kennedy made no decisions; he put yet more questions instead. There were to be enquiries about the legislation needed to provide presidential powers for a mounting crisis. The Department of Defence was asked for its views on preparations for military and civil airlifts, naval measures, conventional ground action and the readiness of Strategic Air Command. The Departments of the Treasury and Commerce were to assess the impact of Acheson's proposals on the economy and balance of payments, the State Department would examine a negotiating position, develop a timetable for the application of counter measures, consult the Germans about a plebiscite and oversee all the other studies. Six months into the Administration, two and a half years after Khrushchev's ultimatum, over two weeks since a new six-month deadline was set for a settlement, Kennedy had still not got his ducks in a row. He was once more asking for thorough review and ignoring long-standing options, expecting novel answers to historic problems, looking for action where a de Gaulle or Adenauer would have recommended doing nothing. And he had given his staff and officials just two weeks to formulate a policy.[35]

Did he have even that long? Public statements and diplomatic nudges from the Soviet Union suggested not. Throughout the month they had marked an abrupt acceleration to crisis. On 10 June Moscow had published the Vienna aide-mémoire. This meant that Khrushchev was openly committed to his demands and it snuffed the last hopes in allied circles that he might back down quietly or let the Berlin matter ride until after the Federal German elections or the October Party Congress. On 15 June Khrushchev announced his deadline for a full agreement or separate treaty on radio and television and backed it with threats against violation of another country's borders: "We have the means to defend our interests." A speech he made on 21 June repeated the warnings and was delivered in the uniform of a lieutenant general. An address to a North Vietnamese delegation in the Kremlin on 28 June dismissed the idea that Soviet resolve could be shaken by western diplomatic or economic sanctions or by the mobilisation of armed forces. He insisted that Soviet demands were reasonable and that he was ready to negotiate, on condition that the status quo was not frozen by time-wasting talks and that the existence of two distinct Germanies was recognised. The Soviet leader's tone was strident, his stance belligerent. That was conventional Kremlin style. Should a western probe have been made to test whether there was some softening under this carapace, whether head-on confrontation could be avoided?[36]

It is very likely that Khrushchev himself was under pressure while he piled it on the Western Powers and on the United States in particular. He undoubtedly felt he had to follow an aggressive policy to please his domestic and Chinese critics. At the same time he must have been aware of the rapidly deteriorating situation in the GDR: 16,094 people had left the country in March; 19,803 went West in April; 17,791 in May. At a press conference on 16 June Ulbricht was unusually frank in admitting to the refugee problem and vowed that once a treaty was signed at the end of the year, the "trading in people" would end, reception camps in the western sectors would have to close and movement from one German state to the other would take place "in a legal manner". The GDR, he added ominously, would control air communications – and most refugees left Berlin by air. Western analysts were quick to spot the risk Ulbricht had taken in forewarning of rigid controls: the chances were that more East Germans would try to get out while the West Berlin route was open.[37]

Hardly any observer noticed an exchange later in the press conference, let alone pondered its significance. In answer to a question from the correspondent of the *Frankfurter Rundschau*, "Does the creation of a 'free city' mean that the state border would be erected at the Brandenburg Gate and have you decided to take into account all the consequences this will bring?", Ulbricht replied stiltedly, "I understand your question to mean that there are people in West Germany who wish us to mobilise the construction workers of the capital of the DDR to build a wall. It is not known to me that such an intention exists. [The construction workers] chiefly occupy themselves with building homes, and their capacity for such work is fully used. Nobody has the intention of building a wall." "Wall". Was the word merely used to suggest that the question was ridiculous? Was it a Freudian slip out of a mind preoccupied with building one? Had Ulbricht told a blatant lie? Or was he deliberately giving hints to East Germans who were so adept at interpreting them: talking about walls, closing camps and controlling civilian movement to encourage a mass exodus so as to wring final approval from the Kremlin for slamming the Berlin exit?

Western journalists at the press conference paid no attention to these comments, nor did anyone else when the full details of the session were printed in *Neues Deutschland* next day. Official cables to the western capitals make no mention of them. One man however, Colonel Ernst von Pawel of the US Military Mission in Potsdam, had been struck by the word "wall". It reminded him of how the Germans had walled in the Warsaw Ghetto. There were plenty of rumours flying around that construction materials were being stockpiled in the GDR – but in a country with a huge home-building programme and new collectives to be provided with fences, granaries and dairies this was not necessarily sinister. However, the two thoughts clicked in his mind. He talked to officials at the US Mission in Berlin about the possibility of a walled frontier across the western sector boundary. They were not very interested. It sounded like another of the wild speculations which so often afflicted Berlin thinking. Everyone was coming round to the view that Ulbricht would have to do something to check the refugee flow soon. But they were thinking in terms of interference with communications to the western sectors, speedy Soviet moves to get sovereignty for the state, tighter border controls. Not walls. Walls were unthinkable.

In any case, attention was concentrated on other, older, threats. On 6 July the East German Volkskammer, broadcast live, discussed a Peace Plan of the German People for settlement by an all-German commission, but mentioned no deadline and stressed the need for negotiation with the West. Two days later the GDR's propaganda chief warned that any attempt to embargo trade between East and West Germany would result in a new Blockade; a few days after that the East German Deputy Prime Minister emphasised that the GDR would take over air as well as land routes once a treaty was signed. In Moscow Khrushchev tried another tack. On 2 July he went to the opening of a season by the Royal Ballet from London accompanied by Gromyko, Mikoyan, Kosygin and Brezhnev and with as much interest in British ballet as he had had in American ice shows. The British ambassador, Sir Frank Roberts, was invited to his box during the long intervals and after the performance and soon realised he was expected to "convey a very serious, solemn and personal warning to HM Government and personally to the Prime Minister": that the dangers inherent in the German problem must not be underestimated. Khrushchev set a chilling atmosphere with his first remark: he had promised Macmillan a hunting expedition this winter but it could not take place if they were shooting at each other rather than at elk. The balance of power, he insisted, had changed; modern wars were fought with nuclear weapons and ten nuclear bombs could destroy Britain and France. If the Western Powers tried to force their way to West Berlin after a treaty, there would be war but surely it was ridiculous to die for a couple of million West Berliners. He rejected Roberts' suggestion that negotiations could be taken up from where they left off at Geneva: the 1959 basis, he retorted, was no longer applicable; there must be a treaty, "free city" and East German control of access. Roberts left the theatre "with the very definite feeling that he had made up his mind and will not easily be deterred by any action open to us".[38]

The message he had been given was no doubt designed to encourage

British pressure on the western alliance through Macmillan, its most nervous member. It served another purpose. It was witnessed by the cream of the Soviet foreign affairs establishment. Next, Khrushchev assured the armed services of the weight he gave to his policy. In a speech on 8 July to graduates of military academies, he announced an increase of one third in the budget of the Soviet armed forces and cancelled the reduction of troops planned for 1961. He railed against recent American increases in defence spending, accused Adenauer of "repeating what Hitler did in his day when preparing for war" and promised that a war would "end with imperialism's complete collapse and ruin". Significantly, however, Khrushchev called on western leaders to "display wisdom in the solution of the German problem", to "attend a conference" and "conclude a peace treaty". Was he trying to avert a showdown or merely trying to shift blame for one on to the West? If there were talks, would he negotiate in some spirit of compromise or was this military escalation another coercive step to get the settlement he wanted? Should the West have probed quietly to find out?[39]

Khrushchev's campaign coincided with the moment when the Washington debate on Berlin policy was coming to a head. Acheson's hard line was backed by the CIA, the Joint Chiefs of Staff and the Berlin professionals in the State Department such as Foy Kohler, the Assistant Secretary for European Affairs. Acheson himself vehemently resented the fact that his 29 June programme had not been implemented immediately. He had long been critical of Kennedy: somehow, he wrote to Truman, he managed to give the "appearance of a President" but he and Rusk were "better when they make speeches than when they act". Now he was broadcasting his disparagement: the British ambassador reported on his "somewhat understandable frustration at finding it difficult to get the President to make decisions" and his irritation with Kennedy's "disconcerting habit of going off at a tangent" in discussions. Macmillan, who had been so horrified by Acheson's first report, jotted: "Does the Ambassador not realise that Dean Acheson's eclipse is likely to be a good thing."[40]

Others who would have been happy to see him blotted out included many of those with easiest access to the President, such as Sorensen and Schlesinger, Soviet experts like Thompson and Harriman, or the State Department Legal Adviser Abram Chayes and Henry Kissinger, a consultant to the National Security Council. They argued that Khrushchev could be blocked by determined diplomatic action backed by a low-level military build-up. Adlai Stevenson, ambassador at the UN, expressed a widespread belief: "maybe Dean is right, but he starts at a point which we

should not reach until we have explored and exhausted all the alternatives"; Carl Kaysen of the NSC put a common fear: the present military
strategy only allowed for a "one-shot response with our nuclear forces", not
for limited actions. On television on 14 June Senator Mike Mansfield
criticised the Berlin hard line and called for an agreement on a free city of
all-Berlin safeguarded by international peace teams. (Khrushchev accused
him of losing a "sense of reality" in including "democratic Berlin", the
"capital" of the GDR.) There was a strong suspicion in Washington that
Acheson, who had been blamed for causing the Korean war by seeming to
dismiss North Korea as outside the American sphere of interest, was now
playing tough in compensation. No one wondered if he was recommending
a version of the western tactics used so successfully during the Blockade in
1948–9 or asked if they might be just as effective again.[41]

Schlesinger later decided that "the early terms of the debate were
artificial": Acheson was not entirely opposed to negotiation, but wanted it
in a context of strong western purpose; his opponents had "illusions as to
what negotiation might accomplish". But on 7 July, knowing that Kennedy
was going to discuss the 29 June proposals that weekend with Rusk,
McNamara and Taylor, Schlesinger put his misgivings about them into
a memo for the President, suggesting that in the Acheson thesis "the test of
will becomes an end in itself rather than a means to a political end". He
raised questions about what specific military and political moves should be
made as the crisis developed, and threw out ideas about so far unpredicted
Soviet actions (such as a separate treaty without interference with access)
and non-military ways to put pressure on the Soviet Union. It seized the
President's attention. Kennedy asked for an unsigned memo on all the
unexplored Berlin issues. That afternoon Schlesinger sat at a typewriter
while Chayes and Kissinger dictated one. It caught the last helicopter to
Hyannis Port.[42]

There, the President was on his yacht and in high dudgeon with Rusk
about the State Department's delay in replying to the Soviet aide-mémoire
from Vienna and about the plight of military planning which left NATO
with only fifteen or sixteen divisions on the entire central front facing
twenty Soviet divisions in East Germany alone. Rusk was given ten days to
come up with a new set of negotiating proposals; McNamara got the same
deadline to devise an adequate plan for non-nuclear demonstrations of
American determination which would give the Soviet Union time for
second thoughts. More ducks to get in a row, and in a hurry, on the very
day Khrushchev had announced a military build-up and intensified the
crisis to which the Administration still had no clear answers after six and a
half months in power.

When the National Security Council met on 13 July it reviewed the range of options prepared in response to the Acheson report. Rusk agreed with Acheson that the United States was not in a good position to negotiate and wanted more consideration of allied economic counter measures. McNamara proposed a programme of national emergency: calling up reserves, extending the service of those on duty, evacuating dependants from Europe and requesting Congress for a further increase in the military budget. Rusk was nervous about a policy dangerously near to mobilisation; Acheson was all in favour of calling up reserves and wanted their training to begin no later than August. There were worries about costs, allied readiness to match the American effort, Congress cutting the foreign aid budget if asked for higher defence expenditure. No concrete decisions were made. Instead, the President called for yet more studies, costings for each and every option, discussions with the allies. Even in a smaller meeting afterwards he was unwilling to state a preference for any of the alternatives available. He told Rusk "there are two things which matter: our presence in Berlin and our access to Berlin"; McNamara was informed that the United States would use force only if West Berlin were threatened directly. Kennedy had either abandoned or never understood the quadripartite status of the city.[43]

There followed five days of feverish departmental activity and hails of memos encapsulating every point of view. Most influential among them was a strong recommendation from Sorensen against declaring a national emergency – he called it later "an alarm bell which could only be rung once". In his paper – short, crisp and action-directed, just as the President liked – he argued that such an extreme step would push Khrushchev to a showdown, might frighten the allies into insisting on disadvantageous negotiations, and encourage critics who accused the United States of being trigger happy. What Sorensen wanted was a series of civil defence measures, allied machinery for applying sanctions, a build-up of West Berlin supplies and preparations for an airlift, plus a strongly worded Presidential public address to explain the issues to the people, make American determination obvious to others and give the Soviet Union an opening for talks. Given this view, plus a suggestion by McNamara that no emergency need be declared before September or October, and recommendations from top advisers at meetings on 17 and 18 July Kennedy was nudged to compromise. He told the Joint Chiefs on 18 July that he must not overreact, that a national emergency must be held in reserve until circumstances justified it, and that he accepted Thompson's advice that the Soviet Union would be just as impressed by firm, low-key moves.[44]

With his basic approach established, Kennedy was now at last ready to make decisions. First in a small group, then at a full NSC meeting on 19 July, they rolled out. Six additional divisions would be steadily moved to Europe, supported by air units, but as yet the National Guard and reserves would not be called up; Congress would be asked for a $3.2 billion budget increase ($207 million of it for civil defence); negotiations would begin with the allies on a matching military contribution and with "no initial indication of any US willingness to increase military assistance" to them; approval was given to existing plans for economic sanctions as retaliation for interference with access; and the President called for immediate allied review of airlift plans and the Berlin stockpile. He would address the nation by radio and television on 25 July.[45]

This, for Acheson, was neither fish, fowl nor good red herring. He was reported to have told colleagues: "Gentlemen, you may as well face it. This nation is without leadership." Later he wrote in despair to Truman: "We shall have to run a grave risk of danger by preparations for ground action . . . to convince Khrushchev that by pressing too far he might force us into a nuclear response" – that was the only way to make him negotiate. But such a prospect filled the President's mind with dread of imminent nuclear war. He had done what he could to avert it as long as possible but had not backed down from a confrontation with Khrushchev over Berlin. His policy ducks were at long last in a row and all pointing in the direction he had chosen.[46]

Was it the right direction? Was an entirely different crisis looming – not the expected one over a treaty, access and western rights in Berlin? Should much more attention in June and July have been directed to events in the city itself?

The situation there had become truly alarming. The cause was refugees: 17,791 had crossed to the West in May; 19,198 in June. That was disturbing enough. But during the first two weeks of July alone 12,578 arrived in West Berlin and in the next seven days there were nearly 9,000 more. On 3 July there was an emergency session of the SED Central Committee with Warsaw Pact ambassadors in attendance. Ulbricht told the meeting of the dreadful refugee figures and admitted that they were rising in spite of all propaganda and stiffer travel restrictions. Speeches from the floor described the effects of this flood on local economies; some blamed collectivisation, others castigated bad state planning in industry. Comparisons were drawn with the catastrophic year – 1953.[47]

The mounting influx of refugees was an immense burden on West Berlin: facilities for screening and medical checks were strained to the limit;

Allied officials at the Marienborn reception camp were working seven days a week; the Senate was preparing barracks for extra living accommodation and asking private citizens to provide rooms. Civilian airlines had so far taken about 800 people a day to the Federal Republic, and could not clear the backlog until they increased their capacity to 1,500 a day. What more could West Berlin do? As Brandt put it, "We cannot sit here in safety and say to the people over there 'don't come'." But Ernst Lemmer, Federal Minister for All-German Affairs, broadcast a radio message to the East German government appealing for better living conditions in the GDR, guaranteed freedom of movement and slackening of collectivisation so as to persuade people to stay put. Instead the regime added to the flow of refugees by denouncing Grenzgänger, East Germans with jobs in the western sectors, as "anti-social elements". An obsolete decree was re-introduced to force them to register their place of employment and apply for permission to go to it or face fines and imprisonment; those from Berlin were told that if they continued to work in the West they would not get new flats in East Berlin; there was a government order that luxuries (cars, motor bikes, televisions, fridges and so on which Grenzgänger could afford because they were paid in West marks) could only be bought on production of proof of employment in the East. The entirely predictable result of the campaign was that in July six times as many Grenzgänger as usual left the GDR permanently.[48]

The West Berlin word to describe the great surge of refugees was "Torschlusspanik" – terror of the gate closing. This sudden rush to emigrate was motivated not by drab living conditions or recent food shortages but by fear that it would soon be impossible to leave. It had been stimulated by government propaganda about an imminent separate treaty and East German control over communications, boosted by drum beating in the Kremlin and the decision to increase the Soviet armed forces. East Germans expected either tighter travel restrictions or war. They wanted to get out and as far away as they could. The Western Powers had offered them no reassurance, no hope for their future in the GDR. The long official silence from Washington had been taken to mean that the United States would accept Soviet and GDR moves passively; perversely, a string of leaks in the American press about contingency plans to reopen access by force, possible mobilisation and the movement of NATO stockpiles to ready positions were enough to inspire panic in themselves.[49]

By mid-July there was intense anxiety in Bonn and West Berlin that the flight of refugees might no longer be an adequate safety valve for discontent: a new East German uprising was likely. The US ambassador cabled to Washington for guidance. The State Department discovered there was no up-to-date NSC policy for dealing with disorder or revolt, but agreed that if Pankow imposed severe restrictions on travel, serious unrest was probable. The Department decided that the United States must avoid any action or statement which would provoke it, for all that staying on the sidelines would damage American influence in Germany and would not necessarily deter Federal or individual intervention to help an uprising. It was conceivable that Khrushchev would allow the present flow of refugees to continue while he pressed for a quick settlement, but if the East Germans acted to stem it there must be no American counter action "so long as these measures do not involve the division of Berlin, and access to West Berlin is not interfered with". (Note the stipulation about division of Berlin. Policy was very different when it happened.) Allan Lightner at the US Mission in Berlin agreed with the "hands-off" approach, but reported Brandt's belief that if a separate treaty seemed likely by the end of the year, up to four million refugees might come to the West; he himself wondered if this would force Khrushchev to back down. Thompson reckoned that the Soviet Union might try to open talks soon, in the hope of reducing the flow. He also suggested – and it was an opinion others were reaching – that if the Communist authorities closed the Berlin boundary, it was "unlikely [that] counter measures could be successful" (he underlined this phrase). Given a separate treaty it was "far better for us that the East Germans close [the] Berlin sector border than that they attempt to interfere with our access by air" (though he did not explain why they would not do both).[50]

Against that background of mounting fear among East Germans and intensifying anxiety among West Germans and allied officials, Jack Kennedy appeared on radio and television on the evening of 25 July to tell the American people and the world of his decisions to call up reserves, strengthen US forces, build fall-out shelters and, if need be, to ask Congress for increased powers and taxes. His speech was broadcast live from his office in the White House (the performance, Sorensen thought, "hampered by the overcrowded, overheated" room), and it was heard in Berlin from 3.00 in the morning. It was grave in its assessment of the momentousness of the crisis, and restrained but resolute in its call for sacrifice, unity and determination to sustain peace and freedom. The President spoke of West Berlin as "a showcase of liberty", a "beacon of hope behind the Iron Curtain", "an escape hatch for refugees", but above all as "the great testing place of western courage and will": the place where "our solemn commitments" and "Soviet ambitions now meet in basic confrontation". "We don't want to fight", the President began one sentence, but there was no Jingoism in what he said thereafter, only steady conviction: "We cannot and will not permit the Communists to drive us out of Berlin, either gradually or by force"; western rights and the people's freedoms must be defended. "We will at all times be ready to talk, if talk will help" but must not "leave it to others to choose and monopolise the forum and the framework of discussion".

Kennedy had laboured on his speech: drafted and redrafted, added ideas and resounding phrases from his advisers, handed it for rewriting to Sorensen, then sat in bed at the last moment with a hot pad to his agonised back while he wrote the final touching phrases about the "heavy and constant burdens" of his office and the dangers of misjudgement in the thermonuclear age. But for all his own care, for all the sharp minds and eyes which had focused on the text, the wording of the speech was perilous. Time after time the President spoke of "West Berlin", not of "Berlin" or a four-Power city; he referred constantly to "western rights" of presence and access, never to eastern responsibilities; to "West" Berliners' rights to security and freedom not East Berliners' wishes; he never mentioned that control of the city by the four victorious allies was the basis of their control over the final peace of Europe. Only one conclusion could be drawn by those listening in the city, the GDR and Moscow: the United States had abandoned quadripartite duties and powers and the heart of the post-war settlement; the Communist authorities were free to do what they liked in the eastern sector.

There is no evidence that Kennedy had intended his broadcast to strike a bargain: "You leave us alone in our part of the city and we will leave you alone in yours." Nor does it seem he was aware of radically changing western policy. Over lunch on 24 July Sorensen had shown the final draft to James O'Donnell, a former *Newsweek* correspondent and long time resident in Berlin. O'Donnell immediately spotted the danger in talking only of "West" Berlin: "West" must be crossed out, he argued; the use of the word amounted to writing off the East. Sorensen seemed surprised by this reaction: he thought the speech said all that was needed; there was little point in claiming the eastern sector when the Russians had been allowed to do what they wanted there for years, especially since it was difficult enough to persuade the American public to defend West Berlin. Anyway, in his opinion, four-Power rights were not the nub of the matter. O'Donnell was deeply disturbed by another aspect of the speech too: a sentence which read "We have previously indicated our readiness to remove the actual irritants in West Berlin, but the freedom of that city is not negotiable." He tried to persuade Sorensen that the "irritants", by East German and Soviet interpretation, were fundamental democratic rights: free press and radio, free elections, free speech and assembly. He made no impact. He took his worries to Robert Kennedy who merely replied: "Jesus, Jim, we just can't be more German than the Germans themselves" – which more or less meant "nit-picking". After seven and a half months of examining every detail and aspect of the Berlin problem, did the Administration fully understand it? Had they decided, perhaps unconsciously, to ignore some of its more intractable elements?[51]

Khrushchev received reports on the Kennedy broadcast while holidaying at his villa on the Black Sea. With him was John J. McCloy, the first American High Commissioner in Germany from 1949, who was said to have been seriously disturbed by Khrushchev's "self-confident, aggressive and at times rude attitude". The Soviet leader denounced the speech as a declaration of "preliminary war", blustered that a war would be won by the biggest rockets and he had them, and warned that as a result, Kennedy would be the "last President of the United States". In quieter, if still unyielding moments, Khrushchev maintained that he believed in the President's "good sense", that the Western Powers would not fight for occupation rights, that there could be negotiations on access and the German problem. So far, at least, the speech had not shaken his position a fraction of an inch.[52]

Its big impact was in Berlin. Here, the refugee flow slackened slightly in the last week of July – about 200 fewer people crossed from the GDR. But no one thought the drop significant, let alone attributable to Kennedy's words, which were thought more likely to feed the panic. It was assumed that would-be refugees were just waiting to collect their pay packets at the end of the month. What was positively frightening about the figures was that so many had squeezed out in spite of a massive police presence at crossing points and railway stations and cuts in the number of trains from East Germany to East Berlin. The regime had loudly condemned those who left as "traitors to peace" and there had been a widely publicised trial of five East Germans accused of "the traffic in human beings" which ended in sentences of up to fifteen years' imprisonment. No one was surprised by a government official's call on 29 July for "temporary restrictions on what one can do and where one can go". All observers in Berlin, East and West, were now convinced that the East Germans would soon close the sector boundary.[53]

Pankow received unexpected encouragement to do so from an unlikely source. On 30 July Senator William Fulbright said on an American national television programme, "The truth of the matter is, I think, the Russians have the power to close it in any case . . . if they chose to close their border they could without violating any treaty. I don't understand why the East Germans don't close their border because I think they have a right to close it." These were staggering words from the chairman of the Senate Foreign Relations Committee – and were taken by the Communists as expressions of official policy. His remarks betrayed complete ignorance of all post-war agreements (there was no treaty to violate but from Potsdam onwards there had been repeated, even if ignored, commitments to freedom of movement). Fulbright called the Berlin sector boundary a border as if it defined two recognised sovereign states and not an administrative division; he gave the go-ahead to those who wished to seal it and implied impotence to stop them. There was an outburst of protest and indignation in the FRG and West Berlin. A Foreign Ministry official called Fulbright's remarks the "greatest mistake yet made by [a] western leader" during the whole Berlin crisis; the West Berlin newspaper *Tagesspiegel* spoke of a self-inflicted "moral defeat" and drew comparisons with Acheson's airy dismissal of North Korea and the outbreak of the Korean War; local politicians called the Senator's comments "morally and politically out of touch with reality". The East German press, on the other hand, carried headlines such as "US Senator Opposed to Slave Traders" and claimed he had called for the closure of refugee camps. Brandt knew all too well what the instant effect of the statement would be: he told the US Mission that the refugee flow would swell.[54]*

Without question, Ulbricht knew that too. On Monday 31 July he went to Moscow. There, it is said, Khrushchev turned down his request to block the air corridors, needed by the refugees to get out to the Federal Republic – such a move might well provoke war. Instead, the East German leader was given permission to close the sector boundary, but told to wait until after a meeting of the Warsaw Pact the following Thursday. Ulbricht's visit to Moscow was secret. But his absence from East Berlin was noticed, and everyone leapt to the same conclusion about where he was and why.[55]

Those who wanted to leave East Germany did not wait to hear what the Kremlin decision would be. On 2 August 1,096 people registered at the Marienfelde reception camp in West Berlin. Next day there were 1,306 more; a day later 1,292. This was a haemorrhage. Without an instant tourniquet it would be fatal to the GDR.

---

* Kennedy never repudiated Fulbright's remarks. The Senator himself, having put his foot in it on 30 July, tried to pull it out again in a statement to the Senate on 4 August admitting that his television interview had given "an unfortunate and erroneous impression", and that freedom of movement across Berlin was "guaranteed by post-war agreements". Too late.

9

Up to the Wire

———⟫●⟪———

As early as 28 June, when about five hundred and fifty people a day were leaving East Germany, a member of the GDR Politburo had called the refugee flow "a national disaster". Yet in the first four days of August 1961 that figure more than doubled; then on 5 August 1,688 refugees arrived at the Marienfelde reception centre in West Berlin, and next day 1,308. The numbers were swollen by Grenzgänger who had been told that from 1 August they must pay in West marks for their rent, gas, electricity and water in East Berlin (a ruling extended to all Grenzgänger from the GDR a few days later). In the week ending 5 August, 505 of them registered at Marienfelde, and these were just heads of family: wives and children were recorded separately. Most families, in fact, split before they crossed the border because they were so easily spotted by the East Germans. Marienfelde had an increasing proportion of miserable women and children waiting day after day to see if their husbands and fathers managed to join them; the S- and U-bahn stations in the western sectors were crowded with anxious relatives peering for loved ones in every train which came from the East. But it was reckoned that two or three men made the attempt to reach the West for every one who succeeded: those travelling alone, and especially young ones, were being pulled off Berlin-bound trains and often turned back with or without proof that they were trying to flee. There were six times as many the usual number of Grenzpos (Frontier Police) and Trapos (Transport Police) on duty in the East, checking papers and luggage; the main routes into Berlin had roadblocks for what was called a "traffic census", and the city sector crossing points were all strongly manned. It was no easy job for the East German police: the holiday season had started so roads and transport were crowded. It was not always a welcome job either: many policemen had every sympathy with those trying to leave and refugees often reported that they had managed to cross because the Vopos (People's Police) turned a blind eye.[1]

While Pankow waited for permission from the Kremlin to build a barrage across Berlin, the authorities used a weapon with which they were skilled. Fear. Vigilante groups were formed: "Fighting Committees against the Slave Trade", to round up anyone suspected of planning flight or helping refugees. In one country district, the names of local Grenzgänger were posted at stations and in shops under the heading "Against Peace"; many who worked in West Berlin were threatened with a new job on a collective farm. On 1 August, the East German Ministry of Health announced that several visitors from the FRG had been taken to hospital with suspected polio and that in view of the West German "epidemic", vaccine had been offered to Bonn but travel restrictions might have to be imposed on all movement between East and West and across Berlin. Fear, though, was a double-edged weapon. Bonn immediately retorted that the interzonal trade agreement depended on free movement; hundreds of people who had been considering flight decided to rush to the West while loopholes remained.[2]

And feeding the fear that those gaps would soon close was the knowledge that in the first week of August Walter Ulbricht was in Moscow. He had left Berlin without publicity on 31 July and his absence was first noticed when he did not appear at a GDR reception for Kwame Nkrumah, the Ghanaian head of state. Suspicion that he was asking for permission to close the border deepened when it was realised that Willy Stoph, the Prime Minister, and Lothar Bolz, the Foreign Minister, were missing too. (Days later news leaked that Andrei Smirnov, the Soviet ambassador in Bonn, had been recalled to his capital at the same time.) For nearly a week officials at the East German embassy in Moscow denied that Ulbricht and his ministers were there. Finally, they explained that he had come to a Warsaw Pact meeting. That meeting certainly took place, from 3 to 5 August. A communiqué was issued expressing the Pact's determination to have a peace settlement "before the end of this year" and promising unrestricted communications for a "free and demilitarised" West Berlin. But no one believed that these had been the only items on the agenda.[3]

Years later a story emerged of what had happened behind the scenes. It is as insubstantial as the account of the March meeting in the Kremlin. Yet again its only named source is Jan Sejna, the Czech Defence Minister, and the corroborative evidence comes from anonymous "western intelligence sources" who may well be the very people who debriefed and believed him or chose to use his version of events. Be that as it may, this account has rung true for many who knew the decision-making habits of the Kremlin and its allies, and the timing of the Pact meeting fits neatly with subsequent events. Conceivably not all of the debate attributed to the meeting actually took place on this occasion; undoubtedly, however, every pro and con was being carefully weighed around this time.

According to this story (small details of which vary according to who tells it), Ulbricht informed the Warsaw Pact leaders on Thursday 3 August of the disastrous impact of the refugee drain on the GDR's economy and warned that it would damage the whole Soviet trading bloc. He appealed to be allowed to seal the Berlin sector boundary. Some of those present are said to have expressed anxiety that closure might incite violence and questioned whether Pankow would be able to restrain its own population. Doubts were raised too about the argument put forward by Ulbricht and Khrushchev that the Western Powers would not retaliate unless the western sectors and allied rights were infringed. (Khrushchev is sometimes quoted as invoking Kennedy's behaviour in Vienna and speech of 25 July as well as Fulbright's remarks to prove this point.) There were predictions of an embargo on trade with the GDR by the Federal Republic and even the whole of NATO, which could injure East German and Soviet bloc economies quite as severely as the loss of labour. Ulbricht was then obliged to traipse back to East Berlin to check with his government on the ability of the police and army to control an uprising and on the availability of labour and materials for closing the boundary through Berlin itself and along the outer perimeter of the western sectors. When he returned to Moscow next day, 5 August, the facts and figures he provided satisfied the meeting that his plan was feasible. Khrushchev, however, would not permit the use of steel and concrete for plugging the border and insisted that only wire be used – presumably to test the reactions of the Western Powers with something that could be rapidly removed if it provoked hostility. A weekend would be the best time to carry out the operation: local and allied officials would be relaxed and Grenzgänger were not crossing. August was the ideal month because politicians, diplomats and military leaders were on holiday. The action could not be postponed for long since the GDR's lifeblood was draining away daily, but preparations would not be complete by the coming weekend. So the date fixed for the final closure was 12–13 August; the time, midnight.[4]

When Ulbricht flew to Moscow on 31 July to warn of the imminent collapse of the GDR, western officials were in Paris discussing contingency plans to meet threats to their Berlin presence and access. As the Warsaw Pact secretly debated and approved Ulbricht's proposal to seal off the sector boundary, the western Foreign Ministers were in the French capital from 4 to 6 August wrangling over the possibility of avoiding an East–West confrontation over Berlin by negotiating with the Kremlin. The allies were not blind to the fast brewing emergency in Berlin. They knew that within days, or weeks at the most, the East Germans would have to staunch the haemorrhage of emigrants. They certainly took no satisfaction in watching the GDR bleed to death. A Foreign Office official had written in late July: "We are not seeking to bring about the collapse of the East German regime through the departure of its most valuable citizens; on the contrary we (and this includes the Federal Republic) are embarrassed by the greatly increased flow of refugees." The disintegration of the GDR would destabilise the whole of Central Europe; the filling of the resultant vacuum would raise tension to a hazardous level for all. Unless Pankow got a grip on its frontiers and population, there seemed to be every likelihood of an East German uprising, possibly aided by West Germany, and with the Western Powers militarily damned if they joined in and politically damned if they stayed out. In Paris Foy Kohler, of the State Department, told his western colleagues that the United States would fight only for allied access to Berlin, for the security of its forces there, for the independence and viability of the western sectors, or in response to any attack on the FRG. Kohler did not refer to refugees or border closure. "Other things might be distasteful but could not be a case for war." Whether "distasteful" or not, his Administration's commitment to Berlin excluded quadripartite responsibility for the whole city and any political or humane duty to East Germans.[5]

When the refugee problem was raised during the first meeting of the western Foreign Ministers on 5 August, no one seems to have mentioned the virtual inevitability of border closure. There was nothing to say, because no one could think of anything to do about it. But by avoiding the issue the ministers had failed to prepare any response for when the time came. Instead they examined their preparations for the crisis they had been expecting for two and three-quarter years. The new Soviet deadline set at Vienna for a treaty "by the end of the year" had certainly concentrated their minds and they made some decisions which unkind observers might think they should have reached long since. For instance, it was at last agreed that the West Germans would be fully associated with contingency planning, economic counter measures and the Ambassadors' Group in Washington. The Americans had come to see advantages in buying time for diplomacy and political manoeuvring with an airlift.* All the Western Powers had gone round and round the hoary old question of whether to accept East German "agents" at checkpoints, and even Brentano now believed that there was no sense in staging a showdown over who wore what hat: East Germans would have to be treated as substitutes for Russians and the allies would try to persuade them to maintain existing checkpoint procedures.[6]

The Europeans preferred the limited four issues over which the United States was now prepared to fight to the undiscriminating gung-ho ideas which had come from the Joint Chiefs over the last months and years. They were reassured too by the new American policy of strengthening conventional forces, and making slowly escalating responses to strain Soviet nerves and give the Kremlin time to change its mind before resort to nuclear weapons. Not that they were ready or able to make much contribution to the strategy. Brentano acknowledged that the Federal Republic ought to have nine combat-ready divisions by the end of 1961 and eleven the following year, but squirmed away from guaranteeing to provide them on the grounds that it was better to wait until his country's elections were over. Couve de Murville pointed out how heavily France was committed in Algeria but thought one good division could be recalled and converted for Europe by September and the tactical air force in Germany put on a twenty-four-hour operational basis; thereafter the best he could offer was to call up reservists within a week should a crisis occur. Lord Home pleaded involvement in Kuwait and the Far East as well as the impossibility of re-introducing conscription so soon after abolishing it. But he promised to form a new division in Britain, including armour, to bring back an armoured regiment from Hong Kong and brigade headquarters from Cyprus and to provide a surface to air guided missile regiment plus two light anti-aircraft regiments to improve the readiness of BAOR (British Army of the Rhine); for good measure Britain would leave three fighter squadrons in Germany which had been due for withdrawal, stiffen a Javelin squadron, and send a Canberra tactical bomber squadron to support SACEUR. If need be, reservists and Territorials could be mobilised within seventeen days. The Europeans were not scrimshanking, but they were more frightened of the political and financial dangers of

---

* There would be a lift, codenamed "Jack Pine I", to supply the allied garrisons if military access was blocked; this might be expanded to "Jack Pine II", with the use of tactical forces to keep the air corridors open and safe; plans would be drawn up for pre-emptive strikes on Soviet and East German airfields, ack-ack and missile sites. Plans already existed for civilian supply by air should all communications be cut and for the evacuation of garrison dependants and categories of West Berliners such as those who had worked for the allies or were politically vulnerable.

increasing their armed services than they were of the Soviet Union. Rusk could only try to impress on them the need for a quick demonstration to the Russians of determination to fight and of units trained and equipped to do so.

The major disagreement in Paris was over whether to negotiate with the Soviet Union. Talks plus military build-up were the two prongs of the new American strategy. Many analysts thought that Khrushchev was ready to talk, and might ease up on Berlin if he got some solid gains elsewhere – he had told the Italian Prime Minister that recognition of the Oder-Neisse Line as Germany's eastern frontier was a fundamental Soviet demand. The Soviet reply to the western Notes of 17 July expressed willingness to come to a conference table and mentioned no time limit for a treaty. All the western ambassadors in Moscow agreed that Khrushchev could show no more of his hand until he got an indication of what was in the West's. The British had never been averse to negotiating (some might say had been injudiciously keen on the idea); Home saw it as a way to help Khrushchev to back down from a major conflict. A recent Foreign Office draft paper for the Cabinet suggested that the status quo in Berlin, Germany and Europe was not unobjectionable; indeed, "we should probably consider ourselves lucky to obtain it". Negotiations could achieve "stabilisation for the next five years or so", without crucial concessions by either side, and must ensure allied and civilian rights in West Berlin, though the West "would have to give up some hitherto strongly held principles" (postpone German reunification "at least for the time being") and the Federal Republic would have to abandon the Hallstein Doctrine so that the West could deal with the GDR even if it did not recognise it. Perhaps there might be a "humane" way to restrict the refugee flow; and "the very fact of a settlement" would act as a curb. The paper ended with a stern warning that Britain's allies must not know what HMG was thinking (a bowdlerised version was prepared – for tripartite eyes only, since most of its recommendations required major sacrifices of principle, policy and territory by Bonn). But, in fact, the Americans would not have been shocked by the uncensored views, indeed would have agreed with most of them. Rusk told Home on 5 August that the West Germans were going to have to "swallow a lot they call unacceptable", and he intended to get tough with them.[7]

He hardly needed to. Bonn had long since made it clear privately that prolonged division of Germany, if suitably sugared for public consumption, was not unpalatable and that the Oder-Neisse Line could be conceded if the Soviet Union paid a high enough price for it. The only West German worry about talks was the timing. They wanted the Federal elections over first: Adenauer could not openly reverse his entire foreign policy just before standing for the Chancellorship; some officials hoped, as did many allies, that he would lose the election and a new government would be much more flexible. So it was not the West Germans who proved a stumbling block to negotiations. It was, as so often, the French. Couve had told a WEU meeting on 1 August that there must be no talks under threat or deadline, that there was no point in them when the Russians would not agree to reunification or self-determination, and that any negotiation over Berlin would inevitably lead to a weakening of the western position in the city. He took the same stubborn line with the Foreign Ministers on 6 August. Rusk tried a direct approach to de Gaulle on 8 August and argued for the need to show the public that every effort had been made before the alliance resorted to force and for an early indication to Khrushchev that the West was ready to talk even if an exact date was not fixed. Predictably the President was implacable. He would not run to a conference just "because Mr Khrushchev has whistled". He had no objection to the Americans probing Soviet interest in negotiations, but he himself would neither join the effort nor feel bound by the result.[8]

That virtual veto did not alter American or British conviction that talks were essential. But they let it stop them tipping the wink to Khrushchev that there would be a formal invitation soon after the Federal elections – the kind of private, reassuring handling of the Soviet leader that Llewellyn Thompson always recommended. What if the Americans and Britain had followed their instinct: gone ahead without French approval, and given Khrushchev a hint of their proposed timetable within days of leaving Paris? Would they have prevented the building of the Berlin Wall? There are attractions to the argument that they would. Khrushchev had a lot to gain from a four Power conference. He could announce it, perhaps at the Party Congress in October, as a triumph for his Berlin policy of threats; he could use it to extract concessions in the city and demand recognition of the GDR and the existing Polish and Czech frontiers; the news of impending negotiations might well make East Germans think twice about emigrating. And perhaps he would welcome the excuse to tell Ulbricht to postpone closing the Berlin boundary. Border closure was, after all, an extremely risky business. Was it worth taking such a risk for a satellite, and a German satellite at that, even if it was one of the most economically and strategically valuable in the whole Bloc? Khrushchev was gambling on western reluctance to fight for "two and a half million West Berliners": if he won and the operation was a total success it was still an admission of Communist failure to win the support or submission of a population; if he lost, he faced personal political ruin and possible national nuclear destruction. On the other hand, it has to be asked whether Khrushchev could have been diverted by an early offer of talks: with

East Germans leaving at the rate of 2,000 a day, the GDR might wither away in weeks. And what a perfect bargaining counter border closure might be: offer to revoke it in return for the Oder-Neisse Line, recognition of the GDR, and disengagement in Central Europe.

"What If" is only a delightful parlour game. What actually happened was that no approach was made to Khrushchev and from 5 August a staff of about twenty officials, crammed into four rooms in East Berlin, slaved away under the direction of Erich Honecker to collect wire and concrete posts from all over the country and distribute them at building sites and barracks throughout their sector, to draft orders for 8,200 Vopos, 4,500 State Security Police, 3,700 garrison police, 12,000 Factory Militia (Betriebskampfgruppen), 10,000 regular troops in the Berlin area and support forces from Saxony. Everything would be ready on the night of 12 August.

Tension in Berlin was high by the end of the first week in August. No details of the Warsaw Pact meeting on 3–4 August had leaked out, but people assumed it would lead to tight border restriction. No one knew about the work of Honecker and his group but it was thought significant that Ulbricht was not seen in public (and did not appear until the second week of the month). There was an acute sense, on both sides of the sector boundary, that something was about to happen. Stories (clearly exploiting Kennedy's 25 July speech) were being officially spread in the East of western military build-up and imminent attack: patriots and loyal Communists drew the conclusion that steps should be taken to defend the state's frontiers; others decided to leave as quickly as possible. Rumours that the boundary would be sealed any day now were brought westwards by taxi drivers, cleaning women and Grenzgänger; relatives crossed to the western sectors to see their families and said they feared it was for the last time. Brandt tried to inject some calm. In his regular fortnightly radio talk, he told listeners that the situation must not be over-dramatised, that he himself had the confidence to leave the city and go off electioneering, but he invited Khrushchev to come and see the "position into which Ulbricht could lead him". The same day the Federal Minister for All-German Affairs, Ernst Lemmer, appealed on television for East Germans not to panic: "The way from and to Berlin stays open." They merely asked themselves "For how long?"[9]

Khrushchev himself broadcast on radio and television on 7 August. It was a great day for the Soviet Union – the astronaut, Gherman Titov, had just landed after seventeen orbits in space in twenty-five hours – and the Soviet leader made the most of it, boasting of technological and scientific superiority, denouncing American "military hysteria" and warning that in a war fought with the "most destructive weapons" the Russians would destroy American bases and render her allies "harmless". Even so, he added an appeal to "meet round a conference table". However, the passage which caught most attention in the GDR referred to western "subversive activities" in West Berlin: "Stop, gentlemen," he ordered; "we are going to sign a peace treaty and close your loophole into the GDR." "Loopholes" can be passed through from either side and East Germans took this remark as an announcement that the Berlin escape hatch was about to be slammed shut. Next day 1,961 refugees registered at Marienfelde, many of them giving this speech as their reason for flight. On 9 August there were 1,650 more, including nineteen Party members. (The week before there had been ninety-one members, eleven of whom were minor officials.)[10]

Conditions at Marienfelde for the new arrivals were appalling. The Senate was calling for doctors and nurses to come and help and was struggling to provide one hot meal a day. There was accommodation for only 3,000. The huge overspill either lay on the ground with one blanket each, or was dispersed to barracks, warehouses and schools, with or without bedding, adequate sanitary arrangements or cooking facilities. Some refugees had had time to plan and sell up. Even so, their money had only a fifth of its value once exchanged into West marks and some people had spent all their savings on return tickets to far-away destinations to conceal from the railway police that they were heading for Berlin. Many immigrants had just grabbed a change of clothing and bolted. Few knew what would become of them once they were flown to the West. Each of them seemed stunned rather than relieved to be in the western sectors: they had left jobs, homes, possessions and families and had been terrified by the crossing.

They had made it, though. It looked increasingly likely that others would not. On 10 August Ulbricht made a tub-thumping speech at a factory, claiming that Grenzgänger cost the GDR a million marks a year, the open border in Berlin a billion, the "trade in people" and "western kidnappings" a further two and a half billion. "Every citizen of our state", he pronounced, "will agree with me that we must put a stop to such conditions." East Germans knew exactly how he would do it and, given that certainty, decided to be one-way "border crossers". On 11 August 2,229 refugees arrived in West Berlin, bringing the week's total to 12,210. That day, after a prolonged spell of warm summer weather, it rained torrentially. The refugees, miserable, fearful and impoverished, were drenched to the skin and had nowhere to dry themselves; some of them slept that night on sodden earth.[11]

Meanwhile Khrushchev, who had been noticeably quiet and calm for several days and unusually abstemious for even longer, abruptly changed mood on the evening of 9 August. At a reception in the Kremlin he gave what Sir Frank Roberts, the British ambassador, described as "an unpleasant and impromptu speech of aggressive self-confidence", blustering that no one could stop him signing a treaty with the GDR, bragging that the Soviet Union could make 100 megaton bombs and deliver them. He was so offensively rude about Adenauer that the Federal chargé thought it best to slip out of the room. Presidium members and government officials were acutely embarrassed by the outburst; one of them came up to Roberts afterwards to say he hoped the Soviet leader had not sounded belligerent in what he excused as a response to recent western military moves, but adding that the sooner East and West got down to talks the better. Khrushchev, however, had not finished letting off steam. He seized the Greek ambassador and berated him about "American bases" in Greece. The ambassador explained there were none. "NATO then," snarled Khrushchev; Soviet rockets were trained on them whatever they were. The ambassador pleaded that Greece was just a small country. Ah then, Khrushchev replied, the Soviet Union had a small hydrogen bomb to deal with it. And as if the poor Greek had not suffered enough, he got another earful next evening at yet another ghastly Kremlin reception (in honour of Soviet–Rumanian Friendship, but showing little signs of amity to anyone else). This time Khrushchev told him that the Soviet Union would bomb the Parthenon if the Western Powers went to war over Berlin.[12]

But the most momentous exchange at this second gruesome social event came when Khrushchev herded together Marshal Grechko, the Defence Minister, and the Greek, Italian, Canadian and British ambassadors. The situation, he informed them, was serious and he was speaking seriously: he had appointed Marshal Koniev to take supreme command of the Soviet forces in Germany. Koniev, he reminded them, had won "earlier victories" there. Then he added, with what Roberts found "odd emphasis", that serving under the Marshal would be General Batov who "had experience in Hungary". The ambassadors did not react. Roberts, indeed, was puzzled by being given information usually gazetted in the official press and given it in such portentous tones. Khrushchev seemed to find him obtuse or rudely unresponsive. The Soviet Union, he shouted, had pinpointed American bases in Scotland and it would take only nine bombs to destroy the entire United Kingdom.* The Canadian ambassador bravely reminded the Soviet leader of Russian bases in Germany,

---

* In a better mood he would have told his favourite joke of July and August: the pessimist says it takes six bombs to destroy Britain, the optimist says nine. Not many people found it funny.

Hungary, Poland, and there was a spat about who had turned down whose disarmament proposals and how often. Suddenly Khrushchev was transmogrified into the genial host, calling for drinks and toasting peace and friendship. Next night at yet another grisly reception he stood in the same company again, downing brandy after brandy, and giving Roberts a "friendly bear hug". (He "is surprisingly strong", the ambassador reported, "and had me in the air with ease". Strong perhaps, but Sir Frank was not one of the most enormous members of the diplomatic corps.)

The news of the transfer of Koniev and Batov was not much commented on in the West at the time, and as a piece of would-be subtle Soviet diplomacy fell flat. The appointments were intended both as a warning of what was to come and a deterrent to western attempts to prevent it. Koniev was the most senior Soviet marshal, well known in Germany as the commander who, with Zhukov, had taken Berlin in 1945. Batov's Hungarian "experience" had been in crushing the 1956 Rising. Together they symbolised full Soviet support for the sealing of the Berlin boundary and readiness to deal with any military measures or civilian unrest which might follow. It seems that Khrushchev had announced the move a few days earlier at a party for high-ranking soldiers and officials, and in very characteristic manner: he just called Koniev over and, according to someone present, said, "Go to Berlin. Scare them." Koniev stammered out something suitably thrilled along the lines of "Thank you for your trust and giving me this great responsibility". Then Khrushchev added "Be careful: not one shot without permission from Moscow."[13]

The news of the appointments was in the East German press on 10 August. And that day the heads of the three western Military Missions in Potsdam were unexpectedly summoned to Soviet Army headquarters for what they assumed would be a routine meeting with the serving general. Instead they discovered that he had been demoted to deputy and Ivan Koniev was presented as commander. He was sixty-four years old, a professional soldier for forty-five years, first under the Tsar then in the Red Army and in command of the Soviet forces in Austria post-war. He was loved by his men whom he addressed not as "comrades" but "brothers". He had a shaven head, a set jaw, and was known as The Tank; he chain-smoked, talked little, seemed morose and was a voracious collector and reader of books on military history. Today he welcomed the allied officers with champagne, asked whether any of them had been on the Elbe when eastern and western forces met in 1945 and suggested founding an Elbe Club. He was wearing thirty-five medals and the insignia of a Hero of the Soviet Union. That laden chest was not a display of soldierly pride or personal vanity. It was a political and military message.[14]

With Koniev and Batov in place as marks and potential instruments of Soviet support, the East German regime had the confidence to make an almost explicit announcement of its intentions. The Volkskammer met on 11 August to be told by Willy Stoph, the Prime Minister, "We are no longer prepared to sit back and watch the wooing away of huge numbers of the people of the GDR . . .". The government, he informed them, must "take appropriate measures against the slave trade, the luring away of people and against sabotage". The members of the Chamber, obedient and unanimous as ever, passed the resolution put to them to empower the government to do whatever it thought necessary. They were not told what that would be. They did not ask. They hardly needed to. And by now the planning for border closure was virtually complete. The first orders would be issued in less than twenty-four hours, on 12 August.[15]

Saturday 12 August was a glorious hot summer day. The city was quiet: many families from both sides were away on holiday, offices were shut, the shops closed at lunchtime for the weekend. People went picnicking in the woods, sailing on the lakes. The West Berlin police were on routine duties and busy as usual at the crossing points, taking names of refugees and giving them directions to Marienfelde. They noted incidents just across in the eastern sector. At 7.30 in the morning a man about sixty years old was stopped at a corner on Köpenicker Strasse, a street running parallel with the Spree as the river turns south-east, at the point at which it was cut by the eastern sector boundary. Vopos pushed him into a car and drove him away from the border. Later, a few blocks to the west where Legierdamm met the boundary, another man tried to drive into the western sectors and when the Vopos ordered him out of his car he made a dash for it. They followed him with drawn pistols, then thought better of opening fire and starting a shooting match with the police on the other side. All in all, it was what the police report described as "a working day like any other, 'without special incidents'". The Allied Military Missions wandered about East Berlin and the surrounding countryside in the afternoon. Given the general expectation that the sector and zonal borders would soon be sealed, they thought they might come across building works, some extra police deployment or troop movements. Nothing; everything seemed normal.[16]

Everything they were looking for was in fact under covers or going on behind high walls and shuttered windows. At building sites all over East Berlin, on police and military parade grounds lay concrete posts, rolls of wire, sheets of mesh, road drills, arc lights, compressors and bulldozers. Stores held extra weapons; lorries and tanks had been serviced. In Vopo barracks the men were hammering together sawhorses to carry rolls of barbed wire for street barriers. In the East Berlin Police headquarters a tiny handful of officials, possibly no more than half-a-dozen, was putting the finishing touches to the orders for the army and police. At four o'clock, Ulbricht gave the word to sound the alert at midnight.[17]

In the early evening officers in the Volksarmee went for a buffet at their headquarters south-east of Pankow and were told what would happen that night, but not yet given explicit orders. At about nine o'clock a Pan Am flight from Munich was entering the corridor to Berlin and noticed troops on the GDR border. An hour later the Sunday edition of the Party newspaper, *Neues Deutschland*, was put to bed; most of the staff wandered home but a chosen few were locked in and began work on a special four-page edition for next morning. At 11.00 Colonel von Pawel, of the US Military Mission, was rung by an informant in East Berlin who could hear tanks. He made off to check, but was turned back by a Soviet officer. At the same time army units in central East Berlin were put on alert and the First Motorised Brigade of the Grenzpolizei (Frontier Police) in barracks near Wandlitz was woken, issued with ammunition, and set off for the half-hour drive to the city; as the men boarded their trucks they could see rolls of barbed wire being loaded into lorries.[18]

In West Berlin, soon after midnight, police headquarters in Tempelhofer Damm on the west side of the airport began to receive message after message that the S-bahn was running oddly: cancelled trains, broken timetables. In other cities irregular public transport at that time of night and at a weekend might not have been noticed. Here, where instincts were acute and any shift in the pattern quickened attention, where tension had been running high and trains ran on time, these wisps of straw in the wind were seized on. Headquarters immediately contacted senior officers at home: something was up. At twenty-five minutes past midnight a West Berlin customs officer reported East German troops gathering opposite his post in Bernauer Strasse, a street due north of the Unter den Linden and along which the sector boundary ran. Groups of pedestrians, wandering westwards through the Brandenburg Gate just before one o'clock, grumbled that they had been turned off their S-bahn train at the Friedrichstrasse station and the U-bahn was not running. Some of them had seen tanks in East Berlin during the day; others had spotted concentrations of soldiers.[19]

Then at one o'clock the ticker tapes of the East German press agency, ADN, began to chatter. The Warsaw Pact countries, they announced, had called on the government of the GDR and all East German workers to carry out such measures "as will ensure that the diversionist activities against the socialist countries are stopped, and that around the entire area of West Berlin, including its borders with democratic Berlin, reliable guards and effective controls are established"; all such measures would remain in force until a peace treaty was signed. Adam Kellet Long, Reuter's correspondent in East Berlin, who had been warned by an anonymous phone call the night before not to leave the city over the weekend, took one look at the tape, ran to his car and made for the Brandenburg Gate. A solitary Vopo stopped him in Unter den Linden: he must go no nearer the boundary. He tried the Leipziger Strasse crossing to the south. Again he was stopped, this time by a soldier, and told the border was closed.[20]

At 1.45 a.m. West Berlin police at the Brandenburg Gate heard the rumble of trucks on the other side. Suddenly the six floodlights on the Gate went out but troops and police could be glimpsed darting across the shadowy open space behind with sawhorses, posts, and rolls of wire. Meanwhile, the 1.10 S-bahn train from Staaken on the city's western border had set out for the centre of town, then turned back again; all the travellers had been ordered off and their fares returned. A regular Royal Military Police patrol in the area, which had spotted nothing unusual for the last hour or so, was stopped by a local policeman to be told that all the station lights had gone out and tanks could be heard nearby. Just before two o'clock S-bahn traffic in both directions ground to a halt at Gesund-brunnen in the north and Schönholz beyond it. Police headquarters woke the deputy mayors, Franz Amrehn and Heinrich Albertz, and the allied public safety officers. By 2.15 on this morning of 13 August all western sector police posts had been put on alert.[21]

And they understood why. At 2 a.m. ADN tapes carried a decree from the East German Council of Ministers: in view of the aggressive policies of the West German government, it declared, and the attempt to incorporate the Federal Republic into NATO to "start another great war", the GDR was establishing "the forms of control which are customary on the frontier of every sovereign state" which included the "borders of the western sectors of Greater Berlin". East German citizens would in future need "special permission" to cross to the West and official passes to work in the western sectors. West Berliners and West German transit travellers, on the other hand, would be allowed to move into the Eastern Sector and East Germany under the "old regulations". "Old document procedures" maybe. But according to new regulations issued at the same time by the GDR Ministry of the Interior, there would be only thirteen permitted crossing points in the city rather than the existing eighty-eight; one day permits for western visitors and travellers would be issued at only four points. U-bahn traffic from one part of the eastern sector to another would no longer stop at West

Berlin stations; passengers for the West must use a line which ran through the Friedrichstrasse station, where they would be obliged to go through document checks and change trains. Crucially, access arrangements for the allies had not been changed, nor had the rules for movement between West Berlin and the Federal Republic. The GDR was scrupulously avoiding any interference in areas where the Western Powers had rights and commitments – and for which they had prepared contingency plans.

While the decree was being promulgated and anxiously analysed by officials in the western sectors, the Royal Military Police patrol in Staaken was watching scores of Vopos, Grenzpolizei and soldiers, all armed with rifles and submachine-guns, unloading building materials beyond the S-bahn station. When its commanding officer, Lieutenant-Colonel Richards, arrived soon after two o'clock concrete slabs were being laid across the railway track and chain fencing slung between concrete posts, with two or three lines of barbed wire on top for good measure. The British and West Berlin police stood there helpless. They knew every inch of this section of border – and the East Germans were well within their own territory. The colonel got on the radio phone to the British Military Commandant, General Rohan Delacombe, and to the Political Adviser, Bernard Ledwidge, who had just been woken by the deputy Public Safety Officer and was about to leave for his office. Richards then made off for the Brandenburg Gate. Here, under arc lights, and again well within their own sector, teams of Vopos in overalls, Grenzpolizei, customs officials and firemen had unfurled rolls of barbed wire the length of the crossing; pneumatic drills were boring a trench about half a metre deep and wide across Ebertstrasse which ran to the Gate from the south; more drills, compressors and bulldozers were trundling into position. Just inside the wire at the Gate stretched a tight line of about fifty heavily armed soldiers and police. It looked very much as if they were ready to use their weapons against their own men: they had their backs to the West.[22]

Whatever their other duties, these guards honoured their international obligations. They rolled back the wire to let Richards drive his official car through to the East. On the other side he found a crowd of distraught civilians being shoved back from the Friedrichstrasse station by Vopos and Trapos. Every street was crammed with armed men, armoured vehicles, every imaginable form of heavy lorry and construction machinery. He checked a main road coming into East Berlin – again solid with military transport and trucks carrying engineers' stores. But not one Russian soldier to be seen. Just outside the East German Ministry of the Interior there were women handing out pamphlets. He was curious, parked round the corner and went to get one. It was a list of all the new decrees and crossing regulations. Grim though they were, they came as a huge relief to a man with military duties and full knowledge of military planning: they showed that all this troop activity was not preparation for an attack on the western sectors, it was an action against eastern refugees. He radioed to his own headquarters (using an open line which was normally forbidden in the East but wise under these circumstances). The good news was passed to the Military Commandant, and was received by the Foreign Office in London by 4 a.m.

Meanwhile information had come to West Berlin police headquarters at 2.30 a.m. that the Brandenburg Gate had just closed to traffic and twenty-three truck loads of Vopos, all armed with machine pistols and guns, had arrived with motor cycle escort at Pariser Platz behind it. There was now a barrier at Hindenburg Platz and the fifteen armoured patrol vehicles which had stood by while it went up had left. S-bahn traffic had stopped at Potsdam, Erhner, Stansdorf, Wannsee and other termini or outlying stations round the city. At 3.05 troops on foot were moving from Potsdam and Falkensee to the border of West Berlin. A heavily armoured unit had been seen on the main road to Staaken – and there were Russians with it. At 3.10 the trench at Ebertstrasse was complete and the road behind it was being ripped up. Leipziger Strasse, running to the south and parallel with the Unter den Linden, was closed. There were Soviet troops with fixed bayonets reinforcing the Trapos and Grenzpolizei at Staaken station. By 3.30 a.m. the police had added up their reports and decided that all public transport had come to a standstill and the whole of the twenty-eight miles of Eastern sector boundary was now a double line of armed men and wire: quite an achievement within three and a half hours of the start of the operation. It was clear, furthermore, that every action had taken place within East Berlin and East German territory. In the view of the police, there was no call to put western security plans and defence measures into effect. Like the Maginot Line, they had been bypassed.[23]

News of what was happening had spread through West Berlin. Off-duty police chiefs had been alerted from 2.15; every man available was at his post by 4.15. The police commander of the Tiergarten section, facing the Brandenburg Gate, had only just got to bed, after rather too good a party given by the British Public Safety Officer at the Officers' Club. It took a lot of shouting and shaking by his wife and mother-in-law and a large bowl of cold water in his face before he could be roused and got into uniform and boots. He left his flat in such a hurry that he forgot his cap and for the next few hours, until it was sent to him, he was more frightened by what a superior officer would do to him for turning up improperly dressed than he was of relatively quick and painless death by a Vopo machine gun. Facing him at the Gate and along the flanks either side were throngs of soldiers and police drilling holes for posts. He and his men bellowed across the wire: "Have you gone mad? What the hell are you doing?" The drills thundered without pause. City officials had been woken and went to the crossing points: police, soldiers, wire everywhere but people from both sides still squeezing past barricades, hopping over coils of wire, jostling through lines of workers and guards. The officials viewed with a professional eye: how long had this huge operation taken to plan? Where had all this equipment and material come from? Where had it been stored in recent days? Why had no information leaked out? Why had no one been warned? Surely, in this city full of spies and informers, the allies must have known? Why had they done nothing to stop it? What were they going to do now? Journalists had been dragged out of bed too. Night staff at RIAS and SFB had monitored the ADN tapes of the official decrees and the first broadcast news of the measures from Radio Berlin at 3.00. They called in their programme heads and news staff; other journalists were phoned by colleagues or by friends returning late from parties in the East who had seen what was going on at the border. RIAS always broadcast music and news through the night. It was just as well that on this occasion a continuity announcer noticed that the record he was due to play after a bulletin was a song "Let's follow the Swallow" – encouraging flight would sound like inciting East German refugees or even calling on West Berliners to leave, so he slipped something solemn on to the turntable instead.[24]

What struck everyone as they came to the wire that night was the contrast either side: noise and urgent activity in the East; quiet in the West with no troops and just a few onlookers who stood mesmerised by the bustle under the harsh arc lamps. The first thought of most of them was: this is no ordinary, temporary tightening of the boundary. One man was overwhelmed by rage: how could Germans do such a thing to each other in his city? Another was flabbergasted: where were the allies? Why were they not smashing the wire? Several journalists crossed to the East – easily done given all the confusion and the flimsiness of some of the barricades. One carried a tape recorder under a mackintosh over his arm – no soldier or Vopo questioned or searched him. When two men from the US Mission crossed at Potsdamer Platz at about 3 a.m. the Vopos obligingly held back the wire to let their car through. They found the streets either side of the Unter den Linden blocked with armoured personnel carriers, half tracks and radio vans; people in pyjamas were leaning out of the windows above watching the ceaseless hurly-burly. Driving round the sector for two hours the Americans saw more army and Vopo units arriving to join the building work, customs officials taking control of traffic and pedestrians. Betriebskampfgruppen, the armed Factory Militia who had been alerted in the early hours by SED officials, had reported to assembly points to collect arms and ammunition and were now being allocated to construction work along the wire, or were searching the upper floors and roofs of nearby buildings. The security police were opening schools and other public buildings to house the night shift who would soon be relieved by the motorised columns of men pouring into the city.[25]

The Americans counted about eighty trucks of police with armoured cars and machineguns at one point alone, then at about 5.30 spotted a light East German tank. In the next hour they watched ambulance crews and civil defence units joining the Vopos on street patrols. Each road up to and along the boundary was teeming with uniforms. There was an occasional Soviet military car touring the sector, but not a single Soviet personnel carrier or tank to be seen. Even so, security would be suffocating by the time East Berliners woke in the morning. If East Berliners rioted or attempted a mass break-out it was going to be up to the GDR to control them and it looked as if they were well prepared to do it. But would West Berliners try to join in? Would their police be able to stop them rushing into the Eastern Sector and on to the East German guns?

News of the night's events had already percolated to the outside world. Dr Hans von Globke, Adenauer's chief adviser and head of his Chancellery, was telephoned in the early hours of the morning by Amrehn and soon afterwards by the Federal press office with reports of the GDR decrees and division of Berlin. He immediately got in touch with the Intelligence services, the BND, to check. Their advice was that this was a border closure, not an invasion of the western sectors. Reassured, he decided to let the Chancellor lie in, and did not inform him until about seven o'clock. Adenauer reacted calmly and decided to go to mass before seeing Globke and the head of Chancellery foreign affairs at 9.00. Brentano seems to have felt no great sense of urgency either: he is reported as telling friends in Darmstadt where he was staying that this was a four-Power problem, and when a colleague rang later in the day to ask if he should break his holiday the Foreign Minister thought it unnecessary. Hans Kroll, on leave from his embassy in Moscow at his country house in Bavaria, heard what was going on in Berlin from the radio; and it was only from a broadcast in the evening that he learned that Brentano was calling on him and the ambassadors in the three allied capitals to return to their posts. (He does not record in his memoirs that anyone had tried to contact him from Bonn – or if he himself had rung his Ministry.) Seemingly Adenauer was not unique in thinking of Berliners as "Chinese"

– and a Chinese wire, if not yet wall, to keep "Chinese" in the East, offered no threat to the Federal Republic.[26]

Nor was the division of the city seen as a threat to the Western Powers. De Gaulle was in Colombey-les-Deux-Églises and decided to stay there, though Couve de Murville returned to Paris on the evening of 13 August and Seydoux arranged to go back to his embassy in Bonn. Macmillan and Home saw no reason to ruin their golf and shooting in Scotland; the Foreign Office issued a press release denouncing East German actions as contrary to the quadripartite status of Berlin, therefore illegal, but that was all. After months and years of dreading a block of western communications with the city and of planning rapidly escalating, frightening military measures in response, allied access and presence in Berlin seemed secure. Of course, ending freedom of movement for Germans across Berlin was a breach of four-Power agreement; of course it was inhumane. Of course, the East Germans had unilaterally substituted a frontier for an administrative division in violation of international law. But that was better than the GDR opening fire on refugees trying to cross the boundary, far better than an East German uprising with all its political and military consequences for the West. All in all, even if it was too shocking to admit in public, a few miles of wire to close the border provided the simplest, safest solution to everyone's problems.

West Germans, French and British had immediately decided that the best policy was to sit back and do nothing. The American response to the Berlin events was no more active and considerably slower. The first news of what was happening in the city reached Washington at about 5.00 in the morning Berlin time (in those days midnight in Washington). John Ausland had taken over responsibility for Berlin contingency planning the week before and was the Berlin Task Force's duty officer that weekend since virtually everyone else was on holiday. He was rung by the State Department with a vague message that a news agency was reporting "something going on" in the city – though by that time ADN had twice reported government decrees, Radio Berlin had carried news of the measures, and wire and barricades had totally sealed the sector boundary. Unperturbed, he went back to sleep for four hours or so until the Department passed on a CIA telegram, just received from Berlin, announcing that movement across the city had been blocked and carrying the coded instruction that the President should be informed. The key words for Ausland, however, were that there had been no interference with allied access or West Berlin's communications with the Federal Republic. So he was not alarmed. He rang the acting director of the Office of German Affairs, Frank Cash, who promised to come to the office as soon as he had put his wife and children on a plane to go on vacation (which took the next four hours). Until he arrived, Ausland read the reports coming in from Germany, checked with the Pentagon liaison officer and with the US European Command near Paris that no Soviet troops were involved and no aggressive military deployments had been detected, then with a couple of other officials he started to get briefed on contingency plans. He could not find one for this specific situation. When Cash finally turned up, he found the planning file marked "Border closure". It was empty.[27]

It was only at about ten o'clock Washington time (3.00 in the afternoon in Berlin) that Rusk and Foy Kohler, the Director of the Berlin Task Force, came into the office. (Kohler's initial reaction to a call had been that Ausland seemed to have everything under control and there was no need to go in – an off-hand comment he deeply regretted later.) They soon agreed that the western sectors and allied access were safe; that the East German border action was purely defensive, and cutting the refugee flow was to be welcomed. There was, they decided, no point in disturbing the President at Hyannis Port. Better wait until there was a fuller picture of what was happening in Berlin.

Surely they should have had one, over fifteen hours after the first East German military units appeared on the sector boundary? But in fact, many American officials in Germany did not have one either. Various members of the US Berlin Mission had been driving round East Berlin and its outskirts for hours and were extremely well-informed; the local CIA was up-to-date. No one, however, seems to have disturbed the sleep of the US Military Commandant, Albert Watson. Plenty of people had tried to rouse Allan Lightner, the Deputy Commandant and chief State Department official in the city, but he did not answer the phone. No one seems to have thought it was worth going round to his home and ringing the bell or shouting at the bedroom window. So the first news Lightner got was at about 6 a.m. Berlin time. (He told an interviewer six years later that he was woken by a phone call, so perhaps it was not off the hook, as callers in the night had assumed.) He did his duty and went to inspect sections of the inner city boundary. All he saw was "building material"; "it looked like barriers were being built to keep refugees in rather than to keep us out." So that was all right, as long as you thought that a barrier did not have two sides and therefore two functions. The first contact between the Berlin Mission and the US embassy in Bonn was made around nine o'clock that morning; the messages were finally passed on to the ambassador only in mid-afternoon, after he had attended a softball match between an embassy team and local West Germans.

From the time Ausland arrived in his office, no one in the State

Department had called Berlin to check what was happening. When a West German journalist based in Washington, Lothar Loewe, heard the Berlin news that morning he had rushed round to the Department to see what the latest information was and what was being done about it. He was told that it was impossible to ring the city because there were no secure lines through East Germany. (Clearly no one had checked to see who in Washington had one or thought to use a coded teleprinter.) Loewe used his nous: went round to the apartment of James O'Donnell, the old *Newsweek* correspondent, rang the US Information Agency in West Berlin, and for a $46 call got a full briefing – and a horrifying story of mounting desperation in both halves of the divided city. That human reaction, and its possible political consequences, was something Rusk and the State Department had not considered at all when heaving sighs of relief at the limits of the GDR operation and the safety of western sectors and allied rights. The possibility that the sealing of the border might incite violence and provoke a backlash against the Western Powers had simply not occurred to them – or to their allies. And when they finally rang Berlin at about noon Washington time, it was to insist that there must be no provocative move, that no local protest should be issued without consultation with the Department and full approval from the three western capitals.

Then and only then was the President contacted. He was setting out on his boat, the *Marlin*, for a picnic and was called back to ring Rusk. The Secretary of State read him a press release he had prepared: the recent measures in Berlin, this stated, were aimed at residents of East Berlin and East Germany, at refugees reacting "to the failures of communism"; they did not threaten allied presence or access though they did violate the four-Power status of the city and were a flagrant violation of the right of free movement; there would be "vigorous protest through the appropriate channels". It was a toothless declaration which merely went through the motions of remonstrance; the very phrasing implied that the United States would take no action since allied rights had not been affected. Yet what else could Rusk say? Kennedy had made commitments to the security of the western sectors and western presence and access but not to the city of Berlin as a whole nor to the seventeen million citizens of the GDR. The President in his 25 July speech had publicly abandoned the bases of the four-Power settlement which had tenuously survived since the war and in so doing had jettisoned the existing formula for eventual reunification of Germany. Logically, therefore, the United States was now obliged to accept the division of Berlin and the German nation even though this had not necessarily been his intention. In practical terms there was no American policy short of war which could deal with this unforeseen Berlin crisis. Kennedy listened to Rusk's statement. "Issue it," he ordered. Then with almost Nero-esque detachment he added: "Go to the ball game as you planned. I'm going sailing."

As the wire snaked round West Berlin from the earliest hours of Sunday 13 August, the Governing Mayor, Willy Brandt, was asleep on the night train to Kiel from Nuremberg where he had spent Saturday launching his election campaign. Like any other Berliner he had been expecting something unpleasant in the city, some tough action by Pankow against the refugees. But he had left for a few days because there was no obvious reason not to, and cancelling a well-publicised election tour might have caused more anxiety than his absence. Subsequently he wrote: "I reproached myself afterwards for being lulled by the thought that it was still far from certain *when* anything would happen." In his Nuremberg speech he had warned that the Russians were "preparing a stroke against our people", that East Germans feared they would be "immured in a gigantic gaol" – words which he explained to a journalist later were purely metaphorical.[28]

On instructions from Berlin his train was held at Hanover soon after dawn and Brandt and his party were given the news. After telephoning Albertz from the stationmaster's office, he flew to Tempelhof and drove straight to the sector boundary, to Potsdamer Platz and the Brandenburg Gate. His arrival was shown live on television and for one family was a moment of sheer delight: the once capless policeman was caught by the cameras standing at the side of the Mayor. "Thank God, Egon is still alive," exclaimed his mother-in-law. Brandt gazed miserable and aghast at the bales of wire and the barricades stretched across the focal points of his city, at the dense lines of soldiers, policemen and Factory Militia sinking more concrete posts, draping yet more wire. "Horrible," he kept saying. "Dreadful." Yet a wry thought came to him: how very orderly it all was, how efficient, how those barriers showed "a true German attention to detail". He was to recall that he "looked into the vacant eyes of uniformed compatriots doing their duty on the other side" and, above all, "I saw concern and despair written on the faces of my fellow-citizens of West Berlin." He had read his own feelings: German had acted against German; the Western Powers, the Protecting Powers, had not lifted a finger to stop them.

Brandt drove to his office and called an emergency meeting of the Senate for that afternoon. Then at eleven o'clock he went to the Allied Kommandatura. It was not an office he had often visited, if ever. The Military Commandants usually came to see him or invited him to their homes. So he was flabbergasted to see on the wall a photograph of Kotikov, the last Soviet Commandant whose withdrawal from that building in 1948 had marked the end of quadripartite administration of the city. It had been hanging there ever since as an invocation of dead cooperation, a fading memento of the hope that one day the four victors against Nazism would create a European peace.

The three western Commandants had already been in conclave for an hour. They had rejected any ideas of military action (though there are suggestions that some of the Americans at the meeting had argued for it). There was to be no tearing down of the wire, no smashing of barriers – a total garrison of 12,000 men could not take on the massive East German deployment along the sector boundary let alone the Soviet support force which was undoubtedly lurking in the background. They had decided that any rash western move would be met by East German fire – whether from a nervous individual or on officer's orders – and once shooting started both sides would be hard put to it to prevent escalation. There was a further restraint: Berliners were beginning to crowd on both sides of the wire, and they were desperate. A sudden military presence might tip them into recklessness. If violence erupted the East German police would open fire to quell it; if shots landed in the West, the local police would return fire. Hundreds would be killed. If rioting continued, there was every likelihood the Russians would send in tanks. Then what?[29]

So Brandt found the Commandants as "disconcerted and disoriented" as he felt himself by the night's events; as "bewildered and at a loss" about what to do. They had plans for countering invasion of the western sectors, but in consultation with the police had decided that these were inapplicable when all action had been confined to GDR territory; on the other hand they were unprepared for what had actually happened and felt helplessly constrained by their assessment of the dangers of any confrontation. Contrary to later stories that Brandt arrived drunk and aggressive, screaming for action, a British witness of the meeting described him as "grave but statesmanlike", an American as "subdued and reflective". Brandt himself was to confess that he could think of no effective counter measures, and the record of the meeting shows that he spoke worriedly about the risk of inciting violence. But he did ask for an immediate protest to Moscow and every Warsaw Pact capital; he urged the Commandants to send patrols to the sector boundary, not to threaten the East but assure the West Berliners that they personally were under protection.

Brandt was a realist. He knew that protest would not open the border again, that force might kill more than it helped. He was also a first-rate politician and knew what Berliners needed at this moment: sympathy, comradeship, some certainty when their lives had been shattered, some physical demonstration that though the allies might concede the East to the Soviet Union they would make a stand for the freedom of their three sectors. When he left the meeting he believed that his views had been understood.

The Military Commandants and their political advisers then settled to preparing a press release condemning the border closure, and a message of protest to the Soviet Commandant. By the time the drafts were ready, Kohler had telephoned the American officials to insist that all public condemnation must be made by the three capitals and that even a message to the Soviet authorities in Berlin must be cleared by them. At 5.00 in the afternoon, Berlin time, Rusk's flabby statement was released and undercut anything the allies in Berlin could devise.

By then, the wire had been slashing through the city for seventeen hours. Berliners knew nothing of the political considerations and military calculation which had gone on behind the scenes. As far as they were concerned, their city had been brutally lacerated and they were isolated from the rest of the world. The Commandants had not uttered a squeak of protest, had not sent a single patrol to the border to demonstrate their presence. Throughout 13 August no head of state of a Western Power spoke publicly about the events in Berlin. Adenauer had called for calm in the city but decided against visiting. He did not bother to telephone Brandt or send a message through others. Brentano did get in touch, but merely said that Bonn and Berlin must "work closely together" – to what end he did not specify. Brandt himself had spoken to Berliners on the radio that day, but it was a terribly inept performance. It was, in fact, tragic. This experienced broadcaster, skilled communicator, subtle politician simply could not find words adequate for the occasion. People wanted to be comforted or lifted as Ernst Reuter had always managed in the darkest moments of the Blockade. From Brandt they only heard the echo of their own bewildered misery.[30]*

No one living along the sector boundary or the East Berlin streets which led to it had slept much that night of 12–13 August. For hours there had been a cacophony of lorries, road drills and bulldozers, stamping boots, clanging barriers, bellowed orders. Small groups had watched all night as the wire

* Friedrich Luft, the distinguished drama critic, had given Berliners what they needed in a broadcast from RIAS that morning. He tore up his usual weekly piece on the arts and instead delivered an eloquent, passionate soliloquy which expressed the tragedy of the city, purged the terror, and exalted the feelings.

stretched between the posts, the tarmac and oblong road setts were gouged out, and trenches were ripped across streets. Then the rest of Berlin began to wake. Early-morning dog walkers strode to the end of their road and blinked at the sight of armed men and wire. Phones rang; friends and relatives spread the news of what was happening. Families at breakfast turned on the radio and could not believe what they heard. People went to the sector boundary to see with their own eyes. Even then many could not understand what was happening: crossings had been closed before, for days and weeks on end, but never like this. It was inconceivable that all the military activity, the guns, the mountains of material and equipment were for "temporary restrictions", "refugee control". They rushed up to the Vopos and Kampfgruppen – just young Berlin lads, many of them – grabbed them by the arm and asked what was going on, shouted at them to stop. Police either side patiently pushed them back. They stood as the morning wore on and the crowds grew, stunned and impotent.[31]

One young East Berliner woke that morning in his girlfriend's bed and switched on the news. He was a member of his factory's militia (he had no choice) and he realised they must have been trying to find him all night at his mother's flat. He had not the slightest wish to be found now. He went straight to the home of a friend where there was no phone. Next day he persuaded a doctor to give him a sick note – he was sick at heart at the thought of the distasteful work he would have to do otherwise. Many people left home before they heard what was going on in the city. When Robert Lochner from RIAS who had been up most of the night reporting the events took Ed Murrow, the head of the United States Information Agency who had come on official inspection tour, to East Berlin for a mid-morning beer at the Adlon Hotel he found hundreds of East Berliners at the Friedrichstrasse station, still assuming that the S- and U-bahn were running. Trapos with linked arms were blocking approaches to the platforms. An old lady asked where she could get her train. "Mut-terschen," the Trapo told her, "you are in a mousetrap": a contemptuous diminutive and callous phrase which horrified the journalist more than anything he had experienced so far. The news of the night's events, and the full sense of being trapped had come early, however, to one man in East Germany, in Bautzen gaol. He was serving a five-year sentence for the crime of arguing in his philosophy seminars at the Humboldt University. He and his fellow political prisoners used to tot up the number of days to their release and say: "And on that date I leave here and cross to the West." Today the prison loudspeakers blared the message: "The border has been closed." They were prisoners for life.

Others were luckier. Two East German footballers, playing a match in

Copenhagen on Saturday, took the ferry to Hamburg on Sunday. Throughout that morning and early afternoon East Berliners went to the sector boundary, saw that stretches were still not blocked, that the wire was lying in coils and could be jumped over, that some houses on the very edge were not guarded and one could walk through or squeeze out of a window. The Vopos were too busy digging, hammering, watching their own men to take much notice; sometimes they deliberately turned their backs. Several people ran over railway lines which marked the frontier and had not yet been barricaded; one man crawled through a cemetery, while his friends in a house in the West signalled to him the whereabouts of the police patrols. A couple took their six-year-old son to a crossing, nudged him through the crowd to the other side, then asked the Vopo on guard if they could go and get him back – and they did not return. Other refugees ran through woods or over fields on the outskirts of the city. At least thirteen swam the river, canals and even Lake Havel; once out of the water, said an official report, they looked "the worse for wear". No one kept count of how many refugees got out on 13 August. The West Berlin police had other things on their minds; Marienfelde recorded 198 but their system had broken down with the arrival of over 2,000 East Germans who had been caught in the western sectors overnight and decided not to go back; most arrivals at the reception centre were asked to go away and come back later. Many more had certainly prepared to cross. But they had been prudent: while the barricades and wire were still low they passed over suitcases, blankets, pots and pans to relatives or passers-by on the other side. By the time they were ready to follow, the barriers were too high to be crossed.[32]

And as the fortifications rose on Sunday 13 August and no help came, no message of support or sympathy was delivered, Berliners' stunned shock ignited into anger. Soon after noon onlookers at Lennéstrasse, at the southeast tip of the Tiergarten, tried to tear down a barbed wire barricade. The Vopos retreated a few yards and fixed bayonets while the West Berlin police dragged the crowd back. Half an hour later about three hundred people at the corner of Köpenicker Strasse and Bethaniendamm began to pull down a barrier. Vopos drew their pistols and again the West Berlin police herded the people back to safety. Later a man in Klemkestrasse, way to the north beyond the Schönholz S-bahn station, got into a fight with three Vopos and was stabbed through the knee with a bayonet. He grabbed a Vopo's gun and hurled himself into the western sector. In a moment of sheer bathos spectators watched the Vopo clamber over the barrier and ask the wounded man if he might please have his gun back. It was handed over.[33]

In mid-afternoon, the mood grew uglier. Ed Murrow sensed it and decided to ring Washington to explain the danger of leaving Berliners to their emotions. By five o'clock a large crowd was gathering on the western side of the Brandenburg Gate. The police blocked the approach roads to motor traffic but pedestrians poured through from the Tiergarten. At six o'clock there were about three thousand people pressing forward to the Gate; respectable, middle-aged couples, most of them, but angry and resolute. They were orderly for a time. Some had placards: "There is only one Germany", "Hang Ulbricht", "Open the Gate". They chanted "Ivan go home", "Germany is still German", "Let the people have their say". The West Berlin police linked arms, extended ropes and poles to drive the crowd away from the wire, the bayonets and the guns. A policeman's wife tried to struggle through with a thermos of soup for her husband; she was terrified by the crush of bodies and the furious faces. And the anger intensified. The chanting rose, the crowd surged forward and suddenly there was a hail of stones thrown at the Gate. East German armoured cars and machineguns rolled into position, line after line of armed men formed ranks across the Gate. GDR soldiers yelled at the West Berlin police to clear the area. The police rammed against the crush, stones flew over and at them. Then at five minutes past seven, the Vopos turned on their water cannon and sluiced the crowd back. It was a miracle, if not divine then of police discipline on both sides, that hundreds had not been killed.[34]

All this while about three hundred young people at the Bethaniendamm crossing, to the south-east, were taunting the Vopos, jeering and throwing stones. Their noise drew more rowdies. The press of new arrivals pushed everyone forward and about forty were shoved into the Soviet sector. One of them at least was thrown into a police van and taken off. When the human weight became intolerable the Vopos opened up with smoke bombs and tear gas, then went at the mass with truncheons. It took nearly half an hour before they and their western comrades-in-crisis could disperse what had become a mob of nearly 2,500. In the mêlée there was a fight between a Vopo and an officer; perhaps the man was trying to escape, but finally the officer shot him with his pistol and he was carted off in an ambulance.

As evening turned to night, the tension slackened. A few refugees took advantage of the dark. About fifty West Berliners hauled away the barbed wire across one street to let four or five of them through, and the Vopos stood by while they did it. Just before midnight, guards at an official crossing stopped a car from the East and tried to search it. The driver stamped on his accelerator and smashed through the barrier: he had a refugee in his boot. West Berliners began to drift home from the Gate, leaving small groups to keep vigil with makeshift torches of rolled news-paper and magazines – short-lived flickers of defiance in contrast to the constant merciless glare of the arc lamps along the wire where uniformed men still drilled and hammered and wove the wire from post to post. The West Berlin police stretched weary limbs, looked for a food van, settled on the ground for what sleep they could get. All day long, they and the Vopos had wrestled against their own people. Those in the West had borne the brunt: they had no military backing, no help from their allies. If they had not triumphed and prevented huge scale riots, not only Berlin lives would have been lost – the Soviet tanks would have arrived and the Western Powers would have been forced to scuttle or fight. No one could bear to think how many would die in a military confrontation.

Monday, 14 August, and at first light western journalists wandered round East Berlin. The border area was thick with armed men, armoured cars, trucks and building materials. Trapos were bricking up two entrances to the S-bahn station in Potsdamer Platz. It was drizzling and in the side streets Vopos and Kampfgruppen were huddled by their lorries, in shabby, ill-fitting uniforms, their young faces stern and white with strain and exhaustion. In the next few hours more lorries rumbled into the city with yet more soldiers, police, Factory Militia. All day motorised police patrols and armoured cars toured the streets – but there was not a Russian uniform or vehicle to be seen. Unter den Linden was closed, and kept closed by pickets with submachine-guns. "Now Unter den Linden is private property?" a man shouted at Kampfgruppen – then made off quickly when he saw the look on their faces. Police with fixed bayonets took up position in the Wilhelmstrasse, later called Otto-Grotewohl-Strasse, which led from the south to Pariser Platz. There was a line of machinegun emplacements running half a mile from the Brandenburg Gate along the Potsdamer Platz. The guard at the Friedrichstrasse station was strengthened: two to three hundred soldiers, Trapos and Vopos manned the entrances and blocked the platforms, and six East German T-34 tanks kept watch over the approach roads, gun turrets swivelling. A few West Berliners were allowed through to go home (an occasional S-bahn train was running); East Berliners and Germans were turned away or sat dismally on their suitcases.[35]

Any East Berliner not on duty at the border or in the streets was expected to go to work. But public transport was erratic and main roads into the city from the suburbs and countryside were barricaded or jammed with military traffic so travellers could not get in and delivery vans were stuck. Most shops kept their shutters up all day. Factory workers found their premises packed with armed Kampfgruppen, and SED officials arrived to give them bracing addresses on the defence of their country or collected signatures to enthusiastic statements of approval for government measures. Little work was done all day.

That morning's edition of *Neues Deutschland* trumpeted: "the power of the Workers' and Farmers' state may be young but it functions with precision". There was no denying that the GDR was being extremely efficient at keeping its would-be emigrants in and the rest of the population down. Touring journalists counted between fifty and sixty tanks in the Eastern Sector, all well back from the border and out of sight to the West but unpleasantly conspicuous to East Berliners. The tanks looked ready to stay: the crews of the six behind the Soviet embassy were putting up tents and laying out their field kitchens. An NBC reporter tried to film a group, and he and his driver were slammed into a Vopo van and held in custody for nine hours without food. Another reporter risked taking a shot. "This is Free Berlin," a Vopo told him. "Taking photographs is not allowed here."

It was quiet in the early hours of the day in West Berlin. No one, however, could have called the atmosphere calm or workaday. West Berliners believed what their morning paper *Bild Zeitung* prophesied: that what had happened in the last twenty-four hours was just the first of many blows to come. Most people struggled to get to work but S-bahn trains were few and far between and it took all day to get a limited U-bahn service to function from the few bits of rolling stock within the western sectors rather than held at outlying stations in the East. What used to be a quick drive or walk for some workers across a spit of the Eastern Sector might now involve a long detour to find one of the open crossings, then a queue while documents were officiously checked. Nearly all telephone connections with East Germany were dead at the start of the day and the East German authorities warned that the rest would be cut by evening; there was no line to Hamburg but the other connections with the FRG were still open and not under threat. The Autobahn was open too for the military, and civilian road traffic was moving to and from the West relatively normally, as was West German canal traffic, though no East German barges had entered West Berlin or the Federal Republic for forty-eight hours and there were heavy patrols on all waterways. Factories were under-manned not least because 50,000 Grenzgänger had been unable to cross for work (though a handful had somehow managed to turn up at Tempelhof).[36]

And the workers, like all other West Berliners, were seething. Why had the Western Powers done nothing, said nothing? They proudly called themselves "the Protecting Powers". What protection had they given? The allies were "Pflaumig" (plum-like), "Waschlappen" (washrags). At Siemens 500 workers downed tools for two hours until known Communist sympathisers were sacked. Mid-morning, men from AEG Turbine marched on the Rathaus, gathering a crowd of about five thousand, and protested that SED and GDR offices were still open in the western sectors, 11,000 West Berliners could go to work in East Berlin for the GDR, S-bahn trains crossed the city with East German personnel. Amrehn took up their complaints with the Military Commandants and asked permission to tear down posters of the GDR measures pasted up in West S-bahn stations, ban the sale of the SED journal, stop conversion of East mark wages into West marks for western sector residents working in the East. The Senate, he told them, was under "severe pressure" from the public for quick reprisals; there must be allied action as well as mere protest. He did not get any.[37]

Brandt returned to the Brandenburg Gate at 11.00. Even if the allies had not yet raised a voice or a finger, he could at last show his people a token of Federal support. He had with him Eugen Gerstenmaier, the President of the Bundestag, Erich Ollenhauer, Heinrich Krone, and Erich Mende, leaders of the SPD, CDU and FDP. A crowd gathered round them denouncing what was happening on the other side of the Gate, begging for action. Suddenly a young man from the other side of massive barriers broke through and ran towards them. "I shall never forget the scene", wrote Brandt, "or the look on his face which was a mixture of joyous excitement and cool determination." "I've been trying to get across for hours," the young man told the welcoming crowd. "When Brandt arrived the Vopos were all eyes. That's when I spotted my chance." If the Vopos had opened fire on him they might well have bagged prize specimens of the entire West German political establishment.[38]

West Berliners flocked to the Brandenburg Gate all morning. And they were angry. The Senate kept issuing appeals for calm. RIAS repeatedly broadcast a recorded message from Adenauer promising that "all required counter measures will be taken" and throughout the day was at pains to give some sense of normality and avoid panic by not interrupting the usual programme schedules with news flashes. Trade union officials toured factories appealing to their members not to make the situation worse, not to provoke the East German authorities with violence. They managed to head off a mass march on the Brandenburg Gate by calling for a protest strike at two o'clock: all work and all traffic in West Berlin stopped for fifteen minutes. But then furious workers demonstrated outside the Rathaus again, incensed by western passivity and what seemed their own city leaders' acquiescence. One of them shouted, "My mother lives less than a mile away and I'll probably never see her again." How many hundreds of others in the crowd could have said the same thing, how many thousand families were split? Then they wanted to march on the Gate. Amrehn and others struggled to persuade them of the futility and danger and at last coaxed them away.[39]

Which was just as well since by one o'clock, there were already between 3,000 and 5,000 people there, shouting, chanting, pressing forward to the wire. West Berlin police and riot squads sweated to force them away. Photographers dodged in front of the lines to film until Vopo hoses squirted them back. Rocks were hurled; the Vopos replied with tear gas and water cannon. The crowd retreated for a moment and the police fought to rein it in behind ropes. Then it burst forward. Rocks flew at the East German ranks; Vopo tear gas was followed by an announcement over loudspeakers: East Berlin forces would open fire. There was a warning shot. And with desperate heaves the West Berlin police shoved the mass a hundred feet from the wire. Their human barricade held until ropes could corral the irate crowd. Soon East German armoured cars moved up to the Gate. Through them a line of armed men advanced to the exact line of their sector boundary. With the menacing phalanx in position the loudspeakers blared again: the Brandenburg Gate was now closed. By 2.30 it was solidly fortified. It would not open again for over twenty-eight years. The thirteen Berlin crossing points had been cut to twelve.[40]

Walter Ulbricht came to the sector boundary that afternoon to view his handiwork and praise his troops. "The most important thing here", he told them, "is that peace is assured." "Some of your opponents think that the might of workers and farmers is not yet strong enough to strike a blow against enemies" – but it had been done. There were Russian tanks in reserve, he promised them, then threw in his idea of a joke: "just so that there are no misunderstandings with our opponents". It took the lads clustered round him several seconds to realise it was their duty to laugh.[41]

The Western Powers had been aware of those Soviet tanks for over twenty-four hours and knew there were none in Berlin itself. From the earliest hours of the border closure they had received reports of troop movements from western border police, travellers and refugees; throughout the following day allied aircraft had criss-crossed the Eastern Sector and Berlin perimeter searching, counting and identifying. By the evening of 13 August it was certain that two Soviet motorised rifle divisions plus a tank division had been deployed on the north, south and west approaches to the city; the east was already held by its permanent garrison of local tanks and a rifle regiment. All intelligence confirmed the early military hunch that Soviet forces had taken up defensive positions and NATO headquarters had been informed that attack was improbable. The units of the 6th and 19th Motorised Rifle Divisions and the 10th Guards Tank

Division were deployed in clusters of three or four tanks with armoured personnel carriers at posts three or four kilometres apart; with the GDR garrison on the east segment they formed a complete ring round the city. Their positions suggested that the Soviet role was to cut the movement of refugees, and indeed all travellers to Berlin, and to forestall civil disturbance, while releasing East German forces for action in the city itself.[42]*

Thanks to police on both sides there had been no major riot that Monday, though the demonstration at the Brandenburg Gate had come perilously close to one. In spite of all the eastern security precautions, however, there were sporadic outbursts of fighting between East Berlin youths and Vopos and Kampfgruppen. There had been scuffles on both sides of the wire at crossing points, too; tear gas had been thrown and two warning shots fired from the East. There was more trouble on the western side of the Gate after nightfall: gangs of rowdies tried to break through the new barriers and get to the Gate itself, but were driven back by East Berlin hoses and dispersed by the West Berlin police. Through the night the Eastern Sector streets leading to the Gate were barricaded. Armoured cars kept their guard at the Gate; 2,000 armed men lined the boundary ahead of them and extended on both flanks. When journalists did a final sweep in the East they found more tanks near Leipziger Strasse and at the Friedrichstrasse station; twenty extra tanks in Marx-Engels-Platz at the east end of Unter den Linden. Armed men were bedding down for the night. Arc lamps blazed along the sector boundary. Road drills and bulldozers roared. The concrete posts and wire twined on and on through the city.[43]

Throughout the whole of Monday 14 August not one allied soldier had appeared on the streets of West Berlin. There was, in fact, a British anti-tank unit in the Tiergarten, but it was so well back from the sector boundary, so well camouflaged and tucked into the trees, that no one saw it, except perhaps Soviet aerial reconnaissance for whom it was intended. For forty-eight hours there had been no western protest against the border closure, not even a message of sympathy from a western capital. If there had been a flood, fire or earthquake, telegrams of condolence would have

---

* Conversations in Moscow in 1992 with a former KGB officer in Germany and with a Soviet staff college instructor who spent a lot of time in East Berlin and the GDR in 1961 both confirmed that Soviet military planning and movement were purely defensive. The KGB man vehemently maintained that defence was needed against western attack and denied any fear of riots or need to assist the GDR which was quite capable of handling the situation itself. The staff college instructor pointed out that any army will have contingency plans for attack, but was certain that these were kept well to the back of the Soviet filing cabinets in August 1961 and there was no talk at all of implementing them.

been sent, promises of humanitarian relief made. But three and a half million people had suffered a disaster, an entire nation had been severed, and there had been neither word nor gesture of compassion. Not even from the Chancellor of the Federal Republic, who was always ready when it suited him to term Berlin the future capital of a united country. Today he had not condescended even to make a courtesy call. Indeed he had displayed unpardonable lack of feeling and disregard for the most elementary good manners. At an election speech in Regensburg that evening he had referred to his rival for the Chancellorship as "Herr Brandt, alias Framm" – in one carefully chosen and disgusting little phrase he had reminded his audience that the Mayor of Berlin was illegitimate and that his name was an alias adopted during the war when he had left his country and joined those who fought against it.

Western officials in the city knew how hurt and isolated West Berliners felt. An American cable to the State Department that evening stressed that popular feeling was of affront at allied inactivity rather than anxiety over the future of the city. A British cable carried the same message and urged that forceful protest at the very highest level was the least anyone could expect: after all, the sector boundary had been turned into a national frontier in contravention of international law and in advance of agreement, it was totally mistaken to claim that the allies' rights had not been interfered with when their free movement in the city could now only be exercised on the say-so of the GDR and through limited crossings, and it must be realised that the Berlin status quo had been lost. Washington and London took no notice. Over the years the capitals invariably thought their officials in Berlin had "gone native", were too absorbed in the minutiae of their peculiar little "island" to see the "wider perspective".[44]

The allied governments were not impressed either by prompting from Bonn. Brentano saw the three western ambassadors in the morning and called for immediate formal protests to Moscow and for suspension of the Temporary Travel Documents needed by East German and Soviet bloc visitors to the West (a form of pressure which had, after all, been very successful in the past). In his view the events in Berlin so far were just a test of western reaction and unless there was a forcible response, the eastern authorities would make further, bigger moves. He made little impact on the British and American ambassadors, Steel and Dowling. They did not see the recent happenings as part of long-term designs on the city but as measures to stop the refugee flow. ("I must say," Steel cabled to London, "that I personally have always wondered that the East Germans have waited so long to seal this boundary.") The Foreign Office took the same view: "our interests are not directly involved"; protest would be futile as it always had been; suspending TTDs was likely to provoke the East Germans to close the remaining crossing points and interfere with West Berlin's communications with the FRG; other counter measures would probably turn into an economic blockade and have an even worse effect on British than West German trade with the GDR. Whitehall's instructions to the Washington embassy were that nothing must be said or done to "increase the tension or to stimulate uprising in East Germany". Formal protest would, of course, be made to Moscow – and negotiations might be proposed, "for which, of course, we are not ready before 17 September" (the FRG elections) and which de Gaulle opposed.[45]

In the United States there was an influential group eager for talks without delay and regardless of de Gaulle's views on them. McGeorge Bundy, head of the NSC, informed Kennedy that the Presidential staff unanimously agreed that there should be a "clear initiative for negotiations" within the next week or ten days, though warned that the State Department was "more cautious" (a pejorative adjective for an already despised group) and "committed to a four-Power process of planning" (which by in-group definition meant "slow and compromising"). He doubted the value of a TTD ban or other "little actions in reprisal against this big one" which were "unrelated to the crime" (border closure). What Bundy failed to understand, what all the western capitals ignored, was the importance for Berliners of a mere gesture. Political calculations were being made but no thought was being given to the feelings of three and a half million people either side of the wire; there was no assessment of the long-term political effect of a collapse of West Berlin's morale and with it the loss of will to cling on to the freedoms of the western sectors. The level of Kennedy's thought was summed up in a memo he sent to Bundy. What, he asked, is being done "to exploit propaganda-wise" the sealing of the border? Recent actions, he explained, had shown "how hollow is the phrase 'free city' ", and how despised the GDR government which the Soviet Union "seeks to make respectable". That offered "a very good propaganda stick". That day the President rejected a CIA proposal to send a combat team up the Autobahn in a display of strength, but he was also dubious about starting negotiations. He was under no domestic political pressure to do anything at all. Senator Mike Mansfield took the view "Let's keep our shirts on . . . Berlin is only one of the many difficulties that confront the President." The American press had not so far criticised the Administration for inertia.[46]*

---

*Journalist Ben Bradlee's memory of 14 August was that journalists were much too busy chasing up a story that the President had been married before, and to a twice-divorced woman.

The President hardly needed to be told by Thompson that border closure had been virtually inevitable – everyone had expected it for weeks past. Nor did he need to feel a duty to act: he had never made a commitment to East Berlin or to West Berliners' freedom of movement across their city. Without a doubt, the private feeling of official Washington and the entire western alliance was that the stemming of the refugee flow had saved them many a headache and was a merciful release from the dread of interruption of their own communications. Few, however, would have accepted one official's view (or at least have had the bad taste to express it): "Ninety-nine per cent of these refugees have not been seeking legitimate political asylum or freedom from real oppression; they have been seeking a better shake economically." Many, though, would have agreed with him that all the West could and should do now was to ensure "the preservation of the security and freedom of West Berlin. Everything else is tangential."[47]

During Monday 14 August 3,213 refugees had registered but hundreds more had been turned away while the staff tried to catch up with the backlog of health and security checks. Only about four hundred of these latest arrivals, however, were formally categorised as escapers; the rest were thought to be East German visitors or Grenzgänger caught in the West and unwilling to go home. On Tuesday another 1,923 were registered (including 482 Grenzgänger), but again barely forty had risked the wire, forests or canals to get there. One of them caught the imagination of the outside world and created a historic image of the city and its division. He was a young East German soldier called Conrad Schumann, who had been a shepherd on a collective farm before being conscripted and becoming a junior officer. He had been looking for a way out all day until finally at the corner of Bernauer Strasse and Kempnerstrasse he found nothing more than a loose roll of wire with vociferous crowds either side distracting the Vopos. He muttered to some young men in the West that he was going to risk it and they tipped off the police (and seemingly journalists and cameramen too). As the Vopos watched the increasing activity in front of them rather than their backs, Schumann did a running jump, dropping his rifle behind him, cleared the wire by inches as cameras clicked and whirred, and dashed to the open doors of a western police van. There were other dramatic escapes that night: two girls who could not swim got across the Teltow canal in inflated inner tubes; two swimmers were shot at in the water. But such incidents were getting rare. The Marienfelde authorities decided to stop publishing the daily refugee figures: they would not give the East Germans the pleasure of seeing how effective their controls now were.[48]

This was a satisfying gesture for those who made it, but too small to placate indignant West Berliners. They wanted action from the western allies. Their mood was caught by local and Federal newspapers on the morning of Tuesday 15 August: western lethargy was explained as either incompetent lack of preparedness or a selfish willingness to see Berliners suffer so long as western interests were not damaged. *Die Welt* castigated western passivity on the grounds that it "both weakened their own starting point for future negotiations" and "increased the aggressiveness of the other side"; *Mittag* warned that the West would accept the Berlin situation as it had the rape of Poland, Czechoslovakia and the Baltic states, and that Federal appeals for calm would fail if the West continued to do nothing.[49]

Since these articles had been written, there was new cause for alarm in the western sectors, a fresh reason to expect allied reaction. Overnight, 14–15 August, the East Germans had decreed that West Berlin vehicles could no longer enter East Berlin without a special permit. This was direct interference with western as opposed to eastern movement (closing crossing points might just about be seen as aimed at East Germans) and it was patently not a measure aimed purely at restricting the refugee flow. West Berliners' mounting anger was relayed to Washington and London during the day by worried but temperate officials. People were not afraid, said Allan Lightner of the US Mission, but "excited and uncertain"; the Senate thought that their proverbial calm had given way for the first time since 1945 to "considerable nervous tension"; some politicians feared that continued frustration with western inertia might erupt into violence. The City Fathers had called for a mass demonstration on Wednesday – a safety valve for the feelings.

But the allied capitals did nothing on Tuesday to neutralise the explosive emotional compound. Unknown to Berliners, allied diplomats in Paris were drafting a joint Note to Moscow. Throughout the day the State Department and allied ambassadors discussed the Federal proposal to ban all TTDs – something must be done, Grewe argued, to encourage West Berlin to stand fast and to deter further GDR measures. The French were in favour but Foy Kohler thought the idea "picayune" and wanted to save other counter measures in case threats were made to western access. Washington and London feared that any move would prod the East Germans to interfere with West Berlin's communications with the Federal Republic. They ignored the day's cables from their embassies in Bonn which stressed that the only preventative against further encroachment was speedy resolute action, that Adenauer had promised it and could not be left in the lurch, that the TTD weapon could be used now even if others were kept in reserve.[50]

Whatever the value of these arguments, West Berliners knew nothing of them. As far as they were concerned the West was taking no interest at all in their plight. The delivery that day of the allied Military Commandants' protest to their Soviet counterpart added to West Berliners' wrath. It was worse than a fiasco: these platitudes of impotent complaint, yet another legalistic ritual of asserting claims no one enforced, served only to remind everyone how unavailing such formalities had been in the past and how indolently overdue this one seemed. Furthermore, the Commandants took no action on written requests from the Senate for permission to stop exchanging local workers' East mark wages and for a commission to consider the future of the GDR-run S-bahn. These two thorns in West Berlin flesh goaded people to attack western Grenzgänger, verbally and even physically, and to call for a boycott of the S-bahn.[51]

The British in Berlin wanted to make a specific protest about the closure of the Brandenburg Gate since Monday afternoon: it had been the only crossing point in the British Sector. Their embassy in Bonn advised against it on the contorted argument that getting the Gate open would look like condoning other restrictions; the Foreign Office was prepared to leave it shut "as a symbol of the repressive nature of the DDR". The British actually held a trump card which could have won this game: the Gate, to the infinite wrath of West Berliners, was still being opened by the Vopos for the regular passage of the Soviet guard at the War Memorial in the Tiergarten. Ever since the early hours of Sunday 13 August the West Berlin police, as if they had nothing better to do, had been obliged to protect the Russian soldiers from being torn limb from limb. British officials wanted to insist on the withdrawal of the Soviet detachment until the Brandenburg Gate was open for all. The most the Foreign Office would concede was that barbed wire could be erected round the memorial, with a gap to admit the Russians, and that British soldiers would mount guard at each corner. This, London fondly believed, would "cheer Berliners". No. It set their teeth on edge.[52]

At least it would take a few ounces off the heavy load of the West Berlin police. Few of them had been home since dawn on Sunday; for two days they had fought back wave after wave of demonstrators against the wire and dreaded the first shots from the armed ranks on the other side. Today they were still on full alert – and on cold rations. They were marginally more relaxed now their barricades were keeping the crowd 500 yards back from the Gate. Even so, a determined mass of rioters might still break through, and there could be violence at any one of the seventy or more wired off crossing points.[53]

In the event, West Berlin stayed quiet if tense all Tuesday 15 August. The only major incident was on the other side, but well back from the boundary, when a crowd of several hundred was broken up on Unter den Linden. Elsewhere in East Berlin the rigid security held. Armed patrols combed the streets, there were armoured personnel carriers at every government building and thirty or forty tanks at strategic points (those at Friedrichstrasse station now defended by rolls of barbed wire), and there was increased vigilance along sector canals and the outer border. Soviet units had not moved. In the afternoon, forces were thinned out slightly – Kampfgruppen in particular were stood down – but there was still more than enough armed presence to intimidate the population. Guns, however, could not change minds. When a deputy Party secretary visited a group of East German railway men on a repair train they pointed to an armed Vopo and group of rifle-touting militia and asked, "Is that what we have to put up with from now on? Is this life in a democracy of the working class?" Another party official, trying to raise the political consciousness of some women railway cleaners, was drowned out with shouts that potatoes and butter were more important than the sector boundary; if things were bad now, what would they be like in the winter? One of the women showed that it was not only Adenauer who knew how to daub a really dirty smear: "Who does Ulbricht think he is? He's not a German, he's a Russian citizen, isn't he?" (And indeed he probably had owned a Soviet passport since the war.)[54]

The *Bild* headline on the morning of Wednesday 16 August proclaimed "The West Is Doing Nothing". That afternoon placards carried by demonstrators outside the Rathaus read "Betrayed by the West", "Where are the Protecting Powers?", "The West is doing a Second Munich", "90 Hours and No Action". Over a quarter of a million people stood in the rain and for over an hour they heard Brandt saying many of the things they wanted saying. He compared the present crisis to the occupation of the Rhineland; "in the coming weeks and months Berlin must not have another Munich". He promised that allied guarantees were as binding as ever; called on representatives of all nations to come and see the Communist "paradise" behind the wire and begged Vopos and Kampfgruppen not to shoot at fellow Germans; "Berlin", he declared, "expects more than words, Berlin expects political action." The meeting had some of the flavour of the magnificent demonstrations of Berlin courage and resolution during the Blockade. Its very size bore witness to solidarity and sent a message of resistance to the East. Several of Brandt's phrases were echoes of the great speeches of his hero Ernst Reuter. But he had only, as one reporter noted, hit the crowd's "uneasy, questioning mood"; Reuter would have uplifted it. Brandt was constrained by his sense of the people's anger; he was terrified of releasing their violence. And indeed, as the meeting ended, there was a cry: march on the Brandenburg Gate. Egon Bahr, Brandt's wily adviser, was ready for it. On his order the Liberty Bell in the Rathaus tower rang out and deafened all ears. The Bell not only sounded freedom but Berlin's endurance and allied support – it was the gift of the American people in memory of the Blockade.[55]

As Brandt told the Rathaus meeting, he had just sent a personal letter to President Kennedy. (Twenty Bonn students had sent a black umbrella labelled "Chamberlain".) It was a grave letter, heartfelt but restrained. In it Brandt argued that the recent boundary measures had "practically destroyed the remains of the four-Power status" of Berlin; western acceptance of them had been tacit acknowledgement of the sovereignty of the GDR; many West Berliners now doubted the will and ability of the allies to react. The Soviet Union had achieved half of its "free city" proposal and "the second act is a question of time"; it would end a haven of freedom and symbol of reunification, and transform a place to which refugees fled into one whose population deserted it. He called on the West to proclaim a three-Power status for the western sectors while demanding restoration of quadripartite responsibility, for repeated public guarantees of allied presence and insistence on a peace settlement in accordance with the principle of self-determination. Berlin, in his view, should be brought before the United Nations as a human rights issue; meanwhile, the American garrison should be strengthened to express allied support and to reassure the people. None of these actions, he admitted, would alter the existing situation – "a deep wound in the life of German people"– but inactivity depressed Berliners and boosted the GDR. He recalled, "not without bitterness", all the western declarations that there would be no negotiations under pressure; now that Communist threats had actually been carried out the allies were saying that it was no longer possible to refuse talks.[56]

The letter was dignified and without rancour. The only words of complaint were reserved for the Military Commandant's "delayed and not very vigorous step" in protesting to the Soviet authorities. Brandt had tried to explain unemotionally the interpretation West Berliners put on inaction and what the likely political consequences would be. Kennedy, however, reacted as if personally insulted. He told his press secretary, Pierre Salinger, "I don't trust this man at all"; Jim O'Donnell reported him exploding "That bastard in Berlin is trying to involve me in the upcoming German election." Stories went round that the President was furious at the contrast between Brandt's lack of suggestions at the Commandants' meeting on 13 August and this "belligerence" now; that he thought the Mayor should have telephoned or flown to Washington to see him (forgetting that he had told Brandt in March to get in touch at any time and ignoring the fact that the Mayor of West Berlin had too many problems at home to spend hours in planes). Even when Kennedy calmed down a bit and learned more about the Berlin mood, his reply on 18 August showed no appreciation of the despair which had prompted Brandt to write, or understanding of the cogency of his political warnings. The border closure, he acknowledged, had been "brutal" but "only war could reverse it" and no one could possibly believe "that we should go to war on this point". He agreed to an increase in the American garrison, but insisted that an overall military build-up was more important. All other ideas put forward by Brandt were slapped down as "mere trifles" compared with what had been done: "the situation", declared the President, was "too serious for inadequate responses". Instead he suggested that "painful" though the rift with the East might be, West Berlin's life was linked with the West and it would remain an "outpost of freedom" and a vital part of the Free World.

Kennedy had entirely missed the points that Brandt had been at pains to make: Berliners did not expect that any specific measure would reverse their present dire situation; they certainly did not want war, or any action which risked war either, not when they could see the armed men and military hardware a few yards away and knew where the Soviet tanks were. What they needed was moral support to come to terms with what had happened and to give the confidence that they could survive it; some proof that they would not be left alone to drift to further destruction. The President as yet could not see the Berlin wood for the western trees. He believed all the arguments in Washington that the wire had gone up not to provoke but avoid an East–West confrontation in Berlin; that the western sectors and allied rights had not been violated and the meagre reprisals would have to be kept for when they were, that sanctions might drive the East Germans to cut the western sectors' communications. By contrast, he had not listened to the advice of his Mission in Berlin or embassy in Bonn that suspending TTDs might look "picayune" in the State Department but was seen as vital in the Federal Republic; that there must be a "combination of actions which individually may not be of great significance" but would sustain faith in the allies. He did not understand that if West Berlin's morale collapsed so would the "outpost of freedom" with its allied presence and access, ties with the FRG and all theories of four-Power responsibility for a city and a peace settlement. If West Berlin was lost by default, the credibility of the western alliance would go with it.

Kennedy's position was, however, already being eroded on 16 August. The Ambassadorial Group meeting in Washington that evening agreed to accept the draft of a joint western protest to Moscow, to be delivered next day, and began to swing to the view that TTDs should be suspended, allied garrisons increased, and patrols sent into the Eastern Sector to affirm allied rights. This Group at least had started to hear West Berlin's cries of distress and to respond. And during the day a cable came from Berlin, not very differently phrased from all the other Berlin or Bonn cables and very similar in argument to Brandt's letter – but this was from a source Kennedy trusted. Ed Murrow of the USIA had been sounding the opinion of local journalists, American and German. He described their feeling "that we are facing a crisis of confidence". What was seen in the city as "the surrender of East Berlin to Ulbricht" had been "a shock so severe that it could gravely affect our future relations", first with Berlin then, as disillusion set in, with Bonn. What was needed, in Murrow's view, was a series of well-publicised if insubstantial steps to express American interest and support; not "violent action, merely some action" to prove that this was not "another sample of Hitler's take-over of the Rhineland". "What is in danger of being destroyed here is that perishable commodity called hope."[57]

Hope was indeed at its last gasp on Tuesday night. All day West Berliners had noticed what the US Mission called the "increased cockiness, smugness and jubilation of East Zone officials and police, many of whom were apparently extremely uncertain on Sunday of [their] ability to get away with [the] seal-off of West Berlin". East German radio and television had been sneering; the joke of the day ran "Did you hear that Brandt called the allies for help?" "Yes, I heard. But the allies didn't." And in the afternoon East German lorries had driven up to vulnerable crossings, to Bernauer Strasse and then across the Potsdamer Platz. Concrete slabs, concrete blocks, bags of sand and cement were unloaded. The GDR was not content with wire. It was preparing to build a Wall.[58]

10

The Wall

=⟫●⟪=

C ould the Western Powers have stopped the East Germans
building the Berlin Wall? In later years many individuals and
a high proportion of Berliners would have said they could and
should. A frequent explanation for western inertia in August 1961 is that
everyone was so taken by surprise. It is a bad excuse: the allies had, after all,
been expecting some form of border closure for months but had simply not
prepared for it, though they had plans for airlifts without really expecting
blockade. The excuse is so threadbare, indeed, that conspiracy theorists
conclude that the Western Powers must have been tipped off about the
wire and wall in plenty of time to agree to accept both. One theory is that
John J. McCloy was warned by Khrushchev during his stay on the Black
Sea (but he always categorically denied it); a more general argument is that
with the whole of Berlin and both parts of Germany swarming with allied
intelligence agencies, spies, informers and double agents it was impossible
not to know exactly what was going to happen and when. A former KGB
agent in Germany claimed that the KGB "knew many western sources in
East Germany" and "sent information" about plans for the Wall – but if
the KGB was alternately as clumsy and obscure in transmitting messages as
Soviet diplomats, no blame can be attached to those who failed to grasp
what was being conveyed. Even so, given the cost of all those spies and their
activities, one might think that the western capitals certainly should have
known in some detail what was going to occur.[1]

But all the available evidence suggests that they did not (and if official
papers reveal the opposite, they are still unreleased). Lieutenant-Colonel

THE LAST DIVISION

Richards of the Royal Military Police said he "was in close contact with every form of intelligence agency in Berlin and also the BRIXMIS (military intelligence) mission based in Potsdam, going in and out of East Germany, and they had absolutely nothing at all". Foy Kohler wrote that the events of 12–13 August demonstrated "a failure of specific local intelligence" and that the President was clearly "deeply disappointed" by not being forewarned. He can hardly have been surprised, however, given the poor advice the CIA gave him over Cuba and the Bay of Pigs; aerial espionage had failed to detect military moves before the invasion of Egypt at Suez, and was just as likely to have overlooked the massing of troops and building equipment before 13 August. Brandt is on record as saying "No hints were conveyed to me by the German or Allied intelligence services, and it genuinely seems that the preparations were camouflaged with total success." Ernst Lemmer, who spent a pleasant evening on 12 August drinking with journalists, remembered that "Even my friends in the press . . . had as little idea as diplomats and politicians of what was going to happen" – and the press had plenty of contacts all over East Germany. Brentano asked Kroll on 13 August whether diplomats in Moscow had heard hints of a wall. If West German intelligence services had been up to snuff he would not have needed to ask. General Reinhard Gehlen, their head at the time, claimed in his very self-serving memoirs that he had "learned from a reliable source that the Russians had given Ulbricht a free hand" and had warned Bonn that the Berlin boundary would be totally sealed (something that was expected anyway). But he added "we could not predict the actual date they would start", and avoided admitting that his office's Friday report which Albertz found on his Senate desk on the morning of Monday 14 August stated "no particular action expected". When Kroll got back to Moscow, he checked with his "usual sources" about how the decision had been taken. They had no idea. Oleg Troyanovsky, very close to Khrushchev as interpreter and foreign policy adviser, knew nothing either. He had merely been told a few days before 13 August that he might prefer to cancel his planned holiday in Berlin; he and his wife went to Bulgaria instead.[2]

To give credit where it is due, the East Germans had run this operation impressively. It was a tremendous feat of planning, co-ordination and secrecy by a tiny group. (What a mistake not to have run the economy with a modicum of that efficiency.) To attribute blame where it is deserved, the allied intelligence services had failed to penetrate those levels of the East German government, Kremlin or Warsaw Pact where such decisions were made, had not themselves observed or had informants to see the vast amount of men and matériel on the way into East Berlin in the days before the wire went up (though East Germans going on holiday just before 13 August found driving slow, thanks to the huge amount of military traffic on the roads). And, since intelligence is only as good as its analysis, it has to be added that the few tip-offs and rumours passed on were not understood in the western capitals or made good use of. Perhaps this was not surprising. Berlin housed so many agencies and garnered so much intelligence, that it provided not information but white noise. The city was also a round-the-clock, mass production rumour factory and a hub of black propaganda, counter-espionage, double agents, and amateurs trying to earn a quick mark: it was usually wise to ignore most of the stories in circulation. When Maxwell Taylor later examined all the intelligence coming into Washington in the two weeks before 13 August he "found only fragments which might have pointed to this event taking place": stories of movements of engineering equipment and building materials. Others remembered hearing of sudden huge orders for posts and wire placed with East German or even West German factories. But they had told themselves that the already heavily fortified frontier needed constant repair, the new collective farms had to be fenced, that East Berlin was a permanent building site. No one was likely to find the significance in isolated reports over several weeks that there were East German surveying teams at various points on the border or that the French had been told by a GDR dentist that several of his SED patients said barriers were about to go up across the city. Even Colonel von Pawel, of the US Military Mission, who had predicted a wall and argued hard for his belief at a Watch Committee meeting on 9 August, always admitted that he had only a hunch and not a certainty.[3]

But even if the Western Powers were not forewarned of the precise nature and timing of the border closure, many would say they could have acted more effectively once it happened. The moment the wire went up, so one argument goes, it should have been torn down: Ulbricht and Khrushchev, confronted by the limits of western tolerance, would not have dared to develop the GDR frontier with concrete blocks. As staid a man as General Lauris Norstad reckoned that if he had been the commander on the spot on 13 August, he would have slung a hook on a rope at the wire, and hauled it away with a jeep. Lucius D. Clay sometimes maintained that all the local general had to do "was to have our trucks up and down the street unarmed – unarmed soldiers in those trucks – and we would never have had a war". Others thought the wire in itself was too trivial to justify action or was too clearly related to refugee control which was in everyone's interests. They talked instead of smashing the first solid barriers with tanks or getting the West Berlin fire brigade to sluice the mortar out of the blocks. Significantly, whatever was said later, such simple forthright ideas were not even considered in August. "I know of no one", said General Maxwell Taylor confidently, "who ever recommended knocking down the Wall." When President Kennedy finally came under criticism for inaction and in January 1962 ordered a review of military planning in Berlin and Germany over the period, there was no evidence of any draft order to remove the wire or wall. Even Clay, who usually claimed that if he had been in charge he would have bulldozed the wire, offered then to testify to Congress that criticism of failure to do so was unfair.[4]

The fact was that western leaders and officials were at first mightily relieved that the sector boundary was being sealed rather than their own communications being blocked. Then, as the gravity and permanence of the closure dawned on them, they were paralysed, like rabbits caught in a headlight. With hindsight, arguments were found to justify that incapacity as sagacity. It became the conventional wisdom that if the wire had been pulled away the East Germans would have retreated a few feet and slung it up again; the same response would have been made to the removal of the first sections of solid wall; the use of tanks under those circumstances would have looked ridiculous and risked the lives of all the civilians milling about on either side. Furthermore, since the East Germans were scrupulous about sticking well inside their own boundary, any action would have taken the allies into the Eastern Sector: a mini-invasion which might well have been met by infinitely superior Soviet armed force. Such explanations ignore questions of whether the sector boundary was legally an international frontier which Ulbricht had the right to fortify or whether it was just the administrative division of a four-Power city where freedom of movement had long been agreed and could not be unilaterally disrupted. They also avoid analysis of what Pankow and the Kremlin may have been thinking on the night of 12–13 August.[5]

It is perfectly likely (though as yet the documentary evidence is not available to test the theory) that they were checking that Kennedy and NATO meant what they said and would only fight for western presence, access and the freedom of the western sectors; that if a determined effort were made to defend the theory of a four-Power city then they would retreat from the brink. The novelist or dramatist could write a scene to show that Khrushchev took to the bottle and bellicosity in mid-August because he was afraid of what might happen when the GDR frontier was sealed. Historians can only spatchcock details to suggest that Khrushchev and Ulbricht were ready to recoil if confronted: the lack of current Warsaw Pact plans for war – the relief of East German soldiers and police when they realised how much they had got away with, the caution with which the wire and Wall went up – and left time to backtrack if attacked. Conversely, however, it has to be remembered that ever since 1950 the experience of the Soviet Union in Berlin had been that the allies never went further than mere protest against encroachment or violation of agreement. So the very gradual building of a border was perhaps just practical tactics: define the frontier with wire, hold back the refugees and protesters from both sides, then have security for a solid construction later – and since all those concrete blocks and sacks of cement were already available, they must have been intended for use from the very beginning, with even the most nervous gambler calculating that the chances of the allies responding with force were only negligible.

As, indeed, they were. Western leaders saw the issues of August 1961 in purely black and white terms. Kennedy was recorded as saying "It's not a very nice solution, but a wall is a hell of a lot better than a war" – and, in view of the inadequate conventional forces, he had to think of quick escalation to nuclear war. But, given all due sympathy for those with the terrifying responsibility for pressing the nuclear button, it is still not unreasonable to suggest that this reaction, shared by Kennedy's colleagues and allies, was not just colour-blind but insensitive to all the shades of grey as well. There were plenty of instant actions, far short of a threat of war, which might have deterred further Soviet and East German encroachments. Why not have allied military patrols in the western sectors, where they had every right to be, to warn against overstepping the sector boundary which in the early hours it was not certain would be respected? Actually taking western troops off the streets looked like a signal of collusion. Why accept thirteen designated crossing points instead of the previous eighty-eight, and seem grateful for them? Why not protest against the closure of the Brandenburg Gate? Maxwell Taylor suggested that the western Military Commandants should inform the Russians that they were coming to East Berlin to discuss the situation and would cross wherever they chose, and by force if necessary. That would have been a perfectly appropriate, not too "picayune", assertion of freedom of movement. It would have been a much more effective, appropriate statement of quadripartite rights than leaving a Soviet guard at the War Memorial. Surely the Soviet Union would not have launched nuclear missiles in return?[6]

And what about all the political and diplomatic possibilities? Is it pardonable that the Military Commandants' protest was delayed until 15 August; that the joint three-Power Note to Moscow was delivered only on 17 August? If the bureaucracy is lethargic, it is up to political leaders to put some vim and vigour into it – not go sailing, golfing or shooting as they did. Even if protest in itself is unlikely to get instant change, it should be made; and the longer it takes to make, the less effect it will have. Allied procrastination in August gave the impression that the West saw no reason to complain and left the East Germans with up to four days to get on with wiring and bringing up the concrete. There was no reason, furthermore, why the Western Powers should not have immediately announced action which would take time to put into effect: for example, an appeal to the United Nations, on the grounds that the Berlin border closure was a violation of human rights and international law, might have given pause to those preparing to restrict freedom of movement with concrete. Again, it hardly matters what the result of the United Nations' debate would have been: there was a case to make, it should have been made, and the process started early.

Thereafter, the Western Powers, who moaned about being taken by surprise, had a whole range of non-military counter measures which they had been discussing to the last detail for months but intending to use for other eventualities: suspending TTDs, slowing or stopping interzonal trade, imposing economic embargoes individually or throughout NATO. If the political leaders and most of their officials had not decided to stay and enjoy their holidays, final approval for some or all of these measures could have been got in days. They did not have to be implemented overnight, but if threatened between 13 and 16 August they might well have made the East Germans a little more nervous about delivering concrete slabs to the sector boundary and given second thoughts to their Warsaw Pact allies who had a lot to lose from economic sanctions. Why not give more than cursory consideration to Brandt's suggestion that West Berlin be make a tripartite responsibility? Or even a Land of the Federal Republic? After all, if the Soviet Union was allowed to incorporate the Eastern Sector into the Soviet bloc, it was logical to establish the final links between the western sectors, West Germany and the western alliance. Yet again: such constitutional adjustments would not necessarily have brought the wire down, but they would have been appropriate tit for tat, and brought home to the East the political price of keeping the boundary closed. Doing nothing was accepting what the other side had done – and encouraging it to do more.

And the western allies did nothing for four days after the wire first went across Berlin. On 17 August Kennedy at last began to understand something of the impact of border closure on Berlin morale. He wrote to Macmillan and de Gaulle suggesting that since West Berliners were "badly shaken by the events of the week" the three leaders might send a joint declaration of their determination to "maintain and preserve at whatever cost" their fundamental rights in Berlin and their "obligations to those under their protection", which included defence of the liberties of West Berliners and their communications with the Federal Republic. De Gaulle had no objections to such a statement in principle, but wanted to add a paragraph to emphasise to the Kremlin that recent events in Berlin "prevent any attempt at a settlement"; that unless there was "a profound change" in the international atmosphere and East–West relations were "marked by a wide and real détente" there could be no negotiations. Kennedy and Macmillan, more convinced than ever that negotiations must begin as soon as possible, dropped the idea of a declaration. The only positive moves on 17 August were the delivery of the three-Power protest Notes in Moscow, the British and French announcements of reinforcements for their Berlin garrisons and the decision of the State Department that its Berlin Task Force would meet daily at 10.30 a.m. But it could well be argued that either a refusal to talk or a threat to uphold rights could have frightened Khrushchev and deterred further moves in Berlin.[7]

To define the events of 13 August, as Rusk and others continued to do, regardless of what happened later, merely as the East Germans using their "right to stop the flow of their own people" was to be blinkered then and purblind thereafter to the enormity of the measures. If the East Germans had only been concerned to block the escape of their citizens, they could have ringed the outer perimeter of East Berlin to stop the bulk of would-be emigrants ever reaching the escape hatch, then doubled the guard on the eighty-eight crossing points to deal with the rest. Sealing the inner boundary was assertion of sovereignty by an unrecognised state, a plug in the last hole in the Iron Curtain, destruction of the chances of German reunification or European détente, a flouting of international agreements, and unilateral imposition of a post-war settlement by coup de main. Two protest Notes were not just an ignominious response to such behaviour. They showed destitution of political judgement and a dearth of political invention.

Berliners (and no doubt the Communist bloc) drew the conclusion that the Western Powers had written the city off. And as a result, on Thursday 17 August Berliners felt utterly isolated and impotent as they watched the next violation of their city by the GDR. Behind the wire the Wall began to rise. Viewed objectively, a row of concrete blocks was no worse than the wire; it merely confirmed the damage that had already been done. But no one could watch this abominable construction unemotionally. As block was thumped on block, images were created which shocked the world. The wire, in reality, had partitioned Berlin. But there could be no more potent metaphor for that pitiless division than the Wall. The wire had been vicious, lacerating, but at least it could be seen through, one could imagine snipping it, dream that something so simply rolled out could easily be rolled up again. Concrete blocks were impermeable, indestructible; a statement that this partition was to endure in perpetuity.

Throughout the day staggered lines of low concrete barriers went up at the twelve open crossing points, forcing cars to brake and slalom through. Vopos and Kampfgruppen piled concrete building blocks at the closed crossings, almost eighteen inch cubes but lightened by pierced channels; as they slopped mortar between them it oozed like runny icing. Prefabricated slabs up to six feet high were interlocked across open spaces and topped with lines of barbed wire. The doors and windows of houses with access on to the sector boundary were bricked up. A few refugees grabbed their last chance: 163 were registered on 17 August, seven of whom were Vopos; one young couple smashed through a barrier in their car and were fired at but came through uninjured. As the Wall rose, East Berliners handed suitcases, blankets, letters to West Berliners; people rushed to hug friends and relatives while their arms could still stretch across. As it got higher, they stood on tiptoe and waved, then brought out step ladders and shouted farewell messages. A bride lobbed her bouquet to her sobbing mother on the other side. By 3 a.m. on 18 August work had begun to block off the whole of the Potsdamer Platz up to a height of eight feet; by noon next day the Wall there was so high no one could see across to the other side of the city.[8]

Not even the most sceptical could now think in terms of "refugee control". This was the butchery of a city. Oddly, it was still possible to get into East Berlin. Sir Christopher Steel, the British ambassador in Bonn, was allowed to drive through and most West Germans, who were now funnelled through three crossing points, had few problems, though they were carefully searched. Yet by 18 August, West Berliners were encountering considerable difficulties: they had been told they could get an entry permit at three of the twelve points, but one of the offices was closed, the next said the permits would take five to six days, and the third announced that only those with a job in East Berlin were allowed to enter.[9]

Faced with the soaring Wall and the shrinking crossings, West Berliners showed none of the passion with which they had reacted to the wire. There were no fights with the Vopos; there were no mass demonstrations on the 17th or 18th, and the police actually reduced their state of alert. Many Berliners had always predicted that worse would follow the wire. Now they saw the form it took, most were too miserable to act. Some were not totally numbed but found non-violent ways to relieve their feelings: there were wild cat strikes demanding the dismissal of Communists from factory jobs,

The first wire (*right*) was
replaced in coming weeks
with (*below*) screens, tank
traps and concrete blocks.
The Wall here has been
built a couple of feet inside
the East and slashes across a
street and the tram lines.

West Berliners demonstrating at their town hall, 16 August 1961.

Ulbricht on 25 August thanks those who built the Wall. Behind him, in a dark suit, is Erich Honecker who planned it.

Bernauer Strasse,
with houses in the
East and the
pavement in the
West. *Above:* in
August 1961 East
Berliners could still
escape through the
windows. *Below:* in
September a Vopo
tries to stop the
escape of a 77-year-
old woman, while a
young man tugs her
down into the sheet
held by West Berlin
firemen. Eventually
all the windows in the
street were bricked
up.

Twelve-year-old Erwin Schake goes to school from Eiskeller with one scoutcar in front and another behind. The grass either side of the track is in the GDR.

Lucius D. Clay salutes the welcoming West Berlin crowd on 19 August 1961. Next to him is Vice-President Johnson. Behind the microphones, Willy Brandt.

Escapes to the West.

Right: a balloon, made of nylon sheets and curtains which carried a four-and-a-half foot wooden platform laden with four adults and four children in 1979.

Below left: a tunnel under the Wall in 1962.

Below right: six refugees crammed into this cable drum in 1965.

When President Kennedy (*far right*) visited West Berlin in June 1963, the East Berlin authorities draped the Brandenburg Gate with red curtains, so that he could not see into the East – or be seen.

September 1989: East German refugees in a camp in Hungary hear that they can travel to West Germany.

10 November 1989. Many crossings through the Wall opened overnight but the Brandenburg Gate is still blocked, though the East Germans who guard it are noticeably unarmed.

By January 1990 the Wall has been broken open, graffiti and the roller bars have been hacked off, and the East German watch tower is no longer manned.

Erich Honecker on trial
November 1992.

The removal of the allied
hut at Checkpoint Charlie,
22 June 1990. Celebrating
its disappearance: the
Foreign Ministers of the
four Powers and both
Germanys, the four
Military Commandants, a
member of the West Berlin
Senate and the mayor of
East Berlin.

and the trade unions began to organise a boycott of the S-bahn, leading to what a police report euphemistically described as "discussion groups at almost all stations". The authorities tried measures to keep the population calm. On 18 August, the police closed the West Berlin offices of the East German news agency and the *Berliner Zeitung*, but that did not satisfy West Berliners who had been calling for such reprisals for days and who wanted the local SED headquarters and the Party's thirteen branch offices closed down as well. The same day the Senate set up loudspeakers along the sector boundary to broadcast news to East Berlin. They scored an instant political success, but only with the Vopos who threw tear gas canisters at the radio vans; in the long run they provoked a Loudspeaker War, with the GDR launching its own news and views at the western sectors and everyone suffering more from the din than they gained from the exchange of information.

A debate in the Bundestag in Bonn on 18 August gave no solace to Berliners: it was a low-key affair, in which the rare moments of passion were almost entirely devoted to criticism of the Western Powers, though Adenauer himself called for solidarity with the allies. He had never been expected to show much sympathy for Berlin and any he might have felt had been muted by a visit on 16 August from Smirnov, the Soviet ambassador, who buttered the Chancellor with expressions of Khrushchev's high esteem and stressed that the Kremlin was ready to discuss all matters and that the Berlin measures were not directed against the Federal Republic. Since West Berliners were offered no protection by Bonn, Walter Ulbricht could really get under their skins on the 18th. He gave a seventy-five-minute speech, broadcast on television and radio, crowing about the success of the recent measures, thanking all who had carried them out, claiming that doubts about the existence of two Germanies had been confounded and that NATO was delighted to have avoided a situation which might have endangered peace, calling Brandt an "inflated balloon" who had "burst at the sight of our People's Army", and making the barefaced suggestion that all those in the West who complained about separation from their relatives should come and join them in the GDR.[10]

After that bitter draught of triumphalism, it was just as well that on 19 August West Berlin received its first expression of sympathy and support from the outside world: a visit from Vice-President Lyndon B. Johnson and General Lucius D. Clay, emissaries of the President himself. For four days Kennedy had ignored advice from the State Department, the US embassy in Bonn and Mission in Berlin that action was essential to prevent the collapse of West Berlin morale and that even a few high-ranking visitors would help. He did, however, listen to journalists. Murrow's cable had hit its mark; another veteran reporter of the German scene, Marguerite Higgins, talked the President down from his rage over Brandt's letter. She it was who planted the idea of sending Clay: a great Military Governor, a Berlin hero, the man credited (however questionably) with defeating the Blockade. The General, indeed, had already recommended himself for the mission: he offered his services in a letter to Maxwell Taylor on 15 August. Kennedy preferred to send Johnson: an obvious symbol of Presidential concern and rather less of a loose cannon than Clay who was notorious for his wilfulness, an extreme example of the Berlin priestly cult and Cold War warrior breed to which the White House was so averse, and a Nixon supporter in the recent election to boot. Johnson was reluctant to go to Berlin (some say he complained that he had planned a weekend's fishing; Kenneth O'Donnell, the President's appointments secretary, claimed he cried "There'll be a lot of shooting and I'll be in the middle of it. Why me?"). But Speaker Rayburn, his fishing partner, encouraged him to go and also suggested taking Clay. So the two arrived in Bonn on Friday 18 August, with Charles Bohlen as diplomatic minder, for a brief talk with Adenauer before flying on to West Berlin on Saturday.[11]

There, the plan had been to take the distinguished visitors straight to the Potsdamer Platz to see for themselves the fearsome new Wall. The streets from Tempelhof airport, however, were packed with excited people, many of whom were shouting "Der Clay, der Clay ist hier". Since Johnson did not understand the simplest German he assumed the reception was for himself and found it irresistible. He stood in Brandt's open car waving, shaking hands, patting backs ("getting ready for his election as the next President of the United States", thought Egon Bahr), and the procession was delayed. At the Vice-President's insistence therefore, and to Brandt's chagrin, they cut the Potsdamer Platz and went straight to the Rathaus, where up to 380,000 enthusiastic West Berliners awaited them and where Johnson, Clay and Brandt all made brief speeches, and the Liberty Bell was rung before Johnson went in to address the House of Representatives. His speech, composed by Walt Rostow and vetted by Kennedy, contained the great phrase from the Declaration of Independence and pledged "our lives, our futures, our sacred honour" to the city; Rostow felt that the "President had to wrap the American Flag around Berlin".[12]

Unfortunately, it was all too obvious that the flag swaddled only the western sectors, and chosen aspects of them at that. Johnson had brought Kennedy's reply to Brandt's letter and it was a deep disappointment. Brandt was far from impressed by the President's rhetoric that the boundary closure had been a sign of East German weakness: it might seem so abroad, he retorted, but "in Berlin it is seen as a demonstration of Communist power". In what Brandt remembered as "a somewhat strained conversation" he pointed out to Johnson that Berlin's unity had been destroyed, it had lost its old role as future capital and as a meeting place for East and West. He criticised the limpness of the Military Commandants' protest, the delay in the Note to Moscow and the fact that it had not been delivered to all the Warsaw Pact countries in whose names the boundary had been sealed; he warned that in view of the GDR's easy victories in the past week, the East Germans and Russians would be emboldened to follow up quickly unless a firmer stand was made by the allies. Arguments such as these, which Kennedy had already found incomprehensible, were not going to sway Johnson who understood the Berlin problem even less.[13]

Next day, however, a practical step was taken to boost West Berlin's security and morale. Carefully timed to coincide with the visit of Johnson and Clay, 1,600 American troops drove up the Autobahn from West Germany to reinforce the US garrison. Kennedy had sanctioned the move on 18 August and was thereafter so nervous about it that he stayed in Washington for the weekend, insisting that the Pentagon make contact with the convoy every twenty minutes, and that he himself must be woken in the slightest emergency. The operation itself was a nightmare for those who ran it. The US Army in West Germany was only given six hours' notice to get organised; they thought it unwise to withdraw troops who directly faced Warsaw Pact forces, and chose instead to send the 1st Battle Group, 18th Infantry which was stationed at Mannheim. So 1,600 men and about 350 vehicles, including an engineer company and howitzers, had to drive via Frankfurt and Kassel to Braunschweig where they bivvied down for the night, and then reformed to reach the Helmstedt-Marienborn crossing on to the Autobahn by 6.30 in the morning of Sunday 20 August. By then, they were a mere eight minutes behind schedule – few commanders of any convoy could claim such a record, let alone with so many over such a distance.[14]

Their troubles were far from over when they got there. The Soviet authorities had been informed of the passage the day before and that the convoy would be divided into six groups or serials – so that if there was an incident on the Autobahn, the whole lot would not be caught at once. That had given the Russian officers at the checkpoint plenty of time to polish the technique with which they were past masters: obstruction. When the first serial reached the barrier, a Soviet captain complained that he could not count the men in the trucks so they must line up on the ground. He then wrote down the numbers and types of each vehicle, counted the troops, and went to check the tally on an abacus in his shed. That produced three more men than the total listed in the American movement order. Recount. The first serial got through at 7.45, an hour and a quarter after arrival. The officer, the movement orders and the abacus produced different totals for the second and third serials. Further recounts. At the convoy commander's suggestion, the fourth and fifth listed their own vehicle numbers in advance and lined up the men in four columns to ease the count. Alas for the best laid plans: the last serial turned out to have an inaccurate movement order – two men, more or less – so did not get through until 1.55 p.m.

By comparison with the crossing, the drive up the Autobahn was sheer pleasure: plenty of Vopos at all bridges and road junctions, but cheering clumps of East Germans in the fields along the way and not the slightest attempt to prevent or delay free access. Babelsberg, the Soviet checkpoint at the Berlin end of the Autobahn, staged its own act: delayed the first serial for an hour for vehicle registration and the next for half an hour, then held on to the third because it contained two extra men (who had been picked up from a broken down truck) until the US Provost Marshal sent the message that unless it went through in fifteen minutes he would order the heaviest vehicle to smash the barrier. That worked. The final remnants of the convoy straggled into the western sectors at 8.10 p.m. Given the fertility of imagination and long practice in procrastination of Soviet checkpoint personnel, this was a miracle of American competence and determination.

And what a welcome the reinforcements got in Berlin. They had proved that communications with the Federal Republic were open and the West intended to keep them open; they had come to help when help was most desperately needed. As the first sixty trucks moved into the western sectors soon after noon, a million West Berliners were there to greet them, every face shining with relief and happiness, every flower and sweet shop stripped for grateful gifts. Johnson and Clay presided at a celebration lunch for them at the McNair barracks; in the afternoon a rapturous crowd jammed a triumphant motorcade along the Kurfürstendamm and Clay reviewed a drive-past of some of the column on the very same stand from which he and General Bradley had saluted the entry into Berlin of the Second Armoured Division in 1945.[15]

With admirable tact, the West Berlin hosts concealed the disagreeable moments which might have marred the great weekend for the majority. Johnson behaved throughout the visit with monstrous insensitivity and vulgarity. He took a fancy to the shoes Brandt was wearing when he arrived, and on Sunday the manager of the shop which sold them was obliged to come to the US ambassador's villa to present him with two pairs. (The Vice-President had unmatched feet.) He kept fussing about wanting to cancel official functions so that he could buy some electric shavers, and made a scene on leaving McNair barracks after lunch because he had been provided with a closed car rather than the open vehicle from which he could milk the applause; when he got what he wanted he made Robert Lochner, who was acting as interpreter, crouch on the floor at his feet so as not to spoil the crowd's view of the Vice-President. On a visit to Marienfelde he handed out biros marked "LBJ" and passes to the visitors' galleries in Congress, though a promise of blankets would have been more suitable. He was furious when told that the Royal Prussian Porcelain factory was closed for the weekend, and when finally offered a dinner service as a token of gratitude from West Berlin, promptly demanded a bigger one; in the evening the manager of the factory was hauled from home to take an order for several hundred ashtrays marked "LBJ". To round off a socially uncomfortable day, he insisted on a jolly fried chicken dinner at the Hilton when Brandt and his colleagues had suggested a private meal to discuss the political situation. Johnson's departure gave relief and a rare moment of laughter: he stood solemnly to attention, hand on heart, as a band at Tempelhof played the popular song "Berliner Luft" believing it was a local national anthem.

The British had bitten their lips during the weekend. They themselves had intended to send eighteen armoured troop carriers and sixteen Ferrets up the Autobahn, but rather than get in the way of the US convoy (or perhaps to avoid comparison of the size of garrison contribution), quietly dispatched them by rail.* No one seems to have commented at the time that the American convoy commander had broken three-Power regulations by agreeing to dismount his troops for the Soviet count at Marienborn. (Perhaps, coming from Mannheim, he was not up-to-date with Autobahn theology.) He had in fact established a precedent which the Soviet authorities in Germany would exploit. There were to be several minor "Tailgate" crises (making "Watergate" or "Irangate" look very old coinage) over the question of whether Soviet officers could see into trucks to count or whether the passengers must get out. These culminated in 1963, when tailgates were admittedly very high, and the Russians stopped all American convoys because the men would not leave their vehicles. Llewellyn Thompson had to come out of retirement and negotiate an agreement before traffic flowed freely again.[16]

---

* De Gaulle, too, had planned to send reinforcements – though only a few hundred men since they would all be lost if war broke out. He postponed their arrival because his gesture would not be noticed amid the American brouhaha, and noted with contempt that the British were happy to send "quelques vieux tanks".

Fortunately none of these upsets disturbed West Berliners during the Johnson–Clay visit. As far as the general public was concerned, the weekend was a magnificent success. The placards carried by the crowds, "Thank you for coming, Mr Johnson", were heartfelt; equally sincere were those which read "Washington is nearer than Bonn", though to be fair to Adenauer he had suggested travelling to the western sectors with the official party but had been persuaded that this would look like American interference with the Federal election. The visitors, and even more the garrison reinforcement, were exactly what West Berliners had needed – a "shot in the arm" as the British Military Commandant put it. A supercilious telegram from the British embassy suggested that Berlin morale was "far too addicted to a diet of gestures". Was anyone ready to offer West Berliners anything more nourishing?[17]

Valuable though the weekend had been for creating an atmosphere of solidarity and hope in the western sectors, it did not slow the building of the Wall. Indeed one wonders if it provoked the East Germans into quicker strengthening of their borders and extension of their claims. The programme now moved into a new, nasty phase. On the evening of 20 August, 600 East German workers, with an escort of twelve armoured personnel carriers and two armoured cars, began to erect a chain link fence north of Staaken. A company of the Welch Regiment, with a troop of four Centurion tanks, lined up to face them, but could do no more: the work was taking place well inside the East Berlin boundary. And early next morning, before the American visitors left, furniture vans arrived in East Berlin streets which faced the western sector boundary, and armed troops and police began to turf out inhabitants and their belongings. In Bernauer Strasse, where the houses were in the East but the front doorsteps in the West, a woman jumped from her balcony, fired at but mercifully unhurt. As the ground floors were cleared, men moved in with bricks and mortar. From the street one could see curtains, flower pots, goods in shop windows; inside, the Wall was being constructed. People in flats on the upper floors were told to leave their doors unlocked so that Vopos could search for would-be escapers at any time. In coming days desperate residents would step on to a high sill and fling themselves into firemen's nets or blankets below. Newsreel cameras captured a horrific scene of an elderly woman dangling from her first floor window while Vopos tried to drag her back and the crowd below tugged to free her. Fifty-nine-year-old Ida Siekmann, who lived on the third floor in Bernauer Strasse, heard Vopos coming up the stairs, knocking at doors and seeming ready to empty the upper storeys. Frantic, she threw a mattress out of the window, teetered on the sill for a few seconds, then jumped thirty-five feet to the ground – and missed the mattress. She died on the way to hospital. That very day the British military carried out five flag-flying tours of East Berlin to assert the western right of access, but seventeen million East Germans had already lost the right or the means of egress.[18]

Adenauer came to the western sectors on 22 August. He went to Marienfelde and to Potsdamer Platz, where East German loudspeakers sneered "You're too late Mr Chancellor; we've acted already" and reminded him "someone else near here bit the carpet" (he was within a few yards of the Chancellery where Hitler committed suicide). West Berliners were polite – there were few catcalls and only occasional placards announcing "Too late" or "At last" – but they were not grateful for such a tardy and seemingly grudging visit and they would never forgive him for not coming in the first dreadful week.* His visit, in any case, coincided with major degradation of their lives. That evening the GDR Ministry of the Interior dared to order all West Berliners to stay a hundred metres clear of the sector boundary "in the interests of their own security". Allied troops immediately began patrols to the very edge to combat this intolerable claim to control western territory but the authorities hoped civilians would keep out of the strip which might well become a firing zone for killing refugees. And to make things claustrophobically worse the East Germans also decreed that three more crossing points would close: in future West Berliners must buy a one-mark permit from the East Berlin police which could be used only at four points (Chauseestrasse, Invalidenstrasse, Oberbaumbrücke and Sonnenallee); West Germans could cross at Bornholmer Strasse and Heinrich-Heine Strasse; all foreigners and occupation forces would be restricted to Friedrichstrasse (Checkpoint Charlie). How could anyone conceivably argue now that Pankow was concerned only with refugee control or even with the defence of its frontier? These new measures were flagrant attacks on the rights of the western sectors and everyone's freedom of movement.[19]

For once, the allies responded quickly. On 23 August the Military Commandants issued a press statement denouncing the latest measures, though their governments could not agree on a direct protest to the Soviet Commandant (as one British official in Berlin put it "a protest to Karlshorst at this stage might well make us a laughing stock"). Berliners, however, were better pleased by an instant reaction than by higher-level formalities. Brandt was certainly delighted, but he warned that if the

---

* After his visit Adenauer several times suggested in speeches that the East had built the Wall to help Brandt in the elections. The Chancellor had few votes to lose in Berlin, but he undoubtedly lost a lot elsewhere by this nasty slur.

new strip was observed, houses within it would have to be evacuated. He took the opportunity to suggest closing East German offices on S-bahn stations in the western sectors which issued papers to prove West Berlin residence, setting up control points on the sector boundary to prevent the entry of "undesirables", which meant SED officials, and closing local Party offices. Mirabile dictu: the Military Commandants neither sucked their teeth nor referred the matters to their embassies or governments. He got the go-ahead and on 24 August the West Berlin criminal police set up tents at the seven crossings to sift East Germans, the SED headquarters and branches were closed; next day the permit offices, five East German trade union and eight youth movement premises were also shut down. Would it have been impossible or dangerous to have done all this before? Might it have had a deterrent effect?[20]

The sad fact was that such moves came too late. They could not now dissuade the East Germans from slicing more salami. And on 23 August the Soviet Union came openly into the month's crisis. In a Note delivered to the allied ambassadors in Moscow, the Kremlin complained of the FRG's "unlawful and inadmissible interference" in West Berlin, citing the presence there of Lemmer, the Federal Minister for All-German Affairs, and accusing him of "preparing provocations" and "directing subversive work" against the GDR: the first attack on the western sectors' links with the FRG. At the same time, the Western Powers were accused of using the three air corridors to Berlin to transport "revanchists, extremists, subverters, spies and saboteurs of all kinds" in violation, it was claimed, of the 1945 Air Agreement which had made the corridors available for "the use of the western garrisons" only. This in its turn was the first threat to western access to Berlin.[21]

The allies did not expect immediate action on the threat. They assumed that the Soviet Union was firing scatter shot: hoping to scare would-be refugees by suggesting that it would soon be impossible to fly to the Federal Republic, to intimidate the western Powers into accepting GDR sovereignty over air as well as land routes, and to frighten them off airlifts for the supply of the western sectors. Possibly, too, the Soviet Union intended to make the corridors a bargaining counter in any negotiations. It was reassuring to find that the Soviet press was playing the Note down and there were no signs of a military build-up to enforce its claims. Furthermore no one worried about flying refugees out of the western sectors. There were now so few of them being added to the backlog: only 631 new registrations on 23 August, 427 on the 24th. Even so the challenge to allied access rights had to be taken seriously – not least because many tripartite "Live Oak" plans for maintaining access, and in particular for substituting military for civil aircraft in emergencies, had still not got government approval. Anxiety provoked action of rare speed: allied replies to the Soviet Note were sent on 26 August, warning the Kremlin that any interference in the corridors would have "the most serious consequences" and adding a protest about recent East German restrictions of movement for good measure. And once the three ambassadors were given a deserved dressing down by McNamara on 25 August for their governments' failure to give instructions to "Live Oak" or to help the Americans in the hard work of its planning, Norstad got full orders for the maintenance of access on 5 September.[22]

A dozen or more West Berliners did what they could for air access on 24 August by jeering at the Soviet representative as he crossed to work at the Berlin Air Safety Centre. He complained and it was decided, against his express wish, to provide him and his colleagues with a military police escort in future. So he complained again – this time that the escort attracted too much attention. There was in fact much more attention being drawn by the relief guards for the Soviet War Memorial: a large crowd tried to overturn its jeep on 25 August and the British began to guard it to and from the border. There was plenty more to incense West Berliners. The Loudspeaker War along the sector boundary was being fought hot and strong and on 26 August up to two thousand people gathered on the western side to protest and had to be driven back by their own police and Vopo tear gas and water. The same day the East Germans set up stalls in two West Berlin S-bahn stations to sell the passes for East Berlin. Someone daubed a sign "Entrance to the concentration camp – one mark" and those who tried to buy passes were sworn at or punched by passers-by until the police arrived to close the stalls down. There was something singularly disgusting about having to buy a permit to move from one side of one's city to the other, especially when there had been two recent cases of West Berliners refused permission to go to funerals in the East. (They left flowers at the Wall instead.) The East Germans, however, had no need to consider feelings or court popularity. So confident did Pankow now feel in its control over its population, so certain that the Western Powers would take no retaliatory measures, that on 24 August the GDR military state of alert was cancelled, and by 11 September all its armour had been withdrawn from central East Berlin. Ulbricht had won; some might say it had been an easy victory.[23]

Within days of the wire going up in Berlin, the allied capitals had more or less taken its existence for granted, and were certainly not prepared to do anything about it. The Wall was a shock, but hardened their belief that retaliation would be dangerous. In the Ambassadors' Group in Washington Kohler was coming round to the idea of a partial ban on TTDs, but there was no enthusiasm for any form of economic sanction: even the Americans, usually keen on a trade embargo, were aware that with many of their firms already working at under 50 per cent of capacity, industry would be hard hit. Instead, everyone now concentrated on the question of opening talks with the Soviet Union. It was as if recent events in Berlin had just been a side-show.[24]

The lasting fear in the West was that the fundamental aim of the Soviet Union was still to squeeze the Western Powers out of the city: "We have to assume," Kennedy wrote to McNamara on 21 August, "that some time in the fall there may be a blockade of a formal or informal kind". McCloy advised that Khrushchev was "not only tough, but a dangerous man in a dangerous mood"; having won a round easily he would try to go a great deal further. Some took the view that the boundary closure had made talks easier: solved the refugee embarrassment, given the West a propaganda advantage, alleviated something of the East German sense of insecurity. At a meeting in the third week in August the NATO countries were virtually unanimous on the need to negotiate – in part, one suspects, because they were so reluctant to increase their military expenditure or face the financial losses from economic counter measures. Adenauer went so far as to announce on television "We do not want a war. Therefore we want to and must negotiate with Soviet Russia", though not, he insisted, over the creation of a "free city" of Berlin or recognition of the GDR.[25]

Only the French maintained the position they had always held, and to which their allies had paid at least lip service in the past: no negotiations under duress. Khrushchev's ultimatum, after all, still held: he would sign a separate treaty at the end of the year unless the Western Powers agreed to a peace settlement. In addition, the French argued, conditions were particularly unpropitious for talks since the West had so obviously been unable to react to the recent border closure. De Gaulle grumbled to his ambassador to Washington on 23 August that the Americans wanted to talk to the Russians but without knowing about what or where negotiations would lead. A conference would be "an act of weakness", "lead to nothing" except conceivably the abandonment of Berlin, and France would not take part in it. This, thought de Gaulle, might be the "Munich Hour", and if war was going to break out, it was just as well if it did now. But "since the Russians do not want war, why not be intransigent?" These were not views he kept to himself. On 2 September he told the US ambassador in Paris that it would be "a grave mistake" to "run" to the

Kremlin for talks but promised, with gallows grandeur, that if "catastrophe occurred", "France will enter it together with the United States".[26]*

Haughty intractability was not going to endear de Gaulle to Kennedy. The American President was acutely anxious about the threat to the western position in Berlin and in a mood to get up and go – alone if necessary. In a memo to Rusk on 21 August he called for "a stronger lead on Berlin negotiations": an invitation should be sent to Khrushchev by September and everyone ready for a full-scale conference by 1 November. "We should this week make it plain to our three allies that this is what we mean to do and that they must come along or stay behind." Characteristically, he called for instant action and for radical reappraisal both at the same time. He wanted fresh proposals – "they should not look like warmed over stuff from 1959" – and was willing to give up occupation rights in the western sectors in return for strong guarantees of presence and access, but still insisted on German self-determination and a free West Berlin. He admitted that Acheson's last paper on a negotiating position was good, but wanted alternatives prepared by "a *small* group", separate from Kohler's people at the State Department and as "nearly invisible as possible", which would report directly to him and Rusk and have everything ready by 25 August.[27]

This young man in a hurry, haunted by the conviction that the true Berlin crisis was yet to come, was made even more impatient by the failure of his allies to provide conventional forces for the military prong of his policy or throw full weight behind its diplomatic spike. Even Britain seemed to be foot dragging. Macmillan was, of course, in favour of negotiation; he always had been. He wrote on 19 August "the situation is tense and may become dangerous", which had been his constant judgement, give or take an extra bout of panic, ever since November 1958. But he did not view the situation as dangerous enough to interrupt his shooting and golf. When caught by newspaper reporters on the eighteenth green at Gleneagles on 27 August and questioned about the Berlin crisis he lost his temper and made the foolish reply "I think it is all got up by the press. Nobody is going to fight about it." He knew this was "a gaffe" but rationalised it in a letter to Kennedy as "sound because . . . the German problem must be settled ultimately by negotiation". But there was a huge public outcry at what he had said; the *Daily Mirror* asked "Is PM Macmillan living in the same world as other people?"[28]

---

* Eisenhower approved of de Gaulle's stance. He thought it was "hard to negotiate with a man who is coming across your lawn with a club and ready to take possession of your house".

One of his officials doubted that he was. Since Macmillan would not come to Whitehall, Sir Evelyn Shuckburgh of the Central Department of the Foreign Office went to Scotland for discussions with the Prime Minister and Foreign Secretary. What he heard drove him to compose one of the sharpest reprimands any civil servant can ever have delivered to his masters. "I have not expressed to you strongly enough", he began, "how deeply concerned I am about the attitude of HM Government in this crisis." He warned that the "carefree attitude of HM Government, the absence of Ministers from London, the absence of any serious military preparations, and the absence of any drive behind Whitehall's preparations for meeting the coming test" was dooming negotiations from the start. He added tartly that it was not, perhaps, "of crucial importance to the UK exactly how much freedom is enjoyed by West Berliners" but it would be fatal if the West suffered a humiliating diplomatic defeat and Britain could be blamed for it. It was all very well claiming to support US policy, but "it cannot be said that we are *in any way* helping the Americans by our example": making a niggardly contribution to NATO, expressing no resolution to the Soviet Union, and failing to explain the gravity of the situation to the domestic public. Kennedy himself could not have put it more forcibly.[29]

But the President's intention of pressing on regardless took a series of hard knocks. On 28 August the Soviet Union announced that it would resume nuclear testing; on 30 August releases from the Soviet armed forces were postponed "until a peace treaty with Germany is concluded" and it was announced that measures had been taken "to raise the combat readiness" of the military; on 1 September the Soviet Union conducted the first nuclear test for three years and there was another two days later. (Between then and 4 November there would be thirty nuclear explosions, nearly all of them "dirty" bombs exploded in the atmosphere.) No one should have been surprised. This was a predictable Soviet response to a President who now knew there was no "Missile Gap" but who maintained his nuclear arsenal while building up conventional forces. Nor was there any reason to assume that the Russians wanted war rather than talks: the Kremlin always preferred to negotiate from every form of strength. But, for a moment, Washington was struck a heap. At what Robert Kennedy described as "the most gloomy meeting at the White House . . . since early in the Berlin crisis", held on 31 August, horror at the resumption of tests was mingled with dread that the Soviet Union intended to force a showdown over Berlin, that "1961 was going to be a fateful one when the Russians could come closest to nuclear war". As the meeting ended Bobby said he "wanted to get off". "Get off what?" his brother asked.

"Get off the planet." And a few days later the President himself despondently decided that, at the very least, nuclear testing showed that the Russians "were bent on scaring the world to death before they begin negotiating and they haven't quite brought the pot to the boil".[30]

The straits were nowhere near as dire as they seemed initially. Khrushchev kept the channels open for talks. He told various western journalists in September that he was ready for a Summit, and even for informal contacts. On 12 September Kozlov, of all people, in a speech in North Korea, insisted that there was no Soviet ultimatum and that the Soviet Union was "ready together with interested countries to discuss and consider any reasonable amendments to our draft treaty". Gromyko then said he was willing to exchange views with Rusk when he attended the autumn session of the United Nations. On 29 September Kennedy received his first letter from Khrushchev – twenty-six whole pages – which included the comment that there was no reason why there should not be negotiated settlements for Laos and Berlin.[31]

What prevented immediate steps to negotiation was, therefore, not the Kremlin but trouble in the western alliance. At a meeting of Foreign Ministers in Washington from 14 to 16 September, Couve de Murville rigidly maintained that there must be no talks, though Home reported to the Prime Minister that French officials looked very unhappy about this, and no one could have useful discussions about negotiating proposals in front of the West Germans. Then, a really disappointing setback: the Federal German elections on 17 September, on which everyone had pinned their hopes for loosening the western line and for which everyone had been waiting before starting the negotiating process, produced the equivalent of a hung parliament. In consequence there were to be nearly two months of haggling until the CDU persuaded the FDP to join a coalition (the price they paid was to sack Brentano). It took until 7 November before Adenauer, now aged eighty-seven, was elected Chancellor for the fourth time.[32]

Bonn's little local difficulties delayed the Western Powers from entering talks but did not prevent Rusk and Gromyko from sounding each other out at the UN. They met three times, on 21, 27 and 30 September. Gromyko was insistent that there were two German states and that the post-war Berlin status had outlived its usefulness but, Rusk noticed, made no boasts of the Soviet Union's military powers, uttered no threats, and seemed aware of the West's determination to preserve its rights in Berlin and the viability and freedoms of the western sectors. Others were startled by Rusk's willingness to go more than half way to meet the Soviet Union. "I am amazed at the pace of the change in the American attitude," Home wrote to Macmillan on 25 September. "They seem to be ready to consider almost everything." "Everything" included not only new written guarantees of access instead of the existing right of conquest, but various inter-German commissions, a declaration on the Oder-Neisse Line, and even thinning out troops in both parts of Germany and possible pulling back of nuclear weapons. The French were indignant: it was bad enough to talk to the Russians at all and infinitely worse to hand them everything they wanted on a plate. The Federal Germans were aghast. Brentano exclaimed bitterly that Bonn would not have agreed to the soundings if it had been realised how far they would go. Kennedy had to write to Adenauer and promise that the United States would never consider disengagement because it would create a dangerous vacuum in the middle of Europe.[33]

While the Western Powers frightened themselves with thoughts of what might happen and argued about how to face it, Berliners, both sides of the city, confronted abhorrent realities: further brutal division of their city and deeper erosion of their rights. Already by 27 August a second concrete wall was being built behind the first across the Brandenburg Gate. In the following three weeks the wire along the sector and zonal borders was steadily, inexorably replaced with solid blocks. Behind them, one, two, three or even four barbed wire fences went up, ditches were dug, watchtowers erected. Not content with multiplying the fortifications, the East Germans had the effrontery to attempt to enforce the hundred-metre no-go strip inside the western sectors: Vopos used tear gas and water cannon against anyone who ventured into it and on several occasions warning shots were fired. This put the allies and West Berlin police in a cleft stick. They were unwilling to allow Pankow to dictate where West Berliners could move in their own sectors; at the same time they were worried that someone would get killed, at which a protesting crowd would get out of hand and there would be countless deaths and casualties. A precarious policy emerged whereby the strip remained open and no public warnings against using it were issued by the authorities, but the police had to try to keep people out of it, and be ready to whisk strays to safety whenever the Vopos were goaded.[34]

And the policeman's lot was already not a happy one. West Berliners were outraged by the East German loudspeakers – up to 183 of them, dozens of which might be roaring in an area at any one time. (In a perfectly understandable incident on 9 September Vopos lobbed tear gas at a western van.) Protesters gathered day after day at the edge of the western sectors to jeer and throw stones at the broadcasting vans until driven back with tear gas and water. It was then up to West Berlin policemen to disperse the crowds. In addition they were trying to keep back, and save from injury, groups at closed street crossings who gathered to protest or shout messages to relatives, and then threw stones at Vopos or tried to tear down barriers. It was particularly difficult to control crowds who gathered to encourage East Berlin demonstrations (there was one involving over 300 on 11 September) or to welcome refugees who still tore gaps in the wire, clambered over roofs or dropped from windows. During escapes like these the Vopos' patience snapped, smoke and gas canisters flew, and sometimes there was firing; West Berlin police had only hand guns and small gas grenades until mid-October so could not give the Vopos as good as they got, and they had to put up with shouts of "Worse than Vopos" as they struggled to drive their own people out of range.[35]

To stiffen morale in the western sectors there were allied patrols throughout August and September: along the sector and zonal borders to create a local sense of security or into East Berlin to assert the right of entry (a demonstration which fell short of the swashbuckling, since western forces dutifully used Checkpoint Charlie). Once in East Berlin, the military vehicles were often tailed, or stopped with demands for identification which according to quadripartite agreement they had no need to present. On 30 August one American patrol was accused of "snooping" at an East German convoy and as the jeep tried to pull away a Vopo smashed one of its windows with his truncheon. Given such hold-ups in the Eastern Sector, or the frequent delays of western vehicles at Checkpoint Charlie, the practice was to sit tight and demand to see a Soviet officer (to emphasise Soviet responsibility and to avoid dealing with an East German). It was very time-consuming since the Russian soldier would take hours to arrive though invariably he allowed the patrol through after accusing it of "gross provocation". This all became accepted routine in the tedium of garrison duty.[36]

By contrast there was real allied alarm on 2 September when the Soviet Union and Pankow delivered Notes accusing the Western Powers of "abuse" of the air corridors by the transport of "revanchists" to the western sectors (another Homeland Day was to be celebrated on 3 September), repeating the claim in the Note of 23 August that the corridors could only be used for garrison supply but adding a new threat that if "misuse" continued, the GDR would reconsider allied access. This was what the West had been dreading all along. To everyone's relief there was no interruption of communications on Homeland Day. But allied fears for the security of their communications were stoked by a series of frightening incidents in the corridors later. On 7 and 9 September a searchlight in the GDR was beamed on a BEA flight, then on two Pan Am aircraft as they came in to land in West Berlin, dazzling the pilots and risking not just the lives of the passengers but of the inhabitants of all the homes packed round Tempelhof on to which an aircraft would crash. A Pan Am flight was buzzed by Soviet fighters on 14 September; so were British Viscounts on 18 and 21 September. After western protests there were no more searchlights, but there was sporadic harassment in the corridors until the end of the year. It reinforced the allied belief that a major push to force them out of Berlin was imminent.[37]

By no stretch of the imagination could the West think that Pankow and the Kremlin were merely trying to frighten refugees by threatening the air corridors: border closure had already achieved that purpose and more. The official total for those leaving the GDR in August had been 47,433 – the second highest since records began in 1949 and only exceeded by the 58,605 East Germans who had crossed to the West in the period of the 1953 Rising. This figure, of course, did not include all those who fled on 13 and 14 August and fused the registration procedures at Marienborn. The vast proportion of emigrants had arrived in the western sectors in the first two weeks of August: once the wire went up, the daily numbers, which had been in the thousands, dropped to a few hundred, and kept dropping – 292 on 25 August, a scant 219 over the whole weekend at the end of the month. The full September figure had dwindled to 14,821.[38]

That huge drop was a testimonial to the strength of the new frontier. Nevertheless, the fact that over 14,000 people should have risked their lives to get out is a terrible index of human misery. It was relatively easy for East German troops and police on border patrol to slip over: in mid-September the West Berlin authorities reported that Vopos had defected "in company strength" – a company being about 150. One day a Kampfgruppen kindly took a jug of coffee to a platoon on guard at the frontier and the moment they had their hands full and their rifles down, he hopped across. Escape was much more difficult for others. On 29 August an East German stowed away on a British military train bound for West Berlin. "We are trying to keep this quiet," said an official report. But desperate minds think alike and two more refugees clung between carriages at the end of the month and arrived safely. A husband and wife were desperate enough to swim across the Teltow canal towing their baby in his bath; a man drove down the Unter den Linden at nearly seventy miles an hour in a delivery van and smashed through the wire near the Brandenburg Gate; three youths crashed a lorry at a section of concrete wall and destroyed fifteen feet of it; some people crawled through drains or ganged together to claw their way under rolls of wire. A twenty-one-year-old man jumped into West Berlin from a house on the border and with friends stretched a net under

324

the second-floor window of his home. His mother jumped into it. Just as his wife and two-year-old son were about to follow, a neighbour shouted for the police. He shinned up a drainpipe, shoved the neighbour aside, pushed his wife out of the window, and leapt into the net with the baby at the moment the Vopos arrived.[39]

Another family did not have that hair's breadth of luck: on 27 September Vopos opened fire on a couple and their child as they tried to climb a mesh fence; the father got over but the wife and child were dragged back into East Berlin. And a few lost their lives. A lorry driver broke his leg as he abseiled from a roof in Bernauer Strasse on 19 August and died later from infections. A man was shot as he tried to swim the Teltow canal on 29 August and the West Berlin police put up placards announcing a reward for the capture of those responsible; the Vopos responded with a notice promising 1,000 marks for Willy Brandt, "wanted as a criminal". Eighty-year-old Olga Segler jumped into a fireman's net from her second-floor flat in Bernauer Strasse on 25 September but injured her back and died next day.

The overwhelming majority of East Germans no longer even considered trying to leave. "I should have escaped when I could," one girl lamented, "but I never thought they would trap us as they did." In what western authorities in Berlin admitted were "intercepted letters" people talked of being "hemmed in", "shut in a concentration camp", deprived of "free air". East Berlin hospitals reported that there used to be an average of one suicide or suicide attempt a day, now there were up to twenty-five. That was a symptom of despair. But there were no longer indications of possible revolt. As one East German told a western journalist "This time the people are too despondent, too cowed. They are helpless and without hope". Not least they had lost faith in the power of the West to help them. "Why", asked a student in Jena, "did the allies not send their tanks to the sector border on 13 August?" That failure to act had revived the bitterness of 1953 when the allies ignored the uprising. "We, especially the young ones, have no more confidence whatever in the promises of Brandt, Adenauer and the western allies. Only a miracle would give us back the hope of any change."[40]

"The entire repressive machinery of the East German state apparatus", an American official pointed out, "is keeping the population quiet and intimidated." By mid-September there had been 600 arrests for criticising the regime or stating a wish to go to the West. Suspected political opponents were beaten up. Five youths who shouted at Vopos building barricades on 13 August were sentenced to three and a half years' imprisonment at the end of the month. There was heavy press coverage of terms of hard labour for those found guilty of "offences against labour discipline" which meant strikes, slacking or grumbling in a factory. Accusations against individuals of disloyalty to the GDR were made in newspapers, on posters stuck up at factory gates or the entrances to their homes; work camps were opened for the "work-shy" or "grumblers"; mass meetings organised for "public education" and denunciation of "slave traders, provocateurs, hoarders". Children were being encouraged to denounce classmates or their parents if they fell into these categories: a ten-year-old was publicly congratulated for giving information to the authorities which led to the arrest of a would-be refugee.[41]

Already hemmed in from the outside world, East Germans were now subject to other forms of isolation. On 26 August Pankow issued a decree to prevent known dissidents from moving out of the area where they lived: that made organisation of opposition difficult. Doctors, intellectuals, academics who had once been privileged members of society were finding it difficult to get permission to travel abroad or receive foreign literature and journals. The young were being drafted into the armed services or reserves: 174,000 members of the East German youth movement were claimed as "volunteers" by the end of September; putting them in barracks was one way of keeping an eye on them and the demand for their military service supported the regime's argument that border closure prevented western aggression. Listening to western radio or watching TV from the Federal Republic was now hazardous: groups from the youth movement were on the prowl to eavesdrop or tear down aerials and in some instances TV sets were confiscated and auctioned or given to the "politically reliable"; persistent offenders who tuned in to foreign stations got up to fifteen months in prison. Church links had been snapped by the new frontier. The Roman Catholic Bishop of Berlin, an East Berlin resident, was forbidden to visit the western sectors; Bishop Dibelius could no longer go to those parts of his diocese which were in East Berlin or Brandenburg.

Physically and psychologically cut off, East Germans tried to come to terms with the regime, or at least to find a private sanctuary where they could hide from it. People looked for a way to live in the GDR without belonging to it. Only 10 per cent of the population were in the Party, and many of these were members not from conviction but self-interest – called "Beet Communists", red only on the outside. Others, however, still clung to the belief that "anti-fascism" was a necessity, that socialism as an ideal was tarnished but not corroded by the means with which it was applied and it was a personal obligation to maintain its decencies and mitigate the brutality. To strive for a better life now seemed more vital than ever. And East Germany was Prussianised and Protestant: East Germans would carry out their duty to the state and hope they could do so without sullying their consciences. Some were fortunate enough to feel a higher duty than that demanded by the state. The young theology student who was on holiday in Sweden when the Wall went up decided that Jesus had always worked among the unfortunate and deprived so he himself must return to his country and serve his flock. He never regretted his decision, though he watched six brothers and sisters leave for the West. The philology teacher, who was at a conference in England on 13 August, also went home. He had a wife, a daughter and a new-born son there. How could he desert them? Thereafter what made life tolerable was his work and his pride in teaching well.[42]

The retreat into self-exile created its own tensions. One doctor, typical of many of his professional colleagues who stayed in the GDR, had argued ever since 1946 that his contempt for his rulers was less important than his service to his patients and any contribution he could make to social progress. His teenage daughter, always distressed by the need to "speak two languages" – one at home, one outside – maintained her love and respect for him but could not follow his course. On 2 September 1961 she got on to an S-bahn train which she knew crossed a narrow neck of the western sectors. When it reached that spot, she tried to jump but was too frightened. Only when she was carried on to the terminus did she realise that the return train was the last that night. This time she jumped. She landed on the track, crawled into a garden and called for help. It was years before she saw her parents again; she was not reunited with her two brothers until November 1989.

No West Berliner could possibly claim that adjustment to life in the western sectors imposed anything like the strain and misery of resignation to the GDR, but it was difficult enough. The wire cut families, separated friends. The brute presence of the Wall, rising higher every day, was a constant reminder of the fragility of communications with the outside world. Before 13 August about eight hundred West Berliners a week had regularly moved to the Federal Republic (a loss partly compensated for by about five hundred West Germans moving in). In September 2,000 a week left (mainly older, more prosperous people) but over seven hundred were coming in – either those who had fled just as the wire went up, or the unemployed who realised there were good job prospects in the western sectors, whatever the other drawbacks. By October morale had steadied. Emigration had levelled at about 1,400 a week and savings which had been removed to the West for safety were returning. Yet the old spirit of "Na, und" had still not fully revived.[43]

Confidence was helped by financial aid from Bonn. On 11 September the Federal government announced a DM500 million fund as a first measure to counteract the economic damage of the Wall. (Existing subsidy to the western sectors stood at DM115 million.) The money would be spent on investment credits, the financing of orders for industry and a major building programme. Brandt was keen to use some of it to increase West Berlin's educational and cultural significance: the place needed a role. It was no longer the future capital or a shop window to impress East Germans, and its enormous industrial importance was precariously balanced on Federal support and eastern control of communications. Brandt spoke of creating a home for one or more UN agency. Moving the UN, whole or in part, to Berlin was a fashionable proposal of the time, and a recurrent solve-all idea which popped up over the years without any of its proponents wondering whether the UN was willing to move, whether the Soviet Union would let it, how much it would cost and who would pay.[44]

A totally new alternative was put in November by Sir David Ormsby Gore (soon to be ambassador in Washington): make West Berlin a member of the United Nations. There were, after all, two and a half million inhabitants (as many or more than in existing members like Cyprus, Mauretania or Kuwait) and as a sovereign state under international protection, it could request the western Powers or NATO for troops and make economic or access arrangements with the GDR, saving everyone else the embarrassment of recognition. It was a witty notion, combining legalism, impudence and a sharp pull of the political rug from under the Soviet Union's feet. The Foreign Office played with it gleefully for days but it was too good ever to be made true. The general public came up with some splendid schemes too. (They were always so helpful at times of Berlin crisis: in 1948 during the Blockade they used to send the Foreign Office enormously long letters, with diagrams, suggesting hundred mile tunnels under the Autobahn or balloon deliveries of freight.) Mr James Moore of Lafayette, California, went to the trouble of talking to the engineers who had built the latest Siemens plant in West Berlin. He proposed dismantling it and moving it lock, stock and barrel to the Federal Republic – the "savings would be stupendous". He was public-spirited enough to offer $2,000 of his own money for a feasibility study.[45]*

Denied the bold and grandiose options, West Berliners had to settle to

---

* His proposal was slightly less ambitious than one solemnly published by the *Guardian*'s defence correspondent the previous year: evacuate West Berlin and hand over the site to the East Germans in return for territorial concession on the FRG frontier. This loony suggestion had given Brandt and Bonn apoplexy. They saw it as a gargantuan offer of appeasement and blamed the (for once) innocent Foreign Office.

the mundane but complex tasks of making their amputated city habitable. Typically, various official bodies still maintained contact with East German agencies – though quietly and at a low level so as to avoid outcry that they were giving the GDR recognition. Whether people approved of contact or not, the technical problems of postal and long distance telephone services, cable and road maintenance, rubbish and sewage disposal all had to be sorted out. West Berlin also had to tackle the inconvenience of roads cut by concrete blocks, tramways which ran into solid walls, surface and under-ground rail links blocked by bricked up tunnels and ripped up sections of line. There was an anxious period in late August when the allies and city authorities feared that the East Germans would remove S- and U-bahn rolling stock from the western sectors. In the event, the GDR maintained the few remaining cross-city routes, no doubt hoping for some Deutsch-mark revenue, and the Senate was able to fill the gaps with bus services and to build a new North–South stretch of U-bahn to jink round a segment which had previously run through East Berlin. Further expansion of transport was needed, however: the boycott of the S-bahn had been so successful that the number of passengers was cut by 80 per cent – they now needed another way to travel.[46]

There were so many other calls for adjustment or reorganisation too. Something like ten thousand former Grenzgänger were now based permanently in West Berlin and needed homes. (Local trade unions had collected money to tide them over the loss of their possessions in the East.) Schools estimated that they had lost about sixty teachers and 3,000 pupils who used to cross to the western sectors; up to a quarter of all students at the Free and Technical Universities had come from the other side. West Berlin cinemas had dropped 27 per cent of their audiences. East Berlin's musical life was suffering: fifty-six out of 166 members of the choir of the State Opera, fifty-four out of the 140 players in its orchestra lived in West Berlin, so did a high proportion of actors and technical staff in East Sector theatres. Planned productions had to be cancelled, the opening of the Komische Oper was postponed, everyone was rejigging programmes and making do with provincial orchestras, amateurs and students, and stars of the Soviet bloc.

Amid the perplexities and practicalities, West Berliners were given a boost to their spirits by the reappearance on 19 September of General Clay, this time for a long stay. His appointment as a token of American support, and as special adviser to the White House on local problems, was Kennedy's own idea. It was clearly intended to capitalise on the general's popularity and the success of his trip with Johnson, but Kohler thought it was also to avert "the possible dangers of having him on the outside as a critic". One suspects that the job was conceived as a public relations exercise, without thought for the political consequences or organisational confusions. Initially Kennedy intended to make Clay a special ambassador with full responsibility in the western sectors. Others got cold feet. Bundy pointed out that Clay's presence, let alone any military duties, would not suit Norstad at NATO, and warned that the general was congenitally incapable of carrying out someone else's policy: "you want no risk of setting up another McArthur-Truman affair". The military in Germany were far from pleased by the insertion of an extra general into their already long chain of command; the State Department was leery about an undiplomatic, nay outspoken, character who would cut across their political adviser in Berlin and ambassador in Bonn and have the right to report directly to the President.[47]

So Clay's powers were muffled in the vague title of "adviser" without ever being clearly defined. This left him enough authority to interfere with the Military Commandant and political adviser in Berlin, but obliged him to work through the military hierarchy in Germany to Norstad, then the Defence Department, or via the State Department. Sensibly, he did not often exercise his right to approach the President directly: "you would soon outlive your welcome". The set-up did not work to anyone's satisfaction. Clay himself blamed the military for all his problems and: "So far as Norstad is concerned, I don't think he was capable of handling anything. But that's just a personal opinion." The State Department was virtually beneath his contempt: "No one wanted to make a decision." He did occasionally apply to Rusk but with little confidence. When asked by his biographer if things would have been different with Dulles or Acheson, he snapped: "That's for damned sure."[48]

The general behaved on his first day in Berlin as he meant to carry on. That evening he and Mrs Clay marched across Checkpoint Charlie into East Berlin without anyone daring to stop them. Two days later he went by helicopter to Steinstücken which was experiencing this year's traditional crisis. The path to the enclave had been wired either side and East German guards would admit or release only residents. But GDR refugees had found it relatively easy to slip through the woods and under the wire to seek asylum – seven of them were now stuck there. Clay's first instinct was to "punch a hole" into Steinstücken with a couple of infantry companies. One whiff of that and General Bruce C. Clarke, US Commander in Europe, was on the train to Berlin. By his telling of the tale, he first asked the Military Commandant, General Watson, "Al, don't you know who you work for?" and told him to take no more orders from Clay; then he instructed the commander of the US garrison to keep his men in barracks;

finally he informed Clay, "You can take your cotton-picking fingers off my troops." Robbed of gun-blazing action, Clay contented himself with posting three military policemen in the enclave to deter invasion by Vopos and with sending a helicopter to ferry out refugees whenever required. (There were six more by 28 September.) The GDR condemned this as a flagrant breach of their air sovereignty.[49]*

Whatever his military and civilian superiors thought of Clay's behaviour, Berliners loved it and him. He was just the fillip they needed at this stage: the city was entering yet another painful division and a further consolidation of Pankow's control. For on 20 September the East Germans had started to evacuate forcibly all the houses which abutted their sector border. Eight days later they began to raze a barren hundred-metre strip right along it: clearing trees and demolishing buildings, to create a Death Zone. It was a frightening, ruthless destruction: one day two houses in a street pulverised, the next day six. Within a few days forty-eight houses were reduced to rubble in Harzer Strasse; homes of up to seventy families in Bernauer Strasse were razed to the ground. Great ditches were gouged out across streets which led to the border, the allotments where Berliners spent their weekends were flattened and the little wooden houses where they slept on hot nights crumbled as they were lifted away by cranes. And the action was not confined to Berlin. An entire village, with five large farms, a café and a sawmill, was destroyed on the Bavarian frontier; a security zone nearly half a mile wide and with anti-tank ditches was slashed across the countryside for 124 miles from Helmstedt to the Harz mountains. Not content with a half-mile-wide cordon sanitaire, Pankow announced in early October that all families who lived within three miles of the interzonal frontier would be moved back "to ensure their peace and safety". Refugees brought the news that a 300-foot-deep no-man's land was planned along the entire Berlin–GDR border; some calculated that this would mean that 20,000 homes would be sacrificed.[50]

The British Communist Party newspaper, the *Daily Worker*, loyally reported that the clearance of Bernauer Strasse involved moving people from "vile old flats to modern or reconditioned ones . . . at public expense"; that people had been asked to leave the area of the sector boundary because they had been "subject to the din and stone-throwing by West Berlin teenagers". Berliners on both sides knew different. Last minute, frantic attempts were made to escape from the East. By now the West Berlin police were in no mood to stand by and let the Vopos

---

* British garrison enclave duties consisted of escorting a twelve-year-old boy to school every day up and down the path from Eiskeller.

prevent them. On 22 September they threw three tear gas canisters to cover the flight of a group of refugees. On 4 October they fired back when Vopos shot ten to fifteen carbine rounds at two refugees which landed near a crowd of about two hundred on the western side; while all this was going on one man leapt from the roof and was killed and the other was arrested before he could jump. Day after day crowds gathered at the boundary to protest and shout defiance. They were met with tear gas, smoke grenades and water cannon. On 27 September 600 West Berliners who threw stones at Vopos were greeted with rifle fire – fortunately in the air. Next day Vopos shot at two people trying to swim across the river Spree: they hit and killed one, the other drowned.[51]

It seems almost incredible that in spite of all the new frontier fortifications, there was a mass escape on 2 October. Fifty-five people, farmers and their families, crossed the GDR border at night with an eighty-nine-year-old granny, twenty-three children and a pregnant woman packed into a cart padded with bundles of clothes to bullet-proof it. Everyone else held on to ropes tied to the cart while a team of horses, whose hooves had been silenced with rags, led the party through the pitch dark down an old farm track to the West.

What little steam there had ever been in the Rusk–Gromyko exploratory talks had evaporated by the first week in October. Kennedy himself saw the Soviet Foreign Minister early in the month; so did Macmillan. Neither extracted anything new from him or found any significant shift in the Kremlin's position. No one could agree what to do next. Kennedy suggested that Gromyko should discuss negotiations with Thompson in Moscow. Macmillan, ever faithful, ever sure that talks were the only alternative to world-wide death and destruction, told his diary "I think the Russians are looking for a way out (as we are) . . ." but few shared his optimism or willingness to look for face-savers for both sides. The Foreign Office opposed Rusk's hints of "thinning out" and denuclearised zones, though recommended preserving allied presence in West Berlin and the freedoms of the western sectors at the price of partial recognition of the GDR and a prolonged division of Germany; "I agree with every word of this," commented Home. Gone were the glory days for Macmillan of Selwyn Lloyd and Sir Anthony Rumbold. The advice from the British ambassador in Moscow was to accept that "the Cold War is likely to be with us for many years and that we should prepare for a long haul rather than a swift tug of war"; since a major settlement was improbable the western Powers must hope for "realistic, if inadequate, temporary arrangements for Berlin and Germany".[52]

French and German opposition to full negotiations was strong and overt. Alphand told the other ambassadors in Washington that the Rusk–Gromyko talks had proved there was no basis for a conference until Khrushchev made reasonable proposals and withdrew his ultimatum. Grewe, his German colleague, insisted that Bonn, whichever party finally formed a government, would never accept a "free city" or discuss basic security questions and that there should be talks only if the Russians conceded in advance guarantees for civil and military access and the status of Berlin. Kennedy and Macmillan had agreed in a telephone conversation on 6 October that Adenauer and de Gaulle must be won over. They had never managed to do so in the past; there seemed no reason now why they should be any more successful.[53]

Khrushchev, however, let the western Powers off their hook. In his opening speech to the Party Congress (17–31 October) he told delegates that the Rusk–Gromyko talks demonstrated a "certain understanding of the German problem" by the West and a readiness to solve questions "on a mutually acceptable basis". The "question of a time limit for the signing of a German peace treaty will not be so important if the western Powers show readiness to settle the German problem". This was a point he came back to in his last speech to the Congress on 27 October: "What counts most is not the particular date but a business-like and honest settlement of the question."[54]

This public lifting of the ultimatum was wonderful news for the West. But it was one in the eye for Walter Ulbricht. Up to this moment in Khrushchev's first speech he had been diligently taking notes and applauding vigorously at all the right moments; at these words, a journalist observed, he "limply padded one hand into the other in his lap". East German officials muttered to Kroll that they were appalled by the Soviet leader's U-turn. In his own address on 20 October Ulbricht dared to emphasise that the GDR was defending the entire Socialist system and that "the conclusion of a peace treaty with Germany is the most urgent task". Many in the audience no doubt agreed with him – and despised Khrushchev for backing down.

Any such criticism of Khrushchev's move would be fed by an incident in Berlin during the Congress – one at which Gromyko hinted when he told the Congress audience on 25 October "things have been happening that are hard to reconcile with a desire to facilitate agreement."

Lucius D. Clay had taken the bit between his teeth. At the beginning of October he informed the British Military Commandant, Major-General Rohan Delacombe, that he expected the recent allied patrols in East Berlin to cause the closure of Checkpoint Charlie, the sole permitted crossing for the Western Powers in Friedrichstrasse. Terming himself "custodian for West Berlin morale", the general announced that this would be a catastrophe and lead to panic flight by West Berliners. Therefore, in his belief, it would be necessary to "confront the Soviets": remove the new obstacles by force and follow in if they were reconstructed further back in the Eastern Sector. Delacombe was not impressed by this rococo programme and reported that the US Political Adviser, Allan Lightner, "seemed both puzzled and perturbed" by it. "We knew", he went on, "that Clay's arrival would be an embarrassment to the American staff here", and he expressed a professional's sympathy for General Watson, who at this meeting looked "rather like a junior officer in the great man's presence".[55]

Clay took no notice of the discomfort of his colleagues. He merely varied his justification for taking on the Russians. On 5 October General Clarke received a telegram from Berlin informing him that since there was a possibility that the East Germans would soon declare their sector boundary an international frontier then totally close it, there would be a probe by the US garrison on 6 or 7 October to assert the right to use all crossings and draw the Soviet authorities into declaring their own responsibility for movement in the city. This message was signed "Watson" but everyone guessed who had dictated it. As Lightner apologetically explained to British officials: Clay "thought up these bright ideas and wanted action taken at once" without any tripartite consultation. Clarke and Norstad did not think the idea bright at all and asked Clay and Watson to reconsider. Back came Clay's reply: "We gain prestige by trying rather than doing nothing." For the moment he was given his head. There was at least one probe: on 10 October an American patrol tried to return from an East Berlin tour by an unauthorised crossing, was halted by a Vopo guard, demanded to see a Soviet officer and waited for an hour without getting one, then tamely re-entered West Berlin by Checkpoint Charlie.[56]

From Clay's point of view his campaign had been very unexciting so far, and it had failed to flush out the Russians. The East Germans were getting cockier, too: on 17 October they stopped two American military vehicles returning from East Berlin and held them for two hours, demanding to see identification papers; later that day two more Americans cars were refused entry because they would not show papers. Then, on 22 October, Allan Lightner tried to cross to East Berlin with his wife to visit a theatre. They were in an official car, with State Department licence plates, but even so the Vopos insisted on identification. Lightner called for a Soviet officer, waited for forty minutes, then tried to drive through; was blocked by a barricade and told he could wait all night. At that he contacted Clay, and an American platoon plus four M-48 tanks and three personnel carriers rolled up to the checkpoint. Thirty minutes later, eight men with fixed bayonets escorted Lightner's car (minus Mrs Lightner who had been persuaded to go into the allied guard shed) into East Berlin. Lightner did a quick circle in East Berlin, returned through Checkpoint Charlie, picked up another civilian member of the US Mission, and then they were both held up by the Vopos until again escorted in by their military. By this time the Mission had been on the phone to Karlshorst and persuaded a Soviet officer to put in an appearance. So the third attempt to cross Checkpoint Charlie without producing identification involved no delay or bayonets.[57]

Several experienced observers decided that the incident was not intentional: that there was an inexperienced Vopo on duty or the kind of swaggering young man who usually picked on nervous visiting school-teachers. Next day, however, the East Germans decreed that only allied personnel in uniform would be allowed to cross without showing papers; civilians must prove their identity. For Norstad the moment had come to stop playing games. He wanted to accept the procedure, which the British and French were willing to observe, "rather than find ourselves involved in shooting over a point in which even we ourselves do not believe". For Clay, on the other hand, the decree was his big chance. US civilian vehicles, sent to test its powers, were held up on the evening of 24 October. Harold Trivers of the US Mission went soon after breakfast next day to meet the Soviet Provost Marshal-cum-Political Adviser at the checkpoint. This man was known as Lieutenant-Colonel Alexeyev, though no one believed the name, and in February 1962 he turned up in civvies on the Glienicker Bridge when the U-2 pilot Gary Powers was swopped for the spy Rudolf Abel. He now told Trivers that he had no authority to intervene. They strolled and talked and ten American M-48s drew up and kept guard while a jeep with four armed military policemen in front and two jeeps with soldiers behind escorted a civilian car through. Clay was straight on the phone to Rusk: there must be more probes. That day and the next several American vehicles went back and forth through Checkpoint Charlie with an armed escort (British and French parties got through unaided but with long delays), and on 26 October when yet another probe was held up until helped across by military police, US tanks again appeared at the check-point. Clay had worked hard for this crisis. Now he was getting it, he was squeezing the last drop out of it.[58]

Norstad briefed the NATO Council on the situation. Nearly all its members expressed deep disquiet and argued that this was a bad issue on which to challenge the Russians. Despite this weight of criticism, and at the risk of precipitating a major military showdown without allied support, the US garrison was given permission to carry out two probes a day by civilians with military escort. And on 27 October when American tanks drew up at the sector boundary to support a crossing, there were seven Soviet tanks facing them. The US garrison was put on alert at 17.45 and fifteen minutes later the East Germans announced that Checkpoint Charlie would be closed until American tanks were removed. Clay had brought his own prophecy true – and Soviet armour into the open for the first time since 12 August.[59]*

Next day all the tanks revved, rolled then braked sharply to bounce for the benefit of the newsreel cameras, while the occasional military vehicle squeezed past them and went in and out of East Berlin as normal. On the morning of 28 October there were ten American tanks packed across Friedrichstrasse so the Russians brought up three more of their own (leaving a further twenty or so on a vacant site just off the Unter den Linden). Berliners were rather enjoying the show, the local press was full of praise and Ambassador Dowling wanted escalation. Norstad cabled to Washington that Soviet responsibility had been proved and the "course of wisdom" was to oblige the Russians to abide by the same access restrictions and document procedures which now operated for the Western Powers. That was far short of Clay's ambitions. As he sat in his "command room" late in the morning of 28 October he was rung by the President himself. He assured Kennedy that the Soviets would soon retreat and was delighted to tell the President that, at that very moment and by an extraordinary coincidence, twenty more Soviet tanks were moving up. (Everyone else knew the twenty were still near the Unter den Linden.) This, he announced, showed that the Soviets were good mathematicians: there were thirty American tanks in Berlin "so they will have a tank for every tank we have". "I know," replied Kennedy, "you people over there haven't lost your nerves." No, said Clay, but he was worried about nerves in Washington. "I don't know about those of my associates," the President told him, "but mine are all right" – a comment Clay was to quote with delight for years.[60]

It was, at best, a disingenuous remark. Kennedy had already decided or actually instructed his brother Bobby to inform the Soviet embassy in Washington that if both sides stood down within twenty-four hours without

---

* No one doubted that it was Soviet armour: the tanks were unmarked, rather like the gang boss who had his fingerprints removed.

loss of face by either, he would see this as a promising sign for political negotiations. That evening the Soviet tanks withdrew, though only to tuck themselves out of sight. The Americans could follow suit.[61]

The confrontation does not appear to have ruffled the Soviet Union unduly. Khrushchev's memoirs are very dismissive about the incident (though his chronology and details over the whole period from August are so muddled that it is not always clear what he is being calm about). He told the Norwegian ambassador a little later that both sides had behaved "like rams with horns interlocking" and likely to pull each other over a cliff, which is why he ordered his reluctant military to pull back, certain that the Americans would be glad to do likewise. The incident achieved little or nothing for the Western Powers. Clay's probe scheme was dropped, though he maintained it had served its purpose by forcing the Soviet Union into the open and admitting responsibility for the border closure – something which surely no one had ever doubted. As a result of the Checkpoint Charlie "showdown", the allies were still stuck with the one crossing point, and American civilians gave up trying to cross into East Berlin unless they had a military driver. Thanks to all the fuss, it had become a matter of pride not to change document procedures, which in practice led to the constant inconvenience of arguments and hold-ups. And right at the end of the year General Watson himself, with an appointment at Karlshorst, was not allowed to cross when he forbade the civilians with him to show their identity cards. When he tried to telephone a protest, no Russian deigned to answer his call. No one sent a tank to help him through either.[62]

How extraordinary that the Checkpoint Charlie confrontation was to be remembered as a major incident in the Cold War, when in reality it had been nothing more than an exercise in military theatricality by a frustrated desk general. The newspaper headlines, "Gun turret to gun turret, eyeball to eyeball", left an indelible image of East–West enmity and the ever present risk of nuclear war, but what had actually occurred was a small fiasco.

The Checkpoint Charlie drama had certainly done nothing to promote early talks about talks with the Soviet Union. Thompson had seen no point in approaching Gromyko until the Party Congress and the Checkpoint fuss were over and, in any case, could think of no proposal which the Russians would take seriously and the French and Germans would accept. Adenauer saw Kennedy in mid-November and stuck to all his objections against recognising the GDR, abandoning commitment to reunification, or changing the present legal status of the allies in Berlin. De Gaulle visited Macmillan at the end of the month and maintained that even the concessions Adenauer was prepared to make, such as acceptance of the Oder-Neisse Line, would not satisfy the Soviet Union so there was no point in talking.[63]*

Hans Kroll, the Federal German ambassador in Moscow, dreamed that single-handed he could launch the negotiating process, and approached Khrushchev on 9 November. He was very excited to be told by the Soviet leader that though the Wall would remain as long as it was needed, it would disappear if there was a new Berlin agreement and an improvement in relations between the two Germanies. Since, however, Bonn was furious that Kroll had acted off his own bat and since there was a widespread suspicion that Khrushchev used him as a stooge because of his all-too obvious wish to be personally credited with a settlement, the ambassador was summoned back to Bonn for a sharp rebuke; everyone was surprised that he was allowed to return to his post in Moscow. Kennedy made his own attempt to stimulate talks on 25 November, by suggesting to Adzhubei, Khrushchev's son-in-law and the editor of *Izvestia*, that there should be international control of the Autobahn. This idea had been going the rounds in Washington and a committee in the State Department had drafted a charter for an International Access Authority. It did not appeal to Khrushchev. At the end of the year he told the British ambassador that he would never ask the GDR to hand over its sovereign rights to a body of this kind. What, he asked, if the UK or United States established relations with Outer Mongolia? Would they press for an international route across the USSR to Ulan Bator?[64]

For the time being, this proposal and all others stayed in their departmental folders. Ever since Khrushchev had lifted his ultimatum at the Party Congress, the pressure to negotiate had eased. The Western Powers had come to terms with the division of Berlin and even if they were still anxious about the maintenance of their own presence and access, there was no sense of immediate danger. Only at the end of the year, when Macmillan and Kennedy met in Bermuda, were negotiations again discussed seriously and instructions drawn up for Thompson to seek an early meeting with Gromyko. France and the Federal Republic had still not approved such talks.[65]

The pernicious effect of such drifting by the Western Powers was palpable in Berlin. Alec Home wrote in late November that the situation in the city

* This visit to Birch Grove made no political progress but was enlivened by Macmillan's cook who objected to her fridge being monopolised by de Gaulle's blood plasma, by the gamekeeper who complained that all the policemen and security guards were upsetting his birds and ruining the shooting, and by the police dog who bit a *Daily Mail* reporter's bottom.

could not be allowed to deteriorate further: if "nothing is done, there is a grave danger that the life of the city will wither away under our eyes". Throughout that month there were frequent tear gas battles along the sector boundary: on 7 November each side threw about seventy gas grenades at the other after West Berliners ripped up East German wire which had appeared a yard inside their own sectors; sixty more grenades were exchanged on the 14th. On 21 November a West Berlin student demonstration to mark the hundredth day of the Wall was broken up by Vopo gas and water cannon; there was a major fight days later when blocks fell off the Wall on to the western side and East German armoured personnel carriers moved up to protect the repair work. There was more than rage; there was mounting depression, too. It was upsetting to realise how refugee numbers had plummeted – and the drop was noticed even though the figures were no longer published. In November the daily total seldom passed thirty. Other attempts had been ruthlessly prevented: a group of about thirty East Berliners who tried to cut through wire was fired at by Vopos on 5 November and only nine of them got to the other side. Spirits dropped even lower when, on the evening of 19 November, the East Germans began to build anti-tank obstacles: a five-and-a-half-foot thick wall at the Brandenburg Gate, six-foot ditches across the Potsdamer Platz and the Wilhelmstrasse, filled with metal "dragon's teeth" set in concrete. By the first week in December there were similar fortifications at all the seven crossing points, leaving just a narrow gap for the passage of a car. Soviet tanks were known to be still concealed in central East Berlin. The GDR was referring to "The Wall of Peace" and claiming that the new defences were needed to stop western aggression; West Berliners felt under siege.[66]

When the British ambassador visited the western sectors he was shocked by the mood – and Steel had lived in the city throughout the worst days of the Blockade. November, he wrote, was always a low period for Berliners, but the month and the weather did not explain "the degree of defeatism which I have found". The British Military Commandant and his staff thought that only the "rich and politically conscious" had given up hope, that people as a whole were "stolid and fatalistic", but it had to be admitted that if the managerial class and its savings moved out, West Berlin could not survive. Lucius D. Clay had decided that the city was "a dying duck". He was miserable in himself, upset by the "disunity and vacillation" of the allies, and convinced that the western position could collapse at any time. He was, thought Steel, "plainly suffering from the common American feeling of frustration, raised to the nth power by his demonic energy and temper". This made him liable to lash out at those with whom he was supposed to cooperate. At the beginning of November there was a disastrous dinner party given by the Delacombes where he noisily accused the British of doing nothing when Soviet tanks were identified in East Berlin. When Delacombe pointed out that he had moved a troop of tanks and five anti-tank guns up to the Brandenburg Gate, Clay flatly refused to believe him. (Macmillan sent a note to Home: "Do you think I might ask President Kennedy to recall General Clay? He seems to me a public danger. He always was an ass: now he is an embittered ass.")[67]

West Berliners' desolation, their doubts about the future, intensified in December. They mourned as a personal tragedy the death of a twenty-year-old student, Dieter Wohlfart, who was shot by Grepos at Staaken when he and two others cut barbed wire to help a woman escape. He lay, mortally wounded, for an hour and a half, while the Grepos held off at gunpoint West Berlin police and British military policemen who tried to help him, then was finally dragged back into the East to die.[68]

Would Berliners have felt better if they had known that on New Year's Eve Herr Joachim Lipschitz, the Senator for the Interior, intended to blow up the Wall? In secret he had built a thirty-yard stretch of replica wall to practise on and tried to acquire plastic explosives; and he intended to use policemen and border guards out of uniform to lay charges at up to twenty-five spots along the intersector border. According to later accounts he hoped to grab the world's attention and precipitate a four-Power conference. In the event, he died on 11 December and word of his plot leaked to the allied Military Commandants.[69]

It is not clear how many already knew about it: there are suggestions that Brandt did but had not yet given approval; some politicians in Bonn were thought to have been aware of what was going on. It was, however, high-ranking West Berlin policemen who passed the information to the allies, dreading that the explosions would set off a chain reaction among West Berliners and lead to a massacre at the border – just the situation they had been risking their own lives to prevent ever since 13 August. There was a stormy meeting of the Military Commandants on 22 December. Watson argued passionately that stopping this action would shatter morale; when he ran up against his colleagues' opposition, he retreated only to the point of declaring that now a practice wall had been built it should be used for experiments to see how much explosive was needed to knock down the real thing. Lacomme, the French Commandant, took the view that morale should be based on confidence not "ill-considered and amateurish escapades". The British were appalled by the whole business, not least because the mock wall was in their sector and they had not noticed it. Delacombe threatened to take unilateral action and smash the offensive object and finally Watson gave up with what was described in the British report as "emotional ill-grace". Brandt and Albertz were summoned by the Military Commandants next day and denied all knowledge of the plot. Albertz later claimed that the fake wall was intended only for "testing weather resistance" and since by then he had ordered it to be demolished, the matter was not pursued.

So Christmas and the New Year passed without incident and with acute unhappiness on both sides of the Wall. West Germans tried to send a little cheer and hope by dispatching Christmas trees to decorate the Wall. West Berliners were reluctant to put them up but felt obliged to do so. They had guessed what the result would be: the Vopos threw stones at them. There could be no reunions with family, no parties for friends who lived on the other side. The gloom was particularly deep in the East where after a poor harvest there was a shortage of food to add to the absence of coffee, soap powder, pepper, matches, salt and rice which the authorities attributed to hoarding. There was only one thing to celebrate: the loudspeakers on the border were silent for a few days. That apart, no one could look back on the past year with anything but depression; and there seemed little hope for the coming year. The GDR and its allies had destroyed the city and any confidence in the future of Germany or the chances of a European détente and settlement. Many Berliners would have shared the view of de Gaulle – and approved the barrack room language in which he expressed it: "Berlin est foutu."[70]

II

Ends

————————————

I n political terms De Gaulle was probably right to describe Berlin as "foutu": the problem of the city had become so entangled in all the other post-war dilemmas and disputes bedevilling East and West that it was totally fouled up. The Wall, in fact, was the nearest the two sides could come to dealing with those insoluble questions: they were now buried under tons of concrete. Until many of the old suspicions and ambitions had dwindled away and the entire European context had changed out of all recognition, the Wall would have to act as a substitute peace settlement. Political and diplomatic processes ever since 1945 had been incapable of resolving the predicament of unifying or dismembering Germany, adjusting disputed frontiers, containing or meshing two disparate social and economic systems, reducing arms. The Wall, crude and cruel though it was, created a Germany for each side, defined the last section of the East–West frontier across divided Europe, and left the two blocs to develop their systems separately on either side while keeping them from each other's throats. It was a twenty-nine-mile-long, nine- to twelve-foot-high, barbed-wire garlanded monument to failure. It commemorated the end of post-war hopes and allied cooperation, the deficiency of statesmanship, the abandonment of rational discussion of mutual self-interest in favour of ideological blinkers and the prospect of mutually assured destruction. Yet the Wall, together with the Bomb, gave Europe twenty-eight years of what passed for peace: an uneasy absence of war.

The building of the Wall proved that Khrushchev could not win most of what he had been playing for since his ultimatum of November 1958, however skilfully he exploited his opponents' weaknesses. In August 1961 the stakes had got too high. His only alternatives to complete climbdown had been withdrawal behind this defensive line or invasion of the western sectors and the inevitability of war. The very way he had played his hand had doomed his game: by issuing threats and setting time limits for the West he had panicked East Germans into leaving the GDR; had he used some of those tactics to oblige Ulbricht to run his state more effectively, they might have stayed. As a result, he only got his minimum demands: he won no peace treaty, no recognition for the GDR, no "free Berlin" weakened for take-over; instead he had to settle for an impregnable frontier behind which Pankow might be propped up and socialism might survive. Of course Khrushchev put the best face he could on this shortfall. He boasted in his memoirs that he had achieved his purpose: "secured for the GDR its sovereign rights", made possible instant economic progress, and enabled Pankow to restore "order" – and, in his complacent view, "Germans have always appreciated discipline." Yet he had the honesty to admit: "We didn't quite achieve the same sort of moral victory that a peace treaty would have represented." And he made the staggering admission that the Wall was a continued and unavoidable necessity because the GDR had "yet to reach a level of moral and material development where competition with the West is possible".[1]

Walter Ulbricht could hardly feel he had scored much of a success by building the Wall, though on the credit side he had finally persuaded his Soviet masters to permit what he had urged for so long and could now hold on to his citizens. For him too the Wall was the minimum requirement; it was a poor substitute for the treaty Khrushchev had promised and the status and diplomatic recognition which would have followed. Many of those in the GDR who tried hardest to believe that the Wall was a justifiable sovereign act by their government had their loyalties strained. The East German writer Stefan Heym remembered that in 1961 "I found that a socialism that needed a wall to keep its people in the country wasn't the right kind of socialism." Later he saw the fortification as an encouragement to further failure: "A wise government", he believed, "would have tried to create a policy which would have enabled them to pull the Wall down as soon as possible." But Pankow never won the acceptance or gratitude of its citizens; given the Wall, the regime came to think that it did not need to. A devoted Party member, Günter Schabowski, finally helped to pull the Wall down, but when it was built he approved of it: "The state which embodied the socialist future of Germany had to be protected from the threat" of the "imperialist opponent"; the people had to be cushioned from the western media, the economy must be saved from bleeding to death. Even in 1989 Schabowski defended the construction of the Wall as "a necessary deed in the self-assertion of socialism". But by then he had reached the anguished conclusion that "the Wall had remained the symbol of a concealed inferiority complex". Perhaps even this bitter judgement fell short; perhaps the inferiority was genuine. Perhaps plugging the last gap in the Iron Curtain with a concrete Wall demonstrated that the Soviet system applied to Eastern Europe was a transplant which was always about to be rejected by the body politic; it could only survive in isolation from the western democratic infections of choice, debate and individuality.[2]

That was a theory often put on paper in the West, but it was never tested. The Wall went up and stood as long as it did partly because of western incapacity. The disunity and indecisiveness of the Western Powers from 1945 onward, interrupted only by forced lurches into action, as with the Airlift or the incorporation of the Federal Republic into NATO, had left East Europe to the Russians. Through the 1950s the allies in Berlin accused the Soviet Union of "salami tactics" while they themselves sawed the Berlin branch on which they sat, weakening their position in the city and their access to it. Their timorous response to Khrushchev's ultimatum and lack of firm policies to combat it had terrified East Germans into flight even before Kennedy caused the final haemorrhage by implying that he was handing over the GDR to the Soviet Union. The Western Powers had prepared for every Berlin crisis except the one which occurred; as the Wall was being built, their blundering and inertia came near to losing them what little they had left in the city. So the West too had to accept second-best in 1961: no more hollow rhetoric about German unity, quadripartite responsibility in Berlin, "rollback" in Europe; just containment of the Soviet Union at the price of East Germany being swept irretrievably behind the Iron Curtain.

In the years after August 1961 western leaders would visit Berlin, stand on a viewing platform at the Wall, and deliver a finely phrased speech condemning this obscene construction. These occasions were not designed for the benefit of Berlin; they were a form of rite de passage, an appearance before the media intended to transform a politician into a statesman. The high-flown orations were so much humbug; Reagan's "Pull down that Wall" was nothing more than gesturism. The Western Powers used the Wall for propaganda, never as a bargaining counter. They negotiated with the Soviet Union, signed agreements and accords, without the slightest reference to it. The Wall became a geographical fact, unalterable and unquestioned. The West, like the East, could not conceive of a world without it.

Even if Berlin as an international problem was "foutu", the city itself was not a write-off. Far from it. Berliners do not give up easily. They have a talent for survival and have learned to make sane lives in bizarre circumstances. Once the Wall went up, West Berliners created a unique city. They turned the western sectors, those stumps of amputated hope for a united Germany, into a metropolis with all the glamour and activities of a major European capital. Two and a half million people carried infinitely more political weight than nations many times their size; Governing Mayors had the stature of significant international figures. The survival of West Berlin continued to depend on the presence and support of the Western Powers yet, paradoxically, the burgeoning of West Berlin was nourished by the sense of isolation born in August 1961. West Berliners decided they must manage for themselves.

Some of them would date the psychological turning point as precisely 17 August 1962. Until then there was bewilderment, and a debilitating pessimism. On that day, Peter Fechter, an eighteen-year-old mason, together with another young building worker, climbed over the wire from East Berlin, dashed across the Death Strip, and reached the Wall at Zimmerstrasse, just west of Checkpoint Charlie. Here the Vopos opened fire. The friend scrambled over; Fechter was hit and lay on the ground, foetally huddled. He called for help. West Berlin policemen clambered up and hung from the metal struts which supported the barbed wire, risking fire from the Vopos, but could not reach him. They threw first aid packets, and shouted encouragement to struggle up the last few feet. West Berliners gathered and were met by East Berlin tear gas. They bellowed to the American military police at Checkpoint Charlie to come and help. The guards lurked in their shed until an officer came out to say "Sorry, but this is not our problem." It was an accurate legal statement. But it burned a horrible political truth into Berliners' consciousness. The crowd stood and watched for fifty minutes as Peter Fechter bled to death and was finally dragged away as carrion by his arms and legs. And West Berliners decided that Peter Fechter was *their* problem. His heartbreaking death had finally brought home the reality that no one would take the Wall away for them, that they must learn to live with it, and find ways to reach across it – to the West, certainly, but also to the East.

They were right to assume that no help would come from outside. The three Western Powers and the Soviet Union were too preoccupied with their own interests in the city to dress Berlin's wounds. Llewellyn Thompson began talks with Gromyko in Moscow on 2 January 1962, but his only concern was with allied rights and his only fresh approach was the proposal for an International Access Authority made up of the four major Powers, both German states, and seven presumed neutrals. Gromyko showed a little curiosity in it at the first meeting and Thompson expanded on ideas for controlling the Autobahn and air corridors, ways to run the Berlin Air Safety Centre and airports, the appointment of checkpoint personnel and the fixing of tolls. However, after the next meeting, Thompson described Gromyko as having "reverted completely to [the] basic Soviet Free City proposal"; by 1 February the Soviet Foreign Minister was saying that Thompson's "approach offers only a very narrow area for understanding, and in fact precludes agreement on negotiations". Even this cautious and barren exchange of views had been enough to enrage NATO: Thompson had launched the Access Authority scheme without prior consultation with its members. Berliners, too, had been displeased: by American willingness to share what had been exclusive quadripartite rights and by the possible inclusion of the GDR in an international body. When in February the Russians demanded exclusive use of the air corridors, then buzzed allied aircraft and dropped metallic chaff to interfere with western radar and air traffic control, Berliners saw the trouble as predictable exploitation of western weakness.[3]

Rusk tried to revive the US–USSR talks when he met Gromyko at the disarmament conference in Geneva in March and it was agreed that he should begin discussions with the Soviet ambassador in Washington. But the US Administration sabotaged this round in April by a clumsy attempt to hustle their allies: they presented them with new proposals for the talks and demanded approval within twenty-four hours. As always, France rejected the package outright; Britain was miffed by the peremptory presentation but accepted it. Adenauer insisted on an extra twenty-four hours for consideration then went along with the proposals only on the assumption they would fail. The new terms proposed by the United States were totally unacceptable to Bonn: GDR membership of the Access Authority, agreements only on military and not civilian access, the establishment of joint German committees, non-aggression declarations between NATO and the Warsaw Pact, and a pledge not to violate "existing borders or demarcation lines", which meant recognising the Wall and the Oder-Neisse Line without Bonn's say-so. To make doubly sure that these talks failed, Bonn leaked the American proposals to the press. Washington came under heavy fire from its allies as well as domestic critics for readiness to give away so much for such minor gains. Rusk pressed on regardless, and talked to Dobrynin over the next three months, but got nowhere. He was not particularly disappointed. He had already admitted to his old colleague Brentano that it "was his ambition to hand Berlin" (as a problem) "to his successor"; he was just talking out his time. At the end of 1962 the Weekend Reading Book for Kennedy informed the President that Mikoyan had hinted that the Soviet Union was "waiting for constructive proposals from the United States on Berlin" but there was an added comment: "I suspect he may have to wait quite a while".[4]

By then, it hardly mattered. The divided city of Berlin was finding its own equilibrium and was free from international pressure. East–West conflict had been played out on a new stage – Cuba – for thirteen nail-biting days in October 1962. Not only had the scene shifted; so had the whole European context.

The details of the Cuban Missile Crisis are well known, and form part of a different story. What is relevant here is that when evidence reached Washington that there were enough Soviet nuclear missile sites in Cuba – only ninety miles from the American mainland – to destroy every American city with the possible exception of Seattle, the immediate White House assumption was that Cuba was a new phase in the Berlin crisis. On 16 October, at the first meeting of ExCom (the Executive Committee of the National Security Council set up to handle the affair) it was reckoned that Khrushchev could gain from this Cuban adventure in two ways: either by diverting American attention while he grabbed the western sectors, or offering to remove his missiles in return for allied surrender of West Berlin. On 20 October, Robert McNamara argued in the NSC that any action taken by the United States in Cuba would provoke Soviet retaliation in Berlin. In a speech on television that day, the President warned the Kremlin against hostile moves in any area where the United States had commitments, especially against "the brave people of West Berlin". Others saw the crisis from this White House perspective. When Kennedy informed Macmillan on 21 October of the dangerous situation and the measures he intended to take, the Prime Minister agreed with his analysis that Khrushchev's "main intention may be to increase his chances in Berlin" and added his own twist of anxiety: if Khrushchev "were stopped with great loss of face in Cuba, would he not be tempted to recover himself in Berlin?" When Brandt received a similar briefing, he advised the President to act as he thought fit without concern for the consequences in Berlin, then warned Egon Bahr that they might be facing a "Long March" so "bring good thick socks", and pondered whether an East German attack on the western sectors might be countered by a call for an East German uprising.[5]

Kennedy's belief that he was fighting the same Berlin war but on two fronts held throughout the Cuban crisis. It endured even when the Soviet ambassador at the UN went out of his way to inform every diplomat he could buttonhole that the Soviet Union would not "fall into the trap" of an attack in Berlin. After one ExCom meeting a reporter found a yellow legal pad at the President's place covered over and over again with the one word "Berlin". Yet he was probably mistaken. Rather than using Cuba for Berlin ends, it was more likely that Khrushchev had abandoned Berlin as a "blister on the American foot" and was looking for a new sore spot to tread on. Be that as it may, it can be argued that Kennedy's management of the Cuban crisis benefited enormously from the long thinking about Berlin and from a readiness he had never shown before to face the possibility of nuclear war while using every political and military device to avoid it.

He deployed full American military might: forces all over the world were on alert, the Strategic Air Command was just one stage short of combat deployment. However, he rejected a JCS call for an air strike on Cuba followed by invasion, and he would not approve limited action against specific Soviet missile sites. He ignored advice to take pressure off Cuba by putting nuclear weapons into Berlin. Instead he announced on 22 October that the US Navy would establish a "quarantine" or "exclusion zone", with an 800-mile radius round the island, to prevent the passage of twenty-five Cuba-bound Soviet ships, some with hatches for missiles, others with delivery aircraft. The word "blockade" was avoided: it might be interpreted by international lawyers as an act of war and, more particularly, the word was so associated with Berlin that its very use was expected to produce a new siege of the city in response. Whatever the exercise was called, it was intended to deter further offensive armament in Cuba while giving the Kremlin time to consider what to do with the missiles already there. While this dangerous strategy was put into force, Kennedy covered his flanks: forty-six ambassadors in Washington and the Organisation of American States were thoroughly informed, personal messages and photographic evidence were delivered to the United States' closest allies, NATO was put in the picture by Acheson, and the Secretary General of the UN was persuaded to call on Khrushchev to halt his ships for at least twenty-four hours – in return for which Kennedy agreed to avoid direct confrontation with them if they stayed out of the interception area long enough for preliminary negotiations to be held. It was a fine repertoire of responses, deftly played, not unlike the tactics Acheson had recommended for confronting Khrushchev in Berlin. It could have been extremely effective in August 1961 too.

Throughout the Cuban Missile Crisis, Kennedy was unrecognisable from the man who had presided over the eight months which led to the building of the Berlin Wall: mature, cool, decisive, able to act spontaneously without first demanding lengthy re-examinations of every aspect, capable of seeing his problems in full colour rather than black and white simplicities, with the courage to face the worst and the finesse to achieve the best. The President had learned lessons in the short period of his

Administration. He now taught the older Soviet leader a crucial one: that nuclear blackmail would not work. Khrushchev, who had treated Kennedy as gullible and weak at Vienna, had suffered a major setback at his hands and felt obliged to recognise his opponent as an "intelligent, sober-minded counterpart". The failure of his Cuban adventure was not the major cause of his downfall two years later. But, like the Berlin initiative in 1958, it contributed to his enemies' belief that Khrushchev the gambler risked the reputation and security of the Soviet Union for debatable gains whilst, at the same time, weakening Communist ideology and alliances by preaching an incompatible "co-existence" with capitalist enemies. He was lucky that no one took advantage of this latest defeat to press for adjustments in Berlin. Perhaps it was not luck but calculation: the West had superior conventional force in the Caribbean but the Soviet Union held the conventional whip hand in Germany, and having so recently peered over the nuclear brink the Western Powers were not willing to take a second look.

While politicians and their advisers had convinced themselves that Cuba was a phase, and not the last one, in the Berlin crisis, one group of journalists in Berlin followed every detail of the story hugging themselves with delight. "Khrushchev has gone too far," they told each other, "and he will lose. He won't try it on with the Americans again. Berlin is safe." That was indeed the real connection between the Berlin and Cuban crises.[6]

Left undisturbed, West Berliners began to make their abnormal lives tolerable. They discovered how to turn their disadvantages into assets: since their links with Bonn were secure but not tight they had freedom to manoeuvre; since they were separated by only a few inches of concrete from the GDR they could make contact; since they were no longer the central preoccupation of East and West they had an opportunity to craft stratagems for their own needs. A policy of Small Steps evolved, gradual and detailed little measures to settle matters of common interest between themselves and the GDR, to alleviate some of the suffering and inconvenience caused by the Wall. The Small Steps were taken along a route Brandt had mapped out years ago but had failed to persuade Adenauer to follow. In 1956 he had pleaded in the Bundestag for the "greatest possible degree of relations" between Germans; for "making life easier in an arbitrarily divided Germany". Now the aged Chancellor's grip had slackened, there was some sympathy for new ideas in Bonn; and since the western allies were not interpreting every Berlin move in the light of threats to their presence and access they would give Brandt some leeway.[7]

The Small Steps were therapy for Berlin and Brandt: the western sectors had been in despair after the Wall was built, the Mayor himself had shown all the signs of clinical depression. Egon Bahr took Brandt's prescription and based a course of treatment on it. In July 1963, he called for "change through meeting". Brandt then defined it: the German problem had international, European, national and security dimensions but human considerations must be paramount; Bonn was wrong to suggest that the West must "always be swift and firm in rejecting any suggestion from the East just because it comes from the East". "If we are ready to serve the interests of our countrymen and bring humane relief, we must be ready to discuss a great deal" and at least come to a private understanding even if a public settlement was unattainable; the very process of argument might bring the Soviet Union "to see that a change was in its own interests".

Radical change might never happen and would certainly take time. For the moment, therefore, Brandt set limited, pragmatic goals. The first Small Step was taken on 5 December 1963 when the West Berlin Senate agreed to explore an East German offer of a brief period with a few travel permits for westerners. The talks which followed give a strong flavour of the political conflicts underlying even minor transactions, the fecundity of Germans from both sides in manufacturing dodges round their own rules, the squeals of anxiety with which Bonn reacted to any dealings with the GDR, and Soviet suspicion, even fear, of "their" Germans meeting the others. (One Soviet official gasped to Brandt "Who knows what you might discuss behind closed doors?") The West Berlin Senate would not deal directly with Pankow because that would advance the theory of a "free city", so intermediaries had to be found; the East Germans wanted to dignify any agreement with the terminology of international law but West Berlin would only accept an administrative arrangement so as to avoid confirming that each side had a separate political existence; Pankow had to be persuaded not to punish visitors previously declared guilty of "flight from the Republic" and merely issued a warning that they would be. The GDR tried to send staff to issue the travel permits, but the Senate refused them sovereign functions in the western sectors, so the clerks were eventually termed "post office personnel". The first permit came into force on 18 December, Brandt's birthday. In the next week or so, until the Christmas season and the term of the agreement were over, 1.2 million westerners crossed the Wall to the East: a staggering volume of visitors which neither side had expected, taking a lot of personal Steps indeed.

Like the refugee tide westwards before 1961, the visitors' flow eastwards was irresistible for a time. Two new short-term agreements were signed in 1964, more visits were permitted at Easter and Whitsun 1965 and in that year a further 36,000 passes were granted for individuals with urgent or compassionate needs; there was a Christmas and New Year opening in

1965 and another for Easter and Whitsun. Then the GDR sealed the crack in the Wall: refused to keep a clause in the standard agreement which set out the differing legal and political positions of East and West. There were no more travel permits until 1972. All those meetings had not yet significantly changed Pankow's views or behaviour. So far, they had accomplished one Step forward and one Step back.

There were, however, other movements across the Wall and a new form of exchange. The "trade in human beings" was renewed – not as Pankow had originally defined it, as the luring of its citizens to the West, but as unashamed selling of East German citizens to the Federal Republic. The trade begin in 1963, when eight political prisoners were released and allowed out of the GDR in return for West German cash. It grew into wholesale commerce: it is estimated that by 1989 nearly 250,000 East Germans had been bought for DM3.5 billion, paid in hard currency, oil or commodities. Unlike other merchandise in the Soviet bloc there was no price control on human beings: their value was decided on the open market, the price rose over the years, and since the West was willing to pay more for a prisoner than a free man, Pankow added value to its goods by putting them in prison first to ensure a good return. Many an individual must have wondered whether committing an offence with a short term of imprisonment might be a good personal investment – a far safer way to get to the West than braving the wire, mines and machineguns at the Wall.

Bonn gradually grew willing to engage in more conventional, less distasteful trade, going round rather than across the Wall, to bypass and isolate the GDR. The FRG set up a trade mission in Warsaw in September 1963; others were opened in Bucharest, Budapest, Sofia in 1964. Once Adenauer resigned in October 1963, the Federal Foreign Minister could state openly his belief that doctrinaire principle was irrelevant to diplomacy and that "no abstract conceptions stand in the way of diplomatic relations with Eastern Europe". That still meant refusal to recognise the GDR, but it permitted relations with those states deemed by Bonn to have accepted the East German regime at Soviet insistence. This step opened new vistas. In the Peace Note of 1966 the Federal Government declared itself ready to work for détente, demilitarisation and renunciation of the use of force against the Soviet bloc. Early in that year Brandt began secret talks with the Soviet ambassador in East Berlin to look for areas of possible agreement which would make self-interest the guarantee of stability and the catalyst of rapprochement.

Brandt himself became Federal Foreign Minister in December 1966. At a press conference in Berlin in June of the following year he explained his basic philosophy: "Europe cannot be built at one stroke"; "The time of grand enterprises is past." These views could have been a statement of the obvious for many years past, but the four Powers in Germany had never been willing to face up to that reality – and in their search for a great treaty, a final settlement, they had constantly stumbled at points where minor, practical agreement might have been found. Brandt's ideas of gradual, pragmatic movement to improve the lot of the individual in a divided Germany meant talking to Moscow and East Berlin and a policy of "regulated co-existence". They also involved easing relations with the rest of the Soviet bloc. In summer 1967 he signed a trade agreement with the Czechs; in 1968 he re-established diplomatic relations with Yugoslavia which had been broken in 1957. In February 1968, in a memorandum to the Soviet Union he used the phrase that the two parts of Germany must not treat each other as "abroad". From this developed his concept of one German nation, two German states: a maintenance of the dream of reunification while accepting present realities without awarding the GDR the honour of recognition.

Small Steps had covered a lot of ground. But they were halted in 1968. The revulsion felt at the crushing of the Prague Spring with the invasion of Czechoslovakia by Warsaw Pact armies, and the Brezhnev Doctrine which justified it by claiming a responsibility to intervene if there was a threat to Socialism, made West German politicians hesitate to establish further contacts and strengthened the voices of their critics who had always maintained that reaching out to the East was a gesture of surrender.

While the first Small Steps were taken to cross the Wall, West Berliners made themselves more comfortable alongside it. At first they felt imprisoned, but at least they had an exercise yard they loved: their lakes and woods. They could not cross into the GDR, unless they could claim an address in the FRG and wangle a Federal passport. But once it became clear that there would be no major interference with traffic to the West, they could also get out to the Federal Republic and from there to the rest of the world. It was expensive if they flew (and city officials and policemen were forbidden to risk land routes right through the 1960s) though eventually Bonn subsidised up to a third of all air fares; it was slow and irritating to go by train and endure lengthy document checks; it was positively frightening to drive since there were no garages through the GDR to recover a broken down car, every tree seemed to hide a Vopo ready to leap out and demand an instant fine for speeding, and the procedures at the GDR checkpoints at either end of a route were deliberately drawn out and intimidating. At home West Berliners gradually stopped noticing the Wall and they overcame some of its inconveniences if not its pain. For hard currency the East Germans were willing to cart away two-thirds of the western sectors' garbage and the rest was incinerated. The Senate paid the GDR DM2 million to be allowed to build two U-bahn connecting lines under East Berlin in the 1960s and over ten years two brand-new U-bahn routes were constructed to compensate for lost lines and the S-bahn service which West Berliners continued to boycott.[8]

A big problem, and a lasting one, was shortage of labour. Seven per cent of West Berlin's work force disappeared in August 1961 when Grenzgänger could no longer cross; young people in the western sectors were sorely tempted by higher wages and plenty of job vacancies in the Federal Republic. To keep the young in Berlin and to maintain jobs and a sense of long-term security, Bonn pumped in money. The Federal government cut income tax for West Berliners (30 per cent below West German rates for some tax brackets) and reduced the local turnover tax; cash bonuses were paid to low earners; special marriage allowances were provided; there were settlement grants for any West German moving to Berlin which included two free journeys a year back to the FRG for single persons and four for married couples; small businesses got credit facilities and exporters bigger ones. Respectable middle-aged West Berliners in the late 1960s were not always happy with the young people who were attracted to the western sectors by Bonn's generosity and the freedom from conscription into Federal armed forces: they tut-tutted at long hair, unpressed clothes, loud music, squatting, the smoking of strange-smelling substances and relationships unblessed by the Church. Young Berliners, on the other hand, were enormously grateful for the introduction of a new culture into the stuffy atmosphere: at last they felt connected with youth outside.

Money, locally generated or invested by Bonn, gave West Berlin a new role and pride in the 1960s. It made the two universities international centres of learning, built housing projects designed by architects of world repute who had competed for city prizes, constructed and subsidised the Deutsche Oper and Philharmonie as homes for a great opera and symphony orchestra, maintained and developed the museums and galleries at a level of content, display and comfort seldom attained anywhere else. For those with a different idea of a good time, there were shops, restaurants, and entertainment as attractive as any in Europe. Enormous sums were lavished on tourists: advertising, good information services, subsidised hotels. Drawing in visitors and impressing them with West Berlin's prosperity, culture and political significance was essential policy. That was why the visit of President Kennedy in June 1963 was so important. When he said "Ich bin ein Berliner" ("I am a doughnut"), they forgave the grammar, understood that he meant he was "Berliner" (a Berliner) and cheered because they wanted the whole world to feel that degree of involvement in their survival. Without it, their city was still acutely vulnerable.

Over the same period, East Berlin began to flourish too. There was destruction and construction to build a capital city. In 1962 the Bauakademie, an 1830s masterpiece of Karl Friedrich Schinkel, was demolished to make way for a dour eleven-storey slab to house the Foreign Ministry – rather a large building for a state with so few diplomatic relations outside the Soviet bloc, but somewhere to work in hopes. The Alexanderplatz, already smashed by allied bombing, sprouted shops, offices and flats in prefabricated blocks tricked out with the coloured panels and mosaic frescos of ersatz international modernism. It held East Germany's largest department store, which always had more selling space than goods, and the Television Tower, from the top of which East Berliners could glimpse the West they were forbidden to visit and on whose brown glass sphere the setting sun beamed a golden cross; a "Pope's revenge" against atheistic Communism, said West Berliners. East Germany's Chief Architect described the new square as "representative of all the merits of our socialist system". Presumably he did not intend the phrase to be interpreted as a summary of the oppressive, unlovable inhuman architecture and the tacky decoration which sat so uneasily with two remaining features of old Berlin: the frivolous, charming Neptune fountain and the Marienkirche, that monument to a long history of Christianity where the bishop was no longer allowed to preach. The building policy was not entirely destructive: some money and effort, though not enough, went on maintaining Berlin's historic opera houses, theatres and museums – the new regime's nervous claim to past German achievement. There was little will and less cash to restore other old buildings; they were left to moulder, still bearing the pock marks of the Soviet shelling in 1945 and awaiting the day when these remnants of imperialism and fascism could be swept away by Socialist progress.

There was always a chronic shortage of building workers and materials in the GDR and precious resources were soaked up by maintenance and improvement of the Wall. Throughout the 1960s wide-bore concrete piping was laid along its top so that no finger or toe could get a grip should anyone dare to try to climb over. Anti-tank ditches proliferated, patrol tracks and dog runs were driven in all directions, watchtowers, floodlights, alarm wires were strewn across the Death Strip. In a massive act of civic annihilation, the whole of the Potsdamer Platz was razed and every East Berlin street leading into it was turned to desert. Rabbits played on the sand which Prussian willpower and husbandry had turned to soil, and across which the traffic of East and West had once passed at Europe's busiest junction.

In November 1961 Stalin Allee was renamed Karl-Marx-Allee. It might be said this was the nearest that the GDR regime came to any political adjustment, even to Soviet bloc norms. The gains of August 1961 as far as most East Germans were concerned were economic not political. Having stemmed the flow of refugees, the government could now set attainable production targets, knowing the size of the labour force, and feel that investment in training would benefit the GDR and not the Federal Republic. The New Economic System, announced in 1963, resulted in the eastern equivalent of West Germany's Economic Miracle: within two years industrial production had risen 43 per cent above the 1958 level. And there was enough spare capacity to produce a few consumer goods. Growing wealth brought social benefits: good medical services, phenomenally low rents, merely token charges for public transport, well run crèches and kindergartens (most mothers worked in an economy where labour was short). Prices of basic foods were pegged – and however harmful this may have been in the long run, for a time it was a contribution to a good and rising standard of living. And each economic improvement had political consequences: East Germans who had known so many years of poverty could now enjoy some of the results of their sacrifice and hard work; a few began to believe that central planning could, after all, deliver the goods, that distribution of wealth did indeed improve the lot of the majority and raise the dignity of everyone. They knew they were different from the West; they were increasingly proud of that difference and more confident that they would catch up materially without losing their sense of neighbourliness and social justice. They knew that whatever the shortcomings of their life styles by comparison with western relatives, they lived very much better than anyone else in the Soviet bloc: "It's certainly not Poland," they said, with vast relief. "It's Russia de luxe."9*

All the same, people still tried to leave the GDR and risked their necks to do so. For a couple of years after the Wall was built it was still possible to find barriers at a few crossing points along the zonal frontier under which a

* "De luxe" but lacking some things which the West regarded as everyday commodities. There is a scene in Billy Wilder's film *One, Two, Three* (for which he tried to shoot location shots in August 1961 in Berlin and found art outstripped by reality) where, in a run-down café in East Berlin, an elderly, seedy band suddenly strikes up with a lugubrious, oompah version of "Ja, ja, we have no bananas". It could have been adopted as the Comecon anthem: An Ode to Fruit.

low sports car could squeeze. (An Austrian brought out his fiancée and her mother that way.) Heavy lorries could smash a barricade or even, as in the case of an East German NCO, an armoured car could ram through. There were organised mass break-outs: over a hundred people wriggled through a sewer in Glemstrasse in 1961 until a young girl could not find the strength to replace the manhole cover after climbing down; once the route was spotted, all sewers and drains were fitted with fixed gratings and alarm wires. Several tunnels were gouged out under the wall in 1962; one was flooded by a burst water main but was pumped out and twenty-six people escaped. Fifty-seven more crawled along a tunnel in 1964 which had been hacked between an outside privy in the West and a cellar in Bernauer Strasse; it lay twelve metres underground, had taken six months to dig and the soil was taken out on a little rubber wheeled cart in over five thousand journeys.[10]

Some people used water or air escape routes: one lad crossed the Baltic to Denmark towed underwater by a small motor intended to power a bicycle; in 1979 two families built a hot air balloon and learned to fly it as they crossed forty kilometres to the West. Others adapted machines: car seats were hollowed out or boots were given false bottoms for hiding places until guards at checkpoints learned to search carefully and to check the under side of vehicles with mirrors. Eighteen people in all crossed to the West in a car whose chassis was enlarged to give a space at the side of the engine; once that trick was discovered, guards were provided with specifications for every vehicle type and measuring rods to check that no alterations had been made. That did not stop nine refugees travelling in the space created by stripping out a car's heating system and shifting the battery. On two occasions in 1965 six people at a time were transported in the core of a cable drum. Alternative skills were put to use: passports were forged in the names of eastern bloc visitors or diplomats; uniforms were made so that East Germans could walk across checkpoints as Soviet or American soldiers. Just as mind-boggling as human ingenuity was human flexibility. How could a girl, however slim, go all the way from Erfurt to the Federal Republic in two ordinary suitcases, placed together and with the touching sides knocked out? How could even a girl who worked in a circus squash into her boyfriend's loudspeaker whose sides measured barely two feet?

Between 1961 and 1989 there were more than five thousand successful escapes from the GDR – 565 of them by members of the armed services. It was reckoned that at least as many more were tried but failed. East German forces opened fire 1,693 times; eighty people died. Each arrest, each shot, each wound or death was a testament to human courage but,

like the Wall itself, recorded the extent of political brutality and bank-
ruptcy.

In October 1969 Willy Brandt became Chancellor of the Federal Republic
– only the second man to hold that office since the birth of the state in 1949
and the election of Adenauer. He made it clear from the outset that his
policy of Small Steps would be developed into a full Ostpolitik: establishing
relations with the GDR and other East European states, while keeping a
firm footing in the western alliance. A survey showed that 74 per cent of the
West German public was in favour of his policy. And he had a fresh
opportunity. The Kremlin was in open conflict with China (which now had
the H-bomb) and did not want confrontation on its western front at the
same time; the Soviet Union had lost technological confidence (an
American had landed on the moon) and its ailing economy needed an
infusion of western aid. Brandt also had encouragement from the newly
elected President Richard Nixon, who on 27 February 1969 called in Berlin
for ways "to end the challenge and clear the way for a peaceful solution to
the problem of a divided Germany". So on 22 January 1970 Brandt wrote
to Willy Stoph, Prime Minister of the GDR, suggesting talks. Since he was
well aware that Ulbricht was likely to oppose West German proposals, he
took the precaution of approaching the ultimate power source: Egon Bahr
was sent to Moscow and on 30 January began discussions with Gromyko on
improving relations with the Soviet Union. With the Russians engaged,
Brandt could then accept Stoph's suggestion of a meeting in East Germany.[11]

It was an invitation with boobytraps. Stoph wanted East Berlin to be the
venue, but Pankow would not countenance the arrival of a Federal
Chancellor via West Berlin. Brandt side-stepped by proposing Erfurt
and it was there, where Goethe once met Napoleon, that the two leaders
of one nation shook hands on German soil on 19 March. They stood under
a banner proclaiming the GDR as "The German State of Peace and
Socialism" while a choir sang demands for the recognition of the GDR and
the crowd cheered the Chancellor as a hero. That evening East German
radio failed to broadcast Brandt's speech: "We cannot simply undo this
division but we can try to modify the effects of partition", by renunciation
of force, cooperation, and an attempt to relieve human suffering caused by
the split. Nothing, however, could mar the psychological impact of this
historic breakthrough at Erfurt. Never mind what each leader had said.
For the first time they had spoken to each other.

And a process had begun which Pankow could only slow, not halt. Willy
Stoph did his best to wreck his return visit to Kassel on 21 May, by
interrupting Brandt's speech of welcome with accusations of interference in

East German affairs and complaints of "neo-Nazi" (in fact anti-Communist) demonstrations outside. The talks produced no hint of agreement. Brandt, however, doggedly put forward twenty detailed ways to improve relations and, most importantly, put a multi-directional squeeze on the GDR. Bahr's talks in Moscow (with occasional direct and secret communication between Brandt and Brezhnev) resulted on 12 August 1970 in a treaty by which each side renounced the use of force against the other, accepted the map of Europe as it stood, and the FRG formally abandoned the Hallstein Doctrine without agreeing to recognise the GDR. In December, Bonn concluded a treaty with Poland, confirming the Oder-Neisse Line, and Willy Brandt knelt on the ground of the Warsaw Ghetto which German soldiers had destroyed.

Meanwhile talks had opened on 26 March in Berlin between the four former occupation Powers to look for a resolution of the city's problems. These meetings carried extraordinary historical echoes. They were held in the old Allied Control Council building, that home of the lost cause of quadripartite cooperation, and they replayed the basic themes of confrontation since Khrushchev's ultimatum of November 1958. They were stuck from the very first session over the western claim that Berlin was an area of quadripartite responsibility stemming from conquest versus the Soviet assertion that there was only a "West Berlin problem" and East Berlin, the capital of the GDR, was not a subject for negotiation. As ever, western access became the bone of contention, with the Western Powers demanding Soviet guarantees for it and the Russians insisting that it was an element of East German sovereignty. By late November, and continuing intermittently to March, there were hold-ups of allied traffic on the Autobahn. For long weary months the negotiation was not so much a move to détente as a trip down memory lane.

Nevertheless, a variety of levers was steadily applied to break the logjam – and the Soviet Union was vulnerable to the pressure. Brandt made ratification of the Moscow treaty dependent on progress over Berlin; NATO insisted that agreement to hold force reduction talks was conditional on satisfactory agreements being reached; Nixon announced a visit to China. The Soviet hard line gradually began to crumble, though steps to a Berlin settlement were still painful and slow – not least because western toes were constantly stubbed on the rock of Ulbricht's obduracy. Egon Bahr, who was struggling to negotiate the practical details of the new Berlin arrangement with the GDR while the four Powers failed to agree on its principles, recalled that it was "much easier to negotiate with Mr Gromyko than with my East German fellow countrymen. They were absolutely rigid, cold and hostile . . . it became interesting to find out if I could meet some people who were, say, 51 per cent German and only 49 per cent Communist." The trouble was that Pankow realised all too clearly the dangers in any discussions; they understood the implications of Bahr's old slogan "change through meeting" and they did not want to change. As the Deputy Prime Minister Peter Florin remembered "There were those who feared that the FRG government, led by the Social Democrats, would somehow try to strangle the GDR by embracing it." But Moscow, it seems, had decided that the Wall, for which the Soviet Union had paid such a high political price, would have to serve as Pankow's only security blanket: the Kremlin could not afford to lose an agreement with the West by giving yet another expensive cover to Ulbricht. Walter Ulbricht was forced to "resign" in May 1971. On 5 September the Quadripartite Agreement on Berlin was signed.

As the Duke of Wellington would have said of one of his own campaigns, it was not an exquisite Napoleon-designed harness; it was a lashing together of bits and pieces, using what was available rather than ideal; something that could be adapted and augmented. That was the Agreement's strength. It was made up of a set of principles, a Final Protocol, four annexes, two agreed minutes, a letter to the Federal Chancellor, and a series of attached notes exchanged by the signatories. This very disjointedness shows the diversity of the problems involved; the vagueness of much of the language (for example it was never made clear if the Agreement applied to Greater Berlin or just the western sectors) speaks volumes for the eagerness to avoid arguments which would abort a practical compact. The four Powers promised to tackle their differences in Berlin by peaceful means and to uphold their own rights and responsibilities while respecting those of others (without defining them). The western allies pledged that their sectors would not be made an integral part of the FRG (the election of the Federal President or full Bundestag sessions would not be held there) and that West Berlin would not become a Land (Federal Ministers and courts would have no authority, though Federal legislation would continue to apply). In return, the Soviet Union guaranteed western access to the city on 1945 conditions and promised that civilian transport would move by the simplest, speediest means: sealed vehicles would pass through checkpoints without inspection and a lump sum annual payment would replace any individual tolls for transit across the GDR. West Berliners would have the same rights as West Germans to visit the GDR; West Berlin would be permitted diplomatic representation abroad; the Soviet Union would set up a consulate in the western sectors. Even the little enclaves were tidied up: West Berlin would give about thirty-nine acres plus cash to the GDR in exchange for a forty-two acre concession which included a corridor to

Steinstücken and the widening of the access road to Eiskeller. If the four Powers could settle the enclaves, surely they could settle anything.

The flesh was put on these bones by a series of agreements on visits, postal and transit matters, negotiated by the GDR and either Bonn or the West Berlin Senate. These involved huge rows over whether the Federal Republic had a right to negotiate on Berlin (seemingly it had, since Pankow kept talking); whether East Germans now in the West would be safe to visit the GDR (they would be ejected but not arrested); whether trains and buses could travel with a single visa (yes); if drivers and passengers could stay in their cars while their documents were checked (yes); whether transit travellers could get out of their vehicles in the GDR to answer calls of nature (not really, and certainly not if they picked up passengers or distributed leaflets while doing so). The East Germans fought every phrase and comma of the arrangements, still trying to assert some independence from the Soviet Union and gain some symbol of status. They would not sign the final agreements until first Brezhnev himself paid them a two-day visit in October 1971 and then Bonn warned in November that ratification of the Quadripartite Agreement and Moscow Treaty still hung in the balance; their signatures were finally obtained at the end of December – too late for Christmas passes for West Berliners' visits. There was a cliff-hanging finale to the lengthy and complicated set of negotiations and the implementation of any of the parts when, in February 1972, the treaties were rejected in the Bundestag in Bonn by a single vote; the CDU held out until a codicil was inserted to state that a German treaty was not pre-empted by pacts with the Soviet Union and Poland and that there was no legal basis to the now accepted frontiers. The full settlement, with all its interlocking ramifications, was only secured by the Final Protocol on 3 June 1972.

With all its theoretical inadequacies, this settlement worked. It was not a peace agreement – a full treaty had to await four-Power negotiation, and it would be an eighteen-year-long wait. But it did much to maintain the uneasy, undefined truce; it established conditions for untroubled living and intercourse which could be built on. The settlement gave the GDR a separate existence and equality with the Federal Republic, which meant it could be recognised by other states (121 by 1976 whereas there were only 26 before the agreements). Both Germanies were admitted to the United Nations in September 1973; they could enter for the Olympic Games and join various international bodies and institutions. East–West tension did not disappear, but it slackened in the area where it had been most likely to snap relations: Berlin. The West had secured its "essentials" of presence, access and the survival of the western sectors; the Soviet Union could retain the frontiers it had acquired for itself and its satellites in 1945.

Brandt and his Ostpolitik had triumphed. He had made a settlement possible by convincing the four Powers that "The time of grand enterprises is past" and coaxing them to take Small Steps towards practical arrangements of mutual convenience instead; he had persuaded his country that "patriotism must be based on what was attainable" and that the rhetoric but not the hope of reunification must be dropped. By reaching to the East he had strengthened the security of the western alliance. He had set up the diplomatic context in which negotiations could be held with some chance of success, then brokered all the agreements. From the practical standpoint which he always took, the 1972 settlement alleviated some of the human suffering which the Wall had imposed: one and a half million West Germans visited the GDR in 1972; over three million in 1976, and almost as many West Berliners at the same time. Each year from 1972 more than 40,000 East Germans would be allowed to visit the West on "urgent family business"; with some difficulty, with a great deal of patience and at exorbitant cost it would even be possible to telephone the West. West Berlin was still an island, but now had causeways: within a few weeks of final agreement, thirty offices opened in the western sectors to do all kinds of business with eastern Europe; over the coming years so many links with the Federal Republic were forged that there were to be more civil servants in West Berlin than in Bonn.

The new settlements "normalised" Berlin, even if the city was in no way normal and the Wall still stood implacable. The Quadripartite Agreement meant that it was left alone by the Powers, except for infrequent squalls of "Berlin Weather". West Berliners prospered through the 1970s and '80s. For a time it seemed that Germans on the other side of the Wall might enjoy some of that ease and plenty too. The statistics looked good: by the mid '70s the World Bank placed the GDR eighth in the rank of industrial nations (and it had a population of only seventeen million). But statistics not only lie, they avoid bigger truths. The GDR was short of raw materials and depended on others for energy. Once oil prices rose after the Arab–Israeli War of 1973 no amount of concentration on exports, no new trade agreements, no insistence on a three shift factory day, could compensate for a chronic imbalance of trade with the West. To afford vital imports, the state had to clamp down on domestic consumption – and yes, they had no bananas. Resources which might have been invested in industry were still diverted to social welfare, but increasingly to the bureaucracy, the military and the activities of the hated secret police, the Stasi. The standard of living was not going to catch up with the West; if anything the gap was widening. East Germans knew it. The Wall no longer sealed them in hermetically:

West German visitors came, were dressed in stylish, well-made clothes and enviable shoes, they snapped up as bargains goods the locals could not afford, they got the best tables in restaurants by a West mark tip which would have bought an entire meal for a resident. East Germans could seldom cross the Wall but they could look at the other side – on television. Eighty-five per cent of all East German households regularly saw western programmes and much preferred them. They seldom watched their own news bulletins at 7.30 in the evening. Instead, as someone said: "most of the country emigrates every night at eight o'clock": they tuned in to the West German television news.

Pankow's life was supported by the Wall but it was endangered by the ideas, debates, diversity which were being channelled into the GDR. The government was made up of elderly men with minds formed by pre-war experience and set by ideology who could not adjust to new circumstances so failed to develop socialism under their protected, controlled conditions. They used the Wall to control people, not to win them. For a brief period East Germans had high hopes of their new leader, Erich Honecker. Sombre, dull, stiff he might be, but he had none of Ulbricht's pretension to be the idol in a personality cult. He had been a member of the Communist Party since 1929 when he was seventeen years old, and a full-time official for most of his adult life, preserved by imprisonment under the Nazis from death in war or from exile in Moscow where he could well have been murdered like so many of his comrades. But he was not a stringent ideologue, even though he wrote that he could not remember a single moment in his life when he "had doubts in what we were about". East Germans welcomed the relative realism of his economic targets, the lack of bombast in his promises or attitude to the West, and expected that the elasticity of his theory might result in some slackening of the Party's grip on their lives and thoughts. These high hopes turned out to be as chimerical as a Five Year Plan.

Certainly pressure on the churches eased, but that went to show that the Party no longer needed to fear the power of Christianity. There was no question, however, of the state withering away: the "leading role of the Party" increased and permeated everything. Party membership was the only assured way of advancement in work or the professions; Party activity be it in the youth movement, paramilitary training or voluntary work was a better qualification for higher education than academic record. Honecker proclaimed in December 1971 that "there can be no taboos in the realm of culture and literature, provided one starts from a solidly socialist position", and since he said that content and style were "questions which concern artistic mystery", writers, artists and intellectuals assumed that censorship would be reduced. They learned in 1976 that "artistic mystery" was still mediated through the Party hierophants: the singer and satirist Wolf Bierman was not readmitted to the GDR after a tour in West Germany and he was deprived of citizenship; those who protested suffered fines, imprisonment and house arrest, were expelled from the Writers' Union or even the country.

Opposition to the leadership grew as did dissatisfaction with the standard of living, but there was no freedom to protest, no choice of party at elections, no right to strike, and the choking tentacles of the Stasi reached everywhere. People expressed their feeling in one of the few areas where the state had no control: they stopped having babies. Live births per thousand of the population dropped from 17.6 in 1963 to 10.6 in 1974, in spite of a lump sum payment for every child produced, twenty-six weeks paid maternity leave, and an optional year of unpaid leave without loss of job or benefits. In a society where 82 per cent of women worked, the state would have been well advised to improve cramped living conditions, to provide labour-saving machines and to spend some of the money spent in political propaganda on persuading the average East German husband to pick up a duster or a tea towel instead of watching his wife do the chores after work while he lolled back as the "Hauspascha".

Faced with dwindling respect at home, Honecker tried to boost the reputation of his regime abroad. He staged international (which tended to mean Soviet bloc or fellow traveller) congresses on every worthy subject under the sun, but even Soviet visitors thought the GDR was the most tense country in eastern Europe and attributed its higher standard of living to "parcels from West German relatives". He travelled to every state which would receive him, establishing diplomatic relations, opening consulates, entering trade agreements, signing treaties of friendship, and proudly put his name to the Final Act of the Helsinki Agreement on security and cooperation in Europe in 1975 – at which his citizens read the human rights clauses and 100,000 of them were said to have immediately applied to leave the country. He never crowned his ambitions with invitations to the White House or Buckingham Palace but he did manage to get the coronet of a trip to Bonn in 1984, in spite of extreme reluctance on the part of the Federal government to receive him and of the Kremlin to let him go.* Scenes of the head of state of the GDR standing on a red carpet and shaking hands with the Federal Chancellor were distasteful to many in both parts of Germany

---

* When Honecker returned from Bonn, it is said, the Presidium asked him what the West was like. "Just the same as here." "What? Exactly" "Yes: you can buy anything you want for hard currency."

(should the man who built the Wall and ordered a shoot to kill policy against all who tried to get over it have ever been allowed into the West and granted some of the trappings of recognition by Bonn?) but the ceremonies blurred the truth that he was a client, the leader of a regime increasingly dependent not just on trade with the FRG but on direct aid.

Honecker took what money he could get from Bonn while struggling to avoid any political change by meeting and to resist Brandt's concept of two German states in one nation. Try as he would, he could not create patriotism in the GDR: a state whose citizens were forbidden to sing the words of the national anthem because they referred to reunification, where there was little allegiance to a regime which had to be propped up by a third of a million Soviet troops, and whose main claim to national individuality was Communism – a creed preached by Marx, who was a Saarlander like Honecker, but permeated by Leninist heresy and forced on the country by foreign invaders. Honecker reinstated the statue of Frederick the Great in the Unter den Linden (after a long exile in the King's palace of Sans Souci), trying to graft pride in Prussian might and culture on to the GDR, hoping that a little of it would rub off on Pankow. He reversed the policy of smashing the past to make way for the Socialist future and faithfully restored the Platz der Akademie with Schinkel's Schauspielhaus and the German and French Churches. To honour the supposed seven hundredth anniversary of the founding of Berlin, he scoured the city for old houses, shops and pubs to create a new/old Nikolaiviertel, a kind of Berlin theme quarter of some charm but of use only to tourists since its shops, bars and cafés were far too expensive for locals. In 1987 on the GDR side of Checkpoint Charlie, the old wooden huts and the oil drums with rusty cables which had channelled cars trying to cross to East Berlin were replaced with buildings in grand motorway filling station style, fit for a national frontier.

The apotheosis of his Socialist town planning was the Palace of the Republic: a people's palace of conference halls, entertainments and the Volkskammer, which at last filled the empty site of the old Prussian Palace, wrecked by allied bombs and finally blown up by Ulbricht. (Its orange mirror glass facings at least reflect images of the Cathedral opposite which are rather more lively than the lumpy original.) But it was all very well pouring money into grandiose projects. Nothing was being spent on the flats and offices of the nineteenth and early twentieth centuries which still predominated in the centre of East Berlin: the wrought iron balconies were corroded and fell off, the stone crumbled away. Nor were resources left for essential services: by 1989 a quarter of all East Berlin's main sewers needed repair and 40 per cent of all households had not been connected to them (the Federal government paid for plant to stop sewage seeping into West Berlin); most of the telephone exchanges were sixty years old, but since there was only one phone for every ten people, perhaps that did not matter; the main electricity transformer centre ran erratically on its 1920 equipment; gas was leaking everywhere. It was an admission of final economic and administrative collapse that in the mid-1980s West Berlin took over the rattling, rusting S-bahn and not only paid to restore it but provided all the electricity to run it.

For eighteen years, Erich Honecker took it for granted that his regime was safe from internal discontent and external threat given the protection of the Wall and the Soviet troops in permanent garrison on East German soil. But those brooding defences only concealed from him the widening gap between his government and people and the danger to the GDR as the Soviet bloc disintegrated under the impact of change. When Mikhail Gorbachev became leader of the Soviet Union in March 1985, Honecker ignored his calls for "glasnost" and "perestroika": there could be no openness or restructuring in a state pinioned by an elderly inflexible élite, a rigid ideological orthodoxy, a stifling centralised bureaucracy, and an all-pervasive secret police. He made no efforts to cover his own political back when the Hungarian Communist leader, Janos Kadar, was toppled in May 1988, or when the Polish elections in June 1989 were a triumph for the opposition group, Solidarity, and resulted in the first appointment of a non-Communist Prime Minister in the Soviet bloc. Indeed Honecker was the first and most enthusiastic Communist leader to praise the Chinese for the massacre of demonstrators in Tienanmen Square: perhaps a case of geriatric leaders sticking together, but also of believing that sending a few tanks was the right way to solve political problems. But Honecker should have seen the writing on his Wall when, at President Chernenko's funeral in Moscow, Gorbachev told Party leaders from all over the Soviet bloc that he would not interfere in their internal affairs. This was not just an offer of independence, it implied that Soviet troops would not prop up tottering regimes either. And he should, most certainly, have heeded the warning from Gorbachev on 7 October 1989, when he came to Berlin to celebrate the fortieth anniversary of the GDR: "Life itself punishes those who delay." On the evening those words were uttered there was a demonstration in East Berlin with the cry "Gorby help us". It was probably too late now for Honecker to change; he had delayed reform too long. And Gorbachev would indeed help the demonstrators – by doing nothing to help Pankow.[12]

Honecker was faced with a new movement of political protest which had coalesced with the oldest form of East German remonstrance: the wish to emigrate. In 1987 small groups, barely a dozen people at a time, had gathered in Leipzig to demand freedom to leave East Germany. They were beaten up by the Stasi. In 1988 there was a routine, officially sponsored, demonstration in East Berlin to commemorate the murders of Rosa Luxemburg and Karl Liebknecht, the patron saints of German Communism. It was hijacked by political protesters to make a very different point. Some of their placards quoted Luxemburg herself: "Freedom is the freedom to think differently"; others read "We want the right to leave". Both groups were beaten up by the police. The result was like beating an egg white: the volume of protest grew.

This tiny tentative East German reformist movement gained the support of people whose ambitions were much more modest: people who simply wanted to travel. Penned inside the GDR, people watched television and wanted to share the West German joy of a holiday in Majorca; the young had the wanderlust of their generation and ached to hitchhike across the world; one East Berlin woman summed up the peculiar frustrations of life in her city: "One day, after work, I would like to go to the cinema in West Berlin." Travel became a major political demand; the government's failure to concede it was seen as the litmus test of its willingness to change anything; as the regime stubbornly resisted calls for any political change at all, more and more people wanted one-way travel and demanded the right to emigrate. Even when Pankow made a few grudging concessions, including permission for visa-free travel in the Soviet bloc, they were not trusted and East Germans decided to get out while the going was good. From January to October 1989, 200,000 of them crossed to the West.

Nearly all of them left to "go on holiday" to resorts in neighbouring East European countries – then sought asylum in West German embassies in Warsaw, Prague and Budapest. In August an embarrassed West German government tried locking its embassy doors, but the refugees camped on the steps and clambered into the gardens until the doors had to be opened. The constant influx of so many East Germans was even more embarrassing for the hard-line Czech government: the citizens of Prague were keen to help the refugees and showed them ways to the West German embassy which would avoid police patrols, gave them food, and longed to follow their example. The Czech regime grumbled at Pankow; Honecker, anxious to avoid any scandal which might mar the fortieth anniversary of the GDR in October, agreed that 2,000 refugees in Prague would be given free passage to the West. This was another decision which boomeranged. Czech dissidents hailed it; as one of them said, it was "the first time when this, the seemingly unchangeable system, was forced to give up", and they knew that they too might force change one day. Pankow mishandled the free passage. The refugees were taken out of Prague in three sealed trains, and routed through Dresden so that the GDR could have the pleasure of stripping those it accused of "trampling moral values with their feet" of GDR citizenship. When the trains reached the city on the night of 4 October thousands tried to board them; riot police lashed out, and there was fighting for the next two days.

Meanwhile other refugees had probed for gaps and weak spots in the Iron Curtain. When they found them, they poured through in packed trains, charter buses, laden Trabant cars with two-stroke engines lurching and belching acrid fumes, or they walked, clutching suitcases, carrier bags and babies. They swept through Czechoslovakia, Hungary, over into Austria, then finally to the FRG, pausing in refugee camps on the way to rest and hear the latest information on openings in frontiers. On 10 September the Hungarian government officially announced the opening of its border with Austria (in return for financial aid from Bonn, it later appeared). That day 6,000 East Germans moved into Hungary; 10,000 more followed in the next twenty-four hours. It was a movement so reminiscent of July and August 1961. Berlin was now sealed but new doors had opened to the West.

Pankow tried to slam them shut. In early October the East German government banned visa-free travel to the Soviet bloc "as a temporary measure". This was wholly counter-productive: its citizens assumed the ruling would be permanent so they left in greater numbers, and without a visa. The frontiers with Communist neighbours were not as heavily fortified as the border with the Federal Republic: there was no point since no East German had ever wanted to move to an even more miserable country. So people walked through forests, and swam rivers or they drove until they found a guard with a blind eye to a blank page in a passport. By early November the West German embassy in Prague had 5,000 more refugees camping in its offices and gardens. This time the Czech government did not bother to consult Pankow. It opened its borders for East Germans to cross to the Federal Republic. Another door to the West was ajar. ·

All over again the lifeblood of the GDR was draining away. Students and soldiers had to be drafted to take the place of doctors and nurses who had left; public transport was halted for lack of drivers; forty Vietnamese took the jobs in a meat processing plant whose staff had disappeared; a fifth of the workers in the largest shoe factory in the country were said to be "absent without leave"; there was a shortage of vegetables and milk products and a restricted menu in the dwindling number of restaurants still open; jewellers ran out of stock as those intending to leave bought anything made of gold to take with them.

There was a marked difference, however, from the refugee crisis of 1961. This time those who did not leave demanded political change as the price of staying. Regular Monday "prayers of peace" had been held in the Church of St Nicholas in Leipzig since the late summer, followed by small demonstrations on the square outside. These got bigger and bigger in September and early October with the demand for legalisation of New Forum, a group calling for dialogue with the regime, freer travel and speech, and change within a Socialist framework. Time after time demonstrations were smashed by the police. But suddenly, the authorities lost confidence – the classic symptom of a regime about to be swept away by revolution. On 9 October Leipzig riot police, army units and Kampf-gruppen were standing by to clear a crowd of 70,000 but the order to shoot was never given. Instead there was a palace coup: Honecker was forced by the Party to resign on 18 October. His replacement as head of the Party, Egon Krenz, had a different face but the same mind: he was a Politburo member, the former head of the Stasi and had gone to Beijing in September to praise the regime for crushing the Chinese democracy movement.

Krenz could not hold the regime together for long. He made vague promises of reform which no one trusted, and the crowds of protesters marched the streets confident that armed force would not be used against them. He made pathetic appeals to would-be emigrants – "Stay. We need you" – but in the first week in November 200 refugees *an hour* were arriving in West Germany. On 5 November he promised new travel laws, to be ready "by Christmas". That weekend over a million East Germans either rioted or left the country; 380,000 Soviet troops in the GDR stayed in their barracks while the leading Soviet spokesman, Gennadi Gerasimov, gave "off-the-record" stories to the press that they would not get involved in suppressing internal unrest. On 7 November Willy Stoph's government resigned; twenty-four hours later the whole Politburo followed suit. Hans Modrow became Prime Minister, with a cabinet of a few new men with smiles and a great many old men with hard faces and views. He personally was a politician of some moderation, by East German Communist standards, but radicalism not moderation was needed now.

By this stage Pankow exercised control over one area only: the border with West Germany and, in particular, the Berlin Wall which was the expression of its authority and the guarantee of the GDR's separate existence. No one ever expected it to come down, not even the wildest of protesters had ever demanded that it be dismantled. The East German regime, which had been floundering for months, proceeded to make a final and irreparable blunder, and threw this last asset away.

On the evening of 9 November journalists from all over the world, who had been chronicling the collapse of the regime, gathered in East Berlin for a press conference given by the government spokesman, Günter Schabowski (who in a previous incarnation had edited *Neues Deutschland* where he had published more pictures of Erich Honecker than any other GDR journal). It was a routine occasion, but enlivened by Schabowski's hint that this one-party state might soon allow free elections. That was a good story for the evening news broadcasts and the next morning's front page. The pressmen prepared to move off and file it. Schabowski, however, did not seem ready to close the meeting. He was muttering to the man sitting next to him and shuffling through the papers on his table. Suddenly he seized a sheet tucked at the bottom of the heap. "This will be interesting for you." Then he read, slowly and hesitantly, an official announcement: "Today the decision was taken to make it possible for all citizens to leave the country through the official border crossing points. All citizens can now be issued with visas for the purpose of travel or visiting relatives in the West. The order is to take effect at once." It was a ghastly mistake. Schabowski had picked up the announcement at a government meeting just before leaving for the press conference; he had not read it or checked it with officials; he did not realise that the policy was not intended for publication until 10 November and would be hedged by stringently tight issuing of exit visas.

The words he had read, without their intended riders, caused a sensation among the journalists. The same question erupted from every corner: "When?" "How soon?" He looked tired and confused, as well he might. "It just means straightaway." There was only one possible conclusion anyone could reach. The whole border, the very Wall itself, would open that night. In a year of dramatic confrontations and upheaval in the GDR and Soviet bloc, Schabowski had just implied the most startling and potentially far-reaching change of all. The journalists rushed to their phones and studios.[13]

12

Beginnings

———————➤●◄———————

The news was relayed with electronic speed. Within ten minutes or so, his statement was broadcast on East German television. "What a cock-up," gasped the man who had been making all the administrative arrangements for the very limited issue of exit visas. Immediately the station's switchboards were jammed: "Is it true?" the callers asked. "Please repeat the news. I can't believe it." "Did I hear right? Is the Wall really opening?" No wonder they had to ask. Whatever else shifted, the unyielding permanence of the Wall was taken for granted. Nor did anyone ever believe the East German media. But the story was quickly picked up by West German television – and East Germans took that seriously. At first the bulletins carried just the bare facts of the Schabowski announcement. The only way to check what they meant was to go to the Berlin border and see what was happening. Small groups of Berliners gathered either side of the narrow crossings. Everything looked normal – or rather as abnormal as it had for so many years. The East German barriers were firmly in place across the road, outside their huts guards were stolidly stamping up and down, from inside binoculars and probably cameras were focused on the spectators. The people waited and watched.[1]

At about 9 p.m. one or two East Berliners put the Schabowski announcement to the test. They went to the guard post at Invalidenstrasse, north of the River Spree, and said they wanted to go into West Berlin. The duty officer gave the usual reply: they must first get their identity papers stamped at their local police station. They turned back. Half an hour later, however, at Bornholmer Strasse to the north-west, a couple made the same request. This time perhaps the guard had been listening to the radio. He said they could cross, but only on condition they returned that night through the same point. They moved past the barrier and stepped over the line in the road to the West. They took the historic step so calmly, so casually that not one of the onlookers grasped what had happened. They only began to understand as first one East Berliner, then another, walked through.

News of the extraordinary events began to spread through the city. At 10.30 p.m. a discussion on SFB (Sender Freies Berlin), the West Berlin television station, was abruptly broken into by a live broadcast from Invalidenstrasse. For a moment it was not clear why there had been an interruption. Viewers saw a reporter talking to a small, excited crowd. Suddenly a young man dashed towards the camera. "They've opened the checkpoint at Bornholmer Strasse." That was a call to celebrate. A Wall was collapsing, a world was dissolving.

Crowds of East Berliners rushed from their homes and converged on Bornholmer Strasse. Some carried sleepy children: "We want them to see." A couple walked into the West for fifteen minutes. "Our boy is at home asleep. So we have to go straight back. We just wanted to put a foot over the line." As people in the East pushed against the barrier at the checkpoint and tried to squeeze through the narrow gap by the guard post, those in the West shouted "Take the Wall down". East German border guards came out. Would they shoot? Would they throw tear gas? No: they heaved aside the concrete road blocks and hauled up the barrier. With a great cheer the East Berlin crowd surged through. "What have I been doing for the last twenty years?" one of the guards asked himself.

News of free passage at last reached other checkpoints. Some of the barriers had not been raised for years; they were rusted in. Excited groups on either side joined the police and wrenched them up. A woman had been telephoned by her daughter in West Berlin: "You can come to see us." When she scurried through the barrier she was still in her bedroom slippers and had pulled a coat over her nightie. As the East Berliners swarmed over, West Berliners rushed to greet them. It was "Cabaret" time at Checkpoint Charlie: the welcoming crowd was singing "Wilkommen, bienvenu, welcome". As word spread through the west of the city – over the radio, by phone, by shouts in the street – the reception committees grew. One cinema emptied mid-film when a man rushed in at the back and bellowed "They're opening the Wall". Who cared about the exploits of Superman on the screen when there were such marvels on the streets? The audience rushed to the border; joined others carrying flowers, chocolate, and sekt, the German champagne. They met inhabitants of houses and flats near the Wall who were running out with coffee, wine, and yet more flowers.

The pedestrians at the crossing had been joined by queues of Trabis, groaning under their loads of passengers, gears screeching even more stridently than usual as trembling hands and feet failed to connect them. The cheers rose, the singing mounted to a crescendo – old Berlin ditties, new pop songs, the national anthem, the Lutheran hymn "Nun Danket alle Gott". The crowds banged on the car roofs, reached inside to shake hands or thrust flowers and wine bottles at the occupants. They sprayed everything with champagne and kissed everyone within reach. The West Berlin police arrived to ask for calm and to promise free transport to the great thoroughfare at the centre of their city, the Kurfürstendamm. But the excited visitors could not bear to wait. They charged on, in hundreds then thousands, and filled the street with one clamorous, delirious traffic jam. The shops opened and distributed fruit and chocolate, the bars laid on free drinks, the hotels handed out hot soup and coffee. "I still can't believe this. Here I am in the Ku'damm." "We've seen the West on TV of course. But this is for real." "Look at the shop windows." "It's so much brighter here. In the East everything is dead."

Crowds from East and West were also moving to the Brandenburg Gate – that blocked artery at the heart of the city, permanently occluded by a double line of concrete, wire and machineguns. By midnight the open areas to either side were densely packed. The throng in the West wore party hats, waved sparklers and chanted "Tor auf", "Open the Gate." Suddenly a young man crouched against the Wall, stepped on to a platform made by a friend's cupped hands, and was raised until he could latch on to the rim. He scrambled, got a foothold, then stood and raised his arms, triumphant on top of the Wall. The spectators roared. They followed him up. Then they danced, they cheered, they guzzled sekt, and twirled their sparklers with joy. For a few minutes the East German police hosed them with water cannon. Cold spray came as welcome refreshment. They danced the more, and the guards joined in the singing from their watchtowers.

The celebration went on all night. Police reckoned that 40,000 East Berliners came to enjoy it. Some of them got too tired or tipsy to go home and they nestled down to sleep in a shopping arcade or under the trees in the Tiergarten. Others forced themselves to stay awake. They did not want to miss a minute of being "Over There", in the West where they had never imagined they would step foot. Perhaps, some of them thought, none of this was true. Perhaps tomorrow everything would go back to dreary, relentless isolation. They danced while they could.

Next morning they joined in an even bigger party. It began at 9 a.m.

with the grinding and rattling of bulldozers in Eberswalder Strasse in the East Berlin district of Prenzlauer Berg. Startled locals watched in amazement as a whole section of Wall was smashed and a new crossing point created. The diggers went into action at four other points along the Wall and bystanders cheered as hunks of concrete were swept aside. In no time at all the ragged gaps were garlanded with flowers. Through them poured hordes of East Berliners. Some laughed and ran into the welcoming arms in the West. Others looked grave as they passed through. They hesitated at the white line in the road which marked the exact point of departure from the East, paralysed with fear or wonder for several seconds before they put a foot across. Then they were overwhelmed with hugs, flowers and drinks. The noise and zeal of the welcome were stunning. The sights were bemusing. At the Invalidenstrasse crossing the soldiers in the East now had flowers in their caps and down the barrels of their guns; the soldiers in the West were the Royal Fusiliers with sprightly white plumes, the regimental band in red jackets, and regimental trestle tables covered with starched white cloths, polished tea urns and plates of biscuits. The visitors were bewildered too by the experience of being in a totally unknown place. Gratefully they seized maps of West Berlin which had been printed overnight for distribution at the crossings. East German maps showed only the east of the city; beyond the Wall was a blank. The West had not officially existed, certainly not for them.

Today it did. Off they went to the Ku'damm and a spree. There were an estimated two million East Germans in the West over the weekend; East Berlin was totally deserted. Here bands played, church bells pealed; cafés, bars and sex shops were open night and day; frankfurter stalls ran out of stock; Dutch girls handed out an inexhaustible supply of white chrysanthemums; the sekt corks fired a constant fusillade of welcome: "Prosit. Let's drink to freedom." As the visitors struggled with unfamiliar public telephones West Berliners reached into the booths and stuffed the machines with coins so that they could ring home and say "I am here, actually here in the West". There were free tickets for East Berliners at the big football match – their favourite team, Hertha, was playing and they had only ever seen them on television. There was free admission to the Opera, and at the Philharmonie, Daniel Barenboim and the Berlin Philharmonic played Beethoven's First Piano Concerto and Seventh Symphony to honour their arrival.

And there was shopping. East Berliners from a land of shoddy goods and shortages were now in an Eden of consumerism. Legally they could hold only East marks and in recent weeks they needed ten of these to buy one western mark, a Deutschmark, on the black-market exchange. This weekend the West German government was giving DM100 as "greeting money" to all East German visitors – there were queues at every bank and hardly enough notes to go round. Even with this sum, East Berliners could not afford much, not at western prices. What they could buy was infinitely precious because so long unobtainable: yes, bananas, bananas and more bananas; and lemons, freshly ground coffee, magazines, a spare part for a bicycle. One woman went home with sticks of liquorice for her children: "Do you know? They've never tasted liquorice." Others sniffed with intense pleasure at a bar of fine-milled, perfumed soap – so wondrously different from the skin-cracking, scum-forming clods they were used to. East Berliners longed for multi-coloured designer-label trainers to replace the ill-fitting, cheap synthetic, white lace-ups which were the best their state factories could produce. One glance at the prices in the smart shoe shops of the West and they settled for window shopping. That was a treat in itself: the quantity and quality, the colour and elegance. The BMW showroom on the Ku'damm reckoned it had 5,000 visitors over the weekend – just to look and marvel.

For many Berliners, East or West, the weekend was not all public festivity but a time for private reunions. They embraced relatives whom they had not seen for twenty-eight years, met new family members, born or married in the intervening time. There were tears of joy, tears of relief and disbelief. Bitter tears too. An old gentleman from East Germany arrived at a West Berlin station. His grandchildren ran to meet him and he stretched out his hands to touch their faces. He had never seen them. Since the Wall was built he had not been allowed to travel. And he had gone blind. He would never see them now. He wept.

To share these mixed emotions, visitors to West Berlin were travelling in from beyond the city itself. The Glienicke Bridge, closed for years to all but western military missions driving to Soviet Army headquarters in Potsdam, had to be opened to cope with the pressure. The Bridge stood at a melancholy spot. Neither the elegant wooded park on the approach from the West nor the glimpses of the exquisite Prussian palaces over the Havel Lake to Potsdam in the East cheered its desolation. It had been such a fitting place for the occasional exchange of spies or release of eastern dissidents. The sinister isolation might have been designed to conceal the covert trade in furtive men; the mists from the lake were a theatrical cloak for Cold War conspiracy. One West Berlin woman had stood here regularly and dreamed the impossible: cycling across to Potsdam. This weekend she witnessed a transformation scene.

A torrent of people was pouring across to the West, choking the pavements and blocking the roadway where the Trabis jolted bumper to bumper. Two policemen stood back to back, sometimes leaning on each other's shoulders to take the weight off their feet. One was in West Berlin uniform, the other wore an East frontier guard jacket. They had been trained as enemies. Suddenly they were united in professional sport: grumbling at idiot pedestrians who would not stay on the pavement and grunting sardonically at drivers who stalled their engines. The irony of their new-found comradeship was accentuated by what was happening below them. Under the Bridge ran a stretch of solid, untouched Wall. Down the sandy path along it strode two Grepos, dog unmuzzled and guns at the ready. They were doing their duty: patrolling the frontier, ready to savage or shoot anyone who dared approach it, while over their heads thousands were "fleeing the Republic" and being urged to "get a move on" by one of their colleagues helped by one of their adversaries.

Elsewhere, the East German authorities had given up the struggle to pen in their citizens. Mechanical diggers were working round the clock to create more channels for the human tide. At 5.35 on Sunday morning they smashed through a segment of Wall at Potsdamer Platz. By 8.20 a.m. a crane was lifting away an entire section. How light and fragile it looked dangling in the air, this concrete block which had once divided a city and a continent. Ecstatic East Berliners rushed on to West Berlin soil, sweeping the East German frontier guards with them, until police from both sides linked arms to hold them back. Now the two mayors of the two Berlins stepped forward and, for the first time ever, shook hands. It was a breathtaking moment. Then came a tremendous, delighted roar.

Meanwhile, as the heavy equipment gouged out slabs from the Wall, pronouncing a government's impotence, small domestic tools delicately picked out fragments to satisfy a very personal need. Berliners had come with hammer and chisel to detach nuggets of the concrete which had bound them politically and physically for so long. On the West side they found brightly painted tesserae from the murals and graffiti which had expressed rage and frustration at its inexorable permanence; on the East there were only flakes of harsh, sterile white. The hammers bounced off the iron-hard surface with a metallic ping; in the cold air sparks flickered like the glittering fireworks on the night of the 9th. Through the night candles and torches silhouetted lines of Berliners in thick warm coats and jaunty German hats solemnly, almost religiously, absorbed in their work of acquiring a relic. Just occasionally a tough let fly with a pickaxe or a group of rowdies jammed a scaffolding pole under the roller bar on top of the Wall to see if it would loosen. Yet there was no real vandalism or triumphalism, and commercialism came later. At this moment people wanted a memorial to their private ordeals or a proof that pitiless durability had succumbed to change. As they worked, dents in the concrete fissured, then cracks widened. They peeped through and saw a different city, reached through and touched hands in what had once been another world.

Yet though the Wall was being breached in so many places and ways, it remained unyielding at its key point, at the most graphic symbol of division, the Brandenburg Gate. Here the pressure of people never slackened. They stood on the Wall until the East Berlin police, indignant at the violation, finally forced them down. They shoved against it until the western authorities, fearing accidents or retaliation from the East, coaxed them back behind flimsy barriers. For weeks to come the crowds stood in an orderly semi-circle in the West, all eyes looking in the same direction, all minds willing the Wall to come down at this last, most poignant point. They were joined by visitors from all over the world. International radio and television teams packed the approach roads with equipment lorries, mobile studios, location catering vans and thrumming generators. Their wires snaked between the feet of hundreds of watchers and round the viewing platforms and the gluhwein stalls. Their arc lamps blazed until the mayor of West Berlin threatened to pull out the plugs: the East German guards were maddened by the glare and by young tearaways who were acting up for the cameras and jeering across the divide – they might well lose patience and open fire. So the lights were dimmed, but the attention of the world remained focused on that one spot until the final glorious moment when the Brandenburg Gate itself opened on 22 December.

After the months of celebrations came the years of hangover. Once the Wall was fragmented, all the old givens of a continent, the familiar certainties of both sides disappeared. A landmark had been demolished and no one knew where they were. And as Ernie Bevin, that great master of the mixed metaphor, was credited with saying: "Don't open that Pandora's box; you never know what Trojan horses will get out." When the Gate opened, every post-war problem which had been enshrouded in concrete came back to haunt Europe.

If anyone had visited West Berlin in 1990 without having first looked at the newspapers and read television, they would have assumed that something dreadful had happened. People were depressed. "This is a great city," one foreign visitor said to a smart housewife on a bus. "Well, yes," was the reply. "It used to be, before the Wall." After a long confused conversation in bad English and worse German, it turned out that she meant "before the Wall came down". From her point of view, its demolition had created clouds of cement dust and sand – everywhere was filthy. But it had also served for years as a gigantic political and economic dustsheet, keeping out scruffy East Germans who now expected West German jobs and handouts, protecting the tidy little island against hordes of scavenging Slavs who were sweeping through the city to sell trinkets in the West, and returning with worn-out tyres, second-hand televisions, reject jeans, to buy bananas before going home to make their fortunes. Other Berliners grumbled that there had never been any crime before the Wall fell (on second thoughts a bit of drug-pushing, "by Turks"); but now there were muggings and murders (all by foreigners, of course). Within a month or so, they had lost their zest for taking a bus ride "to the other side", or driving through the Brandenburg Gate. A trip to East Berlin was dispiriting: the place was so run-down; how long would it take to get it in order? who was going to pay for it? The old joke had been "the great thing about the Wall is that your mother-in-law doesn't come to lunch every Sunday". Now she did, and so did all your brothers and sisters, with their children, and even a man who claimed to be married to a cousin you did not know you had; and they all expected not just lunch but lavish presents because western streets were paved with gold and CD players grew on trees.

These grouses were just minor symptoms of a much graver malaise: "Mauerkrankheit", "Wall-sickness", something East Berliners knew they suffered but which West Berliners imagined they were immune from. Living with the Wall had been a damaging experience for everybody.

On the east side, the regime and the Party had been cut off from the capitalist world and from internal debate. Once the Wall fell and they were exposed to questions, the full extent of their failure was horrifically apparent. Even a long-time and devoted SED member groaned in September 1990 "Half the time we are in a kind of rage, furious with the leadership and furious with ourselves for putting up with them so long. Half the time we are still in a state of shock." Only now could the gap between the government's claims and its achievement be measured; only by comparison with the outside could the poverty and incompetence be assessed. The stupefaction and bitterness seethed as it was revealed that the leadership which preached Socialist morality and called for citizens' sacrifices had had Swiss bank accounts, magnificent hunting lodges, luxury villas with every imaginable furnishing, gadget and swimming pool that could be bought for hard currency. Then the anger boiled over with the nightmare realisation that the Stasi had poisoned every aspect of life: that the most respected figures in political and social life had been informers, that friends had betrayed friends, that husbands had given information against their wives.[2]

Within this sick system the majority of people had rejected the principles

378

of the regime but been obliged to distort their feelings and behaviour to fit it. They had respected some of the GDR's "socialist achievements", like low rents and social welfare benefits, and taken pride in the intensity of friendships, generosity of spirit, openhandedness, the support and care of communal living. Suddenly, at the end of 1989, they were hit by different values, by choice and by the stern rules of a capitalist economy. They disliked much of what they saw: the materialism, the "trained elbows", individual greed. Or, like the physically starved, they were sickened by plenty: a young man who had spent years searching bookstalls to build up collections of Thomas Mann, Heinrich Böll, Günter Grass, saw rows of editions of all of them in a West Berlin bookshop and felt so ill he had to leave. And it was startling to realise how different East Germans were. Lothar de Maizière, the first non-Communist Prime Minister of the GDR, was struck by the fact that there were two German cultures. "West Germans", he exclaimed, "have practically forgotten their grammar. They hardly use the genitive case or the adverb any longer." Over the years "we experienced, heard, and read different things": lived with social realism, absorbed Solzhenitsyn and Akhmatova, even if not more politically approved authors, listened to Shostakovich and Penderecki, while the FRG got used to the twelve tone row and abstract expressionism or adopted American pop culture.

What made contact with this other world so painful was that West Germans seemed to rubbish anything from the East and expressed their contempt for "Ossies" with such arrogance. For the Wall had warped "Wessies" too. Fighting for their own principles had conditioned them to intolerance of other people's; justifiable pride in establishing a sound democracy and thriving economy too easily slipped into conceit; long-held fear that this successful system might be overwhelmed by the Soviet bloc had erupted as swaggering. "The way they talk to us," gasped de Maizière. "The way they treat our past. My God! You would think we never ate with a knife and fork before the Wende" – the Change, the collapse of the Wall and all its consequences. East Germans thought the West Germans did not have to make any psychological adjustments to the Change. One politician in Brandenburg complained "Wessies" had only had to learn one new thing but could not manage it: a GDR traffic regulation which had been taken into the Federal traffic code allowing cars to make a right turn at a red light. "They should consider how they'd feel if it wasn't just the right turn but everything." To be fair, West Germans had had to make a lot of adjustments, even if not on the Ossie scale. It was an unfortunate fact that, as both sides admitted, there was still "the Wall in the head".

It was going to take years to demolish that psychological barrier. By comparison, the concrete Wall went quickly. The "woodpeckers", the souvenir hunters, had chipped off fragments; commercial dealers then moved in with crowbars and electric drills and hacked off lumps to set in perspex for paperweights. The Pope and Presidents Reagan and Bush were given whole slabs each; the CIA erected an entire row outside their headquarters as a victory trophy; the GDR auctioned other sections in Monte Carlo for between £8,500 and £12,500 a piece. The great bulk of the Wall, however, was knocked down in October 1990. As a sign of the new political times, the barbed wire from on top went to reinforce the frontiers with Czechoslovakia and Poland. There was a last-minute emotional surge of enthusiasm for the hideous thing: conservation groups protested against the destruction, Berlin museums grabbed sections for display, the city authorities wired off a stretch to the south of the Reichstag to keep it safe as a monument. Most of the rest, 900,000 tons of concrete, was pulverised to use for road building. Whatever the other deficiencies of GDR industry, it had made first-class concrete and it sold at the top price of £7 a tonne. That left the problem of the 4,000 German shepherd dogs who used to defend it. The chief GDR vet was reluctant to obey orders to put them down. Many householders wanted them as guard dogs, until it was discovered that they never barked, just mauled people to death. Eventually homes were found for most of them, and miserable pets they made: they had never learned to play and clearly felt it beneath their dignity to learn to catch a ball now. A television film showed one being taken for a walk: head down, tail down, dismally walking to heel, until suddenly he spotted a length of Wall. Off he shot and snuggled against it, whimpering.

Which was very much what a lot of humans were feeling. They were lost without the Wall. And no sooner had it gone, than change, like the dust, blew through everything. There was no time to get used to it: decisions were taken in rapid succession which would have been better reflected on and spaced out. Most crucially on unification. Straw polls taken at the opened crossing points in Berlin over the weekend of 9–10 November 1989 suggested that 70 per cent of East Germans were stoutly opposed to unification; only 28 per cent were at all interested. First things first, people thought, in West or East: free elections in the GDR, the build-up of democratic parties and processes, then perhaps some discussion of con-federation (and this time many in the FRG not just the GDR were keen on the idea); thereafter, over several years, the two sides might grow together, the federal constitution could be revised to accommodate the different views and needs of the five eastern Länder. But economic facts swept away political speculation. The Wall had been built to stop refugees getting out, it came down because it could no longer keep them in; once down, there was nothing to prevent the flight from the republic of its entire population and all its capital in the quest for wages at ten times the rate of those in the GDR and all the goods of the golden West to buy with them. There was a "gate-opening panic" with both sides of Germany terrified that the GDR was about to collapse.

As East Germans left in droves and their T-shirts carried the message "Last out, turn out the lights", the GDR held its first free elections – and on a multiple list which included western-backed parties, one of them being the CDU to which the Federal Chancellor belonged. Just before polling day on 18 March 1990 a man in Erfurt summed up a general feeling: "Kohl's is the party of money, so I'm voting for it." No wonder the result of the election was a triumph for Kohl's unification slogans and promises of prosperity, and a disaster for the dissident groups like New Forum who had hoped to build a reformed and distinct East German state. As Günter Grass acidly put it: "The D-mark promised everything. The hard currency. The coin to bring you happiness. The substitute for thought that would glue everything together." That mood pushed all reason and caution to one side. As the GDR gave out economic death rattles, German monetary union came into force on 2 July, with the East mark made equal to the West, a bountiful, but not long-lasting, present. After that, there seemed to be no way to delay the political consequences. On 18 July a treaty was signed to end all the rights of the Second World War victors, in Germany and especially Berlin – a "Two plus Four" treaty for which representatives of the two Germanies moved from the "Cat's Table" to the main seats at the conference and those who since 1945 had claimed exclusive responsibility for any settlement negotiated the agreement with them. On 3 October there was full reunification – or some would say, unification, since this was a Germany which had renounced for ever its lands beyond the Oder-Neisse Line. Finally, on 2 December all-Berlin elections were held: the first since 1946 when Soviet interference had made sure there was not a free vote, and perhaps the first city-wide democratic poll since the Nazis had seized power in 1933.

Yet what a joyless process it all was. The celebrations at each stage were few and somehow false. For East Germans it did not feel like reunification at all: an Anschluss, they found it; a notice outside an East Berlin political cabaret read "Welcome to the Federal German Occupation Zone". It had magnified every anxiety and resentment which had surfaced when the Wall was opened, and it prolonged them. Towards the end of 1994 Jens Reich, a founder of New Forum, reflected that before 1989 "Everything was clear. The politics were clear . . . We knew where we stood with the economy.

Everyone knew what to do." But he recognised the folly of this wistfulness: "we were living like children. Now we are adults" and he revealed the false hope which so many had invested in unification. "I feel free now. But that is not the panacea for happiness." The problem with maturity and responsibility, of course, is that they are difficult to handle and bring one face to face with complicated problems.

Specifically east Germans were confronted with dire economic and social conditions. In 1991 two-thirds of them expected to achieve western living standards by 1997; two years later only 8 per cent of them were so optimistic. In 1990 over three-quarters of them were employed; by 1993 that figure had dropped to 54 per cent; one in ten of all workers had been obliged to retrain, and one in five had changed employer – a series of traumas for people brought up to expect a job for life and a regular wage whether they worked hard or not. By that time, 80 per cent of all east Germans under the age of twenty-five were saying that they felt second-class citizens: despised by Wessies, constantly criticised for lack of management skills and past failure to invest in industrial equipment, for present pollution and civic squalor. They were still earning only 70 per cent of the western wage for the same job, while their rents and food prices rocketed and their crèches and social centres closed. "Ostalgie" was born, with rose-tinted vision of the secure, friendly past; old pop groups who had gone out of favour once western music was available began to get bookings again; smokers gave up west German brands for home-produced cigarettes, Coke was rejected and an Ossie substitute drunk instead; after several years when every bar in the east seemed to sell nothing but fizzy beer bottled in the West, local breweries reopened. Yet the consumer trimmings of Ossie pride could not conceal a significant sign of ill-ease. In February 1995 an east German Professor of Demography announced that "the Vatican is the only place in the world that has a lower birth rate than east Germany." A third of the number of babies was born in 1994 as in 1989. In some ways this reflected what westerners would think were the benefits of choice: couples were pursuing their careers and marrying later; they preferred their jobs to full prams and travel abroad to nappy changing. But, conversely, women had been hit even harder than men by unemployment; with only one wage and costs going up while public provision for child care disappeared, above all with confidence wrecked, there had been a "womb strike".

West Germans were suffering loss of confidence too. For a brief while it had been possible to assume that the problems of the eastern Länder could be solved with money – a lot of it, granted. Unfortunately, once the eastern books were examined, it turned out that the bill would be infinitely higher than anyone had predicted: much of the old GDR economy was irreparable and had to be built from scratch, cleaning up pollution and installing public services would soak up billions, the vast numbers of unemployed were mopping up social welfare benefits and those in work could not pay adequate contributions to cover the costs. Just as these facts sank in, the miracle economy of the FRG went into a downturn from 1992. Many west Germans were also frightened of their new national status: even after so many years of congratulations on sound democratic institutions, plaudits for their liberal processes, they still did not trust themselves. When Chancellor Helmut Kohl cried "Wir sind ein Volk", one people, German ears heard a Hitlerian end to the sentence: "ein Reich, ein Fuhrer". Opening to the East had meant not just to the rest of Germany but to eastern Europe: there was a growing dread of a new refugee flood, this time of impoverished non-Germans and with it the horror of racialist neo-Nazism; as immigrant hostels were firebombed by skin-headed louts, Germans asked themselves if two generations had really changed anything.

Outsiders put the same question. Europeans, East and West, remembered what they had suffered in the past from a united Germany. Soon after the Wall fell, a three-part cartoon in *Le Figaro* showed first two jackboots either side of a chasm, then two jackboots on the same side, finally a jackboot starting to goose-step westwards. The same pictures could have been drawn anywhere in the old Eastern bloc – except that a fourth image might have shown an east-bound jackboot stuffed with Deutschmarks and welcomed with open arms. Even before 1989 West Europeans had begun to doubt the power of the EEC or NATO to contain Germany, merely West Germany; by the time of reunification they were questioning the future role of both these institutions: born in Cold War, suited for life on one side of the Wall, but now lacking an agreed role, a vision of growth. How easy things used to be, how comfortable the slogans, how certain the future when the Wall defined them all.

The doubts, the dilemmas, the worries about the future were, of course, writ large in Berlin. In practical matters, the city coped quickly. Even given its traditions of efficiency and adjustment, it was striking to see the speed with which West Berlin traffic signs and bus stop shelters appeared by 1990, even in the most remote easterly suburbs, the rapidity with which road and rail routes were built to join the two sides, the energy with which eastern museums and monuments were scrubbed and painted and a massive programme of home and public utility construction was undertaken. It was a wonder in July 1992 when the first of 26,000 new fibre optic links connected telephones across the city (for the previous two years the two City Halls had found it quicker to exchange messages by motorcycle than phone; a visitor to West Berlin was well advised to travel to the

Friedrichstrasse station if wanting to call an East Berlin number). At the emotional level, however, Berlin remained divided. And each side was ambivalent in itself.

East Berliners were riled by the perceived arrogance or at best touchy about the patronage of the other side: anyone might have thought they would have been glad to see the closure of the hideous People's Palace with its miles of asbestos, or the re-christening of streets like Otto-Grotewohl-Strasse often with old, prettier names – but umbrage was taken by even the most moderate. Such was the mood of discontent that there was a huge wave of sympathy for Erich Honecker when he was put on trial for his order to shoot to kill anyone who tried to escape over the Wall.* West Berliners, on the other hand, seemed lost now they had ceased to be the embattled defenders of western principles and the centre of world attention. No one was entirely happy when Bonn announced that the capital of the new Germany would be Berlin. The decision may have been inevitable, given all the old claims and constitutional rhetoric from both sides; it may be wise to shift the centre of political gravity nearer to the five Länder and eastern Europe. Yet West Germans worry whether they can maintain their decencies outside the tight restrictions of small, provincial Bonn, and West Berliners clearly fear that their noses will be put out of joint with the influx of national politicians and officials even if they cheer themselves up with metropolitan bravado: "Their daughters won't pass for pretty here as they did on the Rhine." There was some relief when it was realised that the move could not take place as planned in 1994, partly because of finance, partly because of ambitious building projects which could not be completed in time; there was possibly a local belief that the decision to allow the Bulgarian sculptor, Christo, to swathe the Reichstag in white cloths in 1995 would deliver a political message: put the old symbols of German grandeur into store.

Any outsider, anyone who has admired Berlin for its courage and adaptability over the years would agree with Rainer Hildebrandt who built and ran the Checkpoint Charlie museum to commemorate those who suffered and died because of the Wall. "We Germans," he said on the

---

* West Germans finally decided that revenge was not sweet but tasteless if enacted against a sick and senile man and the trial was cancelled after two months in January 1993. Honecker, who had been claiming to be at death's door for years, finally died in Chile on 29 May 1994. He returned to a new life in August 1994 on the anniversary of the building of the Wall – this time as a computer virus. His face appeared on screens, followed by the message that all existing programmes were to be destroyed "by order of the Council of Ministers of the GDR" then by the menacing words "Honni's last revenge – I'll be back". So far new software has kept him at bay.

fourth anniversary of the opening of the Wall, "are not thankful enough for what we got. We think we have problems now, but they are nothing compared with those we had then." Since Berliners savour acid jokes they tell each other "things were certainly no better before. But today they are even worse", yet deep down many of them must remember, must recognise a genuine improvement in their lives. Sooner or later they will accept that they have experienced a turn in the Berlin Weather, a turn for the better, and that they have the experience and talent to live with normality too. Then they can say "Na und".

Bibliography

"The Observer" *Tearing down the Curtain*, Hodder and Stoughton, London, 1990.

Adenauer, Konrad, *Memoirs 1945–53*, Weidenfeld and Nicolson, London, 1966.

Alphand, Hervé, *L'Étonnement d'Etre*, Fayard, Paris, 1977.

Ambrose, Stephen E., *Eisenhower the President*, George Allen and Unwin, London, 1984.

Ball, George W., *The Past has another Pattern*, W.W. Norton, New York, 1982.

Bedell Smith, Walter, *Moscow Mission 1946–49*, Heinemann, London, 1950.

Beschloss, Michael R., *Mayday: Eisenhower, Khrushchev and the U-2 Affair*, Faber and Faber, London, 1986.

Beschloss, Michael R., *The Crisis Years: Kennedy and Khrushchev 1960–63*, Edward Burlingame, New York, 1991.

Bohlen, Charles E., *Witness to History 1929–69*, W.W. Norton, New York, 1973.

Bradlee, Benjamin C., *Conversations with Kennedy*, W.W. Norton, New York, 1975.

Brandt, Willy, *People and Politics: The Years 1960–75*, Collins, London, 1978.

Brandt, Willy, *My Life in Politics*, Hamish Hamilton, London, 1992.

Bundy, McGeorge, *Danger and Survival*, Random House, New York, 1988.

Cate, Curtis, *The Ides of August: The Berlin Wall Crisis 1961*, Weidenfeld and Nicolson, London, 1978.

Catudal, Honoré M., *Kennedy and the Berlin Wall Crisis*, Berlin Verlag, 1980.

Childs, David, *The GDR – Moscow's German Ally*, George Allen and Unwin, London, 1983.

Clay, Lucius D., *Decision in Germany*, Heinemann, London, 1950.

Couve de Murville, Maurice, *Une Politique Étrangère 1958–69*, Plon, Paris, 1971.

De Gaulle, Charles, *Memoirs of Hope*, Weidenfeld and Nicolson, London, 1971.

Divine, Robert A., *Blowing on the Wind: The Nuclear Test Ban Debate 1954–60*, Oxford University Press, New York, 1978.

Dulles, Eleanor Lansing, *John Foster Dulles: The Last Year*, Harcourt, Brace and World Inc, New York, 1963.

Eisenhower, Dwight D., *The White House Years: Waging Peace 1956–61*, Heinemann, London, 1966.

Eisenhower, John S.D., *Strictly Personal*, Doubleday, New York, 1974.

Frankland, Mark, *The Patriots' Revolution*, Sinclair-Stevenson, London, 1990.

Galbraith, J.K., *A Life in our Times*, André Deutsch, London, 1981.

Garton Ash, Timothy, *We the People*, Granta Books, London, 1990.

Gehlen, Reinhard (Translator David Irving), *The Gehlen Memoirs*, Collins, London, 1972.

Gladwyn, Lord, *The Memoirs of Lord Gladwyn*, Weidenfeld and Nicolson, London, 1972.

Gromyko, Andrei A. (Translator Harold Shukman), *Memories*, Hutchinson, London, 1989.

Grosser, Alfred, *Germany in our Time*, Pall Mall Press, London, 1971.

Grosser, Alfred, *The Western Alliance*, Continuum, New York, 1980.

Hanrieder, Wolfram F., *West German Foreign Policy 1949–63*, Stanford University Press, 1967.

Hoopes, Townsend, *The Devil and John Foster Dulles*, André Deutsch, London, 1973.

Horne, Alistair, *Macmillan 1894–1956* and *1957–1986*, Macmillan, London, 1988 and 1989.

Kennedy, John F., *The Strategy of Peace*, edited by Allan Nevins, Harper and Brothers, New York, 1960.

Khrushchev, Nikita (Editor and translator Strobe Talbott), *Khrushchev Remembers*, André Deutsch, London, 1971.

Khrushchev, Nikita (Editor and translator Strobe Talbott), *The Last Testament*, André Deutsch, London, 1974.

Khrushchev, Sergei, *Khrushchev on Khrushchev*, Little, Brown, Boston, 1990.

Kirkpatrick, Ivone, *The Inner Circle*, Macmillan, London, 1959.

Kohler, Foy D., *Understanding the Russians*, Harper and Row, New York, 1970.

Kroll, Hans, *Mémoires d'un ambassadeur*, Fayard, Paris, 1968.

Lacouture, Jean, *De Gaulle, The Ruler 1945–1970*, Harvill, London, 1991.

Ledwidge, Bernard, *De Gaulle*, Weidenfeld and Nicolson, London, 1982.

Leonhard, Wolfgang (Translators Elizabeth Wiskemann and Marian Jackson), *Child of the Revolution*, Collins, London, 1957.

Leonhard, Wolfgang, *The Kremlin since Stalin*, Oxford University Press, 1962.

Macmillan, Harold, *Riding the Storm 1956–59*, Macmillan, London, 1971.

Macmillan, Harold, *Pointing the Way 1959–61*, Macmillan, London, 1972.

Macmillan, Harold, *At the End of the Day 1961–63*, Macmillan, London, 1973.

McCauley, Martin, *Marxism-Leninism in the German Democratic Republic*, Macmillan in association with the School of Slavonic and East European Studies, University of London, 1979.

McCauley, Martin, *The Soviet Union since 1917*, Longman, London, 1981.

McDermott, Geoffrey, *Berlin: Success of a Mission?*, André Deutsch, London, 1963.

Marshall, Barbara, *Willy Brandt*, Cardinal, London, 1990.

Medvedev, Roy and Zhores, *Khrushchev: The Years in Power*, Oxford University Press, 1977.

Mićunović, Veljko, *Moscow Diary*, Chatto and Windus, London, 1980.

Morgan, Roger and Bray, Caroline (editors), *Partners and Rivals in Western Europe: Britain, France and Germany*, Policy Studies Institute, Gower, London, 1986.

Nixon, Richard M., *The Memoirs of Richard Nixon*, Sidgwick and Jackson, London, 1978.

O'Donnell, Kenneth P., and David F. Powers with Joe McCarthy, *Johnny, We Hardly Knew Ye*, Little, Brown, Boston, 1970.

Partos, Gabriel, *The World that came in from the Cold*, RIIA and BBC World Service, 1993.

Penkovsky, Oleg, *The Penkovsky Papers*, Collins, London, 1965.

Planck, Charles R., *The Changing Status of German Reunification in Western Diplomacy 1955–66*, John Hopkins Press, Baltimore, 1967.

Prittie, Terence, *Konrad Adenauer 1876–1967*, Tom Stacey, London, 1972.

Prittie, Terence, *Willy Brandt – Portrait of a Statesman*, Weidenfeld and Nicolson, London, 1974.

Rostow, W(alt) W(hitman), *View from the Seventh Floor*, Harper and Row, New York, 1964.

Rusk, Dean, *As I Saw It*, I.B. Tauris, London, 1991.

Salinger, Pierre, *With Kennedy*, Doubleday, New York, 1967.

Schick, Jack M., *The Berlin Crisis 1958–62*, University of Pennsylvania Press, 1971.

Schlesinger, Arthur M. Jnr., *A Thousand Days: John F. Kennedy in the White House*, André Deutsch, London, 1965.

Schlesinger, Arthur M. Jnr., *Robert Kennedy and his Times*, Houghton Mifflin, New York, 1978.

Sejna, Jan, *We Will Bury You*, Sidgwick and Jackson, London, 1982.

Seydoux, François, *Mémoires d'outre-Rhin*, Bernard Grasset, Paris, 1975.

Simmons, Michael, *Berlin: the Dispossessed City*, Hamish Hamilton, London, 1988.

Simpson, John, *Despatches from the Barricades*, Hutchinson, London, 1990.

Slusser, Robert M., *The Berlin Crisis of 1961*, John Hopkins University Press, 1973.

Smith, Jean Edward, *The Defense of Berlin*, John Hopkins Press and Oxford University Press, 1963.

Smith, Jean Edward, *Lucius D. Clay: An American Life*, Henry Holt, New York, 1990.

Sorensen, Theodore C., *Kennedy*, Hodder and Stoughton, London, 1965.

Thorpe, D.R., *Selwyn Lloyd*, Jonathan Cape, London, 1989.

Trivers, Howard, *Three Crises in American Foreign Affairs and a Continuing Revolution*, Southern Illinois University Press, 1972.

Tusa, Ann and John, *The Berlin Blockade*, Hodder and Stoughton, London, 1988.

Ulam, Adam B., *Expansion and Co-existence: The History of Soviet Foreign Policy 1917–67*, Secker and Warburg, London, 1968.

Weyden, Peter, *Wall: The Inside Story of Divided Berlin*, Simon and Schuster, New York, 1989.

References

━━━━►●◄━━━━

FO371 denotes a document from the Foreign Office general correspondence; PREM refers to the Prime Minister's files; CAB to Cabinet papers and DEFE to the Ministry of Defence archive. All these British official papers are in the Public Record Office at Kew. COB is Commanding Officer, Berlin; AW is the Anne Whitman File (which refers to Presidential papers as she filed them); ACW refers to her own gleanings; DDE refers to Dwight D. Eisenhower files; CAH is Christian Herter (usually on a telegram); "tel" means telegram throughout.

Presidential, Administration and other documents from the Eisenhower period (such as the Herter series) come from the Dwight D. Eisenhower Library, Abilene, Kansas. Those for the Kennedy period are in the John Fitzgerald Kennedy Library, Boston, Massachusetts, including the interviews for its Oral History programme. In addition, the National Security Archive has been a rich source. References to it begin with the number of the piece, then have the number of the fiche on which it can be found.

INTRODUCTION BERLIN: NOVEMBER 1989

1. Details from John Simpson, *The Darkness Crumbles: Despatches from the Barricades* and conversations with Wolfgang and Sigrid Grund.

I: THE DIVISION OF BERLIN, GERMANY, EUROPE

1. Unless specified, details and quotations in this chapter are taken from *The Berlin Blockade* by Ann and John Tusa, where full references and bibliography can be found.
2. Walter Bedell Smith, *Moscow Mission 1946–49*.
3. Clay interview with J.E. Smith in *Lucius D. Clay: An American Life*.
4. Clay in interview 16 July 1974 for the Oral History in the Harry S. Truman Library.
5. David Childs, *The GDR – Moscow's German Ally*.
6. For work of Moscow group see Childs, Martin McCauley, *Marxism-Leninism in the German Democratic Republic* and Wolfgang Leonhard, *Child of the Revolution*.
7. Tedder quoted by Michael Simmons, *Berlin: The Dispossessed City*; Lucius D. Clay, *Decision in Germany*.

8. Leonhard, op. cit.
9. Ibid.
10. Ivone Kirkpatrick, *The Inner Circle*.
11. Refugee figure: Alfred Grosser, *Germany in our Time*.
12. 12 January 1948, Clay teleconference with Washington, *The Papers of General Lucius D. Clay*.

2: ABNORMAL NORMALITY

1. Notes on West Berlin and East Berlin, January 1960, FO371 154006.
2. British and Soviet Zone Weekly Summary, week ending 30 December 1954, FO371 118072.
3. Details from FO371 153975 including "The Relationship between Berlin and the Federal Republic", and FO371 153984.
4. David Childs and Martin McCauley, op. cit.
5. From conversations with Professor Stefan Dörnberg, Professor Achim Hoffmann, Hans Jacobus, Peter Neuhof, Heinz Schweikert, Tino Schwierzina and others.
6. Details on refugees from The Bulletin of the Federal Ministry for Expellees, Refugees and War Victims, FO371 146083; 2 April 1952, Report on the Berlin Refugee Problem, Major-General C.F.C. Coleman, GOC Berlin, FO371 98153.
7. Details about Adenauer from Alfred Grosser, *Germany in our Time* and *The Western Alliance*; Dean Acheson, *Sketches from Life*; Hervé Alphand, *L'Etonnement d'Etre*; François Seydoux, *Mémoires d'outre-Rhin*; Terence Prittie, *Konrad Adenauer 1876–1967*; Willy Brandt, *My Life in Politics*; Konrad Adenauer, *Memoirs 1945–53*; and conversations with Louis Heren and Sir Frank Roberts.
8. Acheson, op.cit.
9. Annual Review for 1950, FO371 93314; Weekly Summaries for weeks ending 2, 9, 16 August, FO371 93352 and Weekly Summaries for weeks ending 25 October and 1 November ibid.
10. This paragraph and the next: Weekly Summaries for weeks ending 26 July, 2 August, and 6, 13, and 27 September, FO371 93352.
11. 24 March 1953, State Department paper, FO371 124497.
12. Transcripts of interviews for BBC World Service series *The World that came in from the Cold* with Lev A. Bezimensky, Nicholai S. Portugalov and Oleg Troyanovsky and the author's own interviews in Moscow with Rudolf F. Alexeyev, Daniil M. Proector, and Daniil Melemit-Melnikov (who drafted the March 1952 Note).
13. 20 March 1952, letter from High Commissioners to Chancellor, FO371 98125; German Interzonal Trade and West Berlin Communications 1952, FO371 98124.
14. 8 May 1952, despatch from GOC Berlin, FO371 98126.
15. Details from FO371 98126 and 98128.

16. 26 and 28 May 1952, records of conversations in British embassy, Paris and at the Quai d'Orsay, FO371 98127.

17. 29 May 1952, letter from Civil Aviation Board to Foreign Office, FO371 98127; 10 June 1952, Air Ministry to Foreign Office and 30 June, Foreign Office to Air Ministry, FO371 98128; 14 June 1952, Berlin to Wahnerheide, FO371 98128.

18. 2, 4, 6, 7, 9 June 1952, Berlin to Foreign Office, FO371 98127; FO371 124574 and 124578.

19. 12 November 1952, Wahnerheide to Foreign Office, FO371 98133.

20. FO371 98132 and 98133.

21. Details from FO371 98153.

22. Leonhard, *The Kremlin Since Stalin*; Andrei Gromyko, *Memories.*

23. McCauley, op. cit.

24. Peter Weyden, *Wall: The Inside Story of Divided Berlin*; Quarterly Report on Developments in West Berlin for Period November 1952 – Jan 1953, FO371 103798.

25. Seydoux, op. cit.

26. Alphand, op. cit.

3: STAGNATION AND SHOCK

1. Details of the Geneva Summit from Stephen E. Ambrose, *Eisenhower the President*; Michael R. Beschloss, *Mayday: Eisenhower, Khrushchev and the U-2 Affair*; Charles E. Bohlen, *Witness to History*; Nikita Khrushchev, *Khrushchev Remembers*; Charles R. Planck, *The Changing Status of German Reunification in Western Diplomacy 1955–1966*; Adam B. Ulam, *Expansion and Co-existence.*

2. Details about Eisenhower, here and later, from Ambrose, op. cit.; Khrushchev, op. cit.; Hervé Alphand, *L'Etonnement d'Etre*; Jean Edward Smith, *Lucius D. Clay: An American Life.*

3. Details about Dulles from Eleanor Lansing Dulles, *John Foster Dulles: the Last Year*; Townsend Hoopes, *The Devil and John Foster Dulles*; Khrushchev, op. cit.; D.R. Thorpe, *Selwyn Lloyd*; Alistair Horne, *Macmillan 1894–1956.*

4. FO371 137398.

5. Berlin and Soviet Zone Summary for week ending 20 July 1955, FO371 118073; Berlin to FO 4 May 1956, FO371 124508.

6. Details in this paragraph from Summary of Changes in Conditions of Access to West Berlin July–December 1955, FO371 124646; 31 December 1955 memo, FO371 124495; Report on West Berlin Affairs for the Second Quarter of 1958 by Major-General F.D. Rome, FO371 130684.

7. 27 April 1956 from Peck in Berlin to Wilkinson in Bonn, FO371 124574.

8. Quarterly Report on West Berlin for the Last Quarter of 1957, FO371 137323.

9. FO371 124514 and FO371 130709.

10. 9 January 1958, telegram from Bonn, 00057 Fiche 10.

11. FO371 118074; FO371 124495; 29 June 1956, report P.W.H. Graebner, FO371 124699.

12. FO371 124506 and FO371 124699.
13. This and details in following paragraph from memos by Graebner, 29 May and 12 October 1956, FO371 124506 and FO371 124699.
14. Jokes from Terence Prittie, *Willy Brandt*.
15. Willy Brandt, *My Life in Politics*.
16. Details from Ambrose, op. cit.; Beschloss, op. cit.; Robert A. Divine, *Blowing on the Wind: the Nuclear Test Ban Debate 1954–60*.
17. 29 and 30 April 1958, Bonn to FO, FO371 137367.
18. Details about Khrushchev from Nikita Khrushchev, *Khrushchev Remembers* and *Last Testament*; Sergei Khrushchev, *Khrushchev on Khrushchev*; Foy D. Kohler, *Understanding the Russians*; Veljko Mićunović, *Moscow Diary*; Hans Kroll, *Mémoires d'un ambassadeur*; Adam B. Ulam, op. cit.; Martin McCauley, *The Soviet Union since 1917*. Sir Patrick Reilly's valedictory despatch, 18 August 1960, PREMII 3121. Khrushchev visit September, 1959(2) Box 48 Ann Whitman File, DDE Diary Series, Eisenhower Library. Conversations with A. Adzhubei, L. Bezimensky, I. Kremer, D. Melemit-Melnikov, O. Troyanovsky.
19. Mićunović, op. cit.
20. Conversations in Moscow and East Berlin.
21. *The Times*, 19 September and 2 October 1958; Weekly Report on the Political Situation in the FRG, 20 and 26 August 1958, FO371 137324; 3 October, despatch from Howard Trivers in Berlin to Department of State, 00214 Fiche 34.
22. FO371 137400; 9 September 1958, minute by P.F. Hancock, FO371 137401.
23. Western replies to Moscow, November 1958, FO371 137404; 2 October 1958, *The Times*.
24. 28 and 29 October 1958, Bonn to FO, FO371 137333.
25. Howard Trivers, *Three Crises in American Foreign Affairs*.
26. 11 November, Moscow to London, FO371 137333.

4: ULTIMATUM

1. Details on West Berlin reactions: 15 November 1958, tel. 341, US Mission Berlin to State Department, 00289 Fiche 44; Weekly Reports on Political Situation in FRG November–December 1958, 13–19 November and 20–26 November, FO371 137325; 21 November 1958, tel. 371, US Mission Berlin to State Department 00355 Fiche 54; 26 November 1958, tel. 409, US Mission Berlin to State Department, 00417 Fiche 63. Details of convoy incident: Report on West Berlin for Last Quarter of 1958, FO371 145683, Fiche 47, and John S. D. Eisenhower, *Strictly Personal*.
2. Details in this and the next paragraph: 13 November, tel. 323, US Mission Berlin to State Department, 00264 Fiche 41; 15 November 1958, tel. 337, US Mission Berlin to State Department, 00287 Fiche 44; 17 November, Berlin to FO, FO371 137335; 15 November, tel. 339, US Mission Berlin to State Department, 00288 Fiche 44; 15 November, tel. 341, US Mission Berlin to State Department, 00289 Fiche 44; Report on West Berlin for Last Quarter of 1958, op. cit.

3. Details in this paragraph: 11 November, Berlin to FO, FO371 137333; 13 November, tel. 323, US Mission Berlin to State Department, 00264 Fiche 41; 15 November, tel. 337, US Mission Berlin to State Department, 00287 Fiche 44.

4. Details in this paragraph: FO371 137342; 00342 Fiche 49; 20 November, Berlin to Bonn, FO371 137336; 25 November, Berlin to FO, FO371 137337; 00393 Fiche 59.

5. 20 November, tel. COB 113, Berlin Command to Department of Army, 00328 Fiche 50; 20 November, tel. 1037, State Department (Herter) to US Embassy Bonn, 00330 Fiche 50; 26 November, tel. 281, State Department to US Mission Berlin, 00406 Fiche 62.

6. 23 November, tel. EC9–6265, 00370 Fiche 56; 2 December, Tripartite Garrison Airlift Plan, following 24 November meeting in Bonn, 00445 Fiche 68.

7. 12 November, Berlin to FO, FO371 137334; 12 November, tel. 332, US Mission Berlin to State Department, 00277 Fiche 43; 15 November, Moscow to FO, FO371 137334 and 135240.

8. Kroll, *Mémoires d'un ambassadeur*; transcript of interview with Sergo Mikoyan for BBC World Service series *The World that came in from the Cold*; 24 November, Sir Patrick Reilly to Sir Anthony Rumbold, FO371 137339.

9. 13 November, tel. 323, US Mission Berlin to State Department, 00264 Fiche 41; 14 November, tel. 1080, Moscow to State Department, 00275 Fiche 42; 24 November, FO minute, FO371 137336.

10. 12 November, W.B.T. Ledwidge Berlin to R.F. Stretton Bonn, FO371 137351; Report on West Berlin for Last Quarter of 1958, op. cit.

11. John S.D. Eisenhower, op. cit. and Dwight D. Eisenhower, *The White House Years*.

12. 13 November, Status report on Berlin for the President from Acting Secretary of State (Herter), 00255 Fiche 39; 12 November, Bureau of Intelligence and Research, Department of State to Acting Secretary of State, 00246 Fiche 38; 13 November, State Department to US posts, 02933 Fiche 449; 13 November, telephone call from Dulles to Herter, 00254 Fiche 39; 17 November, Dulles remarks to Grewe, Fiche 449.

13. 14 November, tel. 1652, Thompson to State Department, 00238 Fiche 37; Michael R. Beschloss, *The Crisis Years*; Sergei Khrushchev, *Khrushchev on Khrushchev*.

14. 14 November, Washington (Caccia) to FO, FO371 137334; 25 November, Briefing on the Status of the Berlin Crisis, AW File, DDE Diary Series, Box 37, Staff Notes, November 1958.

15. Allen Dulles in 386th meeting of NSC 13 November, AW File, NSC Series, Box 10; 12 November, tel. 320, Berlin to State Department, 00250 Fiche 39.

16. Dwight D. Eisenhower, op. cit.; memo of telephone conversation with the President, 22 November, Christian A. Herter Papers 1957–61, Chronological Files, October 1958 (3) Box 6 November 1958(1).

17. 11 November, Bonn to FO, FO371 137333; 12 November, Bonn to FO, FO371

137334; 15 November, Adenauer statement, Weekly Report on Political Situation in the Federal Republic of Germany 13–19 November, FO371 137325.

18. 22 November memo, FO371 137338; 21 November, tel. 1096, US Embassy to State Department, 00353 Fiche 53; 25 November, Briefing on the Status of the Berlin Crisis, op. cit.

19. 12 November, Paris to FO, FO371 137334; 18 November, Paris to FO, FO371 137337; 25 November, Briefing on the Status of the Berlin Crisis, op.cit; 17 November, Paris to FO, FO371 137335.

20. Details on de Gaulle from Charles de Gaulle, *Memoirs of Hope*; Bernard Ledwidge, *De Gaulle*; Jean Lacouture, *De Gaulle, the Ruler 1945–70*; Hervé Alphand, *L'Etonnement d'Etre*; the remark to Kreisky: Willy Brandt, *My Life in Politics*.

21. Details on Macmillan from volumes of autobiography; Alistair Horne, *Macmillan* vols. 1 and 2. Conversations with Sir Edward Tomkins and Sir Frank Roberts.

22. Adenauer's dismissal in 1945: Konrad Adenauer, *Memoirs 1945–53*; comment on Adenauer's grievances: François Seydoux, *Mémoires d'outre-Rhin*; Bruce comments 13 December 1961 to Secretary of State, 02646 Fiche 399. 25 March, Bonn to FO, PREM II 2347; 10 April, Steel despatch to Secretary of State, FO371 137374.

23. See for example: 11 April record of lunch with Dr Ritter, Minister at the German Embassy, by Philip de Zuluetta, FO371 137374; 11 September, FO371 137376.

24. Details on Selwyn Lloyd: D.R. Thorpe, *Selwyn Lloyd*; Keith Kyle, *Suez*; Alistair Horne, op. cit.; and conversations with several of his former officials.

25. This and next two paragraphs: FO371 137333; Lloyd 14 November minute, FO371 137336; 15 November, Secretary of State to Washington, ibid.

26. This paragraph and the next: 28 November, cover letter, FO371 137337; record of 21 November discussion in State Department, FO371 137339; 19 and 21 November, P.F. Hancock to Sir Christopher Steel, FO371 137336; copy of US Embassy, Bonn, telegram, undated but received in FO archives 24 November, FO371 137337; 22 and 23 November, E.H. Peck Berlin to P. A. Wilkinson Bonn, FO371 137339.

27. 21 November, tel. 1096, Bonn to State Department, 2933 Fiche 449; 20 November, Paris to FO, FO371 137336.

28. 19 November, FO to Washington, FO371 137339; 19 November, tels. 2752 and 2753, London to State Department, 2933 Fiche 449.

29. Minutes of conclusions of 18 November Cabinet meeting at 10 Downing Street, CAB 128/32; 22 November draft, FO371 137339.

30. Log of President's telephone call 27 November, AW File, DDE Diary Series, Box 37; John S.D. Eisenhower, op. cit.

31. 27 November, Washington to FO, FO371 137338; Eleanor Lansing Dulles, *John Foster Dulles: The Last Year*.

32. Weekly Reports on Political Situation in Federal Republic of Germany, 20–26 November, FO371 137325; 27 November, tels. 412 and 416, US Mission Berlin to State Department, 00423 and 00424 Fiche 64.

33. 9 December, Moscow to FO Senator Humphrey's conversation with Khrushchev, FO371 137342; 28 November, Moscow to FO, FO371 137338.

34. 28 November, Moscow to London, FO371 137338; 29 November, Khrushchev comments and 30 November, *New York Times* interview by Sidney Gruson quoted by Jack M. Schick, *The Berlin Crisis 1958–62*.

35. Harold Macmillan, *Riding the Storm*.

36. 3 December memo of conversation between Foy Kohler and Olivier Manet, 00448 Fiche 68; 13 December, Paris to FO, FO371 137343.

37. 9 December, Bonn to FO, FO371 137342; Weekly Reports on the Political Situation in the Federal Republic of Germany, 27 November – 3 December, FO371 137325; 28 November, Bonn to FO, FO371 137339; 10 December, tel. Berlin to Secretary of State, White House Office, Office of Staff Secretary, International Series Box 6, Germany vol. 1 of III(2) April 1957–December 1958; 5 December, Brandt interview in *Suddeutsche Zeitung*, FO371 137342; Willy Brandt, *My Life in Politics*.

38. Dwight D. Eisenhower and John S.D. Eisenhower, op. cit.

5: DIVIDED THEY STAND

1. Details in the first three paragraphs: conversations with many Berliners; 2 December, tel. 437, US Minister Berlin to State Department, 00446 Fiche 68; Report on Berlin for First Half 1959, FO371 145700; interview with Brandt by David Schorr of CBS, 13 January, US Embassy Berlin to State Department, 00615 Fiche 94.

2. Report on West Berlin for Last Quarter of 1958, FO371 145683; 10 December, *The Times*; 10 December, Berlin to Bonn, FO371 137329.

3. This and next two paragraphs: 10 September 1953, memo for Lay from Dulles, White House Office, Office of the Special Assistant for National Security Affairs, Records 1952–61, NSC Series, Policy Papers Subseries, Box 3, NSC 132/1, "Policy on Berlin"; FO371 124497 and 124645 passim; 21 November briefing sheet for Chairman of JCS, 00333 Fiche 51; 20 November briefing sheet for Chairman of JCS, 00332 Fiche 50; 25 November, tel. 1111, US Embassy Germany to State Department, 00401 Fiche 61; 14 November, tel. 2659, US Embassy UK to State Department, 00276 Fiche 42; 27 November draft Cabinet paper, FO371 137340; 2 December Tripartite Garrison Airlift Plan (drawn up at 24 November meeting in Bonn), 00445 Fiche 68.

4. 21 November briefing sheet for Chairman JCS, op. cit.; 28 November, JCS, State and Defence Departments, Ad Hoc Working Group Report on Possible Courses of Action in Berlin, 00428 Fiche 65.

5. Details of armed convoy plan and next two paragraphs: Jean Edward Smith, *Lucius D.Clay*; Tusa, *The Berlin Blockade*.

6. 21 November, *New York Herald Tribune* and 25 November and 1 December, *New York Times*; 16 December, Paris to London, FO371 137343.

7. 11 December, tel. 1236, joint message from State and Defence Departments to US Embassy, 00489 Fiche 74; 12 January memo, 00607 Fiche 92; 27 December, Bruce's secret diary, 00567 Fiche 27; 23 November, tel. EC-6265, Norstad to JCS, 00370 Fiche 56.

8. Robert Murphy, *Diplomat among Warriors*; text of Alsop article and comments, PREM 11 2720; memo of conference with President, 11 December, AW File, DDE Diary Series, Box 38, Staff Notes December '58(2).

9. 15 November, Moscow to FO, FO371 137334; 12 December, Moscow to FO, FO371 137343; Twining comment at 13 December meeting, memo USDEL/MC/7, 02933 Fiche 450; force estimates: JCS memo, 1907/157 00396 Fiche 58.

10. 18 November, tel. 1062, US Embassy to State Department, 00315 Fiche 48; 14 November, FO to Washington, FO371 137336.

11. 21 November, P.F. Hancock memo for Sir A. Rumbold, FO371 137336; 16 November, Bonn to FO, FO371 137336; 1 December, Rumbold minute on background to procedural questions, FO371 137342; 25 November, Briefing on Status of Berlin, AW File, op. cit.; FO371 145838.

12. 24 November, Moscow to FO, 24 November, Washington to FO and 25 November, Paris to FO, FO371 137337; 25 November, Briefing on Status of Berlin, AW File, op. cit.; 9 November, Bonn to FO, FO371 137342; 9 December, tel. 1212, US Embassy Germany to State Department, 00473 Fiche 72; memo of conference with the President, 11 December, op. cit.

13. 11 December, Paris to FO, FO371 137342.

14. Details this para and next: 14 December, Paris to FO (Secretary of State to PM), FO371 137343; 15 December, record of Foreign Ministers' meeting on 14 December, FO371 137347; Willy Brandt, *My Life in Politics*; 17 December, Paris to FO, FO371 137345.

15. 16 December, NATO communiqué, 02933 Fiche 450; 20 December, Moscow to FO, FO371 137374; 19 December, Bonn to FO, ibid; Weekly Report, FO371 137325.

16. FO371 137347, 137348, 137349 and 137350.

17. Eisenhower, op. cit.; Macmillan, op. cit.; FO371 145794.

18. FO371 145686, 145687, 146690, 145794 and press conference, FO371 145690.

19. This and next three paragraphs: 2 January, Rumbold minute and 7 January, Hoyer Millar minute, FO371 145819; 15 January, Introduction to a New Policy About Germany, FO371 145821; January exchange of messages between Jebb and FO, FO371 145691; paper on possible interim solution for Berlin, cover note, 18 February, FO371 145695; 19 February, report on Joint Committee decisions on European Security, Interim Berlin solution and Reunification, FO371 145820; 14 February, directive given by PM at Chequers, FO371 145819.

20. Possible New Approaches to Problem of Berlin, 7 January, memo from

Bureau of European Affairs, Office of German Affairs, 00592 Fiche 90; 5 February, Bonn to FO, FO371 145840.

21. 13 January, press conference, FO371 145688; 14 January, tel. 1477, US Embassy Germany to State Department, 00626 Fiche 95.

22. Details in this and next three paras: 13 January, Washington to FO and minute, FO371 145815; 21 January, Berlin despatch to FO, FO371 145816; 27 January, press conference, FO371 145837; 28 January, Bonn to FO, FO371 145691; 14 February, Bonn to FO, FO371 145858.

23. Details in this and next para: 02933 Fiche 450.

24. This paragraph and the next: memo of conference with the President 29 January and memo of conclusions, AW File, DDE Diary Series, Box 38, Staff Notes Jan '59(1); 02933 Fiche 450; John S.D. Eisenhower, op. cit.

25. 5 February record of conversation between Secretary of State and Dulles, FO371 145817; Macmillan, op. cit.; 02933 Fiche 450; Eisenhower, op. cit.; 9 February, J. Killick minute on lunch with US Embassy staff, FO371 145841; 6, 8 and 18 February, Dulles to President, AW File, Dulles-Herter Series Box II, Dulles February' 59; 8 February, memo of conversation between Adenauer and Dulles, 00741 Fiche 113.

26. Details in next 5 paras: Macmillan, op. cit.; Horne, op. cit.; Thorpe, op. cit.; 23 January, FO to Moscow and 24 January, Moscow to FO, FO371 143433; 23 January, FO to Washington, ibid.; 2 March, Rumbold minute on US reactions, FO371 143434; 21 January, Dulles telephone call to President, AW File, DDE Diary Series, Box 38, Staff Notes Jan '59 (2), Telephone Calls Jan '59; 3 February, Paris to FO and Bonn to FO, FO371 145817.

27. This vital matter is covered at length in FO371 143433, 143437 and 143438.

28. This paragraph and the next two: Kroll, Horne and Macmillan.

29. Record of meetings, 22 February, PREM II 2690.

30. Record of meeting 23 February at Kremlin, ibid.; record of conversation, 24 February, between Foreign Secretary and Mr Gromyko, ibid.

31. This para and next: 24 February, Khrushchev speech; PREM II 2690; 9 March, Reilly account of visit, FO371 143439; 25 February, tel. 1686, US Embassy Soviet Union to State Department, 00825 Fiche 125.

32. Record of meeting with Soviet leaders, PREM II 2690; 26 February, Moscow to FO, FO371 145821; Reilly account, op. cit.; Macmillan, op. cit.

33. This paragraph and the next: 26 February, Moscow to FO, FO371 145821; Record of meeting 26 February in Kremlin, PREM II 2690; John S.D. Eisenhower, op. cit.; Reilly account, op. cit.

34. Record of conversation between Foreign Secretary and Mr Kuznetsov, PREM II 2690; 2 March, Moscow to FO, FO371 145821.

35. 2 March, Moscow to FO, ibid.; Record of two conversations between Foreign Secretary and Mr Gromyko, Leningrad, PREM II 2690.

36. Quoted by Thorpe, op. cit., from Reilly's private papers.

37. Record of meeting with Soviet leaders 2 March in Kremlin, PREM II 2690; Reilly account, op. cit.

38. Summary record of discussion concerning the final communiqué, PREM II 2690; 12 March, tel. to UK High Commissioners, FO371 143400; 5 March, minute of meeting between Foreign Secretary and ambassador Chauvel, FO371 143439.

6: GENEVA AND CAMP DAVID

1. H. Macmillan, *Riding the Storm.*
2. Weekly Report 5–11 March, FO371 145683; report of 7 March Khrushchev speech in Leipzig, FO371 145831.
3. 6 April, Ledwidge, Berlin to Wilkinson, Bonn, FO371 145699; various reports in FO371 145695, 145696, 145697 and 145763; 9 March, tel. 778, US Mission West Berlin to State Department, 00952 Fiche 140.
4. Record of 5 March meeting of Secretary of State and M. Chauvel, FO371 145823; Macmillan, op. cit.
5. Details in this and next paragraph: 2 March, Steel to Hancock, FO371 145773; record of 12 March meeting in Palais Schaumberg, PREM II 2676; record of 13 March meeting at German Foreign Ministry, ibid.; Macmillan, op. cit.; record of the confidential parts of 13 March conversation between the PM and the Federal Chancellor in the Palais Schaumberg (Top Secret), FO371 145827.
6. Ambrose, op. cit.; ACW Diary, 5 March, AW Diary Series, Box II.
7. Memo on 6 March conference with the President, AW File, DDE Diary Series, Box 39, Staff Notes 1–5 March '59(2).
8. ACW Diary, 6 March, op. cit. Papers 1957–61.
9. 6 March memo of telephone conversation with Secretary Dulles, Herter Christian A. Papers, Miscellaneous Memos '59, Box 10; Dwight D. Eisenhower, *Waging the Peace*; memo of conferences with the President 17 and 19 March, AW File, DDE Diary Series, Box 40, Staff Notes, 15–31 March '59.
10. Record of 20 March conversation with Dulles, FO371 145860; Dulles memo, 20 March, White House Office of the Staff Secretary, International Trips and Meetings, Box 6, Macmillan Talks 20 March '59.
11. Memo of conference with the President 20 March, AW Files, International Series, Box 22, Macmillan Visit 20–22 March '59(1); Macmillan, op. cit.; Eisenhower, op. cit.; 23 March, Washington to FO, FO371 145860; ACW Diary, 21 March, AW Diary Series, Box 10.
12. Reports from Bonn in FO371 145774 and 145776; 28 April, tel. 2398, US Embassy Germany to State Department, 01222 Fiche 185; record of 28 April conversation between de Gaulle and Herter, 01225 Fiche 186; 31 March, tel. 3645, State Department to US Embassy France, 01071 Fiche 162; 24 April, memo of conversation between Dulles, Herter and others, 01214 Fiche 184; 25 April, tel. 5639, US Embassy UK to State Department, 01220 Fiche 185.
13. Macmillan, op. cit.; 14 April Khrushchev message, FO371 143429; FO371 143430.
14. FO371 145808, 145837 and 145843.
15. 16 February, Hancock submission, FO371 145818.

REFERENCES

16. This paragraph and the next: 21 March, report of four-Power Working Group, FO371 145827; 6 April, Bonn to FO and 4 April, Washington to FO, FO371 145846; 02933 Fiche 450; 24 April report of four-Power Working Group, FO371 145850.

17. 29 and 30 April, Paris to FO, FO371 145851; 1 May CAH US Embassy France to State Department, 01245 Fiche 189.

18. 14 May, CRO to Commonwealth capitals, FO371 145866; 10 and 11 May, Geneva to FO, FO371 145877; 11 May, Herter to President, AW Files, Dulles-Herter Series, Box 10 (II) May to June; 12 May, Secretary of State to PM, FO371 145835; 13 and 16 May, Geneva to FO, FO371 145853.

19. Except where separately noted, details about the Geneva talks come from the printed volume Meeting of the Foreign Ministers, records of proceedings and principal conference documents, summaries of private meetings and verbatim records of plenary sessions FO371 145879. There are other texts or versions of the same texts in FO371 145810, 145811, 145812 and 145813. Various statements and verbatim records of formal sessions can be found in FO371 145870 and 145880–145886.

20. 14 May, Geneva to FO, FO371 145830; 22 May, Geneva to FO, 145831.

21. 16 May, Rumbold to Hoyer Millar, FO371 145866; Kroll, op. cit.; 25 August, despatch from US Army Europe (Office of Political Adviser) to State Department, 01634 Fiche 245.

22. 22 May, Geneva to FO, FO371 145866; 26 May, Geneva to FO, FO371 145867; record of 26 May conversation between Lloyd and Gromyko, FO371 145701.

23. Memo of 27 May conference with the President, AW File, DDE Diary Series, Staff Notes May '59(II); Eisenhower, op. cit.; record of conversation between Secretary of State and President, PREM II 2871; 30 May, Geneva to FO, FO371 145701 and 145868.

24. "Subversive Activities", FO371 145702; 1 June, Geneva to FO, FO371 145701.

25. 23 May, tel. 991, US Mission West Berlin to State, 01298 Fiche 1298; 29 May, Berlin to FO, FO371 145867; Brandt memo, 1 June, Berlin to FO, FO371 145702; 30 July, tel. CAHTO 183, West Berlin to State Department, 02937 Fiche 454.

26. 4 June, Geneva to FO, FO371 145868; 9 June, Herter to President, AW File, Dulles-Herter Series, Box 11, Herter, June '59(2).

27. 9 June, Geneva to FO, FO371 145869.

28. H. Macmillan, Pointing the Way; 14 June, Geneva to FO, PREM II 2685; Eisenhower, op. cit.; Foy Kohler; 9 June, tel. CAHTO "Crisis over Berlin", 02937; 12 June, Herter to President, AW Files, Dulles-Herter Series, Box 11, Herter June '59(2); 17 June, Washington to FO, PREM II 2685.

29. Trivers; 14 July, tel. 68, US Mission West Berlin to State Department, 01530 Fiche 230; 27 July, tel. 111, US Mission West Berlin to State Department, 01565 Fiche 235; 02937 Fiche 454.

30. Memo of 16 June and 18 June conferences with the President, AW File, DDE Diary Series, Box 42, Staff Notes 16–30 June '59(2); 19 June, Geneva to FO, FO371 145872.

31. Details in this and the previous paragraph: Macmillan, op. cit.; Eisenhower, op. cit.; 17 July, Herter to the President, AW Files, Dulles-Herter Series, Box 12, Herter Christian A., July '59(2); 16 July, Geneva to FO, FO371 145880.

32. 20 and 24 July, Geneva to FO, FO371 145882 and 145884.

33. Eisenhower, op. cit.; 23 July, Geneva to FO, FO371 145888.

34. 27 July, PM to President, and 29 July, President to PM, PREM II 2674.

35. 4 August, PM to Secretary of State, PREM II 2990.

36. 25 August, despatch US Army Europe to State Department, op. cit.

37. Eisenhower, op. cit.; memo of conversation 27 August at Palais Schaumberg, White House Office, Office of the Staff Secretary, International Trips and Meetings, Box 7; memo of conversation on 29 August at Chequers, DDE, Trip to Europe (Chronology), ibid.

38. Details in this and next paragraph: Khrushchev, *The Last Testament*; conversation with Alexei Adzhubei.

39. Memo of 15 September meeting, (JFK) President's Office Files, Box 126, USSR-Vienna Meeting Background Documents 1953–61(C); AW Files, International Series Box 48, Khrushchev visit September '59(1); 16 September, *New York Times*, quoted by Beschloss.

40. Details of the tour: author's conversation with Adzhubei; 19 September, State Department memo, AW File International Series Box 48 etc.; 21 September memo of conversation with Cabot Lodge on train from Los Angeles to San Francisco, ditto; memo of 25 September conversation with President, AW Files, DDE Diary Series, Box 44, Staff Notes Sept '59(1).

41. *The Memoirs of Richard Nixon; Last Testament*; 26 September, memo of conversation at lunch, (JFK) President's Office Files, Box 126, op. cit.; Beschloss.

42. Memo of conversation 11.45 a.m. 27 September, White House Office, Office of Staff Secretary, International Trips and Meetings, Box 10, Khrushchev visit Sept. '59(3); memo of conversation between President and officials 12.15 p.m. 27 September, ibid.

43. 27 September, memo, (JFK) President's Office Files, op. cit.

44. Memo of conversation 1.45 p.m. 27 September, White House Office, op. cit.

45. 30 September, Ledwidge, Berlin to Wilkinson, Bonn, FO371 145709; Weekly Report 24–30 September, FO371 145685.

7: THE PARIS SUMMIT

1. 9 October, letters from President to de Gaulle and Macmillan, AW File, International Series, Box 12, De Gaulle, 15 September on (8), and PREM II 2990; 20 and 16 October, President to de Gaulle, AW File, op.cit; memo of conversation with President 16 October, AW File, DDE Diary Series, Box 45, Staff Notes, October '59(1).

2. This paragraph and the next: Macmillan, *Pointing the Way*; 20 October, de Gaulle to Macmillan, PREM II 2890; 15 October, Paris to FO, FO371 145626; 23 October, FO Brief, FO371 145834.

3. October and November Weekly Reports from Bonn, FO371 145685; cables from Paris, FO371 145760 and 145781; record of meeting at Number 10, 17 November, FO371 145781; records of conversations at Chequers, 18 and 19 November, PREM II 2714; 4 December, Lloyd memo to Macmillan, PREM II ditto.

4. Details in this paragraph and the next: records of meetings, 19 and 20 December, PREM II 2991; record of conversation PM, Eisenhower, Lloyd and Herter, 20 December, PREM II 2987; Macmillan, op. cit.; de Gaulle, *Memoirs of Hope.*

5. Review of Events in Berlin and the Soviet Zone for week ending 13 January, FO371 153725; 12 January, Bonn to FO and Berlin, and 13 January, S.J. Barrett to W.J.A. Wilberforce, FO371 153971; 13 January, Despatch, Berlin to FO, FO371 154008.

6. Details of Radio Bill 25 March and 19 October, Bonn to FO, FO371 154222; 22 February and 7 March, Berlin to Bonn, FO371 154307.

7. Details in this paragraph and the next: 11 January, 29 March and 25 April, W.B.J. Ledwidge, Berlin to R.F. Stratton, Bonn, FO371 154208; 13 and 14 May, ibid.; Review of Events in Berlin and the Soviet Zone for week ending 28 April, FO371 153726.

8. Despatch 9, 11 March, from Office of GOC Berlin (British Sector) to Sir Christopher Steel, FO371 154311; 13 January, Review of Developments in DDR for Last Quarter of 1959, FO371 153725.

9. 22 May, *New York Herald Tribune*; 30 December, *New York Times*; and 14 March 1960, *Daily Telegraph.*

10. Various reports, FO371 154311; 26 and 27 April, *The Times* quoting Federal German White Book on collectivisation; The Refugee Flow in the First Months of 1960, FO371 154312.

11. 21 May 1959, *Financial Times* and 12 June 1960, *Sunday Times.*

12. Details in this paragraph and the next: Macmillan, op. cit.; memo of conference with the President, 14 March, AW File, DDE Diary Series, Box 48 Staff Notes, March '60(3); memo of conversation at Camp David 28 March, AW Files International Series Box 23, Macmillan visit 26–30 March; PREM II 2978; de Gaulle, op. cit.

13. Details in this paragraph and the next two: FO371 153904, 153905, 153906, 153907, 153909, 153911, 153913, 153914; de Gaulle, op. cit.; memos of conversations with the President, 24 and 25 April, AW File, International Series Box 12, De Gaulle visit 22–25 April(1).

14. Cover letter and memo Martin J. Hillenbrand, 16 October, White House, Office of Staff Secretary, International Series, Box 6 Germany vol. II of III (2); FO Brief, FO371 154089.

15. FO Brief for Foreign Ministers' meeting 12–14 April, FO371 154087; reports on Washington Group, FO371 154083–8; Report of four-Power Working Group, 9 April, FO371 153784; discussions in preparation for Paris Summit conference, printed volume, PREM II 2992.

16. FO371 154089; record of conversation between Secretary of State and M. Couve de Murville, 13 April, FO371 153784; records of meetings in Teheran and Istanbul, FO371 153784 and 154087; Macmillan, op. cit.; record of meeting in State Department, 12 April, FO371 153784.

17. 19 April, Berlin to FO, FO371 153980; 12 May, Berlin to FO, FO371 153761; 16 May, ibid.; 30 April, Moscow to FO, FO371 153980; Bohlen, *Witness to History 1929–69*.

18. Details in this paragraph and the next: US memo in FO371 154211; 3 February, tel. E-372, State Department to US Embassy Germany, 00704 Fiche 107; 26 March, tel. JCS 956971 to US C-in-C, 01047 Fiche 158; 27 March, tel. 827, US Mission Berlin to State Department, 01056 Fiche 159; Bruce secret diary 01063 ibid.; 1 April, JCS order, 01083 and memo Chairman's Staff group, 01084 ibid.; 3 April memo White House Office, Office of the Staff Secretary, International Trips and Meetings, Box 6, March–April '59(2); 15 April, tel. 2311, US Embassy Germany to State Department, 01150 Fiche 174; 16 April, tel. 2327, ibid., 01162 Fiche 176; 16 April, tel. 5370, US Embassy UK to State Department, 01163 ibid.

19. Details in this paragraph and the next: FO371 154211; memo from Herter to President, 22 January, AW File, Dulles-Herter series, Christian Herter Box 12, Jan '60; 9 February, Berlin to FO, FO371 154212; 16 February, letter Bonn to FO; 4 March, JCS to McElroy, 01829 Fiche 274; memo of conference with the President, 8 March, AW File, DDE Diary Series, Box 48, Staff Notes March '60(3) and 01835 Fiche 275.

20. U-2 details: Beschloss, *Mayday*; Ambrose, *Winning the Peace*; Leonhard, *The Kremlin Since Stalin*; speculation on Khrushchev's reactions and motives Bohlen, Khrushchev, and conversations with Messrs. Troyanovski, Adzhubei, Melemit-Melnikov, Razmenov; 7 and 14 May, Moscow to FO, FO371 153760 and 153763.

21. 9 May, Khrushchev letter to Macmillan, FO371 153760; conversation with Adzhubei.

22. De Gaulle, op. cit.; record of meeting at the Élysée at 2.30 p.m. 15 May, FO371 153787; record of meeting at the Residence at 4.30 p.m. 15 May, FO371 153787.

23. Memo of conference with the President at 4.30 p.m. 15 May, AW File, DDE Diary Series Box 50, Staff Notes May '60(1) or International Series, Box 39, Paris meeting; record of meeting at the Élysée at 6 p.m. 15 May, FO371 153787; Macmillan, op. cit.

24. De Gaulle, op. cit.; record of meeting at the Élysée at 11 a.m. 16 May, FO371 153787; Bohlen, op. cit.; Beschloss, op. cit.

25. Record of meeting at Quai d'Orsay 16 May, FO371 153785.

26. Minute by PM of conversation with President de Gaulle at the Élysée at 7 p.m. 16 May, FO371 153770; ditto with President Eisenhower at the US Embassy at 7.50 p.m., ibid.; D.R. Thorpe, op. cit.; record of conversation at the Soviet

Embassy at 9.30 p.m. 16 May, FO371 153787; minute on that meeting, ibid.; Macmillan, op. cit.

27. Reuter report on press conference, FO371 153770; John Eisenhower, op. cit.
28. Khrushchev, *Last Testament*.
29. Details in this paragraph and the next: record of meeting at the Élysée at 3 p.m. 17 May, FO371 153788; statement by Soviet delegation 10.30 p.m., FO371 153770; de Gaulle, op. cit.; John Eisenhower, op. cit.
30. Record of conversation between PM and Mr Khrushchev in the Residence at 10.30 a.m. 18 May, FO371 153788; record of a discussion at Quai d'Orsay at 10 a.m., ibid.; minute by PM of conversation with President at British Embassy at 4 p.m. 18 May, FO371 153770; 18 May meeting of Chiefs of State and Heads of Government, AW File, International Series, Box 11; transcript of press conference in Palais de Chaillot at 3 p.m., FO371 153770.
31. Horne, op. cit.; Thorpe, op. cit.
32. PM's message, 19 May, FO371 153765; 18 May, Washington to FO, FO371 153763; Eisenhower, op. cit.; Alphand, op. cit.
33. 19 May, Berlin to FO, FO371 153734; conversation with Louis Heren; 21 May, Berlin to FO, FO371 1544073.
34. NSA, *Crisis over Berlin*; Confidential annex to COS(59) 24th meeting, 7 April, '59 DEFE4 117.
35. Paper on Berlin Contingency Planning May 1960, FO371 153770; Maintenance of Air Access COS(59)248 5 October; 30 September, letter from SACEUR DEFE5 95; 27 July memo UK Chiefs of Staff Committee, 01935 Fiche 291; 9 August minute ibid. DEFE4 128; *Crisis over Berlin* 02939; 31 August minute COS(60), 01948 Fiche 292.
36. 3 March, US Mission West Berlin to US Embassy Bonn and State Department, 00869 Fiche 132; tel. SECTO 171 (Geneva) to State Department, 01348 Fiche 204; 4 June, tel. TOSEC 01351, ibid.
37. 28 April draft terms of reference for study of harassment as a Berlin counter measure, White House Office, NSC Staff Papers 1948–61, Executive Secretary's Subject File Series Box 9 (1); 21 April 1959, 28th meeting of Chiefs of Staff Committee, DEFE4 117; record of meeting at Quai d'Orsay at 4.30 p.m. 18 May, FO371 153785; 18 May meeting of Chiefs of State and Heads of Government AW File, International Series, Box 11; record of meeting at Élysée Palace 5 p.m. 18 May, FO371 1537388.
38. Record of Events in Berlin and Soviet Zone for week ending 8 June, FO371 153727; 25 April, P.S. Tomlinson, Berlin to R.F. Stretton, Bonn, FO371 154288; 26 October meeting of Commandants and Governing Mayor, FO371 154010; passim, FO371 154031; Review of Events in Berlin and the Soviet Zone for weeks ending 21 July and 3 August, FO371 153727.
39. This paragraph and the next: 31 August, Berlin to FO and passim, FO371 154270; Review of Events in Berlin and the Soviet Zone for weeks ending 1 and 8 September, FO371 153727.
40. Review of Events in Berlin and the Soviet Zone for week ending 15

September, FO371 153728; 9 September, Bonn to FO, FO371 154271; 10 and 12 September, Berlin to FO, FO371 154772; 15 September, Bonn to FO, PREM II 3343; Reviews of Events in Berlin and the Soviet Zone for weeks ending 22 and 29 September, FO371 153728; 26 September, S.J. Barret, Berlin to P.L.V. Mallet, Bonn, FO371 154276.

41. 15 September, Bonn to FO, FO371 154273; 16 September, Washington to FO, FO371 154274; 18 September, Paris to FO, ibid.; 15 September, Bonn to FO, PREM II 3343.

42. 22 December, Despatch on Berlin 1 July to December 1960, FO371 161076; Reviews of Events in Berlin and the Soviet Zone for weeks ending 6 and 13 October, and 3 and 10 November, FO371 153728, and week ending 24 November, FO371 153729; 5 October, Berlin to FO, FO371 154277; 26 and 27 October, PREM II 3009.

43. 6 June 1961 despatch from Sir Christopher Steel, Bonn to the Earl of Home, FO, FO371 160646; January cables from Bonn to FO, FO371 161136.

44. FO371 154312; October cables Berlin to Bonn, FO371 154010.

45. 11 January 1961, Review of Developments in the DDR for Last Quarter of 1960, FO371 161076; 13 July, Review of Developments in the DDR for Second Quarter of 1960, FO371 153727; General Review of Developments in DDR in 1960, FO371 161109; Review of Developments in the DDR in the Third Quarter of 1960, FO371 153728; FO371 154025; 12 December, W.B.J. Ledwidge, Berlin to P.W.J. Buxton, FO, FO371 154312.

46. Terence Prittie, *Willy Brandt*.

47. Conversation with Manfred Rexin; 23 November, letter from H. Lehmann to FO, FO371 154022.

8: DUCKS IN A ROW?

1. 25 May, Bonn to FO, FO371 153766; 24 May meeting of NSC, AW File, NSC Series, Box 12; 24 May, Macmillan to Lloyd, PREM II 2988; 8 June, Department of State intelligence report on 3 June press conference, FO371 153984; 28 July, Report on Berlin for Seven Months ending 1 July, FO371 153727.

2. 8 June, Department of State, op. cit.; Kroll, op. cit.

3. Details in this paragraph and the next: Arthur M. Schlesinger, *A Thousand Days*; Theodore C. Sorensen, *Kennedy*; Bohlen interviewed by A. Schlesinger, 12 May 1964, JFK Oral; L. Thompson interviewed by Elizabeth Donahue, 25 March 1964, ibid.; G. Kennan, 1964, ibid.; F. Kohler, October 1964, ibid.; George W. Ball, *The Past Has Another Pattern*.

4. John F. Kennedy, *The Strategy of Peace*; Sorensen; Schlesinger; R. McNamara interview with A. Schlesinger, 4 April 1964; Rusk interview with Dennis J. O'Brien, 13 March 1970.

5. J.F. Kennedy, op. cit.; M. Hillenbrand at Harvard School of Government Nuclear Crisis Project, *The Berlin Crisis*, Fiche 460.

6. Schlesinger, op. cit.

7. Rusk interview with Dennis O'Brien, 13 March, op. cit.; J.K. Galbraith, *A Life in our Times*; Rusk interview with O'Brien, 2 December 1969.
8. Kennedy quoted by Beschloss and Schlesinger; Schlesinger, op. cit.
9. J.F. Kennedy, op. cit.
10. Schlesinger, *Robert Kennedy and his Times*; Kroll, op. cit.; *Crisis over Berlin* 02940; 4 February, Thompson cable quoted by Beschloss.
11. Notes on discussion of the thinking of the Soviet leadership, 11 February, Cabinet Room, National Security Files, Box 176, USSR General, 2/2/61–2/14/61; 22 February, Kennedy to Khrushchev, NS Files, Box 183, USSR Khrushchev correspondence 1/61–10/61; NS Files, Box 176 passim.
12. Refugee figures: FO371 160656; 25 March, Berlin to FO, FO371 160534; 23 March, US Mission West Berlin to State Department, 02017 Fiche 303; 28 March, *Christian Science Monitor* quoted by Catudal (with doubts shed on the story by an intelligence source); Jan Sejna, *We Will Bury You*; Weyden, op. cit.; 12 August 1992 article in *Nezevisimaiai (Independent) Gazeta*; RIAS programme, 13 August 1986, *Mauerbau* produced by Manfred Rexin; author's conversations in Moscow 1992.
13. 31 March, Moscow to FO, FO371 160534; 22 April, Berlin to FO, ibid.; 30 April, Moscow to FO, ibid.; 7 May, Warsaw to FO, FO371 160535.
14. NS Files, Germany-Berlin-General, Box 815.
15. 4 April, memo for President from Bundy, NS Files, Germany-Berlin-General, Box 81.
16. 5 April, memo on meeting between President and Macmillan, *Crisis over Berlin* 02940.
17. Washington talks, follow up action (undated), PREM II 3321; 5 May, memo from McNamara to Bundy, NS Files, Box 81.
18. Eisenhower quoted by Ambrose, op. cit.
19. Memo dictated by Taylor for JFK Oral History, 12 April 1964; Ambrose, op. cit.
20. 16 May, memo, NS Files, Box 117, USSR General 5/9/61–5/17/61.
21. Kenneth P. O'Donnell etc., *Johnny, We Hardly Knew Ye*; Thompson interview with Donahue, op. cit.; Bohlen interview with Schlesinger, op. cit.; Rusk interview with O'Brien, 13 March 1970.
22. All in President's Office Files, Box 126, USSR-Vienna meeting, Background documents 1953–61 (A) and (C).
23. 24 May Thompson telegram to Secretary of State, President's Office Files Box 126 (A), op. cit.; 30 May Moscow to FO, FO371 160474 and Thompson cable to Secretary of State, NS Files, Box 177, USSR-General 5/26/61–5/31/61.
24. Schlesinger, op. cit.; Alphand, op. cit.; de Gaulle, op. cit.
25. Harriman according to Abram Chayes in interview with Eugene Gordon, 9 July 1964; Beschloss, op. cit.
26. Memo of conversation 3 June, President's Office Files, Box 126, USSR-Vienna meeting, memos of conversations (1).
27. Schlesinger, op. cit.; memo of conversation in garden and private

conversation, President's Office Files, op. cit.

28. This and next three paragraphs: memos of conversations, 4 June, President's Office Files, op. cit.

29. Horne, op. cit.; Schlesinger, op. cit.; Macmillan, op. cit.

30. 5 June, Bohlen; *New York Times* quoted by Beschloss; 14 June, Sir H. Caccia to Sir F. Hoyer Millar, FO371 160476.

31. Nikita Khrushchev, op. cit.; Sergei Khrushchev, op. cit.; Sorensen, op. cit.; Foy Kohler recorded October 1964.

32. March 1978 letter from John Ausland to Catudal; Kohler recording, op. cit.

33. Text of Soviet aide-mémoire, FO371 160535; allied discussions, FO371 160536 and 160538; Sorensen, op. cit.

34. 29 June report, *Crisis over Berlin* 02941.

35. 29 June, NSC meeting NS Files, Box 313, NSC meetings '61.

36. *Crisis over Berlin*, op. cit.; 29 June, Moscow to FO, FO371 160537.

37. Details in this and the next two paragraphs: FO371 160475; 16 June, Berlin to FO, ibid.; 16 June, airgram C-466, US Mission West Berlin to State Department, 02090 Fiche 315; RIAS programme, *Mauerbau*, op. cit.; Catudal interview with Pavel.

38. 7 July, Berlin to FO, FO371 160538; Slusser, *The Berlin Crisis of 1961*; 3 July, Moscow to FO, FO371 160537.

39. Slusser, op. cit.

40. 24 June, Acheson letter to Truman, 02106 Fiche 317; 7 July, Caccia to Hoyer Millar, PREM II 3616.

41. Schlesinger, op. cit.; 3 July, Kaysen to Bundy, 02131 Fiche 321; Khrushchev according to 7 July *Time* quoted by Catudal, op. cit.

42. Schlesinger, op. cit.; Abram Chayes interview, op. cit.

43. 13 July NSC meeting, NS Files, Box 313, meetings and memos.

44. Range of memos NS Files, Box 81 and *Crisis over Berlin* 02941; Sorensen interview with Kaysen 6 April 1964; Sorensen memo, President's Office Files, Box 116, Germany-General 7/61; memo of 17 July meeting NS Files, Box 88 Germany-Berlin subjects 7/7/61–9/11/61.

45. Memo on meeting before NSC 19 July, NS Files, Box 313; Draft record of action, NSC meeting, NS Files, Box 330.

46. Acheson according to Ausland quoted by Catudal; 4 August, letter to Truman, 02261 Fiche 341.

47. FO371 160656; Catudal, op. cit.

48. Reports in FO371 160509; 21 and 24 July, *The Times*.

49. Examples of leaks: 27 February, *Washington Evening Star*; 29 May, *New York Herald Tribune*; 3 July, *Newsweek*.

50. 12 July, tel. 76 from Bonn, *Crisis over Berlin* 02941; 17 July, William O. Anderson (Office of Soviet Affairs) to John C. Ausland (Germany), 02182 Fiche 329; 18 July memo, Ausland to Hillenbrand, 02189 Fiche 330; 24 July, tel. 87, US Mission West Berlin to State Department, 02220 Fiche 335; 24 July, tel. 258, Moscow to State Department, 02218 Fiche 335.

51. James O'Donnell to Curtis Cate, and to Prittie.
52. 28 July, Moscow to FO, FO371 160540; Beschloss, op. cit.
53. 31 July, Berlin to FO and passim FO371 160656; FO371 160480.
54. 2 August, tel. 252, US Embassy Germany to State Department, 02253 Fiche 340; 2 August, tel. 124, US Mission West Berlin to State Department, 02255 Fiche 341; 4 August, Brandt statement to Senate in cable from State Department to European stations, President's Office Files, Box 116, Germany-General 8/61–10/61.
55. 5 August Berlin to FO and passim, FO371 160480.

9: UP TO THE WIRE

1. 7 August, dispatch, US Mission West Berlin to State Department, 02273 Fiche 344; Berlin situation reports 5 and 7 August, FO371 160480; 3 August, *New York Herald Tribune*; 9 August, *New York Times*.
2. 3 August, report on Grenzgänger, FO371 160509; 1 August, tel. 117, US Mission West Berlin to State Department, 02247 Fiche 339; 2 August, *The Times*.
3. Berlin situation report 5 August, op. cit.; 4 August, *New York Herald Tribune*; 5 August, *Christian Science Monitor*; 6 August, *Sunday Telegraph*; Warsaw Pact communiqué National Security Files, Box 82, Germany-Berlin General 8/6/61–8/8/61; 6 August, Moscow to FO, FO371 160541.
4. Sejna, op. cit.; Catudal, op. cit.; Cate, op.cit; Weyden, op. cit.
5. 30 and 31 July reports on quadripartite meetings Paris to FO, FO371 160540; 2 and 3 August ditto FO371 160541; Draft Cabinet paper, cover note 26 July, FO371 160480; 2 August, Paris to FO ibid.
6. This paragraph and next: 5 August record of meeting at Quai d'Orsay, FO371 160542; *Crisis over Berlin* Part VI 02941; Catudal, op. cit. Footnote: undated instructions for Norstad National Security Files, Box 82, op. cit., 8/29/61–8/31/61.
7. 4 August, Moscow to FO, FO371 160543; 3 and 5 August, Moscow to FO, FO371 160541; 3 August, Thompson to Kohler, National Security Files, op. cit. 8/1/61–8/5/61; draft paper, op. cit.; 5 August record of breakfast conversation between Secretary of State and Mr Rusk, FO371 160541.
8. 6 August, record of meeting, FO371 160542; 1 August, record of WEU meeting, FO371 160565; memo of conversation, 8 August, *Crisis over Berlin* VI 02941; 9 August, Paris to FO and 12 August, Washington to FO, FO371 160542.
9. 8 August, Berlin situation report and refugee details in the next two paragraphs, FO371 160480; conversations with many Berliners; RIAS programme *Mauerbau*, op. cit.
10. Khrushchev speech, Slusser, op. cit.
11. Cate, op. cit.
12. This paragraph and next: 10 August, Moscow to FO and 12 August, Canadian embassy Moscow to Ottawa, FO371 160543; 12 August, Moscow to FO, FO371 160481.
13. Story told to D. Proector and told by him to me.

14. 11 August, Berlin to FO, FO371 160618; 12 August, *The Times*.
15. RIAS *Mauerbau*, op. cit.; 12 August, Berlin to FO, FO371 160543.
16. Report on Happenings, Development of the Situation 13 August, Police Report November 1961; Situation on the Sector and Zonal Border, 14 August Police Report.
17. Cate, op. cit.
18. Cate, op. cit.; Prittie, op. cit.; *Mauerbau*, op.cit; conversation with Robert Lochner; statement by Conrad Schumann, 11 August 1986, Checkpoint Charlie Museum; Weyden, op. cit.
19. Conversation with Günther Dittmann; Police Reports, op. cit.; Cate, op. cit.; Weyden, op. cit.
20. Information from Reuters' historian, Professor Donald Read.
21. Police Reports, op. cit.; Brigadier L.F. Richards at 22 March 1991 seminar at King's College, London, printed in *Contemporary Record*, vol. 6, No I, Summer 1992.
22. This paragraph and the next: Richards and Ledwidge in seminar at King's College, London, op. cit.; *Mauerbau*, op. cit.
23. Report on Happenings, Development of the Situation 13 August, Police Report November 1961; The Closure of the Sector and Zonal Borders on 13 August, Police Report 2 October 1961.
24. Conversations with Margot and Egon Lesnick, Hans Georg Urban, Robert Lochner, Harald Karas, Herbert Kundler, Joachim Bolke, Peter Herz.
25. Ibid.; 13 August, tel. 182, US Mission West Berlin to State Department, 02295 Fiche 346.
26. This paragraph and the next: Weyden, op. cit.; Cate, op. cit.; *Mauerbau*, op. cit.; Kroll, op. cit.; Seydoux, op. cit.; conversation with Sir Edward Tomkins.
27. This and the next four paragraphs: Beschloss, op. cit.; Cate, op. cit.; Catudal, op. cit.; Weyden, op. cit.; conversation with Robert Lochner; Rusk statement, 02287 Fiche 345.
28. This and next paragraph: Prittie, op. cit.; Brandt, op. cit.; conversation with Margot and Egon Lesnick.
29. This and next paragraph: two cables on Kommandatura meeting, 13 August, Berlin to FO, FO371 160509; McDermott, op. cit.; Trivers, op. cit.; Brandt, op. cit.
30. Conversation with Professor Kundler and other Berliners.
31. This and next paragraph: conversation with many Berliners including Barbara Jacobi, Tino Schwierzina, Robert Lochner, Heinz Schweikert.
32. 14 and 15 August, *The Times*; newsreel Deutsche Wochenschau Archiv; 15 August, *Guardian*; 13 and 14 August, Berlin to FO, FO371 160480; 28 August, Berlin to FO, FO371 160656.
33. 14 August, Police Report, Situation on the Sector and Zonal Borders: special incidents.
34. This and next two paragraphs: conversations with Robert Lochner, Günther Dittmann, Margot and Egon Lesnick; 14 August, Police Report, op. cit., special incidents; 14 August, *The Times*.

REFERENCES

35. This and next two paragraphs: 15 August, *Guardian, New York Times, New York Herald Tribune,* and *The Times*; 14 August, tel. 198, US Mission West Berlin to State Department, 02308 Fiche 348; 17 August, Berlin to Bonn, FO371 160512.

36. 14 August, Berlin to FO, FO371 160480; police reports, op. cit.

37. 14 August, tel. 198, US Mission, op. cit.; 14 August, Berlin to FO, FO371 160507; 14 August report on Military Commandants' meeting, FO371 160509.

38. Brandt, op. cit.; 14 August, tel. 198, US Mission, op. cit.; 14 August, Berlin to FO, FO371 160507.

39. 14 August, tel. 198, US Mission, op. cit.; conversation with Professor Kundler; 15 August, *Guardian.*

40. 15 August, *New York Times, New York Herald Tribune, The Times, Guardian.*

41. *Mauerbau*, op. cit.; film in Deutsche Wochenschau Archiv.

42. 13 August, Berlin to FO, FO371 160480; 13 August, tel. 186, 02296 Fiche 347; SACEUR General Movement Situation Reports for 14, 19, 24 August, FO371 1605100.

43. Newspaper and police reports, op. cit.

44. 14 August, tel. 198, US Mission, op. cit.; 14 August, Berlin to FO, FO371 160507.

45. 14 August, Bonn to FO, FO to Bonn, and FO to Washington, FO371 160509.

46. 14 August, Bundy memo for the President National Security Files, Box 82, Germany-Berlin General 8/17/61; 14 August, memo President's Office Files, Box 88, State 8/61–9/61 (unsigned in this version but accepted by National Security archive as from the President 0029 Fiche 347).

47. Memo for Maxwell Taylor for 15 August meeting of Berlin Steering Group from Lawrence J. Legere, 02311 Fiche 349.

48. 15 and 16 August situation reports Berlin to FO, FO371 160480; Conrad Schumann statement, op. cit.; Deutsche Wochenschau Archiv film; 16 August, *Guardian.*

49. This paragraph and next: 15 August, Bonn to FO, FO371 160509; 15 August, Berlin to FO, FO371 160480; 15 August, tel. 210, US Mission West Berlin to State Department, 02316 Fiche 349.

50. 15 August Steering Group meeting, *Crisis over Berlin* VI 02941; 15 August, Washington to FO, FO371 160510; 15 August, tel. 333, US Embassy Germany to State Department, 02313 Fiche 349; 15 August, Bonn to FO, FO371 160509.

51. 16 August, Berlin to FO, FO371 160509; 16 August, *The Times.*

52. 15 August, Berlin to FO and Bonn to FO; 16 August, FO to Berlin; 17 August, Berlin to FO; all in FO371 160510.

53. 2 October, Police Report, The Closure of the Sector and Zonal Boundaries on 13 August; 16 August, *Guardian.*

54. 15 August, situation report Berlin to FO, op. cit.; 16 August, *The Times*; 15 August, tel. 210, US Mission West Berlin to State Department, op. cit.; 17 August report by F. Kaunitz, FO371 160503.

55. *Mauerbau*, op. cit.; 17 August, *The Times*; Brandt, op. cit.; conversation with Egon Bahr.

56. This paragraph and next two: 17 August, *The Times*; 16 August, letter from Brandt to President Kennedy, FO371 160482 and tel. 223, US Mission West Berlin to Office of the White House, 02340 Fiche 353; Beschloss, op. cit.; O'Donnell letter to Prittie; 18 August President's letter to Brandt, National Security Files, Box 82, Germany-Berlin Vice-President's trip 8/19/61–8/20/61; 16 August, tel. 342, US Embassy Germany to State Department, 02322 Fiche 349.

57. 16 August, Washington to FO, FO371 160510; 16 August, Murrow Berlin to Wilson State Department, National Security Files, Box 91, Germany-Berlin cables vol. III.

58. 16 August, tel. 221, US Mission West Berlin to State Department, 02326 Fiche 351; Weyden, op. cit.

10: THE WALL

1. Interview with Y. A. Kondrashev, Moscow.

2. Brigadier L.F. Richards, seminar at King's College, London, 22 March 1991, published in the *Contemporary Record* vol. 6, summer 1992; Kohler, *Understanding the Russians*; Brandt, op. cit.; Lemmer memoirs quoted in *Mauerbau*; Kroll, op. cit.; Gehlen, *The Gehlen Memoirs*; interview with Oleg Troyanovsky.

3. General Maxwell Taylor interview with Mrs Elspeth Rostow 26 April 1964; Richards, op. cit.; Weyden, op. cit.; Catudal, op. cit.

4. 30 September, memo of conversation with Vice-President Johnson, Paris, 02518 Fiche 380; Clay interview with Richard M. Scannon, 1 July 1964; 17 January 1962, tel. 0109–62, JCS to C-in-C USAE, 02688 Fiche 406; 17 January, tel. 1349, Clay to Rusk, 02688, ibid.

5. Rusk interview with Dennis O'Brien, 13 March 1970; Martin J. Hillenbrand interview with Paul R. Sweet, 26 August 1964.

6. O'Donnell, *Johnny, We Hardly Knew Ye*; Taylor interview, op. cit.

7. 17 August, letter from the President, National Security Files, Box 73a–74; FO371 160511; National Security Files, Germany-Berlin General 8/17/61.

8. 17 August, tels. 224 and 238, US Mission West Berlin to State Department, 02341 and 02343 Fiche 353; Deutsche Wochenschau Archiv; 19 August, *New York Herald Tribune*.

9. This paragraph and the next: 18 August, *The Times*; 17 and 18 August situation reports, Berlin to FO, FO371 160480 (all other situation reports for August are in this file); 19 August, Berlin to FO, FO371 160511; Police report November 1961 on Happenings 13 August–13 November.

10. 17 August, W.J.A. Wilberforce record of conversation with official from German embassy, FO371 160511; 19 August situation report, Berlin to FO; 21 August, Berlin to Bonn, FO371 160512; 19 August, *The Times*.

11. Smith, op. cit.; Beschloss, op. cit.; O'Donnell, op. cit.

12. 29 August, Delacombe despatch to Sir C. Steel, FO371 160523; Bohlen, op. cit.; Cate, op. cit.; Rostow interview with Richard E. Neustadt, 11 and 25 April 1964.

13. Brandt, op. cit.; two memos of conversation 20 August, 02369 and 02370 Fiche 357.

14. This paragraph and the next two: 18 August, Washington to FO, FO371 160510; 20 September memo on clearance of 1st Battle Group, 02493 Fiche 376.
15. This paragraph and the next: Deutsche Wochenschau Archiv; Smith, op. cit.; Brandt, op. cit.; Weyden, op. cit.; Cate, op. cit.; interview with Robert Lochner.
16. Jack M. Schick, op. cit.; Alphand, op. cit.
17. 29 August, Delacombe despatch, op. cit.; 21 August, Bonn to FO, FO371 160511.
18. Police report on Happenings, op. cit.; 29 August, *The Times*; 22 August situation report, Berlin to FO.
19. 23 August, *The Times*; 23 August, situation report, Berlin to FO, FO371 160512.
20. 24 August, Berlin to FO, ibid.; The Closure of the Sector and Zonal Boundaries, police report, 3 October.
21. 23 August, Moscow to FO, FO371 160623.
22. 26 August, Bonn to FO, FO371 160623; FO minute, FO371 1610546; National Security Files, Box 82 Germany-Berlin General 8/26/61–8/28/61; *Crisis over Berlin* VI, 02941.
23. 24 August, tel. 317, 02400 Fiche 362; 25 August, tel. 331, 02405 Fiche 3631; 26 August, tel. 340, 02408 ditto; 28 August, *The Times*; Prittie according to information from a defecting soldier; 11 September situation report, Berlin to FO, FO371 160482.
24. 18 August, Washington to FO, FO371 160510; 22 August, Washington to FO, FO371 160496.
25. 19 August, Home to Rusk, FO371 160511; Home minute, 18 August, FO371 160512; 21 August, President to McNamara, National Security Files, Box 331, meetings and memos, NSAM 71–115; 18 August, Caccia to Shuckburgh, FO371 160513; 21 August, UK delegation to NATO, Paris to FO, FO371 160482; 30 August, tel. POLTO 240, 02423 Fiche 365; 21 August, Bonn to FO, FO371 160482.
26. 18 August, Washington to FO, FO371 160544; Alphand, op. cit.; 2 September, tel. 1199 and 1200, US Embassy France to State Department, 03435 and 02436 Fiche 367; Allen Dulles memo for President National Security Files, Box 82, Germany-Berlin General 8/22/61.
27. 21 August, memo from President to Secretary of State National Security Files, Box 82, Germany-Berlin General 8/21/61.
28. Macmillan, op. cit.; 27 August, PM to President, FO371 160547.
29. 27 August, Shuckburgh minute for Home, FO371 160513.
30. 4 September, research memo, State Department Bureau of Intelligence and Research National Security Files, Box 82, Germany-Berlin General 9/7/61–9/8/61; Schlesinger, *Robert Kennedy*.
31. Beschloss, op. cit.; Slusser, op. cit.; 15 September, Moscow to FO, FO371 160551.
32. Telegrams and memos, FO371 160551, and printed volume of Secretary of State's visit to Washington 14–30 September, FO371 160558.

33. 3 October, Washington to FO, FO371 160554; 25 September, Secretary of State to PM and various other cables, FO371 160553; 15 October, Paris to FO, FO371 160557; 13 October, Moscow to FO on Brentano's talk to Couve, 11 October, FO371 160557; 14 October, Washington to FO, ibid.

34. Police report on Happenings, op. cit.; 27 August, tel. 343, US Mission West Berlin to State Department, 02410 Fiche 363 and 28 August, tel. 351, ibid.; 28 August, Berlin to FO, FO371 160508.

35. August and September situation reports, Berlin to FO, FO371 160480 and 160482.

36. 30 August, tel. 375, US Mission West Berlin to State Department, 02425 Fiche 365; 31 August situation report, Berlin to FO.

37. Assessment of Current Soviet Intentions, National Security Files, Box 82, op. cit.; 2 September, Moscow to FO, FO371 160624; 15, 18, 21 September, Berlin to FO, FO371 160625; and 8, 9, 13 September situation reports Berlin to FO.

38. 5 September, British Embassy, Bonn letter to Central Department, FO, FO371 160656.

39. This paragraph and the next: 10 September, *Sunday Telegraph*; 29 August and 8 September, *Guardian*; 7, 8 and 10 September, *The Times*; police reports; 30 September, situation reports Berlin to FO.

40. 1 October, *Sunday Times*; 14 September, *Guardian*; 13 September, *New York Times*.

41. This paragraph and the next: 30 August, tel. 371, US Mission West Berlin to State Department, 02424 Fiche 365; 31 August, *Guardian*; 18 September, External Department Berlin to Chancery Bonn, FO371 160504; 29 August and 13 September, Berlin to FO, FO371 160503; 29 September, FO minute, FO371 160504.

42. This paragraph and the next: interviews with Werner Krätschall, Professor Achim Hoffmann, Barbara Jacobi.

43. 5 November, CIA report 3960/61, 02617 Fiche 395.

44. 12 September, *The Times*; 26 September, Political Department Berlin to Chancery Bonn, FO371 160514.

45. 14 November, Sir David Ormsby Gore to the Earl of Home, FO371 160564; 1 September, from James R. Moore, White House Central Subject Files, Box 55; Prittie and FO371 153985.

46. This paragraph and the next: 22 and 28 August and 10 September, Berlin to FO, FO371 160496; 28 August, tel. 351, US Mission West Berlin to State Department, 02417 Fiche 364; 17 September, Berlin to FO, FO371 160508; 25 September, External Department Berlin to Chancery Bonn, FO371 160654.

47. Foy Kohler recording, October 1964; 28 August, Bundy memo for the President, National Security Files, Box 82, op. cit., 8/26/61–8/28/61; Smith, op. cit.; Catudal, op. cit.

48. Lucius D. Clay interview with Richard M. Scannon, 1 July 1964; Smith, op. cit.

49. Catudal, op. cit.; 23, 28 and 29 September situation reports, Berlin to FO.

50. 2 October, police report on The Closure of the Sector and Zonal Border; 28 September, *New York Times*; 1 October, *Sunday Times*.

51. This paragraph and the next: 22 September, *Daily Worker*; September situation reports, Berlin to FO; 4 October, *Guardian*.

52. Reports on Kennedy and Macmillan talks, FO371 160555; 11 October, E. E. Tomkins, FO to Viscount Hood Washington enclosing transcript, FO371 160556; Macmillan, op. cit.; 6 October, Sir E. Shuckburgh for Lord Home, FO371 160558; 4 October, Sir F. Roberts to Sir E. Shuckburgh, FO371 160558.

53. 24 October, Washington to FO, FO371 160559; 6 October, record of telephone conversation, FO371 160555.

54. This paragraph and the next: Slusser quoting *New York Times*; 19 October, Moscow to FO, FO371 160559; 26 October, External Department Berlin to Chancery Bonn, FO371 160560.

55. Two cables, 3 October, Berlin to FO, FO371 160514.

56. 5 October, tel. COB 434, USAE Berlin Command to USAE C-in-C, 02530 Fiche 382; 7 October, Berlin to FO, FO371 160514; Annual History US Army Europe, 1 Jan–31 December 1961, *The Berlin Crisis* 02658 Fiche 401; 12 October, Berlin to Bonn, FO371 160514; record of events tabs 38–45, October 1961, Lauris Norstad Papers 1930–87, Box 97; 16 October, situation report, Berlin to FO.

57. The above plus Trivers, op. cit.; November 1961 police report on Happenings.

58. Conversation with Robert Lochner; Trivers, op. cit.; 24 October, Norstad to Lemnitzer, Lauris Norstad Papers, Box 86; 25 October, Berlin to FO, FO371 160514.

59. 26 October, UK Delegation to NATO to FO, FO371 160514; 27 October, Berlin to FO, ibid.

60. Deutsche Wochenschau Archiv; 27 October, cable from Office of Special Military Representative of President, 02597 Fiche 392; 28 October, Norstad to McNamara and Lemnitzer Norstad Papers, Box 86, op. cit.; 1 July 1964, Clay interview with Richard M. Scannon.

61. Beschloss, op. cit.; 29 October, situation report, Berlin to FO, FO371 160484.

62. Conversation with Oleg Troyanovsky; 5 December, Roberts, Moscow to Shuckburgh, FO371 160566; Trivers, op. cit.; 28 December, Berlin to FO, FO371 160572.

63. 28 October, Moscow to FO, FO371 160559; 23 November, Washington and 30 November, Bonn to FO, FO371 160517; various reactions and reports, FO371 160565; Macmillan, op. cit.

64. Kroll, op. cit.; 10 November, Moscow to FO, FO371 160562; 29 November, memo JCS, 02637 Fiche 398; 26 December, Moscow to FO, FO371 160568.

65. 21 December, draft instructions, FO371 160569.

66. 21 November, memo by Secretary of State, CAB129 (107) Part 2 End A; November situation reports, Berlin to FO, FO371 160484; 20 November and 5 December, Berlin to FO, FO371 160572.

67. 9 December, Berlin to FO, FO371 160484; 11 December, Sir C. Steel to Sir E. Shuckburgh, FO371 160569; 2 and 4 November, PREM II 3612.
68. Yearly summary of Police Activities 1961; December situation reports, Berlin to FO, FO371 160484.
69. This paragraph and the next: 11 January 1992, *Berliner Morgenpost*; 22, 23 and 27 December, Berlin to FO, FO371 160572.
70. 22 November and 24 December, Berlin to FO, FO371 160504; 2 November, J.W. Russell minute, FO371 160564.

11: ENDS

1. Nikita Khrushchev, *Khrushchev Remembers*, op. cit. and Nikita Khrushchev, *The Last Testament*, op. cit.
2. Transcripts of interviews for the *The World that came in from the Cold*.
3. Thompson–Gromyko talks: *The Berlin Crisis* Fiches 404, 408, 409; 5 February, POLTO 1014 US Mission to NATO to State Department and 17 February, TOPOL 1142 State Department to US Mission, 02706 and 02708 Fiche 409; Annual Historical Report for the US European Command and JCS 02902 Fiche 441.
4. Rusk talks also in *The Berlin Crisis* passim; 21 March, memo on Rusk conversation in Washington National Security Files, Box 81; 7–9 December Weekend Reading Book, 022895 Fiche 440.
5. Details here and next two paragraphs: Beschloss, op. cit.; Ball, op. cit.; Schlesinger, op. cit.; Macmillan, op. cit.; O'Donnell, op. cit.; Brandt, op. cit.; Khrushchev, op. cit.; interview with Egon Bahr; 7 December memo by Deputy Director for Intelligence CIA, 02893 Fiche 439.
6. Interview with Joachim Bölke.
7. This paragraph and the rest of the section: Marshall, op. cit.; McCauley, op. cit.; Brandt, op. cit.; Grosser, op. cit.; Prittie, op. cit.; Childs, op. cit.; Catudal, op. cit.
8. Conversations with many Berliners and especially Hans Georg Urban; Prittie, op. cit.; Brandt, op. cit.
9. More conversations with Berliners; McCauley, Childs.
10. This and next two paragraphs: information and exhibition at Checkpoint Charlie Museum.
11. This whole section on the Ostpolitik: all the works cited in 7; Egon Bahr and Peter Florin interviews for *The World that came in from the Cold*.
12. Details here and for the rest of the section: contemporary newspaper accounts; two-part film by Lapping Associates, *The Fall of the Wall*, shown on BBC Television, November 1994; interview with Jan Urban in *The World that came in from the Cold*; John Simpson, *The Darkness Crumbles*.
13. John Simpson, op. cit.; film of the press conference in the Deutsches Museum *The Fall of the Wall*.

12: BEGINNINGS

1. For this section: as above; conversations with Berliners; newsreels and what I myself saw.

2. This and the rest of the section: newspaper reports, especially 28 September 1990 and 9 November 1993, *Guardian*; interviews by Judy Dempsey, 5 November 1994, *Financial Times*; 6 November 1994, *Observer*; 21 December 1989, *London Review of Books*; 10 and 11 November 1989, *Independent*; 20 November 1989, *Daily Telegraph*; 15 March 1989, *Guardian*; Grass article 20 October 1990, *Guardian*; 2 October 1993, *Financial Times*.

Interviews

———❖———

Professor Ulrich Albrecht, Rudolf F. Alexeyev, Alexei Adzhubei, Dr Ella Barowsky, Stephen Barrett, Lutz Becker, Lev A. Bezymyansky, Mr Bogomolov, Joachim Bölke, Barbara Bure, Günther and Lorre Dittmann, Professor Stefan Doernberg, Egon Bahr, Valentin Fallin, Alexander S. Grossman, Genrikh I. Gurkov, Louis Heren, Peter Herz, Professor Achim Hoffmann, Barbara Jacobi, Hans Jacobus, Harald Karas, Sir John Killick, Yevgeny A. Kondrashev, Werner Krätschall, Ilya S. Kremer, Professor Herbert Kundler, Heidi Leopold, Egon and Margot Lesnick, Robert Lochner, Vicky Lowe, Daniil Y. Melomid-Melnikov, Peter Neuhof, Nicholai S. Portugalov, Daniil M. Proektor, Yuri N. Rachmaninov, Manfred Rexin, Victor S. Rykov, Heinz Schweikert, Tino Schwierzina, Sir Edward Tomkins, Oleg A. Troyanovsky, Dr Hans Georg Urban.

Index

against more negotiations 265, 292,
318–19, 337–8
and new security barriers 277
and the Wall 307
reinforcements 313n
de Zulueta, Philip 210
Debré, Michel 157, 188
Delacombe, Major-General Sir Rohan
273, 333–4, 340
Deutschmark replacing Reichsmark 24
Dibelius, Bishop Otto 191, 326
disarmament 79, 199
displaced persons 14–15
see mainly refugees
Dobrynin, 347
Douglas, Lewis 131
Dowling, Ambassador 291, 336
Dulles, Allen (CIA) 99, 207, 236
Dulles, John Foster 66–8
Geneva 1955 65
and Khrushchev's Berlin statement
97–8
and British reaction to it 114–15
and the armed convoy 129, 130
meets NATO ministers 133–4
meeting with Mikoyan 136
concessions by, 1959 139
confederation idea 139–40
wants talks with Soviet Union in
Germany 142
talks with all parties 142–3
sick 143, 160
against Macmillan's Russian visit
144–5
attack on Macmillan and Lloyd 161
laments Anglo-American
collaboration 163
death and funeral 169
high altitude flights stopped 201

East Berlin:
populaton decline 193, 364, 382
trade balance 193
riots 193–4
after the Wall 322–7
preparation of Wall 331–2
evacuation of houses 331
flourishing in 1962 355

New Economic System 356
after Quadripartite Agreement
362–6
shopping spree after Wall's fall 374–5
East Berlin Rising 55–6
East Germans 352, 366–7, 381–2
East Germany *see* German Democratic
Republic
'Economic miracle' 40
Eden, Sir Anthony 51–2, 57–8
Eisenhower, General Dwight D.:
access to Berlin 6
Russian capture of Berlin 7–8
on Khrushchev 63
Open Skies policy 63–4
as statesman 64–6
and Dulles 68
and Hungary 77
and Suez 78
and Soviet Union nuclear arms 80–1
and Khrushchev's Berlin statement
97, 98, 99
and British reaction to Khrushchev
114–15, 118
note from 132
against armed convoy 141
pro-airlift 141–2
and Macmillan's Russian visit 144–5,
159–60
advice to Macmillan 163
and Geneva Conference 169, 173,
175–6
irritation with Macmillan 175
writes to Khrushchev 175–6
to see Adenauer, de Gaulle and
Macmillan 178–9
visit by Khrushchev 179–85
irritated by Adenauer 195–6
and Paris Summit 199
and high altitude flights 202
and CIA U-2 spy planes 202–6
end of Paris Summit 209, 209–10, 211
and J.F.Kennedy 236
on negotiation 319n
Eiskeller 33, 52
election December 1958 123
electricity cuts, by Russians 50–1
Emergency Reception Law 39